Sgned

WRB
35-

Another taxing book
for Boris
from Ramsay

Sisters of the Brush

Sisters of the Brush

Their Family, Art, Life, and Letters 1797–1833

Ramsay MacMullen

Design & Composition: Windfall Software, Paul C. Anagnostopoulos & MaryEllen N. Oliver

Publisher's Cataloging-in-Publication
(Provided by Quality Books, Inc.)

MacMullen, Ramsay, 1928–
Sisters of the brush : their family, art, life & letters 1797–1833 / by Ramsay MacMullen –1st ed.
p. cm.
Includes bibliographical references and index.
Preassigned LCCN: 97-92193
ISBN 0-9658780-0-7

1. Women artists–New England–Correspondence. 2. Way, Mary, 1769–1833–Correspondence. 3. Champlain, Elizabeth Way, 1771–1825 –Correspondence. 4. Riley, Eliza Champlain, 1797–1886–Correspondence. 5. Miniature painters–New England–Correspondence. 6. Way family. I. Title.

N43.M33 1997 704'.042'097403
QBI97-40691

Published by PastTimes Press, 25 Temple Court, New Haven, Connecticut.

Printed in the United States of America.

10 9 8 7 6 5 4 3 2 1

Contents

Figures

Preface

The letters from which this book was made, wrapped up and stored from the early 1920s in a certain piece of furniture in a house in the Murray Hill part of New York city, had probably not been looked at since 1905 (note 2 in Chapter 1). Then in 1992 I examined and transcribed them and gave my Transcription and the originals to the American Antiquarian Society in Worcester, Massachusetts.[1]

The idea of making a book out of the letters arose naturally from their dramatic focus. At the center, among thirty-odd writers, were the New London trio calling themselves "sisters of the brush" (**no. 95**), accounting for two thirds and more of the pages of the whole Transcription. Their close kin and closest friends account for another considerable portion. Equally marked was the chronological focus: more than 85% of the letters date to a period of only fourteen years, 1817–1831.

I judged that readers (other than specialists) who might pick up the correspondence as a book would jib at certain features of the original: "wrong stops, points, and marks omitted or misplaced, grammatical and typographical errors &c. Serious inconveniences!" as one of the writers says (**no. 90**). I have therefore, in the words of a well-known model, "normalized all . . . capitalization, punctuation, and paragraphing. I have retained the italics of the original letters" where they were not (as too often) "erratic and apparently meaningless," while "silently italicizing titles of books, names of ships" and titles of works of art;[2] and words once separated like "any thing" or "mean time" I have joined by a hyphen. I have only departed from my model in not normalizing mis-spelt words, some of which anyway were less careless or ignorant than oldfashioned.[3] I have added between square brackets an occasional explanatory word or two, or letters or a word or two that are certain but destroyed, or where the writer left out something inadvertently.

Except in one chapter (the fifth), I have disturbed the chronological sequence of the letters hardly at all, since the story flows along intelligibly without re-ordering.

As to the larger problem of somehow reducing the whole correspondence within reason, I cut less than a fifth: most obviously, from the poetry written by Elizabeth

Champlain; next most obviously, from the prose of Mary Way's late letters; and after that, from little business items and greetings often in postscripts, or toward the end of the letters, or from quite tangential correspondents. I have left in much that contributed not to plot (as it would be called, if the whole correspondence were a novel) but to characterization. Whatever my sins in my editing, they can be easily repaired out of my Transcription; the latter itself, out of the originals.

The persons who appear most often I generally refer to as their family members did: "Betsey," for example.[4] It would be cumbersome always to speak of "Elizabeth Way Champlain," too distant to call her "Mrs. Champlain."

Several Kin-charts are offered to help in the sorting out of the connections, which are, it may said in their defense, no worse than you have in a Russian novel. Problems in dating the letters, about a third of which lack the day or the month or the year, or all three, I solved as best I could in the Transcription, with arguments that I need not repeat here except in those few cases where more careful reading produced a better result. I have thanked many people who helped me at various points in my editing, and need not list them here; but I must (as I did in another book long ago) again record my particular debt to SML, ACS, KEP, BSG, MMJ, ALF, PJC, ETC.

Sisters of the Brush

1

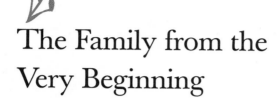

The Family from the Very Beginning

All in the form of letters, like a very big novel but true, about not very important people, three women artists at their center, from a not very important town in a country just emerging from infancy–such is the material at hand.

Of names anyone might know, in all the correspondence there is only Tom Paine, spoken of as a friend in case of need. At a much lower level of recognition, add a certain U.S. vice president, a certain former governor of Ohio, and the Rev. John Murray of fame as the founder of Universalism; also, various painters–Trumbull, Inman, Jewett, Jarvis, Waldo, Rembrandt Peale, Augustus Burr, Ambrose Andrews, and still more–whom the correspondents know and talk about, and a similar number of writers–Woodworth, Halleck, McDonald Clarke, Charles Clinch, James Brooks. But these are not great figures in their respective arts. The Republic had few such to show in the first forty or fifty years of its existence.

Then why the labor of reading this collection of correspondence? For historians by profession, the question hardly arises; or it does so only in a context of subspecialties and research needs of the moment. Let such serious inquirers look in, then, and pull out whatever serves their purposes. For all others, however, answer must be found in the simple fact that (to repeat) the letters constitute a big novel to which, with its flow of people's lives, readers may enjoy committing themselves–especially since those lives are unfolded to intimates in trust and candor. It is an odd fact that one may learn more about long-dead distant strangers through their letters than one ever knows about any but one's closest friends.

And, out of fairness to the correspondents themselves, something should be said of their style, or styles, plural: Mary Way's evoking the best of Vivaldi's bassoon concertos; George Champlain's, a piece for brass band by Poulenc, perhaps; Anna Fitch's, an organ chorale by Sir Arthur Sullivan. However one chooses in one's own terms to define and individualize them, they are indeed individuals, and do consciously address epistolography as an art. They want to move, surprise, amuse, and almost incidentally to inform, on almost every page. To a high degree, they succeed.

It is of course no easy thing to draw a narrative out of a collection of letters. None of them was originally written with a narrative in mind. The writers take up and put aside subjects according to their inclination at the moment, and an equally arbitrary process determined whether what they wrote ever reached a later generation. Almost at the start, some was lost in the mail, or destroyed at some time before 1900 because, perhaps, it was judged uninteresting or discreditable. For the latter reason, in what survives, here and there words or lines or even paragraphs have been crossed out, by whose hand, there is no saying; and, for the former reason–lack of interest–the process has continued in the preparation of this book, though on a very modest scale. About editorial practises, readers probably need to know only that punctuation has been modernized and the individual letters given a sequence in **bold numbers.**[1]

There was a saving instinct clear across the family, so much is evident. The correspondent who contributes the earliest letters, Oliver Champlain, kept what he had from his brother George, sometimes; Anna Fitch likewise, from her dearest friend, Mary Way; likewise, a number of other persons in their circle; but if Eliza Way Champlain Riley, George Champlain's daughter, had not made a project of it, asking people to send her what they had and keeping the collection all together, no doubt this instinct to save would have availed nothing, and time in its usual various ways would have destroyed what is now before us. Eliza was the key, as well as much the most abundant writer of what she saved. Whatever narrative can be drawn from the collection must be in some sense her story. She began it very naturally with her father and uncle at a point in the 1790s, carried it on into the mid-nineteenth century, and somehow transmitted with it a respect for the past that kept it all safe through succeeding generations.[2]

In outline, first regarding the actors in that story: she and her kin, until her marriage to a New York man, were all of New London, their lines going back to the mid-seventeenth century or earlier. Their home town had shaped them all: a seaport on the edge of Connecticut, "land of steady habits" as its people called it. Almost by logic Eliza's father George and uncle Oliver were captains, and her three brothers all thought of following in their footsteps (though in fact they chose other occupations). She herself followed her mother and her aunt, who earned their living through painting; for that, along with school-teaching, paid about as well as anything women could do at the time, independently.

So much for the actors, in outline. But their home has its own story, too, which needs to be told in a little more detail. It emerges from out of the most remote and alien beginnings, Siberia no less. From here, a certain people, tens of millennia past, emigrated to the new world east of them and spread across it till at last some few reached the farthest edge of the land. There, a tiny cluster was seen in 1614 by an observer from the ocean's other side. He returned home with news of their settlement and the name of the inhabitants: statio his percommoda . . . salmones his

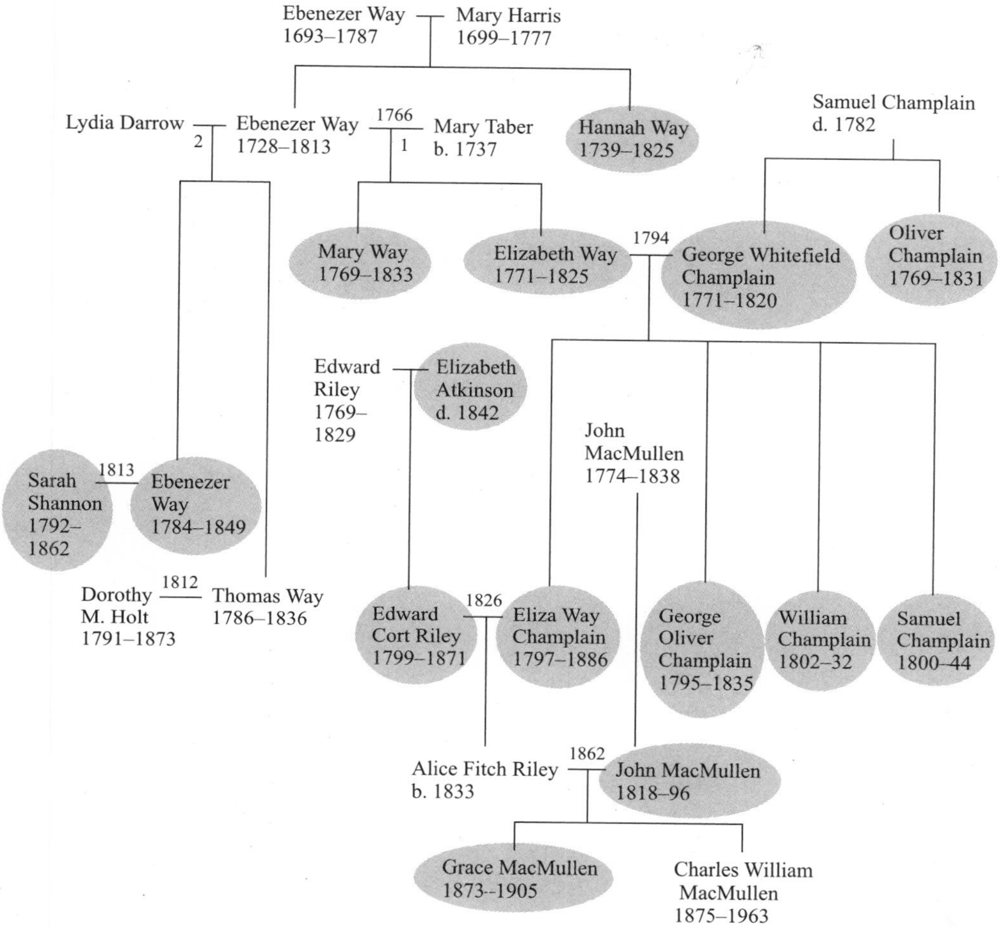

Figure 1. Kinship Lines (the letter writers circled)

capiuntur; barbari Pequatoes accolunt (here in a Latin version of what he reported, for readers who might have trouble with the Dutch).[3]

For the Pequots who thus make their first appearance into written accounts, the meeting with Europeans proved a very nearly terminal affair: the Europeans included not only explorers but armed settlers. A small group come in from Massachusetts, soon after a first encounter with the inhabitants, skirmished with them (1637) and killed as many as they could, helped by a neighboring tribe, the Mohicans. Of the hundred or so captives they took, the women and children were enslaved and the men drowned.[4] Uncaptured survivors lived on in diminishing numbers under the overlordship of the Mohican Uncas, son-in-law to their quondam sachem Sassacus-Tatobam.

Europeans could now enter upon the civilized occupation of the area along the shore. It proved attractive, percommoda, because of its superb great harbor, though the land was not specially good. A plantation was formally organized in 1645/6, at first called after the earlier inhabitants, "Pequot"; soon, "New London." Among its first townsmen were Robert Hempstead, and by 1651 the Indian trader Jonathan Brewster with John Coit, boatwright, and Philip Taber, of Chepstow; also George Denison and John Prentis, respectively soldier and blacksmith. All six were among the ancestry of the correspondents whose letters appear in the pages that follow; and similarly, other settlers in the next decade by the name of Starr, Truman, Christophers. Hempstead's descendants included the diarist Joshua (1678–1758), who in 1739 witnessed the baptism of Hannah Way, first-born or eldest of the correspondents, below.[5]

Among the original New London settlers should also be mentioned a certain Cauken from the same town as Taber, that is, Chepstow near the southern edge of Wales, and a certain Manwaring from Over Peover on the northern edge. The descendants of these two, eventually joining in marriage, brought into the world Frances Manwaring Caulkins. It was through her that New London came to be celebrated in a remarkable *History*, published in 1852.[6]

By her day, whatever had once been remote and alien about the place was now grown quite familiarly American; Siberia, Sassacus-Tatobam, and Latin were all forgot. The superb harbor had accounted for growth beyond the ambitions of farming. New London now had its bustling Hempstead Street, its Coit, Starr and Truman Streets, because it also had its wharves and shipyard. Already in the 1660s a Coit had built a vessel for a Christophers, to be commanded by a Prentis;[7] trade already reached to the Caribbean, and half a century later to Europe, too. True, its bulk was limited: most traffic before the Revolution moved up and down the coast in small home-built vessels of twenty to seventy tons, some plying to Boston, more to New York. Distant trade was conducted largely with the West Indies. In addition to their role as middlemen, carrying other ports' goods from one to another, New Londoners dealt in agricultural products from the hinterland, livestock and especially horses. Their economic activity can be followed through the marine list published in the city's newspaper from 1770 on by Thomas Allen, a new citizen through marriage to a Christophers. Allen's son in turn became by marriage brother-in-law to Ebenezer Way Sr., father to the "Ebb" of this present correspondence and grandfather to Eliza.[8]

The Revolution in its time checked growth. New Londoners suffered great losses, while at the same time diverting their energies to the war very handsomely. Some were rewarded with high positions of leadership. The outstanding example was of course the native son that no one cared later to claim, General Benedict Arnold, whose forces in 1781 landed on the city and systematically burnt down the greater part of it, building by building. The act was long remembered and the savagery that attended it recorded on a monument and in a poetic memorial by a descendant of the victims.[9] Guy Richards' home was spared only because of the illness of a woman resident in it, but Ebenezer Way Sr.'s store was given to the general conflagration. Richards after the war was tied by marriage to the family of George Whitefield Champlain, while Champlain's father-in-law was the Ebenezer Way in question.[10] These, with mentions in Christopher Prince's autobiography, are the earliest glimpses of the correspondents, below, other than the purely genealogical.

A word only on Prince's autobiography: rich in detail on the later 1770s, in the midst of war, the writer being at that time in his twenties and ardently engaged in the most exciting events. It later pleased him as an old man to draw out an account of them from his life's log.[11] His narrative touches the Champlains not only through his marrying of a New London girl but because he worked in and sailed out of the port: sailed as a privateer under the command of Oliver Champlain (who in 1777 made his fortune), met Oliver's brother George (not yet Eliza's father), met various people who were to sit to George's sister-in-law Mary when in the 1780s she took up portrait-painting, and himself and his brother Kimball sat to her as well. There are various other connections belonging naturally to a close-textured little town and its seafaring inhabitants. But their bearing on the letters is too tangential to need retailing here.

Following the war, life must be rebuilt. First, trade picked up promptly. An illustrative notice in Thomas Allen's marine list totals the cattle and horses clearing though the port in 1785: something over eight thousand of them. An Episcopalian church in place of the one destroyed by fire only a few years earlier arose under the vigilant eye of its veteran warden, Jonathan Starr, brother-in-law to Allen and to Ebenezer Way. All three had married daughters of Pardon and Elizabeth Taber, descended from Philip, Eliza's great-great-great-great-grandfather. The new church's pulpit was entrusted to Samuel Seabury, first bishop of Connecticut, who was to join the families of these three men in 1789 through the marriage of his son to the last available Taber girl. Such was the characteristic closeness of society in that time and town. There, and therefore in the letters that follow, the word *cousin* was and is frequent, recall of kin-ties was and is detailed, and the circles that people moved in were defined not only by their wealth and employment, but also by seniority of citizenship. You could be poor but accepted in the Establishment because of your ancestors. Genealogy was more than a hobby.

That father of daughters, Pardon Taber, in the previous decade had had occasion to seize a quite different clergyman by the collar and drag him from his pulpit. Though the victim was in his seventieth year, age could not save him from rebuke for his loose habits (perhaps not *very* loose) and his Socinian principles. Taber was fined for acting as he did on the Sabbath.

The town took right religion seriously, but not all in the same form. By 1789 certain members of that same doubtful church attacked by Taber, the Baptist, had split off to form New England's first Methodist church; and in 1786 John Murray, founder of Universalism, had spoken from the Congregationists' pulpit in New London and won over certain adherents. That was in fact a return engagement. To smaller and less formal groups in other meeting places he had preached a dozen years earlier; toward the end of his life he recalled them again: "I delight to dwell upon the days I have passed in New London. Deshon, Wheat, Saltonstall, . . . Huntington, Champlin, . . . very pleasant you have been to me." All those names, not only Champl(a)ins, recur often in the correspondence; those were the days that began the conversion of an ancestor, Eliza's "dear Aunt Hannah." Looking back from 1820, it was Hannah's boast that no minister of the Universalist faith had ever passed through town without calling on her.[12]

The city took on certain formal outlines as a consequence of the formation of the Republic. It adopted a symbol for its seal, a full-rigged ship with the words above it, divided, MARE LIBERUM. Jirah Isham is seen in the correspondence below, using this device during his tenure as mayor in 1837–38.[13] The mayoralty itself had arisen from the incorporation of New London in 1784, with that office and the treasurer's enjoying indefinite terms, while others were filled annually. Guy Richards was the first and almost eternal treasurer (till 1820). The court-house, burnt, was rebuilt, and the first Federally appointed Collector of Customs, the Revolutionary war hero Jedidiah Huntington, was installed in 1789 in the Customs house. There young William Champlain, George's son and Eliza's brother, was later to serve for a good many years. He had no doubt won the job with the help of his uncle "Ebb," postmaster from 1816 to 1837.

More will be said of the setting for Eliza and her family in the twelfth chapter, below. Enough here to have shown in rapid outline how "Pequot" as it had been at first (and so announced by explorers to a region of the earth that Pequots themselves must have thought of as the Far East) turned into a settlement quite recognizable by any of us today. It had become, in the course of no more than a century or two, part of the West.

Over the same period, New London's history has served to introduce some of the Way-Champlain correspondents. Reviewing them again: they are Hannah Way baptized in 1739 into the Congregational church, John Murray who converted her to Universalism, her nephew the younger Ebenezer Way, postmaster for twenty-odd years, this latter's brother-in-law George Whitefield Champlain (Eliza's father) and in turn his son William in the Customs house, with Jirah Isham set over them all as mayor. Beyond this half-dozen whose hands we have, their relatives at different times have also appeared under the names Taber, Allen, Richards, Starr, and the elder Ebenezer Way; more remotely connected, Brewster, Seabury, Hempstead, Coit, Truman, Denison, Prentis, and Christophers. In terms of no more than this little cast of families in fact a great deal of New London's general history could be written prior to the 1790s, and much of it in their own words; for much survives from their hand quite outside of the Way-Champlain correspondence. They were all of the educated, literate elite, the directorate, as it may be called, of this second-rank eastern maritime center–a city holding, in its loose grid of a dozen streets along the shoreline, several thousand citizens and a good number of schools, churches, and public buildings.

At this point perhaps the principal personalities can be introduced in the order of their appearance in the collection, and in detail, so far as it can be recovered, beginning with Eliza's father, the writer of the earliest letters: George Whitefield Champlain. Apart from his marriage connection with the city's postmaster, something about his background is known: strongly religious, of course, as his name indicates. The preacher Whitefield had swung through town thrice, the last time in 1763, and preached in the Congregational pulpit.[14] Evidently his listeners felt his impact. At any rate, Captain Samuel Champlain and his wife named their youngest son for him. In due course, this boy like his brothers went to sea. The choice of life was inevitable, from the tradition not only of the family but of the general population, among the males of which at least a quarter were seamen.[15] First to go had been Lodowick, just old enough to command a privateer sloop in the Revolution. Some of his winnings he invested in land south of Lake Erie.[16] Then followed brother Oliver, at what date cannot be known, commanding several sloops in coastal commerce (among them, the *Juno* and *Lucy Ann*), and then owning by himself alone the brand-new *Lion* in 1802 through 1804 and the *Juno* in 1806–07, which he also commanded in the latter year.[17] It was more usual for risk in even modest vessels to be split among several investors, and to change hands from year to year or even month to month, as opportunities for freight arose.

In 1794, Oliver's youngest brother George Whitefield Champlain makes his appearance as one such part-owner and, in 1797 and again in 1800 and the next two years, as captain of the *Lucy Ann*, in 1802 leaving it for his brother's *Lion* and in 1804 commanding the same ship enlarged to a brig; at other times, commanding the *Betsey* and *Juno*; by 1807, simultaneously sole owner of this last.[18] The same four vessels appear at various moments in their lives part-owned by members of the Frink, Tracy, Douglass, and Chappell family, who pass command around as teenage brothers nowadays may share a pick-up truck. One of the Allyns commanded the *Juno* in 1801, midway in a long career at sea with many ships under him. One had been the *Thomas Pinckney* which George was glad to use for the delivery of his mail (**no. 4**); and the circle of partners to which Allyn belonged included also George Chapman whom George Champlain again uses to carry his letters home (**no. 5**), as his wife Betsey in turn uses one of the Deshons to reach *him*.[19] The Deshon family was deeply and successfully engaged in maritime commerce, and their connections can easily be shown by marriage into the families of Starr, Christophers, and so forth.

The *Betsey* that George had once captained eventually expired at sea at the ripe age of 24, with all hands aboard her; and he recounts the death of a certain Dickenson, by drowning, and of another captain's son by tropical disease (**no. 11**). All modern readers of the maritime trading records of these times are struck by the risks entailed in seafaring and the heavy loss of life, to say nothing of separation from family and the tedium of hanging about in foreign ports awaiting cargo. Well might it excuse "Father's gloom" (**no. 294**), which his children recalled to each other after his death and which hangs over his letters: "I have ever had hard fortune and what can I expect but a continuation of the same" (**no. 4**), "God!–everything is against me in this world. But I must bear it" (**no. 11**).

In the fall of 1797 he writes to his wife from New York on his way south,

Another oppertunity presents and I verry gladly embrace it, not for the variety of news, but that you may know I have not forgot you. We have not taken in any cargo as yet & I cannot tell when we will begin. There is no freight offers.

It is now Sunday morning & Capt. Deshon & myself is going to Trinity Church to hear the chime of bells there is there. I have not been away from the vessel yet, tho' Mr. Hertell has been aboard to see us & invited us up to see him. They are all well. Good morning, dear girl.

And as a postscript, referring to his two-year old George and infant Eliza,

Kiss them dear little ones ten thousand times for me. O I long to see them but when it will be, I know not. Tell them for me they have a father who will never forget them in this life nor in that which is to come. Why was I born to go to see but O God it is so.[20]

As Christmas drew near (**no. 3**) he wrote again, from Savannah,

With the greatest pleasure I embrace every oppertunity to inform you where I am and what I am about. This is the first I have had since I arived here. It is the ship *Shepherdess*, a New York & Charlestown packet. We arived here from Charlestown on the 19th after a passage of 36 hours. We are now discharging our ballast and as soon as that is over we shall overhaul the ship and take in a freight for London. I am in hopes this letter will come to hand, on account of the two I wrote you from Charlestown dated the 16th of Dec. They were both the same date. One I sent in the Brig *Thomas Pinckney*, Alexander Allyn Master, a regular packet from Charlestown to New York & from New York to New London, some times. With the letter I sent by Capt. Allyn I likewise sent one hundred & twenty hard dollars. I took his receipt to be deliver'd to you in New London. This recp't observe. I enclosed in another letter of the same date of the one I sent with the money, which was the 16th, and put it into the office to go on in the mail, but I find on enquirey that that letter which I put into the office will not arive in New London short of 20 or 22 daays, and I am in hopes this letter will come to hand, mostly on account that you may keep a look-out and not let the letter lie in the office any time after it arives. It was a gret risque to send the money by water, but I cou'd not do otherwise, for I cou'd not get a draught,. as I told you before, and therefore was oblig'd to do as I have done. God send it good luck.

I think I have given you every information about the money that is requested, therefore I will quit that subject & go upon another. In the first place, I must tell you that this is the most disagreeable place I ever was in. I can give you no idea of it, therefore I will not attempt. One thing you may think I have forgot, by not begining my letter with it, which is the letter you sent me by Peter Deshon. But know, I found him here and got it–for which I thank you ten thousand times. He had been here two days before we arived. I found several of our New London folks which came with him. Among the rest was Samuel Packwood. They were all well. There is young Girley. He talks of going with us. Wheather he will or not, I cannot tell as yet. I shou'd like for him to go verry well because he came from New London and he is a steady young fellow, and a man that I can once in a while have some conversation with, as there is no one on board that I can take any satisfaction in talking with.

O God, you cannot tell the trouble both of body and mind that I have had since I left home, and I see no prospect of any less untill I return, which will be, I hope, in May or June, perhaps longer. God only knows when we shall get away from this place. It is entirely out of my power to tell. There was a melancholy accident happened here the night before last. The Capt. of a Charlestown packet together with one or two of his passengers and some Negroes got into his boat to go a-gunning after ducks. As they were lying in the river, and wind-bound–they were bound to Charlestown–the boat was overset. The Capt., one of the passengers, & two Negroes were drowned. The Capt. lost his life in endeavouring to save the lives of the others. He had saved one or two by swiming after them, and attempted it once two often. However, he reach'd the shore, and was so beat out with swiming and so chilled with the cold that he lay down and perished upon the beach. There could be no assistance given him as the vessel had no other boat and no vessels in sight of his. The Capt.'s name was Dickenson, I believe. He was buried this day, at rest. I trust you see what accidents sailors is exposed to; but we have all the same God! . . .

I take no satisfaction in nothing nor never have since I left home. I divest myself of every-thing–I am sure, ten thousand times more than you would wish me to, were you to see me all the time. Believe me–for by Him that lives for ever and ever, I tell you the truth.

One thing I would wish to be at home for: that is, that I might have clean cloths once in a while and be comfortable. I have not had a rag washed since when I sent to you. One reason is, it is verry expensive; another is they do the cloths more hurt than good. God knows I do everything to save a penny–that is, in an honest way.

I did not think of writing so much when I sat down, but I know not when to leave off or where. That, you may see by this letter; for I have wrote the last part of it where the second part shou'd be. I hope you will read it right, if it is not wrote so.

It is now Christmas eve, and I do not expect to have any thing much better for dinner than I had last, when I was on an allowance at sea. But never mind, if you have any thing good I will content myself. Give the little ones something for my share. I long to see you all. So, good night, except of my best love to you and ours, remember me to my dear mother, sisters and brothers, father and aunts, tell them I want to see them all–Polly and Phebe into the bargain. Good night.

I remain, dear girl, your affectionate,

G. W. Champlain

P.S. This is the 19th letter I have wrote since I left home.

And again a fortnight later (**no. 4**), before leaving for London, with worried mentions of his letters that may have gone astray (as in fact most did), and special mention of the money he had sent,

> Beyond my expectation, another favourable oppertunity present itself, which is the sloop *William*, Capt. Geo. Champman, bound from this port to New York, & perhaps from thence to New London. If not, he will forward this by the first oppertunity.
>
> Be assured, the only satisfaction I take or have taken since I left New London is in writing to you. The trouble I have met with this voige is inexpressable. For God sake, let me mention one circumstance that has happened not two minutes past. As I was writing this letter, a large rat came down the cabin stairs &, wheather through fear or what, I cannot say, but he made towards me as fast as he cou'd and run up under my pea jacket as if he was going to take hold of my throat. But as soon as he had got up as high as my breast, I squeez'd him so hard with my arm against my brest that I kill'd him. I was a little startled at it but not so much as to drop my pen, for I still kept that in my right hand, all the engagement. Out of curiosity I have this moment been and measured him before a half dozen men, & he measured exactly nineteen inches from the end of his nose to the tip of his tail. It is really the biggest rat I ever saw in my life, and so they all say who has seen it. But he has lost his life–therefore eternal silence be his doom. This engagement is over, therefore I shall procede with my letter.
>
> As I observ'd before, I never met with so much trouble in my life, and I see no diminution of it before me. There is a report in circulation here that France has declar'd war with America. It is believ'd by a great many, but I hope it is not so; for we are a-going right in the way of them, and I expect no other than to be taken, if it is so. And the first of a war is the worst time to be taken. But my trust is in God. I have ever had hard fortune and what can I expect but a continuation of the same. But I rely on God's goodness to restore me again to them that is most dear to me.
>
> [I]t wou'd afford me the utmost satisfaction to have a line from you, cost what it would, for I desire greatly to hear from home and how you all do–especially my little birds. It is impossible to tell you how much I long to see them. It seems as if I had been a year from home when it is no more than four months this day; but I hope it will not be above five or six months more before I see home, if no accident happens–which may God avert.
>
> Time hangs heavy upon one where he can have no satisfaction–no society, nothing but the old story over again, which is to sit smoking in a gloomy cabin, and nothing to be heard but the noise of the rats, which, to be sure, is not so agreeable as some other music. But I bear up under my troubles, tryals, and tribulations with a Christian fortitude, I think. I thank Almighty God for giving me my health so well as I have had it since I left home, and shall continue to pray that I may still preserve it. I have been more unwell since I arived in Savannah than I have all the voige before, but I have never been so as to lie by, thank God, and at present I feel verry well. It is not unhealthy here at present.

I hardly know what to say next, for I assure you I have almost run aground. O that I had Lydia's tongue that never fails. I would fill a quire of paper. But it is not my good fortune.

More delays, and then (**no. 5**) toward the middle of February departure is certain:

In my last which was dated the 4th inst., I told you we expected to sail in the course of five days, but we have not, as appears by this letter, the reason of which is, we cou'd not get ready. But we are entirely full at present, & have been this three days. Nevertheless, we expect to sail tomorrow or next day at fartherest, wind and weather permiting. To tell you the truth, I am heart-broken with this place & have pray'd ever since I have been hear to get away from it. For never was there a place on earth that was so disagreeable to me, & everything else that I see & hear on board is the same: the man that I am with is the most disagreeable one I ever knew since I drew breath. But, as I told you before, it is impossible for me to give you any idea of the troubles I have met with this voige untill I give it you by word of mouth, which I hope to in the course of four months, God willing. If it was not for the hope of seeing home once more, I shou'd pray that this day might be my last. But as Pope says, 'Hope springs eternal in the human breast'.

Then, close to the beginning of April 1798, and close to the port intended, Champlain's ship was intercepted by exactly what he had feared, a French privateer, and taken into Bordeaux. He had feared this might happen because the threat was on a grand scale and well advertised: over a hundred American vessels sitting in detention in this port at the very time he set sail for the south and then for the east, to Europe; previous to his setting out, several years of noisy complaint and litigation, diplomatic appeal and posturing, about the Quasi-War; and fresher to memory, in the spring of the year he left, report to Congress of hundreds of cases of "spoliations and maltreatment of [U.S.] vessels at sea by French ships of war and privateers," in the words of the Secretary of State.[21] They were widely published. The costs to American trading ships inadvertently involved in the hostilities between Great Britain and France since 1793 should have deterred anyone from venturing into the waters off France, or England, too, for that matter, so long as the war lasted. But, as George Champlain reminded himself, "Hope springs eternal." So he and many others took the risk.

When his ship was seized, he wrote to his brother Oliver who he knew was in Paris, and who replied promptly (**no. 6**) to "le Citoyen G. W. Champlain, in the care of Mess.rs Gray & Hoskins, Rue Cornac No. 5, Bordeaux–Paris 29 Germinal 6 year, 18 April."

My dear Brother,

Mr. Bradbury's favour of the 13 ins't with a line inclosed from you is this moment come to hand. It makes me very unhappy, dear George, to hear you are unfortunate. I don't mind your imprisonment so much because am well assured it is only momentary. If you have property on board the ship, which expect is the case,

I fear it will be very difficult to recover. On reciving your letter I went immediately to Mr. Thos. Paine who is my friend & who is intimate with the government here. He has advised me not to take any measures about your liberation, as he has no doubt but that you would be out if not already, before a letter can go from here to Bordeaux, but should it not be the case, be assured I shall not rest till you are at liberty. Mr. Paine has offered his services. You will not fail to write me every post.

My affairs here will not permitte me to leave Paris as have every-thing depending & my presence is absolutely indispensable, for I do not know if I am worth five pounds in this part of the world–have this very day been laying attachments on the property of a person who is indebted to me thirty-six thousand livres. But it is very uncertain if I ever recover the debt as there is many creditors.

I have taken it extremely kind of Mr. Bradbury, the attention he has paid to you. You must keep up good spirits & try to live comfortable what time you are in prison. Use as much oeconomy as your prudence may dictate, for believe me, Brother, our poor countrymen here are all poverty-struck. For my own part, I have had no money these five months but what have been borrowed of my friends & should I not recover what is due to me here, shall be ruined entirely; but while have a shilling, my dear fellow, you shall be heartily wellcome to the half of it. If I get my money I mean to come to Bordeaux & no doubt I shall be able to do somthing that you may find advantageous to yourself; but you will observe on what all this depends. Write me fully what your situation is. Don't spare pen, ink & paper while your in prison, for it will serve to keep you alive.

Here is another letter handed me from my worthy friend Mr Putnam, who has likewise been kind enough to offer you his services.

Well, dear George, it is comfortable to have friends & I hope you will believe me yours,

O. Champlain

George Champlain wasted no time in passing on the bad news also to his wife at home (**no. 7**), writing in mid-April,

Dear Betsey,

Haveing an opportunity of sending you a line, I verry gladly embrace it. On the 25th of last March we were captur'd by a French privateer and brought in here for trial. On our arrival here we were put in prison where we remain'd eight or nine days and then examin'd by our Consul, Joseph Fenwick, & taken out. How long the ship will be on trial I cannot tell.

Neither can I tell you when I shall be at home. I have found several gentlemen who was verry well acquainted with my brother Oliver. He still resides in Parris. I have sent him two letters desireing him to come and see me, or send me something to subsist upon. I expect an answer in the course of three or four days. One of the two gentlemen was kind enough to advance me some money on my brother's account, or I know not what I should have done, as my adventure is taken from me.

Oppertunitys is scarce to come to America. I expect to embrace the first one that offers. Was it not for the hopes of seeing you and my dear little ones again, I should die, for my heart is broken. I met with Capt. James Peters here, of New London, who has been verry kind to me and serv'd me in every thing he was able. This letter I shall give into his care. He takes passage in the ship *Alexander Hamilton* of Baltimore. I can write you nothing more at present, for I hope to bring the next letter my-self.

Remember me to my dear little ones as well as yourself. I long to sea you all. My love to my dear Mother & Father and all our aunts and all inquiring friends. I greatly desire to see you all.

This from your affectionate husband,
Geo. W. Champlain

When next Oliver heard from his brother in early May (**no. 8**) the situation had changed almost completely:

My dear Brother,

I have this moment rec'd yours of the 30th April by the hand of Capt. Earl. I have been on board his ship these too days expecting to go down the river, but the tides are so low that we have been disappointed and are likely to be detain'd here five or six days longer on that account. We are at present about six miles below Bordeaux and we are waiting for the moveing of the waters to procede on our passage. As I told you in my last, I was going to take passage with this Capt. Believe me, dear Brother, it grieves me to the heart to think I must go away from the country without seeing you, but so it is. Necessity compels me to do it. Believe me, it would afford me pleasure inexpressible to shake a fist with you. But we must dispense with it this time, for I see no way, and my family calls my assistance at home. Was it not for that, be assur'd I should have seen you before this time. . . .

Believe me, dear Brother, your train of misfortunes has dam[pened] my spirits to that degree that I hardly know how to get over it; but as I am well persuaded your spirits are superior to any of your kind, I hope they will not be so depress'd, but that you can rouse them again and try for another. Fortune always favours the brave. Would to God we had made our voige here that I might have had time enough to have communicated every-thing I wish to tell you, every circumstance concerning our family; but it is otherwise, and it cannot be help'd. As for our ship and cargo, there seems to be but verry little hopes of recovering, and if ever, it is not likely it will be this some time; and for the reason, the Consul and the Capt. judges it best for me to go back again to America. This is all I can tell you concerning that affair.

My oldest child is a boy and one of the most finish'd pieces of clay you ever set eyes on–is nam'd after you. It is not only I that says so but everybody that sees it. The other is a girl–is nam'd Eliza–is not flesh and blood, one would think, to see her, she is so much like the angels that we hear tell of. Excuse my extravagance of speech, but really they are two beautiful children. You accuse me of negligence in not writing to you oftener. I think I can with the greatest propriety return the insult–if I may be allow'd the expression–and tell you that this is only the third letter which I have rec'd from you, and this is my sixth which I have sent you. Nothing further at present. Adieu, dear Brother.

On his return home, George Whitefield Champlain's fortunes remained dark, watery, and star-crossed. The final letter from his hand (**no. 11**) finds him nearly a year later at Port Royal in Jamaica, now a mere mate or owner's agent under a captain who drinks too much; himself, in a postscript, down with dysentery:

Dear Betsey,

Since the last I wrote you, which was from Antigua, I have seen nothing but trouble in every shape, and increasing every day. We ariv'd here the 12th of this month [April 1799] and have not had any orders to discharge as yet. When we shall God only knows. The Capt. has been at the point of death since he has been here but has recover'd and has this day gone up to Kingstown. This is the second time he has been brought to death's door since he has been in the West Indias–once in Martinico and once in this place. The fever rages terribly in Kingstown at preasant. Capt. White who formerly liv'd in New London is out here in a ship. His son which was an only child came his mate. He was taken sick since we ar[ri]ved here and liv'd but four days–a heavy stroke to his parents. There is so much trouble of every kind, and death before my eyes, that it seems hard to tell which one had better choose; but yet I would wish to live for the sake of –– and my dear little ones, whom I long to see more than tongue can express. I try to put you all out of my thoughts as much as possible, for were I to give loose to them I shou'd be ten times more wretched than I am, if possible, at present. I have had my health tollerably well since I left home, thank God, and so has the rest of our crew.

There is an American arm'd ship ariv'd here, sent in by the *Surprise*, a British frigat. This American had an engagement with a French privateer. The privateer took her. As soon as the Frenchmen came on board the ship, they murdered three of the Americans and throw'd them over-board. Soon after, this frigat hove in sight and took all the Americans & then took the privateer. They put the murderers in irons immediately and have them on board the frigat at present–all the news I have.

I have not sold any-thing as yet. We lie seven miles from the town of Kingstown. The markets is not so good here as they were at the Windward Islands. Of course I cannot expect to do so well. But Good!–every-thing is against me in this world. But I must bear it. We expect to go from this to the Havannah, which is worse than all. Would to God I could tell you all I know, what I think, &c; but I know not whose hands this may fall into. Therefore shall not attempt. But my letter from Antigua may give you a hint of what I mean.

I am not the same as I used to be. I am quite unman'd. My spirits are low. I think of ten thousand things in a minute. Blast all, I'll say no more.

P.S. Please to remember me to my dear little children. Likewise my dear mother and all our friends and relations–

Remember your friend who has ever been true & faithful in every sence of the word from our first acquaintance. I [know] not what to write nor how to address myself. . . .

His circumstances did improve, though the correspondence does not show just how. There is no reason to think it was through any other form of endeavor than in the past, that is, seafaring. His ownership of another vessel by 1807, the quite substantial eighty-one-ton *Juno*, suggests some little prosperity; but when he retired from the sea at a date unknown, eventually requiring a cane to lean on, he lacked the means for any ease of life, and his need for family was perhaps never assuaged. During his long absences from wife and children they had grown used to getting along without him, and he figures almost never in their letters or, perhaps, in their thoughts; so his settled gloom may be to that extent explained. When he writes to his eldest son away in New Orleans, he reports on his condition darkly: "I was sensibly affected," the son writes back, "at the gloomy forebodings which Father expressed relative to the state of his system. But I fear it is more of a mental than a corporeal malady."[22]

In his late forties his gloom is broken into by the irresistible high spirits of his wife, who describes his whistling and dancing as best he could in accompaniment to her practice; and he tried his hand at some musical instrument, too. There is a joke about it in a letter addressed to him from abroad by an old pal, a Connecticutter, who sheds light on other corners of his character as well–one, well suited to his ready quoting from Pope.[23]

> Dear Friend,
>
> After a passage of 23 days [to Liverpool] and the most pleasant, to, that was ever made over the Atlantic, I find myself safely landed in his Majesties dominions and am now about [to] acknowedge the rec't of the kind & entertaining letter which you favored me with a little before I sailed for the land of our forefathers. I shall leave this place in two or three days for London. I shall not at this time [make] my discourse lengthy, as our great lexicographer of Yale has it. I must not forget, however, to tell you how much pleasure your letter affords me, as I there heard my learned friend speak in his own language and gave me strength to the recollection of the many intellectual feasts which we enjoied in our favored country (New England, I mean); for, since I left the land of steady habits I have found no substitute for our cofee discourses on antient & modern litterature, arts & sciences, & when we made poets, heros, and demigods wince under the [?]wiring thong of our criticism. I am glad to hear of the peace of your dwelling & that there has been no pulling of caps; but don't be too nice about caps if you can save your hair. I yet hope the time will come when I can join you in the concert you mentioned. It is a comfort to me to see that you have chosen the instrument from among the righteous, whereby I perceive that the natural force of your piety is not abated; but, considering your great theological knowledge & Old Testament learning, I wonder you did not mention the trumpet & Jews' harp–the only lawful music of our pious Plymouth ancestors.

Still only forty-eight, George Whitefield Champlain died (1820) after a lingering slide into worse and worse health, leaving his wife with very little except debts.[24]

2

Mary Way

Like her husband George Champlain, Betsey (formally "Elizabeth") and her sister Mary Way were born New Londoners–Mary, the older by two years (1769), then came Betsey. Their father was a store-keeper, under a grander term a merchant. His wife died soon after Betsey was born, and he turned to a female relative to help in the upbringing of his children. After a dozen years as a widower he took a second wife. She bore him two boys, one named after him, the "Ebb" of this correspondence, and then Thomas. She herself was later remembered by Betsey as "that imperious step-dame [who] ruled with despotic sway at the old mansion." Of the girls' growing up, nothing is known beyond their learning to sing in school together.[1]

In due course arriving at an age to marry, Mary Way never did so. How then to support herself? The character that emerges amply from her letters could not abide dependence and inertia. Still, it was not easy for a single woman to live independently. She had only her skill with the needle and then with the brush. In combination, however, they produced what have been called "dressed miniatures," tiny portraits in profile, of which the face and hair are painted on paper and the clothing of the subject is cut out like dolls' from various materials, stitched and glued in place, and touched here and there with a painted highlight or detail. She was not the inventor of this art, but very few attempts before or after her seem to exist, and the total of thirty-six surviving that may be reasonably attributed to her hand command the field.

It was a quite little field, to be sure: limited to a clientele of New London and neighboring towns, especially Norwich. She abandoned it after twelve or fifteen years of practice. Yet the total of this work, aside from the few hundred dollars it brought in, is worth a moment's attention.[2]

Dozens of her sitters have a name, their apparent age and their known dates can be fitted together, and their portraits themselves can thus be approximately placed in time. They belong, all but the first and last two, to the 1790s. Earliest of the surviving must be Polly Carew (Pl. 1.1).[3] In her portrait, both drawing and technique are more primitive than in any of the later ones, and recall another early work by Mary Way now at the Metropolitan Museum in New York, datable to about 1795. A descendant of the sitter shown in this latter portrait places her in New London, where in fact the great majority of Mary Way's identifiable customers resided.[4] Among them, Pardon Taber the elder is only the most explicit: her grandfather. He remembered her and Betsey Way Champlain in his will. Others by name Truman and Devotion, Huntington and Colfax, can be tied in to the several families (Kin-charts A-B) to which the two sisters of the brush were connected by descent or marriage. If there were any further doubt, we have, scrawled awkwardly on the back of one portrait of the 1790s (Fig. 2), in an inscription written over by afterthought, Mary Way's name and that of "Mrs Lizy Champ[lain]," Betsey's mother-in-law.[5] Still another of the dressed miniatures, a particularly fine one, has her business card as backing: "Mary Way fecit, New London Feb. 18th 1800." Charles Holt is the sitter. Set in a survey of her oeuvre, a superb, greatly magnified photograph along with a life-sized one were offered by William L. Warren in the *Antiques* magazine of 1992, making it less necessary to show off this painting (Pl. 2.7) on any larger scale than I do.[6] Of slightly later date is a very similar, striking, and mature piece in profile showing his cousin Giles Holt, born in 1783. His looks and costume belong to the early 1800s (Pl. 2.8).[7] He and Charles were related to Mary through their grandmother Sarah Way Holt.

Figure 2. "Mrs. Lizy Champlain"

The better-documented portraits, of Polly Carew and the Holts, enclose the others about which less is known, and help to explain the whole series. Mary can be seen commencing her career before she was twenty and continuing it in a defined style, though indeed a confined one also, within her small town and within the circle of her own acquaintance or family.

An early commencement to her painting fits with two slightly larger works which, from the costume and fashion of wearing the hair, seem to belong to roughly 1790. These, however, are conventional watercolors, not "dressed."[8] They show a very elderly couple identifiable on the back and in other records as the Perkins of Norwich, and serve as a reminder that Mary could provide her customers with more than one kind of portrait.

Her next step, taken in the spring of 1809, was to advertise the setting up of a school in which she taught "painting, tambour, embroidery, lace work on muslin, reading, writing, plain sewing, &c &c." Students might board there, too, with Frances Seabury–who more respectable than this latter woman, the Episcopal minister's wife, the bishop's daughter-in-law, and quite incidentally Mary Way's coeval and cousin? But there was, alas, another school advertising the identical range of subjects to be taught by another woman, in the same issue of the same paper, and others in the recent past that had disappeared, presumably failed; so whatever business there might be in New London, Mary Way would not have it to herself.[9]

It might be wondered why she did not instead set up as a portraitist in more conventional and better-paid media. Was she not good enough? Claims for her skills can be easily tested, for example, against Anson Dickinson's (1779–1852). Here was a major miniaturist of the time, with whose work, however, some of hers may be compared very much on a level; as also, with those of other fairly well known miniaturists.[10] But New London was not Boston or Baltimore, with any broad moneyed class; nor, as Ebenezer's daughter, would it have been possible for her to raise her charges and pretend she was a really famous artist like Dickinson. Accordingly, before the summer of 1811 was over, she had made her decision: at an age past forty and with only Charles Holt to receive her in New York, where he now lived, she would try her luck in a larger world.[11]

In situations similar to hers, other artists moved about to other markets. Not only were meaner talents than Mary Way's, or the quite primitive, hawked from place to place; but the very best were forced to do the same. Their works were then displayed as specimens to likely customers; ads were hung in the ground-floor window of this or that lodging, or appeared in the local paper, promising, as an instance, "the most striking likenesses," by a portraitist lodging in the Way house in 1797; or in New York, no less than Anson Dickinson's talents for sale; or again, the news that "P. Parisen, miniature painter, will continue for a short time to take likenesses, finely painted, on moderate terms"–this, by the man who painted Edward Riley in New York some years before Riley's marriage to Eliza Champlain (Pl. 8.18).[12] He raised enough business to justify a second ad next month, and then once more on his return to the city four years later. It is not known where he had traveled in the interim. For such as he, subjects must be sought over a range from Atlanta to Montreal. Even those unlucky artists who had families had to move about periodically in Mary's day.

The problem was an economic one, of course, but also a matter of the market's percipience. Americans in the early Republic were so scattered about in such small centers, where any at all existed, and were by the standards of Paris or London so rural in character and so little cultivated, that high art could not look for high rewards. At least, they were exceedingly rare in the period to which Mary was born, and became more accessible only as the next century went on–even then, only in a few of the largest, most educated centers. On the other hand, clearly there was some sort of demand, if not for the little jewels that were so enormously valued in Europe by European artists, then at least on a lower level of artistic discrimination and moved by those most irresistible of impulses: love and pride.

People wanted to show off to their relatives a picture of their new spouse or little child, like the girl in Plate 1.1 or the two- or three-year old on an ivory precisely one inch high, most likely done by Elizabeth Champlain (Pl. 1.2).[13] They wanted to remember a parent or grandparent, and even had portraits made of the deceased stretched out on his or her very deathbed.[14] Their correspondence often refers to such business. Self-love, too, played its part: the young wished to be remembered at every moment of the day by their betrothed;[15] they wanted to celebrate their marriage by paired portraits; and, as appears in many comments exchanged among the sisters of the brush, and most clearly of all in a poem by Elizabeth Champlain (**no. 59**), sitters of all ages hoped to be shown, and forever fixed in memory, as they almost were or almost had been–recognizable, but artfully improved.

Until photography entered on the scene, then, in 1839, a range of human reasons for commemoration thus relied on miniatures. They were given as presents or displayed everywhere, and moved a market of every social and economic level.[16]

Plate 1.2, however, has introduced a very different art from that of Mary Way's "dressed" efforts. However skillful she had become on paper, by the turn of the century, she appears not yet to have ventured on the normal medium for ambitious miniature portraiture: that is, ivory.[17] Proof lies in a letter from her step-brother Ebb in February of 1811 (**no. 14**), in which he thanks her for specimens of her work she had sent him.

> The paintings, though you say they are not your best performance, have received more praise than is in my power to describe from every one to whom I have shewn them, among which are many of taste and judgement. You say, had I named some particular piece to you, I might have been better satisfied, but be assured I know of no fancy piece that could have given me more pleasure & none in which you could have had your work shew to better advantage, considering its being on paper. I have seen many miniature paintings both on ivory & paper since I have been at this place, but they were all miserably done, and for those done on ivory, they pay twenty dollars.

How was she to prepare herself in this far better remunerated medium? About the special methods she would have to learn, there were introductory and advanced manuals, then, as there are descriptions today, calling miniature painting on ivory "one of the most exacting techniques ever devised."[18] Its difficulties were not what one might expect: the extraordinary fineness of the detail and of the brush that must be used (called a "pencil"). To these, artists in oil on canvas, copper, or wooden panels had become accustomed according to a tradition reaching back some centuries, in Flanders or elsewhere. No, it was rather the devilish slippery surface and the translucence, opalescence, luminosity, call it whatever the critics wished, inherent in the support itself on which the paint was laid; and that quality could not be denied, it must rather be brought out and made a working part of the total effect. Betsey Champlain called it "reflection-painting" (**no. 59**). To illustrate the nature of a sheet of ivory, no more than three or four times the thickness of this paper, consider a painting shown in a later chapter (Pl. 4.12, below), where she has applied colors to portions of the back in order to reinforce those of the front clear through the ivory (Pl. 1.3). The same device appears less strikingly on the back of an elderly woman's portrait, one of a pair (Captain Pardon and Amy Taber) of 1817–19 by Mary Way and again, by artistic reflex, perhaps, even on the back of a watercolor on paper (Fig. 5).[19] Any such effect would be lost wherever opaque colors were applied; so water-based materials had to be used in all or most areas, and somehow made to stick, and not to fade (which they were specially liable to do). And, rather than all-over, paint had to be applied discontinuously in thin lines or dots, hatching or stippling.

Ordinarily, this art was learned only because it was taught. That might happen at home, if the home belonged to one of the Peale family. Anna, James' daughter and Charles Willson's niece, is only one case in point (her cousin Titian Ramsay, who did miniatures among other things, by coincidence married the sister-in-law to Eliza Champlain's daughter).[20] All the Peale's, as is well known but never-endingly remarkable, were talented artists down through the third generation and beyond. It was easy and natural for them to take up painting while they were still children, and they all did so. In contrast, and with few exceptions, men and women who were determined on a career in art but lacked any close kin to lead them into it had to resort to some professional in his studio, under whom they could serve an apprenticeship or, more often, from whom they could take lessons.

To explain the latter process, Alexander Robertson in New York may serve as well as anyone on Mary Way's horizon. He had emigrated from Scotland with his brother Archibald (leaving a third Robertson to paint at home). Together in 1791 they had opened the Columbian Academy in Painting. Archibald had published a highly successful art-manual in 1802, the first serious attempt at exposition of this sort in America, destined for many subsequent editions, and in 1808 his treatise specifically on miniature painting was widely circulated among the interested of the city. All three Robertsons often showed their work in the annual exhibitions at the American Academy of Fine Arts from the year these commenced, in 1816, until the end of their separate careers in the 1820s and 1830s. Side by side with his own work, over the years 1819–27, Alexander like many other artists showed the work of his pupils, too: mostly "young ladies"–one of them Ellen Tooker, in 1821, who went on to study with Mary Way's niece Eliza. Finally, it was common also for established practitioners like the Robertsons to show off such pieces as they might own by still better, often "classical," artists like Ruysdael, or dubious Rembrandts, or copies of Titian, which they lent to the Academy's exhibitions and offered to pupils in their studios as models and inspiration.[21] Such were the various means by which a person in Mary's time and place might learn what painting was.

Academy exhibitions and manuals were of course generally available to the public, but more focused instruction could only be commanded by money, which she lacked; and there was the additional obstacle of her sex. It was one thing for young ladies to take lessons in self-improvement and cultivation; quite another, for a middle-aged unknown to set up as a professional in the face of competition by Dickinson or the Robertsons. A visitor thinking to learn from one of the latter was put off by his pomposity: "a proud conceited *huff*; teaches by copying prints &c in water colours. This method may please young misses but can never make an eminent painter." The writer scorns their sex. And elsewhere and at a slightly later date, a woman portraitist recalls how her earliest customers "entered my 'sanctum' with eager looks, to see whither–'a woman *could* paint a likeness?' "[22] But indeed, outside of the Peale family and earlier than Mary Way, it is not easy to instance a single American painter of any consequence or success who was a woman. Through her life and the forty or so known pieces from her hand, to say nothing of the hundreds unidentified, Mary Way must be considered the young Republic's first female professional.

Greatly against the odds, whatever she achieved. Still further: she was from Connecticut, that little farming- and sailoring-state. Where was the cachet in Connecticut, to be set against a painter like "Parisen," also spelled "Parisien," or Louis-Antoine Collas? Or against John Ramage from Ireland or the Robertsons from Scotland, not to mention various others of some fame like John Jarvis from England, the homeland to which the most ambitious of American artists needed to repair, like Benjamin West, to raise their skills and repute and perhaps their very selves, as high as *Sir* Benjamin.[23] It was common knowledge that America by itself could produce nothing of value in the arts. As cause or consequence, "American painters recieve so little encouragement," Eliza was to complain a few years later (**no. 81**). "Anything which comes from abroad is all the rage, while native talent is supposed to live and die in obscurity."

Nevertheless there appeared in five December issues of 1811, in the city's newspaper *The Columbian* (owned and run by that family friend of the Ways and Champlains, Charles Holt) as in the *New York Evening Post* through February of the next year, her comprehensive advertisement of "Mary Way, portrait and miniature painter from New-London, Connecticut. Takes likenesses upon ivory or glass in colors or gold, landscapes or views of country seats, &c &c. Paintings not approved may be returned without charge at her painting room, No. 95 Greenwich-Street, where specimens of her performance may be seen and the prices made known. Hours of attendance from 11 o'clock till 3."

She can only recently have gained enough mastery over the conventional media to claim them as her own. Her show-off pieces only nine months earlier were still on paper (above). Nor is anything at all known about her "landscapes," except two of New London and its harbor done before she left her home (**nos. 100** and **120**). Perhaps, then, she was a little bold in the assertion of her talents; yet on the other hand those talents must be plain to anyone who looks at her work today; so why should they not have been plain and reassuring to herself? Indeed, she declares as much in the letter to be quoted next. She followed up her ad with listings in the city's directory (mostly for businesses) as "Way Miss ladies' drawing school 32 Williams" (1814–15), calling it in 1816–17 a "drawing academy" to make it sound a little classier, eventually expanding it to the form "ladies' drawing academy and miniature painting, 98 Chatham" (1817–19), and, near the end of her career, simply as "ladies' miniature painting, 57 Chatham" (1819–20). By then (1818) she had shown a "Portrait of a Gentleman" and "A Child" in the annual exhibition of the Academy.[24] Her business card while she was living at 98 Chatham with her friends the Fitches, that is, in 1817–18, proclaimed her a "portrait & miniature painter. Drawing taught." She was using the card as backing to her pieces, a purpose it serves for the portrait of the man of Plate 2.9. He makes one of a pair with the elderly woman mentioned above. Judging from its text, Mary's teaching at the end was taking second place in her professional life; yet she still took pupils.[25]

The progress of her professional development can thus be followed through the public record in print. Her aspirations rose and, as will be seen, so did her reputation. But from this same period in New York there also survive three certain examples of what she could do on ivory: the pair of portraits just referred to, her Taber cousins; and, closely resembling the latter of these in the appearance of the sitter, in technique, and in date, a portrait come down as Mary, the wife of Charles Holt.[26] For technical sophistication and sensitivity to character, these three pieces approach the best of American miniature portraiture on ivory at its height, that is, during Mary Way's own later years of work and the ensuing decade or so.

Her letters, it will be seen, present her as a success in her profession. There is, however, an outside opinion beyond that of the Academy, and slightly earlier. We have the diary of a very considerable artist, Ethan Greenwood, socially known to the best of Boston and beyond, numbering the cream of the eastern Republic among his sitters, and in every respect a serious and successful professional. In the spring of 1817 he took a great swing from Boston down to Washington, Baltimore, Philadelphia, and other points along the way, gathering commissions and talking to the local talent. On his way home he determined to spend three days in New York: "Devoted myself to see & examine everything related to the fine arts & called at a number of print shops & gilders, called on Jarvis the painter. Called on other painters. On the 25th [March] I was introduced to Dickinson the miniature painter.

Called on Vanderlin & had a long talk about the arts. 27th. Called on Miss Way, miniature painter."[27] We may judge from these notes of his that he sought her out as one of the painter-elite.

Only two words at this point should be added to explain, first, what success meant in money-terms, and second, to explain whom she got help from.

As to her profits from painting: those grander half-life-size or larger oil paintings on canvas by acknowledged masters fetched $50 or more; by competent unknowns, $12 and up; but miniatures by the absolutely best of the time, only $25–50, while Mary Way charged $6–10, occasionally $20. Her niece when in New York seems regularly to have charged the former price, a few years later; but both niece and sister in New London sold their work for far less while their materials cost them just as much: there, frames and ivory ate up a tenth to a third of their profits.[28]

So: in New York could you produce enough to live on? Evidently–but it was an anxious business and you couldn't count on getting rich. Certain details will emerge, below, among them, the length of time needed to do, or repeatedly re-do, difficult pieces,[29] or unremunerated repairs and updating of past miniatures.[30] We learn of Mary's going sometimes without a customer for two or three months (**no. 85**), Eliza's advertisements still less responded to, later, and her conclusion quoted above, that "the city [is] overrun with artists."

Mary Way in her choice of what to offer her customers followed the conventions of the time, including occasional "fancy" paintings, as they were called, of an allegorical and didactic sort: *Friendship* and *Amabilité* (**nos. 21** and **46**), *Christ Healing the Blind* (**no. 19**), and the flower-nymph *Clytie* (**no. 100**). For the most part, however, she depended on portraiture: friends and kin like the Tabers, two generations of them, the family Holt, Anna Fitch, Mrs. Northam, John Sistare of New London, and a scattering of others.[31] From all nine of her New York years, however, no more than a score of identifiable pieces! Hardly enough to pay the rent. We have too little information to go on, to attempt any inventory of Mary's oeuvre, therefore too little to explain her finances. Perhaps twenty-five or thirty commissions a year would have sufficed for a modest livelihood, added to what her teaching brought in. The itinerant miniaturist Ruth Bascom averaged forty a year over her long career, but hers were only profiles on paper; Anna Peale managed more than that, oils on canvas as well as miniatures; but she simply painted when she felt like it, not only when she was asked.[32]

Given the difficulty in making a living with a brush and the jostling competition of too many artists in New York, it is surprising how generously Mary Way was taken in and helped by the fraternity, as it was: all male. Foremost she mentions Williams, that is no doubt William Joseph Williams (1759–1823).[33] He knew miniature painting as well as portraiture on a conventional scale, he knew the city as his birthplace and again as his residence for a decade in his later career; and he had wide experience in the American art community. She mentions Joseph Wood and John Jarvis, too, both very distinguished miniaturists, though not only that; and in later letters her friendly acquaintance with Dickinson and Waldo appears (**no. 85**).

Of these two men, the former has been mentioned; and as to Samuel Waldo, he too made a name for himself. He had set up his studio in the city only two years before her arrival, after his studies in Europe, but was to become one of the founding members of the Academy. On first sight of his work, Charles Willson Peale judged him the best portraitist at work in the city, and sought him out.[34] Waldo was to prove a benefactor to both Mary and her niece. The latter named one of her children after him.

Despite the kindness of such individuals, however, looking back, Mary could call herself her own creation: "I know much may be learnt by study, observation and practice, without the aid of a teacher" (**no. 155**).

Such was the scene of art in which she had to make her way. Naturally she reported on her progress to her home and kept her sister abreast of what was happening; but her letters were few and unsatisfactory, about which Betsey Way Champlain complained (while also getting Mary to do her art-supply shopping for her). Eventually Mary made amends with a very long account (**nos. 16–17**) written about two years after her arrival and in her most characteristic tone, the didactic; but the greater part is in fact teaching from another artist, author of the book she quotes so liberally: John Payne's *Art of Painting in Miniature, on Ivory*, in one of its earlier editions:[35]

> I sat down now 'in pretty good earnest' to write that wisdom-giving letter (as you call it) or chapter upon painting, tho' I am utterly at a loss where to begin. The first idea that obtrudes itself, is what I have endured in obtaining the vast fund of knowledge I am about to communicate. But of this you know nothing, and care less. Let me tell you, however, three times a day upon your marrow bones you have reason to be thankful you are in New London. There you are Painter General, and after you have taken a good likeness and are sure the outline is correct, the worst is over. You can then set down in peace and comfort and finish it as you please, in your own stile and manner, and no one to say you nay. Far differently situated is your poor sister. The evils I apprehended when I came to New York was debt and a prison, poverty and disgrace its inseparable attendant. The dread of connoisseurs never once enter'd my imagination. This was in some measure owing to vanity, or that self-conceit which you know is a family disorder, as well as to my ignorance of the art, having had no opportunity to study the works of other painters. I had seen but few equal, and none superior to my own–concluding therefore I had nearly arrived at perfection, [I] very modestly set myself down a first rate genius.
>
> Of course I felt no reluctance to enter the lists with Wood, who, from what I had heard and seen, I considered the only painter here worth notice. As soon as I was announced by my advertisements, I found myself surrounded by painters, engravers, critics, and connoisseurs in every shape and form, who flock'd in from all quarters to spy out my liberties and judge of my pretentions, examin my works, question me respecting the course of my studies and mode of practice, to approve and to condemn. They talk'd of painting as a science, a sistem of practical philos-

ophy, founded upon the study of nature; nor would they allow it was possible to paint anything naturaly or as it should be, unless you knew the philosophy of it and understood the nature of things, could trace effects to their cause and tell what occasion'd its appearance, particularly in the doctrine of lights and shades, colouring, &c.

I thought my time was come; and what confounded me the more, they talked in Greek and Latten or which is the same thing, a language I did not understand. There was the dimey [=demi]-tint, the half tint, the local tint, the opposing tint, the harmonizing tint, with ten thousand more tints too numerous to mention, and all I know of the matter was simply this: the meaning of tint was colour. But what the colours were or where they should be apply'd, was far beyond my ken. In the midst of this distress and perplexity, I had the address to conceal my ignorance and preserve appearances, upon which I knew everything depended. This, however, could not have been done for any length of time if I had not had the good fortune to meet with Mr. Williams, to whom, as I told you, I inadvertantly exposed my ignorance in the theory of the art. He had the goodness to assist me in my studies, furnish me with books, and give me instruction, by which I so well profited that I soon began, not only to understand thier language but to see the truth and propriety of thier reasoning, and was as much astonish'd as Williams, when I considered how I had blundered along in ignorance and blindness all my days, that I had hit so near the mark.

One circumstance, however, I must not omit to mention, as it served greatly to facilitate my improvement. When I first arrived here, I found hanging in one of my chambers those three wonderful paintings of [a distant Taber relative] William Saltonstall's, of which you have undoubtedly heard. He requested I would give them house room till he could dispose of them to advantage; and he could not have confer'd on me a greater favour. These superb paintings were Scripture pieces, done by the famous Rubens, painted on copper a yard and a half square, the figures half a yard in length. But I shall not attempt a description, as my feeble pen can never do them justice. Here was an ample field for criticism. The connoisseurs were never satisfide with viewing them, and from thier observation, I gathered much useful information. In the spring they were placed for sale in a picture store in Broadway, and the price affixt was fifteen hundred apiece. These, I had the advantage of studying six months day and night, in which time I may safely say I made greater improvement. and gained more knowledge of the true principles of the art, than I should, had I staid at home, in fifty years.[36]

But to impart this same knowledge in writing is no easy matter, and I hardly know myself how to set about it. I have also conversed much with all the painters upon the subject, particularly Wood, who has show'd and told me his stile and manner and lent me a book of rules which he approves and practises. From this I shall make a few extracts; but, in the first place, I must inform you the gloss or varnish that Palmer told you he made use of for his pictures is neither more nor less than gum [arabic] water, in which he disolves a large proportion of sugar candy–

more than the rule, which is only one third, but not so much as to make it sticky when dry. With this he floats on his colours, draperys, backgrounds and frequently his complexion, or part of it, as far as is convenient, after which he shades it with *handling* as its call'd–what we call touching or specking. He says he floats it on in this manner to give the softness and delicacy, and prevent that dry, hard appearance it is otherwise apt to have.

The book says as follows: 'There are four' modes of working 'in miniature painting, namely, floating on, washing-in, handling, and marking. The first process which is floating and is chiefly used for draperies and backgrounds, is thus performed. Having mark'd . . . ' the outline of your drapery, mix your colour, not puting so much gum water as would make it shine, as that would frustrate your purpose. Lay 'your ivory on a level table, fill a large pencil plentifully with the colour, and lay it quick over all parts of the ivory you want cover'd, seeing it runs on every part equally–which, if in a proper fluid state, it will readily do.' When dry, 'you will have a fine level surface, ready to work the shadows of your drapery. . . . Washing-in is performed when your picture is on your desk, by filling your pencil moderately with colour and giving a very broad stroke, rather faintly, as the contrary would not answer. This manner is chiefly used in begining the hair, backgrounds, and likewise in laying on the general flesh tint of the face. It is also used in the first touches of the dark shadows, which ought to be laid on faint and broad. Handling is the manner in which all the fleshy parts of the miniature must be worked after the first washing-in. And, lastly, marking consists in the sharp-spirited touches given to the different features, in order to give that animated appearance so necessary to constitute a fine picture.' It is to be observed in all painting in water colours, ivory, vellum and paper. Transparent colours only must be used for the flesh, and for draperies, opaque, or body colours, as they set off each other. Uniting them in the same place improves the appearance of both. In all cloth draperies for men's portraits, it is necessary to add some flake white, as it not only gives the colour that dead appearance which cloth exhibits, but likewise gives it body, which makes the flesh tints appear to more advantage.

The next thing to be observed is, in mixing 'your draperies, you are to make them appear several degrees lighter in colour than you want them to be when dry, for this reason–the flake white is a colour so heavy that, after you float on your coat, it will sink to the bottom and leave your colour several degrees darker than when it was wet; and finaly, . . . you are not to' mix your colours 'too thick and heavy in floating on your draperies, but merely to see it is evenly spread over the parts. . . . '

In the next place, the light is to be considered. The painters here will have but one, and that a high light. Wood closes the lower casement with the shutter. Of course, the light strikes with most force upon the temple or side of the forehead which projects most as the head is a little turned. Next, it falls upon the cheek bone under the eye, where a delicate shade tint begins, almost imperceptable, losing the light by degrees towards the lower part of the face. Thus says the book. . . .

And Mary Way now transcribes more of Payne's work which of course was not available in New London, and which need not be repeated here, in a part dealing with the depiction of the sitter's personality. She continues:

> Now, sister, comes the most important of all considerations, without a true knowledge and understanding of which, painting is but daubing, in the eye of a connoisseur–be the likeness ever so good and the colours laid on ever so nice, not worth notice, or serve, as they say, to make the faults still more conspicuous. 'Tis call'd the art of colouring or the doctrine of lights and shade. I write this more for Eliza sake than yours, for tho' you may be too old or too wise to learn, she is not, and if she mind her hits and begins at the right end, she may excell both her mother and her teacher. I therefore earnestly request her to study it, get it by rote, so she can repeat it, and she will sooner or later understand it, tho' she may not at first perfectly comprehend it all. When I return, I can give her any explanation she may require; but to do it in writing is rather tedious and perhaps not quite so intelligible.

Here Payne is quoted on the fact and consequence of light picking up color as it is reflected off colored objects, adding that reflected effect to whatever it then next touches. Once again, the text need not be repeated, except to notice Mary's emphasis added to Payne's words. He says,

> 'There are two manners of colouring, the one depending on habit, the other on the true knowledge of colours. The first is confined, the second unlimited.' 'Tis the first, sister, that we have have always practiced but have just begun to expand. You must alow me to put in a word edgeways, now and then. But to return–and to what is coming I desire you will pay particular attention: 'The harmony of nature in her colours arises from objects participating of one another by reflection, for there is no light which does not strike some body, nor is there any enlighten'd body which does not reflect its light and colour at the same time. . . . '
>
> Now if all this is Greek and Latten to you as it was to me at first, you must not only cry over it, but study it out as I did. 'And where's the profit of this dry study,' says I to Williams, as he was endeavouring to expound and explain the matter to my comprehension. 'Is not the effect sufficient, without bothering ourselves about the cause?' 'The reason is because we do not see them. Without a true knowledge of colours it is impossible for us to disern the beauty and harmony of nature. We see the most glowing colours; but the thousand nice gradations, soft tones and delicate tints escape our observation because we are ignorant they exist.' This I know is true by experience. I once saw a rose painted by an artist, a bunch of green leaves directly under it. It looked beautifuly natural and I copy'd it. I knew not then it was reflection. We do not look for red in green and so we do not see it; but it is surely there, as that the red is near it.
>
> Another thing, sister, in which we have always err'd, shading with the same colour, that is, light red with deep red, light blue with deep blue, and so on. Many a lecture I received from Williams because, as he said, I was loath to soil my beautiful

colours with black, which is darkness, and the proper colour for a shadow. Certain it is, all colours are brightest in the light; ours on the contrary are brightest in the shade and fade away as they approach the light, in direct opposition to nature. The rules [of Payne] say, 'Where the light recedes in the smallest degree, the shade begins, and part of the colour is lost, and a tint is formed, composed of darkness and the colour of the body; and in those places where the light passes totally, because it cannot touch them, it would leave the body quite black if there were no light scatter'd in the air and if the body did not receive any other reflection. Light–this light of reflection–will be tinged either with the colour of the body or of that which causes the reflection, mixed with its own colour, and with the colour of the light. The deepest shades ought to be the colour of the tint of the general harmony, because it is supposed that the air is already tinged with this variety of tints very nearly of the same tone, employed in the same figure and often upon the same part, with moderation, contribute much to harmony. The apparent value of colours in a picture (as in all things) arises from comparison. Several colours which, placed unmixed by each other, have a kind of aerial brightness but when mixed together produce a dull earthy colour–for instance, fine blue with vermilion–or bright green with lake or carmine–colours which by mixture lose strength–become harmonious and are call'd broken colours. These contribute as greatly to the sweetness and softness of tones in pictures as they subtract from thier brightness.' Harmony, accords, tones &c–I suppose you understand. They are musical terms, and apply'd to painting because music and painting are sister arts founded upon the selfsame principles, the colours in a picture, like the notes in a piece of music, should so exactly accord, as to present to the eye that perfect harmony musick conveys to the ear. I remember an observation of yours with which I was much pleased, and have often thought of it since. You may perhaps recollect it. One evening when we were at singing school they was singing a remarkably fine tune with which we was both delighted. You whispered to me, 'How beautifully that tune is shaded,' I thought the remark very juditious, and certain it is, there is a great similarity between music and painting in that respect. Those paintings of Rubens is done in this masterly style: the sweetness of tone is not to be described. Well he understood the doctrine of lights and reflections. Tho' his colours are the most glowing and briliant, they are far from glaring, so compleatly are they softened, mix'd, blended, and as it were melted into each other, as to produce the most perfect harmony. This is what the connoisseurs call the true balance of colours, where no one is alowed to predominate. If one glares, it offends the eye, like a note in musick strain'd higher than the rest. It makes a discord and produces an unpleasant effect. In painting the Holt family piece, I determin'd not to fail in this respect. Accordingly I laid on the reflection with a trowel. The white draperies, arms, face &c next the crimson sopha appear a bright rose colour. The twins who were dresst in scarlet stand near thier brother, and a warm reflection from the colour appears on his dark green drapery. The dark colours cause a shade, and so on, according to the different situations and points of light in which they are placed. These rules are to be duly observed as well in the flesh as in the draperies, which is more or less affected according to the force, strength, and disposition, or situation, of the colours, in point of light, that are placed near it. The most natural shades for the face are purples, blues, and greys, especialy for a delicate complexion. These, however, should be warm'd, more or less, as occasion may require with red browns and yellows, such as burnt umber, burnt terra sienna (which is an excelent colour, inclining more to the orange) or raw terra sienna, which is a deep or what they call a warm yellow; or gamboge mixed with a little carmine will answer for a substitute. But the thousand different tints that are necessary for the face, tis tedious to describe, and the object before you is the best direction.

I will, however, just mention some shade tints, from the book, that I find are most approved and practiced by the painters here. 'Of grey tints there are various kinds, according to the subjects they are required for–a warm grey tint may be made by a due proportion of burnt terra sienna, prussian blue and lake, the more terra sienna the warmer the tint, the more blue and lake the colder. Another grey tint used with success by some eminent miniature painters is composed of prussian blue and vermilion, but it requires a larger proportion of gum than ordinary to make them work well.' Wood is fond of this tint and does plentifully in it. I had observed it in his work, but knew not how it was form'd, and used black with vermilion, which is nearly the same colour, tho' I think not quite so good.

'A third grey tint, which is an excelent one, is form'd of lake, sap green, and prussian blue.' When I first mixed this colour I thought it was black, but when I came to examin it and use it, I found it a much more delicate and proper colour for shades. I don't know as you have any sap green. I will send you a piece, 'tis much used by the painters in the flesh tints. 'A beautifull hair colour, either dark or light according to the quantity of the colours, is made of carmine, lampblack and sap green. The manner of forming it is only to be acquired by practice, but when once attain'd will be found well worth the trouble. That very difficult tint which is often to be met with in children's hair, by the proper junction of these three colours, will be produced to perfection. Some excelent painters make all thier hair tints of burnt terra sienna, lampblack and yellow ochre, the latter being added only when there is light wanted. Burnt amber is a substitute for terra sienna, but care must be taken to avoid the redish cast that it is apt to produce. In painting the face of your picture, observe as a general rule, that it is much easier to warm the shade tints than to cool them–therefore, best to begin with cool greys and purples, and toward the finishing of the picture add the warmth which is necessary to produce the [tin]t of nature.'

It may now perhaps be necessary to explain the terms warm and cold as it respects colours. Yellow, orange, [?]violet, browns, are call'd warm colours, and all the rest–crimson, purple, blue, green and black–are cold. For background there is no particular rules. I have questioned the painters who say it depends intirely on the complexion, colour of the hair, and drapery, to which the background must be suited, but as the use and design of backgrounds in miniature generaly speaking is merely to set off the face and figure to advantage, of course the less showing the better. Jarvis says, in viewing a picture, the background should not be noticed–that is, never be seen or observed till it is look'd for.

To suit the background to the picture exactly requires not only taste and judgement but a true knowledge of the nature of colours. The pearl shade takes it name from colours, which is the same we see in pearl, a very faint blue and red. 'Tis nothing more than the reflection of crimson drapery upon a delicate complexion. The light strikes upon the crimson, which reflects its colour upon the shaded side of the complexion. The red is the reflection, the blue is the shade. You will see it to perfection in N. Payne's picture, on the child's arm and leg next the mother's red drapery. Observe, reflections are always upon the shady side, and more preceptable when the face happens to be against something dark. Then you must have observe[d] a light struck just upon the outline where we once used to make it darkest. This proceeds either from the rays of light scatter'd in the room or from some object on which the light strikes, or (to use a painter term) from some enlighten'd body. If this body has a colour, the colour is seen in the reflection; if not, it shew only the colour of the complexion mixed with that of the light, which, if clear, is slightly tinged with yellow, which is the first degree of colour.

I shall make but one observation more at present, and my pen is so bad I shall not be able to write that intelligably. 'Tis this. Hard lines is always to be avoided in painting. They are much disapproved by connoisseurs. They say there is no such thing as a line in nature. If we examin criticaly we shall find the smallest that can possibly be imagin'd has its shade and reflection, like the colours in the rainbow, mixed and blended with that which is nearest. Of course, the outline should not appear, but be lost, and as it were melted into the background.

If my husband could make a pen as well as yours, I'd keep him at it, and consider my poor neighbors. I've turned and twisted mine every way, hindside before and upside down. 'Tis the best I have, and about as good as a rusty nail, with which I have murder'd out this letter so far, after a fashion; but shall write no more till I have a new recruit.

These thundering rents and winters' wood keeps me in terror all the time, but, poor as I am, I will enclose fourpence half-penny which is all the cash I have to spare at present, for Sam to buy some quills, and get his father, master, or Uncle Tom to make the pens, some time or other. I hope it will be in my power to reward him for his trouble, and all the rest of you. I am sorry to say it is not at present. Send them the first opportunity, if you ever want, wish or desire to hear from me. . . .

I set right about making the two frames you sent for, work'd all day and all night, and have just now compleated them. I have lost the larger circle you sent. I think, however, this is near the size. If it should not fit, it will do for some-one else, and I will make another. I will have more made against the next opportunity. I think I shall be able to supply you with frames at the old price, that is, if it don't cost all nature to get the glass cut and frames made. I brought a number with me which I shall make up first.

One must pay here for every-thing thro' the nose. Wallnut wood is four dollars a load, and not such loads as you have there by one third. I bought an indifferent load of oak yesterday for three. You that have got your winter's wood laid in, and your rent paid (as you inform'd me some time ago) must, I think, feel very comfortable; but your rent is nothing. To be obliged to lug out forty-five dollars ever three months, business or no business, is not a very pleasant consideration, and keeps one in a quandary, as it were, all the while. No need to think of washing to make you sober. I have just been obliged to scrape togather all I could muster for this purpose. Of course I am rather low in cash at present, as my poor fourpence half-penny can witness–except one pair of shoes, not a single cent have I laid out for wearables since I've been here. But this is a secret. Should the world know my prudence and economy, I should lose my credit intirely.

Adieu.

You can't [say] I never direct my *longwinders* to you.

Send back my towel.

3

Elizabeth Way Champlain

By the age at which Mary Way had begun her professional career, so had her younger sister, Betsey, that is, early in the 1790s. We need to suppose so in order to explain Betsey's attainments by 1799, indicated in two letters from John Murray. He was the Universalist minister. First, in February after his return home to Boston from an evangelical visit to New York and points south, he wrote to her Aunt Hannah and the family. His tone is homiletic, perhaps the only tone he knew; but his concern was not spiritual:[1]

> I told you I would write to you on my arrival. It is with pleasure I perform my promise. I know it will give you, every one of you, sincere pleasure to know that, except a cold that had me in the pulpit of Providence meeting-house, from which I have suffered ever since, I got home well, and am as well as ever. I expect to be in this state of things, but there is an other and a better state to which I am hasting. There, well as I am here, I expect to be better, in mind, in body, and estate. Yes, in mind, for my mind will never *there* be plagued with any-thing that will war against the law of it. In my body–yes, in my body, for we are told there is a spiritual body which never be afflicted with pain or disorder of any kind. And in estate, for there we shall be rich, infinitely rich, and what the rich in this state of being never are, we shall be happy–so that, tho' I feel myself beyond the power of calculation indebted to infinite goodness for an immense ballance of *good* in my account thro' life, yet on the whole I frequently look forward with delight to my journey's end.
>
> I am sure it will give every one of you much pleasure to know that I found Mrs. M. and her little girl in good health and, consequent on my return, in good spirits. They are both beyond measure delighted with the likeness Mrs. Champlin took of me. Mrs. Murray thinks that this alone is sufficient compensation for the toils of the journey. She wishes Mrs. Champlin was here, or she and her little girl there, that our little daughter may be taken also; and I wish Mrs. Champlin was here that she may take the mother also. I think it would be a good thing for Mrs. Champlin

to come and spend some time in our house. I have no doubt but she would find her account in it, and she may rest assured of finding from each of a sincere and hearty welcome. These, my dear friends, are not words of course, in the mere complimentary stile. I am persuaded it would be for her advantage, and I wish—we both wish—her to make the experiment. Let me here from you, and tell me she will come.

My society I found rejoiced to see me, but their patience almost exhausted. Mr. B[allou][2] has made much mischief, I will not say by design. I regret that he is not a Scripture Christian and that he is not taught of God. I am greived to find him too proud to submit to the teaching of the spirit that dictated the Gospels and Apostles what they wrote. I am greived to find him destitute of the principle that a Christian cannot live without. In fine, I am both greived and disappointed to find a deceitful Deist where I expected a sincere Christian. I should be comparatively happy never to hear any-thing more of him in his present character, but I fear he will go on deceiving many under the character of a Christian Universalist, and, in the judgement of strangers, one with me.

I pray God to bless you, each of you, by enabling you to hold fast the profession of your faith without wavering. A little while and faith will be swallowed up in full fruition, and we shall be for ever with the Lord. Now is our salvation from sin and sorrow nearer than when we first believed.

Many changes has taken place with us since we first injoyed together the delight attendant on receiving the truth in the love of it. A little while, and one change more will take place that will put us beyond the power of any change that will, or can be, for our disadvantage.

I am not able to say whether I shall ever again be blest with the privilege of seeing you again in this changing state, but I rest in the assurance of seeing you in the mansion prepared for you in our Father's house, where, I make no doubt, are as many mansions as there will be beatified spirits called home there. I trust you will meet each of your dear departed friendly connections, never more to suffer the pain of parting. There in your house, built by your heavenly Father, which you will never see in a mouldering or decaying state, you will injoy the felicity of security, no untoward circumstances ever depriving you of it. Let your poor dear mother remember this, and comfort one another with these reflections, with the assurance that they are real.

Mrs. Murray joins me in love to each of you, and we hope Mrs. Champlin will seriously reflect on what I mention'd, and we wish, if her good man ever comes to Boston, he would let us see him as much as possible.

There at the end is the reason for the letter: the application of Betsey's talents to his own family. But after a few months for her reflection, and no results, Mr. Murray thought best to write her direct, with an even more specific request:[3]

I wish, my dear child, that I had, when I saw you, thought of what I am going to mention to you now. I want to send my mother [in London, John Murray's birthplace] my miniature. This I have is so well liked by Mrs. M. and every acquaintance that I am not permitted to part with it; yet they think it would be still better if it was not quite so good. I believe everyone thinks, with me–tho' some few only say with me–that it is too young and the lips is very little too far out. If you can add a little to my age and take a very little from my mouth, I think you would gain a little more fame still, tho' every body owns it is an astonishing effort of genius.

I have been looking out for a person to send this by hand, and with it the money and a frame to put it in, but I have not yet succeeded, and, fearing that I shall not have it in time to go with the London vessel, I send this by post, requesting you to let me have it as soon as possible. If you know or can hear of any body coming to Boston that you can put confidence in immediately, request such person to call on me for the frame, and if you cannot, as soon as possible send me the picture, as mine was before I returned from [New] York, and I will have it put in the frame here. But send it so as it will come safe, and soon, I intreat you. My mother is old and cannot wait long, and now I have got the notion of sending this resemblance of her son, I am impatient till she has it; and indeed, if you knew how much I suffer every moment while I am writing from pain occasioned by a very large abcess under my arm, which I have been suffering from this nine weeks, you would readily suppose I am impatient to have it. I beg therefore you will let me have it as soon as you possibly can, that I may avail myself of the opportunity of sending it on by a friend going to London.

And he concludes with affectionate wishes to old Mr. Way, to George Champlain, and to the children George and Eliza. His hopes for a second portrait were only to be realized posthumously.[4]

Betsey's painting of other sitters continued, at what rate appears in a tribute from a much later New Londoner,[5] finding "some of the old mansions of the town [still] rich in miniature & others in oil-paintings of the ladies of the period–refined, sweet faces set off by elaborate coiffures & great ruffs. The miniatures painted by Mrs. Champlain at the beginning of this [nineteenth] century, in especial, those of the Coit sisters, have a delicacy of treatment & a purity of sentiment peculiarly suited to the fair young faces of her sitters" (the Coits being, as one might have guessed, her relatives, though distant ones).[6] There is mention of her male sitters, too, from 1811–1812, including her distant kinsman Captain Jared Starr;[7] and Mary Way refers to Betsey's being "Painter General" in their home town (above); but subsequently, nothing on Betsey as an artist till 1816.

Then, on some summer day with leisure for a long effort, and evidently under the spell of the family's favorite Lawrence Sterne, she writes the following to her sister in New York. It is her earliest surviving letter, beginning with some paragraphs of tomfoolery and family news, before eventually turning to her own painting as a business:[8]

I strained my fine-spun nerves when I gave my oration upon your Ladyship's parts, clapping my hand upon my forhead with a significant air of importance, by way of collecting my soaring immagination, as I have observ'd fools, to signify all was not right within, and relieve thier scatter'd senses from the intricate mazes of high-wrought fancy–but shall now exercise (when I come down again) my serious faculties, aray'd in all my native charms of original ignorance and genuine simplicity, and address you in the under-brush stile of home-spun matter, disrob'd of the gorgeous mantle of divine sublimity which flows so gracefully around the parts whose refulgent rays reflect too powerfull for common genious to survive the brilliant dazzle of thier beams or fathom the depth of thier center.

In hoc vocus mutae quae in nulla alia editone hujus. Why don't you cry, you fool, don't you hear my Latin. You see I have rub'd my peticoat against the College, if not against a zealot's brains. Cry louder, Phebe, sufficient for me to hear you. Ah! I talk to the winds. They hear not, answer not–and none so deaf as them that will not hear. Come, Hercules, give us another hoist, if I am not allready out of your reach; for I have got stuck a second time. I have been so long up in my balloon, am in danger of breaking my neck down by too sudden a transition, therefore will slide gently along by a gradual descent. No fear but I shall touch bottom, if you give me time, but must drive you all away while I clamber over the wall, as I don't wish to come down with a jouse and shew my legs. No doubt you see my difficulty. The ropes of my veicle is rather beyond my reach, nor am I as well skill'd in the management of them, being but a raw hand, as Cousin Jess,[9] who once had a design upon my life. And, unless the law is repeal'd or a new one enacted, one may swing for taking the life of a cousin, as well as that of a sister. But I fortunately liv'd through the surfeit, and thanks to the Way blood and strength of constitution that enabled me––

'A fool, she don't understand a word of her [lin]go,' says Congress [=Aunt Hannah]. 'The complement is poorer than the parts, if she thinks so.' 'Tis true, the wind was high–I believe south-east, which involuntarily carried my airy machine rather beyond its limits. But excuse, since conclude it was in persuit of my feather (which will serve for a bore for ages) and is the only two things that accord that is in posession of a poor body. I think the burlesque indifferent good–tollerable applicable, but shall renew my wrench if you escape with life. If I don't desist, take off my top-knots, and descend to my own rank and level. I wish I was down, for I feel like a sailor on horseback, but don't see but I am making speedy work of it. Well, and here I am, safe and sound in wing and limb. Well, Poll [Mary Way], how do you do?–or don't you recognize my features in this home-spun garb. 'Oh! yes says Poll, better than ever.' Now do you see we can shake hands and squeeze heartily without the sublime viel which so disvigur'd me?

We are all pretty well, and Aunt Hannah is the most understanding woman in the world, especially in politicks, and not a grain nor morsel more childish than I am myself. She is making flowers every day after frying pan-cakes is over, the frolick, and she's got a dollar's worth of pork–good pork, too, of Brooks–and a whole liver. But to please her, wish you could help her to more, for as the eye is never satisfied with seeing, so is her mark never cloy'd of her greatest luxury, and the old black hen

> lays an egg in her lap every day, sometimes two, and then she's got the garden dug, or will by fall, and–that is if she can muster rage enough to raise the ready; and she's got good black snuff, and yellow too, and eats a rye gingerbread every night to keep her from fainting away; and got good pig-tail tobacco, and–besides having a clash with Miss Love every day. As you know, after all the variety of good things, clashing upon the affairs of state is the desert, and makes Miss Love shut up her clam shell in a trice, and–and–I wish I was as happy as she–and if pork and politicks was as much my hobby, should be–
>
> 'What an eternal tongue,' says Poll. Well, I shall keep it going, Latemore. 'What a diuc'd sister,' says you again, 'that will not give me time to breathe, imposing such a task that breaks in on my retirement in vollys every trip.' You cannot get rid of my peals– No easier than we once could shake off Palking Pinker, who, upon the excellent quallity of his fowls &c, who wore the skin from the bone in order to prevail with us, in direct opposition to the consent of our purse, . . . was in comparison quite comprehensive, energetick, and interesting–if your cause in evading me proceeds from what you would insinuate, that your cunning fit too seldom comes on (which if I should wait upon, should remain hush-mouth'd, as I am not subject to fits of that description, and am very seldom attack'd)–What do you do with your numerous corespondents whose consequence I should sopose required as severe fits as your sister, who, I can tell you, holds herself in as high estimation as any of the society? And what friend will prop our heads for us, if we are dispos'd to loll them? So far from any such assistance am I, that I have to hold the heads of a number, as well as my own, as erect as my *languid state will admit*.

And at this point, having tried her best to raise the ghost of Tristram Shandy, Betsey turns to a new item of costume just acquired, which lasted her for years and fulfilled all ambition for elegance; for, at the opening of the century, "fancy feathers, particularly the imitation of the Indian plume, were very popular";[10]

> Well, I have worn my feather, and the effect was evident that it had upon the multitudes. The doors and windows were full of heads 'as I did march along,' rank above rank as at a theatre. Some stood wondering, aghast; others observed that the Greens and Hubbards had come; others, that it was a family of the Mohawks, whose husband was an Indian chief; others, that it was a Jewish family in whose train there was one Genteel, and my complexion favouring the report passes currant. And in my evening walks, slow moving to catch the sound of various whispering tongues, through the soft breeze of gentle zephers that play around my nodding plume whose elegance is much enhanced by the full moon's silver rays, striking her modest lustre upon its thousand particles of purest white–among which is (perhaps) the adder's hiss of rankling envy, whose envenom'd tongue, tip't in gall, pours forth her blasting breath that poisons all the scene–but blesst independance that gives me power to pass undaunted by the babbled throng of base and little minds that conscious worth disdains to stoop to hear, and smiles at all thier rancour. Jemmy Lee–you see, I have perus'd Jemmy and Nancy–and old Blue Beard I have by heart, though never see

the cork-skrew––I like a party-colour'd composition, tho' varied and animated by flights of folly, and should be a greater admirer of Heresy, was there not such a sameness in his lines.

But here, having done with the one work of Sterne, Betsey now inserts an anecdote or vignette in the spirit of the *Sentimental Journey*:

Rural Sports

I could not help smiling this morning, though at the expence of ignorance, which by right should only be wink'd at. I sit alone, musing over my paint desk, w[hen] a violent rap roused me from the dull reverie in which I was wholly en[gaged] and made me start a sphere above my station. I answered according to the ancient custom . . . , when a buxom country dutchess, who I should say was as coarse as three threads to an armfull, made her appearance, with all the rural importance attendant upon country refinement–who, from eating of her golden butter, made her cheeks to glow and out-blush (mine excepted) the deepest tints of the cherry or pianny [=peony], snapping her whip in my eyes, demanded to know if I would purchase of her some 'new, sweet, charming butter, as nicely churn'd, she'd warrant it, and as clean, as any of the folkses out our way; and axt but a shilling.' I observ'd by way of banter, if she would take her likeness for some, we would barter. She came sideling up to me, excusing how dirty she was, but came just as she [. . .], which I perceived. 'Why, the dear sees me, what are you doing?', and as was a very [. . .] answer, return'd, 'My business;' and with an awkward curtsey, seem'd to be very desirous I would show her some specimens. Ever willing to oblige, I gratified her Ladyship. 'Dear sees me, for the massy sake alive, how *naatural* they look, for all the world just like folks. What is the name o'these things?' I return'd, likenesses. 'Well now, as sartin as this world, I would buy one if I durst.' I endeavoured with all the skill I was mistress of to make her understand the design, but found my labour in vain. She obstinately persisted in her former state of ignorance, and instantly, with all the fury of a tigress, thrust a fist into my draw[er], no way remarkable for its smallness or delicasy of form–as I should judge, would outweigh a common shoulder of mutton–and without the slightest warning to His Honour or myself grab'd *Nelson* (who in future I shall call Adonis, as he came very near sharing the same fate–who, you recollect, was kill'd by a wild boar) by the hair I had newly dress'd, and totally discompos'd his fine white tresses that added such grace to his manly beauty, unmercifully dragging him like a criminal before the bar of justice. But he, proving himself the gentleman and perfect master of etiquette and decorum, being posess'd of an uncommon share of heorick fortitude consistant with the carracter of a warrior, smil'd in the midst of danger and suffer'd all the indignities of the bitches love pats without a word of reply. I instantly, taking upon myself the arduous task of a surgion, play'd his part with such dexterity and success (stopping the blood with my hankerchief) that he surviv'd the shock with only the loss of his hair and one of his ears; but he won't take upon himself a new carracter and be aprehended for a counterfeit. I made use of all my skill to erase the impression made by the greasy thumb and finger of the dairy maid, and after a few days was tolerably recover'd. It has, however, left his Honour in delicate health, which I am fearful will eventually terminate in a [?]Hic Pic. But to gaurd against a future relapse, shall close my draw[er] against rustic curiosity.

Another funny apearance has come under my inspection of late; but to skreen myself from the carracter of a patter I shall give the name in blank. –, a form alltogeather disgusting, whose eyes, sufficiently projecting to hang a cat upon–but fortunately could neither of them look toward you, which greatly relieves the bystanders–one much larger than its partner, looking steadfastly yonder, the other's attention was call'd off equally ernest in an opposite direction. I made a lower obescience than common out of pure fear. Whose form, so extremely corpulent as scarse a common cloaths-line could, without being stretch'd, make both ends meet around it, and am certain if he should go off, which his appearance seem'd to threaten every moment, you would hear the report and think the Regulars has come–but notwithstanding, report says he is an unexceptionable carracter and stuff'd with honourable parts–tho' from his looks should judge his honourable parts were stuff't.–Throng after throng flies to me for protection of the outcasts of nature, the scum and offscouring of humanity, thinking that my representing them in a favourable light will prevent them from frighting people to death–and meet, too, with very good success, for I would out-lie his Satonick Majesty's self for a cent, in the way of my duty. . . .

I receiv'd your *runt* by the hand of Capt. Denison, wherein you inform me of an oportunity for George to make his fortune. True, to view only the bright side of the piece, appears dazzling. But let me state the case including all the disadvantages that must inevitably be attach'd to such an undertaking: youth, inexperience, and an abundant share of curiosity–which of course would send him to the theatre every night–as also a more populace city which would afford more room for acquaintance, public amousements, and disapation, being free from any master, head or guide which he would consider had any right to inspect his liberties. Not that he has every given me any reason to suspect he is tinctur'd with said difficulties more than any other lad of his years. But ever anxious for his welfare, should not dare to lay temptation in his way.

Betsey Champlain's most characteristic concerns here emerge in this earliest surviving of her letters. First in her mind were her children, of whom only George was as yet out of his teens. All four needed a start in life but not necessarily one of such hazard as awaited them in New York–where of course Mary saw only the promise. Beyond family concerns, there were also the artistic, concentrated in Betsey's business. Portraiture finds some mention in most letters she wrote, if only through her asking her New York correspondents for the paints, ivory, frames, pith and paper that New London never could supply. But literature and music, too, were important in her life. As will be evident, they turn up throughout her corrrespondence, sometimes woven together, as the "fancy" piece *Lord Nelson* appeared casually in the "rural" anecdote, just above. Here, too, may be the best point at which to introduce, a little out of chronological sequence (in fact, belonging to 1819), another of Betsey's efforts at literary imitation, this one likewise taking art as its material or occasion. Her model is the fourth canto of Pope's *Rape of the Lock*, perhaps, or less probably his *1738 Dialogue* II, or Swift's *Verses* on his own death. In any case, classical satire, under the title *On flattery* (here condensed by a good half):[11]

O flattery, how sweet thy healing breath!
  Our love of thee is constant–lasts till death.
All other passions weakens by degrees.
  'Tis thou and thou alone a word can please.
At thy sacred shrine the mitred head low bow.
  Thy magic altar witnesses our vow.
To thee, unrivaled power, we'er beggars born.
  Thy charity inspires e'en hope forlorn.
All court thy favour; at thy feet we sue.
  Who reigns without a foe on earth–but you?
Each other's weakness we with hawk's eye see
  But in our perfect selves find no debility.
A connoisseur I stile myself–and why,
  My benefit is reared upon a lie.
Shew man his real self–where's my resource?
  Returned upon my hands (you know) of course.
Vanity's a general weakness, this I know.
  My heart as well as others tell me so–
Or why this boasting? when I dare assert
  That from the expression can define the heart,
And what the eye by dint of art conceals,
  The nose or mouth with eloquence reveals.
Reader, excuse my satyr, for if they
  Would let me draw them in thier natural way
And prove my skill in the strong marks of age,
  Nor shew a rose bud crawling off the stage,
Then would the artist high my work approve,
  My fame in lofty sphere by merit move.
A lady sits who boast angelic mien.
  She'd have me take her (at the most) fifteen.
Her face she dreams is full. Mistake–'tis thin
  And scarcely held together by the skin.
Her dimples into wrinkles long's been turned
  And nose and chin inseparably curled.

Her elevated shoulder begs the graceful slope.
  Each day's experience proves the words of Pope.
The terms are flown, yet thier amount may see
  Enveloped all in self-pleased vanity.
What does this frosty headed class demand?
  My guilty pencil trembles in my hand.
Where lies my help? A beauty must be made.
  Poor I confirm that time dare never fade.
You are my match–asside–my forehead beat,
  Conclude my patient's–say–is fifty-eight. . . .
Dare I what sits before me ever draw,
  And make the truth my firm established law,
The low'ring brow contract, as nature meant,
  And give each furrow and each deep indent,
How easy were my means of living gained.
  But they the cash detain, were nothing feigned.
Avaunt! my delicate and silly fears,
  Since every touch must bury thirteen years.
They teach my pencil falsehood, and they learn
  Thier graces long entombed in age's urn
Comes forth new cast as purest calcined ore,
  And grants them charms they never claimed before.
The hint is given–received. From fancy's eye
  Produce a Venus, they gobble down the lie.
To hear one fish for flattery: 'I declare
  I'm freckled so from riding, I shan't dare
To appear this eve at such a splendid ball!
  I do not know myself, indeed, at all.
And tan'd so brown–O bless me, what a pickle!
  Yet I must go, or the Esquire will call me fickle.
I know he'l say 'tis caprice. I don't care.
  I may by evening light appear more fair.
Dear Mrs. C–n, I must beg your brush
  To spare my tan and freckles. Lend a flush,
And let your goodness show me what I was.
  My complexion's bright–'tis [?]blouzing is the cause.
I never saw a freckle on my skin.
  My viel of Brussel's lace, so flimsy thin–
'Tis quite a shame. The price should make it fine.
  I feel so vexed, I wish 'twas coarse as twine.
'Tis one my brother purchased when at Rome.
  O frightful! How I wish I was at home!'
Thinks I to myself, I wish you was, and I

Had got my pay in my own custody.
This is Sir Isaac Newton's stile and matter.
For half a day they keep up such a clatter.
Various sensations does such scenes excite–
From deep disgust, the resistless smile invite.
The husband's ushered, introduced, sits down;
Bears marks of age, some wit, and some the clown.
'This mark upon my chin–careless mishap,
Betty this morn in pinning on my cap–
You will omit, Madame. Sad affair.'
The spouse replies, 'My dear, 'twas allways there.'
'Now Fred, upon my word, I'm sure it never–'
'Why, Jane, you must forget.' 'Now, did you ever!
If you lie so, I'll bring you out. Last night
You ne'er came home till just at morning light.'
'We went by water, and the wind came round
And from necessity, lay in the Sound.'
'You would excuse yourself;' and this I thought:
Had you not this, some other must have sought.
'No matter now, my dear. We'l end the fray
Some other time; for you must sit today.
Will Mrs. C–n dare to take my phiz?'
'A pretty one,' the wife replies, 'it is!'
I could not crowd an answer edge-ways here
For hosts of tongues that rattled on my ear. . . .

At the time of this poem, the winter of 1818–19, Betsey's portraits from life which she describes made up the bulk of her painting. She could reach up to Mary Perkins (**no. 172**, of 1824, the year before Betsey's death) as she had to Captain Starr, earlier. These were of New London's bluest blood or highest aristocracy, and presumably paid according to their rank and wealth. Even higher, she got Commodore Perry's brother Nathaniel as a customer, in 1822 (**no. 131**). That was because of his local connections.[12] From casual mentions in the correspondence a somewhat fuller list of her sitters can be compiled than for her sister, but her complaint of "difficulty with as many as six of my last front faces," of whom she names only one, serves as a reminder of the size of her business. The complaint is incidentally contradicted by her results, so far as we may judge from the one work surviving, unidentified of the late teens of the century (Pl. 3.10).[13] When she was less busy, she took on sitters for love or practise: her husband in his declining years, herself at Mary's request (but never finished: Pl. 3.11).

By contrast, her fancy pieces like the *Nelson* mentioned in the first of her letters quoted above, along with her *Lafayette* (**no. 168**), served for advertisement as much as for sale; and she did others surviving only as titles: a *Creation*, a *Hebe*, and a *Happy Father*.[14] She never finished her *Christ Rejected* (Pl. 4.12), taken after the central figures in Dunlap's painting (Pl. 4.13). That huge, splendid, famous canvas had swung through town in 1822. The story of its visit belongs to a letter given in its proper place, but Betsey's copy better fits with the present sketch of her professional life. It may be compared with the original to show what she did with the subject before her: she compressed, focused, and within the tiny surface of the ivory, dramatized. Emended, too (for in the original the central figure is lamentably out of drawing).[15]

Like Mary Way, Betsey listened to better artists when she could; but they were few and far between in her neck of the woods.[16] Again like Mary, she copied assiduously from the best models she could lay her hands on. For the elder sister, it had been the masterpieces attributed to Rubens (above), in 1816 the public exhibitions and auctions and artists' studios (**no. 19**), and in 1819, a portrait of the King of France, evidently a miniature, of which Mary began a copy (**no. 85**). For Betsey in that same year it was an engraving that had come into her hands: the subject, General Lafayette (**no. 57**). Engravings were a common instrument of art-education, as is clear from published manuals of instruction.[17] She later recalls her pleasure in having "copied from a number of portraits that were said to have been drawn by the greatest artists;" but there is a note of uncertainty, here, about just how good and famous they really were. Work by Rubens was certainly not to be had in a town like New London, nor anything approaching such a quality. When she was shown a snuff box with an elegant face on it, again the King of France, she counts it "without exception the richest and highest finished piece of painting I ever saw."[18] The comment shows some naivety. She longed to learn from it, but could afford only a dollar and a half to buy the like "as a model," if Eliza could find them in New York. They turned out to cost far too much and she had to abandon the idea. The next year, 1824, she mentions borrowing some miniatures by Nathaniel Rogers: his *Mr.* and *Mrs. Whistler* painted some time before 1811, plus a third, male portrait.[19] The last she had before her for only four days of intensive work, the earlier ones only in the midst of other commissions so that she had to rise with the sun to attend to its lessons. She is described at the time as "over head and ears in business," perhaps increased by her teaching. She had at any rate had pupils in the past.[20]

So much for the main facts of the case, without the details that the letters in full provide. What emerges is a picture of sharp ups and downs of business, no period of much prosperity, sometimes substantial indebtedness, always resilience, quite essential resilience in the job of making a living. Besides, Betsey Champlain like her sister really loved her art and never tired of studying it so as to improve. After Mary's return from New York, the two discussed it and Eliza's education in it, and shared their experience; local talent in the form of Mrs. Bryant entered the picture, to receive advice and supplies of pith, on which she painted her watchpapers. Watchpapers, however, were beneath Betsey, and they hardly paid.

She could afford to be a little choosy because, to repeat her sister's phrase, she was in New London "Painter General," even enjoying some fame beyond the city. So much shows in the deference offered her by Dunlap in 1822 (**no. 126**). A student was with him at the time and lent Betsey a work on painting by the president of the Royal Academy, which she studied carefully; but there is no mention or likelihood of her attending to book-learning beyond this, and beyond Mary's very copious extracts sent her a decade earlier (above). With this sisterly teaching excepted, Betsey might fairly call herself, like Mary, her own creation. When her *Christ Rejected* is set side by side with even Malbone's miniatures, the comparison shows how remarkable had been her progress in the art.[21]

4

Eliza Way Champlain

She has appeared already in her father's letter above: "Eliza–not flesh and blood, one would think to see her, she is so much like the angels." That was in 1798, when she was a year old. She grew up the only girl in a family with three brothers. The older George and she were good friends when their relationship comes into view; the younger Sam was near enough her age to require a bossy impatience on her part; but toward baby William, five years her junior, she was more relenting. She may be imagined as a talented and high-spirited child, who went to the city's school, read a lot, watched her mother paint, watched her aunt also; imitated both; and missed her aunt when Mary Way departed for New York.

Nearing nineteen, it was time to consider how she would earn a living. Opportunities were scarce at home, and there was her aunt urging George (above) and no doubt Eliza in her turn to try for better luck in the big city. She did visit there and stayed with her Aunt Mary for some number of months long enough to feel settled, make friends, visit public displays of fine art–she later recalled admiring a miniature by Anson Dickinson[1]–and do some painting of her own. So much may be inferred from Mary's subsequent letter of July, 1816, soon after her niece had returned to New London (**no. 19**). The tone is affectionate as always, and didactic:

> Dear Eliza,
>
> Your welcome letter has come safe to hand, and never was anything more exceptable. You are a good girl for writing so particularly, and I am pleased your painting is so much admired. You have only to persevere, exersise your patience. Don't be discouraged by any little difficulties you may meet with as you progress in the art, learn to conquer, to surmount them, and you will soon arrive at eminence.
>
> I don't know what to say about your teaching school. If you do, you will have trouble in the flesh. You must pound it into many a numbskull, and if you find some of such a comfortable thickness you could not succeed with all your pounding, as is likely enough will be the case, you must expect to bear the blame. But don't let even

this discourage you if you think you have fortitude and resolution adequate to the task, and can procure good copy; for this is a main article in the business. Give three lessons a week, from nine till twelve, at five dollars a quarter. This point settled, the next question is what I think of your going to Guilford. I think it a very good plan, and advise you to go by all means, since Aunt Hannah and your mother is willing. I am glad you and Amilia Allen are friends again. Remember what I have often told you, to take offence at triffles shows a mind weak and contemptable. 'Tis only nescessary at first to exersise a little-self command, and reflection will soon convince you how few things are worth your anger. 'Tis a most unpleasant sensation, and what is still worse, no small degree of consequence to the person who offers the affront. This consideration should always prevent your resentment. Never fall out with any one if you can help it, but above all things keep in with your relations whatever you do; your Uncle and Aunt Way, your Uncle Oliver and his wife, Aunt Taber's and Aunt Allen's family. They are worth all the rest in town. Visit them often and cultivate thier friendship and esteem.

Mary Way here breaks off for a word of sympathy about the miniaturist's occupational hazard, eye-strain, and of confidence in New London's leading eye-specialist, Dr. Elisha North. It was in fact this man who established the country's first clinic in New London and earned the title, Father of American ophthalmology. He reappears in the correspondence at a tragic moment some years later.[2]

I am sorry to hear your mother's eyes are in such a bad way, if painting is the cause. I should suppose mine would be in the same condition. I'm sure I've strain'd them as much. I think Dr. North need not frighten her with the apprehension of total blindness, but 'tis his policy to make the case appear desperate in order to enhance the merit of the cure, which I hope soon to hear is effected.

You ask if I have any business. I have now, for the first time since you left me, tho' I don't think it is a very profitable jobb—one of those eligant engravings in Broad-Way to copy on silk for a young lady to embroider: *Christ Healing the Blind*. There is fourteen figures, more than half a yard in length, men, women and children half naked. It will take me at least a fortnight to do the painting. 'Tis most beautiful. I wish you was here to copy it.[3]

I have been much gratifide the week past—feasted my eyes on the most superb paintings. There has been several sales at auction all of which I have attended. The first was in the City Hotell in Broadway. Mr. Northum, who is in his element when he can do good upon *free cost*, knowing my taste for the sublime, came to inform me Maria was here. He offer'd his service to attend us, which we excepted with pleasure, as there was no doing without a beaux. In this case he came fix'd for the business—best bib and band, new hat, big as an old fashioned tea table; his staff like the Club of Herculous which he brandish'd most manfully, for our diffense and protection. He is devoted to me, you know, and positively I never had a beaux in all my days who upon all accounts suited my step so exactly. His high standing in society as a man of property, his known character and respectable appearance are three qualities that don't meet in every beaux. I therefore make much of him. By the way, if the Old Lady [Mrs. Northam] should happen to slip her wind about these days, I would not answer for the consequence. I shall pray against it with all my might, as in that case for the sake of propriety I must fight shy–which would not be so pleasant.

But we have stray'd from the record, as your Speaker [=preacher] says. Let us return to the City Hotell, where I was mightily amused not only with the paintings but ten thousand other elegant curiosities which were for sale, besides viewing the house which is big as a world and most supurb. The next day we attinded a public sale at Waldoe's. Those two rooms we were in when Charlotte Wait[e] was with us were both full–some of the same pieces, but chiefly copys from the ancients. We went next to our old Union Hotell in William Street, where was a large variety of landscapes, and very handsome; but today we have been again to the City Hotell in Broadway to view a collection of paintings and white marble statuary just arrived from Itialy, and I must say they exceed any-thing I have yet seen. One chimney-piece perticularly struck my fancy as the richest thing I ever saw. I requested Mr. Northum to ask the price. It was twelve hundred dollars. He has seen so much of this work in Europe, he calls himself a judge, and thought it was very low; but as I had left my purse at home I did not make the purchase.

I wish'd for you very bad. Yesterday, too, you would have enjoy'd yourself here. There was no need of going out. We had the Fourth of July just under our nose nearly all day, from Chamber street down to the Park. The different Companies and Societies were parading and forming, the new seventy-four built for the occasion mann'd with beautifull boys dress't clean and white as snow with blue jackets. The Temple of Liberty and the Irish Harp hung with festoons of flowers–the sweetest thing you ever saw (I'm sure you would have painted it if you had been here)– with ten thousand other emblems too tedious to mention were parading before the door from nine till twelve o'clock. The house was crouded with company to see the show–the Northums, Fitches, &c, with fifty thousand more.

The sister of Mr. Fitch is here on a visit, which has prevented Anna's finishing *Lord Byron*'s picture that she begun in great snuff when you first went home–work'd upon it three mornings from nine till twelve, and has never touch'd it since. I shall return you the copy you left for her, as Mr. Carter (that is his name) has left these pieces with me–says he has no use for them, I may keep them as long as I please. So if she is disposed to finish hers, she may copy the original. He told me he should send his picture to the young lady to take a copy of, which he expects she will send him, and when she does, I shall see it. He has brought me a number of books, by which means I have discovered his name, and that is all I know about him. I have not seen him since I receiv'd your *Cupid*; but I have touch'd it up as you desired, and am sure he will be pleased with it, so I shall venture to enclose the landscape you made choice off. The reason this does not look as well as the one you painted for Maria Cob is because you have not put white paint on the other side. You should have painted this just as you did hers, and after it was finish'd and press't smooth, breath'd on it till it was damp and then, with thick gum water, stuck it on a card or paper.

You wish to know what folks says about you. I read part of your letter to Anna [Fitch]. She admires your stile, says you write with ease and eligance, desires her love to you, begs you would not hurry yourself in the least about those pictures and only do them when you are quite at leasure. Mrs. Dawson and Hannah sends love by the bushell, and Mrs. Hayden begs to be remember'd to you most effectionately.

Yes, Maria [Sanford] is married–was privately married about the middle of last month (a whim of Hayden's). No one was knowing to it but myself. Captain Hayden was going to the southard, to be gone six months, and it was to remain a profound secret till his return. Before he went away, however, it became absolutely nescessary to inform her father. His answer was, 'I have no objection to you, Sir, tho' by God! she's a fit wife for a Governor' (he spoke my mind fully)–but surely no reason why it should be conceal'd. He took the most effectual method to publish it, by telling [Maria's sister] Eliza. Of course it was a secret no longer. Maria don't care, tho' to please Hayden she had rather it had remain'd a secret till his return. I am sorry to say I shall then lose her. He has concluded to settle in Richmond, Virginia. To me it will be a loss indeed. I shall never, never find her equal! Poor Bradbury! It will be a thunder-stroke to him when he finds she is realy married and he must relinquish his fondly cherished hopes. Well, everyone must have thier trials.

Mrs. Clinch was to see me not long since. In your name I presented her with the little mourning piece. She was delighted. She asked the price and I answer'd, 'Your acceptance.' Oh! she could not think of it. She had requested you to do it and was willing to make you any compensation. I said you did it with pleasure and absolutely refused to take any thing, and as she could make no other return, she praised you, to your heart's content, said a thousand and ten thousand pritty things of you which was echo'd by Mrs. Wait and Charlotte, who was here with her–in short, you had more praise bestowed upon you than could be purchased for double the money you would have ask'd, had the price been what it would. They regreet your absense–that they had not seen more of you, that you had not visited them when they had asked you so frequently and wish'd it so earnestly; desired thier love to you and hoped, when next you came to New York, they should enjoy more of your company.

Oh dear, I have so much to say and no time to write, I ought to be in bed and asleep this moment, that I may be up as soon as light, and attend to business now I have it. Well, then–adieu! and ten thousand bushells of love to every-body I know and those I don't know, no matter, pay it on to them, with a very few exceptions which I don't think worth while to name.

Now don't be getting fitts if you should not receive this letter as soon as you expect. I want to send a book to Aunt Hannah, and I don't think it will do to send it by the mail. I shall therefore leave it at Mr. Baxter's with this letter, the first time I go out. They have offer'd to send letters for me, and have opportunities every day. The book I shall send is the *Life of Mr. Murray*, written by himself, and I think well worth reading. She has liberty to send it to her friends if she has any that are not too stiff and prejudiced to read it. I think no one can give it a candid perusal without receiving both pleasure and instruction. When she has done with it and finds a good opportunity, will thank her to send it back, as I have promised to lend it to several of my friends here when it returns.

Once more adieu! Write as often and as much as possible. Be sure let me know how your mother's eyes are, and Sarah Lee, when they hear from her, how she is, and when they expect her return. And is it Amy who says I am the most obstinate girl in the world? Tell Aunt Taber I say her judgment (in this case at least) is erronious. It is not founded on the principles of true religion or sound philosophy, both of which would teach her things are order'd above. 'It is not in man that walks, to direct his steps.' I came to New York as I came into the world not voluntarily; I had no hand, will, or agency in the business. I remain here, as I stay in the world, because I cannot get out of it till the time appointed; and she may with the same propriety call me obstinate in the one case as in the other. But if she only knew how much I long to see her, she would be convinced it is no fault of mine that I do not return.

July 25th

I have just receiv'd your last letter by George. Since the above was written I have had much affliction, which is the reason you have not receiv'd it. I could not go to Baxter's myself and had no opportunity to send it, as none of my acquaintance know the family. I have been in a peck of troubles with a most tremendous boil upon my leg, which made me heart-sick for fear I should be obliged to show it to a doctor. I should have died but for Maria and Mrs. Dawson, who are the best of human beings. They have done every thing for me. Mrs. Dawson went to a doctor, told him how it was, and asked what was to be done for it. He said he must see it; but that was out of the question, she told him. He must not even see me, for I would not endure the sight of a doctor who knew, or even suspected, I had a *leg*. He thought it was mighty foolish but supposed I must be humour'd, so he told her what was to be done, and his prescription seems to answer every purpose. It is now much better, tho' I don't like to walk much upon it, and have not yet been out.

I will send this letter to Baxter's by George [Eliza's brother]. I am very glad he has given up the thought of going to sea. I hope he will find a good place here and attend to his business. You need not be in such a fever to do Fitch and his wife's pictures. They are in no hurry about it. Take your own time and don't neglect more profitable business. They don't wish it, and would be very sorry if they thought you did. The last picture of Mr. Northum's is thought to be full as good a likeness as the first, and they are very much pleased with it. For my own part, however, I think it has one capital fault, which is the reason you are not so much pleased with it yourself as you expected: the background is too handsome. I have often told you, and now repeat it with tears in my eyes, your 'background should never be seen till it is look'd for.'[4] But this is so bright and gay, it reverses the order of things and destroys the effect it ought to produce. Instead of modestly retiring to a respectful distance, it steps boldly forward and engrosses the whole attention, while the likeness, which should be the principle object, is not notic'd or, if it is, appears to the greatest disadvantage. In short, it is what I call an impudent back-ground and spoils the picture. Had you left the ground white or made it some dark colour, like the other, it would appear much better. This bark paper I find, tho' extreemly beautiful for light and bright colours, is not so good for dark, black hair and drapery. It is very difficult to paint. It is therefore more proper for fancy work than likenesses, unless, indeed, it is some one who has a very briliant complexion, light hair and drapery.

To pause here over details: Mary Way's modesty about her leg recalls the female patient of Dr. North who was unwilling to have him treat even her foot (so long as it wasn't dirty, said he, she should just let him look at it); and there are references to the Baxters in the letter that need explanation, this family being on the edge of Mary Way's circle, with New London friends and connections. They provided her with a mail-route to her home, and Eliza with a sort of suitor, whom she ridiculed privately under the nickname "Lobster"; and Mrs. Baxter and that son also sat for two of Eliza's earliest efforts in portraiture.[5] As to George Oliver Champlain, he is seen visiting New York in July to seek his fortune, though he moves on further south before long. He had apprenticed to a bookbinder and learned the trade at home, as the younger Sam at the age of thirteen was likewise put to a master, in his turn, such a term of training being so common for boys of the time; and then George thought to follow his father's calling to the sea, and tried a voyage to France; but it didn't seem the answer; so here he was on the loose, looking for whatever better opportunities might turn up.[6]

In this present letter, however, the main items that call for comment are those that shed light on the process of Eliza's artistic education. Her development of her talents for painting are the chief yield of her first two visits to the city. What helped most of course was her aunt's example and constant instruction, witness the hammering home of John Jarvis' dictum on backgrounds in the letter quoted above; and there were occasional pieces of advice to be had from establishment figures, too: Waldo not quite alone in this role.[7] A further element in her training was the copying of better works, where possible, by acknowledged masters; and these might be available through engravings like that of *Christ Healing the Blind*, just encountered, or as originals (in the letter that follows) which she saw for sale in the winter of 1818; or again, paintings or sculpture in public places, including New York's famous Gardens, or displayed for sale;[8] and works by her aunt or by friends were not to be despised as models, either.[9] New York had its artists' open studios, its collectors (some of whom were artists) opening their houses to friends and acquaintances, or lending their treasures to shows;[10] in particular, it had its Academy of Fine Arts.

With a loan in 1816 from the Mechanics Bank, the directors of the languishing Academy had been able to lease and renovate six rooms in the commodious and commanding Old Alms House. It overlooked a park on one side, Broadway on the other, and Columbia College no more than a block away.[11] An English visitor recently arrived with his nose in the air paid these new quarters a visit, reporting that "the collection is small; and, upon the whole, very indifferent, with the exception of two or three rustic pieces. Among the casts, there are a Venus, an Apollo, and a fighting gladiator."[12] But it must be remembered that the visitor had in mind a comparison with what one might find in London, ten times the size of New York, whereas what counted for Eliza Champlain and her aunt was rather the difference between the latter's hundred thousand, and New London's mere three. Besides, the Academy's permanent collection which the visitor looked on with such disappointment was most splendidly outshone by its great first Exhibition of 1816: over a hundred paintings then on display by such major or established figures as "Rubens," Copley, and West from abroad; among native artists, Dickinson, Stuart, Waldo, Dunlap, Jewitt, and Jarvis; not counting some sculpture, a score of drawings, another score of paintings by the celebrated, the indefatigable Colonel John Trumbull himself, and close to forty more by artists too shy to name themselves.[13] Giving some idea of the tastes of the time, there was a *Mary Queen of Scots* by each of the locals William Leney and Mrs. Robertson, a *Sleeping Cupid* by the seventeenth-century Pierre Mignard (copied for exhibition by Dunlap in 1819), a *View of the Falls of Niagara* by Archibald Robertson; also, still-lifes, landscapes, scriptural pieces, pieces historical, metaphorical, philosophical, and a great many portraits, of all sizes. To enjoy the show, a crowd of fifteen hundred people on October 16th had paid twenty-five cents' admission each. It was a great success. In the next year, under the aegis of the newly elected president Trumbull, almost equal riches were displayed on two separate occasions; again in the following May, more still, and annually thereafter in that month. What immensely instructive and inspiring treats for Eliza!—without mention of that most notable of all features in the 1818 exhibition: a pair of portraits by Mary Way herself. *There* was New London in New York. As she was fond of saying to the end, "You can do anything if you try."

Beyond the more or less conscious study of all this exemplary material, a second element in Eliza's education was the painting of watch-papers. They were of a size to fit in a pocket watch, that is, an inch and three quarters or so in diameter, or to be displayed in a frame on a mantlepiece. The support for the water-color might be pith, bark-paper, or ordinary paper.[14] Of Eliza's four that survive, one on paper (Pl. 1.4) with the very faint *Veni, vidi, vici* above "Adieu," and another (damaged) on pith showing Iris (Pl. 1.5), give a sense of this field for her art. The latter she painted under the inspiration of a print she saw at an auction (**no. 33**, below). A third (Pl. 1.6) is the most representative of the genre, which was throughout the early Republic specially given to patriotic and commemorative subjects, as here: George Washington.

It is usually impossible to tell whether her "fancy" pieces titled, for example, *Cupid* or *Fame*, *Amabilité* or *Douceur*, *Hymen* or *Love & Harmony*, were watch-papers or not; and if not, whether on paper, like the mourning piece for George Washington (Pl. 1.6), or on ivory like her *Temple of Friendship* (Pl. 7.17).[15] Because of her tone when she speaks of them, clearly watch-papers were a less serious art form. Some she could dash off in ten minutes. She can sometimes be seen turning them out as little presents or as a sort of currency in place of the real that she lacked.[16] All their mentions together, however small a part of her total production, add up to several dozen. They served as a form of practice in idle times, right up to the year of her marriage, and in the preceding letter her aunt can be seen leaning over her shoulder as she worked, or metaphorically doing so, so as to study the good points and praise them, criticize the flaws, and explain the techniques that were lacking. Through this relationship Eliza had what her mother and aunt never enjoyed, years of instruction at the hands of competent professionals. To these two teachers, however, must be added that most important third, New York itself. Here were sophistication and vitality in combination as marked as those to be found anywhere else in the Republic, offering views of a still wider world beyond America and stretching the three "sisters of the brush" (**no. 95**) to the utmost. The titles of Mary Way's and Eliza's "fancy" pieces show as much–even show them stretched beyond their powers, witness their struggles with French orthography, the names of classical mythology, and the bookish part of painting.

Mary continues Eliza's professional instruction in September of the same year, 1816 (**no. 20**). Her reference, incidentally, to "the horrors of May Day" in an early paragraph is explained later: it was the customary moment for new-renting, and as such, under just the descriptive phrase she uses, had been heroically hymned or objurgated a few years before by New York's editor-in-chief, her acquaintance Samuel Woodworth, as it was to be the focus of a play by another acquaintance, Charles Clinch, a little later.[17]

Dear Eliza,

I have so much to say to you, I don't know where to begin, nor which of your letters to answer first, for I have received them all, and more than all–so don't be getting fits again for fear they should miscarry, and all your mighty secrets be exposed to the world, and make it stare with gaping wonder! and astonishment! There is no danger of this, I can assure you, so you may rest contented and write on with perfect freedom, anything and everything you please, as often and as much as possible; and doubt not but I shall receive it safe and sound.

I am sorry for your affliction, and wish you may never meet with any worse than drawing the likeness of a corps. I should like to have such a job every day, for my part, and wish it was as fashionable here as it is there. I should not then want for business, for death and the grave is not half so terrifying to me as the cares and difficulties of life. To be sure, you give a dismal account of your uninteresting occupations and amusements, and, to crown all, you say 'once in a while somebody drops off, fifty thousand years old, is buried, and there's an end of them.' This is discouraging indeed, particularly to one of my turn of mind. Did you say it to induce me to return? Such a lenght of years is worse, far more to be dreaded, than all the horrors of May Day.

For the piece you have engaged to paint: I don't see but it will be plain sailing as it is design'd and the figures drawn, or if you should meet with a few difficulties they will be triffling. I have no doubt you will do it beautifully, if the figures are well drawn, with due proportion, symmetry, ease and grace. If not, some alteration will be necessary. In this, your own taste and judgment will direct you. You know what looks well, and have now a tolerable idea of proportion; therefore please yourself, and you will no doubt please others. To paint on silk you must first lay a ground of flake white. Here, judgment is necessary–not too thick, as, in that case, it is apt to scale off. Wash it on, thin, with a large pencil and let it dry. This do two or three times over, if necessary, but not so as to cover the threads intirely. When it is dry, your outline will appear, or where it does not, you can mark it lightly with a black lead pencil, and after with rubber, the same as on paper. When you have mark'd the feature correct, go over them with a camel's hair pencil, and then *wash* on the complexion as much as possible. The more you wash on your colouring, the better it will look, the quicker it is done, and the softer and smoother it appears. Even the shade should be done in the same way, and receive as few touches as possible. This requires rather more care than on paper. A little more gum than usual is necessary in the paint and it should be laid on with a pencil rather larger than usual, the strokes quick and light so as not to disturb the ground. Never repeat your strokes while it is wet. When it's quite dry it may be finished with touches where it is necessary, but the fewer of these, the better. Don't be sparing of your shades and colours. Lay them on with a trowel till it glows again. Pieces of this kind which are to be viewed at a distance should not be painted fine and delicate like a miniature. They require boldness, force and colouring to attract and fix the attention.

I have done two pieces this summer. The first, I worked upon a fortnight steadily; the last, a week. For the first, I had twenty dollars, for the last, ten. The paintings were much admired and the price thought very reasonable. For a head that is not a likeness I ask a dollar; for one that is, six dollars, the same price I have on paper; and for the other painting at the same rate, according to the time I am about it.

I presented your *Cupid* to Mr. Carter, and likewise your apology. He was delighted with it and thought apology unnecessary. He show'd me another little piece his beloved had sent him, much handsomer than any of the rest–two beautiful doves upon a sprig of wild roses or sweet briar. The doves are white shaded with purple, which has a fine effect. If you can spare *Lord Byron*, I will thank you to send him down upon a visit. Carter has taken away his, and Ann [Fitch]'s is still unfinish'd. She regrets it so much, I promised her I would send for yours. I wish you could see a little piece I have just finished. Captain Hayden presented Maria [Sanford] with an elegant gold watch, and I have painted a paper for it. As you were so fond of mottos, I believe I will send you the design to copy, and perhaps the painting to look at; but if I do, you must keep it but one day and certainly return it by the first mail, after you have receiv'd it. She values it more than the watch and would never be willing to run the risk, for fear it might get injured, tho' she would not refuse if I should ask the favour. If I send it, therefore, it would be without her knowledge. But I will consider of it.

Like you, I cannot help regreting that Maria is married. She certainly seemed form'd for something superior, something more than a mere wife–a domestick drudge. To tread the beaten, dog-trot path of common matrimony requires nothing extraordinary. Any woman, every human will do well enough for this. To keep out of the fire and out of the water is all that's requisite in a wife. But, as you justly observe, she would have been such an honour to the race of Tobias and led apes [that is, taught school] so gracefuly, 'twas a pity she did not go about to do it. She laughed very heartily when I read her your observation and told her I was of your opinion. I thought two or three such as she and I might bring Old Maidenism into fashion, and if this could once be done, it would not appear so terriffing to the girls, and drive them headlong into matrimony, induce them to have any-body, and do any-thing to avoid it, as was too much the case at present.

You have observed the indifference or, rather, dislike sister Fitch has ever show'd to Maria. This I know proceeds partly from her thinking she is a favourite of mine and partly from envy, 'which hates the excelence it cannot reach.' Maria comes every fine day to walk with me, as the doctor order'd I should walk out as much as possible for air and exersise. She has regain'd her health and spirits, her flesh and colour, and is more beautiful than ever. As she is not the slave of fashion, she dresses in the most becoming manner, with taste and elegance. We was out the other day and call'd on sister Fitch–the first time she was even in the house. I introduced her to Miss Fitch [Anna's sister-in-law] who is the exact image of her brother both in looks and manner. She had never seen Maria before, and it was evident she view'd her with surprise and admiration. Ann treated her with cool politeness, Mrs. Northam with all the warmth of friendship. The old lady knew how much she was attached to me, seeing her here when I was sick.

They urged us to stay to tea, but we declined and sayd we should pursue our walk as far as Mrs. Dawsons. Ann said, she and Miss Fitch was just going down there when we came in to make a visit, and would walk with us; so we all set out togather. Down by the park we met Hannah [Dawson] who was coming up to see me, so she turned about and went back with us, and, tho' Ann is cold and stiff as death, and Miss Fitch just like her brother, and Hannah neither one thing nor another, yet between Mrs. Dawson and Maria we had a tolerable warm, sociable time, in spite of isicles and crowbars. Maria and I came away before the Fitches. When we were gone, Hannah told me Ann observed to Mrs. Dawson, that Mrs. Hayden was a great favourite of mine. 'Yes (Mrs. Dawson said) and good reason for it. Mrs. Hayden is very much attached to Miss Way and pays her every possible attention, and love, you know, begets love.' One of the gentlemen observed, Miss Way must be a lady of taste if that was her favourite, for he thought her the most elegant woman, both in looks and manners, he ever saw. 'She is a very *showy* woman (Ann said), she attracted general attention as we came down Broadway, ever eye was turn'd upon her.' Miss Fitch observed 'Such little folks as you and I, Anna, can hardly expect notice, when Mrs. Hayden is in sight.' 'No (he said), such a woman as Mrs. Hayden would take the shine off from a most any one.' Now, I was malicious enough to enjoy this conversation because I knew Ann did not.

The next Sunday I drank tea there–indeed, I have every Sunday since you went home. They pity me so because I am alone, and I had a thousand times rather be alone than be with them, generaly speaking; but they compel me, I cannot avoid it, if I ever refuse and come home, Mr. Northam will come after me and give me no peace till I go home with him. Well and so, when I was there, Miss Fitch said to me, 'Miss Way, I admire your friend Mrs. Hayden.' Every person of taste and discernment must admire her, was my answer. 'She is beautiful.' Her beauty is her least merit. 'I admire the expression of her countenance.' 'Tis the index of her mind. 'I should like to be acquainted with her.' The more you know, the more you will admire her. Fitch sayd nothing. His wife observed, 'She is a very *showy* woman.' Showy (I repeat), if I understand the term, is something that appears more than it realy is. If this is its meaning, it is by no means applicable to Mrs. Hayden. She is *more* than she appears. She made no answer, and her father's coming in turn'd the subject, or I realy think we should have quarrel'd. I was ready, cock'd and primed.

Day before yesterday they all drank with me, that is, Fitch and his wife and sister, Maria and Hannah Dawson. I told Maria, she knew we were a cold, stiff, dead-and-alive set as ever came togather, and I should look to her for life and animation for the whole company. I wish'd her to lay aside her dignity, upon the present occasion, as much as possible, for the sake of general utillity, and only think of preventing ague fitts, and keep us from freezing to death. She promised to do her best, and realy preform'd wonders–drove away the evil spirit, dispell'd the chill that always hangs about them, and so powerful was the effect of her magick charms, that at at last some signs of life appear'd, to my great joy. This encouraged her to continue the business, until her unremited and humane exersions were crown'd with compleat success. Fitch was alive! He was charm'd, he spoke, gazed, smiled, and smil'd again. Even Ann began to unbend, and drew out her crowbar (I don't mean her corset bone) and, to our astonishment, in the most polite and friendly manner, invited Maria to visit her.

Yesterday Mrs. Cob drank tea with me. We were alone and had abundance of chat. Amongst the rest, I ask'd the reason of her aversion to Hannah Dawson, and found it was just what I had before conjectured: Miss Dawson, she said, had the rudeness to contradict her, when she knew she was right, and as a married lady she thought herself intitled to more respect from a girl. I said all I could in Hannah's favour but found it impossible to remove her prejudice. She thinks she is handsome, she says, but don't like her countenance. 'Tis that she always judges by, and never was mistaken. She knows Hannah has a pettish, unpleasant temper, and wants nothing to do with such people. By the way, she has taken a great fancy to Maria, who she saw here, and made her promise to visit her with me.

Our old church goes on much as usual, I think. Nothing new has turn'd up, only Lobster improves in beauty daily, and it is high time for you to come back and draw his picture again, for you did not do him justice before. As to Crab [another beau of Eliza's], he sets so for a head, I don't know hardly how he looks. White continues the business; Giggins is half the time out of town (jug and all), and poor Hannah sighs and looks disconsolate. Mason does not return, and as to Captain French, we fear he is dead and buried in the gold dust he went in quest of. There has been no news of him since he sail'd. But your other beaux, Mr. Cheavlere, has return'd from the country–he walked home with me the other evening from church. Didn't I snowball him. He will not trouble me again, I fancy.

I think I've answered all your questions, and wrote you nonsense enough, if that can amuse you. . . .

Mary's next to her niece, not very much later, continues the cozy jokes about their acquaintances in the city, about her "Lobsters" and "Crabs," and adds a detail or two about their address near Pearl Street and their church; but little else:[18]

Dear Eliza,

I need not tell you your letter was very exceptable, as it contained a variety of *shell-fish* of which you know we are extremely fond. Of course the contents were greedily devour'd. I had only a chance to read it once, the Dawsons grab'd it, and I have never seen it since. It affords a delicious feast to those who, like us, have a taste for the sublime, and can relish a savory dish equal almost to the high season'd mess cook'd up by you and Mrs. Dawson, with which families may be supply'd as usual. Doubtless you remember the precious ingredients that inrich'd this lusious composition, and show'd at the same time the delicacy of your own refined taste.

No, you are not forgotten. The pleasure and amusement your visit afforded will be long remembered. A thousand times a day, 'Oh that Eliza was only here, how happy we should be,' is echo'd from every quarter. It was concluded, when you left us, we should not laugh again this winter; but your letter has once more stretched our jaws. We had a fine frolick over it, I assure you, and Mrs. Dawson shook all over like a pyramid of gelley. You are a great favorite of hers. She thinks there never was such another as Eliza. I tell her all my relations are as agreable. She has her doubts, but says if that is the case we must be a remarkable family. I only wish they would some more of them come down and show how agreable they can be. You must not talk so discouraging about coming again. Be a very good girl this winter, and I hope Aunt Hannah will let you, in the spring, and come down herself with you, which I think will be no bad scheme; and then we will take clear comfort.

As to all your beaus and Belzabubs, big and small, about which you make such affectionate inquires, I leave Mrs. Giggins (who keeps a bright look-out for you, as well as for herself) to give you an account of them. From my own observation I can only say, poor Crab has got the dismals and looks like the juce. He has never smiled nor simper'd since you left the church, and as to Lobster, Oh he has been here, don't you think, and made a bitter complaint to Mrs. Dawson. You know Tholl Baxter. You know the day you smiled upon him so sweetly and gave him that kind look (which he says went to his heart) to induce him to come again in the afternoon. Well, and so he went home in high glee upon the strength of, and hurried his mother to death to get his dinner quick, that he might go to church in season. She, it seems, had procured him some od[..]d[..] soup which is his favourite dish, but unfortunately made it too hot, and he, being very much in love, in a great hurry and confounded hungry, never stood to blow it, but down with it boiling hot. Burnt his mouth, spill'd it on his nice stiff collar, and took out all the starch!–and having but one shirt, you know it was impossible for him to fullfill his engagement. He was very much mortifide and disappointed, but accidents will sometimes happen, and he hopes you will excuse him. A great deal more he said to Mrs. Dawson which she will tell you herself. She pities him very much. I did not see him. She has promised to write you a chapter of nonsense. You may therefore dispense with any of mine, tho' I think I have the nack of writing very prettily myself. Some folks, you know, cannot do it. As Aunt Hannah says, it is a gift. Well then, if it is, let us be thankful for it and improve it to the best advantage. As it requires a wise man to act the part of a fool, we expect whoever reads our letters will give us full credit for all the wisdom we possess, which, if they measure in due proportion to the quantity of folly this contains, I think they must consider me as the very Solomon of the age.

Adieu. . . .

In December (**no. 21**), Mary supplies more news of their mutual friends and some, now, more conventional views of marriage and courtship. Mr. "Chaveliear" (or "Cheavlear" of **no. 20**, above) reappears, as he will again in later contexts, too, and under still other spellings and guises, a member of Mary Way's beloved Universalist church and a Chatham-Street neighbor; and there were other marriageable young men about:[19]

Hannah [Dawson] has got a *real certain true serious* beau. . . . Oh how I want you here to help me torment her! You would die to see her manage with him pretty much as she did with her knitting work–so artless and simple, so unconsious of appearances. No one was ever less calculated to be in love. Like the goose, she hides her head and thinks she is perfectly safe and nobody sees her. There are few men but what would take advantage of such a character, yet I think he will not. He appears to be a man of strict honour and principle (that is, as far as it is possible to judge of such a strange two-leged featherless animal as man), nearly as young as she is and almost as artless, and quite as deep in the mud as she is in the mire.

Now you are getting fits to know who and what he is. Do you recollect two English gentlemen that boarded with Mrs. Dawson when you was here–the brothers of Mrs. Booth, John and Thomas Fenno? It is Thomas, the youngest, she has hooked. You may remmember his coming to church once with her and his sister. They sat just back of us, in White's pew. . . . Hannah is a modest, agreeable, good-hearted pretty girl, and does not want of sense. This is the sum total of her character, and this is nothing extra. I think if it is her good fortune to have Tommy, of which there is every probability, she will do extremely well–not better than she deserves but far better than she had any reason to expect, circumstanced and situated as she is, pennyless and portionless. The question is not 'what *is* she?' but 'what *has* she?'–while he might make pretensions to any lady in New York. A fine person, sensible and agreeable, he has had a liberal education and, in short, possesses every requisite that constitutes the gentleman. Such is Hannah's beau.

What would you have more to make your mouth water? As Shakespear says, 'Is not birth, beauty, learning, gentleness, virtue, liberality and such like, the spice and salt that season a man?' For shame, girl! to set there moping in the chimney corner, and here is Hannah dancing about to places of amusement almost every night–the theatre and conserts, and taking all the pleasure in life. Come, lay aside envy, hatred and malice, and all uncharitableness, and come down here and make your market like a good Christian; for you see, after all, this is the place to do business. Matrimony is all the rage, and if you don't come soon, your beauxs won't keep without salting. Chaveliear is married already, and some of the rest appear to be upon the spoil. Oh, another piece of news I have to tell you–yes, and another to the end of that. But, in the first place, Jane Sanford is married, to a certain Captain Jhonson of the Army–a nice man, they say, immensely rich besides learning and talents; for he is a poet, and has *berhymed* her most unmercifully. There was love at first sight. The first time he saw her face he was so struck with her beauty, he told a friend of his who was present, 'With her he should be the happiest of men, without her the most miserable.' Went directly to her father, made proposals, intreated his consent and permision to visit her, which was granted. In less than two months the business was settled compleatly, and last Sunday they were married. Today Hannah Dawson call'd to see the bride. I could not help laughing to hear her remarks, and the comparison she made between Captain Jhonson and Fenno, much to the advantage of the latter, you may suppose. But this is perfectly natural. The poor thing is over head and ears in love and don't know what's the matter. You may judge of the warmth of thier passion, they can walk togather on the Battery these fine cool evenings and find it very comfortable!

But now here comes the tit-bit–the pith & marrow of the whole. I conclude you will think it worth all the rest. You know the beautiful picture you saw at Walldo's–that mouth that you was, or pretended to be, so much in love with. It is quite at your service. Charlotte [Waite of **no. 19**] has resign'd all pretensions to him. The match is broken of, I find, to the astonishment of all her friends. She spent the afternoon with me last week, we had abundance of chat, she talked of you, wants to see you very bad, and hear you laugh again. In the course of conversation she told me she should soon introduce a gentleman to me, one of my countrymen, that is, a Yankee, of whom she thought more highly than other people, as she considered them much smarter and more intelligent. This beau, however, she should submit to my investigation, wished me to examin him thoroughly, consider him in every point of view. As he would set for a picture, I should have a good opportunity, and when I had criticized, scrutinized, and connoisseur'd him well, tell her candidly my opinion, and if it was worth while for her to set her cap for him. So highly she valued my judgment, she realy believed she should go about to do it. But what will Saydam say? I asked. 'Don't mention him (she reply'd), if he was worth the Indies I would not marry him. I've done with him forever. He is a fool. If I can't have a man of sense I will never marry at all.' Then (I observed) nature was more bountiful to his person than his mind, his picture is so beautiful. ' 'Tis no likeness, Miss Way, it is flatter'd to death. Oh, how Walldo flatters!' Thinks I to myself, you did not say so last winter. Then it was not flatter'd at all. Accordingly, the next day she came and introduced her

Yankee beau. I was pleased with him: fine black eyes, an intelligent countenance, perfectly genteel, sociable, smart and sensible, his manners easy and agreeable. We soon became acquainted. He tells me he was at New London in time of the war, and Mrs. Champlain drew his likeness, when she lived down by the Longbridge. He says Eliza Goddard introduced him. Perhaps your mother may recollect him. His name is Cotes or Coats, he is in the shipping business here. Mrs. Duryea regrets very much the match with Saydam is broken off–says he's a fine young man and does not want for sense. She thinks Charlotte has not used him well, tho' she don't know the particulars. But it's nothing to me. Come down and see to it yourself. I've enough to do to take care of my own business.

The watch-paper you sent is very well as to shade and colouring, and I dare say will be much admired; but there is a certain stiffness about it that does not accord with my ideas of ease and elegance. A fancy figure, and indeed Mother's, to appear well, should be drawn like *Fancy*, light and airy, in a loose flowing robe, and show the form as much as decency will permit–at least, not look like a stick with corsets on and a frock tied round it. Understood?

I found about twenty little pieces of broken green glass in the letter, which I suppose is the palate you sent to mix the shade tint upon. If that's the way you manage, no wonder you can never hit the right colour. Ivory and white earthen is the only things suitable to prepare colours upon. This I have told you a thousand times. I suppose the reason you go back stern in painting, and unlearn what you know, is because you have no one to scold and find fault with you, as I do. You are too much admired. Your mother praises all your works, and others cannot see, or if they do, will not point out your faults, like me, and tell you how to mend them. 'Tis easier to praise than to condemn, and more polite, and flattery is more exceptable than truth.

By all means put a crimson scarf on sister Fitch, which, as the drapery is white, you can throw around the form so as to make a background unnecessary; but if you make one, let it be pretty much the colour of *Lord Byron*'s coat. Don't forget the reflection from the crimson on the face and drapery. Put spectickles upon one of Fitches pictures–which you please. If upon the poorest likeness, it will improve it and make it equal to the best; if you choose to put them on the best, it will be still more striking, and be a suficient reason why the other is not as good. As to puting white paint on the other side, I don't think it's necessary. It is handsomer, without, than any mortal complexion. If you do, it must be a mere wash, very thin, or the space is so large it will be apt to break the paper.

You ask if those doves I mentioned had white paint on them. They had not. Carter says she [his 'beloved' who painted them] never uses it. I borrow'd the doves and copy'd them for a watch-paper which I so[ld] for three dollars. I have painted two others since, one like Maria's, for which I had six dollars, and the emblem of *Friendship*–for that, I had four. I will send you Carter's *Doves* in this letter to look at, and see what treatment they receive and how quick they return, before I dare venture Maria's. If, like Noah's dove, they return *soon* and safe, that is, in two or three days or by the first mail, Maria's watch-paper will come next. If not, perhaps you will never see it. You accuse me of giving a description of it to make your mouth water. I did not describe it at all. I only said I had painted one, and wish'd you could see it. When you do, you will judge for yourself, and perhaps be disappointed in your expectation. I don't know how soon Carter will call for his. You must keep it only long enough to take the outline. The design is simple, and I like it, but I made vast improvements in the copy I took. I don't know but this has faded. When I first saw it, I thought the doves were done with purple, but it now appears the colour of shade tint. I did mine with a bright blue purple, and the wings so much better and more like feathers, that now these look like bats' wings, in comparison. I put white on the other side both of the doves and the roses, which I made larger and double, to represent the moss rose. The branch, buds, and leaves, too, were improved, and also the Latten motto over the doves. It is, in English, *silent eloquence* or *speak with silence*. The *H* at the end is the first letter of her name, only put to fill up the chinks, and should be left out. Carter still keeps your *Cupid*. He has never sent it to his girl–says it is handsomer than any piece she has painted. I don't know but I may set him down for a beau of yours. He is a great admirer of genius and often enquires when I heard from you and how you come on.

Again I must encounter all the horrors of May Day. I have given up the house. The Tylues are the divel. I would not live with them another year if they would give it to me, and so I told him. Where I am to go I know not. Mr. [Charles] Holt will take a house in town this spring, and if he can find one large enough to accomodate his own family and me, for eight or none hundred dollars, which he thinks probable, he will furnish me with apartments. This I should like better than the little four- and five-hundred dollar houses I have lived in these two years past; but I dread living in the house with his children. Mrs. Holt observ'd she had a large troublesome family, but they should not trouble me if she could help it. This I believe, but fear it is not in her power to prevent it. They are not under the best government. But I would willingly risk this inconvenience in consideration of the advantage I should derive from such a situation for business as he will probably choose. But it is not certain a house can be found that will answer the purpose. However, if it is *best*, I know it will be; and if not, I don't desire it. I am wiser than I used to be, and make myself quite easy, knowing there is a house for me somewhere, and tho' I don't know where it is, I know it is exactly where it should be. It may be the *narrow house*, and to that I have no objection, so well assured I am that nothing will take place but what is perfectly right. Tell your good mother I am more confirm'd in the truth of this pernicious doctrine (as she considers it) every day and hour of my life, both from experience and observation, and I am pleased to find that Voltaire (whose works I am now reading), the greatest philosopher and wisest man that has lived since Solomon (so say the learned), is exactly of my opinion. I am charmed with him upon this subject. He says fatality, or what he calls destiny, is one of the elements of philosophy. On a close examination, the doctrine that opposes it appears loaded with absurdities and contrary to the idea of an eternal providence. But, he observes, some are destined to reason wrong, some not to reason at all, others to condemn those that do reason. And this too is right. . . .

I have come through this winter, so far, much better than I had reason to expect. What little business I have had has enabled me to pay my rent, buy wood, and live very comfortably (as to cloaths, I 'consider the lilly's' and wear my old ones). I have a nice little girl that waits upon me and is no trouble. I mention this because I never had any one to wait on me before but what was more trouble than all thier service was worth, and I had rather a thousand times wait on myself than be plagued with them. This was the case with Patty and all the rest I ever had to deal with. But this one suits me. She lives next door, comes whenever I want her, does all my errands and every-thing I wish, and then goes home. I tell her when to come again, and she never disappoints me.

You say you are never happier than when breaking the seal of one of my letters. I know you are happier now, and thankful I have at last come to the end of my paper.

Adieu.

Since I wrote this, Mrs. Cob call'd on me. I gave her the watch-paper for Maria which she admired very much. I made some inquiry respecting this Mr. Stanton you mention. She says he has lately been to New London. He belongs here. He is a fine young man, and no relation to the Stantons there. She says Maria has a ring for you which she will leave with me to send. When she does, you will receive it. I have seen sister Fitch and her husband, and find the law is repeal'd. Anna consents to have speckticles on one of the pictures, but not on the last. That on bark paper she says is for her own privet use. I've told the Miss Holts and Lucy Surtain thier watch-papers were done, and I expected them soon. They were much pleased, and want to see you very bad. Maria Hayden, too, and Hariot Miller make most affectionate inquiry, and many others too tedious to mention.

Adieu.

5

George Oliver Champlain

New London's very stable society was teased, sometimes confronted, by the knowledge of alternatives to its own ways to be found elsewhere. If those New London ways didn't suit you, because they left you poor or cramped or put-upon, you could try some other place where business might be better. It was this prospect that John Murray promised to Elizabeth Champlain back in the 1790s, this that "Uncle Taber" was seeking when he passed through New York in 1813 and again in 1818 with his too-numerous family; for even within the not very large circle of Mary Way at the time, there were those to whom New York itself might not seem to offer promise enough. Off they went, then, to look for their gold still further away–until, at the end, we see the youngest of the Champlain family on his way to New Orleans in search of the living that his home begrudged him. He was to die on that voyage.

In between these earlier dates of the 1790s and William Champlain's death in 1832, at various moments Betsey, Mary, and Eliza had all thought of moving, most often to points south. Two of the three turned thought into action.[1] Perhaps it was to be expected that George too should have tried his luck in New York in the summer of 1816, returned home after a few months, but grew restless again toward the end of the next year. He then renewed his travels south in the company of a young friend and distant kinsman; wrote home after his arrival in Natchez; and, in his mentions of home-town acquaintances and kinsmen there (including the same Holt family that helped Mary get started in New York), indicates how much on the move the youth of the young Republic were.

Besides whatever news he had to pass on, the warmth in his heart and the ill-regulated effervescence in his head together directed the flow of his letters, sometimes beyond easy understanding; but there is at least no difficulty in seeing what were his main concerns: earning a living, and the health of those he left at home, so many of whom seemed to be, in his mind, on the very edge of the grave. His homesickness made him write frequently for a while, beginning in January of 1817 from Natchez, where he was to remain for a year and a half. At the start he might have thought himself lucky to find employment with Andrew Marschalk, a man of considerable prominence in the city, in most years the state printer, and as knowledgeable in Mississippi ways as could be found:[2]

Dear Parents,

After a long, tedious, and extremely difficult journey of 100 & 12 days from N[ew] London, I have at last brot. up at this place, where I conclude to remain for the present, having obtain'd a profitable situation at my business here; and–what renders my prospects still more flattering–I am the only individual binder in the territory. Suffice it to say the situation suits me right well, and I am detirmen'd to remain here for some months. Wm. Deshon has left me to see his brothers at [New] Orleans, from which place I have just rec'd a line from him informing me that my business is very good their and that his brother is about employing him in some capacity or other which he does not mention in his letter. I was very much deceiv'd in his carachter–but 'tis no matter. Experience is the best teacher, as Mother says, and we have parted by mutual consent.

(Understand) the particulars of my journey I shall never commit to paper, but if we ever meet again, shall learn them verbally. . . .

I have just met a couple of my acquaintance here: Henry Huntington (formerly Capt. 37th Inf't station'd and well known at N[ew] London) & Chas. Clark brother of Capt. Arnold Clark of N[ew] London. Clark, however, leaves this place in a few days for N[ew] Orleans & from thence takes shipping for N[ew] York. In him I shall loose a valuable friend. They are both merchants here. Clark has been here 1 month longer than myself, but Huntington has been establish'd a year or better, together with his brother Horace, who has lately married a fortune here, & Henry is about following his example, I understand.

Write me immediately upon the receipt of this and inform me of the situation of Sam'l & Wm. Eliza I am not so anxious about, she having already a trade. Give my love to all kin, both sides the house [Way and Champlain], & to Uncles Ebb'z & Thos. Particularly request them all to write me, as likewise Elisha Stanton if he has return'd from the East Indies yet, & to that unaccountable Scott of Scotts, H[alsey] Godard, who has sent his *non-diagonal* comp[limen]ts to Chas. Clark in the letter he rec'd from him.

And a week later (**no. 23**):

Honour'd Parents,

Being fully aware of the anxious solicitude you are under by not hearing from me of late, an opportunity now offers which I shall embrace, an no doubt the disappointment will be agreeable when you receive this, as I was under the full impression after my leaving you that you had form'd no very agreeable opinion of my destination, on account of the abrupt manner of my leaving you on that never-to-be-forgotten night. But howsomever, everything for the best (as Aunt Hannah says).

After a journey of about 2500 miles I have at last hove too under (Father knows what sail). Immaterial–But suffice it that I am in a dam'd snug berth, which is nothing more nor less than my business at this place, which is to conduct a bindery for And. Marschalk Esq. (editor of the *Washington Repub.*) who has engaged me to carry on the business for him, he furnishing a room, materials & stock, & myself to execute the work and receive one half the net profits arising therefrom.

(this endeth the first lesson, Parson Seabury)

I have commenced, and I assure you my prospects at present look flattering, having a great deal more than I can possible attend to in my line, & an assurance of patronage from some eminent characters in the place. (You comprehend). I have likewise found two or three of my accquaintance at this place, viz. Chas. Clark merch't, brother of Arnold Clark the son-in-law of Stephen Holt Esq., & Capt.s Brown & Huntington–one of the 25th, the other 37th Reg't, U. S. Inf't, formerly station'd at N[ew] London. The first is destin'd for Orleans where he is attach'd to the Ordnance department, but the other is a citizen of the place, having establish'd himself in the mercantile line and about settling here permanently–other-wise speaking, taking an extra rib to himself (now you understand, Father, for no one else can), who is poss[ess]ed (according to common report) of that combustible matter which (to use Master Dow's expression), never fail'd to make the mare go.[3] So much for so much. Success to him, for he is a fine little fellow and a good friend of mine, and that's all I care for. He lost nothing by his first failure (comprenevieue). But Chas. Clark is a genuine true & sincere friend to me, and therefore I desire you to treat him for my sake accordingly. Enough.

But to return. The toils & dangers, trials and difficulties under which I labour'd to accomplish my first grand inland perigrination was great in the extreme, and Oh! I could a tale unfold. But 'tis no matter. A very little time will clear up all and make me learn'd as some is and as close to the point.

I sincerely hope this may find you all well, but I fear some has taken there departure for the *Holy Land* (not Palestine), as I have heard with great regret the death of 2 young men in the public journals at the island of Martinico: N. French & D. Prentis. I am right sorry for their relatives whom I am sensible will deeply feel their loss. Poor John Prentis. . . . I hope none of my blood of either house is gone (either of Montagu or Capulet) to try the undiscovered country from whose bourn no traveller was ever yet permitted to return.

Mr. Clark takes charge of this and perhaps two or 3 more, but possible I may send them a different rout. At any rate, answer immediately uppon the receipt of this and let me know the trouble in the wigwam. My others by the mail will go (that is, when I write) direct to Ebenezer Way Esq., who I hope is well, as also his *rib* & fam. & his rib. No offence, I hope, Sally & Dolly. As for Aunt Polly [Mary Way], she will stand the shock and buffets of this life equal to Job or his turkey or any other sheet anchor man. I beg pardon of you, Mother's sister. To the point. Do for Heaven's sake write me about the boys and of their situation or expectations, for I think more than you are aware of about them and of Eliza's expectations

& health. Tell her to write me as also the boys and yourself, and give my love to Aunt [. . . Uncle] Oliver [. . .] Aunt Hannah and Aunt Polly, who I hope is enjoying every comfort this life can possible afford, for she well deserves it, as likewise give my love to the Old Standards–Grandmothers Champlain & Way, likewise to to Uncles Taber & Allen's family. So now I have the 2nd lesson finished, therefore the peace of the Lord be amongst you, and remain with you always.

And later in the same month (**no. 24**) George writes again, with a not very serious apology appended to the bottom of the page, "(Erratta not corrected till my next, as I never read proof)," and with a word changed and a line dropped out of the poetry he quotes, because he quotes from memory:

Dear Father,

The following extract is from the pen of Lord Byrons', & in my opinion may be rank'd with some of the most grand & fiery similies in the *Illiad.* If you never read his *Corsair,* I will request you now to, very confidant that you will be highly pleased with the poem. It commences from the introduction of Conrad (who is the hero of the piece) into the presence of the Seyd or Sultan at the Divan (or Court), who is disguised as a dervise or pilgrim. During the interview at the pallace which fronts the bay, some of Conrad's crew had enter'd the harbour & set fire to several of the Turkish fleet (Conrad's orders to that effect being executed too soon betrays him). The Sultan descries the conflagration of his ships &, bursting with *horror* & fury at the treachery of Conrad, orders him in double irons & close confinement immed'ly, their to await his punishment, which was to be the most dreadful death. But it being some time since I read the poem, I have forgot the more sinister particulars.

But to the poetry. The Sultan speaking to Conrad (previous to his detecting his treachery) exclaims:

Well as thou wilt, ascetic as thou art,
One question answer. Then in peace depart.
How many–*Ha!* It cannot sure be day.
What light, what fire, is bursting on the bay?
Ho! treachery. Say Guards, my scimitar
&c

Then follow . . .

Up rose the Dervise with that burst of light,
Nor less his change of form, appall'd the sight
–Up rose the Dervise, not in saintly garb
But like a warrior bounding from his barb;
Doss'd his high cap and tore his robe away.
Shone his mail'd breast and flash'd his sabre's ray.
His close but glittering casque & sable plume,
More glittering eyes, and black brows' sable gloom
&c &c–––

As I am no critic or connossieur of poetry, I shall not attempt to judge of the merits of the extract, but I sincerely think it is but little inferior to any of the Father of Verse's (Homer) most chivalric parts of the *Illiad*. However, with me the first impression is always the best, and I assure you that it struck me forcibly the inst. I had finish'd it.

Plenty of work at present, & enjoying excellent health (which God knows I hope you share the same blessing). I shall be along the coast in a year or so, where I sincerely hope that untill that time none of you will have acscended unto the tomb of all the Capulets.

Toward the middle of the next month, with an early mention of the Colonel Green to whom he had once been apprenticed, he writes further about his prospects and plans in his business, bookbinding:[4]

. . . You no doubt will receive news of me ere this reaches you either by the letter which Clark wrote home, in which he mention'd me, or by seeing my advertisement in Col. Marschalk's paper, which I sent on to Col. Green some weeks since, with a request to him for an exchange of papers. I have an eye to windward! and had before I started this journey.

Am in good health and good business. Will probably be along your coast in a year or two. Father, you must not go 'to that bourne from which no traveller was ere permited to return' untill I see you again–that is, if you can possible avoid the summons of that stern & unfeeling sheriff.

Enough nonsense. Tell Sam to write, as likewise Eliza, of everything which has taken place since my leaving their–deaths, marriages *et cet.* Send at least a doz. letters and let Uncle Ebb [New London's postmaster] direct them, as probably I can get them free by that method. Give my love to that ancient relic of Old Clifford's shores, Aunt Hannah–(alias) Congress. Tell her I think we'll see each other ere she takes her departure for the Stygian shades.

Next, in July of 1817 to his parents (**no. 28**):

Your 2. vols. in one have just come to hand (I suppose scarcity of paper was the reason). I could not admire the cold frigid & austere stile of Father's note when compared with Mother's *few* but affectionate lines; but I'll make ample allowances for his eccentricity by supposing that, as he is but just arrisen from a sick bed (which I was sincerely sorry to hear he had been sick), that he is still a little more fretful & irratable than when in good health. My God, it is very surprising that you have not received one out of the numerous letters I wrote you which I sent by my friend Mr. Spencer of this place, who arrived in New York (by the papers of that place) by the 8th of May.

I shall leave this place in a few months for Baltimore or Philad'a, as I have bound up almost all the books they have in the [Mississippi] Territory. I have made *something* since I have been away from you & I intend to make a *greater something* ere I see you again. I would send you on a sum of money if I could devise any safe means of conveyance but I have no accquaintance or friends to take charge of it, and I dare not trust it in this letter, as villany & wickedness had almost if not quite arrisen to its zenith in this world. But however I sleep with only one eye shut, has H. Goddard says; & God knows it stands me in hand to do so, as they are not too good to robb the communion table, 3/4ths of them in this place.

Pray write me about the boys and tell me where and what Sam is about. I feel a deeper interest in his welfare than you are aware of. Give my sincere love to Eliza, Aunt Hannah, Grandmother & Aunt Tracy. I was affraid that one or both of those antient representatives of each house had slip their wind; but they hold it as well as any craft I ever knew. Success to them. I hope I shall see them ere they depart the Stygian shades.

Spelling his family name one way as he signs off, he goes on in the next surviving letter of January 1818 (**no. 31**) to try it two other ways, for reasons known only to a man of many roles and poses, destined later for a second career on the stage. His concerns with health reflect those of his correspondents–but the reality as well. In this year yellow fever, annual in its ravages in New Orleans, cast a shadow on Natchez as well:[5]

Your several letters I have rec'd by due course of mail, for which I thank you, as I was fearful that some of you was or had shaped your course to the other world. I hope Aunt Hannah still is afloat, althoug her bark is very ancient & out of course– some of her timbers if not all in a decay'd state. But as Charles Wheat used to say, she belongs to the family of Methusala, (alias) never-dying breed. You must not think I envy her. On the contrary, I do sincerely pity her case, being obliged to buffet the storms of this infernal gulph of sin & sorrow in her old age and infirmities. However, I hope we shall meet again. If not, 'Peace be with her.' Here endeth the first lesson (Parson Seabury).

I am glad to here of Sam having obtained a situation, although I know it to be only a temporary one, and of course not one that can possible benefit him much; but I likewise know it to be of some benefit, by relieving you of a considerable expence. Bill, I hope, will keep the birth he has obtained, as it will qualify him for other kinds of busines as well as if he was a clarck to a merchant; or perhaps he can obtain a similar situation hereafter, when he may be compelled to roam, as I was, when scarcely 'nineteen summers had matured my thoughts.'

But I hope he may prove more fortunate than I (poor devil). I have nearly closed my business at this place. I cannot yet tell what I shall turn to upon yet or what point I shall shape my course for when I leave it–but probably New Orleans. I have hopes to get into a nother line of business. But I cannot tell yet. I have lost my poor friend Cha's W. Clark, as good a hearted fellow as ever lived. This assertion I have & always will maintain. I likewise lost by the pestilence which then raged here and at [New] Orleans all my most intimate friends & accquaintances. Some of them were of the first respectability in Natchez & all (of which I speak) about my own age. Fortunately for me, my constitution was not quite so delicate as some, which enabled me to weather the squall–and a black one it was, two, I'll assure you. We lost 300 of our citizens of this place in about 8 weeks, and at one time so alarming was the progress of that fatal fever that the city was totally deserted–as much so as ever Babylon was, their not being six families in it. I fled to the country on the 19 October, immediately after I had 'lent a hand' to plant seven of my friends (I make use of the term plant in consequence of the burying ground of this city's being called after the name of a negro fellow who was our sexton–we call it Jones's Plantation) who died that morning. I thought it time then to haul off. I staid in the country one month. Athoug I was in the city almost every day, I was not at all apprehensive on my own account. I can't tell the reason, but so it was. However, I suffer'd a great deal by the loss of so many friends and accquaintance. But 'such was the will of fate.'

Their is no birth here open for either of the boys, & if there were I would be opposed to their coming, as this climate is too unhealthy for a northern citizen ever to live long in. 5 from the 'Land of Shady Habits' (alias) Connecticut died here in the course of 3 days. . . . Poor Guy Champlin is no more.

Of this last figure, a distant but important cousin (Kin-chart C), more will be said later. Here in explanation: George's uncle Lodowick Champlain, 'one of the bravest and most skilful of the New London seamen' who fought to keep the Sound clear of Loyalist privateers in the 1770s, named one of his sons after his father-in-law, a man himself renowned for his role in the Revolution. This son was Guy Richards Champlain (1785–1817), commander of the letter-of-marque *General Armstrong* during the War of 1812, who on a well reported occasion engaged a British frigate off Surinam, disabled it, survived the encounter despite his wounds, and in a later command proved successful in many other engagements elsewhere; he subsequently pursued a military career as a naval captain in service to revolutionaries in South America. Lodowick's brother Oliver was also prominent in the War of 1812, while his second son was Samuel, the "Major" of letters to follow.[6] In Newport, from a distant branch under a different spelling, one Champlin, charming belle of the Revolutionary period, was mother-in-law to Commodore Matthew Calbraith Perry; another Champlin, wife to Mathew's brother Oliver Hazard Perry; and it was a third brother of these two, Nathaniel, whose portrait was painted by Betsey at the time the young man came to fetch his bride in New London.[7] Together, all these persons constituted an extended family of real war heroes whose exploits were published in the New London and New York papers and in honorific resolutions addressed them by civic groups. Young George was understandably proud of being known to them.

When he next writes, he leads off with assurances that he is surviving the epidemic (**no. 35**, of March 1818); and he adds some doodling, "Thompsonary & Dictionary," etc., in the margins:

I am well & in good health. I likewise sincerely hope you enjoy the same.

I earnestly request Father not to address A. Marschalk again on the subject that he has (information respecting his son!). I am in this place in tolerable good business at present, which will more than probable be bettered e're long. A. Marschalk, with whom I have for some months since had no connection with (in consequence of detecting the villain), yesterday morn sent an unsealed letter to me (written by yourself) directed to him, containing an earnest request of him to forward immediately 'any information he may be in possession of respecting his son! GOC.'

I know not the cause which has prevented you from hearing of me at least every two months, as upon my honour, I assure you that I have wrote 5 letters within the time that you assert you have not heard from me. I know not what to attribute the irregular receipts of letters (from each side) to, unless it is to be imputed to some derangement in the run of the mails. I cannot think of their being any fraud practised (interception), as I think our correspondence of two little consequence to a third person to be any inducement for that act; but you may depend that you are in 'arrears!' for nine letters which I have written you and for which no mention is made of (in those few I have rec'd) of your ever having rec'd them. Please direct all your letters to me! hereafter, as I assure you, my dear Parents, that I am not negligent or inattentive to the arrival of the mails. But I have been most severely disappointed of a letter from you, numberless times, which has almost caused me to swear to drop correspondence altogether–but only in my 'irriatable mood' that idea was entertained. I have wrote you at least five-and-twenty letters, and have rec'd seven in return. I shall expect all arrearages to be made up shortly.

I admired that quotation in Mother's last epistle, from Young. The selection did equal honor to her head & heart, & she may rest assured that it shall not be lost on her affectionate son,

G. O. Champlin

To his sister Eliza in April (**no. 37**):

Having received but one letter from you since your arrival in New York (the bearer of which was Mr. Mathewson) and having sent you an answer to it immediately upon its receipt, accompanied with another letter (which of course must long ere this have come to hand), and as it is now better than two months since 'these great transactions came to pass,' I think it about time to jog your memory on this head, hoping by this means to get a second epistle of some kind or other from you. At the time your letter was handed me, by D. Mathewson, I had just returned from the country (about 20 miles in the interior from this place), to which we all were obliged to flee in consequence of a fatal pestilence which visited our city the two last fall months of Sept. & October. For my own part, I narrowly escaped, for the next day after my arrival in the country I was violently attacked with all the symptoms of the disease, which prostrated me for one week; but by the aid of good attendance, & these complying with my prescriptions (which was 100 grains of calomel, in two doses), and a naturally strong constitution to boot, I got the 'weather guage' of my sickness. I have no doubt that I contracted the disease in this city, as I was in the habit of frequently visiting the houses of my sick friends & accquaintances, of whom the majority is no more. Amongst them was my lamented friend Chas. W. Clark, whose loss I have most sensibly felt and which I shall ever regret. He, however, died at Washington, six miles from this place, and was their buried. I am now enjoying as good health as I ever experienced in the 'Land of Steady Habits.' . . .

Please give my most sincere esteem & respects to that truly amiable & charitable lady Mrs. Dawson, as the attention and kindness that she manifested for me when an invalid (alias, salt-water boils) you know will always be remembered by me with gratitude. Likewise, to Miss Hannah and Thomas [Dawson], whom I respect much (as we were port-mates if not shipmates in Bordeaux). . . .

George in July addresses his father for the first time by his nautical title, "Captain G. W. Champlain," testifying to the pride he took in him (**no. 44**):

I leave this place for New Orleans tomorrow. I cannot tell what kind of business I shall engage in after I arrive or whether I will remain there any length of time. This is an unhealthy season of the year to visit that city, but as it is the opinion of old residents of this town that there is but little difference in the health of the two places at this time (there being several cases of sickness here as well as there, now–nothing malignant, however) and it being generally allowed to be as warm in Natchez as N[ew] Orleans, I conceive the risk I run will not be great by the exchange of places. At all events, the particular nature of my affairs render it indispensably necessary for me to go. There is nothing further to be done at my business here, I having done up all the binding which was in the place; and as the book-store here keeps a constant supply of blank work on hand, and a number of the merchants import their blank books from the eastward at a much lower price than I could afford to make them, that branch of binding would be unprofitable to me. I could get into the mercantile line, if I chose, but my situation would not be such as I conceive could ultimately benefit me, nor would it be immediately as lucrative as a birth at my own business in New Orleans; for I have had several liberal offers from binders in that place since I have been in Natchez; but my engagements here prevented my meeting them at the time. Now, however, I shall comply with their request, as I have just squar'd the yards here.

At present I enjoy better health than I have for some months past, for I have just recovered from a severe dyssentery which was preceeeded by an attack of the fever & ague which, with the former disorder, reduced me to 'a tailor's yard or a dried neat's tongue!' (as Falstaff says to Hall). But thanks to the deity, I am now gaining my health and vigor rapidly and am pretty confidant that I shall be more hearty than I have ever been heretofore. If I find upon my arriving at [New] Orleans I can stand the clime, I shall probably remain some months in the city; but if not, I shall be compelled to shape my course for a northern or eastern port.

Please direct no more letters to this place, nor indeed *don't write me* untill you hear from me again, which you may rest assured you will, as soon as I procure a situation in N. O.

Give my love to the boys and to Eliza, as well as the different relatives of either house; tell William his individual letter has never come to hand, but his & E. Stanton's joint epistle was duly received. Samuel's and a note from Uncle Tom

[Champlain] in the same has likewise been received, but I am sure a great number of yours and others from home have miscarried, as well as about a dozen of mine. What cause to impute it to, I know not. Your two several letters, written last and enclosed in a blank envelope to me by Uncle Eben. Way, is received. I was sensibly affected at the gloomy forbebodings which Father expressed relative to the state of his system. But I fear it is more of a mental than a corporeal malady. In either case, God's will be done. I hope I shall be permitted to see all of those whom I left behind me before they 'leave this mortal state.' But should they be call'd hence, may they enjoy that happiness eternal which the poor wanderers through this 'thorny vale' can never know. Adieu.

Duly arrived in New Orleans, and after a long gap in the correspondence, George is prodded into writing to Eliza by her recent reproaches for his silence (**no. 66**, of December 23, 1819):

Your kind (tho' voluminous) epistle, which I like, has just been handed me by Mr. Williamson, whose politeness and attention I am much indebted to, as I suspect he was at some pains and trouble in finding out my residence–which (by the bye) is not a 'stupendous fabric'. He, however, very politely offer'd to take charge of my answer to you and forward it immediately by a ship (whose name I forget) now on the eve of sailing–for the which of course I thank him, &c &c.

To return: in answer to your first inquiry, this must be a satisfactory & conclusive proof of my still being in this 'terrestial sphere.' That you all have had ample cause of alarm I readily admit, from the circumstance of knowing that all the communications from residents in this place (during the summer) to their 'friends in the North' have been more or less exaggerated, relative to the health of this city. That it has been severe is a serious fact; but that it was as formidable as some of your city papers stated I deny. The truth is, there did not exceed 1200 deaths (during the sickly period) by malignant fever, although there were many swept off at the same time by other diseases–the dysentery or Cholera Morbus particularly raged with considerable violence among a certain class of the community (the Kentucky boatmen) and others in that line, and probably from 2 to 300 suffered by that complaint; so that, upon a fair calculation made by some of the best informed citizens (among whom, 2 or 3 are physicians of my acquaintance), it may be safely asserted that 1500 was the extreme number that died during the 'trying months' (as they are familiarly termed): July, August, Sept. & Oct. . . .

After comments on the news from home regarding Mary and Aunt Hannah,

You will please inform Aunt Mary that it is not possible for me to return to you this fall or winter, owing to the nature of my engagements with Mr. Jansen, but that I will make every exertion (consistent with my interest) to enable me to effect an arrangement whereby I may visit you by June or July next, to spend the autumn with you (winter I could not stand, having grown so effeminate in this southern clime) and in 'Old N[ew] London' (as Sam says). Give my sincere love to Aunt Mary, tell her that I have neglected her personally (for the which I have to beg pardon), but that I always intended the letters address'd you should be subject to her perusal–for I always have mentioned her in every letter that I ever have written to any individual in the family since my absence.

I am highly gratified at the 'proficiency' which you inform you have made in your vocation. I have only to wish that you may excell both Mother & Aunt Mary (which by the bye I hardly think possible), and be enabled to convert hereafter into a lucrative business that which was first adopted by you, in early youth, but as an amusement. I should like very well to see the singular 'Non-descript' you mention ["Sandy" Clarke], as I think he must (from your description) be one of the 'modern literati of the present age.' But alass! I have my doubts whether the able tutoress whom he is under will ever succeed in making a 'Raphael' or a 'West' of him. I fear he is one of those 'unfortunate wights' that Gray or Goldsmith describes so admirably.

Knowledge to his eyes her ample page,
Rich with the spoils of time, did ne'er unrol;
Chill penury repress'd his noble rage
And froze the genial current of his soul.

But I have been guilty of 'plagiarism' long enough. Therefore to the point. Please give my sincere respects to Mrs. Dawson, Miss Dawson, and to Tho's D.–a family, Eliza, which I always did and which I always shall entertain the warmest respects & friendship for. I congratulate you upon your good fortune in being placed under the same roof with such an amiable family (would to G . . . it might ever be my lot again) in whose society you canst but enjoy yourself. How different from that in which poor Mother was placed at your age, when that 'imperious step-dame' (which she has often told us about) rul'd with despotic sway at the old mansion. I have no doubt that Aunt M. as well as Mother will admit Shakspear's couplet to have been applicable to her at that time–

She gives the bastinado with her tongue–
Our ears are cudgelled with it.

But to conclude with your own words, 'I suspect I have already wearied your patience–if not, I have my own' (which is a fact with me). I have to request you will in your answer to this short epistle, which I shall expect by the first safe conveyance that offers, inform me of domestic affairs generally in N[ew] L[ondon], but particularly of the situation of the 2 boys and that of Father, whether thier has been any change in his moral character (since my absence) for the better! If not, be silent on the head. I have not heard from him direct for some months. The cause I know not. I always direct my letters to him, altho' I write him & Mother on the same sheet. Be sure and transmit me on all information you can possibly glean relative to the 2 boys. They have repeatedly solicited me to give them some encouragement from this quarter relative to a trade. To this request I have two, and I think both very powerful, objections. They are these. Those mechanics who carry on business in this place generally employ journeyman and but few have apprentices. Those who have, take the Creoles of the country–Colour'd boys! Of course that objection I view as insurmountable. Again, I am positive that their risk would be extreme during the summer months, and if they were taken by the fever here during the first summer, I strongly fear they would both 'bid the world good night,' as 9/10ths of the newcomers here, if they are taken by the fever, never recover. This I know (not by experience, thank God) but by observation. For myself, I consider I am now a Creole of the country, alias, case-harden'd; for I have never known what the disease in the country, for I was initiated in St. Domingo, you recollect. You would not know me, I am positive, were you to see me, as I have undergone a thorough revolution in person & features.

However, I find I'm 'drifting on a lee shore,' and I shall 'shortly be aground' unless I 'come too' by 'dropping anchor.' So 'here goes'!!

By May of the next year (1820) the news of his father's death had reached him, and he writes to his mother (**no. 70**):

It is with sincere grief I learn the fate of poor Father, although I confess I have for some time past anticipated it, as Sam & Bill's last letters described his case minutely. I should not wonder to learn that he hail'd death with joy! from the description given of his situation & sufferings by them. But nature's debt is paid and he is 'where the weary are at rest.' Unfortunate man! I believe he had been long weary of his 'clay tenement,' which has at last yielded up its troubled spirit into the hands of its Maker! Throug him may he receive grace and life everlasting.

I fear your attentions to him and deprivations of rest which you must have subjected yourself to, during his long confinement, may have undermined your own health. God forbid that it should be the case, for if you should get sick, your situation would be more pityable, if possible, than his, in your present circumstances. In your answer, please to inform me of the exact state of your health and your present & future prospects.

Mr. A. J. Robertson is the bearer of this to you; he leaves here to morrow morning in the new steam-ship for N[ew] York, at which place he must arrive in 10 or 12 days at fartherest (barring accidents), from whence he proceeds immediately up for N[ew] London, as he informed me.

Enclosed you will find seventy dollars: a small sum I acknowledge, but which is, I seriously assure you, all the cash I could command at present. It will answer as a temporary relief which you stand much in need of, I suspect, at this time. I have sent the boys all the black clothes I was the owner of, old & new, which they perhaps will have to get altered further, and brushed, or scoured, if they think them worth it. I shall keep the news a secret for some time until I can afford the purchase of a suit, as all my present stock of clothing is of other colours; but I don't know as it's hardly worth my while, being such a distance from home, and it being in itself a mere ceremony or 'outward show.'

Request Eliza to write me is she is in N[ew] London (for I don't know which place she is in, N. Y. or N. L.), as I have not heard from her for some months. I can not arrange my affairs this season as to admit my coming personally, but I will try to succeed next. I have enjoyed remarkable good health during my long residence in this city at all seasons. May the same blessing still be continued to me during the remainder of my stay. Give my love to all, particularly Aunt Hannah. Please let me know what Uncle O. is about there.
– Adieu dear Mother, for the present.

Your affectionate son,

Geo. O. Champlin

NB–Dear Mother. In consequence of not being enabled to procure N. York notes to enclose in my letter, I am compelled to transmit you specie. It is packed up snugly in two stout paper wrappers, and Mr. Robertson has it in charge in his trunk. I should have sent you a full hundred, if I could have raised it at the moment, but I assure you that cash even in this place is equally as scarce at present as honesty is all over the world! –– Please let me know the general habits of Father for the last 2 or three years.

Ever yours,

G. O. C.

Answering the request in the postscript, William wrote back and George acknowledged it, and added some teasing of Samuel under his family nickname "Boreas" (**no. 77** of August):

Yours & Sam's came by due course of mail to hand, in both of which are respectively stated the receipt of 'box of clothes' & 'seventy dollars,' which affords me pleasure to learn came safe to hand, through the attention & punctuality of Mr. Robertson, to whom I feel much indebted. I wish, my dear boy, that it had been more in my power to have given you all a more liberal token of my regard, but alass! the 'iron hand of poverty' still hangs o'er me as well as yourselves. Notwithstanding all the 'court' I have paid the 'fickle dame,' she still averts her visage from poor 'pilgarlick'.

But enough of this.–Appropos–I cannot, however, but admire the animated & (I hear) exaggerated picture you have drawn of the mutual feelings which pervaded each breast upon the sight of 'Boreas' advancing towards the house with that 'tallisman' (the box) under his arm and (set aside 'specie!) the not-a-little mortification you must unavoidably have felt at finding the contents to be–what!–why, 'gentle reader,' nothing but 2 or 3 half-worn articls of clothing. Hardly enough altogether to furnish forth one decent 'suit of sables.' But, my dear fellow, take 'the will for the deed,' and let this apology make up for your disappointment, when I candidly assure you that when I threw them into the box, I threw in the 'widow's mite'–my all (of that colour). Consequently, I now forever take my leave of that subject and of 'beggarly accounts of empty boxes.'

You will accept my thanks, William, for the able & feeling manner in which you have detailed to me the particulars respecting the last moments of our poor parent.

> I can only say, the perusal of your letter afforded me 'a luxury of anguish' which I would not at that time have exchanged for 'a luxury of bliss.'

Enclosed in a box George adds, "Heaven that denies the luxury of bliss shall yield at least the luxury of anguish & teach us the stern pride of wretchedness!!" and, drawing a hand to point to his brother's initials, continues,

> Imitate his virtues but avoid his infirmities: W. C. With regard to myself, I am still enjoying the best of health, a blessing which the Deity has still continued to extend to me in this unhealthy clime during the last four years of my life. (May I fully appreciate this divine goodness.) At present the city is tolerably healthy, although there has been several deaths latterly of the billious fever; but from what I can learn, those who have fell victims to it are all foreigners, emigrants who have recently arrived and who had never resided here during a summer. Of course, they might be considered as proper subjects for it at this period. For myself, the nature of my vocation is such as probably to render me less exposed than any other male individual in the city, being constantly within doors, rarely going out of house oftener than once a week (in the day time); for it is, in my opinion, exposure to our burning sun during the day at this season which destroys human life in this place so fast. The nights here are at this season, in pleasant weather, delightfully cool & refreshing, and it has always been my regular custom (after closing the store) to walk a couple of hours in the evening on the levee or some public walk (throughout the year), and instead of being any detriment, I concieve it to be an advantage to me, as the uninterrupted state of good health which I have enjoyed is a pretty conclusive proof, I think. . . .

Like William, Samuel Champlain wrote of their father's death; he too asks about the advisability of joining his oldest brother in search of work; and he too is put off by George's response in August (**no. 78**):

> I thank you for your kindness in complying with the request I made you, in my last, relative to the particulars attending father's illness, prior to and after his decease, and do not think I flatter ('for what advancement can I hope from thee, who no revenue hast') when I affirm that in my opinion there are sentiments in that letter, together with an originality of thought, combined with nervous language, which I say would do honour to an older head than yours. Sam, I admire your style & diction, the which, with a little cultivation, could be materially improved. I would advise you to devote the leisure moments you have, when released from your daily avocation, to the accquirement of litterary knowledge or some useful historical works. Particularly would I suggest the perusal of Robertson's *America* by you; for a knowledge of one's own country ought to be accquired before that of any other (a mistake which I was guilty of & the bad effects of which is now felt).[8] Likewise acquaint yourself thoroughly with figures, as a good accountant can always be a useful man in any community. I would recommend to you to wholly throw aside all light frivolous works of which the country now teems with–I mean novels & & such-like trash–for I can by experience assure you that by devoting your time to them you are sacrificing

a trasur (which time is) which you never can recover, as I am satisfied that they are productive of more injury (to a young mind of a certain cast), ultimately, than they are an advantage (I am a living witness to the truth of this); &, to use the old proverb, 'they are sweet in the mouth but bitter in the belly.'

I wish you to acquaint me what progress you have made in 'Daboll' since I left their–how far you have cyphered, & whether Mr. Holt gives you charge of his 'books' yet.[9] I should feel proud that were the case, for I know that by a little study & attention to modern forms of book-keeping you could very soon qualify yourself their to fill, hereafter, a higher & more lucrative situation, the which may be open to you (provided you possess those qualifications) sooner than you may be aware of. Assist (in the mean-time, Sam) Mother, as far as lies in your power, which I don't doubt you do, for I assure you their is no duty paramount to that, from a child.

I hope one of 'these days' that I shall be enabled to retrieve in part our name! (you take my idea). If I fail, it will not be from negligence or from lack of exertion, but from Miss Fortune. I hope likewise that I may have the happiness yet to be my brothers' making the same exertions to effect the same purpose. If they do, may they be crowned with success, is my first wish.

Sam, you will excuse this hastily penn'd & badly organized letter, as I am uncommonly impatient, latterly, when I commence a letter, to get to the end of it (as I always did lack, you know, 'patience & thread'); for my ideas flowing so fast, I don't stop to select from among the host in my brain, but commit those to paper which come uppermost–good, bad or indifferent, barber fashion, 'first come, first served;' and if [you] can delve & pump my meaning out of this 'hieroglyp[hic] scrawl' of a hand, you are as profound a scholar as the 'Templar' Brian-de-Bois-Gilbert of *Ivanhoe*'s memory.

He closes with mentions of various friends and kin New-London connected: George Colfax the river captain, Green who taught him his craft, Thatcher and Goddard and others of his age.

Then toward the end of the year (**no. 84** of December 1820) his fortunes for a moment improved:

This is the first leisure moment that I have had for a period of 2 months (as I may say), in consequence of the death of Mr. Jansen.[10] He died on the 4th Oct., not of the epidemic that prevailed at the time but of a liver-complaint. As he died intestate, it was necessary for some one to administer upon his estate, which was estimated at about $5,000. He was not owing me enough at the time of his decease to authorize my acting in that capacity. Independent of that circumstance, I laboured under a further difficulty–that of not being a free-holder or (in other words) not possessing any real estate. Consequently I could not obtain security for 'double the amount' (as is the law) of his estate; and another individual administered. However, I attended the auction sale and purchased in such part of his stock as I wanted, together with the bindery *en masse;* and (as Paddy says) 'I now have set up for myself.' My prospects are pretty good as yet. I have near a thousand dollars' work engaged and as I rent the establishment which he occupied I have a small stock of stationery and acc't books for sale, which must do for the present, until I can effect an arrangement which will enable me to extend my business. I pay $30 per month rent and I let out my back yard and kitchen to a neighbor, who keeps 'bachelors' hall,' and get my board free.

It will be impossible, my dear Bill, to speak with certainty upon my 'promised visit,' altho' I will make exertions to come if possible, the ensuing spring. But, you know, that must depend on circumstances. I live in a 'blasting clime,' it is well known, and altho' you or Sam might, if a situation could be obtained here, make money, still, the risk you would run would destroy my peace, through apprehension by seeing you here. It is a fact (so help me God) what I assert to you. I have been told many times that I have been more fortunate than 999 out of a thousand, and I believe it, for I have lived through 3 out of 4 of the most sickly summers that the country has ever experienced, and not been touched with fever. . . .

I saw Major Sam Champlain (Guy's brother) the other day. We recognized each other at the Meridian Hotel where we met. He is a fine looking man. He has resigned his commission and is here upon his business relative to his brother's property. Let me know Eliza's prospects, wherever she is, as I despair of ever getting another letter from her. Geo. Colfax is here. We lodge together. He is in daily expectation of getting the command of one of the steam boats.[11] Geo. is a smart young fellow and will do well, know doubt. I received four of the New London papers a short time since and I sent yesterday a no. of the *Orleans Gazette* on to you. If A. J. Robertson is there yet, request him to bring out about a groce of Manwaring's best sheep skins, as I will purchase them.

He reverts to the Major in his next of February 1821 to Sam (**no. 90**):

. . . I was at the theatre the other evening and I fell in with your namesake, Samuel Champlain (brother of Guy), formerly a Major in the U. States Service but now resigned. He is, I assure you, a very fine man, perfectly a gentleman. In the course of conversation he asked me if I knew or recollected our family coat-of-arms. I answered, I did not, exactly (having forgotten the 'heraldic bearings' and terms). He requested me to write Uncle O. or some of you for information respecting it and this, in part, is the object of this note. I wish you would be good enough to speak to Uncle Oliver and ascertain from him the 'device' and 'motto', and transmit it on to me, in your answer. For what purpose he made the inquiry I am unable to say, but as I promised him I would satisfy him so soon as a letter could go and return from you. He expressed himself much obliged to me, and would depend upon you for information. Do be good enough to be particular in giving the 'minutia' of the Coat, and forward your answer as soon as written. . . . If I mistake not, Uncle O. has in possession a copy of the coat of arms taken from the original in the Heralds' College, London, which he received when he was in Europe.

In September when George again writes to William it is to reassure him once more of his own health, to report the city so far spared the annual onset of yellow fever, and to respond to good news about the youngest; for Samuel had found a job as clerk with the flour merchants Holt and Quinby:[12]

> I feel extremely obliged to you for the information you gave me respecting Sam'l. It afford'd me much pleasure. I would wish you, however, to enquire out his particular address, as I am as yet totally ignorant of either the name of his employer or the St. I wish him success, which he can't but have, provided he conducts with that circumspection & caution which I fancy he is possessed of–altho' you know him much better than myself, of late years, I having not seen him since almost a child.
>
> I regret to inform you of the decease of my poor friend Geo. Colfax. He died up the river 10 miles above Baton-Rouge. He was Master of the *Ohio* steam boat. The nature of his complaint I have not as yet learn'd but believe it was fever. However, the news is authentic, his owners in this place having received a letter from the boat to that effect. 'Death's shafts fly thick, The cry goes round, & who so artful as to put it by.' God rest his soul, poor boy. He had had a liberal share of misfortunes of late. But he has now 'ceased from his labours.' Now [from Gray's *Elegy*],
>
> The breezy call of incense-breathing morn,
> The swallow twittering from her straw built shed,
> The cock's shrill clarion and the echoing horn,
> No more shall rouse him from his lowly bed.

With apologies for taking close to half a year, he next writes Samuel, in big-brotherly fashion, to congratulate him on his new position (**no. 111** of March). What could account for so long a delay on George's part?

> You must attribute it to the natural indolence of your brother (whose mind has been 'sour'd of late') but who does not at the same time forget what is due to brotherly affection. The fact is, Sam'l, I have been roughly handled by the 'blind goddess' within a few months past; but with 'Percy of Northumberland,' I can now exclaim, 'through the distant gloom I see life peering.' Aye! I believe that I shall have to differ in opinion with the immortal 'Bard of Avon' respecting that 'tide in the affairs of men which, taken at the flood, leads on to fortune.' For that 'tide' waited for me at one time heretofore in this place, but I neglected to 'sail with it.' However, 'brand me for a fool!' if I don't 'clutch it' if it comes round again.
>
> I have just commenced an edition of books to bind (of a thousand copies) @ $1.25 per vol. and by the time they are compleated, a second edition of another work will be issued from another press; so you see, my dear fellow, that their is a prospect of my being kept busy at least.
>
> I hope, Sam, that you will stick to the line of business which you have been educated to or (in other words) that which chance put you into (i.e.) a mercantile man. Rest assured it will be better for you than a mechanical profession at the advanced age which you have arrived at; and, further, I wish you to make N[ew] York your permanent residence, for I think it decidedly preferable to N[ew] Orleans in every respect. I am now so much hurried with my business that it is impossible

for me to 'torture' out this epistle to a greater length, so I must 'e'en conclude,' hoping, my dear brother, that you will pursue a course in life which may become a 'Champlain,' the which name I most solemnly assure you shall never be disgraced in my person.

The press of work he enjoyed, or suffered under, in the latter months of 1821, could turn into failure or exhaust him all too easily. Whatever the ups and downs of his business, and however dispiriting, he prefers not to reveal their details to his younger brothers. Instead he shows a fraternal interest in how their careers are coming along, and responds to the accounts in a warm fashion. He writes to William on the day before Christmas Eve of 1823 (**no. 150**):

Your last, under date of 17th Sept., I received through the medium of Mr. Forsyth, to whose politeness I feel myself indebted. The information you have imparted relative to Samuel has afforded me much satisfaction. I hope that he may 'through future years' be prosperous and more successful than he has been heretofore.

With regard to yourself, you inform me of being still attached to the Post Office in New London and that you 'enjoy many advantages which, in other situations, you might be deprived of.' (I quote your words in allusion to your chance for studying.) It certainly, Wm., is a great advantage you enjoy–and I earnestly beg that, until you receive a direct invitation from some source whereby you are sure of bettering your condition, that you will remain contented in your present, and endeavour by a close application to the perusal of works on useful knowledge to reap the benefit they are capable of affording, which 'after years' will more clearly enable you to appreciate, and which your present station (although humble) allows you.

As to myself, I am still in the possession of the first of blessings (i.e.) GOOD HEALTH. For such I most sincerely thank a gracious Providence. With regard to my success in life, so far as respects the accumulation of worldly wealth, I might (if the comparison will not be deemed presumptuous) with Napoleon say that during my absence from the Northern States I have 'thrice seen fortune within my grasp and thrice has she eluded it.' Destiny forbade it. I am content.

Aye! in the language of the 'mad poet' ['Sandy' Clarke], thrice have I been 'flung on the torturing surge of cold and midnight loneliness' since I've been a wanderer from my 'native land;' but that inherent buoyancy of mind in conjunction with a small degree of philosophy which has come 'to the rescue' has enabled me (notwithstanding the dark & cheerless gloom which at several periods heretofore has clouded my horizon of life) to 'ride out the gale,' maugre the loss occasionally of my 'best bower.'

Wm., depend upon this assertion as truth! I emigrated at too early an age. Had I postponed my departure for foreign parts untill I had attain'd the age of twenty-five years, I feel a conviction that I should now have been in the possession of a sufficient competency to justify returning among my relatives in N[ew] L[ondon] and settling permanently for life; but that 'tide' (which the 'Bard of Avon' speaks of) may 'return again,' maugre his high authority, and should it! by Heaven! (sink or swim) I shall make a 'desperate effort' next time to 'ride on't at its flood.' Enough of the 'dark side of the picture' (as Mother would say). I am yet young and the experience I have bought (it is true) at a high rate will not be lost by me.

I shall conclude with myself and enquire about relatives and friends. Eliza you say is still 'with her old friends the Fitches.' The family name had entirely escaped my recollection until your letter arrived–a faint remembrance of a young lady who was a visitor at Aunt Mary's house in Chatham Street, and whom I once or twice saw. She was an intimate accquaintance of Eliza's, I think, but do not know whether she was married at that period or not; but believe her to have been the intended, the wife, or the sister of Mr. Fitch. Further relative to the family I cannot speak, my recollection having failed respecting them. Eliza cannot too highly prize the situation which her good fortune has given her, in the bosom of so amiable a family as I have understood, from her former letters to me, theirs is, and during her stay among them may her deportment be such as will enable her to command the respect, inspire esteem, and communicate a pleasure to all around her, is the earnest wish of her brother George.

Sam I am satisfied will make a smart man if he applies himself assiduously to the perfect accquirement of his profession (let it be what it may), but more particularly if a mercantile one. For, in case he should be inclined to travel hereafter, he would then see the necessity of his being a master of his business, if he should be but a clerk, as those who are not first rates find it extremely difficult to obtain a birth in our southern merchants' compting houses. I hope he will not give way to those strong incentives and allurements to pleasure and disipation with which New York abounds.

He now has arrived at that age which should enable him to think & act for himself, and methinks he should feel the necessity of pursuing an industrious frugal course, with the view, and to then end, that he may be in possession of means hereafter to assist and be a joint supporter of our mother. The length of time I have been absent should be conclusive proof that 'all is not right' with me.

Attribute the cause of my prolonged residence here to what you list. I can give you no further reasons for it than a continual succession of disappointments & misfortunes. I think therefore that the circumstances should operate with the greater force on his & your mind, and clearly demonstrate the necessity of making those mutual efforts in order to improve your respective situations in life, and not to prodigally dissipate (when in possession) that substance which should in part be reserved for the above strong duty–that noblest of all filial acts, the support of a widowed mother and only sister.

Ever yours,

George O.

Please answer upon receipt and communicate particulars of our family (remember to Aunts Hannah & Mary).

While he continued active and advertised as a bookbinder or 'relieur' at changing addresses in the city,[13] difficulties in his business developed. They were quite at odds with his ambitious ideas for the family coat-of-arms, for the esteem of Major

Champlain, the "Upper House," and all the rest of his ilk in New London. Everything came to a most unhappy ending in the last letter George Champlain wrote from the south, in the following spring (**no. 159**):

Dear William,

I have at length closed my business in New Orleans and am about to engage in an entirely different profession. I shall leave here on or about the 10th June next for Nashville (Ten.) in company with a gentleman with whom I have made an engagement. The nature of my future business you shall be made acquainted with anon. At present I do not feel myself at liberty to communicate it to you; but you may rely on this truth, that your brother George O. cannot engage in any other than an honourable one. Two powerful reasons have induced me to abandon the bookbinding business: first, gradually declining health, attributable to too long confinement at a sedentary profession like mine in an unhealthy clime like Louisiana, and, altho' never having been seriously sick, yet I am well aware 'I am not what I was' in constitution some 4 years ago. However, one consolation is that of knowing it has not been impaired by excesses of any kind, but [is due] solely to the nature of my profession and the injurious effects this climate will produce sooner or later upon a hardy northern constitution, as mine was. A change of air and scene would, I am confident, restore me in a few weeks to original health.

Secondly, my business has become good for nothing of late, and the sole reason which induced me to remain the last 12 months here was the expectations I had of getting the binding of a large edition of a law work which has recently been done here by B. Levy Bookseller & Printer. There is 4000 copies of the work (*Civil Code* of Louisiana) the binding of which would amount to bettween 2 & 3 thousand dollars; but, as the printing and binding was by order of the legislature farmed out to the low bidder, it was awarded to a French binder whose terms were lower than mine, and who had been for some time in the employ of the State Printer, whose influence no doubt was used in securing him the job. However, I have the satisfaction of knowing that he can clear no profits from it, as his terms were entirely too low–beside which, his situation is rather a delicate one, for, independent of the binders being obliged to give security to the amount of 10,000 dollars for the safe delivery of the work, he is farther compelled (by an act of the Assembly of the state pass'd this session) to have it completed and delivered within a very limited time (6 months), under a heavy forfeiture.

I have not informed you of our cousin Sam'l Champlain's being in this place. He is Guy's brother, you know, and was here about 3 years since. He recognized me a few nights since at the theatre, but I think I should not have known him had he not attracted my attention by his earnest gaze at me, separated only by a couple of boxes. He is much older in appearance than when here before. He had but just left the army at that period and was a very fine looking man. He in his deportment is much of the gentleman, I assure you, and I suspect is of the same pluck of Guy 'of noted memory.' He says that I have altered much since he saw me before; but of course you know that will be observed by another which one's self is ignorant of it. I do not know his business this quarter, but suppose it to be relative to his brother's property, which is in the hands of one of two individuals here.

I wish you to address no more letters to me at this place, nor, indeed, until you hear from me again–which will be shortly after my arrival at Nashville. You will please intimate this request to Mother, Eliza, and Samuel (the latter two, by the bye, I have not received a line from these 18 months). Remember [me to] Uncle Oliver (who, if I have not corresponded with, I have not forgotten !), aunts and Co., uncles, &c.

Adieu, *mon frère*–

G. O. Champlain

George turned over in his mind the idea of going west, but decided against it (**no. 175**). He went back to Nashville instead, as he announced he would, in the course of the summer. Word of his arrival there reached New London in the fall; but it was hard for him to go home, now that the two things he long feared during his time away had turned into realities: his employment gone, and someone he loved gone, too.[14] Nor would it have been easy for him, the oldest brother, to come back licked.

6

New York's Delights

Some of the letters thus far suggest what notable sights could be seen by the New London visitor to New York: rich objects for sale, civic celebrations, and a level of human activity bordering on the frantic–not only on May Day. Other observers of the time coming in fact from every point, among them many from Europe, looked about and noted these very same sights among a thousand others, too. What they saw they recorded for posterity; so the city's changing appearance over the first half-century after the Revolution is known in far more detail than that of any American rival.[1]

New York was a miracle. In the two decades since Captain Champlain and his friend had walked up Broadway to Trinity church in 1797, the population had trebled to a hundred and fifty thousand, and was to go on increasing at an extraordinary rate, together of course with an increase in the area it overspread, its housing, streets and government buildings, its shops, dockside and storage facilities, its places of manufacture, entertainment and worship–everything imaginable to support a roaring growth.

Of the whole city, however, Mary Way and Eliza naturally knew only a part; and for the understanding of their correspondence, that part alone needs description. Their sex, sense of propriety, and limited means kept them from the opera and grander assemblies as it did also from workshop districts and the river's edges. They certainly had no knowledge of New York's slums or taverns or its many thousands of prostitutes. A different, narrower world supplied their needs. Essentially, it lay in the middle of the Third Ward, in what is nowadays the financial district, bounded by Cherry Street on the south and Chatham less than a quarter-mile to the north, with James, Pearl, and William Streets included.[2] To this part of town Mary had moved from Greenwich Street, perhaps about the same time as her Universalist church. To this part also the author and editor Samuel Woodworth had moved; here Mary's dear friend Anna Fitch lived out her married life with her husband Samuel, a rising and successful lawyer; here the leading publisher and general purveyor of song,

Figure 3. Eliza's New York

instruments, and musical instruction to the city, Edward Riley Sr., had his home and business; for a time also Charles Holt, publisher of *The Columbian*; and assorted acquaintances like the Titus, Avery, and Weeks families all of the same big merchant house, the Jigginses, the Haydens, Chavalier and his follies, Charles Clinch and his wife (he, the author), the Dawsons who were important to both Mary and Eliza, probably also Anna Fitch's parents the Northams.[3] The latter family Mary may be supposed to have met through the church they both ardently attended. At its doors, too, Eliza later met those various beaux who made her laugh, calling them "Crab," "Lobster" (young Baxter), or, by their right name, young Jiggins who will be seen squiring her about, and White in the pew behind her. Fresh from England, there in White's seat sat the handsome Thomas Fenno one Sunday, soon to appear as suitor to Hannah Dawson. The church was a great social center.[4]

What needs to be noticed is the village-quality of this urban setting, within which changes of lodging might take place from time to time simply because boarding-houses rather than bought houses were so common a residential solution at the time, and the market was fluid;[5] but the coherence of the village persisted. Its welcome was really more friendly than one might have expected to find in New York of the time. Consider the level of social mobility, to call it by its kindest name, which fed the miracle of growth: consider the yield of small towns, the influx of free blacks, the large immigrant population from many European countries especially Ireland "in the most wretched condition"–as the *Columbian* happens to notice on a certain day (February 27, 1818) which could have been any day in the early nineteenth century. They brought a Babel of languages and accents, a confusion of social habits, and, as the *Columbian* also notes, material needs quite beyond the economy's powers to satisfy. Hence, "several large soup-houses." As an additional hardship, prices prevailing were generally higher than those familiar in old or New London, made more painful still by recurrent bad times, and a competitive, scrambling pace of life.

Further, the social and cultural quality of the "village" is notable in comparison with what Mary Way and her niece had been used to at home. The two now found themselves taken up among persons with more money than they themselves commanded, something which Mary could handle without difficulty and in fact hardly mentions, but which at times troubled Eliza very deeply. Her clothes, for instance, not to mention her aunt's–all wrong! Money, however, bought not only clothes but a special measure of taste, education, and polite manners, things she had been brought up with so far as they could be afforded, and which she could admire in others to the point of awe. The books and periodicals she saw in friends' homes, the social accomplishments and cultivation, the response in conversation to higher culture on display in the city, all lay on a level well above New London's. What she and her aunt lacked and would have wished for, they nevertheless looked on without envy; the richness they found themselves in the midst of, whether or not they could possess it, they could enjoy in different ways according to their different ages and experience; and for Eliza, the year or so she spent in New York while still in her teens constituted a finishing school of sorts, not to be scorned by a girl a little too fat, too ready to laugh, too mischievous in her comments on other people's absurdities.

Only five minutes' walk beyond their immediate world lay Broadway, just on the other side of their church and Chatham Street: Broadway indeed broad, a hundred feet across, extending two miles and more down the very center of the city, lined with trees and the best shops and handsomest houses; the strolling-place of high fashion, especially for women in their new dresses and fifty-dollar hats. When Eliza's circle complained of the mud ankle-deep in the streets, when travellers report the pigs that roamed about and the city's general filthiness, they were not thinking of its grand central avenue.[6] Just south of it toward the "village" was a very agreeable triangular park giving its name to the city's premier theater on one side, with Columbia College a block away on the other. In the College there were occasional free lectures and oratorical displays. Vauxhall Garden was close; other places of entertainment, theaters and "gardens," were scattered about more widely, half a mile distant in various directions.[7]

Eliza, as has been seen, visited her aunt Mary for some period in 1816, but toward the end of summer returned home. There, her aunt Hannah Way of her grandmother's generation was in her late seventies and needed looking after. It was, however, a job from which Eliza could sometimes be spared. Mary would welcome a second visit–urged it, in fact (**no. 27**, in June of 1817), not least through a report on all the delights of New York so readily available.

Dear Eliza,

Patty [Mary's Irish serving girl] has just handed me your letter, which I am very glad to receive at last; and tho' 'tis just eleven o'clock, and I so tired I am scarcely live, I shall try to answer it, as it will be many hours before the town is still enough to sleep. The President [Monroe] has honnor'd us with a visit and, to return the compliment, we have honnor'd him with every possible mark of distinction, luminations, fire works, cannon, squibs, rockets, and music of all kinds. I've been walking the streets ever since dark, squeezed and jam'd by the croud flat as a pancake (as you will see by this letter). City Hall is beyond description. I wish you was here to see for yourself. I went through it the other day with a large party and took a survey of this superb edifice and all the wonders it contains; was introduced to a number of gentlemen–among the rest, the Vice President, the late Governor Tomkins, said to be the most polite man in the United States. The attention we receiv'd from him was answerable to his character. He was told I was an artist, and soon let me know he was a connoisseur, and favor'd me with his remarks and observations upon the painting. Oh! those paintings, which I will not murder by attempting to describe. You must come and see for yourself. Yes, you must positively come.

Maria Hayden is here still, and we want you very bad. She will not go till fall, and has begun to paint another piece, to please her husband: a *View of the Niagara Falls*, which will astonish the natives when it is compleated–said to be the most correct view that has ever been taken.[8] Two of our first artists who wanted it to copy offer'd the owner a hundred and fifty dollars, but he would not sell it. They then offer'd him forty dollars if he would lend it to them a month. This he refused to do, but being under obligations to Captain Hayden, he could not refuse him, so here it is, and here it will remain all summer. If Maria does it well (of which I have no doubt), she will immortalize her name. The view is sublime, and when you look at it you can hear the waters roar. It is four times as large as *Crossing the Brook*, but it would not please you as it does connoisseurs. The colouring is not so bright and glaring as it is natural. There is a group of Indians killing a snake, which is much admired, but as I said before, come and see for yourself.

As you inquire so affectionate about my youngest child [meaning, her most recent portrait], I must inform you, he is a beautiful boy of three years old, and wants nothing but a pair of wings and a bow and arrow to be a living Cupid. I have painted him in my best manner at full length on a piece of ivory five inches long and four broad, for which I gave three dollars–a little picture book in his hand and a landscape background. Modesty forbids further comments, but we repeat again what we have said a thousand times before: come and see for yourself. Oh! come, come along. I have a thousand things to show you and to tell you which, unless you do come, you will neither see nor hear. Pray come with Sally, if Aunt Hannah can spare you. Give my love to them both. Tell Sally I depend upon her promise. Nothing could give me more pleasure than to see her here. I conclude her husband will come with her, of course, tho' Patty says he thinks he can't leave his business. But I hope he will think better of it. If, however, he is obstinate, you and Sally can come together without him. I promise to furnish you with beauxs as smart as any you leave behind. Don't disappoint me, and be sure you come before the fourth of July, for you know we keep it here in style.

I am still in Chatham street N[o]. 98, two doors above the corner of Pearl and Chatham streets upon your left hand as you go up, opposite Wayman's. You will recollect where we turn to go to our old church. 'Tis much pleasanter and more public situation than where I lived before. Here is as much to be seen–as much noise and racket–as in Broadway, where I expected to have been at this present writing. I had engaged a house there, as I thought; but the devil of a landlord was afterwards offer'd more rent than he had ask'd me and excepted the offer. I give here a higher rent than at Tyllues. The situation is better, the house is handsomer and more comodious. I have still a dark bed-room (at your service, where you shall be heartily welcome to feast your fishbones and hogg's bristles) with many other conveniences too tedious to mention.

I receiv'd your two watch-papers, and disposed of them according to your orders. The Miss Holts are delighted, return a great deal of love and thanks, and wish they had something more substantial to send. They hope you have not forgot your old beaux Mr. King, who they say was very deeply smitten. He is now in New Orleans, and when he has made his fortune will return, no doubt, and lay it at your feet. Lucy Surtain has call'd with them since–made perticular inquires when and what I heard from you. I suppose she expects to receive her watch-paper about these days. As to the Fitches, I can't tell exactly what they think. They don't appear to be uneasy, however, and I shall not mention the subject again till the pictures arrive, after which you shall see Maria's watch-paper, if I can contrive to send it in safety. But there must be a piece of pastboard–something stiff in the letter in which it is enclosed–to prevent its bending. I will see about it when I've time. I painted another from it last week. It took me from Monday morning to Saturday night, and I had but six dollars, so you see 'twas not a very profitable job.

I return *Lord Byron*. Ann [Fitch] painted one from it that realy look'd beautiful, and proud enough she was of her first born; but all is vanity below! Mr. Fitch must not see it till it was compleatly finish'd, because she would astonish him. When at length that blissful moment came, it was folded in a piece of paper with the utmost care, that it might be convey'd with safety home; but alass! fate had decreed his doom. Before she reach'd the door, she stumbled over one of my little rocking chairs, hit his Lordship's head, and split the skull. All horror struck! she stood, thinking she had given him a death blow. I soon convinced her, however, the wound was not mortal–that, tho' 'the time has been that when the brains was out, the man would die,' it is not so, now, since 'tis discover'd they can live just as well without, and tost thier heads even higher than those who have more weight to carry. So light is vanity!

You inquire about Giggins and Charlotte [Waite] and thier beauxs. I have not time to give you the perticulars at present, but they are not married yet, neither of them. It don't signify. People must wait till thier time comes. 'Tis of no use to hurry the business. Christian fortitude, patience and resignation are the virtues to be call'd into practice on trying occasions. They are those I would recomend in in the present instance and in any similar case.

Mrs. Dawson lives close by here–but a few doors off. She and [her daughter] Hannah sends bushels of love to you and Aunt Hannah and many others that I have neither time nor room to name. Adieu. You see I have gone the length of my chain as usual, tho' I write with my eyes fast shut. Not all the noise in the street can keep them open another moment.

Good night.

My love to your mother. I send her the Antwerp blue and a cake of blue verdeter [vert de terre]. The first is the sort she sent for a pattern and the last is much like it. I should have sent it long before if I had know which way or how to get it to her. Patty has promised to find a conveyance for this. Adieu. Pray write often, don't be so stiff and ceremonious. If I ever get time I will repay you.

In reply, Eliza did arrange a second visit to the irresistible New York. Her aunt Sally and uncle Ebenezer Way brought her down, though he couldn't stay long.[9] She reported on the trip to her old aunt Hannah (**no. 29**) in early October:

I suppose you know before this time, we got here alive. If you had been with us you would have had forty thousand fits. Our vessle took in water at a great rate but we were so sick we did not mind it. We are now taking all the comfort in the world. Aunt Mary has some eligant paintings that I intend to copy before I return, if you don't send for me. . . . All your friends here enquire of you till I am tired of answering them all: the Northams, Fitches, and things. Mrs. Dawson has just been, and sends ten thousand bushels of love to you, and is so sorry you did not accompany me, she is just dead. She is the same good soul she ever was. I love her better than anybody here *except the company*. I have not seen Mr. Northam yet. When I do, I shall expect to have my arm shaken off as usual, for you know when he goes round a room full of company he never leaves them till he has limber'd all there joints. . . .

Aunt Mary sends more love than I can write and says you will soon recieve the book and Mr. Northam's comments upon it. They are already written but she will add something to them before they go. It is only want of time that makes her neglect writing. . . . If you do not understand my York terms, you must get Aunt Way to explain them when she returns. Tell Mrs. Fosdick we shall not open our lips to New London folks when we return, we shall be so mighty grand. She need not expect to touch us with a rod pole. . . . I have not time to write more, for Giggins is waiting to go down to the post office with me. Be sure write soon. My love to Mother. I shall write her tomorrow. And be sure burn this before you have read it.

Adieu.

Aunt [Sally] Way desire a great deal of love to you and Mrs. Fosdick. My love to Uncle [Ebenezer] Way, and tell him that his wife had a real kiss from Edmund M. Blunt so he had better come and see to her or he will lose her.

Very shortly after this, Betsey Champlain sent Eliza some spending money in a non-negotiable form, which was returned to her wrapped up in a worried little note reading, "Mother, pray send me New York bank next time. This won't pass." On the same piece of paper Betsey then wrote in reply, adopting her most parental tone (**no. 30**),

Hearing of your safe arrival in New York has deliver'd me from considerable anxiety, and hope you enjoy yourself as well as you expected–not but what I fear in the main it will rather have a tendency to injure your happiness than promote it, owing to your youth. The sudden breaking in upon your young mind totally unqualifies it for everything domestic and at the same time leaves a void more sensibly than the temperate, sober recluse life to which you have formerly been accustom'd. However, by the exertion of your natural tallants, by limiting your desires, and a firm resolve to not give way to any imaginary want, suppressing every wrong sensation and encouraging every one that arises from a virtuous principle, perhaps you may make the visit an advantage to you. But–observe me–be on your guard at all points.

Lousia Wait call'd on me yesterday and appear'd rather supriz'd that I had sent her favorite *Marquis de Salvo* to New York; but by assuring her that it would be copied there, and could not be here, I satisfied her tolerably well. I desire, Eliza, you will pay attention to that, first–the very first–as she wants it in her school; and you are to have something for doing it, which price I must insist upon Mary's setting.

I am under much anxiety in consequence of the expectation of George being drafted to list in the army. There is to be a number out of this town of his age, perhaps five out of thirty. He will be oblig'd to go. But perhaps he may escape. I shall live in hope of that untill I know the sequel.

I send you two dollars–the one, you sent back.

Betsey's next letter (**no. 32**) was written in January of 1818:

Dear Eliza,

Your unexpected long silence is quite alarming. Is anything the matter? Write immediately as soon as you recieve this and let me know. Or do you wait for cerimony? It would fill a larger sheet than I can write to give my reasons for not answering yours. I have not since I wrote last had but one application, which you might think was a favourable circumstance; but every other work and care sufficient to put it out of my power until now.

Yet through it all I have not been discouraged. I merit immortalization for my faith. The one last I speak of was a five-dollar one only. I have been under the nesessity of giving my note upon interest for the sum of $12 to a certain person whose name perhaps I am not authorized to mention–the note, however, being a voluntary offer, she laughed at and threw under the table; but that will be picked up again by the time the year is up, if I should not be able to cancel it before. But fortunately I have as good a knack at hopeing as any of the long faces I see around me. The cause is still a mystery, but I find I can bear every trial and affliction in life that is laid upon me better than formerly.

We are all pretty much the same as when you left us–only a little older and uglyer is all the difference I discern. Sam'l is yet with [his uncle] Thomas, as no other door is as yet open for him and no chance of a trade in this place, as there is so little business doing that those who have aprentices are readier to send them home than take new ones. We have heard nothing from George since before or about the commencement of the sickness at Natchez. The suspence is one of my heaviest troubles–but as the news has not arrived to the contrary, hope he is still living. Yet should it be otherwise ordered, I am blest in firmly believing that every-thing that is, is for the best, and by the shield of faith am better prepared for the blow than at any former time since his birth. I have long meditated upon the subject and familiarized myself to the thought of death, which I know must come at some period, and find it has a very salutary effect in lessening the fear both in respect to ourselves and that of our friends.

I desire, however, that you will write if but one line as soon as possible to let me know if you are well, and what has prevented you from it before, and give me no unnesessary anxiety–whether you find business, and every particular respecting yourself and Mary, what her prospects are, whether she has turns of gloom and depression of spirits, a disorder so prevelent here, or whether you have power to laugh away the hypocondriac, which owes its origin to the jandice, for I have traced it to my entire satisfaction. I have had three very severe attacks since I moved here, but for two or three months have not even for a day, for which I consider I have much reason to be thankful.

I have not been out of the house except once to Mrs. B[ryant]'s, when I call'd to see A[unt] Hannah, two or three times over to Thomas's, and one evening I spent at Uncle [Pardon] Taber's with Mrs. O[liver] Champlain. Perhaps you will wonder how that came about. She has called to see me about six times that I recollect, and expressed a wish for me to walk with her, and I proposed the plan which she readily fell in with. She was to call me at six, which she punctually performed. We spent a very agreable evening and that was my last visit. I would go there, but cannot without I know [?I can] see her alone, but as that is uncertain, I still omit calling. I would wish to be divested of all prejudice toward every creature, but, exclusive of all respecting you, his neglect of you has been so pointed that I cannot feel a freedom to go as yet untill I posess a more abundant degree of charity, which enables us to throw down all prejudice and fills our hearts with the love of God.

I intended to have fill'd this sheet but [son] Will'm has called and I feel in a hurry to hear from you and Mary. My best love to her. Write as soon as you recieve it and tell me how you both are–all about your expectations. Adieu.

I enclose 10 cents for you to purchase me as much of that drawing-paper that you wrote me one of your letters upon. . . .

While Betsey Champlain was worrying over the lack of news from New York, Eliza had in fact begun an account of herself (**no. 33** of January 7, 1818), at the same time expressing her own concern at New London's silence. Her exercise, like a fair number of others in the correspondence, took her a long time to finish; so it appears to be at cross-purposes with the foregoing:

Dear Mother,

What the plague is the reason you don't write? I have waited centuries for a letter and am now out of all manner of patience. You know you owe me fifty. I wish you would write oftener.

Aunt Mary and I were at an auction yesterday that has almost been the death of me. Oh Heavens! if you could only have been there you would have died. There was millions of the most eligant prints I ever saw, besides ten thousand statues. There was Apollo and the nine Muses. If you could only have seen there faces you would have died. Such heavenly countenances I never saw before; but my pen can never do them justice. There was the three witches in Macbeth that looked more like the divel than he does like himself. Everything about them was forked. There was the *Decent from the Cross*, and *Christ blessing the Children and Healing the Sick*–every one as large as a middle-sized table. But the most superb thing among them was *Echo Personified*, that surpassed every one of the engravings, in my opinion. She was clothed on the same careless manner that [Eliza's own] *Fancy* is, but appear'd to be the child of air. She was wrapped [in a] robe of vanity or something ten thousand times thinner than the thinnest lawn, with ten million folds in it. You could just distinguish her form which was eligant. She was not flying but sailing through the air. You would have died if you had seen it. I cannot describe it for my soul. The mate to *Echo* was *Iris*, goddess of the rainbow. That was superb but it did not kill me like the other did. She was represented flying, and the rainbow appearing through her robe and hair that spread in every direction. I would give the universe you could only see those two pictures.

There was ten thousand other pictures that I can't think of, I was so taken up with those I have mentioned. One I must not forget: the five wise Vergins with those lamps, almost as large as life. The foolish ones did not make there appearance. If they had I should certainly have scraped acquaintance with them. There was Cleopatra applying the asp. I suppose you have read *Anthony and Cleopatra*. She was crown'd and lying on a most superb bed–white marble. She was the most beautiful creature I ever laid my eyes on except Echo. There was two white marble temples and transparent marble lanthorns with a wreath of the most eligant flowers painted on them I ever saw. There was a bust of Acchillus three times as large as life, a statue of Alexander Pope, Homer, and Apollo. You see I mention them just as I recollect them without any regard to propriety. The auction room was monstrous and eligant. There was not an inch of wall to be seen. It was wholly cover'd with paintings, and a mahogany table that reached from one end of the room to the other and cover'd with statuary. There was Centaurs and divels of every description. Oh how I wish'd for you! There was a marble table that was four hundred dollars. If I was to write ten thousand years I could not tell you the half I saw or give you the least idea of the eligance of anything. There I was, wandering about like a troubled spirit, without being able to make the least purchase.

I have ten thousand things to say to you, and have got Aunt Hannah to scratch too now. My little stock of knowledge is quite exhausted and my brain as dry as the remainder biscuit after a voyage. I spent New Year's day with Mrs. Dawson. Giggins and I went to Saint George's Chappel in the morning. It was eligantly dress'd. It was done by nine young ladies. The wreath was festoon'd from the chandeliers abbove the church, and over the pulpit was wrote with a wreath of roses, 'Emanuel'.

In the afternoon Mrs. Dawson and Marriah carried me all over the city and show'd me all for nothing. Oh I wish you was here. You would be delighted; but I suppose you will not want to come as long as 'Miss Way' remains here. Do you have any business now? I am copying the picture of a lady Aunt Mary has been drawing. It is on ivory and my copy is thought to be full as good as the original copy.

For heaven sake, write soon and let me know how you go on. I want to hear from y[ou] very bad.

Adieu.

My love to *Fancy*. Pray be careful of her Ladyship and don't get her injured, for I value her more than anything I ever painted.

Since I wrote all this stuff, I received your letter and was glad enough, you may depend. The paper I send, tho' it's not the same you wrote for. Patty made me a present of four sheets of that paper that you wrote for, and I wasted it on a set of ungrateful creatures that never took any notice of my letters; and in a passion I vow'd vengeance & asked her to take your money and get some more of it; but she said the man had no more. This I send I hunted Broadway for, and I think it pretty good–much better than any Patty's. The paper is enclosed in half a sheet of Patty. You can compare notes and see which you like best.

Good bye.

One or two further exchanges between mother and daughter have been lost, followed by this (**no. 34**) from Betsey of about the same date as the preceding. She (with never a mention of her husband!–but a letter **no. 42** in the next chapter gives a hint how unhappy the marriage was) had recently changed lodging to the house of her artist-friend Mrs. Bryant, probably so as to save money, and is suffering from a recurrent form of ill-health:

Dear Eliza,

You observe Mary is out of health and spirits. What is the matter with her? O I wish to heaven she would return with you. I would risk my chance. I long so much to see her, but think it more than probable I never shall in this present world. I have buried her. I cannot say how my feelings may vary with the return of health and after this place seems like home, but the Keeney scene [in imitation of the actor Edmund Kean] was all acted over. I have been upon the point of dispair from the loss of health and spirits, togeather with the operation of moving, which you know allways kill'd me. I have the jaundice. Some days I am the colour of king's yellow, another, a black, and the third, white as a corpse. I have been doctoring for them, which has thrown it out into the skin; but it will strike in at other times. At present I am taking soot eggs and cider. After this, am determin'd to go through with the whole in rotation–that is, every thing prescrib'd–for I have suffer'd more than I can express. I mind the loss of spirits more than even health, though one depends on the other. I am once in a while animated but it seems a kind of spurious animation without any real cause for coming or going–yet more cause for the latter than former. Uncle [Thomas] Allen and Aunt has call'd upon me, and [their daughter] Amelia. I have promised to return it but have not the spirits which must serve the means of getting me there.

As to your money, I send it but, as before, is borrowed. It has been very dull times for three months–not any-thing to do but work for debt, and retouching for nothing. I am heartily sick of the scene, yet hope my prospects may brighten, after I have been sufficiently tried in the furnace of affliction. As to this world, there is nothing to expect from it but misery and wretchedness, and it is to wean us from it and oblige us to set our hearts upon something more permanent.

Eliza, don't let the above make you gloomy. I am much better than I was, since I have got so as to eat and sleep. I am getting the better of the disorder but feel far from right, yet. Perhaps when you return and divert me with some of your anecdotes, I shall throw off this hysteric gloom that hangs about me. It is moving in with strangers, and every-thing new and strange and the want of the company of people of sentiment that makes me feel like a cat in a strange garret, togeather with my disorder–which, however, I feel I am getting the better of. I have a very good appetite, which seems to be a favourable symtom; as also, I can sleep well, now. I am as much, certainly, if not more attach'd to Mrs. Bryant than you could feel yourself to Mrs. Dawson. She is really one of the most interesting carracters, when you are as intimately aquainted with as I am, that I ever yet met with in my pilgrimage thro' life. She is extremely like Mary. Mary may think I pay her an indifferent compliment, but depend, that woman only wants to be known to be admired and beloved. Her ideas of right and wrong are so just, her penetration so keen, that you find every-thing you want in her, besides amiable candour that makes her appear the real friend. Deception is foreign from her soul; in fact, she is all soul; but nobody knows her worth but my own dear self nor ever will. She is such a recluse. I can't bear she should shut herself up so, and not impart her virtues to the world; but through a delicasy, and not being fond of much society, it must be so. She posesses more than all the cardinal virtues, and has been able to improve me in many particulars, which perhaps you will think that I thought there was no need; but not exactly so. There is none but what we may select virtues from and leave the foibles, if we find them. This world is a school in which a tractable scholar may, if they posess a good heart, ever be able to improve thier minds and manners by putting in practice the amiable qualities of those around them–and even then be far from finding ourselves as perfect as there is need. Perhaps you may smile at this moralizing, but I speak my real sentiments.

I expect George will arrive before you come up, as Capt. Deshon is expected to arrive in New York every moment. I hope the poor fellow is well. I long to see him. He will loan you the sum to pay your passage if he should. I sapose it would be in vain to wait for Lewis Allen. You can come with who you please. Do use your influence with Mary to come back again. I verily think it would be better for her and all the rest of the family. Eben'r has moved a fortnight since. He and Sally both express a great desire for your return. Do make Mary come with you, that I may see her once more. Adieu.

E. Champlain

To this last request Sally Way now joined her voice, in March, in a letter (**no. 36**) from which the more tedious trivia may be omitted, and to which her husband adds a touch of humor at the end:[10]

Pardon me, my dear sister and niece, for this apparent neglect, and be assured it was my intention to have answered your kind letters long before this. . . . Now for the news, for I have bushells–so much that I do not know where to begin. But first, I will inform you that your parents have had a letter from George. He writes in excelent spirits and speaks of returning in a short time. During the sickness at Natchez he retired to the country. He observes that he lost all his young friends by the fever. For further particulars I must refer you to your mother's letter, as I am told she is about writing you. She began one several weeks since, so you may expect a long one before a great while.

I am extremely sorry to inform you that Mr. Blakesley [at St. James church] is about leaving us. He preached his farewell sermon last Sunday and goes to East Haddam this week. I am much afraid we shall have no minister, and if we do, am sure he will not make his place good. Aunt Hannah regrets extremely the loss of them. She says she shall feel lost to have that house shut up.

You ask how she is. I think she is very smart. She has been complaining a little. One of her knees has been lame for some time but has now got quite well again. She takes a walk every day when the weather is pleasant and often mentions you both. She says if she was not so old and good for nothing, she would make you a visit this spring; but I tell her you have promised to make us a visit. And now my dear Sister, I hope you will gratify us. I will exert all my energies to entertain you. Oh if you knew how much I want to see you both, you would come.

I want to see New York ten thousand times more, now, than I did before I went there. I never made so pleasant a visit in my life, and had I been in good health, should have enjoyed much more than I did. How is dear Mrs. Dawson and Hannah? Give bushells of love to them. Tell them I long to have a good set-down with them. And how is good old Mr. Northam and lady? I am very sorry to hear that the old gentleman is unwell. He is a worthy old Christian if ever there was one. Please make my best respects to them, to Mr. and Mrs. Fitch, and my particular regards to Mr. & Mrs. [Charles] Holt and family. I shall always feel gratefull to them for their kindness and attention to me. And when did you hear from that amiable sweet woman Mrs. Hayden? I hope I shall some time or other meet with her again. If you ever write her give my best love to her.

I am pleased, my dear Eliza, that you enjoy yourself so well. Don't you refuse any invitation you may have to balls or parties, for recollect when you return to New London, no such amusements await you. We have had but one ball this winter, and that I did not attend owing to my ill health. I hope now, my dear Sister, you will write immediately or make you secretary do it if you can not find leisure–but at any rate I shall expect a letter from one of you very shortly. Good night. Husband sends much love to you both.

S. S. W.

A true copy from the original Greek written on three or four different pieces of paper.

Attest,

E. W.

Eliza's answer later in the spring (**no. 38**) ignored the calls for her return. She was having a lovely time with her art and all her new experiences:

My dear Mother,

I presume you have received all my nonsense before this, and that it has cured your mark. Lest I should be mistaken, however, I shall now and then send you a dose of fresh, as I prefer it myself to stale. I have a funny request to make which you must not refuse me, tho' before I make it I must give you my reasons. You must know that your fame has reached New York. It was long before I came, so you must not lay it to my charge. A particular description of your dress, manners, and acquirements had preceeded me and astonished the natives. An account of your going to the Methodist meeting accompanied by Mr. O[liver] C[hamplain] and array'd in all your noon-day splendor or sun-flower finery that dazzled and overwhelmed the spectators without their daring to open their lips in their own defence–that the Methodists tolerated your top-knots, furbelows and all your eccentric notions, knowing you to be a privelidged character and such an uncommon genius, and hopeing, I suppose, to turn your poetic vein to their own advantage, that is getting you to write hymns, . . . –for you know self-interest is at every-body's bottom or at the bottom of every-body, which you please–well, as I said before, this is the only way I can account for the strange infatuation of those hitherto incorruptable class of saints and saintesses. Nevertheless, I am afraid you will be excommunicated if you put their unparalleled forbearance to the test much longer, for they must consider you already as one of their 'foundation shakers.'

Now, what I would ask of you is this: Aunt Mary wishes you to draw your own picture [Pl. 3.11] and send her, and she will draw hers and send you in exchange. She has an unconquerable desire to see you in your sun-flower uniform: your yellow turban, yellow gown and black apron with the row of flat-irons across the bosom, for she can scarcely believe me when I tell her what a dashification you cut in your uniform and how much you are admired in it. Nothing will convince her but ocular demonstration; and, that she may have it, she makes the foregoing request, with which I hope you will comply. She says you may flatter it as much as you like provided you don't flatter away all the likeness. Just 'keep probability in view,' and it will answer. And she desires me to give you her solemn promise that as soon as it arrives she will 'commence opperations' on her own. You must not make the least alteration in your dress, and then she will not in hers. I think her dress and yours will form an amusing contrast, tho' they will never be seen together. Her gown is simply a black canton crape with a black lace collerett and a large green bonnet made more for use than ornament, which she is obliged to wear constantly or her eyes pains her so she cannot live. Her eye she will draw bandaged. One eye is as many as Dunlap appears with, who by the way she calls her 'one-eyed brother.' You had best take her at her word and draw your own soon, or her eye may grow so much worse that she will not be able to take it at any rate. You will then possess what you have so long wished for–a specimen of her painting–and I can assure you, you would never recognize her former in her present style, it's so much improved. And I can tell you, it would be a great advantage to your reflection paintings. Don't disappoint us, for we depend upon your likeness without fail.

The miniature of a lady now lies before me that Aunt Mary painted before I arrived. It is finished and set, and is without exception the most superb piece of painting I ever beheld. I would give worlds you could see it. You would believe it the work of the ancients–so much softness and harmony I never saw in any painting. I won't even except Dickison's *Cupid and the Graces* that set me raving when I was here before. The lady in question has her head inclining just enough on one side to avoid the stiffness that a head bolt upright, and exactly in front, is too apt to have; her hair is dress'd very tastefully, tho' without a single ornament and every curl blended and soften'd in such a manner as to produce the sweetest effect imaginable, and cause all the hard lines I ever made in my life to rise in judgement against me. Her robe is of the thinest mull mull and carelessly cross'd on the bosom. The sleeves are loose and fall in large folds over the arms. It has no ruffle except one row of lace round the edge which confines an elegant bouquet. The neck is exposed as much as decency will permit, and their is not a vein but is drawn to the life–so much so, that I sometimes fancy I can see the bosom heave. I never saw simplicity and eligance so happily united before, and never desire to see again a picture loaded with ornament since I have seen this without one, so much superior. I was so much engaged describing the dress of the lady, I forgot to tell you her face is 'beautifull as the creation of genius.'

You must think that with studying such a painting as this, and a couple that Aunt Mary is going to have lent her which she says is fifty thousand times superior, I shall soon arrive at emenence. I am also reading 'A brief account of the lives of the most celebrated painters in every age and country,' and if my noddle is strong enough to hold all the knowledge I am so unmercifully thrusting into it, and to turn it to account, you must not be surprised should you receive before long a learned desertation on the theory of painting by 'Miss Way'–as you introduce me to my 'eternal woe.' Nasty–but then, this same knowledge can not be obtain'd without much tribulation and close application. I must study day and night, 'consume the midnight oil,' and, like all other philosophers, pay through the nose for my knowledge, besides having the satisfaction of beholding every morning an additional line to my phiz; for you must expect the dimples of youth to give place to the wrinkles of age as I progress in this unfrequented path. I assure you it is not strewn with roses, but plentifully with thorns. I can tell by woeful experience, for I have been pretty faithfully scourged, although I have advanced a little way. But I suppose what I have gone through is but the begining of sorrow or, as Sancho says, 'cakes and gingerbread' to what I shall have to go through; for you know he or she (it's a poor rule that won't work both ways) that encreases in wisdom encreases in sorrow. Faith, I have no reason to dispute this. For one has kept pretty equal pace with the other since my arrival. Would you believe it, Aunt Mary has set me down as complete ignoramus in painting as she ever knew. 'Tis fact–and a most provoking one. But if I live, I intend to astonish the natives, and have them all 'set me down, young woman, for fear of mistakes.'

Dear Mother, the foregoing letter has been written so many centuries, I thought if it had been dated I should never have sent it. But as you will never be any wiser than you are at present respecting its birth, parentage, and education, I thought their could be nothing amiss in sending it in its forlornly unintelligable state, as it was written in the dark ages–that is to say, before the world was so enlighten'd as it is at present by brightness of my genius.

But I shall fill up my remaining half sheet with nonsense without ever telling you of anything of consequence. The first and most important is, Aunt Mary's eye is *no better*. The next is, I myself in my own shape and person am drawing the likeness of her doctor. She assists me but he sets to me, and a better likeness you never saw than I have got of him. He looks some like Jim Lee used to, only a thousand handsomer. He is much younger than Lee and is by far the handsomest face I have seen since I came to New York. I never saw so handsome a mouth in my life: his lips are round, red, and full and theirs ten thousand little develish shades around them that puzzle me so to get, but which I'm determin'd shall be got, that I don't know when the picture will be finished. But when it is, I expect it will immortalize my name on earth at least, if their is such a thing as sublunary immortality. I always think I should rather have my trumpet blown in Heaven than on earth, tho' I suppose I may thank my stars if my ears are ever saluted with a blast from it in either place–tho' I shall try my possibles and think I shall stand a chance for it (whether I get it or not) when Doctor Wright is finished. You know it will not be a money-making job, of course. It will only keep my genius in play, which was a necessary evel, for it began to slumber and would soon have snored as if it never was to wake again.

I have been painting a watch-paper that, if you could see it now, would set you distracted. You know I shall never cure my mark with cupids and flying females. I have personified Fame, tho' [similar to Pl. 1.5], as I have drawn a rainbow in the clouds, she would answer as well for Iris as the former. She is sailing (if you will pardon my mode of expression) through the air enveloped in lawn, tho' the symmetry of every turn in her form is display'd. A part of a sky blue scarf streams from one shoulder and is lost in the clouds. Her hair is flaxen and confined with a wreath. Her wings are of the richest purple and studded with gold. She holds in one hand a roll of paper on which is printed in small characters of course the name of *Washington*, and in the other a golden trumpet. Her form and face is perfection. A wreath encircles the whole. It is ten thousand times handsomer than *Fancy*, and *Love and Harmony* is a fool to it.

Do for Heaven sake write soon. I have received your letter at last, after so long a time, and was indeed surprised at your long silence. The Baxters are coming to go with me and get Mrs. Bryant's veil and as soon as it is got I will let you know, that you may send [the New London-New York packet commander] Capt. Lamphere for it.

Now I have a favor to ask of you, that, if you have natural affections, I think you will not delay gratifying. Aunt Mary's eye since I began this letter has grown so much worse that at times I think she will die with the pain of it, and Doctor says nothing will help her but leeches. She has enquired at the druggists' stores and finds they have come but are a dollar a piece and it will take *twenty*. For her to think of getting them at that price in her present situation would be madness, and it is quite impossible for her to think of living in so much pain as she daily suffers. Therefore, she begs of you to send Sam or Will'm to get some out of the brooks that are so plenty in N[ew] L[ondon], and put them in a phial of cold water and send them down as soon as possible. If they don't know them exactly, Uncle Ebb can describe them. Doctor Wright says they are in all the brooks now, but cannot be got here except at the apothecary's. He has very little hope of her ever seeing again, especially if she don't apply leeches very soon. For Heaven sake don't fail to send for them if you have the most remote idea where they can be found, for *delays are dangerous* in her case at least. If you was only here and knew the agony she endured, and is obliged to do many parts of painting that I cannot, you would certainly think that, of all situations, hers was the most dreadful. The pain of her blind eye is at times so severe that it affects the other so much, she cannot set up an instant, and is often quite faint before she reaches the bed. I am so in the habit of receiving refusals for whatever I write for to you that I have not much hope of the leeches, but surely you will after what I have written try to get them in the way I mention'd, and save her twenty dollars. Recollect, this is not a gimlet, and therefore ought to be attended to. I shall wait with impatience for an answer, and she with pain. Pray don't fail if you value her life. Write soon.

Adieu.

[P.S.] Send them soon if at all.

[P.P.S.] Write by the first mail, if it's only a line, to let us know if theirs any prospect of getting them soon. Pray don't fail. There is two sorts of leeches: brown and green. The brown ones are the best, if they could be procured. They have spots or stripes over them. Don't fail, pray, to get them.

The anxious, urgent postscripts produced prompt action on Betsey's part which she explains in her reply (**no. 39**) of May, 1818:

Dear Eliza,

I rec'd your letter with a blank date. It might be known to be a relative of mine. However, I paid as strict atention to contents as they required, and expect the leeches will accompany this letter. I have endeavoured to impress upon Ebenezer's mind the necessity of carrying brook water to keep them on thier voyage and to charge the Cap'n to shift it every 12 hours or they will die–which keep in memory after they have arrived, if Mary wishes them to live. I have suffer'd much for fear they could not be convey'd alive, on account of the particular water and inatention they are liable to meet with, but hope she will find them in perfect health, and that they may answer all our wishes. The account you gave of her case depressed my spirits even unto melancholy, and gave birth to the following stanzas; but was in the hope that your energetic mode of description might have exagerated or given me more alarm than was just. However, I fear not.

As respects the poetry, the sentiments have been cramped for want of the necessary varnish, but are genuine. The triffle I have borrowed is quoted, but the author suffers less by the theft then I from the scandal. I could not but steal a little, it came so napingly. It is my opinion that if all the brotherhood of illuminaries had been as scrupulously honest toward each other as I have been to them, they would oftener have appear'd through an eclipse as I now do; and this light-finger'd propensity is not natural, as Mary's misfortune gave birth to them. Shall expect the benefit of her criticism. It provokes me beyond all things that I cannot have my productions found fault with, and I confess I don't impute so much to thier complasance as to thier ignorance–that's polite, says you–and, after all, have to play the critic's part myself, in which I am most deficient.

Your request of my likeness is as astonishing as unexpected, as the thought has not entered my heart for at least 20 years. Should it ever be in my power to gain time, I will not promise but what I will do it, however difficult and undesirable; for the sake of Mary's alone would prompt me. But I think some person more disinterested than myself should draw mine, as I should be more apt to flatter than ever, and should be liable to make this a plea: that I was so blind I could not see the marks of age–which, as indifferent as my sight is, I have a pretty keen eye toward my own imperfections that it would be pretty difficult matter to persuade me that I looked or acted worse than I really do, however unwilling I might be to own it. . . .

My best love to Mary. I dare not ask her to write an account of her eye, but long for a letter from her. Write often as possible and mention every particular in respect to the success of the leeches. I hope they may have a salutary effect. Be particular as to your health above all things. Never read aloud or sit up late nor sleep with your window open nor any other thing that is imprudent. Good-bye.

I had like to have forgot a most essential thing. If you have one spark of pity for my feelings, send on that viel of Miss B[ryant']s. It has been a great trial to me for fear she would think you neglected her commands. Give ten thousand charges respecting in case of miscarriage. Don't fail.

By mid-1818 at the latest, construction of the new Universalist church which was to open its doors in December must have begun, and gives some chronological setting to Mary's mention of it when she writes Aunt Hannah (**no. 40**). Aunt Hannah was a most devoted member of the faith, fond also of religious verse, which accounts for Mary's quoting from Cowper's *The Time Piece* (lines 161–78). Here, the poet argues that all that happens, happens according to God's wish. The thought is close to Mary's favorite text from Pope, "Whatever is, is right":

Dear Aunt,

Twenty times I have been about to write to you since I received your last letter, but something has always prevented. I will now set it through and write a line in spite of fate. I feel anxious to hear from you, and wish you would write more frequently and longer letters. I want to know exactly how you are, with all the particulars: whether you are comfortable and contented with your situation, if you enjoy your health and are in good spirits, cheerful and happy–in short, whether you live up to your professions. 'Whatever is, is right' is your motto as well as mine. You often say you wish to be consistant. Whoever really believes this must be perfectly contented. They certainly can have nothing to fear, nothing to wish but that things may go on in thier course. Prepared for whatever comes, they take it fair and easey. They cannot be otherways than happy, let the world go which way it will. Now this is exactly my case. I have arrived at this pitch of perfection, and can truly say with Cowper:

'Happy the man who sees a God employed
In all the good and ill that chequers life. . . . '

Now this is victuals and drink and pretty good cloaths–that is to say, 'tis all that is necessary in this world. Heed it again, consider it well. This is my creed, and I am as happy as the full and firm belief of such a creed can make me. This is saying a great deal, but not more than I can prove. Indeed, without this comfortable doctrine,

I could not get along at all–should fret myself into a consumption, and have been in my grave years ago. But this reconciles me to every event of life, both good and ill, stops all repinings, murmurs and complaints, and leaves nothing to desire. 'By thier fruits ye shall know them.' Now, where these effects are not produced, faith must be wanting. I hope, however, this is not your case.

I am much obliged to you for lending me Eliza. I shall endeavor to make a good girl of her, and when you really want her and think you cannot do any longer without her, return her to you safe and sound. In the mean-time, let us hear from you often as possible. Eliza has more time than I and will always answer your letters. I have no news to communicate: only that we are about building a new church at the corner of Duane and Augustus streets.

All your friends desire thier love to you and want to see you very much, and so do I. Adieu.

This little sermon which Mary Way delivered to Aunt Hannah may have been directed as much at herself, given the anxiety she must have felt for the sight of her ailing eye. Meanwhile (**no. 42**, July 17, 1818) her sister was in low spirits, turning her, too, to reflection and poetry. The poetry goes by the title, "On viewing a Comet," and begins, "Hail Heaven's viceregent whose sublimer glow . . . ," to end with the plea that Faith's "chearing power the thought divine infuse/ That higher swells the philosophic muse." On the heels of these twenty-five lines come "Refflections on Life *by the author* (a-hem)," which open with the image, "When exhibiting on the theatre of life, at that bright period when the heart is enveloped in delusive pleasures that appears stamp'd with the seal of truth, aided thro' the power of a glowing immagination, we fondly dream of happiness." Betsey Champlain had entered on the literary period of her life with her usual exuberance, when she turns out a great deal of verse and a certain amount of prose; but she is nowhere more right than when she presses others for criticism. They in turn are right in withholding their opinions, because the verse and prose are at best facile; and that may justify the decision to omit them from the record here.

Dear Eliza,

I have so lately wrote, I have nothing to say that will in the least amuse or edify you, but are very desirous of hearing from you as often as possible, on account of hearing how the leeches operate upon Mary's eye, and whether she wishes more procured or not. As to the manner and means by which they are procured, I refer you to your Uncle Eben'r for information, as he sits here in his own name and person and has forbid my letting you into the secret. 'Tis sufficient that she can have more, and as many more, as she chooses, and may they be blesst to her, is my ardent prayer.

I hope you will write as soon as you have rec'd this, as it is time we heard from you both again. And another consideration: you posess a very happy tallant in putting us in good humour with ourselves; therefore I request an answer the sooner, as I am less apt to be so with myself than others. But at present I am upon tolerable terms with myself and could wish you both here to partake of my good humour. Young observes, or some one equally great (if any can be), 'we are never happy until we think there is none on earth more happy than ourselves.' This is exactly my case, I hear you say–but with what reason? Reason is out of the question when one would be happy. We may, through the power of philanthropy, extract it from even misery itself if we cannot find any thing better to found it upon. I have finally found that composition is the only cure for hypochondriac, which I think I mentioned in my last. I receive a periodical visits, and when attacked find my philanthropy wants an aid, which I find in indulging the Muse or Muses–for there is so many of them, I ought to speak in a plural sense. I have composed a short piece upon the appearance of the comet, and another upon Life, in prose–which is highly embellish'd with tautology. I send it with no other motive than to request Mary's candid opinion, whose judgement I prefer to any one's at the present day that I dare expose it to. I would give more for a candid, sincere critick than Young would have given for a friend, which, as he expresses, are worth all hazards we can run. I write without every nesessary ingredient–pens, paper, time, ideas, criticism, and being in love. I have only ragged elbows and empty pockets to prove I have any title to a poetess. I wish you to read them and she to point to the parts disapproved of and scratch them out, not to substitute them with others; neither do I wish her to act the hypercritick, but according to the best of her judgement condemn or give due merit as she finds nesessary. . . .

So here you have it with all its imperfections on its head. I wish Mary only to lop off every excrescent branch, pointing out, in what is left behind, errors, until she reduces it to proportion without adding any-thing of her own, however superior it might be, as thus it would not be original–that is, my original. Wherever you observe quotations, there I have borrowed, as it happened to fit the rhyme and sentiments were congenial likewise; but I have been honest. Should there be any more than I have quoted, I am totally ignorant, and am ashamed of that; for I scorn to borrow. What I have wrote is the result of experience, and may serve as a lesson to you, my dear Eliza, to teach you that every-thing that glitters is not gold. I would have you seek wisdom at an earlier period than she is generally saught, and profit thereby. I think I would reccommend a single life by all means, alltho' I am sensible that there is no station exempt. Still, you will have but one to be anxious for, and, just in proportion to the happiness you do enjoy, the exact weight of sorrow lies in embryo untill brought to life by time. This is what I know, not merely the effects of faith. If you are so fortunate as to arrive to contentment, that is the very highest feather in our caps. Let me beg of you never to aspire after more; for in reaching more you will loose that. This is truth's creed, so help me God.

And at this point Betsey introduces a figure who will recur often in the correspondence and eventually in the public print: M'Donald Clarke, called Sandy from his first name (of course, Alexander).[11]

Now I give you a taste of Sandy's quality–that is, Alexander Mcdonald Clark. He pops into every body's house and either is or effects to be deranged. There is, however, different opinions respecting him, and for my soul I cannot make up my mind which way it is, tho' I have watched him with a more scrutinizing eye than any-one else. No-one minds him now at all. He has become so common and constant a visitor to every-one in this town that he is esteemed no more than a chair, and all kinds of domestic evils carried on before him, while he appears so wraped up in sublimity as to notice nothing. Just to serve my master, I requested him the other day to compose something upon me. The request was vulgar, I grant, but, as all the rest of the girls had, I thought by that method I should be able to see what he was up to–and is the seperate inclosed. A few hours after that, I heard Mrs. S . . . s make the same request. He observed, I never write for the married ladies. You do not, I observed; why, I thought you had handed me some lines which were very flattering. He looked more arch than I ever see him, and replied, Why, I was afraid to diney least you would lampoon me. Oh no, I answered, I never write satyrs upon anyone.

Now I can say that, 'in the music of truth,' the meaning is too obscure for me to understand it, tho' I allways was of opinion that we could understand our own productions full as well as another's; but this seems to want marginal notes for my ear, which I will thank Mary to assist us to, as she must be my criterion in future–if she will. I think my pride would be gratified by a similiar request. It cannot strain her eyes, as she has only to hear, to play Doctor Johnson.

Now, I am mistaken if your father is not capable of being as good a critic as I need, but will never hear a word of mine; and the reason, I formerly thought, was envy, from expressing such a strong desire to compose, himself. But pondering upon the subject I find it proceeds from this cause–through all my pieces appears a disgust of the world–and conscious guilt, from considering himself to be the source. He turns a deaf ear to it, nor can I offend him higher than to attempt reading it, as he is sure of recognizing his own image in them.

But to return to Sandy: one day our young group had taken a walk, the house was still, and I hapened to carry all my writing aparatus into the parlour. Presently my brother poet calls to see the Misses Dodges, and found them away, and he flung himself into my room, as there is no fasten to the door. I felt rather small, but he was too much of the gentleman to attempt to touch any paper that lay on the table. Says, so you are writing. I answered Yes, I often copy Poets' Corners, &c. Yes, but you compose. So does Mrs. Pool. And, soposing I had diverted his mind from thinking they were my own, I handed him the piece I composed upon the Muse, which I will send you in my next, if you have not allready copied it–and if you have, tell me, and save me the writing. He said he thought it very sublime–whose opinion I do not value very highly–but said it was wrote in a different stile from his own, as he was most partial to Lord Byron's, signifying he copied his stile. I observed, every writer had a stile of their own and that I new nothing of borrowing diction any more than sentiments. He said he knew I was a poetess the first time he ever saw me, when he had his miniature taken. I asked him by what mark they were distinguish'd. He answered, I had a poetical eye. I wished to know wherein it differed from other eyes. He said there was a peculiar brilliancy in one spot on the white of the eye that ever denoted a poetic genius. I rather suspect this was the effect of art, and don't know but he plays upon the public, as many sopose.

I am afraid your tongue will find occassion to sigh in reading all this. Don't omit mentioning whether you have copied the *Ode to the Muse*, and one addressed *to Mirth*. If not, I will copy them and send for inspection.

My love to Mary. Write immediately.

Adieu.

7

Bad News All Around

Aunt Hannah's health evidently required a lot of watching. That meant more insistent calls from home for Eliza's return. Return she must, then, unhappily to New London not many weeks after the preceding letter. It is probably in the period that follows that she painted a portrait of the old lady in her late seventies (Pl. 5.14).[1]

Her first despair on arrival, shared with her aunt Mary, has somehow faded from the record; but she wrote again, perhaps in late July of 1818 (**no. 43**), with a good many crossings-out, because she didn't know how much she could or should complain. She pictures herself among what she could now, after New York, too clearly see to be small-minded people in a small town, who had very little to offer but small talk, and were, some of them, ready to resent anyone or anything of different proportions. Like Sinclair Lewis, Eliza had been spoiled for Main Street by Broadway; and yet she wrestled with her dissatisfaction:

Dear Aunt,

I was determined not to write you again till I felt better but I fear I shall never be happy again [these last eleven words over the crossed-out "had some good news to communicate"], and till I felt in better spirits–which I suppose you know would follow, of course. The good news I alluded to is, I shall certainly send you the money in my next letter. The idea of it has put me in better spirits than I have been in since my return from bliss to misery, for I don't know how otherways to express myself. Never, since the hour you were born, did you see such a dull, dumb, forlorn place as this is: not a grain of business doing nor a soul stiring, and every time I have been down to Mother's I have scarcely met a living creature. At least they did not appear as if they had the breath of life in them. The first week of my return I verily thought I should have died, and Oh! that I had. You can have no more idea of my feelings than I have power of describing them, and only because you have never rèturn'd to New L[ondon] since you quited it. When I was with you and Anna I was not sensible of the priviliges, the advantages, and the happiness I enjoy'd, nor ever should have been had I not been deprived of them. Whenever we said anything, I always found I was a little wiser at least when it was over; but now nothing can I hear but the faults of my neighbours. I am relatively cut off from any source of improvement. After the first week of my return, I was determin'd, as I told you, not to stay at home so much as I used to, thinking that going out would make me feel better. I began this week with visiting, but I could not carry it through. It was too great a task and required more exertion than I was mistress of. It was too 'flat, stale and unprofitable.' I either wish I had never been to New York or had never return'd from there, for it is impossible for me to square myself to both situations, they are so totally different. I believe I have a mind capable of improvement and I know I have a very great desire too improve, and that I have been in an exelent school ten months; and now to be snatched so suddenly away and placed in the hum-drum situation I am at present placed in has been a much greater shock to me than it is to Ann, when she is at the Gardens and they start right out of *Robin Adair*, *Jesse of Dumblane*, and *Love's Young Dream* into *Molly Wodd*.[2] You know how grating that is to her. This is even so to me.

Oh Lord, how I want to see you and her. You can have no idea how I want to get in my element again, for I'm sure I am out of it now. It seems to me ages, yes millions of centuries, since I left you–since I have had a grain of food for the mind. It will starve to death if much longer neglected. If you don't write me something soon, no matter what it is, so that it comes from N[ew] York, I shall be satisfied with it. Oh Lord how I long to hear from you, Oh how I envy you and Ann [Fitch] your happiness there together. You must enjoy yourselves so much. I can't think of you without the most exquisit regret. But I have said enough, for talk does no good.

Last Sunday evening I felt very low spirited indeed and thought I would go down to Mother's to see if I should not feel a little better. As I passed Aunt [Sally] Way's I stop'd. She insisted on my staying till after tea and she would walk down with me, which I did. But we first went into Uncle Allen's, for Aunt Way and Aunt Allen's family are very intimate indeed, and I am very glad of it, for I love them all better than anybody I visit in New London. At Aunt Allen's we saw Capt. Lee and his nephew Frederick Scranton, cousen to Betsey–quite a likely beau. They were all extremely glad to see me, Aunt Allen particularly. I thought she would kiss me to death and eat me up alive. I know she is the best woman in existance and always was. Betsey and Amelia [Allen] were glad enough to see me, but they were more moderate in there transports. Well, I proposed there going down to Mother's with Uncle and Aunt Way and myself. Amelia, John, and Frederick Scranton went with us and a young lady who was visiting there. Betsey was engaged and refused to go.

We spent what is called a very pleasant evening, but as I could not be in New York, I should have enjoy'd myself alone much better. I however tried all I could to be happy, and to appear to be so if I could not in reality; and it is this striving to appear to enjoy myself when I'm in company that has made me so wretched. You must say somthing that there is not one grain of sense in–[above the line:] *your* sort of sense–and then laugh yourself to death at it, or else you are considered cross, ugly-tempered, and odd. Oh! for one of those long fitts of museing that we could all enjoy when in company with the Fitches. There was somthing sublime in that, when compared with the triffling chit-chat I have been doom'd to since my return. The contrast is so striking, I cannot get along with it, and, because I cannot, always conceal my disgust at some of those foolish, low *conversaziones*.

Mother calls me Miss Know-all-things, and has tormented me to death to give her my opinion of her poetry; and, to save me from perdition, I cannot tell what is the nature of my opinion or whether it has any nature in it. I was down there the other day. Don't you think and Mother brought about fifteen quire of paper all wrote as fine as Mr. Northam writes, of her own poetry, which she would, in spite of my teeth, read aloud, tho' I beg'd her not, observing I was not in a mood to hear or relish it. All would not do–she would read the whole of it to me, not one word of which I heard or understood; and when she had got through, I was to give my opinion of it, as I had heard it, in spite of my teeth and senses. I was in an agony, for I could not get off any way, and what to do I did not know. At last I told her I could not say anything for I knew nothing about poetry nor never desired too; but she did not care, she said. She did not want a better judge than I was, and I must give my opinion; that Aunt Champlain had pronounced it exquisite, and that it would pass the most critical review in the world; that she would give worlds that she was blest with such poetic talents; and a deal on't, as Aunt Hannah says, which I can't remember. I was astonished, you may well think, and beg'd her not to show any more of it in my day. But alas! I fear that not only I but you will see some of it in some of the papers ere long; for I find with sorrow my inability to stem the poetic torrent that threatens to pour on our devoted heads from that quarter, in spite of our teeth.

But to go on with my mournful story: I found I should never leave the house alive if I did not do or say something in favor of it. So that I might return home, I told Mother I would take some lines she had made on Young, and endeavor to understand them. I took them and brought them home, thinking them the best of all her productions; but as I don't feel myself competent to the task of criticizeing them, I beg you, as you would value my peace and happiness here and hereafter, to send me your opinion of them. Pray don't disappoint me, as my life depends on your opinion.

I am really afraid Mother's brain is turning, for she acts to me as if she was distracted. Aunt Champlain [=Mrs. Oliver C.] says she is absolutely crazy, yet she cannot live one single moment out of her society. They are forever together. Mother plays on her guittar and flagelet together, and Aunt Champlain dances after it, and I sit looking on and sighing over the 'stench of mortality'–for they smell stronger of it here than they do in New York [these last five words crossed out, and above, "and I sit in perfect astonishment, wondering at their happiness and sighing over my own misery."]

How comes on Mrs. Dawson and Hannah? I hope to hear better news of them than I expect to. I have thought a great deal about them since my return. Mrs. D. stole the hearts of Uncle Ebb and Sally. They think more of her, they both say, than of any-one else they saw while they staid in N[ew] York. Uncle Ebb says she was a *grand fellow* as ever he saw, and he should be so happy to see her in New London,

> and so would Sally. So do you tell her so, and tell her *I* should *not* be glad to see her at all.

To this, Eliza adds longing requests for news of various New York friends, no less than twenty-three of them, whom it comforted her to recall and to particularize on this hot summer evening in her little room down the hall from her Aunt Hannah: "Pray begin down to Gasner's and go up to the corner of Rosevelt St. and be very particular about all the beaux, and you will forever obliege me." Then, changing the subject:

> I was so sorry I could not write to Capt. Lee. I never was so provoked about anything. I understood he was going to New York in a fortnight. Instead of that, he goes off in a tangent three days ago and all that made me write this letter so as to tell you the prospect I have of sending you the money soon, and I wrote this to beg you if possible to get *Amabilité* varnished. Time enough to send by him, as I never shall get such another chance of having it brought, perhaps, in the world. Pray, if it's possible, send it by him, as all of my friends is distracted to see her, after seeing *Lady Douceur*. I have not told them she will be along very soon, and Aunt Way says, if I will lend them to her to hang up in her parlour for some time, she will get frames for them. When you send her, wrapp the muslin shawl round the board first, before you put her into the bag, as pieces are very easily injured by having only one thickness over them. I am so sorry I have had *Douceur* cut off from the board. I don't know what to do, the varnish has cracked so terribly. Mother has been obliged to get another board made on purpose for her, on which she is to be put and secured at her four corners, or she will be ruined; for all creation has been to see her. Her fame spreads like wild fire, and they all hold her by one corner and always crack the varnish some-where.

Eliza's low spirits a little later in the summer of 1818 had risen, despite the weather (**no. 45**):

> I believe in my soul the world is deluged again. The rain has poured in torrents forty days and fifty nights, and the gloomy appearance of everything, together with my own melancholy reflections, have almost unhinged me. I sat here in my little chamber just after dinner, thinking of you and wishing myself in New York, where storms are pleasant; for I can always see Toby's nose in the thickest of it. Well, as I was saying, I was alone and thinking of you all when I was called down by Aunt Hannah, & supposing it could be no one come to see us in such a storm but William, I ran down-stairs in a mighty hurry, thankful once more to see any kind of creeping thing upon the face of the earth, when Oh! Heaven! what was my astonishment, looking like the Devil as I did, on beholding a handsome young widower just made. He arose from his seat at my entrance &, with all the solemnity nessisary on such trying occations, advanced with his hand extended to shake & press mine as hard as circumstances would admit–which he did in great style, I assure you. I was so unexpectedly and so compleatly caught in my dishabille that I turn'd all the colours

of the rainbow &, without knowing what I said, stammer'd out a few inarticulate sentences about my surprise at seeing him. I believe he saw how compleatly I was disconcerted, for I saw a smile playing about the corners of his ruby lips that I by no means like the expression of, in spite of his efforts to suppress it. This made me mad & I was determin'd to show a proper resentment on the occation, which I did, till I made him sorry enough. He asked to see my paintings, I suppose, to make up. I had none to show him but *Fancy*, all the rest being down to Mother's. 'Oh! Eliza!' he exclaimed on beholding her & glancing at the same time at the crape which enshrouded his hat, 'this is too cheering a sight for me. It is long since happiness and I have met. If melancholy, black melancholy was depicted here, it would accord with my feelings better, much better.' Aunt Hannah tried to devirt his thoughts from the melancholy turn they had taken and I would have joined her with all my soul but was afraid to, lest he should set me down a young woman for fear of mistakes. So I fixed my gooseberries on the floor as the safest place for them, while he remain'd. He did not keep me in torture but an hour, & you may depend I was thankful enough when he arose to take leave, which he did exactly in widower style, with the air of a person rejoic'd at their emancipation from their matrimonial shackles, striving to conceal it yet resolving to shackle themselves again as soon as they possibly could. Now, I would tell you who he is, but you always say you do not like to see things too well finished. You like to have somthing left for the imagination because it's more sublime. So I will leave you to form what conjectures you please upon the subject, & proceed to something of more consequence, if I can find anything that is.

Last Sunday I staid home, tho' it was a delightful day; but we had no minister, & when that is the case your dearly beloved cousen Jonathan [Starr] officiates, with the assistance of the *Junto*. Well, as I had no particular curiosity to see or hear him, I staid home & read a box of news-papers which were taken while I was with you. I send you a couple of anecdotes that I cut out. You see I went through the church service in Oliver Cromwell's cannon, and the 'wonderful efficacy of the *Steam Bath*' amused me very much. It brought so fresh to memory the credulity of Old Smith, as the Dawsons call her; and whenever I find anything in the papers that please me I will always send it to you.

I have been reading the *Forest of Montalbano* [of 1812 by Catherine Cuthbertson], four thick volumes, but the words *horrorized* & *terrorized* occur so often I am sick of it. Yesterday afternoon I spent at Aunt [Sally] Way's and in the evening Oh! Heavens, I heard such music as I shan't forget in a hurry. About six or seven o'clock there came along a band and stop'd opposite Uncle Way's. It continued to play there an hour. Oh Heavens you never heard anything half so delightful in your life. There was the base drum, an organ, dorric reeds, clarinets, besides ten thousand other instruments, & I really fancied myself in paradise. They played several tunes which I did not know, but more that I did; several marches; & Oh! they played *Jesse's Smiling*, *Young Jesse*, *The Flower of Dunblane*. Never since the creation of Adam was anything half so delightful. It brought you all to my bodyly eyes as well as my mind's eye. Uncle Way and several gentlemen contributed to keep the band there for as long as they would play, for they would not play without money. They gave us *Kate Karny* alias Paddy [?]Rory–you know that is one of my favorites. Eliza Holt is forever humming it.

If I could make a dictionary of my own, it would be ten thousand times easier for me to write. To save me from perdition I cannot find one word through the whole book half expressive enough to express my feelings when I'm in my high ropes. I don't know but if Mother and I should undertake what we might do, for she is certainly the most singular genius that ever was known, & would you believe it–she makes a conquest every time she appears in public, so say the learned. I believe I told you in my last about our going to Aunt Allen's to spend the evening and kick the guitar. Well, Mother was in one of her happiest moods and performed admirably on her two instruments. Well, General Isham was there, and I thought if there was such a thing as judgeing of the feelings from the countenance, he was very much delighted. He sat as long as she play'd, & when she had finished arose to depart, after thanking her very handsomely for the treat she had given him, and Amelia told me that, as he was going out, he sayd to her he *dare* not stay in the house another minute for fear he should get too deep in love–that she was the most fascinating, the sweetest woman that ever existed, and said so much that I beged Amelia not to tell Mother; for it was more than the strongest mind could stand–even yours. But she sayd she would. So here ends my paper.

This from Eliza arrived too late to be included in Mary Way's letter which now follows (**no. 46**), though she does refer to it as just arrived. It was rather the preceding one (**no. 43**) which she had in front of her to answer, taking up such matters as Captain Lee and *Amabilité*. She still speaks as if she were a part of the Fitch household on Cherry Street, visiting there all the time or receiving Anna at her own lodgings at 98 Chatham Street.[3] The intimacy afforded a glimpse of Anna at cross-purposes with her benevolent father Northam regarding her parody of Samuel Woodworth's poem, *The Bucket*. This latter poem, destined to prove Woodworth's most durable by far, had appeared under his usual pen-name "Selim" in the *Republican Chronicle* and *Weekly Visitor* and *Ladies' Museum* of July, and provoked not only Anna's verses under *her* usual pen-name "Agnes," but his surrebutter again in the *Republican Chronicle*:[4]

Dear Eliza,

With this you will recieve one from Ann, for which you may thank me, if you are disposed to be thankful. She said she wish'd you would write to her, and I told her you consider'd her a critic and was unwilling your letters should fall into her hands. She pretended to take it in dudgeon, tho' I know she would have consider'd it a compliment, had not her feelings keenly smarted from the effects of a severe stroke from one of that honorable fraternity, to which you know painters and poets have naturaly a certain kind of thrilling aversion.

The case was this: she had copy'd *The Bucket* and her answer to it, to send to you, and in the pride and naughtiness of her heart, handed them to her father, requesting he would read them both and tell her which he thought the best. The honest old saint, innocent as a sucking dove, not dreaming he held in his hand and was about to pronounce upon the bantling of his daughter (that is to say, his own offspring and natural grandchild according to the flesh) cooly, calmly and deliberately hit the poor thing an unlucky blow, heavy enough in conscience to 'crush to atoms all the bones' of a much more promising child, by saying very candidly *The Bucket* was the best. This was of course a thunder-stroke to the fond mother, and the more terrible as it was quite unexpected. She stood the shock, however, tolerably well, and in faltering accents modestly confest, she thought so too; but yet, like Jesamy, the fop ventured to ask what objection he could possibly have to her answer. The reply to this question was more mortifying than poetic vanity could well endure. She seized her pen and in the true spirit of resentment and revenge, addressing herself to you, has drawn the character of a critic. That it is done feelingly is evident, and I think a tolerable likeness for one sitting. But the old gentleman is for more substantial blessings. He has no taste for poetry and therefore not a competent judge. On religious subjects and weighty matters, I know no one of whose judgement I think more highly, for those have been the objects of his study; but he has no acquaintance with the Muses. These considerations I offer'd to Ann as a plaster for her broken pate.

In the next place, you must answer her letter, which I hope you will do as soon as you recieve it. Write to her in the same style you do to me, easy and unstudied, just as you would talk if she was present. This is the style she likes, as it is most natural and agreeable. I wish the letters you wrote me were such as I could show her and the Dawsons. Read them to her I must–what I can, that is readable; and it is such a plague and botheration to separate the sheep from the goats–I mean family matters and what it is not necessary for her to see–from those things that would please and amuse her, that, instead of mixing them all up together, a kind of hodge-podge which tho' I like very well myself won't do to treat company, I would rather wish you to serve it up in a genteel way, on different or separate dishes, that I may set them best before my friends and share it with them, which will give it double relish. You understand this, I conclude, and when you write to me again let it be such a letter as you are willing they should all see, for see it they must. They don't like for me to read a little here and a little there. They want to have the whole, and see for themselves–and I want they should. But family matters, secrets and, in short, everything you do not wish to meet their eye (in which I wish you to be as particular now, and more so, for I feel very much interested in what consernes you all) write on a paper by itself and enclose it in your letter. This will save me much perplexity; and be sure you do it in future.

And now for Mrs. Dawson and her affairs. I have the pleasure to inform you she has at length found a house just by, in William St., three doors from the corner of Pearl St. on your left hand as you go down, very near here–the upper part of a pretty little sunny two story brick house, pleasantly situated. Hannah has return'd from the country. They are comfortably settled once more and as happy as usual there. . . .

But now a word or two of myself. You see I'm alive. Of this melancholy truth I think you must be by this time pretty well convinced. Believe me, I have muster'd up all the life and soul there is in my to write this, because your letter was so dismal;

but after all should have been unequal to the task, had I not had an application for a picture in the mean time.

Mary Holt has just handed me a letter from you for which I have only time to thank you, now, and will answer it hereafter. I don't know how it came. I have not seen Capt. Lee nor heard of him before, tho' I should be very glad too. *Amabelite* is not yet varnish'd, so you must have patience till Ann's is finish'd, which will be soon; and then they will be done in best manner possible. I shall be as careful as you would be, and do it as well, and as soon as it is ready, I will write and let you know, that you may send for it.

Adieu. . . .

Mary's next letter of the early autumn (**no. 49**)[5] continues the story of *The Bucket*, now providing the text of the poem which wouldn't have been available in New London; but it also continues her reply to points in the two last from Eliza (**nos. 43** and **45**): "cool off on Mrs. Cooper," *High Betty Martin*, the Lockwood family, and so forth. Toward the end, Thomas Moore's immediately popular tales in verse, the exotic *Lalla Rookh*, is referred to (it had reached the U.S. only in the previous year); and the "*small matters*" being made for Mrs. Sexton are baby-clothes for the "infant" of the next year, referred to archly in **no. 53**:

Dear Eliza,

I have so much to say, I realy don't know where to begin. So many things present themselves and croud at once for a passage to my pen–and such an intolerable memory, too–if I don't set them down directly I shall forget half. 'Tis necessary to take a view of the different subjects I am about to handle, and arrange my ideas, in order to be as consice as possible. First, then, I must inform you your precious packet has arriv'd–how it was receiv'd &c. Next, I must give you an account of your beaux's, particularly Toby's nose ettc. ettcettra; render an account of *Amibility*'s health and wellfare; present you with a parody on *The Bucket* by 'Agnes' alias Anna, and with the answer to the parody by 'Selim' alias Woodworth; offer a few critisims on lines written upon Edward Young, with observations upon your mother's poetry in general; and conclude with such reflections as will naturaly arrise from the consideration of these important subjects. It will give your Speaker much pleasure if she is able to pass thro' the interesting matter contain'd in the brief outline she has thus hastily sketched, in the course of the evening. She will not, however, weary your patience if she should even be oblig'd to defer her comments upon some of the passages untill another opportunity.

We will now proceed to consider the subjects or texts, if you please, in the order they lie before us. And first, with respect to your letters, nothing could be more exceptable to us both. We were dying with impatience for thier arrival. Ann was delighted with hers. I read it. It read very well. No doubt it would sing well, set to musick, provided the musick was good. You ask my opinion of it and request me to point out the faults. I never allow myself to criticise any thing till I have given it a second reading, which I've had no opportunity of doing. However, she's pleased enough with it, and I think it's very good. If it has a fault, it is rather more painstaking than the one you wrote me (which is what I wish you to avoid). You might as well have given her some of the nonsense you stuff into mine, respecting Toby's Nose, and saved me the trouble of answering it. She could give you an acount of it better than I, who never knew he had a nose till you made the discovery and bored it into me. I think it appears rather more comfortable since the cool weather–not quite so high coloured, fever somthing abated. But I can tell you more about your beau Johny, who is married since your departure, to his Eliza. We have had high times here–a tareing second-day wedding in great style, or snuff. You would have enjoy'd it. You know what terrible singers they are. Upon this occasion they all lift thier voices with one accord, and of course a mighty noise ensued which unroof'd several houses in the neighborhood, to the utter dismay of the inhabitance, with other triffling damages that have not yet been estamated. The very carmen stared in gaping wonderment, not being able to hear thier own noise. Painting in fresco and *Lalla Rookh* suspended for a while. Thier warbling strains and even the sweet singers of Hot Corn and Baked Pares

'——made a pause!
An awful pause! prophetic of thier end!
And may the prophecy be soon fulfil'd!'
Young

Little Wixey was here the other day, and enquired most affectionately after you: when you was to return &c. The rest of your beaux's go on much as usual. Lockwood family have moved away and another has taken possession of that suit of rooms with forty thousand children that fill up every window in Chatham Street. Your church beauxs all desire thier love to you, 'Dignity' and 'Wittito' in particular. As to 'Lobster', he has crawl'd off since you went away–no one to take care of him. He has been missing some time; but no matter.

Enough of such nonsense. Ann has finnished her picture and I have sized them both. Never any-thing looked better than they than they do. The colour has not moved at all, for I went carefully over the paint with a small pencel before I ventured the brush. But what will you say when I tell you Ann's picture exceeds yours in beauty far, very far. How far? you will ask. What shall I say? Far as the blushes of Aurora exceeds the shades of night. No bad simile. Quite poeticaly express'd, and true, if it don't ryme. Not your simile, says you. Tell me about the picture. Well, then, we repeat it, it exceeds yours as far as the blushes of Aurora exceeds the shades of night; or, in plain prose, as much as a red nose exceeds a black one. Ah! that sounds more comfortable, you will say (for I know you hate to be outdone), and conclude there's not much to chouse between a red nose and a black one. But you are mistaken, I assure you there's a mighty difference. If you won't believe it, come and see for yourself. Well, I can't help it. 'Tis your own fault. You should have staid till she finished her's, and then it would have been as much inferior to yours, perhaps, as her *Doucer* was to yours, for I should not have trouble'd myself about it. But you went off and left her to bother me, and I was determin'd not to be bother'd for nothing, so, as I was oblig'd to attend to her, I directed her to shade it intirely different from yours, with red altogather–nothing but carmine, and you can't conceive any-thing so fine as the effect produced. It has taken the shine of from yours, everyone acknowledges except Chevalier, who still gives yours the preference, condemns the other, and with his usual wisdom asigns this reason: 'I'll tell you what–I abhor artificial beauty, I do indeed, I do indeed. Yes, yes, yes. I met a lady in Broad-way. Her bonnet was lined with pink. It cast such a sweet reflection on her face. Oh, she looked beautiful. Just so, just so. She did indeed. But take of her bonnet and her beauty's gone. Ha! Pale as death, I suppose. Now, I don't like such things. No, no, no. Give me clear simple nature, I say' (and then with one of those killing *arch* looks, which can only be [?]convei'd but never express'd), 'don't you say so, Miss Way? Ha! What's your opinion?' That your the greatest fool nature ever formed, I mentally reply'd. But I must be civil till these two rotten pictures are varnish'd, and then fare-well forever, and forever fare thee well. Mr. Northam is to carry them to him tomorrow, so you may send for yours as soon as you please. I suppose it will be ready for you.

And now, what comes next? I've forgot. No matter, rules are but the fetters of genius. We feel disposed to travel out of the record, just now, and shall indulge ourselves in making some inquires respecting the general impression with regard to your appearanse and acquirements, in your last visit to New York. Don't they think you look better by all the cost–don't they think you vastly improved, in looks at least if not in manners? I'll tell you something, if you won't tell anybody. There was a certain girl came down to New York, once. Shall I describe her? She was a great overblown fat clumsey country girl, big as ever the pudding bag would let it be–tight!–strain'ed to death–stiff, awkward, ignorant–and &c &c. Well, and so, down she came, a whole packet-load of her, and here she was. We found her very amusing and used to almost die with laughing at her simplicity. There's music in every-thing, you know, if you can only get it out. So we took her in hand, dosed her well with Congress Water,[6] kept her upon light fare, reduced the cumbersome load of mortality that hung upon the vast dementions of her unweildy figure to something like a reasonable size, and by giving her now and then a polishing rub, she became quite another thing, and return'd (comparitively speaking) easy, genteel, refined, and tonish–or Yorkish, if you please. Pray just ask your friends there if they remember any such person and if they should happen to recollect her, let them compare what she was with what she is, and I think they will not be disposed to deny to our exertions the credit they deserve. If, however, they do not yet consider her quite perfect (as I must confess there is still room for improvement), tell them to send her back, and we will give her the finishing touches. In the mean time, it will not be amiss to administer a dose of Congress occasionally, to keep down her flesh. 'Tis cooling, good for the blood, an excelent thing to carry off gross humours.

My love to Aunt Hannah. I hope she will not fat up this *girl* (tho' now I suppose I must set her down young woman, for fear of mistakes) with good cooking, and spoil her figure, which to render tolerably genteel we was oblig'd to scold and starve, as it were, the very flesh of [=off] her bones. I've no wish when she returns to have the job to do over again, therefore Aunt Hannah must not give her pancakes, fried cakes, corn and beans, and all the good things she knows so well how to make.

I dined with sister Fitch the other day (by special invitation) upon corn and beans. Aunt Hannah did not make it, but 'twas very good. 'Tis thought a high Yankee dish here, but they don't make it like she does. I have been invited to a number of parties since you went home, but made none. I've been to several. Some I have refused. Last week Mrs. Clinch and Maria sent for me to drink tea with them (which I suppose was to be considered a flattering testemony of regard from a woman of her superior sense and judgement). I at first declined the honnor on account of Maria's oddity in so obstinately refusing to visit, because I never could prevail on her to drink tea with me; but Ann preswaded me to consent, and we had a very agreable time. In the evening we went to Washington Hall to hear an oration delivered for the benefit of the deaf and dumb by one of your beauxs, Lawyer Clark. Kitteredge, your beloved Kitteredge, was prompter. Oh how we wish'd for you, Mrs. Fitch particularly, to help him find fault. He hates the poor fellow as bad as you do, and for no reason, as I can see. Ann and I defended him out of pure charity. After the oration was over we went to the Garden, took some ice cream, heard the music, and saw the fountain play for the last, last time this year. Alass, the season is over, and for that very reason I felt disposed to linger longer than usual, and tho' it was cold comfort, left it with regret.

Day before yesterday I drank tea with Mrs. Cooper and the Miss Thomasses, who were very particular in thier inquries about you. I told them they were remember'd in your letters, tho' I did not say you 'cool'd off upon them.' They were much obliged to you, of course, and return'd the compliment with all thier hearts. There was several ladies there. Young Thomas and two gentlemen from the South spent the evening with us. Henry is realy a pritty fellow, and vastly improved. You would be in love with him. He has travel'd, you know, and seen the corkscrew, and gain'd as much advantage from it as yourself. He is going to New Orleans this fall, and we are all going with him to make our fortunes. Money is the one thing needfull in this world. 'Tis a grand place. I wish I was there. This town is overdone with every kind of business.

When did you hear from George? Have you written to him? Why don't you write, and when do you expect him? I would like to go to Natches with him when he returns, and take you along with me. We might do wonders there. This is all talk–tho' it might be something more if Aunt Hannah could spare you.

But I must stop, or I shall have no room for the poetry I promised you. So here it comes, from the *Republican Chronicle*, prefaced with the following: 'The author of that beautiful effusion, on which this is a parody, must be sensible that it is no mark of disrespect either to a writer or his production to take this liberty with the latter. Had it ever been so consider'd, the following parody would never have appear'd.

How dear to the heart are the pleasures that ever
    Attend on the cold gloomy season of snow.
Balls, parties and sleighing prevail spite of weather,
    While the bowl, and good cheer, warmth and spirits bestow.
Then within's the bright fire, always sure to draw nigh it
    The merry and gay, who from freezing have fled.
But the comfort most dear was to slumber in quiet.
    Beneath the warm blanket that cover'd the bed–
The soft woolen blanket, the warmth-giving blanket,
    The comforting blanket that cover'd the bed.

That soft woolen cov'ring I hail'd as a treasure,
    For often at night, nearly void of all sense,
I found it the sourse of a life-giving pleasure–
    The purest that nature can ever dispense.
How quickly beneath its warm surface I enter'd
    And soon every freezing sensation was fled,
While thus so delightfully, glowingly center'd,
    I bless'd the warm blanket that covered the bed–
The soft woolen blanket &c.

How sweet 'twas to lie and mild summer believe it,
    So genial the warmth which this covering throws.
No soft downy couch could e'er tempt me to leave it,
    Tho' spread for a king's royal limbs to repose.
But alass! those delights are no more*, for the season
    Which always renews them long since has been fled,
And often in spite of the chidings of reason
    I sigh for the blanket that cover'd the bed–
The soft woolen blanket, the warmth giving blanket,
    The comforting blanket that cover'd the bed.

Agnes'

*This was written when the weather was very warm–since then the following has been written as a substitute for the four last lines, being more applicable to the present season.

'Although every trace of that loved situation
    While summer beguil'd me, from memory fled,
Yet now I experience a strong inclination
    To sigh for the blanket that cover'd the bed–
The soft wollen blanket, the warmth giving blanket,
    The comforting blanket that cover'd the bed.'

Mrs. Dawson and Hannah sends the usial quantity (which is about ten thousand bushels, you know) of love and affection to you all, particularly to your Uncle and Sally for thier kind invitation. You told me Sally was going to Portsmoth. I suppose she has been and return'd by this time. Ask her if she recollects a Mr. and Mrs. Holdredge, who say Captain Way and his wife boarded with them in Boston. They now live in the house with Mrs. Dawson. She appears to be a charming woman. I like her much, and so do the Dawsons. She speaks in the highest terms of Ebb and Sally, and was pleased to find I was a relation–regreted she was not in New York last fall when they were here, hopes they will come again soon, and so do I. . . .

I have taken Eliza Woodward['s] profile on ivory. You will see it, I suppose, when she returns. . . . I must defer critisisms upon your mother's poetry to another opportunity, as you see I have neither time nor room here.

And then follow Woodworth's verses, *To Agnes, in Answer to the Parody on 'The Bucket', in Praise of 'The Blanket'*:

I sang not in vain, tho' uncourtly the theme,
For Agnes the strain has commended.
Her lips as she tasted have hallowed the stream
Which erst from the *Bucket* descended.
But tho' its cool brim has been bless'd with her kiss
(And a sweeter young minstrel ne'er drank it),
It could not afford her such exquisite bliss
As fancy conceives in her *Blanket*.

How richer, how dearer, my lyre is to me
Since prais'd by the Muses' fair daughter;
And since my rude *Bucket* is noticed by thee,
Its contents have become holy water.
Then sip it, dear Agnes, again and again,
For however high you may rank it,
I'll cheerfully yield it, and never complain,
While I share in the bliss of your *Blanket*.

'Selim'

Eliza Holt has just gone from here. She says the parody on *The Bucket* is universally admired. You know what [an] enthusiast she is–Oh she thinks so highly of Ann's talants. She heard you had returned and call'd to see you. I told her you ask'd if she still danced to the tune of *High Betty Martin*. She says, Oh yes, she drank tea with him yesterday over at Hunter's, and it was he told her you had return'd: he saw you at the window, or some one that look'd very much like you. A long mass she bid me say, but she may write it herself–and so I told her. She says you must write first, if it's only a slip of paper, and enclose it in my letter [i.e., a letter to Mary]. She will answer it.

Maria Cobb was here this morning–says she has not seen you but saw your mother and was charm'd with her and her her musick. Give my love to her and tell her I beg she will have compassion on my poor guitar and at least spare its life. I find I have still a kindness for the poor thing. Since I hear of the kicks and cuffs it receives, natural affections begins to work. I regard it as an old friend that has sooth'd many a pensive hour, and am not so insensible as to hear of its sufferings with indifference.

This letter has been written some days, waiting for Ann's, who is very busy writing for her husband and making *small matters* for Mrs. Sexton. I was there last night. She said she would write today and bring it here this evening.[7] She tells me Fitch has realy sent the catalogues he has so long threaten'd you with. You know he attended the book auction and always gave them to you. After you went away he still seem'd disposed to continue the business–such is the force of habit–and every one he brought home, would say, 'I will salt this up for Eliza. I mean to send them to her.' We laugh'd at him and had no thought he was in earnest. You, I suppose, will be surprised to receive a dose of Congress from that quarter. I hope it will cost you nothing, but if he has not directed it to your uncle it may be an expensive piece of of fun. It must be a good joke that's worth paying for, these hard times.

Yesterday I receiv'd a long letter from Maria Hayden. She is not well. . . . She has given up her visit here this fall and is very pressing for me to go on to Richmond. She says Hayden thinks I might make a fortune there in a very short time: have business enough, both painting and teaching if I choose, as there is no drawing school in the place–as many scholars as I wish'd and any price I chose to ask. I shall be at no trouble nor expense. If I will only consent to come, Hayden will speak to a captain of a vessel who will take the best care of me and see that I want for nothing that is comfortable and convenient; and as soon as I arrive, will insure me good business and enough of it, and knowing my pride and dread of obligations, to remove my scruples and relieve me from all apprehensions on that head by convincing my [=me] she has interested motives. She says she wants me to paint her a family piece in the best manner. What delicacy! Oh what a Maria! What can be more generous, more tempting than such an offer, to one in my situation? There is but one thing can induce me to refuse it: Aunt Hannah's old church. I am as loath to leave that as you were, for I shall never find such another, and I will stick by it as long as I can keep clear of debt. . . . I send you a kaleidoscope. It is a little soil'd, to be sure, but you will like it the better as it came wrapt round a piece of soap.

Mary's reference to "one in my situation" is not clear at first. She had her friends, after all; she had her business and her health, excepting only her ailing eye. But in the several months since Eliza's return to New London, her sight had in fact deteriorated seriously, through glaucoma.[8] The evidence emerges more and more clearly in the correspondence, but here first in the marginal doodling that she added on the blank pages of Eliza's next-to-last letter (**no. 43**): "asilum asylum assilum Holdredge alth. allth." She was practicing "although," the first word of the poem she was to copy, and testing the spelling of the family-name, too, which she was charged to mention.

Then she attempts a philosophical essay, getting no further into it than the opening sentences,

> The doctrine of fatality, prescience, and the origin of evil has more or less engaged the study and employ'd the pens of men of the greatest tallants, the most learned and able philosophers. It is indeed a subject that affords an ample field for speculation, reasoning and argument.

Finding, however, that the intellectual discipline involved is of no use in controlling her fears, Mary confronts the "asylum" of her idle scribbling in another sort of exercise. Its beginning is somehow lost, and many of its words and whole lines have been added or struck out in re-writing; the person addressed is unknown, perhaps nonexistent, or in fact herself; yet the theme is clear. It is total blindness:

> . . . dreadful hour, a thought struck me. It was a comfortable thought. It saved me from despair. So the poor benighted traveler, lost and burdened in the mazzes of the pathless wood, perceives his sad condition, sees the dangers that surround him, hears the wild beasts prouling for thier prey–the dreadful roars, the contending elements. He feels the pelting of the pitiless storm that pores in torrents on his unsheltered and deffenceless head. Hope dies within him, he gives himself up for lost, and with anguish and dismay awaits his doom. But [crossed out: "should the"] amid the storm a dim beam of light from a neighboring cottage meets his eye. Imagen what are his sensations! Hope revives in his bosom, he springs forward in his ardor and renovated strength. [above: "with"] Can he at this moment (he well) breath the sigh of regret that it is not a palace–that it is not built of marbel and studded with deamons? Or will he fear that it may not altogether suit his convenience and accomodate him as well as he could wish? Is it possable such a thought could enter his heart at such a time? No, never! 'Tis a shelter from the storm, a place of safety, a reffuge from greater evils–this is all present necessity requires, and already he enjoys by anticipation the warmth and comfort of [?]brillows. So to my benighted mind appeared the *Alms House*.
>
> Start not, my friend, nor think me crazy when I assure it was my fix'd and settled purpose to remove there rather than be a burdan to my friends, in case I should be blind, and unable to persue my business. Think not this a whim of the moment, a freak of fancy, the effect of a gloomy and disturbed imagination. No, 'twas the most deliberate purpose of my soul, founded on principle, approved by reason and confirmed by judgment. So be not surprised if you should hear that it is my place of residence. I know (if you come to New York) you will visit me even there, and I have friends here who I think would not scruple to do it. I mention'd it them. I believe they thought me deranged. It did not meet thier approbation, however, and they try'd to reason with me upon the subject. But I had reason'd before them and knew every argument that could be brought against it. It is the duty of the publick to support those that cannot support themselves, and I consider it far less degrading than a state of dependance upon the bounty of private individuals, even tho' they should happen to be friends and relations. I had therefore determin'd to sell my furniture,

pay my rent and what few debts I owed, and with the remainder purchase a few nescessaries such as edurse[=eiders], comfortable clothing, suitable for the occasion, and remove to the Alms House (or Poor House, if you please) as soon as possible.

I foresee some difficulty [above: "some obstacles"] in the exertion of my plan from the opposition of my friends, which, however, tho' thier influence was great and my obligations to them infinite, I had no doubt I should somehow overcome. I even pleased myself by prepared my mind for the treat and pleased myself in considering the firmness, courage and patience with which I should support the hardships and privations which I must natchraly and necessarily expect in such a situatation. As to the shame or disgrace attach'd to this recepticle of wretchedness, poverty and misfortune by an unfeeling and misjudging world, I view'd it with contempt, despised it too heartily to give it the smallest consideration.

Bless'd be heaven, blessed be the god of my salvation! I have not been compell'd to carry this scheme into effect. I have still one eye left, and tho' with that I see imperfectly, I am still able thro' the goodness of devine providence to continue my business; and tho' I proceed but slowly at present, I shall double my diligence and hope if possible to make up lost time and extricate myself from the difficulties and embarrassments in which I am involved by this, to me, most terrible misfortune. I have not paid my last quarter's rent, but my landlord, who knows my situation, has agreed to wait. Heaven bless him and grant him patience, for I have some other debts that must first be paid–debts of honour–and I shall not sleep sweetly untill they are discharged.

This brings me to the point–the dear, the dreaded subject, a subject I enter upon with reluctance, this subject upon which my full heart dwells with pleasure, my tong would wish to be forever silent, the kindness, the unexampled goo[d]ness of my friends. I delay'd it as long as possible, I put it off to the last moment, nay, I had even half determined not to mention it at all, conscious as I was of my inability to do justice to my own feelings and thier deserts: love and gratitude–the most delightful of all sensations, and not easily expressed. To the glow of sentiment, language is cold and vapid. What more than mortal eloquence can give it utterance? It seals the lips, and those that feel it most say least about it. How then shall I proceed to tell thier goodness and retale, in common words, uncommon acts of kindness and benevolence? I can only say they have done everything for me, more than I desired; far more than I deserved. They have prevented my want, prevented even my wishes by thier unwearied attention, without the least regard to thier own ease or convenience. But this is generally speaking. Allow me then to introduce you to Mrs. F[itch] (the lady I mentioned to you in my last letter) to whom I have particular obligations. To draw her character with one dash of the pen, she is the counterpart of my Eliza (can I say more, and gratitude forbids me to say less)–I mean in essentials, in humanity and benevolence, in principle and practice. The strict principles of morality and virtue are rather solid than showy–an understanding of superior order, a warm feeling heart. With manners cold, distant and reserved, she would not perhaps attract the admiration of a stranger, but from those that know her she will ever command respect, esteem and love. This is a rough outline and certainly needs some corection, and many nice touches to finish the picture; for, did you know the original, you would say I flatter as little in characters as in faces; but remember, it is unfinished, and make the nescessary allowance. In this state they appear to disadvantage, and should not be exposed to the vacant stare of the vulgar and ignorant, but reserved for the designing eye of a conosiour in the business, such as I consider you, or should not submit it to your inspection.

So the same pages of **no. 43** were used first to record the lament of a young woman denied her chance in life, as she saw it–Eliza, denied New York with all that the city meant, and sentenced to New London–and then re-used to record the hidden pain of a woman in her fiftieth year also denied her chance in life. Mary had challenged the competition of a larger arena, she had won. The previous year, her works had hung in the Academy, the year to come she would be, even with but one eye, "the only painter in New York, either portrait or miniature, who has any business" (so, Eliza, in **no. 65**). Now, however, just at the moment of entering upon the rewards of all her effort, she could foresee or reasonably fear they would be withheld. Her response was the envisioning of the worst, an asylum of some sort or spelling (the city had a variety of refuges for the helpless).[9] Her picture of it could hardly have been very pleasant, given what everyone knew about poor-relief and given especially the highly moral, or moralizing, view of poverty held by a woman from the "land of steady habits."

Our glimpse into the private corners of Mary Way's mind reveals more than she usually allowed to appear: a true perception of her younger friend, the stiff, devout, literal and almost humorless Anna Fitch whom she nevertheless loved faithfully; also, her estimate of Eliza, whom she praises and thanks quite in passing, but with no less affection. Notice, too, how Mary keeps in balance the thorough good cheer of her letter to Eliza (**no. 49**) and the despair of her private musings (**no. 43**). The two were written within a few days, perhaps hours, of each other. And she balances her very lively imagination, addressing the unknown friend of **no. 43**, with the disciplined academic intellectuality of her essay on free will.

Some two months after these communications Mary spoke of herself more frankly to her family at home. Her letter (**no. 51** of December 6th) was addressed for her by somebody else. Her closest friends made a point of stopping in on her every day to help and cheer her. Mrs. Lee from New London, on a New York visit, had recently paid a call and afterwards reported on it to those at home, Ways and Champlains all; but news of this report was carried by parts of the correspondence that have not survived.

Dear Eliza,

I write you with my own hand, tho' without seeing, not to give an account of myself and my forlorn condition–that, Mrs. Fitch will do for me–but to tell you (what I know she will not) her own goodness and benevolence. Of the Dawsons' goodness you have already heard. Mrs. Lee has sounded thier trumpet, and she has said no more of them than they deserve; but she knew not Mrs. Fitch, from whom I receive every possible kindness and attention. She visits me frequently, often two and three times in a day; reads to me, and trys every way to amuse me and keep up my spirits, which, but for her exertions, would sink below the grave.

Write as much and as often as possible, particularly to her; answer her letters as soon as you receive them; assure her of my gratitude, for she will not allow me to express it, and if she would, I feel more than I can express.

Today is Sunday. They have all gone to take leave of our old church. Next Sunday the new one will be open'd, but whether I shall ever see it, God only knows. Here I set alone, with my eye blinded, like patience on a monument–I cannot add, smiling at grief. I am not stoic enough to smile at this moment. My neck is now broiling and smarting with blisters, and literally speaking I have my part in the lake that burns with fire and brimstone, for I can compare it to nothing else. But what is this to mental suffering?–when I reflect upon the certain consequence of even a suspension of my business, for any length of time. But I must not think. It is useless, and complaints are unavailing. It is, it must be, *right*. I will not repine, but hold fast the faith. I will not renounce my principles in this hour of trial when I most need thier support.

Adieu.

My love to your mother and Aunt Hannah, your Uncle and Aunt Way, Aunt Allen's family, and all friends. I am sorry to hear Aunt Hannah is so afflicted–can only recommend what I am obliged to have recourse to myself, patience, till deliverance comes. Thank heaven it will come at last.

I write more by feeling than by sight, and don't know as it is readable, but that's your look-out. My friends will read your letters to me, so don't spare the pen.

About the time this was written, Eliza was addressing Anna Fitch in a rather self-conscious style, as was usual when she wrote to this older friend of hers:[10]

My dear Anna,

I am thankful Mrs. Sexton's frocks are done. They have kept you so long silent, I sincerely hope that nothing now may prevent your writing much and often; for nothing in creation gives me more pleasure than letters from you and Aunt Mary, who I suppose e're this is better, or we should have had letters from Mrs. Dawson or Hannah, who Mrs. Lee informed us would certainly write to me should she continue the same or grow worse. Your letter was a great relief to us, as Mrs. Lee brought very discouraging accounts from there. Aunt Hannah, Mother, and myself were very uneasey about her being alone and ill, but Mrs. L. seem'd to think Mrs. D. and Hannah was everything to her, and was pleased she had such friends.

I was rejoiced once more to receive a letter from you, after your long, long silence, but grieved to hear of the affliction which in part occasion'd it. Mrs. Titus I was unacquainted with, having only seen her at church, but have frequently heard her spoken of in the highest terms by those who knew her. Her death must be a dreadful stroke to her friends, and her leaving so young and large a family makes it the more distressing. Aunt Mary mention'd her death in her last letter but she did not particularize. I hope her friends bear the loss with fortitude. I think that a genuine Universalist ought to bear everything laid upon them with fortitude. . . .

I thank you for your opinion of Sandy and his poetry. I have never seen or heard of the poem you mention written by Oliver Waite, although I have frequently heard he was a genius; neither have I seen Job Taber's *Progress of Society*, tho' I have heard it as you say spoken of very highly. These poets formerly flourished here but, alas! the former is no more, and the latter does not live here now. Sandy also is absent, and as you appear to consider New London the favorite residence of the Muses, I believe I must exert my energies or it will lose the high opinion you have formed of it. I don't think I shall ever be quite so aerial as poets generaly are. Aunt Mary thinks I '*smell*' too strong 'of *mortality*.' But I believe on the whole I may as well relinquish the idea altogether, as I feel I should never become anything more than what you so much despise: a poetaster. Therefore I shall crush at once all those air-built structures I have spent so many nights in forming. I don't think Aunt Mary's theory is correct. I am sure I desire to become a poetess, but it will not be, and I must destroy your expectations 'forever and a day.'

I am thankful Aunt Mary has had resolution to resist one [Maria Hayden] whom I had not faith to think she could. She wrote me her determination some weeks ago, and it instantly brought to my mind what she said in a former letter in answer to my unsuccessful solicitations for her to come up once more and make a visit. 'These things are ordered above. It is not in man that walketh to direct his steps.' I cannot be angry with you for not threatening Aunt Mary as I requested. You give such good reasons for not interfering, tho' I think your advice would have had as much weight with her as Mrs. Hayden's. I don't see why it should not. I too had very little faith in the arguments I made use of to turn her from her purpose. Still, I could not help saying what I did. I assure you I take no credit to myself on the present occasion. The church deserves all our thanks, and I think we ought to belabour it with them. It is more dear to me now than ever, for I see it has more power over Aunt Mary than her 'soul's far dearer part,' Mrs. Hayden. Yet, since I think of it, I don't know but Amasa has had a finger in the pie. I suspect he has found out her weak side by this time, and knowing his power over her has doubtless promised, if she will consent to remain longer in New York–that is, as long as he wishes–he will transport her in the twinkling of an eye to Richmond; for one of his steps when taken for a beloved object must travel faster than thought.

I am now reading Byron and am in love with him. I never was more distracted about a poet in my life. Aunt Mary may say what she pleases against him, but I won't believe it, and so I intend to tell her. She says he won't wear well, but I say he will. He'll wear till 'time shall be no more,' if future generations admire him half as much as I do. Oh! he is a sweet writer. I have read the *Corsair* over fifty times and always find new beauties in it. The *Bride of Abydos* too is beautiful, but Aunt Mary won't acknowledge he possesses any merit–which quite offends me. The perusal of good poetry imparts so much pleasure, the composition of it must afford the man or woman of genius a far happier gratification. Oh! what ecstatic delight it would give me to be able to write like some poets; but I can't and so may as well hold my tongue about it–and that I cannot do. You bear the insults *The Bucket* receives with much more sweetness than I can. A 'Swill Pail' was what I never admired and shall now like less than ever. . . .

Oh! that I could spend one of those delightful, never to be forgotten hours I enjoy'd when we were painting *Douser* and *Terribilite*. The recollection makes my present situation the more irksome. I cannot bear to have my tongue confined, and writing don't relieve me half so much as talking to you would.

Aunt Hannah continues much the same. At times she is perfectly easey, and then in torture. It is very tedious tho' not dangerous. She bears it with more patience than *I* should, as she does everything else.

I am very glad Mrs. Sexton has got through some of her difficulties. You say nothing of her husband [jailed as a bankrupt], so I hope he is at liberty before now. . . .

Pray write soon, for you cannot think how highly I prize your letters. The last thing I do every night after I'm in bed is to take the last letter I have received from you, and the last one from Aunt Mary, and re-peruse them ere sleep, and then Fancy witches me down to New York, where she makes me the happiest of mortals for a few hours. Alas! too soon I awake and find it but a dream. My happiness has always vanished 'like the baseless fabrick of a vision.' . . .

Excuse tautology and all other -ologies.

Since this letter was written I have received one from Eliza Holt. She says Aunt Mary's eye is no better. I am distress'd about her. Pray, the instant you get this, let me know the worst, for anything is better than suspense. If you send only a line, just to let me know how she is. Pray don't fail.

A letter from Anna Fitch (**no. 52** of December 12, 1818) indeed came promptly, by chance. It crossed Eliza's, just quoted; for Mary's anxious friends were now exchanging more up-to-the-minute bulletins. Most of them appear not to have survived. The mention of Mary's painting of Clinch, and of Eliza requiring ivory from New York, shows the sisters of the brush still working, though perhaps Mary's part was not recent.

I should have answered your last long ere this had I not heard that Eliza Holt had written immediately on the receipt of yours, who I thought would inform you of your aunt's situation. There is no apparent alteration in her since that. Her eye is still in a disagreable state, though I trust not a hopeless one. She has gone through the usual routine of bleeding, blistering &c. The fourth blister was applied to her neck last Saturday night; but though her eye is almost entirely deprived of sight, I cannot renounce the hope that she will regain it. I was glad to find that Mrs. Lee had informed you of Mrs. Dawson's & Hannah's attention to her as it must have relieved you from the terrible idea of her being alone & sick.

I have this morning been from one end of the city to the other in search of ivory. I found it very scarce & dear. I at last bespoke some (at the place you formerly bought it) to be finished this afternoon.

Your aunt has written you a letter [**no. 51**] which I hope you will value very highly, as it was penned almost without looking. She has also written to Mrs. Lee, expecting her son to call for it. As he has not, I shall enclose it. . . . You say, as I do not mention Mrs. Sexten's husband, you hope he is at liberty. He is not. And I think (and was going to say hope) it will be a long time before he is. I called to see her today & found she had been summoned to take up her cheerless abode in a jail, with her infant; & I suppose it will be long ere I see her again. Poor unfortunate woman! Her 'drops of joy' are small indeed compared to the draughts, the bitter 'draughts of ill' she is condemned to drink. . . .

I suppose you remember James Clinch. Whether you do or not, he is going to be married next Thursday week–Christmas eve–to the lady for whom your aunt took his picture, Miss Nichol of Stratford.

I write in haste as it is time for me to pay my accustomed evening visit to your aunt, in order to cheer her up, that she may enjoy pleasant dreams during the night; but before I conclude, let me entreat you not to distress yourself about her. She has a phisician (whom we consider skillful) attending her constantly, & her friends often call & aid her in keeping up her spirits, to bear with patience this tedious indisposition. . . .

Mrs. Hayden is in town. Her husband is ordered to reside here instead of Richmond. I am very glad on your aunt's account, though she will not be very near the Arsenal, being two miles out of town. She arrived on Saturday evening & called on your aunt yesterday morning while we were at church.

Apropos of church: the new one was opened yesterday and, large as it is, was as much crowded as ever you saw the old one. In the morning, when you know there are generally fewer than the other parts of the day, the pulpit stairs were full, & the people obliged to stand in the aisles; but last night it was still fuller. It is a very neat commodious building, and is said to hold three times as many as the other. It was very gratifying, I assure you, to see that effected which had been so long desired, but as it is my misfortune never to experience real happiness while conscious of another's pain, my gratification was much diminished by your aunt's absence, knowing the disappointment it must have been to her. How far this is consistent with true philosophy I leave wiser heads to determine, while I endure all the pain or pleasure it produces.

Your aunt says she wishes you would write to Eliza Holt, as she calls almost every day & is very impatient for an answer.

From Eliza on New Year's day (**no. 53**) a full page of thanks went off to Anna Fitch, for her truly generous attentions of all sorts to Mary, and a second, less elaborate, more chatty page about friends and acquaintances. Of the Clinch's mentioned here, James and Charles sat for their portraits to Mary and Eliza respectively. Charles attained some fame through his literary career.[11] The family, seen in previous letters, will recur in later ones as well. Captain Jeremiah D. Hayden deserves a slightly fuller introduction, since he and his wife Maria Sanford were to play a large part in Eliza's life in the years to come. He first appears at the time of his marriage in 1816 (**no. 19**), a New Jersey man. Because of his profession he is forever disappearing over the horizon, to Richmond, Pensacola, Washington, New Orleans, at the same time changing jobs within the army, or quitting the army, until his death quite young, as a major, in 1826.[12]

My dear Mrs. Fitch,

. . . Eliza Holt told me you was with her [=Mary] a great part of the time and read to her and try'd to keep her spirits from sinking. She also told me of Hannah Dawson's goodness in staying with her nights. She says Aunt Mary has the patience of Job. I am thankful for it, as I think she needs as much as he had to support her through this dreadfulest of all misfortunes, loss of sight.

I was greatly astonished to hear of the arrival of Mrs. Hayden. It will be a great gratification to Aunt Mary, I'm sure, at this time. I hope Capt. Hayden will be stationed in New York, at least till she is recover'd, as a flying visit from Maria at present would be such a disappointment to her–tho' your kind attentions to her since her illness have render'd Mrs. Hayden's almost unnecessary. I should be delighted to see Mrs. Hayden.

I am pleased your new church is at last completed and attracts so many, but what are you going to do with the old one? My predilection for that still continues with unabated ardour, and I shall be very angry if those who have the disposition of it suffer *negro*'s to have it, as was talked of before I left you. I can't bear it should be so insulted. You ask if I remember James Clinch. I do, perfectly well, and his brother Charles, and their sisters. I don't think you could mention a person whom I saw while I was in New York that I have forgotten. Everybody made too deep an impression to be easily erased. I recollect hearing you mention the lady to whom he is married at the time he sat for his picture, but I had forgotten her name. We were much surprised to hear of Patty's marriage, Aunt Hannah particularly. I believe she had set her heart upon Patty's following the example she herself had set, and living a life of 'single blessedness;' but, as she always has said 'Whatever is, is right,' I will not let her renounce her principles now. I hope she has married well, as I think she deserves a good husband if she has any. . . . Poor Mrs. Sexton is unfortunate indeed. It is dreadful to think of her being in a jail at this inclement season with her infant, and more terrible still when we see no prospect of her being restor'd to liberty. . . .

I had forgotten to ask you if you would join me in endeavouring to persuade Aunt Mary to come up here. My mother and aunts are all of them so anxious to have her here–they told me to urge it with all my power. I have told Aunt Mary what they say, but I am positive, almost, that it will not have any effect on her. I wish she was with us and do not wish to leave any means untried to have her here. I wish you to insist upon it if you think it is best, but if you think her phisician is more skillful than she could have here, pray don't urge it. I leave it all to your superior judgement and I hope you will exercise it. Write as soon as possible.

From New London, the insistence increased that Mary should come home. Still in January, Betsey writes (**no. 55**),

Dear Mary,

We have been much alarmed about you from Mrs. Lee's report, but, since that, Eliza has rec'd a letter from Mrs. Fitch who spoke more encouraging. We regret that we cannot offer you any personal assistance–any but Eliza. They seem to think it possible that she might be spared, could she be of any real service; or rather, it is the opinion of Eben'r and Sally. But I see no possible means of A[unt] H[annah] doing without her. If she could be of advantage to you, you can mention it to Aunt Hannah, who might find some elderly woman for society. She is still afflicted with the rheumatism, other-ways as usual. I am indifferant as to health, but have suffer'd greatly of late from an atack of hypocondriac which I believe originated from a supression of business, since I find, by a new suply, it has worn off. But in my despiring moments, I wanted nothing so much as to recieve my passport for a 'greater and better world' than this. My feelings were in some measure reliev'd by the compossition of a few simple stanzas which at my darkest season restored me to a degree of chearfulness. I hand them to you in their native simplicity, void of embelishments. Beauty unadorned is admired the most. *Ahem.*

Come Death, thou last, best friend that man can boast! . . .

And (omitting 40 lines),

The prasalogy nor rhyme cannot recommend it, and there is no doubt in my mind that Young or Pope and many others even among the modern poets might have been happier in conveying thier ideas; but the sentiments are original and divine and proceeded from the very 'heart's core,' as Shak'r expresses it–a fortunate circumstance that I inherit from the Deacon, that weak vien that blunts the edge of my share of human miseries (but perhaps the thought is enviously sugested). A double share, if I am not altogeather mistaken. They are your own sentiments, which was my only motive in copying them: whoever does posess them cannot utterly dispair, as this short scene will soon be o'er.

I enclose one dollar for the purpose of purchasing a couple of plates of ivory. . . . One is [for the portrait of] Capt. Mc'dowel. I will omit the description of his features, but he may thank his stars for falling into my merciful hands, as I am certain it his not in the power of any human limner else to give him such a picture (as would please him) with his likeness attach'd to it; and I am not such an advocate for truth as to tell it at my peril. . . .

and here Betsey offers twelve lines of the satire quoted in a previous chapter and later to be developed into its full form, beginning "O flattery, how sweet thy balmy breath! . . . "– after which her letter tails off in confused effervescence and marginalia.

Mary answered in a few weeks (**no. 56**), using some friendly amanuensis and attempting to stem the tide of poetry that flowed south from New London. The joke about the "deacon" which she responds to is obscure[13]–as also, the fact that Eliza's return to New York had been settled on in lost letters, was indeed imminent, and was to take place in May.[14]

Dear Sister,

I have received your letter and executed your commission by proxy. Mrs. Fitch, who was so good as to offer her services, had a wild goose chase after the ivory. She could find none in town of that size under a dollar or six shillings a plate. Mr. Tryon, who supplys me, had sold all his that was good, but was prevail'd upon to cut these, which I think are excellent, tho' I can see but with *half an eye*, as your sister Lydia says. Indeed, I am in a sad condition at present; but of this, Eliza's letters will inform you, for I am tired of complaining and telling the miseries I suffer both in body and mind. Envy is a passion that never yet disturb'd my repose, but I think I should envy the Deacon-Westcot talent you so justly boast, if I thought it would produce on me the effect you ascribe to it. But alass! nature has form'd us differently: you, in her happiest mood, light, airy and elastic, in a reverse humour (unluckily for me) she cast into my composition some more weighty materials which heavily tend towards the centre. You might as well attempt to raise a millstone with the feather that lightly waves in your hat or turban, as my spirits with whipt sillabub [i.e., satirical poetry]. No offence, my dear sister.

Now, I beg you will not misunderstand this, as you did my last letter, and think that more is ment than meets the eye. Believe me, I mean no reflection's on the charming art that affords you and the Deacon so much amusement and gratification. The two effusions your letter contains are not intirely destitute of merit, they come in quite appropos to the subject, and some of the lines are very pretty. You know I never flatter, and will not expect me to say more, especially as you seem sensible, yourself, they are rather inferior to the productions of the ancient poets.

You say you are not such an advocate for truth as to speak it at your peril. You see I dared do even that. But it often requires more firmness and self-possession to hear the truth than to speak it, particularly when it comes in contact with our own vanity or meets us full butt in our Hobbyhossical carrier. This I know by sad experience; yet even these trials and tribulations are not altogather without thier use and advantage, as they will either unhorse us at once, and induce us wisely to give up chase, or else we are improved in our horsemanship and, by being obliged to handle the reins, we acquire skill in managing the unruly animal, and fix ourselves still more steady and firmly on the saddle. Which of these is most desirable in the present case it is not for me to decide. I would not deprive you of what beguiles your care and, as you say, blunts the edge of your portion of human miseries. Humanity forbid I should advise you to dismount. Go on, my dear Sister, success attend you! A pleasant jaunt to you and your Hobby. Don't look so sly and suspicious upon the word of an honest chastiser. I protest my conscience absolves me from the least wicked or malicious intention. I really feel a kindness for the animal (as Stern did for the Ass) whenever I meet it, and sympathy for the rider, and would not willingly hurt a hair of thier heads.

I am glad you have recover'd from that most terrible of all disorders. I am much afflicted with it at present. 'Tis the natural consequence of a suspension of business. When I think on my deplorable situation, then, in a fit of the blues, poverty and dependance with all thier dismal train pass in review before me. Philosophy fails here, unequal to the trial. I can suffer pain and sickness, I can meet death with pleasure; but from phantoms such as these I shrink agast. Here, faith is put to the test–that only can support me. God grant it fail not.

My love to Aunt Hannah. I cannot wish to deprive her of Eliza, tho' her company would give me pleasure. I know she is sick and infirm and needs her assistance still more than I, for I have the best, the kindest of friends that ever a poor blind soul was blest with, and I want for no assistance it is in her power to give.

Adieu.

Brushing aside Mary's words intended as a shield against more poetry, and moving hastily through certain requests of her own for New York purchases, Betsey copied out for her daughter (and sister) her satirical piece "On Flattery." It was quoted at length in the third chapter, above. Betsey's pride in it is not well hidden, and there survives another fair copy of it which she sent to New York at some date unknown, later. The date of the present version (**no. 59**) is July 22, 1819:

Dear Eliza,

I wish you to attend to my *commands*. . . . I send two sizes for ivory which I wish you to be very particular respecting. The largest is the size of Capt. Jared Starr's which I drew eight years since. Elizabeth Saltonstall has sent for his likeness. They wish it the same size. The other is the size of a couple of frames I have for sale, but never happened to have an ivory large enough to fit them, or might have sold them long ago. I send two dollars for this purpose, and the other two doll.'s I send you, agreeable to my promise that when the [?]Craswells paid for Mrs. Baxter's likeness I would send it to you. But the times are bad–consequently, cannot afford to give them to you without reward. I have sent two crape hankerchiefs for you to paint; but this is for your comfort: you never will have the task repeated, as they will last three years, and that term of time will bring me to my fifty-teens, and then the yellow flag must give way to a more sable tint–that is, if my feelings acquiesce. But if not, I shall finish my century in streamers gay; for I value not the worlds opinion in any thing that is untinctured with vice.

But I have such a ballad to write that I must not try to comment too long–only to desire you to purchase the thinnest, whitest, and freest from grain. I wish one the large size, and two the smaller. What remains of my 2 dollars, get as many a size less as it will procure. The hankerchiefs I beg you would do them slightely as possible, for your sake and mine. Don't on any account send either the ivory or them (when done) by mail, but by Capt. Lamphere. The former I am waiting impatiently for. You will not disappoint me, as I have used my last plate and, should any one apply, I must lose the job.

This ballad as I term it on account of its length is nothing more than the picture of fancy, yet a good general likeness of human nature, or at least such as have fell under my inspection–believing it just to include the whole, as variety is our predominant passion. It is not founded upon any particular facts, as appears. Yet so near is the dialogue between Frederick and Jane to what I have seen, that my conscience never even frowned at me for writing it. As to the stile, it has more of the original tint than if it was truely sublime, since its bluntness savors of the Way [for instance, the Hannah Way] carracteristic that labour would have destroy'd. You can even discern three sorts of cake, and a charming great piece of gingerbread for the desart artter dinner. Speaking in carracters is no scandal. She is a dear old soul as ever lived and is as innocent of it as a lamb.

On Flattery

O flattery, how sweet thy healing breath! . . .

Was it not that by writing so much I have learned to write as fast as common people can read, I should never have endured the idea of putting so much togeather upon so triffling a matter, particularly as I have introduced so much little low chatter; but allways being under the influence of Fancy, who from her fickleness soars, or descends, as her variable sallys direct, but happening to be very happy in rhyming, thought I would humour her whim, and went on exactly as an unambitious horse will repeat his steps around a cider mill–which I think quite a bright emblem–as I had run out of matter. Repetition gives it length–or rather, the effect of habit: could not stop when I had done. This is the first and only satirical piece I ever wrote. My conscience begins to blister a little now. I don't like satyr: it is allways productive of enimies and it seems to display an envious mind. But mine does not proceed from that. I have been so fretted with affectation in age, it was to give vent to my feelings. It has, however, one good tendency: by supressing whatever it points at. I would not have it exposed to any eyes but yours and Mary's. She will soon see that I shall never excel in this branch.

I have two matters of joy. Aunt H. tells me John French and wife called on Mary upon some occasion [when they were in New York recently] and that she was much better from applying the leeches, which made me quite happy. Let her not suffer for them as long as our tributary streams will afford them. Another source of pleasure is we have heard from George. His letter was dated 25 or 7th of July–we never rec'd one more expressive of good health and spirits, though he speaks nothing of visiting us, as in his former letter. William intends copying it and sending it to you. It was directed to him. He makes rather to high encomiums upon his mother, which has been the only preventative of your father's exhibiting it to the public, tho' afterwards he smooths it up as well as apologies will answer. But it his[="is"] quite at its ease and the only one I have had in my posession three minutes after it arrived. . . .

Send me word in your answer, whether you have copied the pieces upon *The Muse* and *Mirth*. If not, I will fill another sheet. I wish Mary's criticism; and mention in your letter the parts disapproved of, which I believe may cost you a groaning, as there will be so much to recite.

I will return Mary whatever is the cost of a little light green paint such as you will find a sample on a small palate. I want it for back-grounds, as I can find no colour so becoming to the hair, and indeed every part, except the white part of drapery, which by being too much of the same tone is rather trying; yet if the piece is delicately shaded I find it the purest, and has a pleasing effect on the whole–and so much quicker done than any other back-ground. O I would not exchange my reflection painting, not for the world. Therefore provide me the thinnest plates. I wish I could destroy her prejudice against it. I save, upon a just calculation, one half my time, and the work appears more like paint upon glass, which is allowed to surpass any. But every man in his humour. Don't neglect one of these articles, if you wish me to live. I have but one engaged at present, but may have [more?] and I dare not be destitute of ivory, applications are so rare.

Give my best love to Mary and write a bonny mess.

Adieu.

Above all things, take care of your health, nor lace too tight. The next letter, mention your father. He always asks me if you did.

E. C.

Toward the beginning of August, when Eliza replied (**no. 60**), she could tick off her various commissions for crape to make turbans, thread for darning, and ivory to be bought from the comb-maker,[15] all desired by her mother at the smallest possible prices. The articles were readied for passage on Captain Lamphere's packet, which regularly plied between the two cities.[16] Summer heat required comment, and thanks for the regular supply of leeches, the operation of which did bring relief:[17]

Dear Mother,

. . . Aunt Mary desires you to give her best love to Uncle Ebb and tell him she is ten thousand times obliged to him for the leeches, and that she is willing to make him any compensation for his trouble and whatever expense is attached to the getting them, as it was impossible for her to live without them. Her eye is perfectly easey provided it's drawn once or twice a week–not else, as it's the congeal'd blood that causes such intolerable pain. It has never been one quarter so easey, since she was first taken, as it is at present, in consequence of having them draw it. Uncle Ebb sent nine, four died on the passage, and the remaining five added to five she had makes ten, of course. They are very active and lively at present and I hope will continue so. We pay them every attention and feast them once a week, which I should suppose ought to content them. Capt. Lampheer promised to take the two bottles when he calls tomorrow for this letter, and if you will set more a-foot so that they may be forthcomeing in due time, you will confer a lasting obligation on us all.

I'm obliged to stop almost at every word to take breath and yet hardly feel life to hold my pen, I'm so overcome with heat. I suppose their will be no connexion in my letter, but it's no matter. If you only understand the heads (of department, I was going to say) of my subject, it's all I expect.

Aunt Mary sends you a cake of this French green. It has turned considerably since 'twas prepared, tho' it's never been exposed to the air, but wrapped up in several folds of paper to prevent its turning. It comes off very hard and I suppose you must use it with gum. Perhaps that will brighten the colour. At any rate, I think I should mix it with gum; but you can do as you think proper.

The turbans I will do as soon as possible, which I hope will be before Lampheer returns; but, by the by, I don't like to be under ten thousand obligations to him without any means of paying him. Money is out of the question, for I know if I had it to offer him he would not accept it, and he will not, or has not time to, set for his picture, which makes me feel rather unpleasant whenever he brings me or takes from me a bundle or anything of the kind; for, tho' he's the most obliging mortal in existence, still I don't like 'to ride a free horse to death,' as the saying is.

I would send you Aunt Mary's criticism on *Flattery* if she had had time to criticise it, but I suppose you are sensible it is a work of time to go thorough stiel with a peice the length of that. I never copied the peices upon *The Muse* and *Mirth*, tho' I should like to see them very much; also, that upon *The Crucifixion of Christ*. I have told Aunt Mary of it and she wishes to see it; and I believe I have never seen 'all the birds in the air,' as Uncle Ebb calls them. Send as many peices as you can muster and we will criticise them at our leasure, as you are in no haste for our animadversions. There is many parts of *Flattery* I like very well–that is, certainly very natural and very true. Still, I think you a better reader of your own poetry than any one else, for, to save me from the gallows, I know not how to make right stops, and of course could not see the sense or (pardon my mode of expression) the nonsense of it; for such a dialogue is certainly a nonsensical peice of business to be carried on between man and wife. I think I should be tempted to slap both their chops for them had I heard it.

Sandy's peice upon you is very much admired. He is thought by geniuses to possess a very fine fancy. . . .

In your last letter you paid me a compliment that I'm sure you will never be at the trouble of paying again: you said I had the happy tallent of making people pleased with themselves. I am very glad to hear it, and wish I could kill two birds with one stone and make them pleased with me at the same time; but I feel so cross since the hot weather that I neither give nor receive one particle of pleasure from any of the sons or daughters of Adam.

Later in the same month of August 1819 Eliza received further comments on the subject of small purchases and small expenses from her mother (**no. 61**):

Dear Eliza,

. . . I have just been running over your letter, and could but smile at the excuses you make for purchasing a ball of thread, to which you know needed none. Permit

> me to observe without offence that there seems to be a tincture of temper blended with the most scruplous honesty in many things you say and write, which denotes the C[hamplai]n trait. It is enough to be honest without enthusiasm.
>
> I meant to have had an epistle ready for Lamphere, but as I never can think of writing except Sunday to you, and one has insensibly slip'd away after another, untill now, and he sails in the morning, I have no time to attend to ettiquette. I send your two dollars 12 cents, which is for no commands of mine but your own, observe me—tho', as I happen to be out of money just now and it is not probable I shall receive any before Lamphere goes, I inclose the only brass wire string my guitar could boast, which is broken and can't be mended, as a sample for another or two like this, which I want you to purchase and pay for: two strings like this a little over, to tie, which it will take up. And let me know how much they come to, and in my next I will refund it, besides being much gratified. There is none of this description to be sold here, or would not give you the trouble.
>
> Composition, flagellett and guitar is all the holidays I have, and cannot think of being deprived of them. I have composed several pieces since I last wrote, but have no critic. I shall not be able to copy but one at present. If I only could recollect what number and which they were I have sent, I should know how to avoid recopying them. I have wrote so much since you left here that I think it is a less tedious plan to send you a book of them by Lamphere than to undertake to send you them severally. I should like to hear the opinion of Mary upon this and another that appears to me I have wrote in a former letter, but can't recollect it. I did not think of giving you half the nonsense when I commenced writing, but the Muse has favoured me with one of her fetch-fire calls, which she merits the praise, or I dispraise, of wholly herself, as I have had nothing to do with it, in a certain sense, but lend my pen, and regret that it was not in my power to have furnished her with a better. As she is very excentric, you will look for her on the superscription side, but she is hawk-eyed, and conclude she found every inch of paper occupied before her arrival, and was under the necessity of making Hobson's choice.

There follow two poems called *Pity's Tear* and *Thoughts on Immortality*, of which the first is very oddly said to be inspired by "your quotation from *The Bucket*," while the second, beginning "I see the portrait of my fate that's wove in Fancy's loom," later stumbles on the problematic line, "Affliction's calcinating power confirms that God's our friend." With these pieces, Betsey supplies her own criticism as a model to her obstinately silent audience in New York, before adding yet a third poem, untitled:

> Permit me to speak with the amiable candour of those who are in the habit of talking to themselves, and see how far my opinion harmonizes with hers [Mary's] and yours. Ahem. I think (pardon my seeming arrogance) that the first borders upon the sublime; the second displays a small degree of wit; and the last, if it can boast of any beauty, lies in its simplicity. I know not what has given me those ideas, but they read so to my ear. This last piece originated from a frame of mind bordering upon a pleasing melancholy, and was sitting by the front window and happened to

observe the grass in the yard waving to and fro, which inspired me with matter, though perhaps not so happily expressed as my betters could have handled it. It was the best that a poor body might do, labouring under similiar difficulties, if there ever was that being. I shelter myself under the skreen of poets being call'd priviledged carracters for every term ungrammatical, and I find it very accommodating. For instance, *calcinating*: for the sake of its sounding better to the ear as it happens to be applied. Its meaning you cannot be at a loss for: purifying, cleansing, tried in the fire of afflictions &c. But so bright a genius requires no explanatory notes. I would ask Mary's opinion, as I would wish her to enter into the minutia of the present subject, whether, in regard to the first line, she would prefer 'I see the portrait of my fate high wrought in Fancy's loom,' or as she finds it. Her answer will be acceptable. I am sensible I have an eye to see the faults without the power of remedying them but in a small degree.

Bright *Fancy* guides the pencil while I draw,
Who spurns at mechanism's servile law,
And as she soars inspired with ideas new
(Not so uncommon, neither, but to few)

Inhales a breeze of pure etherial air,
As breathed in paradise the blooming pair.
The science most in pleasure's service spent
(Requiring higher power than man to invent)
Is composition. 'Tis a tallent given
To sooth the soul, when near to madness driven.
E'en music in her softest cadence charms
Not more the lover who with folded arms
On the fair form of the loved object bent,
His only means to give the passion vent.

O joy that surely crowned with highest test
And speaks the nearest what's termed happiness,
Posessed of wine's exhillerating power
That lulls the pang and sooths the lingering hour,
Enchanting Muse who tinctures with a joy
Life's keenest woes, and freeest from alloy.

Eliza didn't reply to her mother until September 20th (**no. 62**):

I suppose you are surprised at my long silence, and, lest you should be alarmed also, I now write. You have without doubt heard of the yellow fever's being here, and that the inhabitants are flying in all directions to escape the plague, pestilence, and famine that is shower'd upon them for their disobedience in the days of Noah, as Aunt Hannah says. It so happen'd that Aunt Mary and myself should be in the country on a visit when the fever broke out in town, and that there is but a faint prospect of our being able to return again soon unless we wish to go into the midst of it. She is very willing to go and take it and make a finish of herself at once, but as I wish to sell my life as dearly as possible, I don't feel disposed to go at this present writing.

We are visiting Mrs. Hayden, she that was Maria Sandford. Her husband is Commanding Officer at the Arsanal and a verry fine man. I like him verry much now I'm accquainted with him, which would never have happen'd, had I not been an inmate in his house, in ten thousand years; for he is one of the most singular characters I ever knew; and yet with all his eccentricity he is continually reminding me (strange as it may appear) of Uncle Ebb. His manners are verry much like his, and think I can see a slight resemblance in his person. He is call'd verry handsome, and I think him verry graceful. He has a noble soul–indeed, he is generous to a fault, if you think such a thing possible. You know my opinion of Maria, so I need not stop to eulogize her.

I have been dangerously ill since I have been here but am now as well as usual. I had not felt well for some weeks before I came, and thinking the excursion might be beneficial I was pleased with the idea; but it had a contrary effect. I was billous without knowing what ail'd me, as as soon as I came I drank verry rich milk just like cream every morning and evening instead of coffee or tea, as I always drank it in prefference to either whenever I could get it. Well, it had the effect that might have been expected: it sent me very ill to bed. Capt. Hayden insisted on sending for Doctor Boyd, his family physician–a measure I strenuously opposed, knowing my inability to discharge any debt, be it ever so slight (for the two dollars you sent me were already disposed of or, which was the same thing, I owed them); and a visit from the doctor would have been five dollars. So, as I had rather die than be under such an obligation to a stranger, I took what Aunt Mary told me was the best thing I could take–a couple of Lee's pills; and as I never could swallow anything, you know, I scraped them to a powder and mixed them with molasses, and amediately afterwards I threw them up again. Well, there I was just where I was before, as sick as death and unable to raise my head from the pillow and growing worse every minute when Doctor Boyd was announced and immediately, without my leave or licence, usher'd into my bedroom. I was scared to death. He felt my pulse, pronounced me in a fever (which by the by the sight of him raised), and order'd me a dose of siena and manna. I took it, it *squddled* round and clear'd the bile out of my stomach in a few hours, and I'm convinced, had it not been for that dose, horrid as it was, my disorder would have turned to the yellow fever and I should have been dead, and spared you the trouble of reading this letter.

They told me Doctor Boyd was riding past to visit a patient who had the yellow fever (and was further out of town than we are), and stoped to see how little Emma was–Maria's child that I have wrote you about before. I have told you the particulars so circumstantialy because I never was so sick in my life before as to faint at raising my head from the pillow for two days and a night successively. . . .

Aunt Mary's eye is much as usual. There is no material change in it. She has three leeches remaining but they are too few to do any great good. She could protract her stay in the country, I fear, for a long time to come, for all the business she gets or had for a long time before she came; and now the fever is there, our prospect is dreary indeed. . . .

I begin to feel so low-spirited at sight of the carts of furniture [in flight] that are passing every instant that I believe I will not write any more at present, nor till I feel much better than I do now.

And now I must give you an account of the two dollars you have given me. Long before they came I was under the necessity of borrowing fourteen shilling from Mrs. Dawson for a pair of shoes, or I should have gone bare-foot now. I was as loath as death to do it, but there was no alternative, and I took the offer'd money without the most distant idea of how I should pay her, or whether I ever should. She told me she would wait till it was convenient for me to return it, and if that time never arrived, she would never sue me for it. That debt is now off my conscience and I owe nothing else except my old debt to Aunt Mary. . . .

Tho' Aunt Mary has promised to critecise your poetry, it is with difficulty I can drag out an opinion of any kind from her, so you must write and battle the watch with her yourself. She don't like your having so many words and so little substance. She says her stomach requires something stronger and more substantial, while I tell her its the verry thing for me, for I have been kept up on slops so long thats that the sight of hartier food, whether in prose or verse, quite upsets the bile. I like *Pity's Tear* very much, so you see I have not got to critesize it; and *Thoughts on Immortality* are very good, though I prefer the other.

And now, what else have I got to say? Day before yesterday Capt. Hayden and his wife carried us out to the country seat of a gentleman about three miles from here. It formerly belonged to an English gentleman but is now the property of the family we visited. I was delighted with the family. They paid us every attention that was possible and insisted on my staying till my health was perfectly reiestablished, as they knew I have been sick; but I could not bear the idea of staying alone, and I knew that the rest of my party would go home as soon as the carriage came for them–else I should have been delighted to have staid. Their was two young ladies about my own age that were all attention to me and carried me all around their paradise, for it is a perfect one; and I should have been delighted with the idea of never leaving it again. It would have been impossible for you to have taken a step without writing twenty quires of paper at every one, full of poetry–the surrounding landscape was so sublime, so heavenly. I can give you no idea of it. You must come and see for yourself. I walked as far as I dare after my recent illness but half as far as I wished. I went on top of a small pleasure house at a little distance from the family mansion, and was entranced with the prospect. O heavens! how I did hate to quit that place. But I was obliged too, most probably forever.

Adieu.

This communication from Eliza did not arrive in time to allay her mother's impatience, who wanted help in caring for Aunt Hannah and moreover supposed there was some agreed date for Eliza's return to New London. Eliza's letter in fact was mailed about the same time as this next one that follows from Betsey, where Betsey is speaking quite at cross-purposes with her daughter:[18]

> Dear Eliza,
>
> What in the world can be the meaning of your not returning? I am allmost tempted to believe you have rec'd counter-orders from some source or other. We expected you six weeks ago. Aunt Hannah's age and situation requires your company and assistance, as well as my situation; but as to age, I yet wear the infant cap. And you have droped the correspondance, which I can't account for. It appears as though something had absorbed all you thoughts and time. Surely Mary must be settled in the country before this. I wish from my soul she would come up with you. Try to use your influence with her. Perhaps it is not improbable that you may go again in the course of the summer or fall with Aunt Hannah, if she could dispose of her house to her mind, as respects tenanting it. She is old and failing, as you know has been the case for some years. Though she is as well at present as usual, still, there has been several sudden deaths of late, and we feel rather concern'd at her being without anyone–only those who are in the house, which it is a very lucky circumstance there should be. But let me tell you, in case of her droping away suddenly, which she is as likely to do as another, it is prophesyed you and Mary will be utterly cut off from all hopes [of bequests].
>
> As to myself, I stand newter. I have no design in wishing your return but to act upon principle, for I sincerely think it is a duty you owe her and yourself, and me. Still, could I act as if she were gone, I should advise you to remain where you are, if you and Mary are both agreed upon the matter. But I am a great advocate for practicing self-denial–Heaven knows I have been in the habit of it for a number of the last centurys–and have practiced it till I like it. You would not pass your time so wretchedly as perhaps you form an idea; for, as I every day renew my age, you would find me very excellent company, I assure you. I am now, just as I have entered my forty-teens, commenc'd dancing, in which I make no inconsiderable proficiency and figure. I can plainly see that nature design'd me with abilities to glide with all the ease of a light-heel'd ghost; but unfortunately the effects of a Way education hath rather suppressed my shining qualities, and like a dandalion in the forest, blooms to die unnoticed. But no matter: my dancing now amuses myself, and would do no more should I perform before the multitude–unless it should excite their merriment. I am my own musician and have learnt the five positions. I suffer for a partner to walse with. You are the one I have pitched on. What first put me in the figary[=vagary] was this: Maria Alleyn requested of me, previous to her leaving town, the greatest favour I could confer upon any one, that of letting her come afternoons when she could attend long enough to take a copy of that English painting, as also she copied General Lafayette, which I have taken a profile of upon paper from an engraving. I have done mine extremely well. It is one of the most natural pictures I ever drew, and meets with the general approbation of the learned world. His whisker is a grove

of trees and shrubbery that meets the mouth. She copied both those pieces well, for her, but at the time of her painting, which commenced for several days previous to my moving and two or three weeks after, I was allmost sick with the jandice. She recommended my jumping the rope, but as I had no rope and felt then if I had, I might probably put it to another use–that of hanging myself, I felt so depressed in spirits–I hit upon dancing, thinking I might add a gracefulness of person to my exercise, all under one, which I have diligently kept up, and find myself at present in an extraordinary state of health, which I wish I could feel sufficiently grateful for. I have had thoughts of commencing circus rider to show my remarkable agility in horsemanship. I veryly believe the devil is an enemey to dancing, as it drives him out of your father as soon as I enter upon the first position, and is so good he will let me hall him around–that is to say, as well as his helplessness will admit, but won't let go his cane. That too must dance if he does, and it understands it full as well. I believe I might make a scholar of that sooner than him. They are inseperable friends. You would laugh your soul out to see him enter into the spirit of it–whistles with all his heart and moves with all the animation a dead man is capable.

One person mentioned to A[unt] H[annah] to write express for you. She observed she had wrote two expresses and felt hurt at your still remaining there. Don't desert her. To hear her mourn every day about you kills me much more than my want of you. I am confident you would get practice. I do none under two dollars, designing the one-dollar ones for you, and another branch you can have, if you wish it: that of drawing from corpse. I have been taken allmost by force to take several, but my want of health was all that saved me. I was, however, in spite of all opposition, obliged to draw Abby Mercer, of whom I am drawing three, and gave more than common satisfaction to the friends. Betsey Allen came up with power, her being a relation and engaged to sit before her death, and answred to excuse me to the world and those who I had refused. If you can put in practice half the self-denial your mother and Mary has–I know you have the power–you would find that branch much the most lucrative, as you can ask what you please. Be sure you come in Capt. Coit, by whom I send this. I have never received a line from you since I sent you that two doll.s, and a short time after Aunt Hannah sent you the bunch of roses you sent for, and we know not whether you have received them or not–

Now the correspondence between New London and New York resumed its regularity: toward the end of October, Aunt Sally Way offered the highlights of local history, the marriage of Sandy Clarke and the landing of a stray balloon near Norwich;[19] and toward the beginning of the same month, Betsey took up *her* pen again (**no. 63**). Once more she exposes herself to criticism by copying out her latest compositions, two twenty-four line love poems which are here omitted:

Dear Eliza,

I cannot express how happy I was at receiving a letter from you, as it as reasonable to sopose I was anxious particularly at such a crisis, and knowing you never enjoyed as good health in New York as in the land of steady habits. I intreat you to be very careful of your health if you have recovered it. Let this caution be impressed upon your mind. I wish you to write as soon as you receive this and let me know how and where you are at present, and respecting Mary's health and prospects. I think a great deal of you both–and George, who I have rec'd a verbal message from. A Mr. Minor has lately arrived from New Orleans who told young Dodge he saw him, and that he was very well and sent his love to us, perhaps a month since we rec'd this intelligence. Your Uncle Eben'r brought me the letter, who, according to his usual custom, waited for me to break the seal and express'd hurry at the commencement. But it consumed considerable time to stop and laugh. I opened it upon uncertainties, not knowing but you might have said something respecting a certain step-mother;[20] but as he would not wait for me to read it myself, I e'en run the hazard (as that is all the pay he requires) to read it out. But instead of that, I found it very congenial to his feelings–that is, if he is like all the rest of Adam's young ones–where you describe Capt. Hayden's person and manners to be so uncommonly engaging. I was pleased, myself, as I was aprehensive of of meeting a bear, and met a lamb. We laughed at the *squeedling* of the physic as well as at many other happy expressions, and to hear my poor composition run down–it was with such good justice to its merits that I can truly say it even pleased me, who, one would think, would be the last in the company it would have pleas'd. I don't in the least wonder at the observation (so like her, too), especially the one upon Jane, Corydon and Delia.

There was a curious circumstance attended that adventure. I had partly wrote it–not a copy, but coming right from the mint–when Mrs. O[liver] C[hamplain] came in, and her husband was to call her in a few moments. It was mail-night and I had previously told Will'm to call down and take my letter without fail. He comes allso Satan-like and, as Mary says, I never could rush when anyone was waiting for my tick. I left (every two of them, as Mrs. O. C. says) together to finish composing what I had begun–and it was bad enough. I believe now I am mistaken, it was at any rate one of the piecies I last sent, and I think you may distinguish it by its being the worst. I have since altered and suited my own taste better–and here it is or some other:

'Corydon. . . . '

'Delia. . . . '

I have done just as I thought I should–throw myself out of every inch of room for prose. I have got so berhymed that I cannot write prose, as this letter will demonstrate. I want Mary here more for her judgement than of any other service she could be to me; and that makes me write so much poetry to send to New York. Still, I hear nothing particular mentioned–only that her stomach requires stronger food. If the whole creation is not sufficiently hearty, I shall dispair at her voraciousness, and she must in future feed upon her own fire of genius. Eben'r laughed till the tears ran in showers at that observation, as well as the C[hamplai]n temper, and I confess you had the better of the argument; but 'tis time to wind up since I have crowded myself out of doors. . . .

Your speaking of your dreary prospects, for which I am sorry to hear, but I am in the same situation. I have finished *Capt. Starr* at last,[21] and 'tis called my masterpiece, but all that don't help towards new aplications, which I have not one of no price or description. A long cold winter coming on, and, to take a temporal view of my case, dispair with all its trains of horrors stares me full in the face. Still, am easey and contented as I ever am. . . .

[Your father is n]ot in a good state of heath, neither poorer then he has been at stated periods. . . . You will gratify me by enquires after his health whenever you write. . . . The piece intitled *Creation* I call'd the best of my productions, but attended with [more] difficulty than any that I ever attempted. Never shall I undertake another. . . .

and here the letter tails off in some damaged lines and various little afterthoughts.

The danger to George Champlain's health down south, which worried his mother, was on Eliza's mind also when she wrote to him in November of 1819 (**no. 65**).

My dear George,

Are you in the land of the living, or have you taken your departure for another and a better world? We are all very much alarmed at your long silence, particularly at this time. If you are well, you certainly ought to write to quiet Mother's fears if no one's else. In her last letter to me she spoke very discouraging about you. It has been so long sickly in New Orleans, you must naturaly conclude we feel more anxious about you than ever. The accounts for that place are very alarming indeed, a circumstance that you must be sensible of, yourself, if you ever look into a paper. Be assured I shall think you very unfeeling and ungrateful if you enjoy good health and neglect writing amediately on the receipt of this, as I am certain I wrote you last. The last time I heard from home, Mother wrote me she had been very sick but was then much better. The family were all as well as usual–that is, I suppose, in good scolding health, as Aunt Hannah says.

By the way, I must tell you this same aunt of ours has sold her house to Uncle Ebb and he has moved into it and taken her better for worse to take care of, so long as she lives. She has given all her property into his hands for him to dispose of as he thinks proper, as that wiseacre Mrs. Pinvert invested a certain amiable relation of ours with power to rule over her with a rod of iron for the rest of her days–a duty which I know he has faithfully discharged, as you know ruling is his forte. Do not imagin from what I have said that I disapprove of her (Aunt Hannah) proceedings. On the contrary, I highly commend her–as she is unable to take care of herself–for resigning her goods and chattles into the hands of those who will be so willing to take care of her the rest of her life. She was very unpleasantly situated, previous to her making this proposal to Uncle Ebb, and her situation was daily growing more and more unpleasant. Therefore I think the conduct of one old lady deserves the highest praise, while that of the other deserves the highest censure; but the one is a wise-woman and, as I said before, the other is a wise-acre.

I understand the shop [in her house] is converted into a post office and the house itself will undergo a thorough repair. You know what a delightful situation it is. I think they will make a perfect paradise of it, and when it is finished I think you ought to return to see the house, tho' you don't care a cent about those who inhabit it.

The boys are still at home. I have now told you all the news I can think of respecting home. If, however, I can think of any thing else from there as I progress with my birds-egging, I will not fail to set it down for your perusal.

I have been in New York since May and expect to spend the winter here. You know I'm very partial to the place. I think if all my friends were here I should never desire to quit it again, but alas! that cannot be. Aunt Mary's eye is entirely blind. It is not painful since the application of the leeches, but the entire loss of it is a heavy stroke. The other will not bear near as much straining as it would before it lost its fellow. She still paints, but is much longer doing a miniature than before she was deprived of her right eye. Otherwise she is as well as usual. She told me me to give her love to you and tell you she she should be very glad to see you here this fall if you think proper to visit us. If not, I suppose we must give up the idea of seeing you till the next.

I have lately taken the likeness of a very striking face, consequently the picture is esteem'd a very striking likeness. You recollect I always used to excell in caricatures. I was determin'd to conquer my passion for them and have so far succeeded that my pictures are now thought to look at least as well as the originals; but I find, before I can give general satisfaction, I must learn to make them look a little better. I did not know how sweet to the soul flattery is till lately, but experience has taught me that with men and women, old and young, gentle and simple, rich and poor (as your sister Lydia says), it is the sweetest draught that can be administer'd; so for the good of the Loo I think I shall dose them plentifully with it for the future–I mean in painting, nothing else, as I find nothing else will go down. I find Mother has adopted the wisest plan. You know she always makes angels of devels. It is the only food that is palatable in this degenerate age. The gentleman I have been drawing wished a front-face on ivory. I assure you I exerted my energies and have far surpass'd my own expectations. It is call'd my master-peice and, considering it's the first effort of genius (for I have never had a gentleman set to me before) I think I deserve a great deal of praise; and on this occasion could not forbear being my own trumpeter. I wish you could see the original and the picture, but it is very improbable you will ever see either, as they both leave the place within a month, and whether they will either of them ever return again to this place is beyond my ken.

The gentleman who takes this letter on for me is an intimate friend of your favorite 'chap' Thomas Dawson. He is going to reside in New Orleans for the present, and you will doubtless have an opportunity of adding him to the list of your acquaintances if you have any desire to enlarge the circle. He is a very fine man, I am told. I have not been long acquainted with him, but what little I know of him, I am pleased with. His name is Williamson and he is lately married to the sister of a young lady whom Thom's Dawson is courting. Aunt Mary has been taking him and his wife. She is also doing John Sistare at this present writing. She is the only painter in New York, either portrait or miniature, who has any business to do at this time, and it's very astonishing to every-one that with her blind eye she should be an exception to the general rule.

You would die if you should see a scholar she has taken lately to teach the art of painting. It is a young man, the queerest animal that ever had existance. I almost laugh myself to death whenever he comes to school. He is a very great genius, but Poverty, who is, you know, the constant attendant on Genius, has hitherto frustrated all his designs. He has had an excellent education, he understands all the *-ologies* that ever I heard of and ten thousand that I never heard of; he is an astromomer and I believe a ventriloquist–there is nothing but what he can do, except take miniatures. But he is determin'd to excell in that line as well as every other, and for that purpose applied to all the artists in the city. But they all–I suppose, seeing what a queer chap he was–refused him except Aunt Mary. But she, you know, always patronizes genius whenever it comes under her thumb, and seeing more in him than met the eye, upon the strength of her [fa]ith, she took the strangest animal in creation and [I believ]e in time she will make a human creature of him. But Heavens! if you could only hear him talk and see how he dresses, you would die at his incongruities.. He [is] brother to the Princess Rusty-Fusty and talks like an emperor. He has invented a machine for taking likenesses for wh[ich] he intends getting a patent, and if he does, his name will [live?] forever.[22] When he gets upon any of those sublime su[bjects] that he understands so well, I never saw anything fla[shing] of genius like his eyes. In short, take him for all i[n all, I'm] sure I ne'er shall look upon his like again. But y[ou must] see him to have an idea of his looks and manners, fo[r ? I'm sure] I cannot describe anything so uncouth.

I am now painting a peice, a very large one, that will be most superb when finished; but I won't undertake to describe it, for I suspect I have already wearied your patience. If not, I have my own, and it is time for me to think of winding up. But not before I charge you once more to write as soon as you receive this and let us know where you are and how you are, and what your prospects are at present. . . .

Mrs. Dawson and Hannah desires to be remembered to you. We have taken a house together again and I assure you we live very happily.

Good bye.

George's answer was written just a month later, the day before Christmas Eve (above, chapter 5, **no. 66**). In the interval, the sight in Mary's "good" or better eye deteriorated suddenly. Eliza's now-lost report of the situation in January of the new year threw Betsey at last into real despair. But she roused herself to respond promptly (**no. 67**), addressing Eliza care of Charles Holt, on Chatham Street. It was the Holts with whom Mary had first made contact when she moved to New York, the Holts whose portraits she had done, of family and individuals alike, and the Holts who had entertained her home-town kinfolk on their visits to the city; the same who had taken her and her niece for strolls about the city; and the Holt daughters Mary and especially Eliza who had maintained a steady friendship with Mary Way, visiting her daily as her blindness gathered and providing extra links to New London.[23] In

New York the Holts all filled the same role in times of trouble that Aunt Parsons was expected to fill for Betsey in New London, simply because blood was thicker than water:

> O God, thy ways are unsearchable and past piecing out. The shocking account you gave us, dear Eliza, in your last letter, obliterates all idea of self, and every fear and doubt that before hung heavy at my heart has fled or suspended. My anxiety for Mary sets them all at naught and I have thought of nothing else since. It is the last theme that occupies my mind when I sleep and the first that presents when I awake. But what is still more agravating is the impossibility of alleviating her distress by anything that lies in my power. Betsey Allen tells me Eben'r called her at her father's the preceding evening of the day your letter arrived, and Aunt [Sally, his wife] is so much distressed for her and sent word to me she intended to write immediately to Aunt Parsons respecting her case–who is abundantly able to assist her.[24] But there is but one who can restore her sight, to whom I hope she looks to in faith–who [? . . .] those to sight that were born blind, whose arm is not shortned and power is the same as when He was upon earth. But if it should not be His will, I ardently pray that she may feel a perfect resignation to the divine will. Refflection will teach her she is not the first or only one in a similiar case. Samson was blind among enemies, Milton wrote his best productions after that period, whose name is immortalized; and thank God she is not spiritually blind. Should it terminate as your fears express, depend upon this truth: she will by being accustomed to a deprivation of sight become more and more resign'd, particularly after the first shock is past, could she fix her mind upon some interesting subject, and from principle she ought to endeavour to. It must of course gradually grow less irksome, untill habit has made it tolerable to suport; and in regard to the means of living, her chance is I believe equally good, perhaps better, as every friend and aquaintance will exert themselves to see that she wants for nothing. And she merits if any-one.
>
> But how weak are arguments against unfiegned distress or real misery. I do not speak thus at the expence of truth and merely to comfort, but have an idea that, was it my case which I have and do still tremblingly anticipate, I should not be left without a source of comfort. 'Lorenzo, the world shut out, thy thoughts call home.' Surely we may enjoy communion with God uninterupted. I have passed through much sorrow of heart and am still passing through it, but mine were more common evils of life, and I dread what I may have to encounter before I reach a happier shore. 'He builds too low that builds beneath the stars.'
>
> Your father has been confined to the house 6 weeks next Saturday, which is tomorrow, except four days in the time in which he took a relapse and has been poorer, in consequence of which I have become a nurse and have not left him to go out any where. He coughs and raises beyond discription; but his case is doubtful. It has been strongly impressed upon my mind that he can-not survive it, and believe him to be in a consumption. But it may prove otherwise. He has pined away to a skeleton but seems to think he shall get up again. Let it be as it will, I feel that I am

resigned. I could wish you to enquire after his health in your letters, because I know it would be a satisfaction to him. When he feels discouraged, he thinks something is decaying inwardly, which I make no doubt of; yet should he be raised I shall think it for the best, as we cannot stay beyond our time.

I have had but two likenesses on ivory and one two-dollar one since last fall—I believe the first of October—but have lived upon it with a five dollar bill added to it, which was a voluntary offer of the loan of it by my friend Mrs. G[oddar]d.[25] Her kindness I shall never forget. We have at last been under the necessity of calling upon Sam'l for his mite, 3 dollars a month, as allso he sold his gun and watch, and two better sons never existed than he and Will'm. They do all in their power and were they able we should lack nothing. William has never missed one night since his father's confinement—been down regularly to bring wood and water, errands of every kind. We have wrote on to George, or rather Will'm has, and have some expectation of his assistance; but if not, we shall be carried through. I have faith to believe now tho' faith had deserted me for a season—which gave birth to the following lines. It may serve to amuse.

Invocation to Faith

O Faith thou precious gift of Heaven, where hast thou fled? O stay!
O'er my sad heart throw one devine, one solitary ray.
Throug desert isles or Java's coast I'd joyful fly with thee.
'Tis thou exhillerates the soul and sets the captive free.
Thou canst e'en prison walls illume and soothe the mind to rest.
Return, thou dear effulgent joy—reign, monarch of this breast.
All earth is but a barren waste nor can the faithless mind
Enjoy one glimmering beam of bliss if once from thee disjoined.
Darkness and gloom usurp thy seat with all thier tearful train
And fill the thought with future wars to rack the tortoured brain.
If then from Heaven thou dost descend, one spark of mercy show.
Assuage the heart that inly bleeds and check the tears that flow.
How sweet Aurora's blush to view when spring unfolds her charms—
When nature's God speaks in each plant, the hills and vallies warms.
I see the golden sun-beams play amid thier nectar'd leaves.
Yet dull the scene without thy smile; for all things cease to please.
My present fears and future doubts thy power shall melt away,
If thou wilt hover o'er my couch and chaunt thy angel lay.
Thy presence gilds the bed of death—defies his keenest dart—
Till the faint lamp of life has fled and chill'd the throbbing heart.
Blest evidence of things unseen, in thee we yeald our breath,
A radiant moon beam piercing thro' the midnight gloom of death.

Give my tenderest love to Mary and Mrs. Dawson and daughter. Tell your aunt to keep up good heart, for in this world we shall have tribulation but in God we shall have peace. There yet may be hope when warm weather returns and leeches are more active. Cannot philosophy sustain the shock? Do all you can to make her happy or at least comfortable, which I doubt not you do, neither dispair, yourself, but believe (as I do) that all that is is for the best alltho' hid from our eyes.

> 'Never did I see the rightious man forsaken
> Or his seed begging bread.'

Let us hear from you as often as possible, if you only write three lines, just to inform us how she is. As you must supose, we are unusually anxious. Pay her every attention and trust God with the event.

While Mary's tragedy was entering into its latter chapters in New York, in New London George Whitefield Champlain was entering on the very last of his life. He died in April of 1820. Betsey communicated the news to Eliza through Anna Fitch, in a letter now lost, and Eliza replied (**no. 68**):

New York May 2^{d} 1820 from the Arsanal

My dear Mother,

I hope you impute my not writing before to the right cause: *trouble*. I assure you we have seen it in its most terrific forms lately, though it has not appear'd to us in the shape of death as it has to you. Indeed there has been times lately that the idea of death was as welcome to me as the most pleasing thing you can concieve. I recieved your letter last Saturday at Mrs. Fitches where I was staying a few days. She, it seems, knew the contents of it before by the newspaper, and withheld her knowledge from me. I thought nothing on earth could add to the heaviness of my soul a few moments before your letter arrived, but that gave the finishing stroke and I envied my father. I think I shall never again regret those who are at rest. It is selfish in the extreme, and if we reflect a moment we must see the inconsistancy of it, knowing as we do how much happier they are than those whose lives are spared a little longer in this 'vale of tears.' But never while life remains shall I forget the shock I experienced when I open'd your last letter. It was dreadful–prepared as I was. I did not think the news could have produced such a feeling; but it's over, and I will dwell no longer upon it, tho' I have much more to say.

You wish us to return and live with you now all is over. Alas! you know the obstacles that are in the way. As I wrote you before, we are deeply involved in debt and our moveing has added to them considerably. With house-rent we have no more to do, after we have paid our last quarter rent, as we have not taken a house. But to Mr. Fitch we owe everything and more than everything, for had it not been for him we should have died. He has spared no trouble or expense to render our situation more comfortable, and for the present, thanks must be our only pay. Mr. Fitch and Dr. Wright think Mary's physicians are very much interested for us and are trying all in their power to get us business, which, if they can do, we had much better stay till our debts is paid, as when we once come home, we shall never return again, and Aunt Mary is confident, she says, that we shall never get sufficient business in New London to pay them–else we should not hesitate to accept your offer, for I am very sensible you must be lonely. But in a case of such importance we must consult our own interest before anything else. What we have concluded upon is this: Aunt Mary is to stay out here to the Arsanal for the present. Our sign is to be put up at some respectable boarding house either public or private in town, where I am to board, provided any one applies for a picture–of which friends have no doubt, as they are all interested for us and will leave no means untried to get us business. And, after that great object is accomplished, we shall have nothing further to stay for. As for my assisting in Mr. Judd's school, if I can get likenesses to take I had ten thousand times rather do it, as I never had the art of teaching any more than yourself, and at the time that affair was in agitation before, I died with apprehension for fear I should be obliged to accept his offer. There is nothing so repugnant to my feelings as teaching a school, because there is nothing but what I am better calculated to do.

Surely, after what I have written, you can no longer be surprised, as you appear'd to be in your letter, that we did not urge you to come down, when we have no home of our own. If such an event should ever take place that we had one, Heaven knows there is nothing we should desire more ardently than to have you with us; but at present we are dependant on ourselves. Mrs. Lee has never influenced us to expect you for we have never recieved a line from her since Aunt Mary's blindness, neither have we seen Dr. Lee who, I understand, brought your last letter and left word at the house where he left the letter that he should come out to the Arsanal to see Aunt Mary as soon as he returned from Albany. If he does, he will bring you a verbal message and her final determination, if I have not given it. And now I must bid you adieu. I have nothing more to say than that I labour under the greatest depression of spirits, and shall, probably, for a long time to come. So pray write often.

8

Necessary Adjustments

A period of recession in New York had been, as the letters make plain, particularly hard on the sisters of the brush. While it eased, over the course of 1820, Eliza found herself deprived of the support of her aunt and reduced from friendship to a condition very like dependence on the Fitch family. Mary's dependence was to become utter and abject, in New London. There Betsey, emerging from her husband's death with nothing but debts and herself dependent on what her sons could raise by selling their most treasured possessions, would have her blind sister and a septuagenarian aunt on her hands. In continual mentions of small economies and small sums, of obligations and doing without, the previous correspondence makes clear that there were no resources on which the three women could now fall back even to maintain the level of disciplined contentment they had enjoyed. They must re-order their lives.

But how? They argued anxiously about the best plan (**no. 69**, of May), a letter from Betsey first:

> Dear Eliza,
>
> Be not suprized at my informing you that we all think you distracted for planning your business in the way you have. The consolation your letter afforded us was that you did not compell me to join you there in New York. I had however made up my mind to go in case you both wished me to; but be assured it would have been the greatest cross I ever took up. I now feel released from my fears, both in hearing from you, and your being situated so that I could not go. But understand me in the right sense: we are all exceedingly disapointed, Eben'r full as much as me. He brought me down your letter and told me to write immediately, and observed that he should also write to entreat you to be reason'd with, and come on. We concluded that it was impossible for you to leave Mary, but if you board in town, of course you must be seperated from her; and it is certain that your board must be paid, whether you find business or not. You did not inform me how nor by whom that was to be settled for.

If Mary sees no way to cancel the debts, I think returning here would be the only safe plan to save obligation. As Eben'r says, she shall never want if she will return, as long as it lies in his power to prevent it, which in all probability will be as long as she or he lives. As to staying where every-thing is so high, when we can live here almost for nothing, we confess we do not see the philosophy of [it]. It is a very common thing at the present day to be involved, and you would find as much kindness from your creditors as others, in waiting untill you can [repay]. We think you must both be plunging deeper and deeper in debt by continuing there. I cannot bear very well to have y[ou be a] tax upon your friends there, as you informed me, when I cou[ld] assist you here and not feel it–and her also. My selfish r[easons] are, I want your society more than I can express. Remember, I mean *both*, and if not both, and you can be seperated, then you. If Mary cannot hear to it–which Heaven grant, if it is best–she may yet be prevail'd upon. I know the world is selfish; but, if I could be made to believe it was best for you both to stay, from principle I would set aside self and dispense with your society, as I wish to do right. And who knows what that is? None but those who can see into futurity. I can say no more. I hope your uncle will add what I have omited in endeavouring to persuade.

As respects my own prospects and affairs, they are as follows: to sum up all I owe, it amounts just about to a hundred dollars. I was blessed in having two aplications as soon as I moved. One I have finished at last, through much labour and sorrow of heart, which, happening at this crisis, sunk my spirits still deeper, being a difficult subject, and taken the side I am unacustomed. But I have got through, and need the money, which is but an introduction to paying my debts. The next will do a little more, and perhaps in the course of a year I may find myself free from debt. At any rate, I trust Providence, which has carried me through many many distressing scenes. I have two or three more engaged but am not to receive money, as they are to pay Canady's house rent. I am rich in faith. That is the best news I can give you.

Mrs. Lee is one of the best souls in the world. She is here often and begs me to come to see her–says she will send for me. I told her not to, as I had nothing of mourning fixed–till I had done up my painting, could not attend to it. But then I intend it. I have reasoned with her, notwithstanding all she has written Mary, to think it is best for you both to join me instead of reversing it. It appears to me that there is no one posessed of reason but what would view the matter in the same light–but we all feel our own obstacles. I know not what to say more to persuade, and must leave it to Heaven, that I know will plan right; yet do come with Mary, if possible.

'Though strong our oars, still stronger is our fate.'

You observe that in such 'a case of importance you must consult your own interest.' Certainly, my dear, it is what I would have you do–or you would not show yourselves rational creatures. But your friends here view it in a direct oposite light of view. It appears as though you were still taxing those friends that has been angels of light to you, and still involving yourselves more and more. If it is not so, I shall be happy. That that you know to be best, that do. Let us hear immediately from you, nor keep us in suspence one moment longer than is necessary. At any rate, I shall expect you both when you are free from debt.

I will give up to your opinion and consent to your doing that which will make you the happiest.

I inclose a few lines suited to my feelings and dictated from principles of truth.

The promised poetry has not survived, alas, nor perhaps some further request from Betsey for art supplies, for when Eliza next writes in mid-June (**71**) she seems to have in mind some communication that has been lost:

My dear Mother,

Don't be concerned about the ivory or us. The former, I suspect, is on its passage to New London and the latter are still in the land of the living, to both our sorrow. It was only day before yesterday that we recieved the leeches, for which we are more obliged to you than we can express. Aunt Mary's whole dependance rests on them, and if they fail–but I won't anticipate ill. We are staying a few days at Mrs. Fitches on a visit, and as she understands putting them on, they were applied yesterday–twelve of them, and they drew astonishingly. Her [=Mary's] eye was so swell'd with the bites that it was almost entirely closed. To-day it is better, and I trust by the constant application of them it will continue to grow so.

And now, pray let me tell you not to send any more letters or anything else to Doctor Wright. Whatever you send, direct to 96 Cherry street, and we shall be sure to get them in a quarter of the time and with much less inconvenience to the parties concerned, as I am frequently at Mrs. Fitches and seldom at the Doctor's, and therefore he has to send a servant two miles and a half out of town with whatever you send, which is a liberty I have no business to take with him, tho' I know he sends them to me with pleasure, particularly the leeches. Yet I would rather not give him that pleasure again. I know the reason the leeches were sent to him was because you none of you could find any other way of sending them to us, but in future I beg you would observe what I have said and direct as I tell you. Pray don't forget.

And now I have a piece of news to tell you that I suspect will surprise you very much. The Academy of Arts is to be open to-morrow afternoon and evening for the benefit of *Aunt Mary*. Are you not surprised? I assure you I was very much surprised when Mr. Waldo call'd at Mr. Fitches last week to enquire into her situation and to say that the Board of Directors of the Academy wished to show that respect to an unfortunate *sister*, as he feelingly called her, provided she had no objection to having it done, and if she did not wish. Nothing could be more delicate than the manner in which he made his proposal, and as nothing can be more honourable in the opinion of her most fastidious friends, she could of course have no reason for declining such a mark of respect; and Mr. Waldo was desired to conduct the business as he and the Manager thought proper, which I have no doubt will be as it should be. At any rate I will leave the subject for the present and tell you more when I know more myself, which will not be until the exhibition is over.[1]

Well, the exhibition is over and I was present at it. I suppose you will be astonished at that. It continued a day and an evening. In the evening the Academy was brilliantly illuminated for the purpose of attracting an unusual concourse of spectators and it had the desired effect. It was most uncomfortably crouded. The collection of paintings were exquisite, many of them done by the oldest masters and many by the artists in the city. The chandaliers were veiled with white crape or muslin which had a fine effect. I did not like to go at all, but Mrs. Fitch said she would not stir a step without me and that she depended on my going–that it was highly proper I should go and I must. So I gave a most reluctant consent and accompanied her and a small party much against my will.

Well, now it is all over and the child named Anthony the great, the immortal Trumbull as you would say, has just call'd on me with Mr. Waldo and Mrs. Trumbull. Waldo introduced me to them and I recieved their bows and courtsies without being struck of a heap, as they say–which is what I am surprised at, as I never was in the presence of such great characters before or recieved so many compliments in so short a time. I began to think more of the genius I possess for painting than I ever did before when I saw Trumbull take up the outline of Doctor Wright's wife (whose likeness I have begun) and say to Waldo, 'The proportions of this face are excellent and the sketch extremely delicate. But, Miss Champlain,' said Trumbull, 'you labour under the greatest disadvantage by painting in too strong a light, and if you will permit us' (turning to Waldo) 'to arrange your light for you, we will assist you with a great deal of pleasure.' Waldo had before asked me if I would accept his assistance, so when Mr. Trumbull proffer'd *his* services I of course made as suitable acknowledgement for the honour they confer'd on me as was in my power; and they then took their leave.

But I have talked so long of what they said about my painting that I have neglected what I suppose you will consider the most important part of the business. Col. Trumbull's errand, as he is President of the Academy, was to deliver into the hands of Miss Champlain, Miss Way's niece, the sums that were recieved on Saturday last in manner and form, and Miss Champlain alias Miss Way recieved from his hands the sum of a hundred and forty-one dollers 53 cents, accompanied with a letter from himself to Aunt Mary expressing the profoundest respect for herself and commiseration for her irrepairable misfortune.

And now, after settling all the weighter matter of the law, will you start at a proposal I am about to make? I wish to know if you would be willing to come to New York, as you proposed yourself some time ago. It is the opinion of the learned that it is by far the best plan that can be adopted for you to come down and for us to take a house and commence operations while the public mind is interested for Aunt Mary, and, as they vulgarly say, strike while the iron's hot. Doctor Wright has just gone from here and has just told me that Waldo told him, when he show'd him his own picture, that if I painted like that he must take me under his patronage, for that the genius display'd in that peice might be carried to very great lengths. Aunt Mary owes more than a hundred dollers, but how much more I cannot tell till after her debts are paid, which I suppose will be in the course of this week. It is the opinion of her friends, then, that with the money that remains a house had better be taken, and you and I commence operations, as I said before, as soon as possible, and that we shall doubtless get plenty of business, as the town is filling with strangers and Waldo, Trumbull, Doctor Wright and Mrs. Fitch have in a manner taken me under their protection. Now all I beg is that you will return an answer to this letter by the first mail that goes after you recieve it, as I wish to know what course to pursue as soon as possible. I do not urge you to come because I well recollect the reluctance you express'd in a former letter; and if the fears and apprehensions you then felt should be realized, I should never forgive myself for being the cause of it–tho' I think there is very little ground for your fears. But, as I said before, act as you think proper, for I dare not advise. I have stated the case exactly as it is, and I must leave the rest to your decision, and pray it be as speedy as possible, for if it is not very quick, I must act without knowing your determination, which would be rather disagreeable in a matter of such importance. As I am determin'd to steer clear of censure in this affair, I refrain from giving my advice. It is a very critical time of life with us at present, or I would come up instead of writing to you, as I know the business would be settled more speedily with tongues, and more satisfactory, than with pens. But circumstances forbid it, and we must bow to fate.

Adieu.

Trumbull's letter is indeed delicately expressed, and copied with much satisfaction to be shown around Mary's circle.[2] One copy, on a back page, was used by Mary as scratch paper in the drafting of her reply:

Miss Way
New York 19th June 1820

Dear Madam,

In the name of the Directors of the Academy of the fine Arts, I have to beg your acceptance of $141.35, being the amount received on Saturday last at their Exhibition.

It must afford you some consolation in the deep calamity with which it has pleased Providence to afflict you, to receive this testimony of the interest which so many of the inhabitants of the city take in your unfortunate situation.

Heartily wishing the restoration of your health, or, if that may not be, patience to endure your privation,

I am faithfully your
servant & friend,
Jn. Trumbull

and Mary's answer,

Sir:

I have rec'd your letter with $141.35 from the Directors of the Academy of the Fine Arts. For this act of unsolicited generosity I beg them to accept my warmest thanks. Should it please Providence to continue my present affliction, the memory of this disinterested act will cheer the darkness of my future days. To the public I feel much gratitude for the promptitude & liberality with which they aided this generous design. I have been obliged to employ an amanuenesis. My present situation prevents me from writing. Accept, Sir, on your own behalf my thanks for the friendly solicitude you express for my welfare, & my sincerest wishes that you may be preserved from the gloomy situation to which I am reduced.

I remain your oblig'd & grateful servant,

M. Way

It was a very dignified acknowledgement, and a human one as well. The city's well-to-do had responded well for their part, too. And the pathos of the moment was put to a further good use. The *Ladies' Literary Cabinet*, a weekly that reached many of New York's educated readers, especially women, announced in two of its summer issues: "Miniature painting. Miss Champlin, pupil of Miss Way, paints and finishes miniature likenesses in any style that may be preferred, at No. 96 Cherry-Street. We furnish our readers with this information the more cheerfully, as every order given to Miss Champlin, will benefit her unfortunate instructress, who is bereft of sight." The address is the Fitch's, no doubt the idea also. It is unlikely that it brought in much business.[3]

In reply to the idea that she should move down to New York, Betsey wrote in early July (**no. 75**):

Dear Eliza,

I cannot give you a more prompt and suitable answer to the present question than to give it in your own words: upon some occasion 'it is a great thing to know when we are well off.' This answer would not indicate that I am happy, but as much or perhaps more so than I ever shall be again in any shape whatever. That my situation may vary, I am thankful from my soul; that your happiness does not in any degree depend upon my coming to New York–for was that the case, I must go–you have had the goodness to leave it to my choice, for which I repeat my thanks. You recollect my weighty reasons: loss of health, and leaving Sam and Will'm. The last reason will weight light with any person but a mother; but frequent opertunities of giving them admonition, whether they receive it or not, is a privilege. They would feel more lost than you immagine, and Sam is extremely set against it. You have been with those who were the same to you as a mother; but it would not be thier case, and they are the two best boys, I believe, in the world. That is, they are so to me.

Another reason: I have taken a house for a year. I am also in debt and must pay them before I run away. If I could see into futurity I should know better how to conduct, and would certainly do that, that would terminate in the best for us all; but as it is, we ought to act as our best judgement directs–which is, for me to remain here and keep house alone, which I can hire for a triffle. Then, in case of what may happen to you or Mary, here is a home. I want your society more than anything. Still, it would be madness for you to come merely for that, if you can do better where you are. The time, too, may come that I shall have no means of hireing a house. Then necessity may make me joyfully accept your invitation, as we none of us know what lies in the womb of fate. But at present, think it expedient for me to stay where I am, and for you to take a house. To me it would certainly be more agreable than to board. You will feel more free from restraint and do more exactly as you please.

I thank Heaven for Mary's good fortune, and view a Providence in her going to New York, as such a benevolent act could not possibly have been performed here. But above all things, don't suffer yourself to be elated at any prosperity that may smile upon you, for when we are ascended upon the mount, we know we must descend into the valley. This melancholy truth I have experienced so repeatedly that it would scarcely be in the power of all the combined hosts of Heaven to prove to the contrary. 'Tis this refflection cements me here alone, or would wish to be so forever.

I have but three associates in this place: Mrs. B[ryan]t, Mrs. Lee and Mrs. O. Champlain. All else puts me in tortoure. I am in a fair way to be excentric, if I am not so allready. Thier society is indeed such. All else is dross. Yet there is times I would prefer my own even to thiers. Now I can write, read and refflect–a priviledge I never enjoy'd as at present; and though at intervals gloom and depression of spirits will overshadow my mind, still, how much heavier would be the burden had I a family to attend to–visits, calls and ettequette to observe, which now I am excused from. It is indeed a great thing, attaining to great wisdom, to know when we are well off. I dare not aspire after any thing greater. I so much fear losing the little I now posess, and have become such a proficient in the school of adversity, which has taught me knowledge. That is my treasure, as I have dearly earned it and shall endeavour to make the most of it. I renounce the world from my heart. The less I see of it, the less I know of it, the less I am injured by it; and every thing that tinctures of pleasure has a penalty annex'd to it. This is my boasted knowledge. This truth has not only been proved by me but by one mightier. E. Young is the man after my own heart. One of his lines is a text for the day. There's none can find that test in his writings like the unfortunate. His sentiments come from the heart, his sufferings made him eloquent; for he holds up the mirror to the child of sorrow.

I send you my last composition. You see it breathes the same sentiments I have expressed in prose. I can convey my ideas better in rhyme, however faulty it may be. Write soon and give me your opinion.

You cannot tell what a blow you gave my feelings when you bid me send *Fancy* (Pl. 6.15, with the text, 'Fancy, who from the Bow that spans the sky/ Brings colours dipt in Heaven! that never die' [Cowper, *Table Talk* 702f.]). You must–since you have become so famous–either send her back or some other to substitute her vacant place. There never was any thing so much admired. Don't disappoint me, since 'tis the greatest ornament my room can boast. Every stranger that comes allows that to beat all the others. Make me good, I say.

Give my love to Mary. Tell her I congratulate her upon her good fortune and hope it will be continued. Your Uncle E[benezer] as well as myself is disappointed, every letter, that you are not more particular in mentioning the state of Mary's eyes, whether she is totally blind or not, whether she can paint any or only discern objects about her. We are very anxious to be informed those particulars–to know what degree of blindness it is. Tell us in your next. . . .

Soon afterwards Mary went back home to stay with her sister, or rather, at first, with her sister-in-law. Just how the move was settled on doesn't appear in the letters remaining, but it was accomplished by mid-summer. Mrs. Northam and her daughter Anna Fitch were her companions for the journey, and stayed to visit for a brief while. Betsey told Eliza how it all went, including the visit of Dr. North. It was a lucky coincidence (except that it made no difference) to have in New London the foremost ophthalmologist on the American continent.[4]

You insist on an immediate answer to your several questions. To relieve you from your nettles, I therefore write at an early hour, and quite unprepared, as I have not been able to collect my scattered senses since Mary's arrival, on account of my anxiety for her and the number of years that has elapsed. The great revolutions we have past through since we last met has excited both painful and pleasing sensations. She has been a little ill, and I have just returned from there. Be not alarmed–it was a slight indisposition. I slept badly, arising from the tumult of my thoughts, fearing how the case might terminate when brought to a crisis. She has applied simple means to her eye but (as yet) has not had time to give it a fair trial. Doctor North has examined it and gives her but little hope; but we should indeed be miserable, was there not a hope beyond what man can give.

Her spirits are as good as we have reason to expect, and her friends on all sides have made it thier study to divert her from that dispondency that must effect anyone in a similar situation. The doctor will give us his final opinion in regard to the propriety of operating when he returns from a short journey of a fortnight's absence; but endeavour to be as calm under the presure of suspense as possible, desiring resignation to the devine will. The eye that was first effected he pronounces as past recovery, but that circumstance now she would consider triffling, could the other be restored, and I have strong faith that it will be. I intended to have her brought here as quick as she landed–had requested Mrs. Lee and Mrs. Champlain to come when the operation was performed. But Sally insisted upon her being there, to which I consented, if she might come afterwards. I am expecting her in perhaps two weeks but it depends on circumstances. I shall go up every evening untill she is with me, when the weather will admit.

We are extremely pleased with Mrs. Northam and Mrs. Fitch. Mrs. Champlain is in love with the latter and I with both, but I should be very cautious in giving my opinion of the two ladies (so candidly) if I thought you could have the presumption to devulge it to them. But truely, if I do posess any skill in phisiognomy or manners, the delicate sentiment of which they seem to be posessed could not bear it without pain–like Mrs. ___ (but don't you tell whom), being entirely under the dominion of that predominant weakness, can swallow monstrous quantities of merit pulverized like a sugar'd pill.

But this is scandal, and my heart condemns me. All therefore that I deem prudent to say of our friends, is, to desire you to endeavour to pattern after them, and by well-doing, shew your gratitude to Providence for placing you in so worthy, so excellent a family. . . .

For all Mary's resolve in the letter that follows (**79**), not to complain about her blindness, and again and again not to complain in other letters later, the self-control she sought was quite beyond her powers; or, one may say, it would have been quite alien to the openhearted relations she was used to in the circle closest around her. She is indeed more openhearted than ever. In the particular things she now regrets the loss of, one can read the particular features of her character, prominently, her zest for challenge. Moreover, no revisions in her text were possible as she used her slate, so she must compose only in her mind; and the reader can gain a better sense now of her raw, or rather, her long developed literary capacity. She was good at turning over words in her mind, she loved eloquence. It was that quality which she notices from time to time in her Speaker, the Reverend Edward Mitchell of her church in New York, and which she emulates, sometimes in the correspondence calling herself "your Speaker" and joking about the formalities of homiletic convention. Emulation, she says, was in her nature. So she responded to every art and quality that she admired, eloquence most obviously and often, composing great sermons, organ-toned paragraphs and pages to Eliza especially, but here also to her friend Anna:

Oh for one comprehensive word or sentence that would at once express all I think and feel. Twice before I have attempted to address you, but feeling got the better of reason and my tears blotted what I had written. But I will say nothing of myself or my situation. It is a sad and gloomy subject. I will talk of my friends.

We were much disappointed in the pleasure we promised ourselves in seeing you here on your return, but, as it was to be so, we are glad to hear that you have at length arrived safe and sound after all your fatigues and difficulties, and hope you will never have reason to repent the journey.

I am impatient to hear more of your little favourite [Cornelia Fitch]. You only say she is the daughter of one of the first of women. May she inherit her mother's virtues and may they prove a rich reward for all the care and labour I know you will bestow upon her. Let me hear in your next letter all the particulars respecting her name, age, temper and disposition, to say nothing of her face and form. Fancy has been busy in sketching the outline of her portrait, but must suspend her pencil till further information.[5] You know Emma [Hayden][6] was my model for children—indeed, bating her high temper, I can conceive of nothing more perfect; and even that, far from being a fault in my opinion, with proper management, well regulated, and under due controul, it might be sublimed or sublimated, if I may so express myself, into the most exalted virtue. How delightful the task, to cultivate a flower so fair, so beautiful and fragrant. Well would it repay the fostering hand of care.

Eliza's letter gave me much pleasure, as it relieved the anxious solicitude I felt for my ever-dear Maria. I rejoice in the happiness little Gustavus has difused around him [born in August, Gustavus Vasa Hayden]. Long may it continue! May his amiable mother find in him a reward for all her sufferings [through her first daughter Emma's death] and may heaven shower its choicest blessings on them both; but, tho' he were an angel of light, I shall never love him as I have loved his sister.

I determined to answer your letter myself, and, as it is impossible for me to dictate, I write this with my own hand upon a slate. Sad work I make of it, to be sure, bitterly do I lament the difficulties I have to encounter, and laugh as heartily at the blunders I commit. We have had quite a frolick over this letter, it reads so funny. 'Tis impossible to help it: one word wrote upon another, broken disjointed sentences, some up and some down. In short, it is the work of darkness, and requires no small show of ingenuity to render it intelligible. My sister Sally has the patience and goodness to pick out what little sence there is in it and put it together, that it may be readable; so you may well think it is attended with some trouble and difficulty. From these circumstances duly considered, it plainly appears that this one letter must and ought to answer for all my friends: for yourself, Mrs. Hayden, and Eliza in particular, and more-over also, it ought to procure me at least half a dozen letters from each of you–you that can write with so much ease and pleasure, and read it when you have done. An amusement to me, and so delightful, and which, alas, I now enjoy no more.

I do not see as well as when you was here. I can scarcely distinguish light from darkness, and have but too much reason to think my case is helpless. I feel all the horrors of my situation most sensibly–deep and heavy at my heart. The gloom of death overspreads me, yet I still live, I am still enabled to support the burden of existence, I know not how nor why, but for some wise purpose, no doubt. They may exhort me to keep up my spirits, preach patience and resignation; they may talk of force of habit, and say that time will reconcile me to my sad destiny; they may tell me of those who have been blind for years that are cheerful and contented, that were never known to breathe a murmur or even wish for sight. Go to the wretch condemned to waste his days in a dungeon deprived of life's best blessings–light and liberty. Assuage the anguish of his soul with words, tell him to be cheerful and contented–that time will reconcile him to his fate! No, my friend, it is utterly impossible to sit down easy and contented under the heaviest of all human calamities, knowing it to be so. There may indeed be those who view it in a different light, those who think the loss of sight inconsiderable, provided they enjoy every other gratification. But their feelings, disposition and character must be widely different from those I am unfortunately destined to possess. They can have no taste for those pursuits which made the happiness of my life, but now constitute my chief misery. They know nothing of those feelings, those ardent hopes, desires, & that enthusiasm that inspires and animates the soul to contend with obstacles, and triumph over difficulties–that spirit of emulation, that enthusiasm that whispers to the soul, 'Nothing is impossible. Go on. 'Tis bright before thee. Pursue the track and thou shall be a Star.' They know nothing of those feelings, nor the pleasure–the inexpressible, the inexhaustible delight–they afford; pleasures that wove the charm that bound me to existence, now lost to me forever, and which I shall never cease to regret while memory retains her seat or life remains.

Is this the language of despondency & dispair? Say rather it is the language of feeling and nature if not of resignation. Do not suppose I shall sink under the weight of misfortune. No, I will rise above it and will bear it as I ought. Think not that I have renounced my faith and principles. Severe indeed has been the trial, heavy the shock they have sustained; but in vain the 'rain descended, the winds blew and the floods came and beat upon that house. It fell not, for it was founded upon a rock. Fixed on the rock of ages, firm and immoveable, still they stand amidst the tempest of the mind, the wild rage of contending passions, unhurt amid the war of elements, the wreck of matter and the crush of worlds.' Fully convinced that what-ever is, is right, I trust the wonder-working hand of heaven. I know that toil is necessary and good must finally be the result. He that wounds will heal, 'sorrow may endure for a night but joy cometh in the morning.' All this I know, and wait impatiently the dawning of that day that shall know no night, and darkness be dispersed forever.

Adieu, my dear friend. Please to present my respects to Mr. Fitch and Capt. Hayden and my love to Mrs. Johnson and the Miss Sanfords–I feel truly grateful for their kindness and attention–to Mrs. Dartenell, Mrs. Tylle, Mrs. Avery, Miss Clinch, Mrs. and the Miss Mitchells. We much regret not knowing Mr. Mitchell was here. Aunt Hannah is half offended with him–she says he is the first Universalist minister that ever passed through town without calling on her, and hopes he will be the last.

Once more adieu, and believe me yours truly,

M. W.

From a certain nobility, to the chatter of a small mind: from Mary's letter, to Sally Way (**no. 80**) writing later in the same month of September also to Anna Fitch:

My dear friend,

Your kind letter was received with much pleasure, but we were much disappointed that you did not return by the way of New London. I had made great calculations upon seeing you. I had procured good help and it would have been in my power to have paid you more attention. We had plan'd several pleasant walks that I think you would have been pleased with. I had not given up your returning this way untill I received your letter.

You will have the goodness to excuse my silence for such a length of time. I have been waiting for sister Mary to finish her letter which has been a lengthy piece of work, as she could write but a little at a time. Doctor North has examined her eyes again a few days since and says he can be of no service to her, as there is nothing like cataract on either eye. He told her frankly it was Gutta Serena and that [she] could never expect to see well again, but might probably see a little better than she now did. She bore it much better than I expected, but at times is very dull and much depressed in spirits.

We are happy to hear of Mrs. Hayden's good health and congratulate her on the birth of her son. Please to remember me to her and tell her nothing would give me more pleasure than to see her in New London. My best respects to your worthy mother. Tell her I shall ever remember her with sincere affection. Your pencil case I have never seen, therefore think you must have left it on the road. Give my love to Eliza. Tell her I intended to have written her but believe I shall not have time, and she must take the will for the deed; but I shall write her next week. Tell her I wish she was here now to take the likeness of one of her old beaus, who is now in town and looks more interesting than ever. My respects to your husband, in which Mr. Way joins, and believe me yours affectionately,

S. S. Way

In November, it may have been, Eliza sent the following undated letter to her aunt (**no. 82**), giving the first glimpses of a sort of poverty she had to endure, a shabbiness, which caused her much distress in times to come:

'Tis now about the witching time of night, I am alone, and have been reading till my eyelids dropped. I am not fond of being surprized into a nap and will therefore tell you why I am up at this late hour, when all creation is asleep except a few sons and daughters of disappation. It will keep my eyes open till Mr. & Mrs. Fitch return from a party to which they have gone, and I hope drive away the blues–who have lately become extremely fond of my society. And as I have not a single idea and must write, am glad of anything tho' ever so triffling to communicate.

We were napped up this morning between nine and ten by little Wixey (don't the name sound like old times?) who came to invite us all to a party at his house this afternoon. The families of the firm of Avery,[7] Titus and Weeks, together with all the Abeels, Dunscombs, and the devil knows who are to be there. I bowed without speaking to my part of the invitation, being determined not to accept it, as my costume is neither the most modern or the most splendid that is going now-a-days; but if I had ever so superb a suit, I should not have accepted the invitation.

I can tell you, Wixey has become quite a great man since his husband- and fathership. He is a great favorite with both the Universalists and Presbyterians, the first of whom his partners in business belong too, and the last, his partner for life. So the poor little fellow, whom you recollect Sally and you talked of *trimming* when you were here, is between two fires and, I suspect, gets pretty well *trimmed* by this time. He lives in great snuff–his wife is a terrible dasher.

I was invited also to a large party at Ann Augusta Thorn's yesterday, which, on account of my shabbyness, I was obliged to decline. I was plaguy mad, for this is the second invitation to a party of hers I have refused without being able to give any reason, and I like her very much. For a dasher I never saw a girl I liked better. I suppose you recollect her. She is cousin to Mrs. Fitch.

I suppose you will be surprised when I tell you I have never drank tea out of this house since you went to New London, but such is the fact. I was invited last Monday to a party at that little Mrs. Curtises who was married last fall, and Mrs. Fitch and Betsey went to the wedding and brought me a piece of cake which had been through the ring. Do you recollect? Mrs. Fitch has been to all the partys and I have staid home to amuse myself as well as I could; but perhaps my day will come before I die. The wheel of fortune goes round and the poor devils who have so long lain groaning under the weight of it may at length get to the summit themselves.

The Mitchells sent us tickets the other day to go to Columbia College and hear the students speak, as two of their sons are in the College and as a ticket was sent particularly to me; and, as the Fitches and Mrs. Northam would not take No for an answer, I was oblig'd to go in spite of my teeth, tho' I had rather been horse whipped. However, I did not repent going as there was one piece, on genius, spoken by a very young student that I think display'd fine tallents. I was distracted about it and so was Mrs. Fitch. I talked so much of it that she told me she would draw up a petition and send him for a copy of it, provided I would sign it. I told her I was always ready to sign anything she would write, but I found out she was quizzing, as it's all evaporated in smoke. John Mitchell spoke on emigration, and spoke very well, but as that is a subject I do not care a fiddle-stick about, I did not pay much attention to him. The chapel of the college was crowded to suffocation, the Lavertys, Tookers, Douglasses, and many other great affairs were there. I was very much pleased with what I heard and saw.

She also remembered her brother George and writes him at the time (**no. 83** of November 25th):

It is so long since letters have pass'd between us that I really don't know which wrote the last–but conclude it was you, by hearing from Mother's letter that you are surprised at my long silence. Be assured it is not neglect. I have often thought of writing but have so long labour'd under the greatest depression of spirits that I was unwilling to damp yours, if you had any, as much as my own were. I have pass'd through, during this last year, more than all I ever experienced before, which has rendered me incapable of attending to anything or any-body but what was ammediately connected with my troubles.

I suppose you have heard the deplorable situation of Aunt Mary, tho' I have not written it. I was with her during the whole course of her sickness, which was severe indeed. Still, through it all, she cherished hope, and as Doctor North was recommended by all her friends, she quit New York and a skillful physician who attended her, to have him examine her eyes. He look'd, and amediately pronounced to her the most awful of sentences: he told her she would become totaly blind. She felt it deeply, but felt also the truth of the assertion, as her sight daily grew more and more dim. From Mother's last letter I find his prediction is fulfil'd. She can see no more! She is with Mother and I expect will remain with her in future. Directly after she recover'd from her sickness and was able to go out with leading, I recieved news of the melancholy event which has lately taken place at home.[8] Unpleasant circumstances of almost every description have follow'd each other so closely for this last six months, it has made me unfit for almost everything, but more particularly for writing.

I have staid in New York for the purpose of getting business and have been, and am still, boarding with one of the finest families in the city. I suppose you recollect Mr. Fitch who was setting for his likeness at the time you was in New York. It is at his house I am staying. I don't think it will be possible for me to remain here much longer. This city is so overrun with artists that it is impossible I should ever get business enough, particularly as American painters recieve so little encouragement. Anything which comes from abroad is all the rage, while native talent is supposed to live and die in obscurity.

I have taken several likenesses which were thought excellent. Waldo was so pleased with one of them that he said he would take me under his patronage if I would recieve instruction from him. I was verry much obliged to him, of course, but as I did not get much business I have only call'd at his rooms twice. He appears to be a very amiable man and has ever encouraged and assisted Aunt Mary as much as was in his power, and was the instigator of her benefit, which I suppose the boys or the papers have informed you about before this. I should have written myself an account of the splendour of the exhibition, but for the reason I have before given.

I think New Orleans would be a good place for my business, and I have such an ardent desire to have work, I think I should be willing to run the risque of my life for it. I should like very much to have your opinion on the subject, as you have been there long enough to be a judge of the matter and I am quite a novice in an affair of so much importance. You put off your long-promised visit so, from year to year, I almost despair of its ever being paid. I realy wish you could make it convenient to come and see us soon, and perhaps you would have me for a companion back. I hope you will write soon and not destroy my castle-building, for, tho' the thought has struck me since I commenced this letter, I am not a little pleased with it. So be sure write soon and let me know what you think of the affair I have in agetation, as it is for you to decide on.

I conclude your business is good as I don't hear any complaints from you. I hope you have plenty, as it's of more importance than anything else in the world.

Adieu. . . .

A few weeks later, in a different, depressed mood, Eliza turned to her aunt twice in quick succession with her laments. Her appeals have not survived, only their answer (**no. 85**) at great length, a full-dress pastoral composition, in which is woven also a picture of a changing relation; for, as Mary's own career ended, she could no longer serve as a professional example to her niece, while her niece must henceforth be her surrogate in emulation:

The following lines appear before you, not for the beauty or sublimity of the poetry, but for the truth they contain. Mark it well.

'Virtue never loves to roam
But sweetly hides herself at home
And on her bank of native turf sits gently down.
But should tumultuous storms arise
And mingle earth, and seas, and skies,
Should the waves swell, and make her roll
Across the line or near the pole,
Still she's at peace, for well she knows
To steer the course that duty shows
And make her home where e'er she goes.
Bear her, ye seas, upon your breast,
And waft her, winds, from east to west.
On the soft air she cannot find
A couch so easy as her mind,
Nor breathe a climate half so kind.' Wats

Feeble and timid minds are but ill calculated to contend with the common evils of life. They are easily depressed and discouraged. Ease, peace and happiness is the exclusive priviledge of wisdom and virtue–wisdom, I say, for even virtue itself, separately considered (if that were possible), cannot afford it, let our circumstances be what they may, in whatever situation Providence may see fit to place us. Happiness may be found, not perfect felicity. There is no such thing on earth. I mean only happiness in the common acceptation of the word. In all circumstances and situations it may well be found. Tho' pride, obstinacy, ignorance and folly shut their eyes against it, wisdom may discover and virtue may enjoy it.

These, my dear Eliza, are not idle speculations. I ask not impossibilities nor require that of others that I cannot or will not do myself. This doctrine I not only preach but practice; and here I stand on incontestable evidence of its truth. Trials bring us to the test, and show what stuff we are made off. Pray, where is the merit of being easey, when there is nothing to disturb us? Any fool may be happy when happiness lies before him and there is nothing prevent it. A weak mind (Hannah Dawson, for instance) may enjoy it when circumstances are favorable, tho' the happiness that depends on circumstances must of necessity be transient. They change, it flits away, vanishes like a dream and is gone, perhaps, forever. But there are minds of another description that will not give it up for lost, minds that cannot be subdued, that 'scorns to be a pipe for Fortune's finger to sound what stop she pleases.' Her malice only serves to wake the dormant faculties, call forth the mental powers, stimulate to action, and nerve with energy the soul. Happiness is the object, and ardent the pursuit. They dig for it as for hidden treasure, they search for it everywhere, they grope for it amid the gloomy shades of darkness, they hunt for it in the depths of misery, in the regions of death, and tear it (as I may say) from the very jaws of despair.

Only shut your eyes, and for a moment think they are forever closed in darkness; consider how dreary are my prospects. Is your case desperate as mine? Surely not. Then take my advice, following my example, and be happy in spite of fate. Nothing is impossible. This is an essential article in my creed, it has enabled me to triumph over difficulties apparently insurmountable. We may do anything we try. You often laughed at the assertion, yet my faith in this doctrine has saved me from despondency, animated my exertions, and crowned them with success. Once determine, and the thing is done, the rest follows of course, patience and perseverence carries us through, be it what it may. It is true, we cannot control events, but we can practice self-control, we can subdue our feelings, restrain our passions, correct our habits, strengthen and fortify the mind by reasoning and reflection, and square ourselves to present circumstances, however untoward and adverse. This is wisdom, virtue, merit–and what is its reward? That calm enjoyment, which depends not upon the caprice of fortune, that sunshine of the soul, known only to well regulated minds. We have much to learn, and much to suffer in this world. 'Hero's in battle, pilots in a storm, good men in adversity,' command our admiration. Then why not follow their example, and be what we admire?

I am sorry, my dear Eliza, to find your spirits so depressed. I am not surprized at this. Full well I know what you must feel–the distress of mind your letter exhibits forcibly recalls what I have suffered on similar occasions: in debt, and out of business. These are indeed serious evils–evils which in my opinion rank high in the catalogue of human miseries. It is, however, a common calamity; but I hope your case is not so deplorable as you immagine. I trust business will again revive and your debts be all honourably discharged. Had you taken my advice and accepted Mrs. Hayden's warm and pressing invitation (to stay with her whenever you was at leisure, and be in town no longer than business or necessity required) you would not now have been so deeply involved. This, you will say, both pride and delicacy forbid. You cannot bear dependance. In that, you are perfectly right. But let us investigate the subject.

What is dependance? But of that by and by. We will begin with pride and delicacy. I am not disposed to quarrel with either of these qualities. The first is not only necessary but, under due restrictions, laudable. It answers many purposes. It is a substitute of dignity where dignity is wanting, and even for virtue itself, where occasions requires. But pride is an unruly passion, must be restrained, nor once allowed to pass the bounds prescribed by judgement. And, for the last, true delicacy is unquestionably requisite, particularly in the female character. But there is a squeamish delicacy extremely troublesome to ourselves, and others, which ought to be exploded. A certain young lady of my acquaintance abounds in this commodity. I say not who it is lest she reply, 'What makes you hate me so?'–as she has done before, when I pointed out her errors, while I ignorantly immagined it was a proof of my regard.

But to be serious, Eliza: Truth, tho' sometimes unpalatiable, is nevertheless wholesome; and now my hand is in, I must say you do wrong to neglect Mrs. Hayden in this manner. She deserves better things. I am both sorry and surprized to hear you have seen her but once since I left you. You have not wanted leisure, therefore your conduct is without excuse. However, it is not too late to repair your fault. I hope you are now at Captain Hayden's, and will remain there while you are out of business. I know Maria, and from the knowledge of her character, I can assure your welcome. Her sisters are seldom there, she is alone, and your company will be acceptable. When you are disposed to make yourself agreeable, you can amuse her, and besides this you may paint, sew, &c, and by a thousand little services and nameless attentions (which would give you pleasure to perform) render yourself useful, without lessening your dignity in the least. Usefulness is the foundation, aim, and end of society; far from degrading, it raises and exalts the character. Mutual benefits cancels obligation. Then where is dependance, that terrific phantom, that frightful bugbear, that so alarms your pride? A girl of your talents and abilities ought never to be discouraged. We need not fear dependance while we can be useful to others. Then why should you dispair? Keep up your spirits, be chearful and happy. Your trials are but light and transient. Prove your fortitude, bear them with firmness, and be thankful they are no worse.

Business is fluctuating. You know I have sometimes been without for two and three months together, and then again had more than I could do. You cannot expect constant employment in the first of your career, untill you are more known and established. In the meantime, be indefatigable in your exertions, go on, improve with all your might. If it is possible to borrow good paintings, study them well, copy their stile, and endeavour to exceed them. At least outdo yourself, if you cannot others. Let your last performance excell all that you have done before. Fear nothing, hope everything, be firm and resolute, and doubt not that patience and perseverence will ultimately insure you success.

But suppose the worst: should even these sanguine hopes and expectations fail, what then? Here you have a good home, and friends that will be happy to receive you. But you say you cannot bear to sneak off and leave your debts unpaid. Here again you are right. This objection however is easily obviated if Mr. Fitch can obtain from Thomas Dawson the money his mother owes me.[9] With this sum discharge your debts, and when you returns we will settle the matter between ourselves to our mutual satisfaction. Did your friends consult only their inclinations, without regard to your interest, we should advise and urge your immediate return. Your company would certainly be acceptable. You could read and write for me, you could assist your mother in her business, and, if you chose, teach painting in the Female Academy: three lessons a week, half a day, a salary of one hundred dollars a year, to be increased according to the number of your pupils.

On the other hand, in New York you have a better opertunity to improve yourself in this delightful art. There you can visit and converse with painters, examine their work, shew them yours, request them to point out your faults, attend to their observations and instructions. Here too you meet with works of the greatest Masters. This is an important consideration; and these advantages, justly estimated and duly improved, are incalculable. But to remain there, you must have some business, sufficient at least to defray necessary expenses. Your prospects are at present dreary. Soon their aspect may change and they appear bright and flattering. This, however, is not certain. We cannot lift the veil that hides futurity. Why should we wish it? One thing is sure: there is a Power whose will controls events, that watches over us, directs our steps, and orders all things right. Then dismiss your useless fears, that tormenting, that anxious solicitude that preys upon your mind and makes you wretched. Give it to the winds and be at rest. Whether you remain or return, time and the advice of your friends will decide–friends whose zeal to serve you has been so fully evinced, friends you so highly esteem, so worthy of your confidence, and on whose judgement you may with safety depend. Consult them upon this and upon all other occasions, take no step without their advice and approbation, attend implicitly to their counsel and instructions, and, if they have the goodness to reprove your faults, receive it with gratitude, as the greatest favour friendship can bestow. You may indeed esteem yourself fortunate, and cannot be too thankful to the Providence that has placed you with such valuable friends.

Give my best love to them all, and tell Mrs. Fitch I am sorry she can give no better reason for not answering my letter than the one you mention. But I am inclined to think there is a more powerful reason for her silence. The truth is, I shrewdly suspect this same little daughter of hers [Cornelia] has engross'd all her time and attention, to say nothing of her affection. The friend is lost in the mother. This is at least a probable conjecture, and so provoking that I feel disposed to assert my rights and priviledges and quarrel with the little saucy monopolist, notwithstanding the charming picture you have drawn. You say Mr. Fitch is of opinion it requires the talents of a poet to describe Cornelia, and you advise me to apply to her Mama for this favour. This I have done without success. I may as well therefore content myself with the piece your talents has produced which, to say the truth, is highly finished; and, making all due allowance for flattery, the vivid colouring of immagination and ornaments of fancy, I think sober judgement may venture to pronounce her a promising child.

I admire descriptive pictures, and, since you are so clever at the business, suppose you give us the unvarnish'd, unembelish'd portrait of Gustavus Vasa [Hayden], plain and simple, just as nature made him. Is he handsome and engaging? Is he troublesome? Does he cry much? In one word, is he as interesting a child as Emma? No, it cannot be. I don't expect, do not even wish it; but may he not bear some faint resemblance to 'her I laud so well'? Her frown, her smile, or some particular feature, surely a mother's watchful eye will trace it out, drawn it with her tears and smother it with kisses. Poor Maria! Hard was the fate that mark'd thee out for suffering. I have witness'd thy severe trials, the anguish of thy soul, thy patience, and tenderness, and I have shared thy sorrows. What a sad thing is a heart like hers in such a world as this. Still she is a wife, a mother, and still has much to suffer. God bless her and preserve her child. Smiling tho' her tears, in painful extasy, methinks I see her press him to her bosom, throbing with hopes and fears, with joy and apprehension. I see her watch his peaceful slumbers, each varying look and motion–hear the sigh of fond solicitude as she listens to his feeblest moan and every breath he draws.

'O ever beauteous, ever friendly, tell
Is it in heaven a crime to love too well?'

This pretty poetic question of Mr. Pope's is easily answered: 'Love not the world, nor the things that are in the world.' Maria sins indeed. She loves too well, she is guilty of idolatry, and, tho' severe, her punishment is just. 'Keep thy heart with all diligence, for out of it are the issues of life.'

But it is time to close. I have worn out my slate and pencil, and your mother's pen and patience, with this tremendous letter. Adieu. Write often, and more cheerfully, tell me all the news. Do you see or hear anything of the Dawsons, does Thomas Dawson take part with his mother or with those that were once her friends–for neutrality in this case is out of the question? I should like to know how he and Miss Mason agree at present, and whether he has sufficient skill in navagation to steer his vessel safely into port amid the rocks and quicksands that threatens the destruction of his hopes. Write all about it, write anything and everything but such a woebegone epistle as your last.

Adieu.

Just as the end of the chapter, another doleful ditty has arrived, which if set to music and well performed might answer for a funeral dirge. But where is Eliza? What has become of her whose once sprightly and animated letters so much amused and pleased me. For shame, girl! Be yourself again, rally your spirits, be chearful and lively as you used to be. I am surprized at you. Where is your fortitude? You have not resolution sufficient to effect your own purposes. In your other letter you said you was going to the Arsenal next week, to draw Hayden's picture. This I was pleased to hear and supposed you was there still. Instead of this, here you are, shut up, moping in the house (because you say you have not life nor spirits to go out), brooding over your own immaginary miseries, and painting watch-papers that you cannot sell for half their value. This is poor business indeed, and you may as well be here as there, for all the improvement you will gain by such wise management. You ought to walk–and every pleasant day. Call upon Waldo, Dickinson, and all the other artists, and see their works. It would be for your health, raise your spirits, and afford you both amusement and instruction. To instruct you is no longer in my power, and you have much to learn. My object in wishing you to remain there, is that you may obtain a more perfect knowledge of the true principles of colouring, painting and shading the face. This is best done by exercising your judgement, seeing and comparing the works of other painters, and varying your stile by copying those paintings most approved by amateurs; and here the *King* and *Queen of France* stands foremost on the list. These you have seen and studied. But this is not enough. These should always be before you when you paint a likeness. You may posess this (to you) inestimable treasure, by copying them exactly. It was my intention to have done this, but fate forbid. I began the *King*'s, I was deprived of sight, and there it lies unfinished. These pictures have taught me more than all the other paintings I ever saw. Posess'd of these, you need not tremble before the connisseur, nor dread the critic's lash.

Allow me therefore to advise and earnestly exhort you to lay aside your watch-papers (at least!) till those are sold you have on hand, and improve your stile by copying these invaluable paintings, now you are at leisure. Consult Mrs. Fitch. I think she will be of my opinion, that it is the best thing you can do at present, if you conclude to stay. In the first place, go out to Captain Hayden's, draw his picture as you proposed, and when that is finished, borrow those paintings once more and take an exact copy of one, or both of them if possible. If you do this, it will be the best winter's work you ever did, and in the spring (if not before) the probability is business will be more brisk. Then you will be ready for it, and have those pieces to show as your own handy-works, which will be sufficient to establish your reputation as an artist.

I don't expect this scheme will meet your approbation exactly. I know and am prepared for all you will have to say against it: the difficulty of procuring, the danger of keeping and the trouble of copying them. Formidable objections, to be sure! This is as judge, as Doctor Wright says. My dear Eliza, I know it can be done, and was I in your place, I know it would be done without delay. Why make mountains of molehills, if the object is desirable, why search the regions of immagination in quest of impediments and obstructions, to damp the ardour of pursuit. Why heap difficulty upon difficulty, obstacle upon obstacle, till the top reaches Heaven–then, astonished and agast at the mighty pile you have raised, sit down discouraged, and say, 'It is impossible,' because it is difficult to surmount them. Has my judgement deceived me? Where are those traits of genius, that warm enthusiasm and energy of soul I have sometimes fancied I could trace in your character, upon which I placed my hopes of your success? Is it only in words, in triffles, in things of no acccount, and is it wanting in essentials? Answer these questions, if you can, to your own satisfaction. Your happiness, my dear girl, is the first wish of my heart. Would to Heaven I could promote it, fain would I awaken in your soul those aspiring hopes, that spirit of enterprize and emulation, which the necessity of your case requires; but if this cannot be, I can only say, the sooner you return, the better, and relieve your mental sufferings, which I know must be severe.

God bless and prosper you.

Adieu.

Either Mary's exhortation worked or Eliza's resilience asserted itself, so that she could write back in her usual tone (**no. 86**). What had perhaps also helped to rouse her from her low spirits was her visit to a huge, splendid painting by a famous artist of the time, Rembrandt Peale (1778–1860). This was first displayed in New York at the time with an explanatory text, needed by the work's complex imagery. At first neglected, it received some needed publicity from the city's council in December, and then proved a great success. " 'The Court of Death' exhibited at the Academy of Fine Arts will be closed" in a week after a tremendous long run, so read an advertisement in the *Commercial Advertiser* so late as March 13th, adding that "evening illumination has become much more effective & interesting by an improved arrangement of the light." Then, the day after the announced closing, behold another advertisement: "In compliance with a wish very generally expressed, the exhibition will re-open on Wednesday night," in benefit of the city's deaf and dumb, with a lecture on the work by the superintendent of the Academy's pupils. America had discovered art as circus, art in overwhelming size and popular impact that moved about from town to town as a road show. The inspiration had been the late paintings of Benjamin West, devoted to religious narrative on a grand scale and seen in London over the second decade of the century by hundreds of thousands; but in a city of such a size there had been no need to take the paintings to the audience–let them come to it in West's own home, at a shilling a head. His pupils like Rembrandt Peale might well imitate their master in this profitable performance. Hence the notices in the New York papers to prepare the public, after a first showing in Philadelphia; and again at the time of its renewed exhibition it drew not only a generally favorable review from the editor of *The Minerva*–that literary miscellany in which Anna Fitch and other acquaintances published their verse–but also a poetic tribute from the artist's son-in-law.[10]

But, to return to Eliza, on the second day of January 1821 she writes:

> Ten thousand thanks for your letter. It was indeed an unlook'd-for New Year's treat. I was invited yesterday morning to accompany Mr. & Mrs. Fitch to the Academy of Fine Arts to see the *Court of Death*. I went, was delighted, and when I returned found your invaluable letter. I snatched it, flew up stairs, and was crying most merrily over it when I was summon'd to dinner. I hastily 'wiped my tears' but not so hastily my 'old men's fears,' for I was obliged to descend to the dining room with eyes and nose not much improved by the 'soaking' they had recieved. As soon as the meal was despatch'd I flew back to my room and read your letter over and over again, and I think I prefer it to the best sermon Mr. Mitchell ever preached.
>
> Would to heaven I could follow all your advice, but I cannot. I can give up painting watch-papers but I cannot ask Doctor Wright to borrow those pictures for me again, after all the difficulty he had in procuring them for me before. You don't know how much people think of granting favors. If you did, I am convinced you would not urge me to do anything so repugnant to my feelings. Recollect, those paintings are matchless and that they were somewhat the worse for the wearing they recieved while in our possession–also, that he did not own them himself and consequently lent them with greater reluctance. I would give an estate, if I had it to spare, to own them, but as that is impossible I may as well resign them without a sigh, particularly as Mrs. Fitch don't think it would be possible to procure them, and to request them and be refused is what I cannot bear the idea of. This I suppose you will call squeamishness or skittishness. Be it so. It is something of which I cannot divest myself. Don't think I make no effort to conquer my squeamishness, as you are pleased to call it, for I am continualy doing it; but in the present instance I think it would be wrong, as it would not be doing as I should like to be 'done unto.' I never should be willing to lend to strangers such incompareable paintings, and I am more unwilling to ask the loan of them.

This point settled, we will now go back to the *Court of Death*, from which we have travel'd without intending it, as a description of it was what I intended to have commenced my letter with. A description, did I say? No, that is impossible. I never could convey to your imagination an idea of the sublimity of it. But I will enclose the Catalogue I brought home for your amusement. It is of course a much more able description than could be expected to flow from my pen, yet notwithstanding, we cannot resist the inclination we feel to make a few comments on the subject.

In the first place, imagination cannot concieve of anything more exquisitely beautiful than the face and form of Pleasure. If she has a fault it is the chastity that breathes through every feature. I at first thought if it had a defect, that was it; but when I look'd and 'look'd again' and thought more deeply on the subject, I found it was the master stroke of the artist. To attract virtueous hearts she must not wear the semblance of vice, and to the eyes of the beholder always appears in false colours. Nothing can be more chastely beautiful than the attitude in which she is placed. There is not the least shadow of indelicacy in any one look or action, which, considering the subject, I think is something remarkable, as there never was a wider field for the display of impurity if the artist had been disposed to represent her in her true colours. But he is a man after my own heart. I don't think Hinkly[11] could have excell'd him in this respect. As she is the most prominent figure in the piece, the light strikes with most force on her face, which I wish to heaven I could sketch upon this sheet; but although it can be concieved it cannot be described. It is perfectly present to my imagination but not to my pen: her hair is the brightest auburn you can imagin, her eyebrows arch just enough, and the colour and expression of her eyes are inimitable. Her nose is exquisitely turn'd, and her mouth is perfect; her form is in profile, her face in front, and rather elevated than otherwise. Her right arm is raised in the act of pouring incense into a vase or something prepared to recieve it, and the shadeing of the arm is beyond anything I ever saw. It is most heavenly! But why should I go on? I cannot paint like Peale. I feel I cannot describe the surpassing loveliness of Pleasure, and I will leave her without making another attempt. We have been too long strangers to each other for me to do her justice.

The next most prominent feature in the piece is 'Virtue.' If I had not seen 'Pleasure' I should have pronounced her unequalled, but of course she was far eclipsed. Her eyes of 'heavenly blue' are raised to heaven, she is supporting the figure of green old age. Nothing can be more venerable than the figure she supports—the bald head, the snow-white locks that are here and there scattered about it, and the heavenly peace that appears to dwell within. Her left arm which supports the stooping form of age is finely turned and, tho' not in such strong relief as that of 'Pleasure,' yet the light which strikes from the torch of 'Desolation' full upon it gives a life and soul to the flesh that I never saw equall'd. The dignified countenance of 'Old Age,' contrasted with the seraphic expression of hers, is fine indeed.

But I must leave the bright parts of the picture (tho' ever so unwillingly) for the dark, with which I must be brief, for I have dwelt longer on it already than I intended and am freezing to death into the bargain. Next comes the Warriour. Nothing can be more fierce and terrible, more heart-appalling, than his countenance as he tramples his victim beneath him. Not a muscle of his ruthless face is relax'd at the woeful sight. Desolation rushes on before him with a torch which, striking on the helmet, the shield of Medusa, the blood stain'd sword, and the ferocious countenance of the destroyer, has a fine effect. Close at his heels follows 'Want.' Nothing in existence can be more wretched. Her meager fingers and the squalid misery that speaks in ever part of her is done to the life. 'Dread' is shrinking behind 'Want.' On the left lie the victims of 'Pleasure.' The remains of beauty were very conspicuous in the countenances of 'Fever' and 'Consumption,' but in none other, and the poverty, the forlornness of their situation compell'd the eye to turn with disgust from 'that part of the picture.'

I could go on till the sun set 'did the limits of our opportunity permit,' but I have so much else to say, it will not do. To make a long story short, I think we ne'er shall see its like again. We may. It's not impossible, for the artist has promised to produce more pictures if he recieves sufficient encouragement for this; but I think it's doubtful. The common council have interested themselves about it at last and his prospect is more smiling, but I don't know how it will terminate. I hope to heaven such tallents as his will be encouraged, particularly as he is a native artist and brother of the brush.

As we were looking at the picture he enter'd. The name of Rembrandt Peale was instantly buzzed round the hall and several of our most distinguished characters instantly surrounded him, I suppose to pay him the compliments of the season or, what is much more, the compliments due to his painting. As soon as I could discover 'an opening in the thicket,' I looked with all my might to see if I could discover those traits of genius and talents in the countenance of the artist which were so conspicuous in every stroke of his pencil; but I found his genius was too mighty for the eye of the vulgar. Except in a very penetrating blue eye, there was no appearance of it. He was quite plain. I must confess I was somewhat disappointed, as I should suppose such tallents would show themselves in every look and action; for he is indeed a great man. But I suppose if they had he would be too perfect. So I will let the subject rest.

Since this was written, Mr. & Mrs. Mitchell drank tea with us, and Mr. Mitchell said that at the Academy the other day he had an hour's conversation with Peale, who told him that if he recieved sufficient encouragement for this picture he should attempt the painting of Christ; and if he does not fail there (said your Speaker) he will do more than was ever done before. But I must leave the whole of it, tho' I have much more to say, for other subjects.

With respect to my mind, I am sorry you do not like the stuff it's made of. I am sensible the materials of which it is composed are not of the most masculine kind. If they were, I would certainly have on breeches before the sun set, as I think that philosophers in petticoats are rather out of character, and you know I am at present between two ('saving your presence'). Fortune or whatever you may please to call it seems, I think, desirous to spread a strengthening plaster over my 'brain pan,' by her placing me where she has, to repair, I suppose, the work of Nature, which she saw was so miserably deficient in Sampsonian ingredients. I pray that I may at length attain the wisdom of Solomon and the strength of Sampson, as I shall never please those under whose petticoats I flourish until I have. In the mean time let me entreat you not to withhold your letters, for if you do I can tell you, you will never add another petticoated Socrates to the list which are flourishing about the period of the Christian era–which, to the rising generation, would be loss indeed. Seriously, tho', I entreat you not to discontinue your letters that you know are so highly prized by both Mrs. Fitch and myself; for, tho' I don't send a regular answer to the weighty arguments you make use of, be assured I swallow them all and sense the truth and propriety of them as deeply as you could wish.

If you wish to know what has given me life and soul to write this letter, I can tell you what will, perhaps, surprise you as much as it did me. Mrs. Hayden call'd here the last week in the old year to see us and enquired about you. Mrs. Fitch then handed her the letter which she recieved from you so long ago and which, never having seen Mrs. Hayden since, had never shown it to her, of course. Before she read it, she said, 'Eliza, when are you going to New London?' As that is of all questions the most puzzeling about this time, I did not answer very readily. I hesitated some time and then said I did not know. 'Not know!' she repeated, 'Don't you think you will go in the spring?' 'I should be very much pleased too,' I replied, 'but all things are uncertain.' 'I will tell you why I ask,' she then said. 'It is my intention to visit New London in the spring to see your aunt, and I wish you to go along if you will.' At first I thought she was jesting and told her so, but when she repeated it in her most impressive manner it left me no longer any room to doubt. I never was so struck in my life, and instantly demanded how long her resolution had been formed. She said she was setting with Hayden the other evening after tea with her eyes fix'd on the fire and her thoughts on you, when Hayden (slapping her on the shoulder) requested she would tell him what she was so busily thinking of. 'I was thinking,' she said, 'how much I would give to see Miss Way. I don't know anybody in existence I should be so glad to see.' 'Don't you,' said he, 'then my dear "Molly," you certainly shall see her.' 'Shall I,' says Maria, 'why, will you go to New London with me?' 'No,' he said, 'you know I cannot leave my post; but you may go without me.' 'How?' said Maria. 'Why, Eliza Champlain will certainly wish to see her Mamma by spring and will accompany you with a great deal of pleasure, I have no doubt, and she is quite as good a beau as I should be. In the mean time I will keep batchelors' hall till you return.' 'Now, Hayden, are you serious?' said Maria. 'I never was more so, my dear Molly. Nothing but death need prevent your going.' 'Then be assured I shall hold you to your word,' said Maria. 'To be sure,' said he. 'So now, my dear Molly, be easy.'

This is the sum and substance of their discourse, and whether you wish it or not, you will probably see us both in the spring. No doubt it will be agreeable all round. . . . In the mean-time I shall endeavour to make myself easy in the few remaining months of winter here. I expect soon to take Hayden's picture. At present I am drawing Mrs. Fitches. As for Gustavus Vasa, I have not much to say of him, more than that he is a fine boy. He has neither Emma's smiley frown nor temper. He weighs a thousand pounds moderately speaking. He is a great laugher and sometimes you can catch a little of his mother's expression about his eyes. But in general his face is very unlike either father or mother, and their is not a trace of Emma. He has a sweet disposition, and Maria appears to be almost happy. . . .

As for the Dawsons, I never see any of the female part of the family except at church, which they constantly attend with the greatest devotion, and are at present in deep mourning for their brother and uncle Bacon. Thomas (strange as it may seem) remains neutral after all our conjectures respecting him. He has call'd here several times and spent one or two evenings besides. He has been out to the Arsanal to settle his business with Hayden, which I believe is done not much to Hayden's satisfaction, tho' I don't know the particulars. He has call'd on all his mother's mortal enemy's except the Sanfords who have given him his cue by meeting him in the street, where he recieved turn'd-up noses instead of a return to his bow–which I believe did not set well enough on his stomach to induce him to call there. He won't hear a word on neither side of the question, as he thinks it's a piece of folly all round and makes a point of silencing whoever attempts to speak of it. Mr. Fitch applied to him as soon as was possible for your 'Wrent' but he had not a cent to give, as his mother demanded all and ten thousand times more than all, and she was perfectly thunderstruck that you should expect such a thing. What a hussy! But Thomas has promised you shall have it when he returns from his next voyage, so that jig's up that you proposed. I think it will be a pretty difficult matter to get a cent from him while his mother holds the reins. Poor Thomas, I pity him.

Cornelia has become quite familiar with the title of 'Aunt Mary.' She talks much of you and her innocent prattle I am sure would amuse you could you hear it. She is such a sensible little hussy, I wish you could hear her talk. I just now asked her what I should say to Aunt Mary, as I was writing to her. She says, tell her Cornelia Northam Fitch wants to see her very much, and tell her how many papas and mammas I have and how many brothers and sisters and how many new clothes I have and a thousand other things which I cannot remember. Her picture has gone to her Mamma Shearman together with four watch-papers to four young ladies of Mrs. Fitches acquaintance. As Perry is their idol, I painted for one a monument hung with willow, the initials of his name on the monument, and a scroll resting carelessly against it on which was written his letter, 'We have met the enemy and they are ours,' implements of war in the background, and the whole encircled with laurel. For another I painted 'Silent Eloquence' with a gilt wreath; and the last and I think the most beautiful was my sleeping Cupid. It was so handsome on bark that I made a copy of it and sent two alike. We have not heard from Newport since they went but are hourly expecting letters.

Adieu

The hurt expressed by Mary (**no. 85**) at not hearing from Anna was anticipated by her friend, who matches it (**87**, of January 3rd) with her own hurt that Mary prefers another child to hers; but amends enough are made by the end of the letter. The large part played by the church in their relations appears here not only in the comforting thoughts that Anna applies to Mary's situation but in gossip, here omitted, about members of the congregation: two young people who met there are married, another deceased, and so forth.

My very dear friend,

I fear long ere this I have been accused of ingratitude, neglect, & everything that is bad, but I depend much on the dislike you have always manifested to judging by appearances, and making up too hasty an opinion. I assure you there have been few days (I doubt if any) in which you did not occupy a portion, & often a large portion, of my thoughts; and as often, for some time past, has my conscience reproved my seeming neglect. But I really think you must forgive me, however unworthy I may appear.

Your letter gave me inexpressible pleasure, for I hardly expected to receive your ideas clothed in your own words.

I trust you still continue to rest on the Rock of Ages. Surely we have much need for such a foundation on which to repose securely in this changing scene, when 'all is shadows,' and for the blessed assurance that 'all beyond is substance.' The implicit belief of this, & the knowledge that the great Governor of the World will do right, is the only consolation which can ameliorate the sorrows of a sad-sick soul; and this is enough.

Though I cannot tell you how much I sympathize in your afflictions, your situation does not appear to me so deserving of pity as many, whose sufferings are far less; for, tho' you suffer, you have a divine antidote. You know that ere long all that now causes our misery shall be removed forever and that more than the mind of man can conceive shall be enjoyed.

Think for an instant how deplorable would be your situation if mental as well as natural darkness surrounded you & enveloped the grave in an impenetrable gloom–if, while enduring what you considered the greatest misfortune in this world, you anticipated still greater in the world to come. These advantages I would hold up to you that you might continue to look beyond the things of time & sense, at the blessings you possess as well as those of which you are deprived. Differing a little from the words of scripture, I would say, 'though darkness lasteth for a night, light cometh in the morning'–that morning which ushers in eternity.

Eliza's letters have doubtless gratified your curiosity respecting our little favourite. The information you have received in this way is probably much more correct than any you would receive from me, for partiality, you know, is apt to throw a veil over every defect & magnify every virtue. You say Emma is your model. I assure you there is no similarity whatever between her & my little darling. She can neither boast of Emma's temper or looks, but a disposition & face to me inexpressibly better & handsomer. And was there not a large share of prejudice enlisted, I am sure you would think so too, did you know. But Cornelia would stand a poor chance, after the declaration, that though Gustavus were an angel of light, you could never love him as you have loved his sister. . . .

Indeed, my friend, you are much mistaken: maternal affection has not extinguished the feelings of friendship I have long experienced for you. In my sleeping as well as waking moments my absent friend is oft remembered. Once in the visions of the night I beheld you, & awoke, with the idea of fainting in your arms at the astonishment & pleasure your unexpected appearance produced.

I assure you, Eliza's letter caused me to break the last commandment, though it produced pain as well as pleasure. Had my feelings at reading some part of it been expressed, they would have broken forth somewhat in this way. So her warm hearted, generous Maria is the only true friend who feels interested for Eliza's welfare, & therefore Eliza should seek a refuge in her generosity from those uninterested creditors with whom she now stays. Pardon those perhaps unreasonable remarks, but the part to which I allude breathes such an air of frigidity that I think the feelings which gave birth to them justifiable. If I do not much mistake, neither Eliza nor you have a friend on earth who feels more warmly interested for your happiness, although the manner of expressing those feelings gracefully is denied. As to Eliza's debts, I think it probable she has multiplied them, after her usual manner. She has employed a considerable part of her time in working for me, & has now begun a likeness of Mr. Fitch. As she had no other business, I was pleased that she was thus employed, to relieve her mind from the deadly weight of dependance. . . .

You know not how entirely my life is changed since I first knew you. Then, I was so constantly alone that I had sufficient leisure to attend to any thing I chose; but now a mother & child occupy that portion of my time which was formerly devoted to reading & writing. You will perhaps be surprised to hear that I have neither read one book nor made one visit since I saw you; indeed, I have never finished the play which I began on board the packet. I assure you I am frightened at times to think what a heathenish life I lead; but hope points to the time when my dear child will be able to renew those pleasures which I once experienced from books, when her innocent prattle, which now amuses, will be exchanged for solid conversation, which shall instruct as well as amuse. This, you will say, is looking forward to a very distant period. It is indeed–for long before those hopes can be realized, she and I may both be far beyond the reach of earthly joys. But should even this occur, I 'know that we have a building not made with hands, eternal in the heavens.' Though these earthly expectations may prove fallacious, they serve to gild the present hour, & must therefore continue to be cherished. . . .

You know to 'err is human, to forgive divine.' Therefore I hope as soon as you receive this, you will sit down & write to me sufficient to fill the largest sheet of paper that can be procured. . . .

Adieu, my very dear & much respected friend.

Anna J. H. Fitch

The Dawsons are such a hateful subject that I have left Eliza to discuss it.

Next, at mid-month, Eliza wrote her mother a particularly inconsequential letter (**no. 88**), confessing at the outset, "I had emptied my budget" in her previous one (so much here may be omitted):

> . . . Your poetry has produced something like a hearty laugh, which is more than I can say of anything else for many a long and tedious day and night. I quite enjoy'd it and instantly set down to reply in verse; but I found I required so many notes to my poem (as I so seldom court the Muses) that I gave it up at once. I am convinced I never was born a poet, nor can all the digging in creation ever produce poetry when that is the case–tho' it may rhymes. . . .
>
> By the by, I would like to know what Aunt Mary thinks is best to be done with her goods. I believe that some of them are spoiling, as they are in a grocery story where I suppose the dampness penetrates the closest crevice. I have never hinted at it before because I knew money was necessary on such occasions and from your letter concluded you had not much to spare; but I often feel uneasey about them, and the other day Mrs. Fitch mention'd them to me. I waved the subject, as I did not like to give what I suppose is your reasons for not sending for them: a carman must be paid, and I have every reason to suppose the person in whose store they are deposited will expect some remuneration for his trouble. . . .
>
> I should not have shown your letter to Mrs. Fitch if so many enquiries had not been made about you, but I fancied she would not like it should I only tell her what I had to say; so I gave her the letter to read. The next night in a dream you presented yourself and apparently in no very pleasant frame of mind said to me, 'Eliza, how *could* you show that letter to Mrs. Fitch? I did not expect such a thing of you.' I have no very great faith in dreams but I must confess I have thought since you did *not* wish it shown. If so, let me know, and I will endeavour not to repeat the offence in the future. . . .
>
> Mrs. Fitches expected letters from Newport arrived night before last. They contain many elegant compliments on my painting and (to use her own words) 'a mother's blessing for the semblance of a fondly beloved child,' and an assurance that she felt deeply interested for my future welfare. She is a most elegant writer on all subjects, and Mr. Fitch thinks her letters ought to be published by all means. I forgot to tell you, after I finished the likeness of Cornelia I painted a small stool under her feet to represent a painted velvet cricket. The roses on the cricket were the handsomest I ever painted. . . .
>
> Send back the enclosed Catalogue [of Peale's great painting], if you please. I wish to preserve it.

Meanwhile (still in January of 1821) there remained some patching up to be done between those two strong-minded women and dear friends Mary and Anna, a situation to which Mary addressed herself in her characteristic style. Apparently a lot of her very long letter was suppressed in later years.[12] What remains begins in mid-sentence, or at least mid-subject:

–not that the creature [Eliza] is altogeather disagreeable, for there are times when she is tolerable good company and even quite amusing. But then, in such a caracter, one meets with so many ups and downs, ins and outs, odd points and sharp corners, it hardly can be call'd plain sailing. Yet after all, to say the truth, we must allow she has many good qualities. Among these, I will venture to point out one or two in which I think she excells. No one that knows her I believe will pretend to deney that laughing is an accomplishment in which she stands unequall'd, and, notwithstanding her modesty, your discernment has perhaps discovered she can cry as heartily and upon as triffling occasions. But I am glad she has recovered her spirits, and I hope and trust the precepts and examples of those she so much esteems and admires will not be lost, while she is conscious there is room for improvement.

And this leads our attention to a certain passage contained in your letter upon which we now beg leave to offer a few brief comments. This passage demands our serious consideration. It is as follows. You say my letter to Eliza caused you to break the last commandment–that it produced pain as well as pleasure and that the air of frigidity it breathed justified in your opinion some (allow me to say) eroneous conclusions. To all these accusations I plead *Not Guilty*. I had rather suffer myself than give pain to others, especially to those I love, and therefore must have express'd my feelings and sentiments in a very uninteligible manner; but surely Eliza understood me, and ought to have explain'd my meaning. I have so often seen and felt the sad effects of judging by appearance, that it has taught me a lesson I never can forget. And every day's experience serves but to convince me how nesessary it is that we should learn to suspend our judgement–that we cannot be too cautious nor use too much deliberation in forming an opinion in any case that will admit of the least doubt or uncertainty. There are so many things to be taken into consideration, that requires time to investigate and examine–so many circumstances, some perhaps unknown to us and others known imperfectly–that to decide hastily or even (we had allmost said, to decide at all) would be rash or arrogant. In fact hasty decisions ought allways to be rejected as the prime source of error, the cause of all the blunders of life, the foundation of jealousies, mistakes, and misunderstandings, the bane of love and friendship.

But to the point. That letter that gave you pain was written to *Eliza*. I knew *she* would understand it, and that was enough. Not that I have the least objection–but, had I thought you would have seen it, I should have been more explicit. It was in answer to one I had rec'd from her, fill'd with direful forebodings, dismal apprehensions, and bitter lamentations least she should never be able to discharge the obligations she owed your goodness–obligations that were dayly increasing. And in her earnest and distressingly emphatic manner she described her mental sufferings and beg'd I would advise her what to do. This, as far as I can recollect, is the sum and substance of the letter. . . .

Thus honourably aquitted by the Supreme Court of Conscience, there is nothing more to fear; and now Mount Sinia's broken law appears before us and claims our due regard–the tenth commandment, namely, 'Thou shalt not covet,' &c. There perhaps a note of explanation would not have been amiss, but it was omited. In order to understand the subject more fully, we must consider it in connexion with the context, where we find an illusion to Maria, in which was included a backhanded compliment on your own merit, as well as to my taste and discernment–a pill that vanity is not much inclined to swallow. Of all my friends and aquaintance, I think you ought to be the last, and have the least temptation, to covet your neighbour's goods. Was I disposed to envy, *you* and not Maria would be the object. 'Tis true that I admire and love Maria, but never envied her. I mean I never wish'd to look or act or think or feel like her. No, not for the world. You have advantages and enjoyments she knows nothing of. And she has sufferings of which you have no conceptions. She has not your religion nor your philosophy to support her under them, but she has patience, the gift of nature (for she is nature's child)–patience to endure without a murmur, to hide beneath a smile the anguish of a wounded heart least it should give pain to others. Our destiny must be accomplish'ed!

How often when speaking of you to my friends have they ask'd, 'Which do you love the best, Mrs. Fitch or Maria?' My answer is, 'I don't know.' I put the same question to my own heart and have not been able to decide. Eliza says I love Maria best, but if I do, 'tis more than I know myself. That I loved her *first* is certain, and four years ago should have said I loved her best, for I did not know you then–though I had seen you often. But now pity [for the death of her first-born Emma] must be thrown into the scales, to turn the balance in her favour.

Were we at liberty to choose our travelling companions through life's thorney vale, we might forget that higher joys await us, perhaps still wish to linger here, and dread our journey's end. 'Tis better so: to know we meet at last is happiness enough. Tho' intervening obstacles devide us here, tho' those we love are lost to us on earth, we know we have a home, a Father's House, where we shall find them all. In that bright mansion of felicity we shall rejoice togeather, and dread no more the pangs of seperation. This world is lost to me. I only live while I anticipate that blissful period, for nothing else is worth the name of life.

Here perhaps it would be proper to close this volume; but my sister is too busily engaged to write for me, and so I scribble on till she is more at leisure. She has had no time to copy this, or you would have rec'd it long before. . . .

And here I stop again to pay a grateful tribute to the unexampled patience of my sister, who, tho' she sees the task that lies before her, still urges me to write, because she thinks it will amuse me. If self-preservation is the first law of nature, in extreme cases magnanimity may be laid aside, and I shall only say I find it nesessary to take advantage of her goodness–and yours also–notwithstanding you inform me your time is so devoted to family duties, you have not read a book since we parted.

Is it possible! I recollect I was considering this part of your letter [**no. 87**] when, by a torrent of ideas, I was hurried away to other subjects; for I was only just going to express my sympathy, and how much I felt for you, in spite of the malice of misery. 'I have no time to read' is a common excuse and passes well enough with common folks. But trace it to its source, and you will find that rather taste than time is wanting;

for you may observe such people have time to waste in frivolous ammusements. A taste for allmost any thing may be acquired, but whether it can long exist in unfavourable circumstances or stand its ground against our natural propensities, I have my doubts. Of these we cannot divest ourselves. They are permanand and durable, and the taste which nature has bestowed upon us may, like the diamond in the quarry, appear rude and unpolish'd, or may be improved and refined; but it cannot be lost or eradicated. It is imperious and demands gratification; and for this, time must and will be found. Strict oeconomy will be observed, even the very shreds and pareings of that most precious talent will be saved to gratify the darling propensity, till by undue indulgence it becomes a passion, and then we stick at nothing. I speak from sad experience. I loved it better far than sleep or food. Time must be had to read, at any rate; and when I could not gain it honestly, made no scruple to steal that which should have been devoted to other purposes. But you–you that can say to your inclinations, 'Thus far shalt thou be indulged, and no further'– why should I be suprized (I who know and admire the propriety and consistency of your carracter) that you should do exactly as you ought. I have often queried with myself whether you was born a philosopher or whether you have acquired that self-controul, that command over your feelings, which I have allways considered so desirable–that sets my own faults and absurdities in the most glareing point of view, and which, as I think it possible to be acquired, I blush to own I have not yet attained. But to tell the truth, there is a certain virtue call'd self-denial. . . .

To this of January from Mary, Anna made some prompt answer; but it is lost. Then Mary replied in February 1821 (**no. 91**). The end is lost; the beginning, as usual abrupt and without salutation:

'One cordial drop, Heaven in our cup has thrown
To make the nauseous draught of life go down'

Friendship, that Heaven-descended drop, renders life with all its miseries supportable, sweetens and gilds the bitter pill, to cheat poor mortals of the peaceful grave. This truth I felt in its full force, when I rec'd your letter. I feel it still. Its chearing influence revives my drooping spirit. The impatient captive longs to drop the galling chain, to quit this dungeon of mortality, and spring to life, to light, and liberty–but longs in vain!–restless and sick with hope delay'd.

The dye is cast. The fatal blow is given–the mortal wound that death alone can heal. Yet the pain may be assuaged or suspended, and perhaps even for a time forgotten. Such is the power of friendship and such the balm that sympathy bestows.

Next to receiving a letter from the friend I loved, to answer it was once my greatest dearest pleasure. Once, did I say? It is still more dear than ever–one of the few, the precious few, that have escaped the general wreck. But it is now a painful pleasure, and when I take my slate and pencil (fool that I am) my tears flow faster than my words; for it is one among the many counsellors 'that feelingly persuade me what I am.' So the wretch that fears to die when he views the deep damp vault, the coffin and the shroud, feels the chill of death strike cold upon his heart.

The strict moralist may condemn me when I say I can excuse a fault but I dispise a weakness. I hold it in contempt while I indulge it, and will conceal till I can conquer it. To cheat the vulgar and elude thier pity, I play the fool and the philosopher by turns, for 'all the world's a stage;' and tho' I am no very graceful actress, I pass among the crowd–I cannot say, without applause or censure. Some compliment my wisdom for making the best of my misfortune, and some thier own sagacity, in foreseeing time would reconcile me to my forlorn condition. Others consider my spiritual blindness far more deplorable. We are surrounded with Methodists. I have some contention with those good people, as well as those of other denominations; but I stand my ground pretty well. 'Tis easier to silence than convince. I have been once to church, and once to Presbyterian meeting, and that is all. I am indeed a spoil'd child. Well may Mrs. Avery pity me [for being now denied the hearing of Mr. Mitchell's sermons], for in this respect I am truely an object of compassion.

Need I say, Mr. Mitchell's call [when on a visit to New London] was highly gratifying, tho' but a momentary pleasure. How much we did regret his time was limited. 'Twas too bad–one solitary sermon, but such a sermon as has not been heard in this place since Mr. Murray preached here; and be assured it has rec'd due applause; for there are people of taste and candor in all denominations. The admiration of those that heard, and the regret of those that did not hear for want of timely notice, together with that spirit of acrimony that vents itself in the revilings of opposition, made great noise, and furnished a subject for conversation in all companies for many weeks, which is not forgotten even unto this day.

We obtained from your Speaker more than half a promise that he would visit us next summer. May we hope your exertions will not be wanting to forward the business–that you will employ your interest to favour and support the charitable purpose. I am aware of your objections, and allow it requires a degree of self-denial few are disposed to practice. But is it presuming too much upon your goodness to suppose you capable of such a sacrifice? Oh! my friend, how does your cup overflow with blessings. Religion in her brightest form has strewn your path with roses. The liberal hand of Heaven prevents your very wishes. What more could you desire? Were you like me, deprived of the happiness you now enjoy, you would justly estimate its value. Where will you find a church so highly favour'd? Such doctrine, and such a preacher? Where will you find another Mitchell? But while you 'feed in green pastures, and by still waters,' remember there are other 'sheep that are not of this fold.' While you indulge in the bounty of Providence, consider the poor, and such as are ready to perish. 'We ask but the crumbs that falls from the rich man's table.' Charity cannot refuse. Therefore, my dear friend, you are requested to remain a few moments after the congregation are dismiss'd, and use your influence with the Committee in our behalf. So may Heaven forever crown your wishes and all your undertakings with success.

'Tis some time since I wrote–careless and negligent, too indolent even to amuse myself, like the unprofitable servant who posess'd but one talent. I feel more disposed to hide it in the earth than to employ it to advantage. Thus from him that hath not is taken even the inclination to make the best of that which he hath. An idle useless thing–'Why cumbereth it the ground?' This is the question. Ah! who can answer it? Time was, felicity's gay visions danced before me, and this deceitful world once wore the mask of bliss. Smiling hope brightened the opening prospect, and all around seemed paradise. Yet I was not deceived, even then. I knew it was a world of trouble and could not suppose I was exempted from the common lot. But with all my future trials and the tribulations that awaited me, I promised myself a liberal share of consolation, and many pleasures in the words of the poet,

'Haply, my path may lie through barren vales
   Where nigard fortune every boon denies.
E'en there, shall fancy scent the ambient gales
   And scatter flowrets of a thousand dyes.'

My pen, my pencil, and my books–these were pleasures of which fortune never could deprive me, and posessing these, I might despise her malice and defy her frowns–pleasures that time would improve and chance could not destroy. Vain boaster! Where are they now? And what is thier amount? Like the miser that perished for want amid his hoards of treasure, I starved in the midst of plenty. Devines, historians, poets, and philosophers lie in piles around me. Those once dear companions of my leisure hours that have so often charmed my cares away and banish'd for a time both pain and sorrow, useless now they lie, silent, and deaf to my complaint.

And why do I complain? My friends are kind and attentive, I have every comfort my situation will admit, every gratification and amusement they can devise or I enjoy, except reading, and that is more to me than all the rest. But one has weak eyes, another has no strength, a third has no leisure. In short, one and all would rather talk than read. And besides, I am so unreasonable, not content with hearing a passage or two now and then, if they don't make a business of it and read for me as I would for myself, I am never satisfied. So, the case being fairly stated (you see), my friends have more reason to complain of me than I of them.

I am ashamed of my letter. Eliza may return the compliment I paid hers, and call this a *doleful ditty*. 'Tis indeed the reverse of what it should be, but I cannot help it. Here again, the doctrine of destiny stares me in the face. I mean, it is the reverse of what I intended it should be; but I cannot help it. Whenever I blame any one or find fault with any thing, my conscience reproaches me with speaking unadvisedly, while at the same time I am consoled with the idea that it is right I should do so. And truely there are things in this wide world of wonders which even the Wise Men of the East, with all the philosophy they have scraped together since the flood, cannot account for (to my satisfaction) upon any other principles. If I am a free agent, why is it I cannot do as I please? Why is it I can no more controul the operations of my mind than I can the elements? Why can I not change my opinion when I choose or alter in any way my mode of thinking? And why, when I would do good, is evil present with me? Consider these things and for a while suspend my condemnation, excuse my errors, and forgive my faults.

There is a time for all things, a set time for every purpose under Heaven. So said the wise man, or to that effect. When I rec'd your letter, it was my intention to answer it immediately as you requested. The time was not arrived and my designs proved ineffectual. Moreover, it was my desire and intention to be very agreeable and amusing, to offer some return for the pleasure your letter afforded me. Fancy had wove her flowery wreath. But when I took the slate, thier colours faded, misfortune claimed it for her own. She snatched the pencil and pour'd forth her complaint–fruitless and unavailing.

But although by some strange fatality your letter still remains unanswered–tho' I have not yet acknowledged my approbation of your sentiments and the justice of your observations–I have felt thier force. Yes, my dear friend, I do indeed posess this devine antidote and feel its power and efficasy. That faith we rejoice in with joy unspeakable, that hope full of immortality like the angel of mercy, smiles away my sorrows, promises thier thier final termination, my release from this house of bondage, this clay-built tenement, the prison of the soul, and in that blest assurance gives me all my boundless wishes can require–eternity! Sublime exalted pleasure, joys unutterable, 'A far more [? . . . ?] exceeding an eternal weight of glory.' Transcendant goodness! When we contemplate our high destiny, thought swells to rapture and earthly consideration dwindles to insignificance.

Sally and I have rec'd letters from Eliza, full of fun and nonsense and are very entertaining. I am glad to find she is herself again. Tell her to write on, her letters are in high demand and much approved, if laughing is a mark of approbation. Even Aunt Hannah could not refrain, tho' at the same time she groaned in spirit, and said Oh! *Liza*, *Liza*, when will that girl have common sense? I was in hopes (she continued) the precepts and examles of Mrs. Northam and Mrs. Fitch would have learned. Here a deep sigh stop'd her utterance, when, recovering herself, many wise observations followed, which, as Eliza has often heard them all before and doubtless will again when she returns, 'tis needless to repeat; and since we are speaking of Eliza, I must own I have not been entirely free from apprehension least you should repent your bargain. . . .

Reverting to passages toward the beginning and middle of Eliza's letter of early January (**no. 86**), which Betsey must have read aloud and read again, Mary writes to her niece on February 17 (**no. 92**):

You have no opinion of a philosopher in peticoats, so I should suppose. Indeed, it appears pretty evident there is no doublet and hose in your disposition, and more is the pity. *You* say fortune has kindly spread a strengthning plaister for your pericranium to supply the deficiencies of nature. *I* say, success to the application; but, ardently as I wish it, I must own in this case my faith requires a strengthning plaister also, before it will be able to remove mountains. I see the glance of suspicion fall from those gooseberry orbs on these momentous words. Ponder them well, weigh thier vast import. Are they to be taken in the litteral sense? Perhaps more is meant than meets the eye, and perhaps nothing at all. A question of such mighty consequence, who shall decide? Go back, run it over again, I will stand still and wait till you return. Well, what think you now? Does it smack of Congress cordial? You know I deal largly in this wholesome article, and it is a pity you should lose your relish for it, as it is probable it will be administred in double doses when you return. We calculate much on Mrs. Heyden's coming with you in the spring. Sally is not a little pleased. She told me she would write to you, but if she says she's as glad as I am, don't believe a word of it, for it is impossible. I have past many a sleepless night in anticipated pleasures, and when I slept, my dreams were all about it. The other night I heard the voice of Mrs. Fitch as plain as I ever heard it in my life. I heard her say, 'If I was a widow and had no family, I would go too.' I thought much of her, and of my dream–if it was a dream. But to me it appeared reality.

Now you must know, we are great dreamers here in Yankee town, and we have great faith in dreams also, and in the interpretation thereof. So I determin'd to interpret my dream in the manner most agreable to myself, which is in the words of Brutus: 'Not that I loved Caesar less but that I loved Rome more.' As this, however, is not exactly applicable to the case, I prefer a more plain and simple exposition which runs thus: If it was perfectly convenient she would come too. And most devoutly do I wish it was. I should then enjoy at once the company of those I so much love and value, those two dear friends that share my best affections. But 'tis time to stop. I have wrote much more to you than I intended, as I have no thought of answering your letter at present, and began this only to inclose a few lines, which I will thank you to hand to Maria and likewise to tell Mrs. Fitch it is necessary I should write to you before I answer her letter.

My reasons are as follows. In the first place, I have a great deal to say to her. Of course it will require a great while to say it, in the manner I am obliged to murder out my letters; and before it was finish'd and sent, you would die in a fit of the fidgets; for tell Mrs. Fitch (if she has not already made the discovery) that patience is not to be numbered among your virtues. Moreover, you may also add that you are mighty chaste, precise, formal, and particular–that you are fond of starch and ceremony and the like. Whence follows the necessity of sending word. We should be happy to see you, for well I know, untill you recieve it in black and white, 'There is no peace to the wicked.' For this reason I should have written before, but we have had cold weather and company chatting, reading, and music, togeather with a few other ettcetra's, which you know are a great hindrance to business, and poor business it is, I must confess, to write nonsense in the way I am obliged to do it. Yet poor business is better than none at all. It serves to ammuse, it answers for a change–any thing to cheat and cheer the lazy paceing hours.

The exhibition you mention must have been a great treat to you, from your description. But I think the artist miss'd it in his representing Virtue less beautiful than Pleasure. To have distinguish'd them by the air, manner, and (above all the different expressions of countenance that marks the carracters) that expression which is independent of beauty or symetry of features, I think would have been more for his credit both as a moralist and painter. . . .

Cornelia Fitch seems to be a great favorite with you. No doubt she is a fine child, though perhaps rather too perfect to please my wayward fancy. A fault is wanting–a fault, or at least an amiable weakness, is necessary, you know, to render a carracter interesting. But I prefer the fault, and in this case I think a little spunk is rather an improvement than otherwise. Observe, I only speak of children. In those 'of larger growth,' temper unsubdued is a weakness not amiable but contemptable. I am a great admirer of nature, and admiting the id[ea] of Christian perfection is true, we are certainly not born perfect. But though she is a little too good, I feel disposed to love her, if it were only for the Yankee trait, as I may call it–that spirit of inquiry that goes to the bottom of a subject. There, she is a girl after my own heart. Tell her Aunt Mary sends her a hearty kiss, and commissions Miss Champlain to lay it on her handsomly.

Adieu. . . .

9

An Excursus on Culture

At the conclusion of her next letter of March 12, 1821, Eliza pronounces herself "in so much better spirits." The necessary adjustments had evidently been made by all three women–herself, mother, and aunt. Debt, death, and disability had been confronted, and they were now settled in to the work of living. Among the three, however, it was Eliza that had the best of it: she could still enjoy the delights of New York. Her report indicates what they were, so far as her circumstances gave her access to them. It invites, furthermore, some gathering together of mentions regarding her circle and the city's cultural activities, so important to her.

First, however, the letter in question (**no. 93**): "My dear Aunt," she writes to Mary, in reply to Mary's last of mid-February,

> I recieved your welcome letter last Monday and have read it over at least fifty times. I find you don't intend to produce satiety in the stomachs of your correspondents by the frequency of your letters. Mrs. Fitch, notwithstanding your apology, was half inclined to be offended at not getting a letter with mine, although she was conscious she did not deserve one at your hands. . . .
>
> I suppose you will be surprised when I tell you I have not been out to the Arsanal to pass a night yet. I don't know why. I have been thinking and talking of it for an eternity at least; but something has ever prevented me just as I was on the verge of going. So I suppose untill the time appointed I shall not get their.
>
> To-day is four weeks since Capt. Hayden came down in a sleigh to carry me out. I had just commenced Mr. Fitches picture and just dressed myself to see company which Mrs. Fitch expected that afternoon; so of course I refused to accompany him. He asked me when he should come for me again, and, without giving him my reasons for not going then, I told him to call on the Saturday following. He promised he would, bowed and withdrew. I then went to work on Mr. Fitch with all my might to get it done before Saturday, lost the likeness in finishing, got discouraged, heartsick and in a fit of low spirits wrote to Mrs. H. not to send for me untill further orders as

I felt that I had a work of time before me. The next week Mr. Fitch carried us all four miles out of town, sleighing, and as we return'd stop'd at the Arsanal a few moments. They were sure I came to stay and began to strip me for the business; but I told them I had commenced a Doctor-Wright background (as I knew they were well acquainted with the delights of that business) and that they must not expect to see me again untill it was finished. It has been in hand ever since and was completed yesterday, to my great joy, for I have groan'd in spirit with it. I don't understand colouring as I wish, and his complexion has been on and off fifty times. The picture is thought a better likeness than the one taken by [George] Freeman but in my opinion it has a capital fault: I don't think it as handsome as Mr. Fitch, and I had rather be guilty of almost any other error in painting than carricature. I think it a handsome picture but I think him verry handsome indeed, you know. Don't you?

I suppose you know Mrs. Avery's house is at length finished and thrown open for the reception of company. It is built and furnished in most superb style: folding doors, marble tables and everything to correspond. The two rooms are furnished exactly alike and cut a most brilliant figure. I was invited to a very large party given by her not long ago, but as I had nothing decent to wear I could not accept the invitation. I was very sorry, as there was to be several ladies there whom I very much wished to see. Mr. & Mrs. Fitch went between 8 and 9 o'clock and return'd at midnight. All Mr. Mitchell's family were there, Mr. and Mrs. Tooker, and the paragon Miss Ellen [Tooker] honour'd the party with her pressence and even condescended to partake of the diversions of the evening. They sung and danced, played battle-door and shuttle-cock, and cut all sorts of capers. They had music of various sorts and, as dancing and shuttle-cock set off the much-admired figure of the aforesaid paragon to the greatest advantage, it was of course her favourite amusement. Mrs. Fitch regretted extremely that I was not there. She said there was so much laughing it was a pity I could not join the chorus.

I went with Mr. & Mrs. Fitch the other night to Woodworth's benefit. You know he has resigned [the editorship of] *The* [*Ladies' Literary*] *Cabinet*, as the proffits arrising from it was not sufficient for the support of the two families. He found it necessary to give a concert. I was quite as much pleased as I should have been at the theatre. The music was admirable. I wish you could have been and heard G.-of-New Jersey recite his own supplement to Collin's *Ode on the Passions*. It was most admirably done; but I believe the poor fellow is in a consumption. You know it must always attend genius. Our seat was surrounded by geniuses: S.-of-New Jersey, young Crommeline, who you know signs 'Rollo' for the *Cabinet*, and poor Sandy [Clarke] stood by himself like a speckled bird. I don't know when I witnessed such an assemblage of geniuses as on that night. The hall was crouded, the band of music fine, the audience delighted, and Woodworth rouged. Several of his friends appear'd and spoke in public on that evening to oblige him that never did on any former occasion. The majority perform'd their parts extremely well and were well clap'd—a few got hiss'd. Woodworth himself appear'd very well on the boards, particularly in *Raising the Wind*, as it was written for the occasion. We return'd at twelve very much pleased with our evening's entertainment. I will enclose our play-bill for your persual.

I forgot to give any account of our sleigh ride, tho' something remarkable was attached to it. We pass'd near a convent of most singular appearance which Mrs. Fitch told me was formerly inhabited by the monks of La Trappe–the most rigid order. Each night at twelve o'clock they rose from their cell and dug a portion of their graves with their nails. They were doom'd to eternal silence and, to expiate their offences, suffer'd what in my opinion would have surpassed the tortures of Hell ('pardon your Speaker'). As she went on with her story I began to think I should prefer being buried alive, which you know was always my devil. The last rays of the setting sun shining full upon a building of such uncommon appearance, hearing its history, and being in rather a contemplative mood, I must confess fill'd my noddle with some very romantic ideas, and if I had been alone I dare say I should have dragg'd it head and shoulders into my novel, as I like to make people's hair stand on end once in a while, and my heroine 'Addeliza' you know might have been confined in one of the dungeons of the convent till rescued from captivity by her champion, 'Fitz Clarence.' I assure you the work has lost a treasure by my not being able to 'strike while the iron was hot.'

But enough of nonsense. I have yet much more to write, and time flies apace. The country round was most delightful. We pass'd the penetentiary. I suppose Sally remembers it if you don't. It was where Mrs. Holt made us walk our gizzards out, and walk after they were out. The instant I saw it my wrath kindled at the reccollection of that eternal, that soul-sickening, walk, and of the wounds, bruises, blisters, and putrifying sores upon the soles of my feet occasion'd by the rotten walk. We pass'd also the country seat of Waite, and Charlotte has now one of her own–a mighty splendid affair, I can assure you. We saw several very superb buildings besides, and return'd home about twillight.

Mrs. Fitch has been very much plagued with her help since you went home, but has at length got Sally again, after having about fifty different servants. I suppose you recollect Sally's history–what you heard of it. We have learn'd more since she return'd, not from herself but from one of the servants that was here last. She was born in Albany. Her parents were poor and she went out to service. She was very beautiful and very young. Her husband, John Barry, saw, fell in love with, and married her against the consent of his family, of course, as they were very haughty and very rich. She had a son and daughter when her husband (who it appears treated her very well) died, and her child was taken amediately from her by his relations, acknowledged by them, and educated in the first style. No expense has been spared on their education and Ellen the daughter is beautiful and very much attached to her brother. She is young, lovely, and a fortune–excells in almost every accomplishment, particularly music. She is now studying astronomy and I suppose I may set her down as a paragon of perfection with the other. At the time Sally's husband died and her children were taken from her, she was striped of everything and thrown destitute on an unfeeling world by his merciless relations; and, not content with that, his fiendlike mother in a fit of passion that her son should have married a *servant*, flew at her in rage, thrust her hand into her eye and put it out! Was there ever a more devilish act? Would not hanging be too good for the deviless? How I should like to see her treated in the same way. I long she should be murder'd. You know something of what Sally has suffer'd. She was obliged to have the ball of that eye extracted, and as their is such an intimate connexion between the eyes, the other suffer'd beyond description. She told me the other day that at times she almost loses her reason with the excruciating pain of the other eye, and at such times there is thick mist before it. I think her history extremely romantic and interesting, and thought I would fill up the chinks of my letter with it.

I must not omit telling you we have a singing-school establish'd amongst us–a Universal one. They have got the head singer in Johnny Mason's church to instruct them at two dollars a quarter in the school, but five dollars if he teaches at the house of the patient. Mrs. Fitch, choosing to learn, prefer'd having him at her own house. Mr. Fitch spoke to him about it and he is comeing this week to teach her; so if their is anything misical in my composition, you know I can learn 'upon free cost.' I am prepareing to be pretty well fa-la-sol'd. His name is Allen. He has considerable dignity and raises blood, sometimes. . . .

I suppose you recollect 'Caroline Matilda' and 'Harriet,' whose poetical effusions so long graced the *Ladies' Literary Cabinet*. Mrs. Muzzy is Harriet's name and Mrs. Thayer, Caroline Matilda's. They each used their Christian names alone. Let me know if Mother signs 'E. Champlain' when she publishes. I saw proposals for publishing by subscription in the last *Cabinet* the works of Harriet Muzzy by her friend Caroline Matilda. It seems the former is in a quick consumption and closely followed by 'the grim-visaged monster' who your genius complained so bitterly of, poverty, who eternaly follows the footsteps of *genius*, nor leaves them till they *dies*.

Ann has learn'd Cornelia the name of Capt. Hatch, so she came to my desk and asked if I was writing to him. I told her no, I was writing to Aunt Mary. Have you anything to send? Yes, said she, imprinting a kiss on the paper, I send her that to pay for the kiss she sent me. You know how mad spunky children make me. I am very glad Cornelia has none, for if she had she might possible get a shake now and then from my fair hands, as others have before her. . . .

I don't know why I feel in so much better spirits than I have for a month or two past. My circumstances are not changed for the better. I have no business nor any prospect of it; but I certainly feel very different, and it's well I do, for I should have been long dead if I did not. I am well assured that I have not truer friends in existence than the family I am now with, nor any that would go greater lengths to serve me, nor any that I value so highly. But all this will not produce business, I fear, and that is the one thing needful about, those days.

Adieu. . . .

It needs no pointing out that Eliza in this account of her recent doings finds herself on the edge of an active literary circle. If she had not been introduced to all of them, at least she knew this or that friend who had been, and so was familiar with their pen-names and published works. There is no difficulty, either, in deriving her claim to inclusion in this group: it begins at least with her father. He made intelligent use of the tedium of his calling, the hours with nothing to do in his cabin: quotes Pope (**no. 6**, the *Essay on Man*, "Hope springs eternal"), could be counted on to relish a long extract from Byron with which his son presented him (**no. 24**). He read and wrote to a degree quite surprising. His wife speaks of his being under "such a strong desire to compose [poetry] himself;" and just in the year before his death, from an old friend of his, he received an affectionate letter recalling their mutual pleasure in learned discourse over coffee. The passage was quoted at the end of the first chapter, above.[1] The picture that emerges from its words is rather different from that which appeared in Captain Champlain's letters to his Betsey, there also in the first chapter. But then, in the ships' logs hailing out of ports he well knew along the New England coast can be found a liberal sampling of verse among the conventional entries composed by mariners of his own day, in story-telling or sentimental mood. For instance,

> "Bounding billows, cease your motion!
> I will tempt your rage no more.
> Cease your roaring, foamy ocean!
> I will tempt your rage no more. . . . "

Or there will be other signs of a love of literature: a daily quotation from Blair, Campbell, Shakespeare (*Romeo and Juliet* 6.9) or some more current favorite, verse or prose at the bottom of the working page.[2] Perhaps the most striking indication of the level of learning that could be found on the sea occurs much later in the correspondence (**no. 247** of 1828). It is a moment of reminiscence by George the son, apropos his mention of Byron a line earlier: "I am amused often at the recollection of a droll expression of my nautical friend, Bill Grant, on the passage. In a severe squall one night while giving some orders on the forecastle, as the men were in the act of letting go the foretopsail halyards, Bill's leg accidentally got caught in the coil of the halyards and it jerked him half way up to the 'cat-harpins.' So soon as he recover'd his pins, however, he with great 'nonchalance' sings out to me who was near, 'George?

> The midwife hauls us in, and the Devil hauls us out.
> O! good God! how are we haul'd about.' "

It is as surprising that the friend Grant should assume George's knowledge, as that he should recall in a moment of terror exactly the right line of verse.[3]

Enough said of father George Whitefield Champlain: enjoying scripture as his foundation but acquainted with literature far beyond that. As to his wife Betsey, for at least a period of her life she had so much poetry in her, the outflooding of it was quite uncontrollable. She acknowledges her special debt to her favorite Edward

Young, especially his *Night-Thoughts* (1713)–real poetry, that, with a capitalized noun or two in every line, italics and exclamation points in every other, and a generally strident dramatizing of topics which modern times hardly respond to.[4] Her verse, when it is less under the spell of this writer, looks to Pope or to intermediaries: to the enormously popular Susanna Rowson, perhaps.[5] Otherwise, her knowledge of literature seems to derive from what other members of the family are fond of and pass around. Her daughter can say to her a little doubtfully (**no. 33**), "I suppose you have read *Antony and Cleopatra*." Betsey's love for verse was thus rather second-hand and imitative, however exuberant; and she appears less likely to have played much part in Eliza's education than her sister Mary, a second mother.

As Mary says in her assessment of her own blindness, books had been her dearest companions all her life. Her laments over the loss of direct access to them, and her difficulties in getting others to read aloud to her, recur often in her later correspondence; and these laments are entirely convincing, given the range of literature she shows herself familiar with and the amount she slightly misquotes, proving she quotes from memory. Her mind, however unsatisfied its appetites after 1820, was remarkably well-stocked. First in her affections was scripture, from which her letters recall no less than fifteen books, not to mention the Book of Common Prayer.[6] She seems to like the qualities of comfort and of oddity almost equally. Shakespeare comes next–above a dozen of his plays, with *Hamlet* and *Macbeth* special favorites.[7] Mary shares her sister's liking for Young's *Night Thoughts* but finds him "a gloomy writer," which is no more than the truth. She adds Thomson's *Seasons*, and eighteen lines of Cowper (which Betsey later quotes, too); also the obscure John Wilmot, the better known Gay, Milton's *Paradise Lost*, Gray's *Elegy*, Collins' *Ode to the Passions*, Byron's *Corsair* and *Bride of Abydos*, the *Enigma* falsely attributed to him, Watts' *To the Discontented*, Thomas Moore's *Lalla Rookh* (just out), James Montgomery's descriptive poetry, but Pope most of all.[8] Sometimes she obviously has a book open on her desk as she quotes, but more often it's in her memory. Before she sends some current verse to Eliza, she memorizes it (**no. 149**). Most in her mind and letters is the line, "Whatever is, is right," on which much of the *Essay on Man* builds, but which also served a theodicy of great importance and comfort to the family. Aunt Hannah quotes it as does Eliza, many times.

So much for straight verse. Of drama recalled in Mary's correspondence, there are Goldsmith's, Sheridan's and Congreve's plays;[9] fiction by Sterne, Scott, and Cooper, a Bulwer Lytton novel the year after it was published (sent her by Anna Fitch), and two ephemerae of the same title, *The Recluse*, respectively by Porter and d'Arlincourt;[10] heavier stuff, the *Life of John Murray*, issues of the *Gospel Herald*, Irving's *The Broken Heart*, De Quincy's *Reminiscences of an English Opium-Eater*, some Voltaire, a travel book by the Reverend William Berrian of Trinity Church, and Fontenelle's astronomical philosophizing.[11] Thirsting for books in New London, she got periodic infusions from Anna (for example, in **no. 262**).

By the early 1800s, New London must have had what other much smaller towns certainly possessed, a public library. What couldn't be borrowed there might be had from a friend next door or elsewhere in New York or Boston.[12] Weeklies offered to their subscribers their Poets' Corner in which quotations from Byron and other greats of the day, but also greats of the past, were reprinted, and to which native talent was admitted. Occasional short novels were serialized. Whatever was especially enjoyed might be copied out and sent around in a letter.[13] There was even what might be called some local New London literary society: "Sandy" Clarke before he offered his genius to a larger sphere; the daughter of a local physician, Betsey Laskallas, who translated the wildly popular *Recluse* from French; three reputable local poets, one of them a Taber relative.[14] But very small potatoes compared with what could be found in New York.

In the next generation, all of George and Betsey Champlain's children indicate in their letters that they liked and knew literature. We would expect as much of the home they came from. At school they enjoyed some additional introduction to the classics of their own language, plus a little beyond that through translation. In the classrooms of the previous generation, children would have read no more than the New Testament, for sure.[15] That might of course account for a good deal of scriptural quotation in Mary's and Elizabeth's letters, too, but nothing beyond that can be certainly attributed to their formal education. By the turn of the century, several good Readers had come into print and within a decade teachers were using them in all towns like the one Eliza and her brothers grew up in. Besides their prose selections such collections contained very much the same roster of writers that the correspondence favors, in little bits and pieces and with some variation in what was left out or put in.[16] By far the most widely used almost from its beginnings in 1799 was Lindley Murray's *Reader*, published on Pearl Street in New York (the author giving his name, incidentally, to a part of the city, "Murray Hill"). Here were Gray's *Elegy*, Goldsmith's *Deserted Village* and a lot of Young's *Night Thoughts*, including a line that the Way-Champlain family specially liked to use humorously.[17] There are other particular coincidences of taste between the *Readers* and the correspondence, from Cowper, Watts, and Shakespeare. American talent wasn't anthologized until after 1820 or so; of course the classroom would be conservative; but otherwise, the tastes among that part of the population that liked books appears to have been remarkably homogeneous, from childhood into maturity and from small town to big town.[18]

Among the four Champlain children, Sam quotes Moore, spins out a long piece of word-play to William, and with his New York friends enjoys learned jokes; but his reading plays little part in his letters.[19] Brother William has bits of Shakespeare in his head, though not much beyond the family favorites; he has by heart some lines from a quite obscure work to which perhaps the title drew him, *The Shipwreck* by Falconer.[20] George comments on his own fondness for Byron, amply demonstrated in quotations;[21] adds Gray and Goldsmith; reads occasional prose works; but really loves and has continually in mind the plays of Shakespeare, which drew him to the theater and so in turn to a still larger knowledge of them.[22] He leaves Scripture to his elders and betters.

As to Eliza, since her contribution to the correspondence is by far the largest, her reading is bound to make more of a show. It seems, however, to be at least a little more eclectic than her siblings', not merely better displayed: besides the Bible, Shakespeare, Pope, Goldsmith, Moore, and Byron, all familiar fare, with De Quincy, Congreve and Porter whose names appear in her family's allusions,[23] and besides Milton, Blair, Burns, Cervantes, Sterne's *Sentimental Journey*, and Mme. de Staël when she was "quite a child,"[24] she tried Mrs. Hemans' *The Voice of Spring*, Lady Morgan's *St. Clair*, and a dreadfully long work by Cuthbertson, *The Forest of Montalbano*; she knew Washington Irving's *Broken Heart* and Scott's *Waverley* novels;[25] even Wollstonecraft's *Vindication of the Rights of Women*, of which something more may be said later.

A copy of that book was handy to her at Anna Fitch's. Here was a household with more money than Eliza and her family in New London ever commanded. No doubt the Fitches boasted something of a private library: there were Sheridan and Pope in the house, and a recent copy of the little romantic novel, *Werter and Charlotte*; recently published novels by Caroline Lamb and Charles Brockden Brown (Anna's favorite), with others in abundance, borrowed or more likely bought.[26] Brown, Eliza liked a lot. He bulked very large on the literary horizon of her lifetime, partly due to his championing of native talent in accordance with a sentiment common in his day, but most of all for his novels. They naturalized the taste for the Gothic, especially his *Wieland*, and stimulated a flood of imitation.[27]

Conversation about books arose among the members of the correspondence out of genuine interest and critical reading in which everyone joined. It was not only Betsey who wanted other family members to tell her what they thought of her efforts–Anna did also. Eliza in the letter with which this chapter began makes light of her novel "Addeliza." She had at least dreamed of being an author. No doubt she flinched from the attempt only because she could estimate her own talents too well. For another illustration of the exchanges of critical opinion within her circle, James Brooks' verse received a close reading which happened to be a very favorable one from the family friend Mrs. Lee of New London after one of her visits to New York; Mary tried two of his compositions and compares one of them to the better work of another poet; and Eliza read and copied them for distribution, and admired them too.[28] Or again, Gothic fiction: good or bad? William thought it ridiculous, and parodies its conventions for Sam; Eliza laughs at its straining to scare its readers out of their wits.[29] Or again, she and her fiancé discuss a poem passing as Byron's, which they think isn't up to his usual style (**no. 208**). They were right.

As has been and is ordinarily the case in western societies, position depended mostly on money but took account of taste, too: if you showed a natural attachment to things that poorer people were generally too busy to bother about, or had no access to, you could pass for richer than you were–pass among your "betters." It was no doubt the salvation of Mary and, a few years later, of Eliza in New York that their conversation revealed them for what they were, well spoken in the sense of literately educated. Besides her love of her faith, Mary shared with Anna Fitch a genuine love of books and ideas. The first gave her an entree to the Universalist church and its after-service chats by the door; the other admitted the bearer to a certain set of people within the congregation, notwithstanding some drabness in her costume.

A love of books, yes, but also of writing. Father Champlain's wish to write, his wife's dozens of pages of verse and some of prose, Mary's start of an essay on free will, even Sam's well-handled little piece of fiction and Eliza's dreams of a Romantic *Addeliza* all show the urge; likewise her own and her aunt's highly colored, conscious "dreams" which were much admired and copied around.[30] Scattered throughout the correspondence are all sorts of incidents and anecdotes worked up in a more or less consciously literary fashion, which could be picked out today and listed as "Gothic," "sentimental," "satiric," or "homiletic" and edifying. Their authors, in their itch to respond actively and creatively to their favorite models, were quite of their times.[31]

Anna Fitch, however, alone pushed her way into print. She contributed to periodicals under the pen-name "Agnes"; later, as "Ally Croker." "She is eternally scribbling to the printers."[32] She appears to have been addressed by poems of "Sandy" Clarke,[33] and swapped honorific apostrophes in verse-form with another pseudonymous writer like herself through the pages of a city literary periodical, the *Ladies' Literary Cabinet*–he, "Florio" who was James G. Brooks, and who went on to become editor of another similar periodical *The Minerva*, in 1823. There, too, Anna who was "Agnes" published both before and after he took over, as she did again in *The Literary Gazette* to which he migrated in 1825; and there, the poetry of young Chavalier, one of Eliza's beaus, sometimes appeared. He was, for example, the author of "Lucy Ann–A Song in the Manner of Lord Byron."[34]

To sample in particular the poetry-pages of these ephemeral publications is to enter another of New York's villages, one not of streets but of printed columns. The image may be pursued a little further, and a central figure introduced. Of the three publications in which "Agnes" appeared, the first had been started by Samuel Woodworth, New York's most indefatigable literary entrepreneur.[35] Indefatigable, yes, but in vain. Eleven periodicals he opened or joined, eleven closed, all but one before attaining its second birthday: for example, *The Halcyon Luminary* born of his conversion to Swedenborgianism (1812–13) while he was simultaneously editing *The War* and contributing pseudonymous verse to this as well. Or again, *The Republican Chronicle* which as a semi-weekly he wrote for and then edited during a good eighteen months, his duties there overlapping with others on a daily paper of almost the same name, till both collapsed in 1819. As his friend Halleck exclaimed poetically, "Poor Woodworth! His *Chronicle* died broken-hearted." His *Ladies' Literary Cabinet* proved the most nearly successful, beginning in that same year and hanging on, though not under his editorship, till the end of 1822, whereupon he began his second Swedenborgian periodical. Et cetera.

During intervals in the middle years of his editorial career he managed a good deal of publication of his poems in others' periodicals under the pen-name of Byron's hero in *The Bride of Abydos*, "Selim." With more poetry later he filled the pages of his own *Ladies' Literary Cabinet*. His early work he then drew out into a volume preceded by an autobiographical introduction in 1818. Its contents (to give some idea of their occasional nature and inspiration in works originating in England) included "To Miss H*****, with a miniature volume of [James] Montgomery's poems, as published in 1807." Woodworth also liked to set words to music, especially in tandem with the city's leading music publisher, the elder Edward Riley (1769–1829).[36] And he contributed fiction to his own periodicals, some of its pseudonymous.

There is something almost frenetic about this career of Woodworth, churning out weeklies and novels and editorials, with short verses as an accompaniment of which he was, perhaps, not very proud. For many years he withheld his own name from them; yet it was one of these offerings that gave him final fame: his *The* [*Old Oaken*] *Bucket*. Again to quote Halleck, "Great Woodworth, the champion of Buckets and Freedom . . . !" He had hit the city's taste. His other writing nevertheless was at least marginally successful, witness the bare fact that his poems ran through various collections and editions. It was only in his editing that he continually failed, and had thrice to apply to the literary community through a benefit, once as reported in the letter above and again in 1829 and 1837.[37]

A number of writers contributed to Woodworth-edited periodicals, but none more often than "Sandy" Clarke. He has been seen in his New London beginnings, above, where his eccentricity stands out. He never made any secret of his character, calling himself "The Mad Poet" in his first volume, challenging criticism with its title, *Elixir of Moonshine*, and offering a portrait of himself with an odd arrangement of his hair and posture (Fig. 4). New York readers were perhaps intrigued. No doubt they liked his description of "Castle Garden," "The Battery," or "Broadway," the last beginning, " 'Tis pleasant to lounge along Broadway, between/ The hours of one, two and three, and behold/ The elegant girls that flit over the scene. . . . " He could boast an abundant output and many reprintings far down into the nineteenth century; but long before that his true madness had asserted itself. He had become involved in money difficulties, his friend Halleck had to bail him out. He died insane.[38]

As to Brooks = "Florio," an editor with whom Anna published and who himself published under Woodworth, he did not suit the city's taste so well; but we may correct the reception of himself and Clarke through the comments of Mary, George, and Eliza: they expressed much admiration for Brooks, little for Clarke, though he published so much more.[39]

Another to be added to this circle of poets was the truly gifted Fitz-Greene Halleck. As a teenager from his home in Guilford, Connecticut, he had submitted his verses to Charles Holt's New-York *Columbian*, in the winter of 1810. Like Woodworth and Clarke (and Brown, fifteen years earlier) he then followed them to the city to make his fortune; lodged on Greenwich Street where Mary first settled; and, like her, applied again to Holt, not as a family friend but as an editor. His still-pseudonymous contributions appeared in the *Columbian* in 1813–14; his new lyrics for *Jessie of Dumblane*, in 1817.[40] The tune was hugely popular and, it may be recalled,

Figure 4. "Sandy" McDonald Clarke

Eliza's favorite. Two years later he and Joseph Drake poured out three dozen short satirical pieces on topics of the day which they had partly written recently, partly produced as the series went along, in the poetry-columns of the *Evening Post*, with tremendous success. The authors called themselves "Croaker" and "Croaker Junior." By the time their identity became generally known, Drake had been carried off by an early death; so Halleck got most of the credit of authorship.[41] He followed up this success with a more substantial poem, *Fanny*, in the style of Byron which received some attention even in England. Within a few years his reputation in his adopted city had become established, he could be found among its arbiters of literary elegance, and his verses were recited at the opening of the rebuilt Park Theatre (1821) and again, honoring this newest composition, in 1828. Connecticutters could be hugely proud of him.[42]

He and his collaborator of 1819, Joseph Drake, had met at the house of a rich patron of the arts, whose confidential secretary, young Charles P. Clinch (1797–1880), was himself a writer, and where the table was always spread for literary men. Clinch and Halleck became fast friends, the Clinch dog being honorifically named "Fitz" and Halleck contributing a song to be inserted at some appropriate point in Clinch's dramatization of a Cooper novel, *The Spy*, when it was performed in 1822. It had a long run, from March till at least November. Still later it enjoyed a revival.[43] Though Halleck had won out over Clinch and Woodworth, Clarke, and other literary lights, too, in the competition for the honor of opening the rebuilt Park Theatre (1821), they all remained friends. From 1831 survives a warm little piece of occasional verse by Halleck to Woodworth's daughter.[44]

Their circle was joined by other lights requiring mention: for one, the Connecticut poet James Percival, whom Anna was vastly excited to recognize on one of his visits to his New York publishers;[45] for another, the author of the novel which had inspired Clinch's drama, James Fenimore Cooper. He too came to the city as a young man (1822), found lodging at the corner of Broadway and Prince Street half-way out to Vauxhall Garden, and made a place for himself–a very large one–with his pen. He and Woodworth concerted the floating of yet one more periodical, *The Mirror*; he and Halleck became intimates and could be seen side by side in the best seats one night at the Park Theatre listening to one of the city's early experiences in Italian opera.[46]

Woodworth personally knew the elder Riley and his son, music publishers–that much can be demonstrated. He could be seen in one or another of the less exclusive groups of literati that met in a certain tavern or a certain hotel. His lodging with Riley, Clinch, Holt, and other such folk in one neighborhood was noted above (chapter 6 at note 2). And Woodworth could hardly fail at some point to make the acquaintance of the regular contributors to his publications, Clarke, Brooks, and (why not?) Anna Fitch. When *The Bucket* came out over the name "Selim," Mary knew its real author, surely admitted to the secret by her friend Anna. Eliza knew the secret behind the pen-names "Croaker" and "Croaker Junior" within a year or two of their appearance–even the name that Halleck went by among his intimates.[47] She and Mary alike puzzled over the identity behind other pen-names in the literary periodicals they read, not only that of the *Waverley* novels so much in the press;[48] and in the letter at the start of this chapter two more pen-names emerge from the pages into real life: the friends Harriet Muzzy and Caroline Matilda Thayer, regulars in the *Cabinet* under their first names only. One of them addressed a poem to a third friend on the same street as the Fitches.[49] As to "S.-of-New Jersey" whose poetry Eliza and her circle discussed (**no. 205**), he was seated near her and her friends at Woodworth's benefit, as she mentions in the letter with which this chapter began, and she recognized him as well as another writer whom she could connect with his pen-name, "Rollo." She was by this date established friends with Clinch and his wife, thanks to Mary's prior connection with them, and had done his portrait (as Betsey had done Clarke's).[50] Finally, a little later Eliza was actually to meet and shake hands with the sister-in-law of Charles Brockden Brown (**no. 129**), thanks to a connection through her minister, the Reverend Edward Mitchell. A liberal man, he attended a benefit for Clinch at one of the theaters, which Eliza notes was "fill'd almost with our church folks" (**no. 114**).

In giving time and space to this collection of little facts, the object should be clear: simply to show the shape of the literary "village" of the day, at the edge of which Mary and Eliza were privileged to have a place and so to join the opening scene of native American literature. Their acquaintance with living authors is almost as surprising as that with the dead, and in their letters can be felt their reward: a pleasurable excitement in being a part of what all the world–the not so little world of the nation's largest city–talked about, read, listened to or stared at.

The particular juncture at which they were present has been naturally discussed a great deal, since it has particular interest. Having separated itself from its mother-country by revolution, politically, a new people can be seen at this moment trying to separate itself culturally as well. Despite a quite remarkable level of literacy throughout all classes, despite a quite remarkable number of newspapers in which writers could experiment and show their work, the job was not easily done. Native themes and the genius to elaborate them could hardly be commanded by mere act of the national will. In modern criticism none of the writers active in the city during the years thus far covered by the correspondence is taken very seriously; in competition within the general Anglophone world, meaning London and so forth, only Cooper made much of a mark for himself. At home, there was scepticism such as a prominent editor expressed upon learning the American identity of the "Croakers": "My God, I had no idea that we had such talents in America."[51] But there was also a ready and generous reception for what little of promise did emerge, like Halleck's and Drake's, combined with some protest against an unchallenged dependence on England. This protest has been noted in the realm of the fine arts (above, chapter 2 at note 21).

The result in literature of the time was exactly the mix of English and American that registers in the reading of the Ways, Champlains, and Fitches. In New York's theaters as elsewhere throughout the young nation, Shakespeare reigned unchallenged; in churches, one need hardly say, the Bible; and so too, scripture and Shakespeare provide the bulk of the correspondents' literary allusions.[52] Next, it is striking how great a favor Byron had won: imitations of his verse were advertised as such by Clarke and Chavalier, a pen-name taken from him by Woodworth, Halleck imitating him and going on later to edit his works; and similarly with all the correspondents' quoting of him or naming him as among their favorites. Anna posed for her portrait holding a copy of his works in her hand.[53]

Another favorite among the correspondents was Edward Young: top of the list for Betsey, cited by her to George, set to be copied by the nine-year old sister-in-law-to-be of Eliza's daughter in a pretty sampler belonging to just these years (1823):

> "In human hearts what bolder thoughts can ray
> Than man's presumption on tomorrow's day?
> Where is tomorrow? In another world.
> For numbers this is certain; the reverse
> Is sure to none."

And if the connection appears remote, let Woodworth speak more directly through his *New-York Mirror* and *Ladies' Literary Gazette* of the same year, where he offers extracts from the same work and adds, "it may seem like literary *heresy* to call in question the excellence of such a celebrated poem."[54]

Pope, too, was a general favorite, with seventy-seven editions in New England during Eliza's lifetime. There were thirty-five American editions of the *Essay on Man* alone in the decade 1810–20, and the lines of this poet that the family liked best to quote were just those that other Americans preferred likewise.[55] Similarly of their other preferences: shared and absolutely representative of their place and times, so that they may be taken as a mirror of the reading public as a whole in their liking for Blair, Goldsmith, Moore, Thomson, Burns, Sterne, and Scott from overseas; Brown, Irving, and Cooper among the larger American authors.[56]

Among the correspondents, too, the three miniaturists were further representative in the way they wove their literary tastes into their painting. There is Eliza's rendering of Anna Fitch holding Byron's poems. It belongs, however, to the most familiar of traditions in portraiture. More striking is Robert Street's choice of a poem by Thomson for the inspiration of a painting he exhibited for sale in 1822, along with the depiction of "a relapsed madman." Why choose to paint anything so bizarre as this last? Why, the next year, should a painter-friend of Betsey's in New London try her hand at the same subject, and Betsey herself and perhaps Eliza?[57] Why should the deranged lover encountered in the closing chapters of *A Sentimental Journey* take form for Eliza in this little painting (Pl. 7.16) of about 1816?[58] Or why quote Cowper to explain *Fancy* (above, Pl. 6.15)? Surely because these were subjects first to be found in the "best" literature. For the same reason Henry Inman, an Establishment artist, chose Sterne's *Maria* likewise; and the veteran librettist Pelissier did an opera on the same subject. Betsey copies out for Eliza a poem by Mary Lockwood of 1815, *The Maniac's Song*, bearing the same title as another of the 1820s by the Guilford (Connecticut) poet John Brainard. In the exhibitions of the American Academy of Fine Arts, as was noted above (chapter 4 at note 12), one could always find pictures that reflected what people were reading, for example, a *Mary Queen of Scots* matching *The Life of Mary Queen of Scotland* just arrived in the bookstores, and a little before, John Agg's drama on the same subject; the local artist John Quidor's *Money-Diggers* matching a poem on the same subject by Brainard, both drawing from Washington Irving's well-liked *Tales of a Traveller*; and of course and inevitably, Woodworth's *Old Oaken Bucket* was put on canvas again and again, as the poem became an American classic.[59]

The speed of these interconnections across the various arts is important to notice, as it was important naturally in explaining the market. It made things "relevant," in today's vocabulary; it created a buzz, or as we would say today, celebrities. And it contributed to the process of separating the culture of the new country somewhat from the old, which had its own interconnections, its own relevance. Let London then focus on Drury Lane, weekly reported still in New York's *Albion*. A time had come for Broadway, too. Therein lay the reward for the witty verses of the "Croakers," the cityscapes chosen for his verses by Clarke, the intriguing secrets of semi-anonymity under false signatures and initials: "S-of-New Jersey," and the like.

They were in and of the village, in and of the moment. Nowhere but in New York would there have been an audience for five hundred and thirty lines on rental habits, Woodworth's *Quarter-day, or, The Horrors of the First of May*, beginning with a well-aimed parody of the versification so much favored by Betsey:

> "While sylvan bards awake the tuneful strain,
> Responsive to the murmur of some rill
> Meandering slow along the rushy dale
> Or, deep embosom'd in the sweet recess
> Of fragrant bower, by the feathered choir made vocal. . . . "

Eliza quite a few years earlier in her young life, had she been in New York, might have responded to the pathos of Sterne's *Maria* in yet another form: not in verse, not in a painting, but in an opera of that title written by the father of this art form in America, Victor Pelissier.[60] He had performed in the orchestras of the city first at the New York Theatre, then more regularly at the Park Theatre where music had its most distinguished home, and, throughout his long career in the city, had been engaged also in arranging and composing "melodramas" as they were called, ballets, harlequinades, and operas. A tireless talent. He and his like in the next decade or two supplied demand through pillaging the London and to a lesser degree the Paris stage, adapting and rearranging and plagiarizing with more or less skill (some, very respectable); and they sometimes included in their reach the authors most familiar among their audience, Goldsmith, Scott, the Gothic novelists Radcliffe and Monk, besides *A Sentimental Journey*. Here could be found a plot, a character, even a whole text, ready-made. The results on the stage contributed much to that close cultural texture, those interconnections across the arts, to which attention was drawn a moment ago; and they did so in a setting peculiarly suitable: New York's theaters and pleasure gardens. In those agreeable institutions were united all the various threads of which the culture of the city was woven. On a given spring evening they provided to Eliza (**no. 93**, above) a band and various elocutionists, the recall of a piece of classical poetry of Collins and the introduction of another piece composed for the occasion. Other sources report political tableaux or "panoramas," one for example with "the figure of the Goddess of Liberty feeding the American eagle [which] is particularly beautiful."[61] *The Albion* for July 22 of 1822 tells its readers about the paintings then on exhibit at the Vauxhall Garden, along with singing and acrobatics; on other days, comedies, tragedies, plays with interspersed songs, musicals, operas home-grown or imported, lots of band-music, dramatic recitations, handsome statuary, occasional extravaganzas like Lafayette's appearance or the balloon ascent of Mr. Guille. On the glorious Fourth, always fireworks; on every day, ice-cream, always. Every art was represented, all of them jumbled together.

It was not youth alone that accounted for Eliza's recovery of her spirits.

10

Ending in a Proposal

With Mary gone from New York, her niece hadn't the money needed to live on and so had to depend on her friends. They did what they could to help her, the Universalist minister Dr. Mitchell playing an active, useful, sensible part in finding her work. A place to live was even more necessary. Here it was the Fitch and Hayden families that made it possible for her to remain in the city. The former were settled into a comfortable life on Cherry Street. Samuel Fitch earned enough as a lawyer to buy a certain ease for his wife, and the two of them were generous and fond of Eliza. Captain Jeremiah Hayden was introduced above (chapter 7 at note 12), at one of the many points of change in his posting. His assignment to the Arsenal on the edge of the city included ample quarters so that it was easy to put up a visitor, and he too had money enough to live with some ease. The account of the sleigh ride in the preceding letter, and much else, makes that quite clear. A warm friendship united his wife Maria with Mary and then with Eliza, and resulted in the two younger women spending much time in each other's company. For example, in April of 1821 (**no. 94**):

> My dear Aunt,
>
> I return'd yesterday from the Arsanal where I have been spending a week. The family are all quite well except the young soldier, who is cutting teeth. I suppose you will smile when I tell you he has dropt the jaw-cracking name of Gustavus Adolphus for the more harmonious one of Julius-Wallace-Hayden, after his eccentric daddy's friend and 'pitcher,'[1] the tall and graceful J. Wallace. He is a sweet boy. He has elegant dimples, his mother's blue eyes when he laughs, and now and then an expression that reminds me of your idol Emma. I think he grows more like them both, but I see no trace of Hayden in him. Mrs. Fitch thinks him a beauty. Mrs. Hayden sends ten thousand bushels of love to you and says she would certainly write if it was possible, but it is not, and I must say a great deal for her. She desires her best respects to my mother who she is very anxious to see–also, to Aunt [Sally] Way who you know is

a great favorite of hers. She says she expects to be delighted with her visit to New London and I sincerely hope she will not be disappointed.

Capt. Hayden has recieved orders to disband his men and scatter them to the 'four winds.' I suppose himself expects to be ordered somewhere else within four or five weeks. Whether his wife will go with him or stay where she is will depend on the place to which he is ordered. She is more desireous of settling in Boston than anywhere else, but that depends on circumstances. At any rate, she must quit the Arsanal within six weeks, as it will be filled with officers and 'armed multitudes,' which will render it a very unfit place of residence for a lady. [?While] Cap't Hayden remains in the Arsanal his wife will board some[where] as near as possible. At present they are in a state of uncertainty. I suppose all this fluster will take place just about the time we contemplated visiting New London; but we are determin'd [to] fight our way there like good soldiers if we go sword in hand. Capt. Hayden told me the other day at dinner, he believed he would wait upon me to New London and pass for my beau, provided I gave consent. I very soon gave him to understand that, tho' his company would be very agreeable, his wife's would be more so. I suppose we shall come some time in May.

The affectionate little 'bless-your-dear-heart' (Mrs. Aymar) is no more. She had a complication of disorders which were expected to finish her before they did. She had been long confined to her room with no prospect of ever leaving it again. When taking a freak into her noddle to see company, she forthwith sent notes of invitation to every one of her most stylish neighbors, not excepting one–whether she knew them or not 'twas all one, come they must. She dress'd herself in superb style, left her sick room for the drawing room, exerted herself beyond what she was able to bear, got a relapse, and in a few days sunk into the arms of the pale messenger of mortality. I always thought the little woman would die a martyr to company, but did not think it would be quite so soon. Her husband is gay as a lark, gallanting all the young girls about as if nothing had happen'd. Her dwarfish little daughter Mrs. Roff bore her death with the apathy of a Stoic. She was no more affected at it than if a kitten had died–which she would have to pass for sheer philosophy. With those who knew her not, it might, but not with me. Whoever gets Aymar will jump into a fine estate, they live in such splendor; but I think they will pay for their whistle. . . .

Mr. and Mrs. Fitch are going to Saratoga this summer. Mrs. [Fitch's sister-in-law, Mrs.] Shearman is expected here about the time that, if I'm alive, I shall probably be in New London. Mrs. Fitches sister Mrs. Weed is expected down this month with her husband. I have been taking a sketch of Mrs. Northam from the one you took on ivory, for Mr. Ashmeade to take on to Jamaica with him. He insists so much on it. He took also the one I painted on bark for Mr. Northam, and was very much pleased with them, he said last Sunday. I copied it first on a bit of broken ising-glass[2] which, not looking fit to be seen, I recopied it on bark. That look'd ill, and I took another on ivory, which I finished at last. I was a long time about it.

Adieu.

I beg ten thousand pardons for my apparent neglect of your caps. I assure you it is not real. I have been waiting so long to see Mrs. Hayden and ask her about the tabs, whether they had better be long than short. She said long, so I finished one out there and I shall have the other done this week, when, if I don't bring them, I will send them, together with the sermons which I have likewise fresh in memory. . . . Mrs. Hayden has call'd here since this was written to carry me out with her again, but I was expecting the carmen to call, and could not go. She says Capt. H. expects a company of artillery on in three or four weeks, and is now making arrangements to recieve them. She looks well and happy. She says, tell your aunt I will stay as long as I possible can–if it is possible, a fortnight. But I don't believe she will stay half the time, as she will have Julius Gowan along to bother her gizzard out. Whoever goes to New London must always have something to hurry them back again.

This was followed in a few weeks by a longer report from Eliza (**no. 95**):

Dear Sisters of the Brush,

. . . I suppose it will be expected that I give you a correct account of my looks and actions before I visit you. Of the former I shall say no more than that they are not improved by misfortune and consequently are indiscribable; of the latter, I can only say I will come and you must 'see for yourselves.' Perhaps you will think I look somewhat older than when you last saw me, and should pass with a better grace for Miss Way, by which title you must know I expect to be introduced, as we are all girls together. I mention my looks and actions that you may not be shocked at any alteration that may have taken place in either since my departure from the land of 'steady habits' and blue lights.

Since I wrote to you last, Miss Mason has requested me to take a two-dollar miniature from the portrait of her mother which was painted by that non-descript Mrs. Eustice, who took at the same time Mary Ann. I have taken it. It is esteem'd a very exact resemblance of the original–[the] family are all delighted with it. I should not have had it to do if Mary Ann had not disappointed me about another picture. She had long promised me one of her beaux. You know she has a great many strings to it. The puppy has appointed the day and the hour that he would call and sit. She held herself in readiness to accompany him here, when the rascal call'd and told her he has relinquished the idea altogether of having it. She said she had a great mind to knock his head off, and I wish she had. I told her I would have lent a hand with all my heart. However, that I might not be disappointed of a picture, for she saw how much I had depended on his word, she immediately engaged her mother's miniature, which is just completed. She often enquires particularly of you, as do all your other friends–tho' I omit mentioning it. [Mary Ann's sister] Rebecca is well, her son grows finely, they still keep up a sort of hollow truce with the Dawsons–that is to say, they are neither friends nor enemies.

We stop the press to announce the arrival of your letter to Mrs. Fitch. From my soul, I am thankful to hear from you once more, for, when I commenced this epistle, I thought it doubtful whether I should or not. I am much obliged. We commenced cleaning house this morning and Mrs. Fitch was as busy as a bee cleaning plate; but she flew at your letter with her hands cover'd with whitening and never stirr'd till it was finished. She then gave it to me. I am much obliged to you for the compliments it contains on my character. I must confess it is a flatter'd piece, and if you draw a few more carricatures of me in this style, I fear I shall die of vanity. Understood! At dinner the merits of your letter were discussed, when Cornelia, whom nothing escapes, asked me very abruptly what Aunt Mary said about her. I had not time to speak before her mother said, She does not mention you, my child. I suppose she thinks you of too little consequence. Then, Miss Champlain, said she, tell Aunt Mary I think it is very naughty of her to forget Cornelia. And now I'm about it, I wish you had mentioned Mr. Fitch. I did not like your forgetting him for I like him very bad. Be more particular in future, as I cannot help resenting any neglect he recieves, particularly if it is from you.

I don't know what I write, for I am surrounded with painters, glaziers, white-washers, floorscrubbers, chief cooks & bottle washers, whose tongues all running at once, each in a different dialect, reminds me of the languages of Babel; and the divel of it is, I cannot get out of thier noise, for there is not a spot in this house that I can retire too and call my own till these nuisances have accomplished the work which they came to do. So you may think we shall rejoice when we are purefied from our uncleanness. I think you cannot have forgotten the horrors of the first of May. Never!–tho' I should live to the age of Methuselah, will May return without bringing to my mind the agony I have endured in this city at that time, and may still endure. But from futurity I turn without daring to think for an instant; for my prospects are dim as the grave, dark as yours, tho' a different kind of darkness.

I have recieved a proposal from Mrs. Cowdry seconded by Mrs. Mitchell. Mrs. Fitch was the bearer of it from a party at Weekses, where she saw both these ladies. It is to teach a school–a thing that I think I am utterly incapable of, as I do not understand the founding system, and to teach school without having ninety and nine num-skulls out of a hundred schollars is impossible. Add to this, a considerable sum of money is absolutely nessassary to begin with, to defray necessary expenses, and I am pennyless. If that was not the case, I think I should make the attempt, as I think I could consent to teach the Divel to lop ashes, provided he paid me handsomely for it. (By the by, I don't wish this made a song of). My poverty and not my will consents to it. Mrs. Fitch thinks it's all I can do, and how I'm to do that, heaven only knows. She also thinks I was mad for giving up watch-papers in my present situation, although I felt I was injuring my eyes by painting them. I have had six applicants for pictures since your departure, not one of whom I have ever seen since they engaged thier likenesses, nor ever expect to in this lower world; but one comfort is, in the other I shall not need them–and I heartily wish I was there. Mrs. Cowdry, you know, is a woman of consequence. She wishes her daughters taught painting, and thinks she could get me several schollars if I will consent to teach. I feel I am not adequate to the task, but do something I *must*. Imperious Necessity commands, and her mandate must be obey'd. She eternaly has been my mistress and eternaly will be, I fear.

I have lately recieved seven dollars! for twelve watch-papers which I painted last winter and painted as *I* paint them. Mr. & Mrs. Fitch both urge my painting them, they are so much admired. He likes to take them to the different jewellers with whom

> he has dealings. He is a good soul, isn't he? I prefer anything to 'teaching the young idea how to shoot.' Unless I had the patience of Job, the meekness of Moses, the strength of Samson and the talents of Raphael, I should not feel quite clever about commencing a school. But what is to be, will be. So I may as well let the subject drop till I see you, as I cannot make one hair black or white by my clack. I am at present streaming in all the glory of rags and if they are not soon dismiss'd I shall be scatter'd to the four winds, or taken in the first whirlwind to Heaven; and to that I have no objection–tho' I should prefer going decently, or I fear you will not own me for a relation when we all meet in the mansions above–think you will?

This from Eliza had not yet been received when the next was begun to her by Mary (**no. 96** of May 18th):

> Why are you not here? I want you *very bad*, if it were only to read over your own amusing letters and answer them for me, as at this season all are employed and seem to find as much as they can do. No one is at leisure now to read to me or write my nonsense. Spring gives nature a jog, and sets the world in motion. A busy plodding pace, such bustling and rattling of dry bones. Even Aunt Hannah has begun to make flowers again, and pursues her business with all the avidity of a girl of fifteen. She says, 'My neighbors tells me I renew my my age–that I grow younger every day; and I really think I am very smart. Why, there is Mrs. Tilley who is many years younger than I am, and I could thrash the ground with her.' Did you ever hear such a boaster? There she crows over the poor old lady, who has been very ill in consequence of a fall. She is better now, tho' entirely helpless, and the doctors are of opinion that she will never be able to help herself again. Poor Rebecca has to teach a school and attend her helpless mother. I hope her rich relations will consider it, and afford some assistance. . . .
>
> Your Aunt [Mrs.] O[liver] Champlain has been confined all winter in a distress'd condition. Her case is singular, and the Faculty are at a loss what to make of it. Her right cheek is swoln and very painful. It was thought at first to be the ague in the face, since it has been supposed to be an ulcer tooth; but now they fear 'tis something still worse. Her face has been lanc'd twice and three teeth extracted, and Doctor North still continues to exercise his skill in surgical operations. He is now about to put a Seaton [= Ceton, suture] in her cheek, and if there should happen to be any face left by the time he has done cutting and slashing, so much the better for the patient. But her friends are very much afraid she never will recover.
>
> Sally has just rec'd news of her father's death, [Richard C. Shannon]. 'Tis not long since she was here with a thousand apologies for not writing to you–hopes you will not think 'tis neglect–that you must still continue your entertaining letters, which afford us all so much pleasure. She says you know her aversion to the pen, and besides, you are such a critic, she is now allmost afraid to write, after the basteing you have given poor Will'm only for being a little genteel, or so, and 'stitching To's about your letters' when 'tis fashionable at Court: My Lord Castlereah and the English nobility direct '*To* James Stewart Esq., British Consul &c&c.'

But enough of nonsense, and now for business. The furniture arrived safe and sound and in as good condition as I could expect, all things considered. But Capt. French forgot to pay the carmen. If Mr. Fitch discharged the debt, let me know, and the amount, and I will send the money. I requested you to keep all the articles that would be useful to you or Mrs. Fitch. You mentioned five only: a hair trunk, the paint desk and stand, the long box and looking glass. These are all you say you have reserved. Some others are missing, which must have been left at the store or lost by the way, or on the passage. The tea-spoons, one set of small knives and forks, one large tea tray, small Dutch oven, one little rocking chair, two school benches, a thin mahogany drawing board, a box of crayons, a box of coloured pencils, and Uncle Taber's picture, hose and all; besides, the most valuable books is missing with the above mentioned articles. Perhaps the carmen may be able to give some account of them, or it is possible they may have been left at the store. But after Mr. Fitch has allready had so much trouble with the old trumpery that I should be sorry to give him any more.

Just as I was drawing to a close, Aunt Hannah brought me your letter, and one to Sally, in which you gave her such a handsome drubbing for her blunt honesty that she really thinks she will answer it herself. And so she may. I too would answer mine, and all the rest I have rec'd from you. . . .

My love to all our good friends–Mrs. Northam, & Mr. and Mrs. Fitch, not forgetting [their daughter Cornelia] 'Tweedle Dee', the little paragon of perfection. To send her kisses would be sending coal to New-castle, as I doubt not they are plentifully bestowed upon her. But the dear little hussy seems determined to make me love her, whether I will or not, and she could not have taken a surer method to effect her purpose than to reproach me with my faults so prettily. Tell her I did not forget her. I know I am very naughty, I ought to have mentioned her particularly in my letter to her Mama, and that I did not was owing to a feeling that I shall neither name nor describe, occasion'd by a certain passage in her mother's letter, where she speaks [of] my favourite. She says her little darling 'is infinite[ly] better and handsomer, and, was there not a large share of prejudice inlisted, I am sure you would think so too.' This I could not allow; and rather than dispute the point I chose to pass it by in silence, little expecting to be call'd to an account for it by so young a monitress. Tell her, her reproof has convinced me I did wrong. I am very sorry, but she is a good girl and will excuse me. I promise her henceforth her pretty name shall allways grace my letters.

Adieu.

The enclosed pieces is for isanglass & ballance due for guitar strings. If you have any thing further to offer, sift it out.

W[illiam] C[hamplain]. . . .

Later in the month Eliza answered in a letter home (**no. 97**), at the end of which she takes up certain concerns of her aunt over the household articles sent up to New

London, comments on the news from home, a question to William; but these may be omitted:

> Well, the incompareable Mrs. Shearman has arrived at last with her son Ebin and her daughter Laura. She is indeed a superlative character. There is as much dignity and grace in her composition as can be blended with the most affable deportment. She appears as if born to sway the world–with half Maria's dignity, she has a vastly superior mind which, operating together in the same person, produces a very powerful effect on the spectators. You like originality. There is much in her manner of expressing herself. I think I never heard eloquence equal to hers, except Mr. Mitchell in his highest flights of fancy. Well has Mrs. Fitch chosen her friend, for if she had searched the world over she never would have found her equal, and of that she's well convinced herself. Tho' Cornelia is a fine child and I have no doubt will make a fine woman, she never will be her 'Mah Shearman,' as she calls her. She plays and sings with exquisite taste and is I think the most accomplished woman I have ever seen. I was out to the Arsanal taking Hayden's likeness when she arrived, so I did not see the 'meeting of the waters,' tho' I believe they paid each other a watry tribute, and the little hussey Cornelia had lost all recollection of her mother, strange as it may seem. She has examined and complimented my painting in such terms as they never were complimented before or behind, and from some cause or other has express'd more affection for me than ever any person (even my nearest relatives) express'd for me since I was born. This melancholy truth I do not speak from vanity but to make you perfectly acquainted with the first stranger who ever said and appear'd to take such a deep interest in my concerns. She certainly is the greatest woman I have ever known, and to hear continually expressions of regard from such a character would certainly raise my vanity to the highest pitch, if that passion together with all my other soaring ones had not been so cruely 'pelted by the pitiless storm.' But my enthusiasm together with 'everything of the kind' has been crushed to the earth, never again to rise to the pitch it has!
>
> I must stop here and tell you that since I commenced this letter Capt. Hayden has been ordered to Pensacola, where he says he will not go–that he will sooner resign than go–and has now gone on to Washington to battle the watch with the heads of department. They moved from the Arsanal last Thursday, and a son-in-law of General Macomb's now has the command there. Maria and her child are now at her father's, where they will remain till he returns and the question is decided whether to go or not to go. She beg'd me to write amediately and tell you how sorry she was to be obliged to defer her visit so long, as we might have been and returned e're this, if it had not been for this unlook'd-for removal. Hayden is very mad about it. He had no idea of being removed, and had improved the place very much, and at his own expence. In his garden he has toil'd night and day, and made a paradise of it, for the enjoyment of those who will never thank him for it. The reason asigned for sending him off is the place is too important for a Captain; so a Lieutenant is placed

in his stead, and the place to which he is order'd, I believe, has five times as many to command. So much for the honor of wearing an epaulet.

In the mean-time, while my visit is in suspense, I am going to take Mrs. Shearman's likeness on ivory. She will make a most elegant picture. She has a very fine face. There is a nobleness about it that looks as if she was incapable of doing a mean action. She has a great deal of expression and an elegant mouth (my favorite feature, you recollect). Her form is large, dignified and commanding, and she dresses with a great deal of taste–more than I ever saw a woman of her age. She is thirty-six, but she does not look so old. I have selected the dress in which she is to set. It is the most heavenly sky-blue crape you ever saw and she looks much better in it than in any of her other dresses, tho' they are all very handsome indeed. A very tasty turban and lace colerett. And I intend to 'cut all crazy,' as Maria says, unless my evil genius directs the pencil.

I have had about five hundred and fifty invitations to Mrs. Mitchell's this winter, all of which I have refused because I could not accept them. You know [the Mitchell daughter] Margaret always took a sort of fancy to me. Mrs. Fitch has laughed herself to death to see her fasten upon me as the leeches used to you, and not quit her hold till she had extorted a promise that I would visit her–which I never intended to do even while I was promising. But they have long contemplated having a sewing party, more for the purpose of bringing together the sheep and the goats of the church, that they might get acquainted, than for the assistance they would be. Accordingly the day was appointed and I recieved such an invitation as I knew, if I refused, I should offend them. So I packed on my duds in high style and sallied forth with Mrs. Fitch and Mrs. Shearman, late in the afternoon of a rainey day, to exert my sewing talents for the good of the [?]loo. Well, we were the last who got there, of course, and might as well have been call'd the 'standing committee,' as almost the whole congregation were assembled and we were obliged to stand till seats were procured; which, however, was not long. First the folding doors were thrown open and both rooms, which you know are verry large, were crouded. In the drawing room and in the highest seat in the synagogue sat Lady Tooker at one of the front windows like a three-tailed bashan, and at the other sat the paragon Miss Ellen and Mr. Pierson's daughters, two very pretty unaffected girls, if I might judge from their conduct. Then came the Marquands, the Clinches, and all the ice-creames of the church. From them, the row extended across the house till it got down to the Degraws and the Sagars and similar skim milks. I thought it was queer that, instead of the company's mixing promiscuously as they always do at large parties, that the small fry should stick by themselves, but I thought of the old saying, 'birds of a feather &c.' I got by chance next to Cornelia Clinch, who you know is near-sighted. The room was verry dark with curtains and blinds. It was near night and I could not see an inch before my nose, when I had some stitching brought me to do. Poor Cornelia had a collar at which she had been fumbling all the afternoon, and 'such a pitious tale she told me' of what she had undergone that I laid down my work and had a real old-fashion'd laugh at her. I then commenced afresh and murdered out a wrist band of the finest linnen, and that was all. Cornelia is very good at descriptions and she gave me such a humorous one of her proceedings that I thought I should have died with laughter. Indeed, I don't know when I should have stopped, had I not caught three or four pair of very penetrating eyes fix'd upon me that seem'd to repove my levity. So I smoothed my risibles as well as I was able because I was at the parson's, tho' I wished the cross old duennas to Jerico who fixed their gooseberry orbs on me when I felt in a funny humour.

Mrs. Shearman attracted the attention of both rooms, as she was shown to a seat beside the aforesaid three-tailed bashan. A general buz of '*who* is she' was heard from all quarters of the room as she majesticaly walked up and took her seat. She loked so grand that even Lady Tooker deign'd to speak to her and, growing more and more pleased with her, enter'd into an earnest conversation with her which ended in a pressing invitation for Mrs. S., Mrs. F., and Mrs. Northam to visit her on the following day–that she had contemplated cleaning house the next day but could on no account deprive herself of the pleasure a speedy visit from Mrs. S. would afford her, and she must not disappoint her but certainly come without more cerimonious invitation. But Mrs. Fitch expected company herself on the following day, and invited them [the Tookers] here, which invitation was accepted and they came, in the evening. My paintings were introduced and even royalty itself deigned to pronounce them adequate. A proposal was instantly started for my opening a school, and insisted upon so warmly by Mr. & Mrs. Mitchell that I did not know but I should be obliged to open it before they quit. They were very anxious indeed. The Paragon with *Fancy* in her hand was hopeing I would consent to teach for she would instantly come to school if I would. They desired me to fix the time that I would commence, but I did not choose to, as I don't know when I shall or whether ever. She has had two or three different drawing masters, and I am told paints elegantly. Her present teacher is Robertson.[3] I had as lief die as think of it but I don't know what to do. Heaven only knows. . . .

At this point as at many others, the ultimate keeper of the correspondence who was Eliza served her own immortality better than others': an anxious letter of late May from her mother was not kept. It would have explained the next (**no. 98**) of June 9th from Eliza:

I have just recieved your last epistle and am sorry to find you so alarmed at my silence. I find you have not learn'd as much patience as *I* have, waiting for letters, or you would think nothing of waiting twice as long. But the truth is, I have not time to breathe, between seeing company and jaunting about. I suppose you are surprised at this confession. Visiting gives me no pleasure, but I go that I may not be call'd queer and odd for staying home so much.

Last Monday we all took a paddle down to Staten Island in the *United States* steam-boat. We set out from the Battery and had a very pleasant sail. I believe we rode down in a coach as Mrs. Shearman could not walk so far without blistering her feet. We went on shore at Staten Island and wander'd round for an hour. We then went to a public house where the piazza, which extended from one end of a large house to the other, was fill'd with gentlemen. There we had some sangaree and, after resting ourselves again, went on board of the steam boat and return'd. I saw Capt. Cahoon on board. Mrs. Fitch introduced Mrs. Shearman and me to him, as we said we knew him. He knew us both and scraped acquaintance with both of us. He had both of his children on board. One of them is a little beauty. On the wharf we found a carriage in waiting, which we rode home, and this terminated our expidition. Tuesday evening we went to Chatham Garden for the benefit of the Orphan Asylum. No ticket was used, only the money which was recieved for refreshments given to them. The Garden was brilliantly illuminated with varigated lamps. The fountain played a variety of tricks, there was an elegant band above it, and a very fashionable singer who sung several popular airs. Mrs. Shearman was delighted but I had seen it before.

Wednesday we were invited to a party at Mrs. Clinches, but before we went, took a ride up to Vauxhall Garden to see the balloon, which was just going off. At the hazard of our lives and the lives of thousands around us, we press'd thro' such a croud of men, women and children, and horses as I never saw before. Fourth of July and Montgomery's burial was nothing to it. We got a very excellent situation and soon saw the aerial machine pass over us, with its inhabitant swinging his bottle over our heads as he pass'd. I was not sorry I went, as it gave me more pleasure than anything I have seen since I can remember. It was made of a variety of colour'd silks elegantly painted, and in the sun made a most splendid appearance. It sailed gracefully through the air without turning to the right or left till we could see it no longer, and as it disappear'd such a murmur of regret arose from the populace as I never heard before. We then proceeded home.

On our way we saw Mrs. Hayden and [her unmarried sister] Eliza [Sanford], Mr. Schoolcraft, and [the other sister] Harriet walking up towards the Arsanal. It was impossible for me to speak to them, of course, at that time. They cut a mighty dash–every eye was upon them. We then went to Mrs. Clinches where we found Lady Tooker and young Mrs. Clinch, Mrs. Avery and Mr. and Mrs. Mitchell, beside several others too numerous to mention. In the evening they urged Mrs. Shearman so much to play and sing that she at last consented. She play'd on all their instruments to the admiration of every one, which consisted of a harpsichord, a piano, and a lute. She was much admired. Thursday we went to a party at Mrs. Avery's, where we were verry agreeably entertain'd with vocal and instrumental music. Mr. Avery plays better on the German flute than any-body I ever heard, and I think him quite agreeable, beside. Mrs. Avery c[a]rried [her son] Walter's picture round the room to show it to those who had never seen it and to gratify me, I suppose. It was verry much admired, particularly by Mrs. Shearman. Mrs. Avery says as soon as [her daughter] Mary Amelia gets as old as Walter she intends to have her taken exactly like it, 'if I'm alive.' The likeness is excellent now. I think he grows more like it as he grows older.

Well, I have told you how the week has been spent so far, but the best is to come. To-day I expect a lady to set for her likeness. She wishes it done in the best manner. She has a verry striking phiz. I can hit but cannot miss her. She is to be dress'd in black with a lace ruffle and a straw-colour'd silk scarf thrown over one shoulder, her head with a great many combs, curls, and braids–and I am delighted. So good-bye for the present, for I am in a woful hurry, in the midst of taking Mrs. Shearman's likeness, which bothers me to death on account of the regularity of her features. This delay in our visit, tho', is plaguy provoking. Adieu. . . .

Eliza's plan of a visit to New London with Maria Hayden was somehow conceived under the wrong star. Delay followed delay. Even her apologies, begun on June 9th, waited till July 17th actually to be put on paper (**no. 99**):

My dear Aunt,

I did not expect to write to New London any more before I visited it, but as I cannot control events, 'tis possible you may yet get another letter before I come. As I have some news to communicate that may perhaps give you pleasure, I instantly set down to write. In the first place, you may depend on our visiting you before a great while, tho' when I cannot tell you yet. Mrs. Hayden call'd here day before yesterday to tell me she had recieved a letter from her husband who is still at Washington and should remain there till December. The letter contain'd only three lines. He requested she would not write to him again untill she recieved another letter which would be soon. She is to let me know the instant she recieves it and I am to let you know then when we shall be ready to come; for if he remains as long as he expect too she will of course be mistress of her time till he returns. I am sorry for the disappointment, as the season will probably be very sultry when we leave here, and traveling unpleasant. She was quite out of spirits and I believe she thinks Hayden means to leave Washington without letting her know where he is going. Her child is well.

In the next place, I have to inform you that Mary Ann Mason has at length enter'd into the holy state of matrimony! Not with Thomas Dawson, who I am convinced loved her sincerely and who she said she loved better than any body in the world–but to be related to his mother and sister, she could not, as she should be the most miserable wretch in existence for life if she should. She has married a Mr. Blauvelt, a verry warm admirer of hers and I believe (tho' don't know for certain) he is the verry same man she once refused. I suppose you recollect the story. She says he is the person whom her parents wished her to marry before they died and that he is a very fine man. I have never seen him but I think if she could do it she was right, as everlasting misery would undoubtedly have been the consequence of a marriage with Thomas. Hannah and her mother are most wofully disappointed at this unexpected stroke. They say if they had thought that they (themselves) had been the obstacle to the match they would have 'begged their bread from door to door' but what it should have taken place, as they are very much afraid that Thomas will never return to their place again now Mary Ann is married, as he gave them a hint to that effect before he went away in consequence of their ill treatment of him while he was here. Poor fellow, I hope he will meet with better friends in his progress through life. If he don't he will be unfortunate indeed. Mary Ann's husband is a capt. of a vessel. You know she always had a great many of the sons of Neptune in tow, besides as many land-lubbers. She has now reduced her train of adorers to a 'select few.' Among those that are dismiss'd is the Solomon Hoogland and a few others of his description. She was married three weeks ago and her husband has now gone a ten months' voyage. Her sister Ellenor is married to George Clinton Sitcher, the little fool that was so in love with her last winter. She lives at his father's, Col. Sitcher, a man of some consequence in the city. He lives in Greenwich Street in considerable style.

Mrs. Williamson is well. Isaac they think is in a consumption and as soon as Blauvelt returns they are going to buy a farm and give up business altogether, as it don't agree with him at all and they think the country would. Mrs. Shearman has gone, and left a void in our family circle that will not soon be fill'd up. A few evenings before she left here we all went to the theatre to see the tragedy of *Richard III* perform'd. It was Barns' benefit and poor Shakespeare suffer'd for it, for he was torn to tatters by that indescribable genius, as he was cut out for anything but gravity.[4] Through the most serious parts he kept the house in a roar with his grimaces. There never was anything so completely burlesqued; and until humpy was slain and the curtain dropped, I could scarcely think for the noise. Almost instantly after he was borne off the stage his reserrection took place: he appear'd out-side of the curtain in the same dress in which he died, to inform the audience what would be the next play, and return his thanks to those friends who were present, which he did in so humourous a manner that their mirth was as boisterous as ever.

The next evening we were all at a party given by Miss Abeel on Mrs. Shearman's account, where I saw little Wixey who had likewise been to the theatre the night before. He said he understood it was the intention of Barns to do his best if the audience would let him, but as soon as he saw disapprobation in his auditors, Shakespeare should suffer for it, as he would directly turn the tragedy into ridicule. He never was cut out for anything but comedy, and for him to attempt tragedy was a great piece of folly. But O how I laughed. I got the hystericks at his drollery.

I have lately had an application from a brother of the brush for his miniature. He is a genius and of course must be queer. He has left his card by which I have discover'd his name is Augustus Burr.[5] He has a fine face and if he had not so much diffidence that he can scarcely set for his picture I should think him quite a fine fellow (that is, if I ever see him again). He has sat twice and I have never seen him since, nor never expect to again, as wights of his description I think of all others are least to be depended upon in this degenerate age. He brought two or three specimens of his painting which I think very good indeed. He studies with Stuart who taught him to use only three colours–carmine, indigo, and raw terra seenna. Those colours will paint a likeness, but the painting is very cold, and for a lady it will do, but for a gentleman of a warm constitution it is rather too delicate. Tho' he makes them 'do with an onion,' he says in general he never uses but three colours; but upon very extraordinary occasions he sometimes uses four. He has taken the De Wolf family who I suppose you recollect hearing Mrs. Fitch talk about. They are acquaintances of Mrs. Shearman's and live in Newport. The likenesses are very handsome and do him credit, but he makes *light* backgrounds because he says he has not patience to make dark, which I think is a disadvantage to them. He admires some parts of my painting very much. He says he thinks my 'labour is verry chaste,' particularly those pieces that are in 'strong relief.'

I have taken the lady who I had told you was comeing to set some time ago. The likeness is thought an excellent one and full as handsome as she is, which for me, you know, is a great deal. A lady call'd here last week–an acquaintance of Mrs. Fitches who talks of having her little boy's likeness, who is about the size of Walter Avery. He is quite a pretty little fellow and I am in love with her. She is also an acquaintance of Doctor Wright's and one of the most agreeable women I have seen since Mrs. Shearman went home. Mrs. Fitch sent for Walter's picture to show her and see if it would not induce her to have one done in the same manner. She thinks it beautiful but has not yet concluded to have one of those kind or a miniature.[6] I am in hopes, however, that she will have the former, if she is sufficently urged, and the family I am with says and does every thing in their power to get me business.

You say we do nothing but from interested motives. I must exculpate them from the charge, for Heaven knows, if they are not disinterested in all they do for me, I am ignorant of the meaning of the word. I deserve nothing at their hands and they do every thing in their power for me. But talking is useless. They all go to Saratoga Springs the first of August, and I shall be again left mistress of the house till they return, which I suppose will be in about a week or ten days. I did not expect nor do I wish it, but as I said before, we cannot control events.

Capt. Hayden, instead of writing to his wife as I told you he was going too at the beginning of this letter, has return'd and will remain here till the last of August. I was down to see her yesterday. She was in excellent spirits but extremely sorry that she should cause us so much disappoint-ment by not being able to go when she said she would. She says she would have gone through fire and water if it had not been for Hayden; but you know there is no dependence to be put in the male sex, particularly one of his fly-away description. He told me yesterday that in all probability he should waite upon us to New London. His wife and I stared with astonishment at him. He laughed and with one of his most incomprehensible looks assured us it was more than probable that he should go with us, as he liked of of all things to wait upon the gals. I told him I should be happy to have him go and then took leave of them; so how the affair will terminate I do not know. A spell seems to be set upon our ever going or ever knowing when we shall go. She was out last week, looking for green crape to make a traveling veil of, when, in steping from one flag to another, she turn'd her ankle in such a manner as to sprain it very bad. She has not worn a shoe since. She is very busy sewing, and her child has the summer comp[laint]–three good reasons she told me to tell you for her not comeing yet, till the weather gets a little cooler. Patience is a virtue, you know, which we have all to put in practice very often, as we murder along through life; but I need not preach to you. . . .

Fourth of July I spent just as we did the one before when you was here–that is, I never went out of the house and saw nothing in it. In the evening Mr. and Mrs. Fitch and myself went up to Vauxhall Garden to see the fire-works, which were very splendid and would once have given me pleasure. The Retreat, Tammany Hall, the Museum and Chatham Garden were all brilliantly illuminated, but I had seen it before and behind.

I often see Miss Moore returning from church, Sundays, who always stops and enquires particularly about you. The beautiful Mrs. Crocker whose likeness you took when you lived in the Thomas house is no more! She died after five days of illness, but with what complaint I don't know. Maria Clinch has had a very severe fit of sickness and is not yet quite recover'd, but is much better. Eliza Mitchell is in very ill health and has gone to the country. She has very consumptive symptoms. Mrs. Fitch is not in good health tho' she makes no complaints, as she despises stooping to complain, you know.

Mr. Fitch paid two dollars to the carmen for moving the furniture. He is well–also Mrs. Northam and Cornelia. They all send their love to you. Cory says Walter's picture 'is superb.' It is very much admired by every-body and is still an excellent likeness of him.

The paragon Floyd is now in town. He boards at the City Hotel but is often at Sandford's. Lagnell is now boarding there. The poor fellow has lost the sight of one of his eyes and the other threatens to leave him. He says if it does he will certainly blow his brains out, as he cannot survive the loss of both. . . .

I have just seen Maria. She tells me that she thinks of boarding in New London instead of here, if she can find anybody that you are acquainted with and will visit with. Her own family she don't like on account of the noise. . . .

Eliza now at the age of twenty-four had had some years to think about marrying, and plenty of guidance on the subject if she chose to listen to it. It was Maria Sanford's marriage that had brought on the first discussion with Mary five years earlier, when the two of them had measured the merits of a single life against that of "a mere wife, a domestick drudge," and found the latter wanting. A few months later, however, a more ordinary choice had asserted itself and Mary was holding out to her niece in New London the great advantages of New York in the matter of beaux: "come down here and make your market . . . if you don't come soon, your beauxs won't keep without salting."[7] For her part, Eliza's mother could say seriously to her, "I think I would recommend a single life by all means," but offered this view in a context of glum Edward-Youngian ruminations. At other moments she was decently flirtatious; and after all, she had not lived a spinster. Eliza herself, if she is judged by her inquiries after Jiggins, Chavalier, or Wixey in New York and an occasional New London man like Halsey Goddard, inclined to marriage like other young women. On the feminine role her views were conventional, too, witness her remark "that philosophers in petticoats are rather out of character."[8] Thus much as background to her reading of Mary Wollstonecraft's famous *Vindication of the Rights of Women*, which is encountered in the letter that follows. Characteristically, Eliza finds little in the work to her taste. Wollstonecraft offered opinions surely approved by Mary about women's intellectual powers and the sort of education and employments which should properly acknowledge those powers; and her general point of view and social sympathies were not incompatible with Mary's and Anna's; but the two must have been shocked by the course of life the author had chosen, and for that reason thought the book unsuitable for a young woman to read.[9] The letter is **no. 100** of August 13, to Mary:

> I have this instant recieved a visit from Samuel and must confess I was never more surprised in my life. Tho' William had told me he was comeing, I had my doubts about it, as he is in the habit of writing nonsense. But when he actually stood before me and I had studied his phiz long enough to be convinced it was himself, I soon gave him the right hand of fellowship. I think him altered very much, and he warmly returns the compliment. He has been yet but six hours in town and is as home-sick as death. He walked about the room as if he was very much agitated but would tell me nothing that I wanted to know. There was a young man with him whom I wished further, as I could not ask him a single question about his affairs before a third person, and am now as ignorant of his situation as if he had not call'd. All I know is that he felt pretty bad; and, as I have so long been bless'd with the same feeling myself, I knew how to pity him. His companion tried to cheer him 'but nothing could a charm impart.' I would give the world to see him alone, as I am dying to know why he is so disappointed; but I fear I cannot, as he don't know the way alone. I begged him to come this evening again, but it's so far advanced I suspect I may give him up. As soon as he comes and lets me know about his business, I will continue my epistle. In the meantime I thank you for yours, but I wish it was longer, as you know a short letter was always my aversion.
>
> The whole family left here for the [Saratoga] Springs last Saturday, so I am entirely alone except a servant in the kitchen and clerk in the [law] office [of Mr. Fitch]. They will stay a week or ten days and as soon as they return, perhaps, I shall set out for New London. Capt. Hayden call'd here last week to tell me that as soon as the family return'd from the Springs, himself, his wife and I would turn our faces towards New England, as it is his desire to see her comfortably settled before he makes his exit; and, as New London is the place which she has pitched on, he bows acquiescence. So, if we are to come we shall come. For my own part, I have done calculating upon any-thing in this life but disappointment, and am fast getting so enured to it that any thing else will frighten me. 'Tis the lot of mortals, and he or she who bears the evils of life with the most fortitude is the best fellow. So I say no more about it than telling you what he says, and shall wait with Christian patience and resignation the moving of the waters.

Mrs. Cob call'd in to see me the other day. She said it was by chance that she found me as she has call'd at the house we used to live at but could not discover my place of residence. She said it was with difficulty she recognized me, I was so much alter'd–if she had not gazed at me in at the window till she traced a resemblance to my mother in my countenance, she never should have known me; and she observed, that was the highest compliment she could pay me. So good night. I wish I could see Sam.

August 20th

Well, Sam'l visits me often but has not yet got a place. I think his prospect is much clearer than it was the first day he call'd, as he is sure of one place, tho' from his account it must be forlorn; but to be sure of anything under heaven like business is a great thing in this place. If, as he says in his letter to William, the man sells butter by the gill, tobacco by the chew, and keeps shop open all night as well as Sundays, I think he would be a fool to go there if he could possibly get a situation in any other store in the city, as I am convinced there is not another that conducts business in this way. So I don't urge his accepting the man's offer, as I should if he could not possibly live without going. I am thankful he has met with Henry Holt (tho' I fear we are doom'd to plague the Holts to death), for a powerful friend was what he stood very much in need of at this time, and I find he has interested himself very much for him. Mr. Fitch has not yet return'd from the Springs, and when he does I have not much faith in his ability to procure him a place in a flour or grocery store, as his acquaintances do not consist of such characters, I believe. But when he comes we shall know. In the mean time he is boarding at 69 Pine Street and not much pleased with his situation. All I am afraid of is that his purse will get empty before he is ready for it, and that does not produce the most pleasing sensations in the world.

I have been laughing at him about the size of his hands. They look as if one of them would cover one third of the city; and he is very fat; so he says he intends to write Mother that I will not let him rest till he has drank a hogshead of vinegar and cut off both his hands. He is a queer dog and has made me almost die with laughter two or three times since his arrival, notwithstanding his low spirits. I wish he was not quite so Champlainish, as I think he would appear to more advantage with less of their 'Ways and means,' and am trying all I can to pound it out of him; but I fear what's 'bred in the bone' won't be pounded out. He, I believe, has many good qualities and I believe faithfulness is one. I think I should place more dependence on his word than on many of the name–I would say, all, for fear of giveing offence. But generally speaking they are an unstable set and I have no very great affection for them. Reccollect, I don't mean those that are nearest related to me. 'Tis merely for grandmothers, uncles, aunts, cousins and the like that I feel such a comfortable indifference that their weal or woe cannot excite my joy or sorrow.

Don't start and look aghast! at what perhaps you will call my unfeeling 'confession of faith,' for I cannot conquer the dislike I have concieved for some of them.

Neither do I wish to. But enough of this till we meet. I will only add, I wish all the boys well, from my soul; and 'further' the Chapter (I believe it is) 'saith not.'

I write this unknown to Sam'l, as he desir'd I would not send a letter till he had got a place, but as I had commenced opperations I was determin'd to go through. Mother, don't be distress'd about him, for I think he will do very well. He wants to suit himself before he engages anywhere and in that I think he is right. Meanwhile you will undoubtedly hear from him often, and I hope, soon, better news.

And now all I have to say is that what you so greatly fear'd has come upon you. I have committed the unpardonable sin of reading Mary Wolstoncraft's *Vindication of the Rights of Women*, contrary to your orders and those of Mrs. Fitch, who, I suppose, both thought my perricranium was not sufficiently strong to stand her thundering reasoning. But I can tell you it is. Indeed, Mrs. F. went so far as to tell me I had no business to read it. As I am 'easier coaxed than driven' on some occasions and as this happens to be one, I made no reply, but took the book and, setting down, commenced it. I know it was not a very palatable dose; but, as I sometimes like to administer unpalatable ones, particularly when I am mad, I never did anything with a better will. I soon got very much interested, so much so that I forgot it was anger that made me take up the book. I think all that ail'd the woman was, they put petticoats on her when they ought to have put on pantaloons–a misfortune which sometimes happens to some of the daughters of Eve ('saving your presence'), to their 'eternal woe,' as cousin Natty says. But perhaps 'whatever is, is right.' At least I will endeavour to think so. But 'tis realy a misfortune that the lady in question, as she had such a strong prediliction for pantaloons, had not been put into them. I should have liked to have had the buttoning up of them of all things. For my own part, I confess I have no doublet and hoes in my disposition, and where that is the case I am convinced a taste for the said articles can never be acquired. Thus endeth the first lesson. . . .

I don't reccollect whether I sent you an account of a Mr. Tainter who preached in the church about a month ago. At any rate I intended too, and if not, here it is. He was a young man and pretty good looking. I however did not like the cut of his jib nor the roll of his eye, which wandered round on the fair daughters of Universal Salvation with what I consider'd an un-Christian-like expression; but when I got home and express'd my opinion, I was consider'd uncharitable. A few days after, he visited with Mr. and Mrs. Mitchell at Mr. George Ire[land], Mrs. Clinches brother, who you know has a house full of handsome daughters. Well, the consequence was, he fell in love with the youngest and handsomest of the set and on the following day sent her a letter requesting her to meet him that evening without the knowledge of her parents on the Battery at 8 o'clock. The moment the letter was recieved, Mr. Ireland took it off to his brother Clinches, who amediately carried it to Mr. Mitchell. It spread like wild-fire among the pillars of the church, and the most approbrious epithet thought too good to be bestowed on the said Mr. Tainter. It provokes me that every fool must be asked to preach in our church who come here and call themselves Universalists, and then turn out as great rascals as ever existed, like Chevalier and a number of others of the same stamp. 'But it's none of my business, Mr. Dunham.' So I will leave it for wiser heads to settle and go on with my birds-egging.

August 22d

I have this instant sent your looking glass, *New London*, *Clytie*, and two band-boxes of mine on board of Capt. Howard to go up by him, as I shall have so much baggage to bring up myself that I thought it was best to send the most critical things without heavy baggage with them. Sam'l has got a carman to carry them all by hand and has himself gone down with them to see them safely deposited, and I sincerely hope they will reach home in safety, as I have spared no pains to make them. I have given Sam ten thousand charges and the carman as many to be careful of the glass & *New London*, as they are the easiest destroyed. *Clytie* has a substantial back-board to guard her and the band-boxes contain nothing but two old hats of mine which I send to make rubbish less, when I go. Mother, I don't think it's worth while to open the pictures unless you want to see them very bad, as it took me 79 thousand years to sew them up and I would not do it again for as many dollars. Reccollect, I want the glass again, or any article of furniture which has gone home. You must let me have them as I have no cash to spend on such articles and it may be absolutely necessisry I should have them, particularly if I keep school (as that is the fate of all such unfortunate wights as me). I shall undoubtedly need many of them, and I mention it to prepare your mind to part with them in case it's so ordered above.

Adieu.

As I wish this to go before the mail closes I must stop my clack, much against my inclination, I assure you, as it's just got cleverly a-going. But, Mother, I have one request to make of you that I hope you will attend to, as it worries me considerably, and that is, that you will cure some of the warts on your hands, as Sam tells me their is 999 thousand on both of them and if their is half that number it will scare Capt. H. and his wife out of the world, they detest them so much. Pray attend to it if you love my life.

I desire you will keep Sam's situation a profound secret, as he don't want it lisp'd in New London, where he is at present, or anything about it. But I knew you would be distress'd to death if you did not know exactly all about him. . . .

"Sam's situation" required some help. It was quite normal, however, that a young fellow should turn to a kinsman to get him a job or at least to recommend him to someone who would steer him in the right direction. Accordingly Sam wrote, no doubt at his mother's urging, to his paternal uncle Oliver, the richest Champlain there was; and Oliver Champlain could at least offer advice (**no. 100** of August 17th):

Dear Samuel,

Your letter of the 14th inst. was duly received and according to your desire I made immediate inquiry of the gentlemen you mentioned in your letter. They told me their intention was to take a boy and bring him up to the business. It appeared to me from their conversation your age [of twenty-one] was the only objection.

I think you had better look around you before you decide on going to sea, for that is a business like most others–if it is not close followed, you will do nothing more then learn to be a sailor, which I presume is not your object. Perhaps it would not be a-miss to drop a line in the news-paper offering your services as clerk to a wholesale dealer. You may have a call from some quarter. Inclosed is a letter to a friend of mine. You will call and hand it him. He is a very worthy gentleman and may find it convenient to assist you. I must remind you of one thing which young men do not think of, that is, altho' you are in a large city, the eyes of the respectable merchant is upon you and will most assuredly know if you are steady or not. Wishing you may enjoy health, prosperity, and a good reputation,

I remain your affectionate Uncle

O. Champlain

By this point, indeed since mid-August, it had become fixed and definite that Eliza and Maria Hayden would truly visit New London. Eliza sent home her things needed for a long stay and followed them up in the company of her friends not many weeks later; but the Haydens then cut short their visit unexpectedly. After they had returned to New York Eliza received the following from Anna Fitch (**no. 103**, of November 17, 1821):

My dear Eliza,

Being disappointed in going to church this evening, I shall embrace the opportunity of beginning a letter which I ought to have begun & finished long since. When I received your first letter I intended to sit down immediately & give your brother William a good scolding; as I expected it was through his means that your letter was so long in arriving. It was ten days after the date that I received it. As time the great restorer has caused these feelings to subside, I shall say no more on this subject at present, if this said brother of yours will promise to be more attentive to my concerns for the future.

I have received three letters from you since you went, not one of which is answered, though I have written. Therefore, in order to begin at the right end, which you know is of great importance, I have laid your first letter before me, open, that I may answer all that is answerable in it.

The account you gave of Sandy [Clarke] proves more in favour of his rationality than I had ever before heard. His opinion of S-of-N. Jersey is correct, he does indeed write & write & there is no end to his writing. We have the rejected addresses, among which is Sandy's.[10] It is very well written & has fewer unintelligible expressions than is usally met with in his productions.

'Aunt Mary was afraid you had forgotten her.' This is another proof how imperfectly she knows me. Where I have once professed affection or friendship, it requires much to make me cease to love, or forget. I never can. I feel grateful for the long letters she has written me, & know that my conduct has not corresponded with such feelings; but procrastination is one of my besetting sins. Do mention in your next if she is still able to write. Thus endeth the first lesson ––.

Secondly, you ask what I shall think of Mrs. Hayden's return. Before your letter arrived, all the thoughts & feelings which her unexpected return produced were over, & it would now be almost impossible to describe them; but this I know, that I have seldom been more surprised than when I heard it, which was at church. Mr. & Mrs. Sandford, Mrs. Johnson, Harriet, & Eveline were there, the first Sunday evening after her return, which I think was a Friday. The next morning I called on her at a boarding house on Broadway, in hopes of finding a letter & to inquire after you all. She told me that you had written some time before she left N[ew] London, which–pardon me–I thought must be a *Sandford*. I do not mean that I thought it was a wilful falsehood but a mistake such as you have sometimes observed yourself. All these evil thoughts I feel obliged to charge to William's account, as they would not have arisen had the letter been received in season.

After recovering in some measure from the surprise I felt at the news of Mrs. Hayden's return, my first idea was that it was entirely the Capt'n's act & that he had probably urged her against her will to return; but according to her own account she did not wish to remain in New London. The people she said she liked very well, but the place she disliked very much. This I think must gratify Johnson, as he will esteem it a corroboration of his doctrine. For the honor of my sex I cannot avoid hoping that she has acted only in conformity with her husband's view. If this is not the case, fickleness & woman might almost be used as convertable terms.

The morning that I called on her, she told me that Capt'n Hayden was to go the next Saturday to Washington, that he had now a permanent situation there as Assistant General, & that she expected to move on in the spring. He had these orders the day after he arrived from N[ew] London. I heard no more of them until last Monday when I met them both together in Broadway. They had just come from Belville where she told me she had been staying for some time.

You say you are home-sick. Actions, you know, speak louder than words, so I expect to see you return ere long, unless you should find some skillful physician who has power to cure this mental malady. I am sorry to hear you speak in the uncertain & unsatisfactory manner you do of returning. According to your own account there is but little prospect of business where you are. Then you would find as much advantage in being here, painting watch-papers & occasionally likenesses. Besides, you were to ask the advice of your friends on the expediency of your teaching. But this you seem to have entirely forgotten.

As to obligations, for mercy's sake, say no more about them. You speak of all you owe. I wish you would not think of it, but as I suppose you will, I will endeavour to show you that the all is but trifling.

Dec. 24th

Precisely at this spot I was interrupted by the return of our folks from church, & have ever since been prevented from finishing this letter. . . .

I suppose you will be surprised to hear that in three weeks I was at the theatre three times. Last Monday we went to see Sandy's former wife–for you must know that they are no longer one flesh but twain. She has procured a divorce, a copy of which has been twice printed in the *Sentinel*. I shall send you the paper with some others which contain some of Sandy's best poetry, & which prove that the fellow has no ordinary portion of genius, accompanied with an extraordinary share of immorality.

Mrs. Baldwin took her benefit last Monday, when Miss Brundage danced a hornpipe. This was what induced me to go. Never did I see any-thing more exquisitely beautiful. I could think of nothing but the houries of Mahomet's paradise–such luxuriant beauty, such artless gaiety, which seemed to show 'a mind at peace with all the world, a heart whose love was innocent.' She entered dancing, with a gun over her shoulder, stopped dancing for a moment and fired it off, then shouldered it & danced off the stage. She understands, as Sandy says, 'the poetry of motion' perfectly. I wished for you all the evening, as I always do when I am much pleased.

I was interrupted a few moments since by a call which was very unexpected. Mrs. Hayden did me the honour of returning the call I made her a few days after her arrival from N[ew] London. I told her I was writing to you & was going to tell you how sociable she had been, had she not entered when she did. I shall give you but the heads of her discource, as I find, if I do not come to a close speedily, my paper will. Capt'n Hayden has a furlough for the winter. Her father, mother & family have moved into the country. I cannot avoid here making one comment: How delightful this must be to the girls! Mrs. Johnson & husband are gone to Savannah. Gustavus, or rather Julius Caesar, is cutting his teeth. His mother intends writing to your aunt soon. She has made the attempt two or three times but did not succeed; & lastly, she is 'as women wish to be who love their lords,' which perhaps you know already. When I told her that I was writing to you she desired me to give her love to you. . . .

Skunk (I feel rather at a loss how to spell this word, as I believe it is the first time I have ever attempted it–however, I shall proceed with my story, right or wrong). Skunk-eyes is married. His other name is Mr. Epaphras Holmes, merchant taylor.[11] This information I gained from the Mitchells, who think quite highly of him, and information you will doubtless consider far more important I derived from the same source. The Knight of the Needle had been introduced there. His name is Goodwin (not the one who stabbed Stoughton). They believe he is recently married &, worse even than that, he is indeed a taylor. They were as much struck with his Knightship as everyone else. His voice & manners they mentioned as being extremely pleasing, and concluded after many fruitless regrets for his unlucky fate by agreeing with me that it was fortunate his situation was no other than it is; for, if being a taylor (which is universally allowed to be nine times inferior to any other occupation) he is so great, what might not have been expected had he been any thing besides? So you see his being a taylor is nothing but 'a blessing in disguise.'

Crab-Apple has again vanished, gone perhaps to seek some warmer clime, to comfort his poor withered shrivell'd frame. Mr. Willis, Mrs. Brown (alias Consequence), and all the other unknown worthies are as usual. You perhaps will be surprised to hear that I attend singing school. I was strongly persuaded to go, and moreover, notwithstanding the *injuries* I received from Mr. Allen last winter, with a truly Christian spirit of forgiveness, felt disposed to assist him. My husband told me yesterday that some time last week he met an old friend of yours in the street. Now who do you suppose it was? Does not your heart whisper Hinckley? Does it not beat high with delightful anticipations? But whisper & beat as it may, it was not your demigod, but no other than the redoutable & unaccountable Cap'n Hatch.

I assure you I have had my own troubles since you left me, with respect to help. I was a whole week after you went without a soul except little Richard for an hour each evening. At last, grown desperate, I applied to the intelligence office, a plan which I have always opposed, & procured a woman, the like of which I never saw before, & trust I never shall, *be*. . . . . . . You know where. After being obliged to turn her out of doors forcibly, I had another who I turned off a day or two before her month had expired. And now I have Jane. She is recovered & was very anxious to return, and I assure you I think more highly of her now than I ever did before, she is so far superior to any one I have had since she left me. I have also Richard, her cousin, so that I feel much more comfortably situated than I have for some time, and, notwithstanding these troubles, I have done some things not very customary with me. I have worked a pocket handkerchief for myself, read three novels, and nearly finished the fourth, & played for the last month nearly every day; so you see I have taken care that your fears should not be realized & that my mind should not be overcome by the deep thought which solitude engenders. One of the books I have been reading is *Women*, a description of which you may perhaps remember Mrs. Mitchell once gave us, while she was setting to your aunt for her likeness. It is extremely well written & is well worth a perusal. If you can, get it and read it to your aunt. I think it will interest you both. The one I have now in hand is *Glenarvon*, which has interested me much, as the character of the hero at first was supposed to be intended for Lord Byron and, if I mistake not, this report was laid to the occasion of his lordship's leaving Italy & returning to England. The author, Lady Caroline Lamb, afterwards denied having had any such intention, but there must have been considerable similarity in the two characters to cause such a report.

I hope you are not in a hurry for your books, for I have not yet been able to read any except the *Progress of Society* [by Job Taber], with which I was much better pleased than I expected to be after your remarks. I read it in haste but did not observe the frequent recurrence of the word 'sublime.' I think it contains many fine lines.

The arrival of *Charlotte and Werter* was very unexpected and rather unwelcome, as I had never the least desire to become acquainted with beings whom I always regarded in so insignificant a point of view. I can swallow a love story with considerable zest if it is served up to my taste, but if not, it does not sit well on my mental stomach. Such I have always esteemed the book now in question, & have of course avoided it; but you recommend it for the style & I must therefore read with a view to that, without considering the folly of the narrative.

A Sunday or two after you left this, Mr. & Mrs. Palms came to church, & a few Sundays after, Mrs. Bradford & Catharine Fox. I was surprised to find the former tall & quite handsome, as I had heard much of *little Judy* hopping along. I wish you had seen her, as I cannot help thinking that you have as incorrect an idea as I had.

There is one piece of news which I must not forget to mention. Fate has put a stop to the breed of Hawks. But though I jest (& who would not, if they had the opportunity?), I am really sorry for the cause of this wonderful effect. The vessel in which Mr. Hawk sail'd was shipwrecked in the September gale, & he, lost. His wife & children were greatly affected by the news and one of the boys, who was our nocturnal visitor, was quite deranged. It was with difficulty they prevented him from plunging into the water, as he said, to meet his father who he imagined was calling him. Such an instance of strong feelings I should not have expected from a Hawk, as I never considered their nature very sensitive.

But all this nonsense must not cause me to omit mentioning something of more importance. I took your watch-papers the day after I received them to the Mitchells. They received them with pleasure & gratitude–pleasure at possessing what they considered so beautiful, & gratitude at being remembered by you. Mrs. Mitchell admired them exceedingly. The girls were eager to show them to their father as soon as he entered, & handed them with, 'See, Pa, what Miss Champlain has sent us.' He examined them a long while without making any remark & then said, 'Well, I don't know when I've seen anything that pleased me so much. They are really beautiful. There is so much taste in the design, besides the fineness of the painting.' You know his manner when pleased. He said they were too handsome to be put into watches, & he would get them framed. And I hear they are now placed over the mantlepiece in a frame. Besides the consideration of preserving them by this means, he thought it might be serviceable to you, as they would be conspicuous & of course attract the attention of every one who entered. And when seen, the question would be, Who painted them? And your talents would by this means be brought into notice. Margaret's I thought much the prettiest, & I was afraid they would think so too; but Eliza appeared quite as much pleased with hers. I never in my life saw people who felt trifles so sensibly as they do. They know how to appreciate the motive, & value trifles accordingly. They were at first too much delighted to think of thanks, but Eliza mentioned to me, the other day, to give their love to you when I wrote, & say that they were much obliged to you for remembering them in the way you had. I wish you had had time to finish them off a little more, as they are exhibited as the specimens of your painting.

You inquire about Cornelia's friends. She says she has given them up, though I often hear her talk of Mrs. Bodkin. She continues as amusing as ever, & often impresses me with the shrewdness of her remarks. Whenever she accomplishes anything she thought very difficult, she always says, 'You know what Aunt Mary would say, "We can do any-thing we try." ' She has not forgotten you & says she would be very glad to see you, & so would we all, Eliza.

I have received your aunt's letter, & as soon as I have made the necessary inquiries I shall answer it. I find by that, that you are very desirous of returning on none but what you call honourable terms, but I can see nothing very dishonarable in your returning to me on any terms. My husband has frequently urged me to write & tell you that he says you must come immediately, and had I supposed that his words would have the desired effect, I should certainly have obeyed him sooner. Mrs. Strang came here to have her husband's picture altered, & was surprised to hear you were gone. She was in mourning, perhaps for little Joseph. A young man has also called & was anxious to know when you would return. He wanted a likeness taken, so you see you have lost one already. I trust the result of my inquiries will make you willing to return. My risible muscles have been very seldom moved to excess since you went. I have no one to laugh with, and what is perhaps still [worse], I have no one to laugh *at*.

I was much gratified at receiving your aunt's letter (though it contained some chiding), as I feared she was unable to write. Give my best love to her & your mother. Remember me to Aunt Hannah & tell her that we should all be very glad to see her. When you write, do mention how your Aunt Champlain is. I saw in the newspaper, some time since, the death of a Mrs. Champlain, which I supposed to be your grandmother. . . .

Mrs. Tyler has been very ill but is now recovering slowly. Young Mrs. Clinch arrived from Hartford last week with a fine daughter. Charles Clinch is on the eve of departure to some of the other states, where he expects to appear on the stage. Mr. Ballou preached here last Friday evening.[12] We went, mud little less than knee deep, to hear him, and as a reward met with disappointment. In almost every sentence he unmercifully murdered the King's English, nor had he any superior advantage to palliate these crimes. He laboured hard & brought forth little. Mr. Mitchell read the closing hymn & never did his voice sound more harmonious. Mr. Allen gave a concert in our church, the end of Oct'r, at which Miss Clark &c officiated. Miss C. & the others now sit with Mrs. Whitehead, which improves our singing considerably. Remember to write as soon as you receive this. Adieu, my dear Eliza.

Affectionately yours,
Anna &c &c &c

Your brother brought me your first letter & was surprised to find that you were gone. He promised to call again but has forgotten to fulfil his promise.

Sam now enters the correspondence in his own person for the first time. Perhaps he avoided it as much as he could because, from sister or uncle, it so often produced a scolding or a sermon. Or a joke about his big hands (**no. 100**). In any case, he appears still at twenty-one an awkward teenager in his conduct as in his letter (**no. 104**, December 9th):

Dear Mother, Eliza, Aunt Mary, Bill & the whole scrape,

How are you all? I am particularly anxious to hear from you at this present, as I have not rec'd but about 5000000 letters from you since my arrival, so pray write 66 thousand reams apiece per week. I am at present with Holt & Quinby[13] & I'm in good health & shall remain there until I quit. That's all the news about me.

My paws are rather larger than when Eliza was here (I forgot to mention that before). When they grow up I'll send post-haste to inform you about it, i.e. the particulars. I have but just rec'd Eliza's letter enclosing one to Mrs. Fitch, which I shall carry up tonight, so don't let that worry you. I don't go often to Mr. Fitch's, 'tis true, but I imagine I go full as often as I am wanted. The last time I was there I was introduced to an old lady by the name of Northup, or Northrup, or Northeast, or some such name–I cannot remember it exactly. I (on arrival) enquired for 'Miss Champlain,' & found her ladyship had been gone about 3 weeks to N. L., without letting me hear a word about it.

How is Aunt Hannah? Let me hear, as I have not hear a word about her since I have been here. As for that 'bundle for Mrs. F.,' I carried it more than 970 centurys ago, so that's safe. The newspapers I could not get. I went to the *Commercial Advertising* & bothered the printer for one of the date you mentioned, but could not find it. I did not know but that it was a case of life & death by your letter: 'Sam, do for the Lord's sake, for Heaven's sake, &c, get the *Com. Advertiser*.' I concluded that the whole human race was just expiring, and went directly. . . .

I wish to hear exactly what you are all up to. Let me know how the rooms look, especially the kitchen–whether that old round table stands in the middle of the floor yet or whether it is cut down, whether those sticks of wood (which Bill & I bored holes through & suspended from the ceiling) are burnt up or whether they are still there, like the coffin of Mahomet, till Doomsday.

I expect to have an answer to all that's been requested, & don't expect to be disappointed. Give my love to Aunts Everybody, Uncles ditto, Cousins Anybody.

I am all of yours, truly,

Sam'l Champlain

I wrote George 3 or 4 days since.

P.S. I would thank some of you to read this letter upon the 'house top.'

This to his home indeed got a reply, in the form of further requests for errands to be run, accompanied by reminders of his procrastination in the past. Principally he is directed to Riley's music store, where the elder Edward and his son of the same name, with competent help from Mrs. Riley in the background, sold everything a music-lover could ask for–in this case, a rare and marvelous sort of xylophone with glass instead of wood, tapped by hammers and variously called a "glass piano," "harmonica," or "musical glass." Properly it was called a "sticcado-pastrole."[14] Young Edward, just a year older than Sam, was evidently a friend of the Fitch household; his father was a friend of Woodworth's. So much as background to **no. 105** from Eliza, likewise of December:

Dear Samuel,

I wish you to carry the packet in which this letter is attached immediately to Mrs. Fitch. I entreat you not to neglect it a moment, for whatever I send to her is of the utmost importance and is always five thousand years reaching its place of destination. Pray let me know as soon as she has received it, that my mind may be at rest, and be sure offer to take letters for her to send by the packet if she has any to send. And write me every word that passes between you while you are there. Your watch-paper you may depend upon, tho' it has not been possible for me to finish it by this trip. When you received it you will not be sorry you have waited so long, as I shall take pains with it.

I am much obliged to you for attending to my commissions, and upon the strength of it I ask another favor that you must grant immediately, or Mother will have fifty thousand fits. Enclosed is one dollar and a half which I desire you as you value our lives to take to Mr. Edward Riley's store in Chatham Street, that is nearly opposite the 'Free School' (I don't know the number of the store, but enquire the name that you may be sure) and purchase just such a glass piano as you saw me playing on at Mr. Fitches the last evening that you spent with me there (Pl. 8.18: Edward Cort Riley).[15] The gentleman you saw there that evening is the same who sells them, and be sure request him to pick out a good one, as he is of course a better judge than you, and send it safe and sound by the first packet, directed to Mother, as it is a case of life and death. Now I desire you to write to me myself, for I don't like this proxy'mation business; and don't make me waite a hundred and fifty-nine million years for an answer to this, as is your usual practice. Let us know what are your prospects and how soon you expect to make your fortune. We are all well, particularly 'Congress' [Aunt Hannah], who hopes you will not forget her 'old black hen.'

Yours affectionatly,
Eliza

A week into the new year, 1822, Anna addressed Mary (**no. 106**) in answer to one from Mary that has not survived:

My very dear friend,

As my last letter was not altogether to your taste, I feel almost afraid to make another trial, for this, like the former, will probably be written in haste. I have acquired a habit, which I acknowledge to be a very bad one, never to begin a letter untill I am absolutely ashamed of my remissness, and then hurry through it as fast as possible to make up for lost time.

And now, having confessed thus much, which is doing a great deal for me, who am never very fond of confessing my sins to mortal man or woman either, we will with your permission proceed to business.

I was pleased to find by your letter that Eliza had not forgotten to mention to you the advice she received from her friends here, & consulting you on the expediency of taking it. The plan you proposed is now set on foot and I have no doubt will end as we could wish. Your views respecting Eliza I laid before some of her warmest friends—Mr. Mitchell's family. They were instantly interested & desirous of doing all in their power to benefit her. After thinking what was best to be done, Mr. Mitchell called here to-day & said that, in order to ascertain how many scholars could be procured, it was necessary to fix upon the terms and the time of commencing the school. The terms he advised should be low at first, untill she has a school established. Margaret he said was so eagerly interested that she insisted Eliza should get $10 per quarter, as her abilities were far superior to Mrs. Fowler, & she had $6; but he had lived longer in the world & thought it would be for Eliza's advantage to ask only $5 at present.

As to the time of beginning the school, he proposed the first of March. He fixed on this time as many would probably leave the city during the summer months. It was also suggested by Mrs. Cowdrey, who has taken Margaret's watch-paper (which is elegantly framed) to show Mrs. King, a lady who has several children. Mrs. C. thought it probable that some of them might become scholars if the school opened in season, as they left town in summer; and this would probably be the case with others. Therefore, after all these considerations, it was concluded that a paper should be drawn up, specifying these things, which I accordingly did in the following words: 'We the subscribers, desirous that Miss Champlain shall commence a school for fancy & miniature painting on the first of March next, offer her the following terms: $5 per quarter for each scholar, three lessons a week, three hours each lesson.'

As you mentioned nothing about the price I thought it best to take Mr. Mitchell's advice. He took the paper & with my husband called this afternoon at Mr. Whittemore's (an acquaintance we have formed since Eliza left). They subscribed for one scholar & Mr. Mitchell for two. He has offered to do all in his power to procure scholars among his friends, and I know of no one who can so effectually accomplish what they undertake. I am desirous of giving the honours to whom it is due, & therefore mention the exertions Mr. M. has begun to make, that, should this plan succeed as I expect, you & Eliza may know who to thank. Mr. M. thinks that twenty scholars may be got, but if only ten, with occasional likenesses & other painting, I think the prospect will be quite favourable. His plan was, if as many scholars can be procured as he expects, to have them divided into two classes, to be instructed on different days.

I have been able to say nothing of landscape painting as I have never seen anything of the kind done by Eliza. I hope she will not be offended at having all these preliminaries settled without consulting her, but dispatch seemed necessary, & you know it is always best to strike while the iron is hot. The watch-papers she sent to the girls has prepared the way for the present measures, for they are known to every-one who calls, and admired by all. Margaret's bears the palm & is thought far superior painting, which is rather surprising, considering the little discernment & taste people usually discover. Mrs. Tooker was quite in raptures about them, which was probably caused in some measures by their frames, and said, if Eliza was here, she would like to have Ellen's picture taken by her. Margaret told her she was expected, & would remind her of what she said, when she was here. I should have waited until I had more information to send, but I thought it best to tell you what had been done & what was expected, that Eliza might hold herself in readiness for a call, which she will be expected to answer by appearing, in spite of everything but death and marriage; or, as you would probably render it, death & destruction.

I was at a loss how to understand what you say about my aversion to long letters until I recollected that you were formerly famous for administering large portions of *Congress*. If you really believed what you said, I think by this time you feel sensible of your mistake, as my letter to Eliza has probably been received & perhaps read. I say perhaps, as it would take some centuries according to Eliza's mode of calculation, to finish it entirely. Ask her if she had not better undertake to teach this, with painting. It certainly would have novelty to recommend it. My pen is so bad that I must leave you a moment to mend it.

Your ideas of genius are too true. I verily believe that in proportion to the quantity a person may possess of that indescribable thing called genius, so will they suffer. It in one respect resembles sin, for it is ever accompanied by suffering. Nor is it the evils that result from poverty alone to which I allude. Though blessed with the smiles of friends, fortune & health, the possessor of this strange ingredient would never enjoy that happiness which might be expected to arise from such fortunate circumstances. Who knows but fate may for this reason have decreed their portion to be penury, seeing that they would be unhappy in prosperity, & that they could be no more, in adversity. . . .

Ever your affectionate friend,
Anna

For this long letter, Anna Fitch was doubly rewarded, first by one from Eliza which contains responsive comments and mention of her recent reading in Scott, Lady Morgan, and Charles Brockden Brown (**no. 107**); then by another from Mary. Of the first, the more interesting part naturally concerns the prospect of Eliza's starting a school:

. . . Your letter to Aunt Mary has arrived and of course put me in a great flusteration. I am infinitely obliged to you all–yourself, Mr. Fitch, and Mr. Mitchell for the trouble you are taking on my account. I am very much pleased with the arrangements and, as soon as a sufficient number of scholars are obtain'd, shall be happy to obey the call; and when I return we will have frolics again. Laugh with me or at me, which you please, I care not. If I have business, good spirits will not be wanting, I promise you. . . .

You know Aunt Mary's passion for astronomy. I have been reading to her Fontenell's *Plurality of Worlds*–rather reluctantly, I confess, as the style is not exactly to my taste. But she don't care for that if she can get among the stars. We want her genius [described in **no. 65**] here to attend our aerial excursions and adventurous flights, and guide us through the Milky Way. Heavens! how the fitful, flickering flame of genius used to flash from his dark eyes when he arose to declaim in all the majesty of rags and dirt, his cloathes being none of the best or cleanest, as you may remember. With what sang-froid he warm'd his muddy stockings, regardless of the surprise or amusement it might afford spectators.

Aunt Mary's guitar has been alter'd and vastly improved. It sounds now 'like the soft warbling of the Eolian harp,' and forms a pleasing contrast, while it admirably accords, with my mother's flagelet. Of course we have music wherever we go, as Cornelia says. How I want to see the little hussey, and your mother–in short, all of you. I am much obliged to Mr. Fitch for his invitation, and shall certainly accept it if I can. My respects to him, if you please.

Your affectionate friend,

Eliza

Mary in the same post and month wrote also (**no. 108**), describing Eliza's reception of Anna's letter and her enthusiastic building of castles in Spain–a school set going, and New York once more all around her. Mary herself reserved room for disaster. She too offered thoughts on talent, or 'genius' in the vocabulary of the day: it seems to be fated to suffer, and in the end, anyway, what is most to be preferred "is the less dazzling but more sure and steady light of reason, the basis of judgement and noblest faculty of the human mind." In sum, hers is a serious letter. Crossing it on the waters of the Atlantic, in Captain Howard's packet going north as Captain Lamphere's packet went south, so we may imagine, was a second and somewhat sharp-edged reminder from Anna that people had been busy planning for Eliza, and she should really do her part in the educational enterprise (**no. 109** of January 27, 1822):

My dear Eliza,

I have written both to you & your aunt and have been expecting an answer for more than a week. I hope neither of the letters have miscarried, for yours contain'd so much nonsense that I am sure the writer will be set down for a fool, & I expect the person addressed, not much better for having such a correspondent. But there is one consolation in case of a miscarriage: no uninterested person would take the trouble of labouring through seven pages of illegible writing to gain little or nothing.

Your brother called here about two weeks since with a letter & some watch-papers. Your letter was dated the 18th of Dec'r, which was nearly a month before I received it. Four of the watch-papers are at Mr. Whitney's. He says he can get 75 cents a piece, but a dollar people think very high. Miss Cowdrey called here the other day. She seemed to have acquired some of the interest which every-one feels in your favour. She was going to make a number of calls, & wished to get a paper to take with her, mentioning your terms &c, in hopes of procuring scholars. I showed her the box of watch-papers which she admired very much, & begged me to let her take them with her, which I did. She disposed of one at $1. In your aunt's letter I mentioned what had been done–that a paper had been drawn up to the following effect: 'We the subscribers desirous that Miss C– shall open a school for teaching fancy & miniature painting, to commence the first of March, offer her the following terms: $5 a quarter, half to be paid at the commencement and the residue at the expiration of the quarter. Three lessons a week, three hours each lesson.' I repeat this as my other letter is perhaps lost. I also mentioned that the Mitchells were using all their endeavours to procure you scholars.

Margaret & her father called here last week (one of the coldest days we have had this winter) to get another paper, as the first was lost. They took it & went to a number of places. The next day Mr. M[itchell] went alone, & yesterday Margaret was out morning & afternoon, as her father said, *forraging*. The names now set down are–Isaac Peirson (certainly one, perhaps two); Samuel Whittemore, one; Isaac Marquand (probably two); Jacob Clinch, one; Edward Mitchell, two; Samuel Cowdrey, two or three; [Rev. William] Berrian, one; William Thorn, one; so here is ten already, at least, & your friends are still continuing their exertions. There is therefore no doubt but more will be procured. All the specimen which they have had to exhibit was Margaret's watch-paper, which they have taken with them wherever they went. Mr. Mitchell regrets that he has not some-thing larger to exhibit. I think *Fancy* would do much execution. Margaret is desirous that you should not only have a large school but a genteel one, and you will perceive that all the scholars which are engaged are of this kind.

The next great thing is the place in which the school is to be opened, which at first appeared the most difficult part of the business to settle. But I think even this will be according to your own most sanguine wishes. My husband proposed that Mrs. Dartnel should be applied to, for the use of her room three hours in the day; that a reasonable compensation should be offered her, and Jane admitted into the school. This would prevent the necessity of getting benches &c. My mother mentioned it to her. She appeared very well pleased with the proposal & said she would think of the price. I think the plan is an excellent one as it is always difficult to hire a room in this way without giving a high rent, and even then, the people from whom you hired it might be rude & disobliging to you or the scholars.

Your aunt [in the November letter not surviving] mentioned boarding among the many things to be considered. We shall certainly expect you to stay with us as formerly, if you can encounter the many difficulties connected with living in the same house with so odd a being as I am. It has always been my practice to inform any-one with whom I expected to have much communication, of what they might anticipate; and, though my information has ever been doubted at the time, longer intercourse has proved that I knew myself far better than any one else. To you this information is unnecessary, as experience has taught you of what rough & impliable materials my character is formed.

And now for a word of advice. Leave behind you everything which will not be serviceable to you in your new undertaking, to wit, timidity, irresolution, want of confidence in your own powers, and [any]-thing else which your good sense may suggest as unnecessary appendages. Remember that you are to assume a new character, that you are to be looked up to as a teacher; therefore bury in one common grave all those qualities which will be a disadvantage to you in this character. Excuse the liberty I take. I would not run the risk of being considered severe, or even putting to flight your good-humour, if I had not your happiness in view.

As soon as you receive this, be so good as to write, for it would be a sad thing if the measures we have taken should not agree with your views after proceeding so far. And remember, as the school is expected to begin the first of March, it will be necessary for you to be here next month. I suppose you will want all the [painting-examples or] copies you can get; therefore bring with you every-thing in the shape of paintings which you have ever done. If *New London* itself could be transported here, I think it would be well. Your brother told me he had rec'd a letter from Aunt Hannah some time ago in which she sent considerable love. Had it been of a perishable nature, I expect it would have evaporated before we rec'd it, which was only a few days since. Remember us all to her, your mother & Aunt Mary. Tell the latter she must remember that I wrote last.

I have often thought of Cornelia since I began this letter, but could not find room to introduce her before. To-morrow she completes her fifth year. She is very much occupied at present about your drawing school & often talks of getting names. She begs me to send you two of her little pictures, which I shall enclose. She thinks they will assist you in painting watch-papers. I asked her if she was glad you were coming. She answered, 'Yes, Ma'am, I wish she was here now, that I do.' . . .

Yours affectionately,

Anna &c &c &c

I shall send Sunday's peices which I promised in my last. I hope you will not consider the postage more than they are worth, as I have no other way of sending them. I cannot help remarking that Caroline's & Eliza's addresses are doubtless by the same pen (I mean Sandy's [i.e. McDonald Clarke]). The peice said to be written by McD–Cl– is an imitation by the author of *Fanny* [i.e. Fitz-Greene Halleck]. Be so good as to save the peices & bring them with you.

When the preceding, with its urgency, produced no action from the recipients, Anna dispatched a third report on the preparations for Eliza's return (**no. 110** of February 28th):

Well, I am really surprised to find that three packets have arrived this week & you are not here yet. When I observed the arrival of the two Howards on Monday, I thought it very strange that you had not embraced the first opportunity & come with one of them. I however accounted for it by supposing that you were waiting a day or two for your favourite Capt'n Lamphere; but when I saw by last night's paper that he had arrived, I was entirely at a loss to account for your absence. My husband thought it probable that you had waited until I had again written, but this appears to me impossible, after the explicit manner in which I last wrote–that ten scholars were engaged, that the school was expected to begin the first of March, and that if you were not here at that time, we should feel in rather a disagreeable dilemma. My constant answer to all who inquired, when I expected you, has been, 'as soon as ever the river is open.' The river is now open & you are not here. I hope sickness is not the cause.

Since I wrote, two more scholars have signed their names & others are expected. Mrs. Dartnel's room has also been engaged. Miss Berrian who lives next door to Mr. Mitchell's took the paper containing your terms to the school which she attended. Her teacher offered to give you the privilege of teaching in his school-room Wednesday & Saturday afternoons, when he had no school, & said he would mention it to his scholars, if any chose to attend, the terms to be the same. After this, Mr. Mitchell & Mr. Fitch called on him to learn the particulars. He said you were very welcome to make use of his school room on these days but he felt bound to consult his partner, whose consent he had no doubt of obtaining. We have not heard from him since. As you would have rent free, & but two lessons in the week to give for the same price, I think were you to have but two or three scholars it would be worth while to undertake it. Being in the afternoon, it would not interfere with your other school; and, as Mr. Mitchell observed, if you got nothing by it, it might be of great use as it would make you better known.

Mr. Fitch called at your brother's house yesterday but he was out. He left word for him to call last evening; but, as he did not come, I suppose they forgot to deliver the message. I thought he might be able to throw some light upon this unaccountable business.

I shall not mention the arrival of so many packets without you to Mr. Mitchell's, for they have felt so interested & sanguine in their expectations that I cannot bear to chill their ardor by perhaps unnecessary suspicions.

If you do not set out as soon as this is received, be so good as to write.

I think all imperfections which this letter may contain will be excused when you hear that it was written on my knee, without even a book, & in a very few minutes.

My husband is going to the Post Office & I wish this letter taken.

Love to all–

Yours affectionately,

Anna &c

Eliza did now respond to her friends' arrangements, arriving in New York in about a week, in time to write the next (**no. 113**) to her mother and aunt:

'Miss Champlain is in town and informs Miss Thorn she intends opening her school on Monday morning the 18th at 9 o'clock at 95 Chatham Street–requests Miss T. to bring with her a pair of compasses, a sheet of writing paper, a lead pencil & India rubber.'

March 12th

The above is a copy of a note I sent to each of my scholars last week. The following is a copy of an advertisement Mrs. Fitch sent to the [*Republican*] *Sentinel* on Saturday last.

'A Card

Miss Champlain, miniature painter, informs her friends and the public that she has returned to the city and resumed her business. Any commands will be punctually attended to at 96 Cherry Street.

March 16th'[16]

This came out yesterday–and last evening a conceited dandy call'd to see my paintings. He said Eliza Thompson sent him to me–niece to Mrs. Eldridge. She is one of your call-again devils, I presume.

Your friend Mrs. Cooper is at last at rest. She died three weeks ago of consumption. Fanny Berdan is on the eve of distraction at loseing her husband. He has been building a house exactly to please her with 'folding doors and marble chimney pieces'–two things she prized above her existence. Just as the house was completed, he died. The shock has been so great as to threaten the destruction of her reason. The house is rented, as she is utterly incapable of taking charge of it. Thus are her prospects blighted. Mary Holt keeps school.

I have been waiting ever since last Monday (and it is now Sunday) for Sam'l to call and take your musical glass on board of Lamphere, as he faithfully promised me he would, long before this. I fear Lamphere has gone and that this glass is fated never to see New London. I wish you would write and kill him for his negligence. If I had any way of getting it on board except sending it by him, I certainly would not think of asking him to do anything about it–but that is impossible. Don't blame me, as I purchased it the morning after my arrival, and have been in a fever ever since about its not going.

And the very next day, March 17th (**no. 114**), this was continued by Eliza:

As my school is put off untill Monday I have time to write again before it commences and tell you a few of the particulars. Mr. & Mrs. Mitchell proposed to Mrs. Fitch my teaching Ellen Tooker, the paragon, at her own house, which is down to the Battery. They thought, as 'every little helps,' I ought by all means to accept every-thing in the shape of business. As Mrs. F. knew, that plan would never succeed. She said, to oblige me, she cut the matter short at once by telling Mr. M. that, to that proposal she knew I never would consent. I suppose it depends altogether upon what is offer'd her, said Mr. Mitchell. No, said Mrs. Fitch, I don't think Eliza could be hired to teach Ellen in this way. Eliza has a school with many as genteel scholars as Miss Tooker, who are not too high to walk or ride to her school. They said Ellen was very anxious to learn but could not think of *going out to a* teacher, as she never had done it. Oh, very well, said Mrs. F.; then the matter is at an end. Eliza is very determin'd when she undertakes anything & I know she will set this through. She repeated this conversation to me on Saturday morning as soon as I arrived, and I assure you I thanked her most cordialy for supporting my digintry so handsomely. Mrs. F. then related Laverty's treatment and Eliza Mitchell said she thought I should be perfectly right, if only to resent such conduct, not to go. Mrs. Fitch informs me Miss Tooker is very intimate at Doctor Handy's, that the girls are as thick as spatter.

Yesterday I employ'd in writing notes to each of my scholars informing them of my arrival, and the place and hour at which I should commence school. William Mitchell took some of them to the young ladies, and some I sent by other hands. I have one scholar who is an assistant in Mr. Sloakem's school[17]–the school which I am to have Wednesdays and Saturdays if I choose, which I shall, of course.

Charls Clinch has been writing a play call'd *The Spy*, from a book of the same title written by a Mr. Cooper (not the actor).[18] Charls had a benefit here in the first of March. The play is highly applauded and has been re-acted since my arrival. Fitz Hallock alias Croaker wrote a song for his 'friend and pitcher' to be sung on the occasion, call'd *The Harp of Love*. The theatre was fill'd, almost, with our church folks. All of them were there, even the Mitchells! He was advised to sell the tickets himself, as is customary for those who have benefits, but the haughty dog refused. He said, let those who wish tickets get them at the box office. His friends urged him to it, knowing his benefit would be twice as much if he would consent to it, but he said no, 'What I loose in money I shall gain in dignity.' He is now at a fencing school preparing for the stage. He has been introduced to Mr. Cooper (the author), who thinks highly of him. The novel is thought equal to any of Scott's, and is all the rage here; so you see he has quite got into literary society without fishing for it.

Mrs. Dawson is quite sick and has been for some time. Mary Ann visits her now. I don't know the nature of her complaint. I have not yet had the time to call on Mrs. Hayden. Capt. Hayden & Harriet Sandford call'd to see me about 3 weeks before I arrived. They understood I was in town from the Benjamins, whom Mr. Mitchell inform'd with every-body else, and were anxious to see me. Mrs. Hayden boards in the next house to Mary Ann [Mason] in Chatham Street.

I got your harmonica last Monday, but am afraid Sam'l will not call to take it on board Lamphere in season. You must not put the cork within the instrument when you leave it, as the pressure on the keys is too great with the top shut. The price of them are two dollars every-where but at Riley's, where they are fourteen shillings. The man who made them is gone away, which has enhanced the price. Mrs. F. has been buying another of them lately for a present. She reminded him of this that he might cheapen the article. It had the desired effect. He let it go at 12 shillings. You must strike sudden and quick for the keys with the sharp point of the cork, and not very heavy. O how I wish I could bring it to show you how to play it. I have had a feast at it since I came. It sounds best in damp weather although dampness is injurious to it. . . .

William, aged twenty and the last of Betsey's four children to enter the correspondence, now adds to the list of errands Sam must run. The letter (**no. 115** of March 18th) has a male and fraternal tone suggesting how the two boys got along together, quite different from the tone of William in his letters to Eliza, below. Within its offhanded paragraphs, however, is literary criticism of a sort directed at the early attempts to establish an American Gothicism, none more in readers' minds than Charles Brockden Brown's: witness his faith that "the caverns of America's hills supplant the Gothic vaults of Europe."[19] William's letter also provides an indication of how works of popular fiction circulated to the provinces through installments; further, comment on early American interest in natural science, such as the Peales'; not quoted here, an inquiry for work in New York for a mutual young friend; and a closing jab at Freemasonry, in which people at the time were ready to see a conspiracy of the Haves against the meaning of American democracy.[20] Perkins and Starr whom William imagines as co-conspirators with Hamilton were names to reckon with, or resent, in New London society. Indeed there is a good deal in the world that William is at odds with:

Sam,

Ha! Ha! I swear I can't help laughing. I have just been trying to give a romantic description of the country around the Stone House mountain, where I had read a long yarn of craggy precipices, ponderous rocks, huge piles of granite, picturesque scenery, caverns in the mountain, meandering streams, majestic Thames, purring (-ling) brooks, barking winds, profound abysses, destructive quicksands, towering eagles, & screeching owls. I say, when I had read this long string, I haw-haw'd (as Gilbert used to say). What nonsense, pure nonsense, for a letter; for a letter should be in an easy familiar style. I think for a story as Fred has written his, it will do very well, & I must confess that I never saw even among the Aw-boo-ba-tucks & Whack-mi-pac-rey mountains any place which would so well answer the purpose of a legendary narrative; & Fred has done it justice. I think he deserves credit for calling our native shore into notice.

Here I am before my story. Excuse me. After having read the legendary narrative, I proposed to my friends to visit the Stone House. Accordingly Daniel, Ric'd, Ralph, O. Avery & ourself started. When we arrived there we entered on our hands & knees and descended into the square room, where we struck a light & read the legendary narrative–that is, as much of it as I had (oh, by the way, I have not rec'd No.18 or 19–what's to pay? can't I have 'em?). We then emerged from the bowels of the mountain & amused ourselves by examining & crawling into the clefts of the rocks & clambering up their rugged sides to view the surrounding country. . . .

On the shore of the little point of land leading towards Jacob's Rocks, I picked up & selected 62 stones of various forms & sizes which I wish you to give the American Museum or deposit in your private cabinet of curiosities, among those which I presented you when in this place. I think it's a shame–I do, & so there now–to keep the letters when there is so many Lampheers & Howards, carts & things running away daily. . . .

Here comes John L. Havens. He says he wants Tom to enquire, at Riley's or some musical instrument establishment, the current price for a flageolet top for a flute, & write me next packet. John does not want to buy one in New York but to know the price. There is Harry Smith has one to sell which he can have. . . .

This crossed with one from his brother in New York (**no. 116**) in which Sam reported on his work at Holt and Quinby: "Two of us have pack'd about 700 1/2 bls in about 8 days' time, besides 3 or 400 that we have pack'd, say, 50 to day 70 tomorrow, and so on, so that I've not had time to do any-thing else. I could not get the instrument ready by the *Juno*, so I send it by Coit. I suppose Aunt Mary understands playing on it. If she does not, she will soon learn, for it is one of the most simple constructed things of the kind that ever fell under my observation." His reference is to the glass harmonica, intended for Aunt Mary. She had long known how to play the guitar, but never took it down to New York. Now in her blindness she picked it up again (**nos. 53** and **107**, above), and her family tried also to relieve the tedium of her condition by this other musical instrument which in fact she did learn (**144**). Further, Sam copies out for William some current popular songs, starting with Moore's "Believe me, if all those endearing young charms, . . . " and going downhill from there.

In the same week Eliza wrote home, too (**no. 117**), much agitated about the supplies she needed for her school but which she had forgotten to bring with her—papers and such:

> . . . I wish you also to look in that case which contains Aunt Mary's cements, and find a machine to hold crayons with. If you don't know what it is, she will tell you. I saw several in it before I came away and will thank you to send them all, as I cannot sketch fast enough for my school without using crayons. If their is any other material for drawing in crayons with the things I have mention'd, pray send them along. You must make a bundle of them, as I have the key of my trunk with me.
>
> I wish I had time to write you a long letter, as I have much to say, but not an instant's time to say it in. Aunt Mary's prediction is fulfil'd: I have one numskull that I cannot pound the least thing into. I wish she was in Tofit, for she will plague my soul out. Some of them are quite clever at the business, particularly Miss Marquand, Miss Pierson, Miss Whitemore, and one of the Miss Cowdreys, who have all been to drawing schools before and behind. I commenced Monday before last. I went to Mrs. Dartnell's on that eventful morning and had the tables set out with their patterns spread over them. I had just finished the business when Mr. Mitchell came in to say that all my scholars were at his house, as they had not been able to find the number. He said he would wait upon them over instantly. I had only time to thank him when he vanished and immediately re-entered followed by ten young ladies dressed in great style, whome he introduced to me one by one as they enter'd. That ceremony ended, he called me into the centre of the room and said he would do what remain'd to be done on his part. He then took out five dollars and presented them to me, said he believed I could now do without him, and immediately quit the room. This I suppose was to set the others a good example, but it was one that neither of them followed. That part of the business they forgot altogether. But I believe he has since reminded some of them of it, as their has been a few of them paid. Mr. Mitchell and Mr. Fitch settle all my business for me. They went togther to Mr. Sloakem's school the other

day to settle the hash about my teaching in it. The gentleman and his partner said they would be very happy to have me teach in their school on those days I chose, for nothing, as their school would be empty on Wednesday and Saturday afternoons. I have since attended there on those days and have one excellent scholar. I wish I had time to say more but have not just now, as my hour for beginning school has arrived. . . .

Next, Sam again, switching jobs to one less terribly demanding than he had at Holt and Quinby (**no. 118** of April 13, 1822):

> Mother, how do you do? I think it is almost time to send you ONE letter. Perhaps I had ought to have sent 49,000,000,000 (as Eliza says) before this time, but you know I write to Bill or at least direct them to him, although they are as much for you as for him–that is, if you choose to read them. Probably the next letter any of you get from me will come from 36 Peck Slip, as I expect to go with Mr. Gross by the 1st of May.[21] I have enquired of several persons who are acquainted with him, and they all tell me he is a very liberal man and much of the gentleman. I've no doubts but we shall agree very well. . . . I shall write Uncle Thomas as soon as I am with Gross. . . .

Eliza's **no. 119** of the same week as this, after mention of letters from New London that have not survived, supplies news about business, her mother's and her own at her school:

> Dear Mother & Co.,
>
> . . . I have procured your ivory and it is now waiting for an oppertunity to go; but as this hopeful son of yours, and brother of mine, is my only dependance in cases of this nature, I can promise you nothing about it, as I know not wheather you will ever get it unless you come for it. I purchased it of the same person from whom I always get ivory, as I consider him much cheaper than the fancy stores. All the enclosed sheets are smaller than the paper you sent. He charged half a dollar for a plate that size, and, as I did not feel disposed to give 2 dollars for four pieces, I got them a smaller size. The six largest sheets came to fifteen shillings. The small one he threw in for the odd shilling. The small one and one of the others has considerable grain. It was impossible for me to get them all entirely free from it. I think the other plates are most excellent. I wish I could afford to purchase several plates like them. He will let you have a larger size than the enclosed for three dollars a dozen provided you will take them for better, for worse–that is, ring-streaked and spekled and perhaps not one out of the dozen that you can use. I told him that would not do. Verry well, said he, then we must charge accordingly. Let me know soon if you think I have made a good bargain, for I have almost forgot the old prices; and let me know if I have reccon'd it right (he said they were 2/6 a piece), for you know I am not a very cute arithmatician, and ivory always bothers me to death with its countless sixpences. But as I think I have said enough about it I will turn over a new leaf with something else.

I have at this instant so much to say and so much to do that I really don't know how to proceed with my birds'-egging. My school occupies every instant of my time, when I am in it attending on my scholars and when I am out of it drawing and colouring patterns for them. I assure you my leasure moments are 'few and far between.' I have now sixteen scholars who I understand are all very much delighted with comeing to school and eager for the day to arrive–much more so than I am, for there are few things that I do not anticipate with more satisfaction than school day. Not that I am much disappointed in any of them. In general, they draw better than I expected and there is three that paints very handsomely indeed. They never miss a lesson unless the weather is absolutely intolerable, and even than the chief of them come. *I* must go all weathers, of course. I don't find teaching so verry disagreeable as I expected, but still it is an amusement that I never should choose, as I have one most intolerable fool that I would willingly give five dollars if she would quit it forever. She has been drawing now ever since the quarter commenced and her last piece is worse than the first. There is no pounding any sense in her. But enough of her. . . .

Maria [Hayden] looks very well indeed. She boarded next door to Mary Ann's and as it was so near my school, Mrs. H. said she should expect me to call often. I did not let much time elapse before I repeated my visit and the last time saw the Captain. It is a long time since, and, as he has not done me the honour to show his face at 96 Cherry Street, I think I shall postpone going again untill I hear from them. Maria enquir'd about you all very particularly. She has, I hear, since taken lodgings in Greenwich Street–I don't reccolect the number. . . .

I attended the theatre a few nights since with Mr. & Mrs. Fitch to see the much admir'd play of *Lochiel*, with the much more admired interlude, Coronation of Henry V, which is a very exact representation of the coronation of George IV. I never witnessed anything more splendidly superb. They have the coronation every Thursday night at the theatre. I never saw more elegant scenery. I will send you my play bill. The author of *Lochiel*, Mr. Agg,[22] is a friend of Charles Clinch and Fitz Hallock; but the *Spy* is now all the rage. Charles is thought quite a genius, I assure you, and is rising in the world. . . .

She closes with irritated grumbling about Sam's unreliability, little suspecting that her letter would bring down some criticism on her own head in a reply from Mary (**no. 120**). The hand and the spelling there are Betsey's, but the tone and thought are of the Mary-sort that defined the writer and bound others to her:

There is a certain stiff formality that I abhor, the offspring of Pride and Suspicion. Ill-Nature nursed the pouting brat and Folly named it Dignity-of-Manners after a lady much admired (the lovely daughter of Magnanimity) and try's to palm it off upon the world for a relation of hers; but the cheat is too obvious for imposition, as no family resemblance can be traced. They are in fact the striking contrast of each other: one stiffer than ten thousand Lobster Collars, made up of starch and ceremony, the other ever easy, graceful and condescending. Such is true Dignity. As to that unsocial, consequencial, apeish Dignity–away with it from among friends. Give it to the 'moles and the bats.' Not that it is any thing to us who have no faults ourselves, or none that we are sensible of, which is the same thing–though perhaps it were not amiss to keep a bright look out for this trait of carracter, and, should we see it gaining ground, spare not: distroy it utterly, tear it up by the roots 'and cast it like a loathsome weed away.'

To be sure, there is a certain passage in your letter that smells of it a little, but this was mere chance, perhaps, and therefore stands for nothing. You say you have call'd on Maria, that she is well. Once you saw Capt. Heyden. He has not returned your call. They have removed to Greenwich Street, you have forgot the number, and shall wait to hear from them before you call again. This account is rather more brief than satisfactory. Maria, you know, is not in a condition to go out, and surely you cannot expect Heyden to return your visits, unless indeed you allow him to place them to his own account. But perhaps the Captain was not so polite and attentive as usual–never mind his capers. You know he is a singular, excentric being. Whoever expects to find him twice in the same humour will miss thier reconing. To say nothing of myself, you have ever found Maria a kind, obliging friend, and have rec'd from her every mark of attention and regard. This I should say demands some small return, and I shall be sorry if she has reason to suppose you either negligent or ungrateful. I hope therefore you will try to recollect the number and call on her as soon and as often as possible. Let me know how she is from time to time, and when they are to go to Washington.

I am glad to hear your school is like to prove successful and that teaching is more pleasing and less difficult than you expected. Experience will convince you my creed is correct: we may do any thing we choose–any thing we set about in earnest. Only 'screw your courage to the sticking place.' Once begin, and difficulties vanish before you like clouds and vapors. Consider then how much may be attained, go on and prosper. Say not it is enough, never rest self-satisfied nor stop short of the mark.

Remember the aim and purpose of your undertaking was not to teach only but to learn. This is the grand object. Sixteen scholars is pretty well for the first quarter. I think you may now afford to treat yourself to a few lessons from a more skillful and experienced artist. The time and expence is but a triffling consideration and bears no proportion to the incalculable advantages that will probably accrue from such a measure. That you cannot begin too soon, is my opinion. Advise with your friends upon the subject and abide by thier decision. Should it meet thier approbation, they can best direct you to whom you must apply for instruction. . . .

As to Mary Ann, it is needless to say I admire her. There is in her conduct a spice of magnanimity that exalts her carracter and raises her above the common level. She is a generous girl and acts upon the true Christian principle, one of those Mrs. Dawson reprobates, that packets insults and forgives injuries; that returns good for evil and punishes her enemies by heaping coals of fire upon thier heads. This heavenly disposition I adore, nor is it any sin to worship what is so justly intitled to divine homage–which I most willingly and most devoutly pay, let me find it where I will. Alas! that it should be so rare. But it is beyond the compass of narrow minds. How then should they admit a sentiment so vast? . . .

May 16th

The above has been written some few centuries according to your calculation—that is to say, five or six weeks. Your mother has had not a moment's leisure to bestow upon it, or you would have rec'd it in season. I am sensible it is no small task to translate my long letters, which they say resemble Greek and Latin—pot-hooks and trammels—or any thing but plain English. If the translation of Miss Lascallas has immortalized her name, surely much credit is due to the translators of a language neither dead nor alive, tho' the work itself perhaps may meet with approbation, or be consider'd so 'wildly beautiful.'[23]

But a truce with fun and folly—for here comes sober earnest. We have just rec'd your letter and I feel more inclined to scold than jest. So now for plain dealing. Among all your faults, Eliza (and they are not a few) there are none so glareing and none that I so utterly abominate as that stiff ceremonious formality which, I am sorry to observe, appears in your manners and conduct. I don't know how you come by it, for, whatever may be the faults of your relations, I am happy to say this is not among the number. I think Captain Heyden was very polite and friendly. He certainly would never have taken the trouble to enquire about you if he was half as precise and ceremonious as yourself. For my part, I hate the very word, for the sake of your friends—for your own sweet sake. Lay it aside, my dear Eliza. Divest yourself of it, if possible, and behave like a Christian. Visit Maria without delay, apologize for your negligence as well as you can, but don't let her know the cause unless indeed you own it as a fault, which you mean to renounce forever.

But no more of this. A word to the wise is enough; and, upon the unwise, words are but thrown away.

Give my best love to Maria. I am glad to hear she has a daughter. I hope she will call it Emma and that it will supply the place of that dear last object of her affection. Let me know all the particulars respecting them—why Heyden has changed his purpose and goes to Pensacola, and whether Maria is to remain in New York. . . .

My love to all my friends but especially to the household of faith. Cousin Jonathan [Starr] is to be married next Monday in the church!!! Your Uncle Eben'r (being a pillar) is particularly invited to attend the ceremony.

Since I have rec'd permission to fill the page I will for your amusement relate a mis-step of my own. You must know, about three weeks ago, I took the lover's leap (rather out of season, I confess) down fourteen stairs into the entry, much such a topsy-turvy caper as you cut at the Langly house, only worse, as the distance was greater. I had the *View of New London* harbour in my hand and was going to put it in the front chamber closet. It had been carried down the day before for company to see. Your mother had just brought it up, and with her usual sweetness was telling me how much it was admired. Not feeling in a very good humour (for I like to own my faults) I said I was willing it should be seen by people of taste, whose opinion I valued, but those were few; but to have it exposed to flies and dust and, what was

> worse, the stupid stare of fools–mere ignorant common observers, incompetent to judge the merits of such a piece or estimate its value–I had rather it was distroy'd. 'Oh Mary, you will be punish'd for your pride,' was her wise remark; and even Aunt Hannah herself could not have mad[e] a more just and more prophetic observation.
>
> I had forgot to count my steps as usual, and she had scarcely done speaking when I fell. After much noise, clatter and confusion, which I can compare to nothing but the crackling of a thunder-bolt, I found myself quietly (tho' not very comfortably) seated below, near the front door. Your mother was frightened out of her senses. I had some difficulty to persuade her I was alive, and laugh'd heartily to convince her I was not much hurt. However, I found it more painful to ascend the stairs the stairs than to fall down; but her assistance and a good share of resolution supported me untill I reached the bed, where I was confined with bruises, wounds and battered limbs for some time. But I am now much better and tho' my foot and ancle is still swell'd and painful I make shift to hobble about very decently.

The above, after its first installment in correction of Eliza, was pursued in the same mood to Sam, separately (**no. 112**, of May 7th, 1822). Mary addresses him at Dennis H. Doyle's on Front Street down on the lower east side, where later he found employment:

> Your mother is displeased with your conduct, and, being too delicate to reprove you herself, has imposed the task on me. I believe you will not thank her for this, neither do I expect what I am now about to say will exactly meet her approbation, for I admire honest plain dealing and hold truth and candor in too high estimation to proceed upon the smoothing plain principle, I assure you. So much by way of preface. Now to the point.
>
> Your mother is distress'd on your account, thro' your carelessness and want of consideration. She is grieved to hear complaints of you from all quarters, and to feel as she does now the sad effects of your negligence and inattention to your duty. William will write no more. He says you have done answering his letters, and Eliza has not seen you for more than three months, tho' she has sent for you repeatedly. This is too bad. Your mother is out of ivory. Two months ago she sent to Eliza to purchase some, which she did, and a frame for a picture she had drawn and cannot recieve the money untill the frame arrives, and tho' she has applicants for pictures her business must stop for the want of ivory, because there is no one to put it on board of a packet. This is not doing as you would be done by. You may need the obliging attention of others as much perhaps as she now suffers for yours. It is no pleasure to me to know 'the measure you mete will be measured to you again;' for this is sacred truth, tho' you may not believe it till experience brings it home to yourself. You neglect Eliza shamefully. You ought to see her at least once a week. You know how she is situated–that she often stands in need of little services which you can, and it is your duty to, perform; and for you to refuse to go when she sends for you, and deny her your assistance, is unnatural and cruel. You would not like such treatment. Business is no excuse for such unwarrantable conduct. You might call on

Sundays, if you staid but for a single moment. You have done writing to us and seem to have forgotten all your promises, friends, and thier past favours. You have not answered your Uncle Oliver's letter as your mother requested. You promised to send your Uncle Thomas a screw-knife for his gun. He has talked much about it, set his heart upon it, and expected to recieve it when Isaac Crannell came from New York, as he thought that was a good opportunity for you to send it. Why will you make promises that are never to be performed, and raise expectations that must end in disappointment? Nothing makes your mother so unhappy as to hear complaints against her children, and I am sorry to say she has but too much reason to complain of you, herself. For your own sake, my dear Sam, try to retrieve your carracter. Do as you would be done by, and you cannot fail to do right. This is the only safe mode of conduct, and when we depart from this rule we lose our friends, create enemies, and are sure to injure ourselves more than we do others. Think seriously of these things,

and believe me your affectionate Aunt,
Mary Way

Some time ago Mary wrote the above at my request and I have had no oportunity to send it before. It is a truth that I have suffered greatly for the want of the above mention'd articles, but they have arrived at last, and with them letters from Mrs. Fitch and Eliza. They both complain that you have not been there this winter. Mrs. Fitch observes, she is sorry you are so very unsocial, and it is the greatest trouble I have. Pray, my dear Sam, do better in future. I entreat you to take the advice of your friends. Write to William at least. Answer Oliver's letter. I heard of it from his wife, it being some time before her death. I imediately wrote you upon the subject but you never acknowledged the receipt of my letter. But above all, don't fail to visit Eliza more frequently. You well know my fears about you all, under eternal apprehensions least some of you should go amiss. Pray for Heaven's sake be steady in all things, that I may never hear anything against you.

Your ever affectionate,
E. C.

Next, of about the same date and handling some of the same material as Mary's—but in a different way—this from Betsey, too (**no. 121**). It indicates, incidentally, that she did her portraits directly on ivory without anything preliminary in any other medium, despite her use of the word "sketch." Hence the need she indicates for her magnifying glass; and descriptions by Eliza of her own work confirm this:

My dear Eliza,

'Tis vain to spend time and thread to make repeated apologies for my long silence. 'Tis as well as true to say that it was impossible to write since you rec'd my last letter. You recollect when you was home, it required our greatest exertions to make both ends meet, and can judge when there is but one, whether they will find much leisure, with the ten thousand calls that (I am sorry to say) I am honour'd with. Yesterday Mr. Parker, wife, Mary Perkins, Mary Winthrop call'd–Betsey Coit, Katherine Thomson, the others I have forgot, but these were more day before–Sally, Mrs. Gaits, Mrs. Burbeck, a little sister of Mrs. Gaits, Mary Prescott, and every moment I am call'd upon by some-one.

The principle part of those call'd to see the sketch I have taken of Augusta Deshon, of whose death I suppose you have been inform'd. She had been confined about two months before her death. Her sister Mary and Elizabeth call'd yesterday, and if I ever saw sorrow depicted upon any countenance, it was upon Mary's. She has so much changed since I last saw her, I could scarcely recollect her–the day I went to take the sketch, was sick as death–and what should they do but send Elder Dodge after me in a carriage. But as I never stand upon triffles, in such a case, went without a murmur. He asked how my family was. I answered, my family consisted only of my sister and myself. He then enquired if she was a widow. I might have answred, she had never had the misfortune to be married. Then he asked how old she was. I said about fifty. Then, if she was older than myself–which was the only lucky question he put to me, I next expected he would enquire my age, and pop the question.

When I arrived at the house, fortunately no one came to the door nor was in the front part–and have great reason to hope they were ignorant of the circumstance of his being my escort. He enquired what time he should call for me. I told him that was impossible for me to say, but should be detained some hours, and should prefer walking home. I bid him good morning and laid him down softly. The first that appeared was Mrs. Ben Richards, who desired me to walk upstairs; in the entry chamber, met the widower. He was not in tears as I expected to find him but look'd like sadness in dispair. He followed us into the chamber where the corpse was, and I ask'd him if he thought she look'd natural–but forgot his answer. He soon went out, and I desired to be left alone. Mrs. Richards assured me I should not be interrupted again. Everything seem'd to work against me. Her mouth was so far open as to expose her front teeth, which destroy'd the line of the face, and I found I had left my magnifying glass behind. The position of her mouth made me think it useless to go back for it, and I did the best I could under such circumstances; but it is approved of by the majority, and I have no doubt but from such of her relation as resembled her, togeather with a faint recollection I retain of her features, I shall succeed. . . .

I must inform you of a misfortune that happen'd to Mary, as one of the many reasons why I [have] not written before. Three weeks ago last Friday night, she fell from the top to the bottom of fourteen stairs, with all *New London* at her heels, knock'd entirely off one of her great toe nails, and bruised herself in a most shocking manner. She has never come down to her meals since, and it has almost worn me to a skeleton to attend upon her up chamber. I presume I go not less than forty or fifty times a day. As to the number of her bruises, the goodness, or badness, of them, I have no more [idea] than you do–except one upon her shin, which has been swell'd and greatly inflamed. I was first advised to apply bruised catnip and spirit with campher; next, poultice; next, spirit water and salt-peter disolved. This she thinks has help'd her more than any thing, and she now begins to walk from one chamber to the other. I am in hopes in a few days she will be able to come down stairs. . . .

The time of her fall, we had sit up till between eleven and twelve o'clock at night. I had that day carried her *View of New London* down to show some person and brought it up and left it in our chamber. She ask'd me for it. I told where it was and that I would carry it in the other chamber, and she said no, I had rather do it myself. She took it, I conclude, in her right hand, which prevented her from feeling along the wall as usual. She went at random and, instead of steering towards the front chamber, went towards the stairs. I was panic struck with a noise as if the roof of the house togeather with the chimneys were ratting about our ears; but before she reach'd the foot of the stairs, I discover'd what it must be. The fright almost took away my senses, it was so strongly impress'd upon my mind that she had kill'd herself. I scream'd, but what, I know not; but fortunately found her alive, and directly began to hush me. I beg'd her to permit me to call up Mr. Culver and his wife. She says, Not for the world. Her cap, wig, and socks flew in different directions, and [I] confess [she] would not have appeared to so great advantage as usual.

The other family it seems heard the uproar, but, having a degree of fear upon them least we should consider them as intruders, waited to be call'd. I beg'd her to let me call upon them to assist her in getting up stairs but she was fix'd as the law of the Medes and Persians that altereth not. I intreated her to let me lead her but she refused even my feeble assistance, and would go up alone, a mummy [= pulpy mass] as she was–but afterwards told me it hurt her more to go up than to fall down. So I advised to allways fall down in future.

I think I have given you as particular a description as time and paper will admit, so don't schold so hard, next time we fall down stairs, at my neglect of you.

The ivory suited exactly, and had I laid out the money myself, should not have done so well. Write soon; and if Sam will not or cannot call upon you as often as we think he might, excuse him, since you know the cause is diffidence. If you can gather anything of his situation, health &c, inform us.

Adieu. . . .

In mid-May another letter from Eliza (**no. 122**). She mentions her pupils set to painting native flowers from examples of her own that she put before them. This had become a part of the curriculum of a good painting school over the last decade or two. A home-made decorated cardboard folder survives with twenty of these models of hers, counting a wreath, in still brilliant watercolors on paper. One has a Cupid, incredibly small, concealed in a rose-blossom; another titled in pencil, "Crown Imperial."[24] With these are several little pencil drawings and paintings as well, unfinished or not thought worth framing. Eliza writes, first:

As a rainey Sunday happens to cross my path, I think I will devote it to writing home, though I have lately sent you a long letter with your ivory, to which I have recieved no answer, and I think it is impossible but you have got it e're this. I can tell you both, I do not like such inattention and if some of you do not write me soon, I shall myself give up the business.

My school comes on very well and some of the scholars improve fast in painting. I have three, painting heads; three painting watch-papers; and the others drawing landskips and flowers. They are all extremely fond of it and of going to school. I find it so far much easier than I expected, as I was prepared to meet with much dificulty, and may yet–only the time has not come.

I think I told you in my last that I had not call'd lately on Mrs. Hayden and that it was not my intention to do so soon. If I did not, I tell you now. Mr. Fitch met Captain Hayden in Broadway last Monday. He inform'd him that he expected to leave New York for Pensacola on the following Friday; also, that Mrs. Hayden had a fine daughter [Emma, second of that name] and was pretty well herself. He enquired very particularly after 'Miss Champlain,' but has never done her the honor to call, although she has been here almost three months; so as soon as 'Miss Champlain' can ascertain that Captain H. has left the city, she intends calling on his wife and not before.

I have much writing to send you of Mrs. Fitches, Sandy [Clarke]'s, and other poets' & poetesses' of the day, but have not time to copy it. I regret it much as there are some very fine pieces amongst them, particularly one by 'Florio' alias Brooks, who is consider'd a very superior genius and is universaly admired. If I do not send this letter immediately and can steal time to copy a few pieces I will enclose them in this letter.

To Cora

Beyond the wave, beyond the wave,
Beyond the stormy ocean's roar,
Thy form hath found an early grave,
Thine eye is closed, to beam no more! . . .
Entombed with thee still be that love
Which unto thee in life was given.
Still may its fond remembrance prove
My charm on earth, my hope of heaven!

Florio

Well, how did you like the foregoing piece? I think it's most beautiful; but perhaps you have not as much taste. I suppose you recollect his piece on 'Greece' that you admired so much. I like this better.

I have now to inform you that Ann has exchanged the signature of 'Agnes' for 'Ally Croker,' so whatever piece you see with the latter name, you will know the author. The reason why she did this was, the name of Agnes had become universally known and she is determin'd to write incog. She is eternally scribbling to the printers and has given them two or three such drubbings that some of them hate her with a mortal hatred. By the by, she don't put 'Ally Croker' to her prose pieces. It is only her poetical effusions to which this name is attached. As it's the fashion to dramatize everything that appears nowadays, I don't know but you will one day hear a play of Ann's, mark me. I say I don't know, but you will. ' 'Tis all conjecture here below'–'and you are sure of nothing till you get it in your throat'–so 'you cannot say I told it.'

I hope you have got all the numbers of the *Recluse*. 'Tis a most wildly beautiful thing. If you have not, make William get them for you, for it's well worth a perusal. The *Spy* also is in great demand. I wish you to hear them both if it's a possible thing. The *Recluse* is translated from the French by the only daughter of your old friend Doctor Laskallas. I hear she is a girl of talents. At any rate this work has immortalized her name. I have as usual five thousand things to say and have not an instant to write, so of course they will remain unsaid. . . .

I should also like to know who visits you now-days and, as Aunt Hannah says, what they visit you *for*. . . .

I expect soon to change my school-room for another, as it is now quite too small for the number of scholars and I expect more soon. Mrs. Fitch expects Mr. Fitches sister Sally (now Mrs. Weed) with her husband and child from Albany, the first of June, to make a visit here, and immediately on her return, Mrs. Northam and Cornelia leave New York to pay *Mah* Shearman a visit, of some length, I presume. . . .

I have not seen Sam'l for six or eight weeks till about an hour ago. I took a walk with Mr. & Mrs. Fitch and Cornelia up the Bowery and met his lordship with another gentleman. I 'stopped–went on–stopped again,' and condescended to speak to him. The inattentive puppy looks in very good case and said he was just thinking about comeing to see me. I know not where he stays or whether he stays any-where, or when I shall see him again or whether I ever shall.

In a letter from Eliza not preserved, she asked the natural question, in Mary's tumble down stairs, what ever happened to the miniature she was holding. Mary cleared up this question in hers still of May (**no. 123**):

The picture suffered less than the original, and has been thoroughly repair'd by your Uncle Ebenezer and Thomas. It feels very smooth and, they say, wants nothing but the finishing touches from your pencil. I hope after you have practised landscape painting some time in your school you will be able to do it.

'You wish to know what company we have and what they visit us for'? To the first I answer, the best the place affords, and to the last, for our good company, of course. You know all the town is in love with your mother, and I am very agreeable (when I choose to appear among them), considering my crabbed uncouth stubborn disposition, and the perfect indifference I feel respecting their good opinion.

Eliza Lee has return'd, full of New York, theatre parties, Handy's, Laverty's and (above all) Amelia [Laverty]'s thousand-dollar harp, which like the lyre of Orpheus charms stocks and stones. Eliza, you know, has not one spark of enthusiasm about her, tho' she is a girl of taste, and she admires it. She saw Mrs. Fitch at Mr. Mitchell's church, but saw nothing of you–talks much of the poets and poetesses of your renowned city, is acquainted with Brooks, thinks highly of his poetic tallant, that he rivals all of his competitors of the masculine gender; has read his manuscript poems;

and told me of the *Requiem* and that it was much celebrated. I conclude this you have sent me is the same. 'The tender sweet plaintive strain' reminds me of Montgomery, and is allmost as beautiful. But [Brooks'] *Greece*, I think, displays more nerve, energy, and strength of genius. It smacks of the sublime, and I have a taste for that. One is relaxing, the other bracing, both good of their kind. You may laugh at my critical review, but I know what I mean.

I am glad to hear Charles Clinch has brought forth [his *Spy*]. I should like to see the bunting–a promising child, no doubt, but I am a little surprized that he should condescend to build upon another foundation. From him of all beings I was prepared to expect something original. But the more's to come. I conclude this is but the commencement of his career.

I have not seen the *Recluse of Norway*, tho' William has promised I shall have it.[25] He is a pretty good boy, has read to me [Cooper's] *The Pirate*, and has begun *The Spy*. Don't fail to send the pieces you have mentioned. Everything that can amuse will be acceptable. . . .

Then, as a bombshell casually tossed into the latter part of Eliza's next letter home (of June 2nd), a piece of news–her engagement to young Riley–which evidently took her family as much by surprise as the reader of the correspondence today. Certainly in the surviving letters there is no forewarning of it; and now, despite the hints in which the revelation was wrapped, her aunt and mother seem unsure just how to interpret it. Eliza had been very discreet:

Dear Mother & Co.,

I have not a moment to spare, as every atom of time is employ'd in the service of my school, but as I have much to say I shall take time to say it. Mr. Fitch has subscribed for all the numbers of the [New York Universalist Church's] *Gospel Herald*. The first volume has come out and Mrs. F. desires me to say, if you have not seen it and would like too, that I may send it up for your perusal. I thought I would ascertain whether you had seen it before I sent it up, for if you have, it would be useless trouble. . . .

Mrs. Fitch and I have at last call'd on Mrs. Hayden and had the satisfaction of hearing her ladyship had left town the morning of the same day. She has gone to reside with her parents at Bellville untill Captain H. returns from Pensacola, and, as I don't know when that will be, I cannot of course give you any information on the subject. She boarded with Mrs. Coals in Greenwich Street (she that was formerly Mrs. Bennett). I am sorry I could not see Mrs. H., tho' I had no desire to see her husband and took measures accordingly.

Mrs. Avery call'd on me last week to know when she should bring Mary Amelia to sit for her picture, as she is at last of age to match Walter's picture. It is to be done the same size and a full-length figure just like his, with a landscape back-ground. She is to be dressed in white or sky blue, whichever I choose, as she wears both. She is to hold a doll, a rattle, or some toy or other in her hand, and I am expected to do my 'prettiest.' She is not handsome, and is humoured to death, so I who never flatter and am not overstocked with patience may prepare to meet with some difficulty before the task is accomplished, for she is ten thousand times more unmanageable than Walter was at that age. Mrs. A. is the first applicant I have had since my arrival, although my advertisement has been continued ever since I came.

I suppose you have heard by the news-papers that the widow of the late celebrated Guy[26] has lately had a benefit. Her husband's paintings were exhibited for that purpose. She is poor and old, and Mr. Mitchell requested the church (from the pulpit) to go and see them. Mrs. Fitch had determined on going and had invited me to accompany her, which invitation I accepted with great pleasure, when a most provoking rain set in just in pudding-time for no other purpose (that I could see) but to spoil our sport. I assure you I was mad enough to be deprived of such a great gratification. The next day Mrs. Fitch sent the price of three tickets to Mr. Mitchell requesting him to send it to Mrs. Guy, without mentioning her name; but as he never transacts business of this kind under the rose for anybody but himself, he makes a point to puff those well who take this method of concealing from their left hand the deeds of the right. . . .

July 2d Long since the foregoing was written, your letters have been recieved and it has been quite impossible for me to answer them before or I never should have neglected doing it for such a length of time. Be assured I thank you sincerely for your 'amiable candor;' but I need not have expected a more flatter'd likeness from your pen which has never yet painted me decently. This is not the first caricature you have had the goodness to sketch for me, and I suppose will not be the last with which I shall be honoured from your ladyship; yet notwithstanding my stiffness, formality, starch and ceremony, lobster-collars and the ten thousand brickbatish epithets with which you thought proper to swell your pokerish catalogue, together with my unsocial, consequential apeish dignity of manners, with five hunderd yards of buckram to sweep in the train of all those fascinating qualeties, I have been so fortunate (some would say) as to hook a serious beau–that is to say, one who has 'pop't the question,' Toby or not Toby.

Now I suppose you would give all your old shoes–aye, and socks into the bargain–to know what I answer'd; but as you have provoked me so, I think I shall suffer you to 'burst in your ignorance.' He is quite handsome and plays devinely on the flute and piano. I am sure if Mother was to see and hear him she would lay violent hands upon him in an instant, and as he is not quite so much older than myself as I wish he was (you know my passion for 'old stick,' as H[annah] D[awson] says), he would be just the thing for her. So tell her to look out when I bring him up to New London. I send this warning as I am sure from my knowledge of her disposition she could never resist a musical beau, and I would rather in such a case have her look well to her going.

I have had a harty laugh about your leap in the dark. I think you must now agree with me that the Way and Champlain skulls are composed of uncrackable materials. If their possessor was hurled from the summit to the bottom of Mount Etna, I am very sure their pericrainm would remain safe, tho' every other part was batter'd to a mummy. But I had as lief die by the sword as famine. I hope it's your last lover's leap.

I am in such haste to get through with my letter (as ten thousand pieces are now waiting me to give the finishing touches) that I tumble out my ideas much in Sam's style–who by the by is as inattentive a puppy as ever, and calls to see me once in 3 months. He is now in a grocery store, but in what part of the city I am utterly ignorant. He boards in Market Street and passes our house six times a day, but without ever stoping to see us. He looks very well indeed.

As soon as my first quarter was ended, I removed my school to 43 Chatham Street, as Mrs. Dartnell's was altogether too small for the purpose. The apartment I now occupy is taken for a year and is one hundred dollars, a most enormous rent but one that I must give, I find–let me go where I will. 'Tis the same that every one asks for letting a furnished apartment, tho' ever so miserably furnished. I hire the one I now occupy of Mrs. Milliss, Mary Ann [Mason]'s sister, whom you doubtless reccolect. I am much better accomodated than at Mrs. Dartnell's and keep the key of my room, a priviledge that I was deprived of when with her, as the room was in constant use. I am at school almost constantly repairing the girls' pieces.

I have had two heads go out of school that I wish you could see. They were really beautiful. Miss Marquand did them both–one was the Princess Charlotte, diadem and all, and the other was as near a match for it as I could find in the city. It was the head of a beautiful French belle that looked exactly as Maria Hayden once did. She had a white lace veil thrown on one side, a variety of flowers intermingled with the most beautiful curls you ever saw, crimson drapery and naked neck. Miss Pierson is painting flowers, fruit, and watch papers (O what a develish pen), and Miss Thorn, Miss Steven, and Miss Cowdery have copied *Amibilite*, and Miss Witermore *Douser*. The other scholars are painting landscapes, flowers and fruit, but there is not one that could take a likeness if it would save their souls; so miniature painting might as well have been left out of the proposals.

The Haydens I have never seen since they went to Bellville, and don't know whether I ever shall again; and I have neither time nor inclination to hunt them up, and they of course care still less for me, in spite of all your preaching ('and you had to preach'). . . .

11

Art, Music, Literature (Through 1823)

The period that now opens for the family is not one of any special drama. For this no doubt the correspondents silently gave thanks. But their accounts to each other tell much of their times and the flow of life in detail of two cities.

In New London writing to New York, Betsey is for the moment easier in her mind about her children. She commends even the delinquent Sam before going on to the mention of errands that would serve her music (**no. 125** of late June, 1822). There lay the principal relief of her life: "To drive away old care, I take my flute," a line of her verse declares. She is seen attacking this diversion in a flurry of experiment, evidently also with some considerable talent such as she had shown for poetry over the preceding twelvemonth–a gifted person, Betsey, but caught in a world too small for her and buzzing about like a fly in a bottle. In her poetry years, a thousand lines and more; now, a thousand instruments.[1] First, there was Mary's guitar and her own flageolet, on both of which she played continually and became quite expert, so as to win compliments from her friends; then a whistle added, the glass percussion instrument as we have seen, an English octave flute, and even a harp, says Mary. Eliza boasts, "We have fine music here often." Nor was Betsey's talent alone. Her friends the Whistlers visited–he, expert on the flute, his wife singing. They all had a lovely evening. Or Ebb would visit and sing, and, when Betsey was boarding for a while in a house large enough to have a piano, Miss Stammers would perform on that instrument (it was her means of livelihood, through her giving lessons). William's friends played the flute and flageolet; extending the circle beyond the family entirely, there was a young Boston man who married into New London and, in the days of Betsey's youth, made a name for himself through the repertory of songs, some forty of them, which he added to social gatherings of the young: "I could bring in a new song in every evening."[2] In the year with which this chapter begins, there was the remark offered in the Boston press by a young suitor seeking "an ideal wife. . . . She must love and cherish *music* above all other arts and sciences, . . . and when she sings her music must be such as will excite joy and grief."[3]

The sum of it was home-entertainment, in New London but also in Boston or anywhere else in the country from the days of Betsey's girlhood to the 1820s, the present juncture in the correspondence. It was entertainment on a relatively high level by accident of talent in the Way and Champlain circle; but it was no monopoly of theirs. As time went on into the 1820s the taste for singing as a means by which people could enjoy their own and each other's company had penetrated steadily from the more privileged to the less privileged households, and become ubiquitous.[4] With it went dancing, too, in which Betsey's half-halt husband and his cane once joined; but there were occasional balls even in her not very pretentious town, and she took it up for therapeutic reasons, herself.[5] All this by way of background to various mentions of musical activities and instruments in past letters, as now in this present one:

Dear Eliza,

. . . Sam is very attentive. He writes as often as I can expect, for which I feel myself under obligations to him. I hear from him oftener than any of you. How does you and he carry sail about those days? Has he grown any more neighborly?–than formerly?

You will find enclosed two dollars rec'd of Mr. Trott for the watch-papers that are sold, and I have given him one watch-paper and your Uncle Ebb another, to pay them for thier trouble. I hope I have not done amiss. There remains 3 unsold. I also inclose three dollars for ivory, and as the last you sent suited exactly, I send one patern of the largest sheet, which is sufficiently large, but wish you to make the bargain as you want for yourself. You recollect the old charge, 'No bone in it,' free from grain and thin. The other six dollars inclosed is for two instruments of music that probably will be the last I shall trouble you to purchase. I have sold my harmonica, and wish you to purchase one of the larger kind which you said was three dollars–those that are played with two corks.

I send you the patern of a flute which was purchased at the Rileys' store. His name is upon it as you will see. The piece was three dollars. I wish you to buy for me one of the same kind the size of the patern. I did not think it necessary to cut the shape, but the length and distance of the notes. This ought to be particularly attended to by measuring the paterns upon those of that length and observing whether the holes in the paper come exactly upon the notes. Should there be a hair's breadth's difference, 'tis of no consequence, but as the one I took the dimensions from accorded exactly with the guitar, should prefer one just like it. The greatest difficulty lies in selecting the best out of such a number. I think the safest method is to ask Mrs. Fitch to go with you. Beg her not to refuse, as it is my particular request, and as you are speechless. Let her ask Riley to pick out two of the best instruments he has in his store of that price, and listen with a critical attention to observe if there is no false notes. That will of course produce discord. Perhaps Sam will go with you. I wish he would. He can try them all and choose the best. It may be, as you take two instruments, he may let you have them cheaper, as he did before; but in case they should be higher than I calculate, take it from money I send for ivory. . . .

I shall write to Sam to take charge of the instruments. All I wish of you is to purchase them, and pack them up ready to send at a moment's warning. I will thank you to pack them up the instant you have bought them, and let that be as soon as possible, that I may receive them soon,

and greatly oblige your affectionate

Mother. . . .

In Betsey's next (**no. 126** of June 30th), it is another art, her painting, with which she is most concerned. Among major artists of the time, the practice of supplementing their income by putting real crowd-pleasers on tour–canvases of broad popular appeal with some grand theme–had enjoyed considerable success. An early (1800) Ralph-Earl rendering of Niagara Falls had been sent on its travels; likewise, Trumbull's historical pieces; and Rembrandt Peale's *Court of Death*, encountered above in the eighth chapter. Now Dunlap's gigantic dramatization of *Christ Rejected by the Jews* had reached New London, all one hundred or more agitated faces in two hundred and sixteen square feet of it rolled up like a rug en route and unrolled to the admiration of thousands in Philadelphia first, then to New York where Eliza is expected to have seen it, thereafter New London in the same month, June, and so on up to Boston. It is last heard from in Lexington, Kentucky in 1827.[6] Its central detail was shown above in Pl. 4.13 along with Betsey's improvements, Pl. 4.12; and a note should be added to explain young Ambrose Andrews whom Betsey met in company with the painting. He was as she says a Dunlap student, then just turned twenty-one, from West Stockbridge, Massachusetts, who was to spend his life at his art without achieving great success. An itinerant, his first datable work emerged two years after this present date with more to follow over the course of many years, miniature portraits or landscapes.[7]

But now to the letter:

My dear Eliza,

. . . I will thank you to write as soon as you receive this. My general business obliges me to omit writing untill I grow frantic with fears that something has happened. I have often acknowledg'd to you and others how much more considerate you are in writing than the rest of the children, and I conclude that whenever a longer space of time elapses between your letters, that there is a cause, and that you are by no means blameable. Mary desir'd me to apologize for her also. She is and has been with Aunt Hannah about a month. She now sleeps with her and is a sort of substitute for watchers–which she [Aunt Hannah] had for perhaps a week after she was siezed with a paralytick shock; but is now more comfortable, though we never expect her to walk again. She is got up and down with less pain than formerly, but appears to have lost her reason–only at intervals for a few moments will seem to be rational, except an unfortunate ray of reason that has inform'd her of the loss of her faculties, which appears to hurt and mortify her feelings very evidently. Mary tells me she had been in the habit of reading a few pages every day, about a week previous to her having had this fit; but afterwards seem'd to have forgotten the use of letters. The first time she attempted to read, being asked, she paused and hesitated a long time, and could not articulate a syllable. She began to count, and counted a hundred. She then began a second hundred and stop'd short, and began and finished a sum in multiplication completely–so says Mary, who you know was always an adept at the business. You would be astonish'd to see her. She is nothing but the shadow of a shade. You cannot imagine how much I sense the change, recollecting her when her mind was in its full vigour; but now the palsy has shattered the small remains of reason and added the finishing touches to faculties once so bright. But it is all right or it would not be thus.

About five weeks since, Mr. Dunlap arrived here from New York with a very large and superb historical painting entitled *The Christ Rejected*. 'The picture represents the events which took place when Pilate brought forth Jesus from the judgement hall to the pavement, crown'd with thorns and in the gorgeous robe with which he had been arrayed by Herod.' This piece was exhibited at Lewis Allen's where he put up. I think, however, 'tis very probable you have seen it, and what I am telling is an old story.

Mr. Dunlap had the politeness to send me a season ticket. I was sick at the time I rec'd it and of course a great trial to me to go; but unwilling to return absolute rudeness for such brotherly civility, felt as if I could not dispense with going, whenever I found myself able. Mr. D. made many enquiries concerning us both. A young man by the name of Andrews, who has been studying with him for about six months, call'd at the post-office to learn further particulars of us, where William was introduced to him by Doctor Swift who happened there at the time. He there presented him with a ticket, which obliged me to go up and see the piece. I was at this time waiting to feel disposed to go, and one afternoon–a violent hot day–Sally came down for the express purpose of forcing me to go before I was ready or had a mind to, and was fairly compell'd by entreaties, threats and every other provoking inducement used by Sally and Mary. After having given abuse sufficient for each party to vent ourselves in the true Way style, Sally and myself went up to Allen's, where, in going, I express'd all the bitterness I felt at her and her colleague for driving me in such rude manner; but after viewing the piece, natural affection began gently to operate, and I loved her old black hen–at least I felt more friendly towards it than I had done. We arrived there about four, but found Mr. Dunlap gone from town, and was not expected to return untill the following year, when he calculates to come on with another Scripture piece for exhibition, and I hope then to see him if I live.

I was introduced to Mr. Andrews by Ebenezer, a deeply interesting carracter to Mary and myself. He appeared to be not much rising twenty; remarkably slender and delicate form'd; very gentlemanly and easy in his manners; but O my soul! there is in embryo that, that will astonish the natives when it is hatch'd, whoever lives to see it. After the spectators were gone, all except Eben'r and 'a Sall I know,' I requested him to call down and see us, for he had express'd a great wish to see Mary. After having been inform'd of the particulars of her case and carracter as a painter, he appear'd to feel a degree of sympathy uncommon to his years, and I was pleased with his phylanthropy. He thank'd me, observing he would do himself this pleasure, but was ignorant of my place of residence. I told him that William would call upon and walk down with him. He engaged to come at eight o'clock the next morning. Accordingly, he came and staid an hour, as the [exhibition] hall open'd at nine; but in this short hour he did [not] let the grass grow under his tongue. We were delighted with so much enthusiasm, for never did I see it in so great a degree. His discourse naturally turn'd upon the sister arts and sciences, and this was cakes and gingerbread for us. We asked him to come and finish his visit in the evening and he appear'd to accept the invitation with his whole heart. We requested him to come at six, but unfortunately there were company call'd and he came not till eight (Mary declares he is the echo of her genius, were he ten years older).

When he came he brought a book which he said that he kept 'as a precious little morsel,' entitled

Rhymes on art
or
The Remonstrance of a Painter
by Martin Archer Shee[8]

We were highly entertain'd, and he staid till after ten. Will'm was here and went away with him.

I borrow'd the book and spent all the forenoon the following day, to write out the most interesting passages that my eye glanc'd upon; but a thought struck me that I would go up in the afternoon and take a sketch of the principle figure in the piece, if haply I might ever purchase a plate of ivory sufficiently large to introduce the whole figure without reducing it so much that I could not do justice to the face. I succeeded so well in re-copying the sketch of Our Saviour and a ruffian who is in the act of dismantling him that, together with what I retain'd in my mind, I have taken them both remarkably striking, as also the same style of painting, as that part was riveted upon my mind. Mr. Andrews gave me a sheet of the ivory paper, but I felt as paper of however superior a kind was unworthy of so sublime a subject. The figure is dress'd in light blue, shaded off into a light ash colour, a scarlet drapery shorter than the robe, with something that had the appearance of a gold trimming–though not very brilliant, no doubt for fear of destroying the effect–; the feet with sandals fastened with a blue ribbon. The crown of thorns was hardly perceptible enough to assertain what it was design'd for, and I am better pleas'd with that part in the copy than in the original painting. I was under the necessity of re-copying it, on one of the largest sheets of ivory you last sent me, while the recollection of it lingers upon my mind, and have infused into the countenance more benignity and devine composure than I expected, as I could not see to do everything there but make a rough sketch on paper with a black lead pencil–a thing you know I never use, but cannot upon so small a scale make it appear so interesting. The ivory is not long enough to bring in view the hands which are tied with a cord. I regretted this circumstance exceedingly, and, from being so cramped, shall not be able to show but one hand (and that, the left hand of the ruffian) that is clench'd in the scarlet robe and parallel with the lower part of the face. The pencil sketch is very accurate in its proportions in every part, if I could only procure a plate of ivory large enough for the figure. I therefore beg your attention to this part of the subject, but without making you any trouble, as I think you can recollect whether you have ever seen a plate of ivory as large as the length of the strip of paper inclosed; but if not, would prefer to finish on the one I have begun it upon. Just answer this question in your next. I have never heard of any larger than a saucer, which would be too small, as I want sufficient space over the head to admit of the rays of light, and sufficient under the feet to represent pavement of some distance. But not having at the moment proper apparatus, and then being oblig'd to quit it (which was a great cross) and turn my attention to 'pot walluping' business, has in some measure suppress'd the ardour of my enthusiasm–yet not so much either but what, as soon as I am over my present hurry, shall again commence operations.

Mary and Sally has been here this afternoon and spent an hour or two with me, and brought me the letter you wrote Will'm, and am sorry to find you so much distress'd. The girls tell me that she [Aunt Hannah] now is, and has for some time been, very comfortable, placed [=placid] and tranquil, much more so than for several years, and easy to take care of, and so pliable that she will do any thing they propose. They nurse her according to their own judgement, as they cannot tell any-thing from her answers. They ask'd her this morning if she disl[i]ke to being call'd or thought old, and Mary ask'd her how old she thought she was. She says, 'Not so very old.' 'Well, what age do you think–seventeen?' 'O yes, I am more than that, you know.' 'Twenty, then?' 'About that.' I was up to see her a few evenings since, and I found her very wild. She did not know me, though she insisted that she did, but could not recollect me, she said; and presently Mary ask'd her if she could not sing a verse to us. She said Yes, and seemed to be very willing, and began to sing *Blow ye the Trumpet*, with as much command of her voice, except being weaker, as I ever heard her.

They often ask her, are you in any pain. No. Are you not comfortable and happy? Yes. And seems to be perfectly resign'd to everything that comes, much more than she was; and I am certain that she has lost all her former fear of death–that is, 'the mode of going.' How often this has been repeated.

I must close my letter immediately and carry it up to put in the box, or wait till Monday night, as I wish to get it to you as soon as possible. I wish you to write upon the receipt of this.

Adieu. . . .

No sooner finished with this, Betsey had to copy out Mary's long answer to Eliza's of six weeks earlier (**no. 124**). The two sisters in the interim had been thinking about Eliza's proposal of marriage and had decided it must have come from young Edward Cort Riley, two years her junior but evidently estimable in their eyes. It remained to be seen what Eliza thought of him. Mary writes (**no. 127**):

> Nothing would be more acceptable than the *Gospel Herald*. My love to Mrs. Fitch, and tell her I will be much obliged to her. I have only seen a few extracts from it in the *Religious Enquirer*, and should be pleased to read the whole. I will thank you to send with it those pieces you mention'd in one of your letters. If you have not time to copy them, send the original. I will return them safe with the book, or sooner if you wish. You forgot to leave the pattern of my caps (alias Mrs. Fitches night-cap pattern). I will thank you to send it with the above-mention'd articles, as soon as possible. . . .
>
> I am very sorry you did not call upon Maria [Hayden] before she left town, but regrets are vain! I think you must be sensible, in this instance, your conduct has not been quite correct. There are those who think it a mighty piece of condescension to own a fault. Be it so. Condescension is one mark of a superior mind. When we rise up in judgement and condemn our faults, we show our superiority; but when, from selfish partiality, we would excuse them, we sink in our own estimation as well as that of others. When we vindicate what is wrong, we degrade ourselves, and are no better than the thing we justify. It is easier for a camel to pass through the eye of a needle than for the modern slave of fashion and folly (screwed up in corsets) to stoop for a purse of gold, and humanity shudders at the bare idea of such a painful operation. Yet even this is far less difficult, far less impossible, than it would be for buckram dignity to own a fault. No–where that presides, such 'amiable candor' and condescension are not to be expected. I am sorry you don't like the picture I have drawn of this darling trait of carracter. To call it names–a 'brickbattish carracature'–was rather uncivil. I think it merits a better appellation. 'Tis true, the painting is somewhat coarse and hard, but the likeness is the main object, and you know that is strikingly correct. My honest pencil never learn'd to flatter.
>
> 'It gives each muscle all its strength,
> The mouth, the nose, the chin its length.'
>
> And hold the mirror up to nature. So, if the picture does not please, the fault must be in the original; and for this I am condemn'd to burst in ignorance, in spite of all my old shoes and mogasons–tho', by the way, I would not give the latter for all the beaus New York affords.
>
> But perhaps I am not quite so blind as you imagine. But certain it is, I can see as far into a millstone as if I had twenty pair of eyes and could at this moment draw his picture, music store and all. You appear inclined to send him to your mother, and I think you could not dispose of him to greater advantage. In musical taste and tallants she far excells her daughter, and can better estimate his value; and besides, it may save you many a wearisome trip to his store, after musical instruments. Doubtless these considerations will have thier full weight; yet after all, should you conclude to keep him yourself, as his age seems to be the only objection, having set your mouth

in order for forty-five, you know 'our greatest strength is shown in standing still.' Try your strength in this way, and wait with patience till that happy period arrives, and then he will be all your heart can wish. . . .

Mr. and Mrs. Mitchell arived here this morning [July 11th] on thier way to Norwich. I saw them but for a moment. He has promised to return in about a week and spend a few days with us, but I dare not depend even upon his promises, for, whenever I calculate upon any common pleasure, it is sure to end in all the bitterness of disappointment–witness Maria's visit. Oh! Can I ever forget what I suffered on that trying occasion. . . .

Mary's reference to the Haydens' quick retreat from New London on their one visit there is explained by Anna's letter, above (**no. 103**). There is no saying, from the surviving correspondence, just what had gone wrong on that occasion. But now a second visit fails, too: one proposed by the Fitches in September in connection with that family's plans to escape the threat of yellow fever in New York. The disease was a recurrent spectre, invited by the city's inadequate water supply, terrible crowding, filthy streets with only pigs for scavengers; so from the 1790s epidemics came and went, and the population who had the means also came and went, from their homes down to Greenwich which was deemed safe, or to some further point in the suburbs. The authorities directed them to move and closed off precincts where the disease was reported. A particularly severe epidemic hit in the late summer of 1822, lasting for a couple of months.[9] Alarmed by it, the Fitches proposed to quit the city for a time, and commissioned Eliza to write her family about that; to whom Mary replied (**no. 128** of September 2):

It is a happy circumstance that prejudice is not altogeather so contagious as the yellow fever. If it was, yours would be dangerous to your friends, for it appears to be equally malignant and incurable, and I think (as the mind is more delicate [than] the body) is of the two most to be dreaded. I am glad Mrs. Fitch has escaped the infection–that she does not despise New London so heartily, or feel for this poor place the deadly hatred you express though our houses are not painted nor our streets are not paved. But Mrs. Fitch is not so proud as Miss Champlain and Captain Hayden, nor (I presume to say) so difficult to please; and, bad as it is, I hope she will not find it so intolerable but what, in case of life and death, it may be endured for a few weeks at least.

Your letter was laid before the Upper House [Ebenezer Way] and there the only difficulty is the want of lodging-rooms. They have a boarder, Miss Salter from New Haven, who teaches music and painting in Mr. Judd's school. She occupies one room and the other (which is all they can spare) will accommodate only two persons. And, though you don't mention Mrs. Northam and Cornelia particularly, we conclude they have returned from New-Port and will be of the party. Sally regrets exceedingly that it is not in her power to accommodate them all, and I should be most happy if she could, for then I should be with them. But in this world few things accord with our wishes.

Your uncle [Ebenezer] has made enquiries, and applied to several families that he thought would be agreable, but has not as yet succeeded to our satisfaction. There are many public houses, but since Aunt Taber left the place (I am sorry to say, but it is a melancholy fact) there is no genteel boarding house, and it is inconvenient for private families to accommodate more than one or two boarders. But we don't dispair. I know one stone will not be left unturned. Your uncle, William, Aunt Hannah and Sally are all engaged in the persuit, and Heaven grant they may be successfull. As for me, I am lame as well as blind, or I would not sit scribbling here, racked with doubts and fears, and all the torments of suspense, and cannot make one hair white nor black. To-night we shall know the result, but 'tis an age till then. I am a fool to feel this anxious solicitude, when I know these things are ordered Above, and all is ordered right. Maria's visit has forever cured me from anticipating mortal pleasures. Indeed, why should I? The world is lost to me! Nothing remains but to divest myself of its cares, hopes and fears–to give them to the winds and meet every event with perfect indifference. There is still too much mortallity about me, and I feel most sensibly my imperfection.

Well, William has returned and now my hopes are fled and all my fears confirmed. There is not a private family family in this town (that are genteel and respectable) who are willing to accommodate four persons as boarders. Thus ends my dream of felicity! I know a public house will not be agreable. In William's letter he mentions Captain Prentice. His house is very respectable. You know the Frinks family–there cannot be a better. With them, they can be as retired as they please. Thi[e]ere price for board is three dollars per week. Fail not to write by the mail.

Adieu.

We have just rec'd news of Doctor Allen's death. The family is in great affliction.[10]

Meanwhile, as Eliza tells in her next (**no. 129** of September 24), the Fitches grew more anxious, and could at last wait no longer for New London to receive them:

Dear Mother & Co.,

Well, we have at last been obliged to fly ourselves from plague, pestilence and famine, battle, murder, and sudden death. We laughed at our neighbours for some time before we took our own flight into Egypt, thinking them uselessly alarmed; but when the yellow 'messenger of mortality' took up his abode within three doors of us, we thought it high time to look to ourselves and accordingly began to stir our stumps merrily, that we might clear out, bag and baggage, with only half a day's warning–which you may be sure was quite as short a time as we could conveniently pack up our duds and be off. As a number of houses have been broken open in the infected destrict, apparantly more for the purpose of destroying their contents than to commit thefts, our folks thought it most prudent to move everything very valuable that the house contain'd, which has accordingly been done, and we are now the inhabitants of a large house at the 'corner of Stanton Street in the Bowery.' I don't know the no. or whether it has a number. At any rate, this direction is sufficient, so I hope you will not forget it and send any to the old number in Cherry St. If you do, I shall never get them, as the house is locked, of course.

Now I have told you where we are and how we are, I will proceed to another part of my story. I was not in the highest spirits when your last dolefull ditty arrived, as I anticipated something of that nature. I was not so completely surprised as if I had not known what home was and that there was nothing too homely & discouraging for me to expect from it. But at the same time, I assure you it was not till I had muster'd all the ressolution I possessed that I could put into Mrs. Fitches hand a letter from one of *my* relations which said, 'You cannot come amongst us, tho' your life is in danger,' particularly when I knew that she had great hopes of flying in that direction & I suppose did not dream of a disappointment; but it had to be done, and *I* had to *do* it, & I *did* do it, tho' I suspect with not a very good grace, as I could not speak. 'What could I say' in such a case? I could only feel–and Heaven knows I did feel.

Heavens! How vividly it brought to my mortified immagination that infernal Hayden scrape, that I can never think of without wishing I had never been born. But bad as it was, I had sense enough to know that it was cakes and gingerbread to acting over the aforesaid scrape, which perhaps would have been the case if I had not from the beginning of the affair turned with the most decided repugnance from the hateful subject whenever it was introduced. Mrs. Fitch saw how I felt about it and has given me two or three broad hints upon the subject, not thinking it possible, I believe, that it was necessary for me to behave apparantly so ungrateful. Would to Heaven not. O! that she could know how little my actions corresponded with my feelings, and how willingly I would undergo every privation that it was possible for a mortal to, if by doing so she could have been accommodated at New London in any shape whatever; for the countless obligations which I am under to this family I am sure I can never half return, even should my debts be all honourably discharged–which at present, without one scholar, there is not the most brilliant prospect of. If I could have found a packet on the eve of sailing for New London when I was packing up my things to move with the family here, I should have consulted my interest rather than my inclination, and steped into it, as my conscience gave me a few twinges for continuing here with such a dubious prospect. But seeing Sam'l the morning of the day on which we moved and hearing that there was no packet nor no more expected, I decided at once to share the fate of my friends, and in a very few hours from that time was in the carriage which convey'd us to this delightful part of the city. I think the purity of the air has already had an effect on my spirits, as they are much better than they have been for some days past, and without any reason that I know of, as fear was not the companion of my flight. Indeed, if it had been possible, I should much rather have staid in town, but that was impossible, situated as I am. I hope this is a sufficient reason for not comeing home, is it not?

I am now doing Mary Amelia [Avery]'s likeness, which close attendance on my scholars prevented my finishing before. Her mother is extremely anxious for it. My school-room is given up (conditionaly) untill my scholars return to town.

Mr. & Mrs. Mitchell have located within three quarters of a mile of Drake's paradise,[11] where we went with the Haydens and which I am sure you cannot have forgotten, if you are human. We all went out to see them last week by special invitation, and I don't know when I have enjoy'd a visit half so much as I did that. As a coach would not hold all our party, Mr. Fitch took a stage for the purpose. We fill'd it and had a fine frolic, I assure you. As every inch of country houses now contain very stylish inhabitants, we had the honour of being introduced to a Mrs. Keys who resides in part of the house with Mr. Mitchell. She is the youthful widow of a lawyer in this city and own sister to the lady who married the celebrated Charles Brockden Brown, author of *Wieland*, *Ormond*, &c &c &c.

I thought I should have died with laughter on first being introduced to her, for of all the fools that ever existed, 'thinks I to myself,' you surely are the greatest. Her conversation evidently showed she had been genteely educated, yet notwithstanding all that, she was the counterpart of Bett Harris; and, setting aside the superior style in which she talked, anyone who had ever seen the other would swear they were more alike than two eyes. I can give you no idea of the closeness of the resemblance, they were so completely one and the same person. It was not Bett in her ordinary mood, but only when she is spewing out her wildest flights of fancy. About thirty of us went to take a walk up much such a hill as we used to climb on Fisher's Island, and we were all disposed to enjoy ourselves. Mrs. Keys was one of the party and, if ever my soul was sicken'd with the word romantic, it was then. I thought I should never wish to hear it again. She talked of Ophelia in *Hamlet* and acted her all up the hill, which was completely perpendicular and not a soul but her could go up without two or three to assist them. I think she was quite as 'alert' and 'vigerous' as Bett, and quite as great a fool, and when she had at last reached the top, then we had it. I assure you she gave us a most sentimental harangue on the beauty of the surrounding landscape. We were all struck speechless and listen'd in mute astonishment at her folly. How do you suppose Mr. & Mrs. Mitchell like her? I assure you she is not a very great favorite with either of them, tho' of the two Mr. M. likes her the best.

I saw in last evening's paper the marriage of Eliza D. Holt to Mr. Dummer, a gentleman who has long admired her but who, I am convinced, she does not care half so much about as she does her cousen Henry Dobbs. I have been in company with him and don't think I should fall in love with him, tho' I believe he is a very fine young man. He is a crockery merchant in Broadway and I believe quite rich, so she has the one thing needful these hard times. . . .

Refuge from the plague proved no very harsh exile, as Eliza's next report indicates (**no. 130** of October 10th):

It is now two months since I have recieved a line from home and as your silence is totaly unaccountable to me I thought I would write for an explanation of it. Although I am not at all superstitious, a dream that I had last night may perhaps be the cause of my writing to day. I fancied myself in a house opposite to the one in which you live, and that I saw a coffin brought out from your house and placed in a hearse that stood waiting at the door. It moved slowly round the corner and proceeded to the grave-yard followed by more people than I thought New London contained. As the last of the train disappeared from my view, I looked up and beheld the air filled with angels each having a golden trumpet in thier hand and thier perfectly 'symmetrical' forms loosely enveloped in a robe of the most transparent texture. I can give you no idea of the grandeur and sublimity of the scene, or of my sensations while gazing on it. It appear'd to me that thier errand so near this 'lower world' was to waft the spirit of the deceased to the 'mansions of eternal rest,' and I felt as if I should have been nothing loath to accompany them back to the celestial regions, the only place of rest provided for us.

Last week John Mitchell came to invite me out to thier country seat to spend a week or two with them. I did not feel any disposition to refuse and accordingly accepted it. I found all the [Mitchell] family well except Cornelia, who I think is in a decline. She is very thin and has a constant cough. Mrs. Cowdry lives in a part of Drake's house at Bloomingdale about three quarters of a mile from Mr. Mitchell's, where, the day after my arrival, we were all sent for to spend the afternoon. I went more for the pleasure of seeing that delightful place once more than the family, tho' I had no reason to object to seeing them, as I recieved every attention and was urged to stay some time with them–which I, however, refused. The day was too cold to walk much or I should have gone down to the water. . . .

Since the foregoing was written we have returned to town and Samuel has call'd on me with the pleasing intelligence that a letter from you has been sent to me and is lost. Also, that the said letter contained money and 'what not' I know not, that it was delivered to Stephen Peck–and that is all I know about it. I should like very much to learn the fate of it, as I have been long anxious to hear from home and at length began to conclude that you had forgotten there was such a being in existence as I am. Mrs. Fitch also is surprised that her letter is not answer'd which was written so long ago.

My school will recommence tomorrow morning, as the scholars have all returned to town and many of them anxious to begin again. I have had one ten-dollar miniature since my arrival which is so well approved of that it is prophesied it will get me some more from the same quarter. I hope it will, as there is need enough. Mary Amelia's is finished and called an excellent likeness. Walter's frame is re-gilt and a fellow to it made, in which hers is set, and you never saw such a dash as they cut in Mrs. Avery's drawing room. I have seldom seen any thing more superb than the pair. She is dressed in a white frock very beautifully worked, with pantaletts to correspond, red morocco shoes. Her hair which is the most delicate gold colour falls in rich ringlets over her shoulders and mingles with the trimming of her frock and sleeves. Her right hand holds a basket fill'd with every kind of flower that I could think of which would look pretty in painting. Her left is extended to show a sprig which she has taken from it. I thought, as Walter made such a parade with his book, she should be equally vain of her flowers, and had almost concluded to strew her path with them when I fortunately recollected what an ugly phiz she had and immediately desisted from the pleasing task, as it would render her face less bearable. I raised the flowers with white paint first, then coloured them to my taste, and I assure you I have got the credit of possessing a very pretty fancy (saving your presence). As I did not wish the landscape to differ widely from yours, many parts are simmilar, though nothing is copied. There is a sheet of water extends across the piece, in which a pink and blue sky is reflected for the purpose of animating the face of nature. A point of land on one side, not quite so distant as yours, with a weeping willow whose longest branches just kiss the waves (if waves they may be call'd) on the other side; a grove of poplars more distant still, with a white cottage peeping from among them and hem'd in by a white fence that runs along the edge of the water. Mr. Fitch admires that part very much. He says it reminds him of a view in the garden of Versaills which was exhibited at the Rotunda and which he thought inimitable. I have introduced an elm tree to throw out those parts that required a dark ground to set them off, and have scatter'd shrubbery wherever I felt disposed. This I believe is the sum total of what I have done and you must acknowledge is a very brief description of my youngest child. In return I shall expect a long account of your youngest children and yourselves, as I think I deserve it after this eternal silence. . . .

This was soon answered (**no. 131**) by Betsey:

Dear Eliza,

I have but a few moments to write, just to inform you that we have rec'd your letter datted 10th and return you many thanks, as we were unusually anxious concerning you. Your making mention of Sam was also a happy circumstance, as he had neglected writing for a long time. If I might now be so blest as to recieve one from George, I should feel relieved from my heaviest burdens. I however still continue to hope he is well. I intend writing to him soon, and wish you to write if you have not since the report of the sickness at New Orleans.[12] I fear he will grow indifferent merely from our neglect.

Our not writing to you proceeded from thinking it very uncertain whether you would recieve the letters, not knowing whether you were in the city or not, and having lost one that contain'd some money, thought best to wait to hear from you. I regret it has cost you so much inquietude, but these were our reasons. The sum that we suppose lost with the letter was only one dollar 25 cts, with a guitar wire as a sample to purchase a hank of the same. The dollar was to pay you for what you paid towards the English flute, which suited extremely well. The 25 cents was for the hank of wire above mentioned.

Your dream was truly sublime, and though death is call'd the king of terrors, there was something so soothing in the *symphony* (excuse me for giving it this term, as I know not what else to call it) that it seemed to ballance those terrors which perhaps are altogeather immaginary. I can only say with some degree of faith that we shall have no more laid upon us than we can bear.

You have displayed your discriptive talant to advantage in giving us an account of the picture you have drawn of Mary Amelia Skeggs. I can see clearest from discription, the tints appear more brilliant. My own fancy gives the finishing touches to admiration, adding embellishments that even Raphiel or Angelo could scarcely equal, discreetly throwing every error into shade, and can at this moment see her glittering tresses, light and wavy, bespangling her face and falling in golden showers over her shoulders, from the reflection of the sun (that is, if you permit his rude beams to visit such perfection) intermingled with the superb embroidery you know so well how to discribe.

My youngest child [i.e., most recent portrait] is Nathaniel Perry, brother to the Commodore. He came with Doctor Brainard, to whom he had given a large snuff box. Upon the lid was the likeness of a French king who is said to have reign'd in the 16th century–which is all the account they could give of him. He was drawn with a long grey beard, open neck, a crimson velvet turban decorated with a white feather. The rich reflection from the turban upon the forehead and ear is inimitable. It is a profile view of the face. A bottle green drapery, confined across the breast by a gold chain over a couple of gold buttons. A dark back-ground, which was the greatest beauty of the whole. It is without exception the richest and highest finished piece of painting I ever saw. I did not like to be too inquisitive before the giver, but, self interest giving me a sly pinch or two, taking the hint, enquired the price. Perry indeed did not know. It was a compliment from his brother. The Doctor's politeness must of course keep him in ignorance; and I might never have been the wiser for my interogations but that Richard Palms happened to be one of the company–informed me they were to be had in New York at the store of Mockwiser at the corner of Liberty Street and Broadway, at the price of a dollar or a dollar and 50 cents. I will thank you to call there, when you are out shopping, and see if there is any you think will answer as a modle for a painter. If they are equal to the one I have discribed, I should like to pur[chase]. I should by all means choose a front face, dark and richly shaded, but if a female, with ringlets. But I must leave it to your judgment and fancy. If you can find a better judge than yourself, take them with you, and if you find any that will answer the purpose, give me information respecting it. . . .

The year 1823 revives the correspondence after some lapse of time and the loss of a letter or two from the surviving numbers. Mary writes by Bestsey's hand to Eliza, giving advice on how best to use her talents in New York, if she chose to remain there: "Improve your style," she had urged her niece repeatedly, three years earlier (**no. 85**), as she now does once more (**no. 132** of January 12)–for style, she then saw and still believes, is a businesslike investment:

Excuse me, my dear Eliza, for not answering your letter immediately as you requested. I was at your uncle's on Christmas day (where I had engaged to pass holidays) when it arrived. To write amid the hurry and hustle of visiting and company, I found impossible, and equally vain to strive against the stream, or return before the time appointed. It has at length arrived, I am at home, and have nothing now to do but answer your letter; yet I am utterly at a loss what to say or how to proceed in the difficult task before me. You intreat me not to advise you to return. Your mother thinks it best you should–begs and prays I will advise you to come as soon as possible. And I should not hesitate a moment to comply with her request, was you any thing but what you are. 'Alas! poor ghost!' I know thee well, and have but too much reason to apprehend thy 'perturb'd spirit' will never rest here.

I cannot say I have ever had much faith in the durability of this school establishment–not that I pretend to an uncommon share of foresight, for it was natural to conclude the rage for learning to paint would subside when the novelty was over and it was proved how very few are qualified for the task, whose talants and patience is equal to the persuit. Therefore I am not surprised at the falling off you mention. I was prepared to expect it. It is true I could not but approbate the measure, as I considered it a great though a temporary advantage, which would afford the means whereby you might obtain a more perfect knowledge of the art as well in theory as in practice. This was the object I had in view, nor did I at that time imagine you would fail to profit by it, sensible as you then appear'd to be of your own deficiency in this respect. It is not, however, the first time I have been mistaken, nor will it probably be the last. But could I reasonably suppose, my dear Eliza, you would neglect so favorable an opportunity to improve yourself in stile an[d] colouring, by the aid and instruction of some able teacher, and thus, as it were, lay a solid foundation whereon to rest your hopes of future success? Doing this in season would have secured to you one permanent advantage which never could be lost. Possessed of this resource, you would, comparatively, have nothing to fear though your school might fail. It could not blight your prospects or materialy affect your interest.

But I have preached volumes upon this subject before. 'Tis in vain you plead poverty and prudence. Both are in favour of the measure, and both should have compell'd you to adopt it. No doubt you found a use for every cent you have recieved, and might perhaps had it been twenty times as much; & still, my dear girl, to be strictly economical, from the little you recieved you should have reserved a certain sum sacred to a purchase so indispensibly necessary. 'What!? (you will ask)–leave my debts unpaid?' Yes, certainly, if it were only for the benefit of your creditors, that you might be able at a future time to discharge the whole amount with interest. Money is often hired for less important purposes. I hear you say, ' 'Tis too late to remonstrate.' Perhaps it is. I only hope, should another oppertunity ever again present itself, you will not let it pass unimproved.

'But now what is to be done?' That's the question. I am not wise enough to answer it. You say I must not advise you to return, for what can you do here? And I must not advise you to remain, for what can you do there? Yet something must be done. You ask for one of my strengthening plaisters. Alas! I have none to suit your case. You must apply to some more skillful physician, some more able counsellor, to advise and to direct you. Mr. & Mrs. Fitch, Mr. & Mrs. Mitchell have wiser heads and not less friendly hearts. Of this they have given sufficient proof. But I need not remind you of the many obligations you owe them all, particularly the two former, for the uncommon interest they have ever taken in your concerns. Certainly they are too sincere and candid to flatter you with false hopes or advise you to remain a moment longer than the prospect of success will justify, as they must be sensible your proud spirit will never rest under pecuniary obligations. Ask thier advice, on thier judgement rely implicitly. They will direct you what to do and how to act.

I know you are easily discouraged and hope your case is not so desperate as you imagine. You are fighting low spirits for amusement. This is doing well. I admire practical philosophy.

Your mother says there was a time when you was happy here, and she regrets you ever saw New York. I have done with regrets, but should be glad if you was now content, like me, to vegetate at home. It is indeed 'to live the life of a cabbage,' that is, a life of ease and comfort (so call'd) which it requires only patience to endure. Therefore lay in a plentiful stock of this precious commodity (against you return), with an equal quantity of chearfulness and good humour, and I will insure you a hearty welcome and as much vegetable happiness as you can enjoy.

Now the question is, whether this dull humdrum mode of existence–calm, still and monotonous–is not upon the whole preferable to the stormy life of enterprise and adventure, 'out at sea upon a shattered plank?'–trembling with aprehension, the sport of chance and every tempestuous passion, tos't about with hopes and fears, cares and disappointments, from transport to torture, now ambition 'boreing the moon with her mainmast,' now sunk to the lowest depths of misery with mortification and dispair. Would it not be wise to avoid these calamities–to escape these threatening dragons and fly for shelter to a quiet, peaceful home where you may rest secure and shut them out forever? . . .

The Handy's past the summer here at Doctor Lee's. Elizabeth is a genius. She plays devinely. She performed a piece upon the organ–it was Italian music, and I thought I was in heaven. I have just read Berian's *Travels through France and Italy*. He is one of the assistant ministers of Trinity Church. Perhaps you have seen it. Whoever has taste for reading, painting or music will be delighted with this book.

Mr. Waldo was here last summer, but too devout to visit any but the Methodist Connexion. Doctor Swift told me he compell'd him to dine with him, but he was quite too religious to be good company. Betsey S. says his partner Jewet[13] was in a still worse condition, mad with the same disorder when she left New York, and confined in the lunatic asylum. Now this is dreadful!–while it lasts. But that will not be long. This is my comfort upon all occasion, both for my own afflictions and that of others: the world's a perfect whirlagig, forever shifting scenes, and scarcely worth a serious thought.

Your prospects may have changed, and this letter find you in as good spirits as it leaves me. I sincerely hope it will. If not, come laugh and sing with us. We have fun and music here, such as it is–pretty good for homespun–especially the latter. We manufacture it in a variety of ways so as to suit all customers–pound it upon the glassy chord, drum it upon the harp, thrum it on the guitar, blow it upon the flute and flagelett, and want nothing but a hand-organ to grind it and complete our assortment.

Now, will not all this induce you to return? And besides, we have assemblies here this winter. Your uncle and aunt attends, and if you come in season you may dance away your cares; for what's the use of being sad in such a merry world?

Adieu!

Whenever it was that Eliza began the next letter, it took her weeks and weeks to finish, clean into March (**no. 133**), so its relevance to points raised by her mother back in October can only have been minimal:

Well, the guittar strings are at length purchased, but when they will be sent is beyond my ken, as I know of no opportunity by water, and by mail they will cost more than they come to. The price is eighteen pence. I have at length received the long-lost letter which contains money for the guittar strings and that foolish dollar for the flute together with the pattern of a whistle to be added, and a thousand directions with a request at the end of the letter, by Bill, that I will not attend to the whistle, as the person who told you of it was a num-skull. So when I know who I am to obey, I will 'go about to do'–and not before. I am sorry to tell you I have never call'd to see about your snuff-box yet, and the more so as I can give no good excuse for not calling. I will however call some day, and if I can find one that I think will suit your step will purchase it and send it on. . . .

Well, we have all been at last to see those famous pictures of the Lavertys, and admirable paintings they are, I assure you, as well as excellent likenesses. With Ellen's I was particularly struck. It looked as it would speak and ask me if I had found 'Mary Robinson,' as you may recollect the fair original did when sitting for her miniature. By the way, she show'd me that same picture the other day. Ellen & Hester Ann are dress'd in marine blue with broad lace tuckers turning over a low neck frock. Amelia is dress'd in crimson with velvet cape and cuffs, and a more exquisite imitation of velvet I never saw in my life.

Last Wednesday Mr. & Mrs. Fitch came down to my school for me to go to Waldo's and see the pictures, as soon as I had dismiss'd my flock. As I had long wished to go, it was with much pleasure I took the opportunity, as I felt sure I should remain unrecognized by Waldo–which was what I wished, of course. For if I had had an idea of being known, I would sooner have died than gone. But as Aunt Hannah says, 'it was to be so;' and I found I might as well make the best of it.

Unknown to me, Mr. Fitch put a half-finished miniature of his wife in his pocket which I am now doing, and, as soon as we got fairly in and engaged with looking at the paintings, he took his wife out of his pocket and handed it to Mr. W. as the work of Miss Champlain. Had a spectre stood before me, I should not have been more surprised and thunderstruck than at that unexpected maneuver, for the last thing on earth that I should think of doing would be taking a sketch or unfinished piece of mine for Waldo to criticize. However, there *it* was & there *I* was.

'And is it possible this is the work of Miss Champlain?' asked Mr. W. 'Well, I am really astonished. Miss Champlain, you will allow me to criticize this piece in the presence of your friends, I hope?' 'Certainly, Sir,' was my answer. 'Well then, I will begin with the face, and of that I shall say that if it was as perfect as the drapery I should have to fly my country–for I never saw anything more exquisitely beautiful than it is.' (And here I suppose I must stop to describe it). She has on a very tasty French cap with pink bows and tabs that accomodate themselves very much to a thin face. The hair that appears from under that lace is not only fashionably but handsomely arranged. A plain white robe and a zone with a drooping lace ruffle, a handsome Scotch-plaid cloak lined with green silk, with a crimson velvet cape, is thrown over the right shoulder, and a small part appear under the other arm. Her right hand holds Byron's *Poems* handsomely 'bound in calf, & gilt but not letter'd.' The lace ruffle falls partly over the crimson cape and green lining of the cloak, which has a fine effect by giving a liveliness to the picture which it would not otherwise have. This part Mrs. Fitch thinks inimitable & Waldo praised till he had nothing further to say about it. He looked at Mrs. F. and said that I could not have had a worse subject, and then preached volumes on the strong light I used for painting, which he said he supposed it would be agony to work in, and has promised to call and regulate it. I thanked him & Mr. Fitch handed him his address. He said nothing could be more beautiful than one half of the face, but the demi-tints on the other half he did not like, and that it was altogether owing to my light which, if he did not regulate, would lead me altogether astray. So I expect a visit from him soon. I did not see Jewitt. Laverty was sitting for him. . . .

While the above was being slowly hatched on Eliza's desk, her New York brother had first called on her as he says (**no. 135**) and then dispatched the following on February 4th to William in New London–proving that he could be a man of action when it suited him:

Dear Bill,

Your newspaper & letter came to hand this morning while I was out, which has been the case for 2 months past. Every letter from N[ew] London or any-where else is brot in to the store while I am at dinner, supper, or some-where else (it's very singular, but so it is–it won't average one hour thro' the day that I am out, either). So I don't have an opportunity of seeing the bearer of them.

I carried the letter to Eliza this forenoon. I rap'd at the door & it was opened by the servant. I went into the parlour. None of the family were in. As I was passing thro' the hall I hear some one running up-stairs, which I thought was Eliza. I then spoke to the servant and ask'd if 'Miss Champlain was in.' 'Yes, Sir.' 'Request her instantly to come down (said I), as my business is of importance.' Upstairs flew the girl & told her that 'there was a gentleman waiting to see her in the parlour who appears to be in a great hurry & wish'd to see her instantly.' Miss Eliza as it happened was in her deshabilles, so she had to shift her dress (not knowing but that it might be the Prince Regent) and after a lapse of 10 minutes she came down. I was standing with my back towards her, muffled up in my cloak. As she came into the door I turn'd around very abruptly. She had a smile upon her countenance, I could distinctly see, which instantly vanished as soon as she recognized my preface, & instead of 'Your servant, sir,' it was 'Rot your picture, Sam, you've frightned me to death.' I laughed most heartily for a few minutes, to see the confusion I had thrown her in, & then came out with her wishes, that the letter, money, fiddle strings, & me were at the 'Old Boy.'

You'll be careful that this letter is not seen by any but our family.

P. S. Tell Aunt Hannah that all Mr. Fitches family are well & send on love by the wholesale to her, which she must reccollect & remit to them.–'O they are lovely' people always so 'kind, so sociable, so friendly, & so obleegin'! How are Aunt Hannah's daffys, tulips, vilets, &c? Have they come up yet? Does she still continue to make artificial flowers & buy 'gum marrer buck' down to Doctor Thompsonses, or over to Doctor Coit's? Don't let her see this, for she'd 'protest' I was a 'naggibone' in good earnest. . . .

Betsey's place of lodging in New London is often unclear. She seems to have moved around from time to time both before and after her husband's death. The next letter to her from her daughter (**no. 137** of February 28th) introduces a new name as her address, "Care of Daniel Thatcher."[14] The Thatcher family was old and prominent in the town, and one of them, a pal of William's:

. . . Ellen Tooker, you know, has been dying ever since she saw the Mitchells' watch-papers to learn painting of me, and has even gone so far as to express a wish to come to my school–a thing which I believe she has never done yet to any school in the city. This her mother refused to let her do, giveing as a reason that she was out too much already and that, if she went to school, she should [be] entirely deprived of her society–a thing she by no means wished, valueing it as highly as she does. Accordingly she told me that, if I would consent to go there and give her ladyship two lessons a week, she would give me $10 per quarter. To this proposal I told her that I could not possibly accede, the distance being so great, it was much more than her ladyship was worth; but that, if she would procure one or two more scholars at the same price to commence with her, I should then think her offer worth accepting, and would go, but not else. She said if that was the case, as Ellen was so extremely anxious to learn, she would exert her influence to get more scholars and send me the earliest information. The next morning Mr. Tooker's nephew called to tell me that his cousen and another young lady were ready to commence & that there was a prospect of more, but they had not engaged themselves yet. This information I did not like, and don't think I should have agreed to go upon those terms. Although I had said I would for one other, I thought it was too little. But Mr. & Mrs. Fitch both thought I had better accept than reject the offer. As I feel bound to take their advice in every thing, I told him I would go, and accordingly sallied forth after dinner to give them their first lesson. I found them expecting me with impatience and delighted with the watch-papers I took for patterns, which by the by were those I paint in the space of ten minutes. Of the style I leave you to judge.

She [Ellen Tooker] told me that her father, Laverty, her two sisters & herself were all setting for their portraits to Waldo, & that she had that morning sat from ten untill 1 o'clock, and asked what I thought she had better be dress'd in. I said if it was mine I should certainly choose white, but that crimson looked very well. 'That is the colour on which I had decided,' she said, 'untill I found that both my sisters intended to be drawn in it, and I of course instantly gave it up.' She them slipped on a very superb mazarine blue dress with a more superb lace tucker and asked how I thought she would look in that. I told her that the frock was certainly very handsome but that a white mull was ten thousand times handsomer, particularly as I was not partial to that colour; but as they were all to cut such a splash, I found she had not taste enough to agree with me and be dress'd in anything so simply elegant as mull and lace would be–for dash and glare is the order of the day there.

I find her a very apt scholar. She will paint two watch-papers at a lesson and do them almost as good as I could myself. She has as much vivacity as it is possible for one person to possess. In short, she is the counterpart of Mother. If she had any more *life* she would die.

And here I cannot but lament that when I was fashion'd, this same mother of mine had not infused into this salmagundyish composition of mine a particle if no more of those spirits which enables her, like an evergreen, to laugh & dance thro' life (if, by the by, this plant ever cuts such capers), while her less fortunate daughter, who cannot so well bide the pelting of the pitiless storm during a visitation of the blues, has not a word to throw to a dog, and, as so much 'goes by favors,' in this lower world, finds that a [?]Mum Chance is not half so popular as a Crazy Betty.

Mother, you must excuse my impudence. I begin to suspect you are half mad with me by this time for giveing my tongue such license; but as I don't exactly like all the materials of which I am composed, and as I think the maker of anything the most proper person to complain to of any fault in the thing made, I have made bold to write the foregoing nonsense. . . .

Cornelia Clinch has a serious beau to whom she is shortly to be married. He is now in Ireland but is soon expected and as soon as he returns the match is expected to take place.

Mrs. Fitch & C. send love. She has lately dramatized *The Recluse*, but won't publish it. It is a beautiful thing, only she thinks it too romantic. But, faith, if it was mine it should come out if I knew it would be refused.

Ellen Tooker told me the other day that Jewett, Waldo's partner, begged her to bring me with her the next time she came to set, and she told him she would if I could be prevail'd on to go; but that it was somewhat doubtful whether I could. I told her that I should like to go provided I could go incog., not else. He said he should suppose I should like to see the portraits, and he had a very great desire to see me, he has heard so much of my painting. I told her that Mrs. F[itch] talked of calling and that I should accompany her, but I should take a day that she was not setting, that I might remain unknown; so I intend to call as soon as her portrait is finished.

Adieu, adieu, I have much more to say but no room.

Some hitch in communication accounts for the offended tone in Eliza's next (**no. 138** of March 17th), referring back to an errand on which Betsey had sent her in October of the previous year; so the offense seems a little mis-taken. Now, however, the order has been filled and a boast added, that her painting improves. One of the pieces she describes finds a match in a sketch that survives, showing her usual sentimental playfulness (Fig. 5):[15]

Dear Mother & Co.,

I have just recieved a visit from Sam and am not a little surprised to hear my silence complain'd of. If I had not written volumes since I have recieved a line from any of you, I should of course expect to hear complaints of the kind; but as I have, I will will be much obliged to you for an explination, as I don't see what can have become of the letters I have written and the guitar strings I have sent. I will thank you to let me know if my letters cost any thing, for if they do I will either discontinue writing or pay the postage myself, as I am very sensible that the nonsense they contain is not worth the money that it costs if it costs any. And the sooner I am enlightened on the subject, the better I shall like it.

I have just given the finishing touches to two of the handsomest watch-papers I ever painted. They were to present to Mr. & Mrs. Michell, with a request that they should take the place of those inferior ones which they honour'd with such beautiful frames. Mrs. Fitch has taken them with my message and brought back word that there was plenty more frames to be got in the city and that those also should be framed. As Mr. Mitchell is an Irishman I have painted him the *Harp of Erin*, with

Figure 5. The *Harp of the North*

many alterations but the same verse [from Sir Walter Scott's poem], which I suppose you recollect. It is much handsomer than the first but not any too handsome for *him*. For Mrs. M. I have painted the much admired form of *Fame* with all her apperatus and the word 'America' on the scroll which she holds in her hand. On the faint outline of the rainbow I have written the words 'Let Fame sound the Trumpets.' Her dress, you recollect, is a lawn robe and a golden zone, and you can concieve of nothing more delicately beautiful than the shading of her her figure and drapery. But I pay through my eyes instead of my nose for such fine work.

Last Monday evening I was at the theatre with Mr. & Mrs. Fitch, Maria & Sophia Clinch to see the celebrated Mathews perform for a whole evening alone.[16] He is certainly the most astonishing actor that I ever saw in my life. To be able to support every character through the whole piece without the least assistance or the least blunder, I think requires no ordinary talents–and keep the house in a roar the whole time. You have no doubt heard of him. He has made more noise than any actor we have had here in an age. Caroline and Elizabeth Handy set in the next box but one to us, but I believe did not reccollect me, as it is many years since I have seen either of them before.

I have a few scraps of news which I will tuck in here if I can find room. Florio, the inimitable Florio, has ceased to write! He finds that his writings, elegant as they are, will not support him and has in consequence turned his attention to the more wighty matters of the Law. He is now courting a young lady who, it is supposed, will soon die of the same complaint as did his celebrated Cora. I suppose you remember her.

Our Jack-of-all trades and good at none, the Chevalier De Ninny,[17] has now turned surgeon-dentist and is becoming a great man. Your cousen Laverty has bought a pew in Grace Church. On being asked by Mrs. Tooker why he chose that church in prefference to any other, he replied, Why Madam, there is more carriages attends that church than any in the city, and I wish my daughters of course to exhibit there. This I think was an answer worthy of Laverty.

We had a wedding in church on Sunday last. Mr. Mitchell has now gone to Petersburg and is not expected home in less than three weeks. His place is to be supplied by others. David Dunham (the father of the young lady whose mouth opens like the bud of the rose) was drown'd in that last dreadful storm. As he was a very useful man his death is consider'd a great loss to the city. Two hundred dollars was offer'd to any person who would find his body. It was found, and buried from his house in Broadway. I cannot help smiling at the manner in which I have mixed up my news. I am not sure that you can make any sense of it. But it is not worth copying, so I shall send it as it is. Adieu, I am in great haste.

Eliza

I have call'd at Wreakmaster's about your snuff boxes but can find none of your description. He has a great variety but they all look like the apostles and not at all like kings. Many of them are two dollars and half, and he says have sold for four and and five dollars a piece; but I saw none for which I should be willing to give so much money. But if you will tell me how to act, I will do accordingly. . . .

Betsey in her reply to Eliza's two last letters, toward the end of April (**no. 139**), has picked up yet another young genius, on top of Sandy Clarke and Ambrose Andrews: John Raymond. But this one proves impossible to find in other sources than the correspondence itself, below:

My dear Eliza,

I never rec'd a letter from any one that was more acceptable than the last you wrote. I was just upon the verge of dispair when it came to hand, but I am very willing to excuse you, if you will not let another three months elapse before you write again. We were all pleased with its contents, and happy to learn your prospects were better than when you wrote before.

Has Mr. Waldo call'd to see you yet?–fixed your light, given you instructions respecting the demi-shades, as you mention'd? If so, give me the outline of all he said and did. Perhaps I may take the hint without the kick. I have seen and examin'd the paintings you describe, and am delighted with them, as also Mrs. Fitches miniature, admire it, and could take a copy of each. I am particularly pleased with her scotch plaid, with the lace falling over the crimson cape and green lineing. I think there was great taste display'd in the drapery.

So far I had wrote through fire and water, for want of time, when I rec'd your letter dated March 17th, which, like all your others, were a welcome one. You accuse us of neglect. What is the use?–when you know I cannot help it. No one had any right to complain of you, as I was sensible it was my duty to answer the other before I had reason to expect another; but I have heard from you again, and you well know that selfishness is the predominant trait in all flesh. Your letters costs us nothing, I assure you, so don't let that idea be any bar to writing when you can spare the time; and if they did, there is nothing I would spend money sooner for. In respect to the box, I am glad you did not make a purchase, as they come so much higher than I expected: two dollars and fifty cents is more than I am able to give. That sum would procure sufficient plates of ivory to last me a year, and that I must have; but if you should ever find one for one dollar fifty cents that you think would answer for a modle, as well painted as the kings and queens I have heard so much about, take it and I will send you the amount. Otherwise omit it, as I should prefer borrowing a good painting to copy. I shall leave it to your discretion and judgement, as I am sensible you know I want the best stile and colouring of a front-face.

I have had very little business this winter as also for three winters past, but it now begins to revive. Among the rest of my patients I have lately met with a 'Genius so rare as beggars all description.' 'Why, he could thrash the ground' with your Aunt Mary's that you have talked volumes upon. He is tall, thin, dark complexion'd, with rather a pensive air, an uncommon degree of of awkwardness in manners, wearing the appearance of a farmer or a shepherd, as he seemed to have a crook or something like it–that is to say, a crooked stick–in his hand, a large bundle tied up in a flag hankerchief. He applied for a front-face on ivory. He was dress'd in blue with a short blue jacket, by way of a Spencer, as was fashionable some centuries ago. As he threw it off, I observed the sleeves were lined with ticken or some kind of striped homespun cloth (every mark of genius). It appeared tarnish'd and as if he work'd in it. His hands looked like a labouring man yet not a match for a pair I could name. Light blue eyes, prominent nose, dimples in both cheeks and chin, rather a small mouth, lips inclining to thinness (what I never liked); small white even teeth, a coarse yellowish cotten shirt which from the open bosom exposed a fine worsted gersey frock; no ruffle, a pink or party-coloured vest with those open work'd buttons as is, or was, fashionable for indispensibles; rusty shoes, mixed coarse yarn stockings.

He appeared greatly embaressed on first sitting untill engaged in conversation, which was as great a relief to me (you know how I hate these awkward, silent painful pauses). Conversation at such crises has a salutary effect as talking the turn of a tune, after having commited a thousand blunders in playing the first part–or the same thing, when having performed the first part well, and know that blundering will succeed, or be the fate of the turn. I then find a tongue very accommodating.

I shewed him a couple of pieces I had partly finished. They were both on paper. He observed that he had seen a miniature of Miss Cox and another of Mrs. Sheffield, and many others of my drawing, that he thought admirable; that he had seen the painting of different artists but never any that would equal mine for likenesses and stile (now this, you see, was 'complementing full well,' but what would he say to see my youngest child's performances?); that he had resided in New York nearly four years; that he attended all the book auctions, presumed to say that he owned the largest library in the United States; as also and moreover, better than three hundred elegant engravings, some of which excell'd any he had ever seen; four large magazines of the heathen mythology fill'd with emblematical engravings; as also those of all the principle carracters of the British and American officers that were kill'd in the last war.

I was greatly amused; and never did the Israelites long for the leekes and onions of Egypt more than I for such treasures. It is sufficient to say that books, poetry, painting and musick were the subjects, and such as are not easily worn out. He also introduced his musical talant–that he play'd upon a violin, a flute, a harpsicord which he had invented and made himself, which he valued at seventy-five dollars, which was equal to the best piano ever heard. I observed I had an English octave flute that I wish'd him to try, and never did I know the value of it untill he perform'd. I desired to know his opinion of it. He said it was an excellent one of the kind but that he owned one of the best German flutes he ever heard. I answered, I should be pleased to hear it. He said he would bring it the next time he came; and sure enough he did. Such musick and such tunes I never heard with my ears. I was so sick of all my *Peggies* and *Mollys* that I never desired to play them again. He observed that he never danced a step in his life (which I can readily believe)–that, while others were amusing themselves with dancing, cards &c, he was at his studies, as also he was a single man and had nothing to prevent or disturb him from his pleasing reveries; and further, that he was a ship-carpenter by trade, that he was born in Columbia, was going on to your famous city, there to reside. I expect to see him again before he leaves the place and perhaps I shall give him your street address and number. It may be (as strange things frequently take place) that he may have a snickering. I hope you will treat him with attention, for, recollect the harpsicord.

Sally is very sick or she would have answered your letter before. If she does not recover soon, William will write for her and send Owen. She gave her sister Harriet *Crazy Jane*, but Mrs. Bryant will send you hers to copy. I need not tell you to be careful of it. . . .

"Dear Mother & Co.," replies Eliza in May (**no. 140**),

I have recieved your last letters and pictures, for which I am very much obliged to you. I will return the latter as soon as possible. I hear Mrs. Lee is in town. She told Ellen Tooker the other day she should like to call and see me before she left town if she could discover my number, which I suppose she has not been able to, by her not calling. Mrs. Fitch said if she could ascertain her place of residence she would certainly call on her, as she treated her with much attention when in New London.

I was much amused by your account of your genius, but entreat you will not give him my number, as I should be sorry to see him here if her even brought a letter. I think the kind of genius that he and many other unfortunate beings possess is a curse rather than a blessing. . . .

Let me know if you have recieved the [Rev. Edward Mitchell's] *Excommunication* of a member of [the Rev. Gardiner] Spring's [Brick Presbyterian] church. Mrs. Fitch desired Sam to send it you. It has made a great noise here and does not redound much to Spring's credit, as you may suppose.[18]

This letter has been written for such a length of time that I have entirely forgotten when I commenced it, and should of course have committed it to the flames (the most proper place for it) had I not yesterday recieved a call from the very fellow I have been talking about: your Genius [John Raymond]. He call'd, he said, at your request to see me and show me his picture, which in due time I had the honour of seeing, tho' not till I had given up all hope that he ever would pull it from his pocket. I think it a tolerably good likeness, tho' I have seen better of your doing. As you appear desirous of having him for a son-in-law and I wish to crush all such hopes in the bud I shall only tell you that there was no 'snickering' (as you are pleased to term it) on either side of the question. I think I must have appear'd with all the starch of Queen Elizabeth, after his seeing and conversing with such a limber-jointed Mah as has fallen to my lot. So it is my humble opinion that you forthwith strike up a bargain with him in my place.

He looks and talks as if he had lost every friend he ever had in his life, and I think some-one ought to take compassion on him. He brought some music for me to send on to you, which I shall do as soon as I get an oppertunity of sending *Crazy Jane*, as it is too large to enclose in a letter. He says he has forgotten the names of the tunes you wished him to write for you and desired you will write me and let him know, and he will send them on. As I did not feel in very good spirits, I could not have appear'd to very great advantage; and as I was not so smitten with him as you appear to be I did not ask him to call again; so I suppose our acquaintance has terminated. . . .

Adieu, the end has arrived.

The painting of a maniac, referred to in the ninth chapter above where also *Sterne's Maria* was shown as Pl. 7.16, passed back and forth between the two cities. So did other paintings at other times, inviting comments. An exchange is mentioned by Eliza at the outset of the previous letter. What was sent now does in June receive her comments (**no. 142**) which she hadn't had time to offer earlier, and she goes on to explain various commissions given her to purchase art supplies, ivory, brushes, and "the new-fashion'd pith for Mrs. Bryant" (intended for watch-papers):

. . . Give my love to Mrs. Bryant and tell her I am very much obliged to her for her *Maniac*. She has recieved no injury here. I hope she will be as fortunate on her passage home. I shall pack her *up*, if possible, with as much care as William packed her *down*. More I cannot, for I was three hours by the watch undoing the planks, papers, lables, ropes, and rattling-traps in which he had enveloped her, besides smearing her all over with sealing wax. I hope his lordship will take no offence at what I say, for if ever I have bundles to send home again that are of half the value of those which I once sent, he may certainly expect to recieve a summons down here to pack them for me, as I think his talent for that sort of thing unequal'd. He does it with all the neatness of a spinster.

I have this instant recieved a call from Capt. and Mrs. Hayden, who leave here on Monday next. The Capt. has got a situation in the War Office at Washington through the intercession of his friends, and they are now on the eve of departure. I think I never saw either of them look better than they do at the present writing. Maria has another daughter which they both say is the counterpart of their lost lamented Emma and is call'd after her. She is thirteen months old and resembles her as much in disposition as looks. More she cannot, from their account–a circumstance which by the bye I should not greatly rejoice at, tho' I have no doubt but you will, although it at once condemns you as a false prophetess, that another phoenix should arise from the ashes of the first, when you have so often declared that while the world stands there never would another 'Emma' enlighten it.

Tomorrow we call on them to see the paragon of perfection, and I shall then of course be better able to give you a description than I am at present–so I shall throw aside my letter till after that important event has taken place.

Well, our first and last call has been paid to the Haydens. They start for Washington tomorrow morning, and I shall pehaps never see them again. In the course of our visit Mrs. Fitch asked Mrs. Hayden if she intended to visit New London at any future period, a question which I did not care to ask her. 'Never while I breathe,' was the answer; and a long pause ensued which was at length broken by Maria's saying she never expected to see any of her friends more when she got settled at Washington. Maria then left the room and soon returned with her child in her arms, and of all the beautiful children that I ever saw it certainly is the handsomest. It is as much like Emma as a little angel and a plain child can look alike. It certainly reminded me very strongly of Emma but is ten thousand times handsomer than ever Emma was, or would have been. This I suppose you will doubt, but I assure you it is true as the gospel. The first Emma was only beautiful to her mother and you, the present one is to all who see her. Her eyes have the most heavenly expression you can concieve of, her skin is fair as a lily, and her hair which is of light gold colour falls in the most beautiful ringlets over her neck. She looks as arch as a little devil can, and has dimples in both cheeks and chin; but her mouth surpasses all the rest for beauty. I can give you no idea of her so I might as well not attempt it. She is very mischevous. She got first Mrs. Fitches purse and emptied its contents on the floor, and, while all hands were scrabbling to get together the cash she had strewed over the floor, she made a dive at her red morocco card-case, the contents of which soon shared a similar fate. Maria says Julius is ten thousand times more mischevous. He was then at Newark. She was hourly expecting him.

She enquired very particularly about you all–said she had made fifty attempts to write to you but they had all been unsuccessful, desired me to leave with her my street and number that she might write to you and enclose it to me. She was very friendly, much handsomer than when she was at New London, and in better spirits than I ever saw her before in my life; so I suppose Hayden's situation at present is more lucrative than it ever was before. I shall of course forward letters as soon as she writes.

I enclose Raymond's tunes and will thank you to send me word what others you want as soon as you can; for, although I did not ask him to call again, it's very possible he will, and I should be sorry to not have the names to give him.

You enquire about my situation. As I have no satisfactory information to give I believe I shall withhold all. Ellen Tooker is painting a most elegant pair of skreens: the wreath which Miss Lord painted, with Fancy for the centre of one, and Cupid playing on a golden hoop for the centre of the other. On the other side of *Cupid* is *Sterne's Maria*. They are both beautiful and admired very much.

Mother, as you are so fond of making a dead set at the gentlemen, I think this Asa Spencer scrape[19] would be a pretty good catch and advise you by all means to strike up to him while the iron is hot. You know he is fond of widdows, particularly if they happen to be old–for I suppose Bill and [his daughter] Charlotte will make a match, and you would be a mother (as the saying is) to the whole concern at once–no bad speck, if report speaks true about the talents of the artists, so I entreat you will not delay to do it and I will come to the wedding. . . .

I suppose you have heard of the death of Capt. Cahoon's son, a lad of fourteen. I presume it's the same son whose likeness you took when on Fisher's Island, and thought such a beautiful boy. . . .

Further mention of art-supplies opens Eliza's letter later in the month. She adds a copy of a "beautiful poem, 'The Savage of Averyson,' " and the news that Cornelia

Clinch is about to be married, and is in the interim "at the theatre, the circus, the Gardens or some place of amusement every evening, and enjoying herself in high stile, I assure you." To this (**no. 143**) Mary writes a reply (**no. 144**) which she had in fact begun as answer to Eliza's May-letter but didn't finish until September! She explains why. The "pamphlet" referred to is that by Mr. Mitchell in support of an excommunicant from the Presbyterian church, above (at note 18):

> I return the *Gospel Herald* with my best love and thanks to Mrs. Fitch. I hope she will have the goodness to lend me the second volume, if I have not too far trespassed on her patience by keeping this so long–which indeed is not my fault. I could have read it through twenty times at least, and Aunt Hannah has only read it to me twice in course, with many a tedious pause and pinch of snuff betweens. She would rest every five minutes, and as often said, 'Mary, I wish to read this book as much as you wish to hear it, but I must stop and take breath'–good soul as ever lived, and I am determined to twist all I can out of her in this way. I have not many reading friends, and those I tax severely. They think me selfish and unreasonable and perhaps a little tirannical, for I often compel them to read to me against thier will, and scold it out of them when I cannot otherwise obtain the favour. It has become at length my ruling passion, and, 'like Aron's serpent, swallow'd up the rest.' They are all subdued but this alone I cannot, will not, conquer. Even my rage for painting and music is in a great measure abated. I can listen to the description of a fine picture without the sigh of regret, I can hear music and feel that I am still on earth surrounded with the infirmities of mortality. But I find my taste for reading is not to be diminish'd by time. I had rather have one meal a day, and that bread and water, than be denied this intellectual food. But here the body is feasted while the mind is left to prey upon itself, and I am half my time in a state of mental starvation. I have learn'd to knit and sew. Indeed, I can do any thing that comes within the bounds of possibility; but I can never learn to read, and it is a sad thing to be dependent upon the whims and caprice of others for the only true enjoyment earth can give–the only pleasure that is not attended with satiety. But enough of myself. Now for something better.
>
> I am sorry for Maria. I feel for her 'a mix'd sensation hard to be described.' I am glad to hear she is well and in good spirits; that she is like to be pleasantly situated; and if she has another Emma, I am sure she is happy as this world can make her, and but the more an object of compassion. What is human happiness? At best, imperfect and precarious–'An odour, fled as soon as shed.' How I pity those whose views are confined to the narrow limits of this miserable world, those that lay up for themselves treasures on earth, that place thier affections on any thing below no matter what it is. Sooner or later it will be snatched away, and what will support them in the hour of trial? I shall see her and her Emma, but not here. For a little season I am deprived of many pleasures and many dear and valued friends, by absence and by death; but they will soon be all restored to me again. They may forget me here, but I know they will remember me when we meet in happier regions and amidst the hosts of Heaven,

celestial spirits, and superior beings. I shall be partial still to those I knew and loved on earth.

Tell Mrs. Fitch I long to see her there, where all my hopes are fixed and this pleasure (great and unspeakable as it is) I can safely anticipate without the fear of disappointment or dread of future separation. What more can I desire? That one delightful thought dispels my cares and makes me, even here, the happiest of beings.

The pamphlet I rec'd is a proof I am not yet forgotten, and I feel grateful for every testimony of her regard in whatever shape it may appear. Many have been edify'd and instructed by this little book. I have lent it often, and every one is pleased with it. I think Doctor Spring & Company must feel very cheap. Mrs. Townsend's letter to him is excellent, and your Speaker has given him a handsome dressing, but he does every-thing handsomly. Mrs. Lee was there when it first came from the press. She says it made a great noise. She heard more of that than any-thing else while she stayed–that Mrs. T. was spoken of in the highest terms of approbation, and his Reverence universally condemn'd.

It is in vain to contend against pride and prejudice, but I am sorry you did not call on Mrs. Lee. Though she is no favorite of yours, her friendship for the family intitled her to this mark of attention. Had you taken the trouble to enquire, Ellen Tooker could have told you she was at Doctor Handy's in Murray Street. She wished to see you and Mrs. Fitch, and had determined to wave all ceremony and call upon you both; but, the day appointed for that purpose, it rain'd and she had no other opportunity.

Thus far I had written sometime last July, and it lay very quietly on the slate, waiting for the moving of the waters. Your mother had promised to write it off the first leisure moment, and I had engaged, as soon as it was finished, to spend a few weeks with Sally. In the mean time, I was sent for to Doctor Lee's. I went sorely against my inclination, well knowing I should not enjoy myself nor her society in the eternal round of company with which she [Mrs. Lee] is infested–strangers from all parts of the Union, those I never saw nor never wish to see. She would take no refusal, so I went for good manners, as Aunt Hannah goes to church. All the world was there, as I expected. I shall not trouble you with the list of names and different carracters that came under my observation (for you have no idea how much may be sensed without eyes–it appears to me I have seen more of the world since I lost mine than I ever saw with them, and for this plain reason: my attention was otherwise engaged, I was then an actor in the busy, bustling crowd. I am now only an idle spectator, and have nothing to do but observe the movements of others).

Mary Parsons was there with her train of admirers, for she has many, though she is twenty-seven and has begun to fade. The girls read to me, sang, play'd and tried all they could to amuse me, and I tried as hard to be amused; and as we may do any-thing we try, I thought I should succeed; but this was not the case. For I soon became indolent and ceased to persevere. 'Twas flat, stale, and unprofitable. The books they read (chiefly novels) were uninteresting to me, I was tired of music, and glad to make my escape.

I went from there to your uncle's. This did not mend the matter. They have a great deal of company, Sally [Way] is fond of society, and they live in such a sociable neighborhood that, what with calls, visits and visiting, there is no peace to the wicked.

Colonel Walbank and family from Boston have lately come to reside here. He is appointed Commander-and-Chief of the garrison–a man of large property, of course, of course a popular carracter. They have taken the N[athaniel] Richard's house, keep thier carriage, and live in great stile, give dinner and tea parties &c&c. He and Ebb were old aquaintance in the army[20] and his wife is a particular friend of Sally's. I was quite pleased with her. She appears to have an equal share of dignity and affability. They have heard much of Mrs. Champlain and wish to be introduced here, but she has declined the honour, at least for the present–I conclude, till she has compleated her assortment of musical instruments. She has now only five to flourish upon; but John Raymond is hard at work making another dulcimer. She has one already, and it is a pretty piece of music; but that, he is about to manufacture is of a superior kind and will no doubt do credit to his genius. 'All on Hobbies:' she has discarded the Muse and mounts another–music is all the rage, and she enjoys it so much and plays so well, 'tis a pity she should not be gratified. I hope the new instrument will fully answer her high-raised expectations, for I like to see every one happy in thier own way. I may prepare for a drubbing when she sees the above stroke at her hobby, as she will call it; though I declare before evidence that it was only a love pat, so gentle that the most skittish animal of the kind might recieve twenty times as much without flinching. And write it she must, or I will never play for her again or accompany her again on any instrument in future. And I know she will do it rather than dispense with my services and assistance on these occasions.

Your mother has improved surprizingly on the flute since her first aquaintance with John Raymond (I like to give the whole name). She has caught something of his stile and manner, but can never hope to play as well, for he is unequall'd. We laugh'd very heartily at the description you gave of his appearance when he call'd to see you. You have compleatly drawn his likeness with one stroke of the pen. You say, 'He looks as if he had lost every friend he had on earth.' We conclude he has been (most woefully) cross'd in love–I think his awkward diffidence and the plaintive tone of his voice is interesting. I am a great admirer of oddities (when they are really so), but affected singularity is disgusting.

Sam'l says Cornelia [Fitch] had him tell your mother 'you was a queer girl, and laugh'd half your time.' We are glad you are in such good spirits, and very much obliged to her for the intelligence, as you don't seem inclined to say any-thing of your own affairs. As to Master Sam, we have not had a line from him since he changed his quarters. I expect he is now too topping to write to his poor relations. No matter–I am glad his situation is improved and hope he will not forget the early impressions and precepts he recieved in the Land of Steady Habits. We have heard from George since I wrote last. He makes many enquiries about you and complains that you don't answer his letters. He enjoys good health and is doing very well. He has promised to visit us in 18025, unforeseen contingencies excepted.

I have been home but a few days. It is now the third of September, and about a month since I rec'd your last letter–which gave me unusual pleasure (I was then at your uncle's, or I should have answered it immediately). It has raised you in my estimation. I approve your candour and am happy to find you have obtained a victory over yourself. Prejudice, tho' strong, is not unconquerable. We are all subjects to like passions. Leave this to little minds. We should never harbour it for a moment, did we reflect that it is but a compound of the baser sort such as 'pride, envy, hatred, malice, and all uncharitableness.' It is founded on ignorance, and when that is removed, it falls to the ground. Point out to me, among the miserable race of man, the object of envy, and I will show you an object of pity and heartfelt commiseration. What is the riches and honours of the world? Can they shield the posessor from pain, disease, and death? How contemptable is human pride! What tho', like the butterfly, it may bask and flutter for an hour in the sunshine of prosperity, and perhaps look down on others. We are all at last but partners in affliction. We may pity but cannot hate even our enemies when we consider 'they are but dust–the worm shall eat them'!

I believe with you that Mrs. Tooker has many good qualities. I am sorry for the loss she has sustained, but I rejoice for her husband. He has made a happy exchange, and she has every consolation a Christian can desire.

Remember me to the household of faith, where you reside, one and all.

Adieu!

Mary's closing comment on Mrs. Tooker answers Eliza's account (**no. 145** of August 4) of the death of Mrs. Tooker's husband, in whom "our church has lost her foremost pillar and Mr. Mitchell, one of his best friends." He died just at the start of a family expedition for Niagara and other points of tourist pleasure. His wife had followed through on the undertaking to get Eliza a few more pupils as company to her daughter Ellen, at ten dollars each, and had proved in other ways obliging; so she earns Eliza's warmer estimate and warm sympathy. Sam, too, is mentioned on account of his new employment with Denis Doyle, "a man of some consequence in the city, has his country seat, his town house, and a number of high-sounding conveniences beside, and is, I should suppose from what I have heard of his character, the very person of all others whom Sam'l would fancy."

Sam was awarded at this time, by the volunteer firemen's Company No. 13, a most handsome engraved and painted certificate crowned with several classical figures at the top, a cityscape below displaying the terrors of conflagration confronted by gallant figures in helmets, and in between, the text, "These are to certify that Samuel Champlin is pursuant to law nominated and appointed one of the Firemen of the City of New York by the Common Council, J . Morton, Clerk."[21] He thus joined a force of some two thousand divided into a couple of dozen companies, quite inadequate to protect the city from almost daily, at least weekly, fires which were sometimes of wide extent; but the volunteers were one of the most approved spectacles in the city of this time, and wonderfully energetic and spirited. A description of Sam in action appears later with a part of the certificate (Fig. 7).

Eliza continues the correspondence (**no. 147**) with responsive comments on the *Gospel Herald* and other items from New London, offering in return some New York scenes of September. They include a reference to the New Church that followed the teachings of Swedenborg–on which Eliza, had she known her future, would have commented less caustically:

> . . . I read as much aloud to Mrs. Fitch in the evening as time, inclination and eyesight will permit; but that is not much, as I have generally something else to attend to. I have not heard from the Haydens since their departure for Washington, but about three weeks ago Johnstone and Eliza Sandford call'd here with Jane [Johnston]'s picture, for me to repair a slight injury which it has lately sustain'd. Our afternoon service is discontinued untill the return of cool weather, but all the female part of our family are so devout that we never fail to improve Sunday afternoon (as we are dress'd in our best bib and tucker) by going to some other church; but Mr. Fitch (who by the by I think is the wisest of us in this respect) prefers surrendering himself to the arms of Morpheus, in his office, to doing the deed within the pale of any church. So as we had all gone, except Mr. Fitch, to hear the New Jerusalemites preach a doctrine that I am sure they cannot understand themselves, I miss'd seeing Johnstone and Eliza. As you know, Sunday is the day to make calls. Mr. Fitch entertain'd them as well as he could while they staid, and Eliza had the politeness to fly to my paint desk and ransack every hole and corner before she left it, without even asking leave. As it happen'd, it contain'd no secrets, but if it had, it would have been all the same. Her female curiosity would have been satisfied. Johnstone left an unseal'd note with Mr. Fitch for me (you know how fond he is of showing his parts in this way) stating that Mrs. J–'s miniature had a fall from the mantle piece which broke the convex glass to pieces and defaced the painting, and requesting me to repair it. I examined the painting very criticaly and find that the glass in breaking has cut an atom of the shade that throws out the point of the nose. The underlip is also slightly grazed, and she had one bead less to tell. This I find is all the injury she has sustain'd and which I find I can repair in five minutes. I write thus particular least you should have a fit on learning that my brush was going to contaminate the best effusion of yours, particularly when the child is of royal descent. But fear not, you know she is only an imitation shawl; but were she the queen herself, I have the family vanity to think I should not disgrace her by the touch of my pencil, as I have improved without any of Neutral-Tint's assistance[22] sufficient to feel confident I could take an exact likeness of the queen if I could once more get her in my possession. But alas! she is beyond my reach. My eyes have looked there last on her, and I must be content.
>
> September 24th . . . For my soul, I could not help smiling at the artful manner in which you have attempted to pump out of me my 'love secrets,' as you call them. And did you realy suppose me fool enough to divulge them by letter? Be assured,

you don't exactly know your man, if you suppose me capable of committing this piece of folly. I respect not only myself but those who are concerned with me, too much, to comply with your pumping request. I must entreat you therefore to bear with more patience the 'starch of Queen Elizabeth' (as you are pleased to term it) on this, as well as one or two other subjects, untill we meet–and perhaps *then*.

I am sorry to say this letter will in all probability depart unattended by the second volume of the *Gospel Herald*, not from Mrs. Fitches unwillingness to send it (as she says it would give her much pleasure to do so) but from her utter ignorance respecting its fate. It is not to be found in the house, and she is positive she has not lent it to any member of the church, as they are of course all in possession of one. She, however, is not so sure that she has not sent it to Newport for Mrs. Shearman's perusal, tho' she has no reccollection of doing so. As the thing is possible, she has written to Mrs. Shearman to know, and if she has it, Mrs. Northam will bring it home with her. If she has not, why, you must wait with patience till it comes to light, and then I promise you it shall be sent. Mrs. Fitch has sent you in place of the *Herald* three newspapers. I have not had time to look over their contents but suppose they contain something worth reading or she would not send them. I suppose they are to be returned, as she did not say they were not to be. I shall therefore tack them together, that they may not be lost. They will be very useful to protect the ivory and tooth-brush from the rough hands of whatever jolly son of Neptune they might chance to be entrusted too. You know I have not too much faith in their carefulness, and consequently like to have whatever is entrusted to their paws well secured. . . . I looked as desired for a soft brush and could not find one except this that would not tear your 'jaws off,' as you express it, and this you will observe has lost one tuft of its bristles; but still I thought you would prefer it to a perfect one that was hard. I think it is pretty soft and hope it will answer the purpose.[23] . . .

Mrs. Fitch has commenced a letter to you that I suppose will accompany this. At all events it will not stay long after it. I have received your instructions for varnishing, for which I am very much obliged to you. I should have ruined the pieces I intended to varnish had I not got them just as did. I have been painting a couple of pieces for patterns for the scholars to copy and, without varnish, I knew I might as well throw them in the fire at once. Mrs. Fitch also has been painting a box for varnishing and is now painting another, which will keep the varnish brush going some time. . . .

Still in September Eliza then started another letter home (**no. 148**), put it aside till October, repeats what she had said before about Sam and his good job at Doyle's, and then moves to the Cherry Street scene:

. . . Mrs. F[itch] and Eliza Mitchell commenced going to school to a lady last week who teaches the much admired art of lace-work. It is now all the rage for married and single ladies to learn of her. She gives ten lessons for five dollars, and has as many scholars as she can attend to. Mrs. Fowler has sent a niece of hers to learn it and now has it taught in her drawing academy with music and, I believe, dancing. Mrs. Fitch and Eliza are each working a superb veil with which they intend to decorate their

> noddles at the time appointed, which will be, I suppose, about Christmas. I have a great desire to learn but have neither time nor materials, so must give up the idea. Catherine is working just such a veil as Mrs. F.'s from her teaching, and I could do the same without paying for learning; but, as I said before, I have too little time and it is too expensive. The lace alone costs four dollars. . . .
>
> I suppose you recollect I had another of the Reeds to take [a portrait of] for the 'wrent'. Mrs. Reed called on me yesterday to see about it, and after the business was settled and she had concluded to send [her boy] Addington for me to opperate upon, she very mournfully enquired how long you had been dead. I felt somewhat disposed to box her ears for being such a nincome, but, suppressing the inclination I felt to laugh in her face, I answer'd with a phiz as long as her own, that you had not been dead a great while. She said she understood it was about two years. I hesitated an instant whether to undecieve her or not, but on the whole I thought if I did not she might report me as a liar; so I took the trouble to bring you to life–at which she was much astonished, and said that it was currently reported that you had closed your eyes on all sublunary things. So now I expect soon to see some posthumous publications, and you will have the advantage of evry other writer of this description that has ever come out, as you can hear thier criticisms incog.–a thing I should admire of all others. Come, pray begin as soon as possible. I have no doubt they will go hand in hand with the *Waverly Novels*, and if I could say more to induce you, I certainly would; but I have no more room to talk nor no greater inducement to urge; so on the strength of this I will bid you *adieu*.

With its lace-schools and house-guests, with ivory and *Heralds* in ready supply, the New York scene contrasts brightly with the shadows of New London, from which Mary writes one Sunday in the latter half of November (**no. 149**):

> I am thinking how happy you are, or ought to be, on this day and this hour, in church with Mrs. Northam, Mr. and Mrs. Fitch, and at this very moment enjoying the highest pleasure New York affords. 'O! that I had wings like a dove'–then I would be there and take my old seat between Mrs. Northam and you, where I have so often listened with delight to the 'music of truth' in the glowing, animated, energetic language of your Speaker, whose impassion'd eloquence commands attention while his subject interests every heart and rivets every eye on his expressive countenance. What a preveledge is yours. Consider this and be thankful, while I sit mopeing here alone, and, to beguile the tedious hours, I conjure up the ghosts of my departed joys and try to wait with patience for those that are to come. The present scene is a mere blank; but smiling Hope has placed a rainbow here, and though the tints may fade, the promise cannot fail.
>
> I have lately met with a poem intitled 'A Russian Poet's Anthology.' I think it very fine, and inclose it because I don't remember ever to have seen its equal. If you or Mrs. Fitch has, please to tell me when and where, and send it to me if you can. This exceeds even the most admired passages of Milton for sublimity of thought. I have heard it read several times, and so strong is the impression it made that,

notwithstanding the worst of all bad memorys, I can repeat every line, and never shall forget it while I live.

The *Gospel Herald* is recieved with its accompaniments, letters, ivory, &c. We are very much obliged to you for them all, and also to Mrs. Fitch for the main article. Since its arrival, Aunt Hannah seems to have renew'd her age and strength. She is here almost every pleasant day. The good old saint stands to her text: she loves to read as well as I do to hear, and proves it by her works. If she goes on all winter as she's begun, we shall take clear comfort. You may laugh at this word as much as you please, but I like it. It conveys an idea I can find in no other, and sounds so comfortable, especially when applied to the enjoyment of books by a winter's fire-side. Pleasure is so transient, and happiness, a name; but comfort, valid comfort, is a reality which we may all enjoy more or less, even under the most unfavorable circumstances. For my part I take as much as I can in one way or another. I am partial to the word and will defend it against all opposition.

So then, my modest enquires respecting beaus and business are completely thrown away, and poor Aunt Charity may die of a Frenchman before you will lift a finger to gratify her curiosity. Very well, keep your choice secrets and I will keep mine. I have my secrets too, and some that you would give the world to know. But 'silent eloquence is the order of the day.' I conclude you mean to take us by surprize, and when you have made your fortune or married Halsey,[24] which is the same thing, let the mighty secret burst out at once and astonish the natives. But as there is some danger his amiable candour will induce him to publish it too soon, and thereby prevent a sudden explosion and spoil the effect, perhaps it would not be amiss to give him a friendly caution on this head. You know, a word to the wise is enough, and therefore any further explanation is unnecessary.

I am happy to hear Mrs. Fitch has begun a letter to me. I hope she will go on and write if it is only but half a dozen lines now and then, whenever she has time to spare and inclination to bestow it on the charitable work. I will wait her leisure, fully assured I shall be amply rewarded for my patience. The longer it is in hand, the more it will contain, and the more it contains the greater will be the pleasure it affords. 'Go thou and do likewise.' But though I am willing to execise patience to the bat's end for the sake of a good long letter, still you are to understand that the sooner it comes the better. Remember this and make all possible dispatch.

Adieu!

And with this effort of Mary's, her cheer lapsing into sadness and reminiscence, the year 1823 closes on the correspondence.

12

Good Old New London

Contrast with the delights of New York needs to be drawn a little more carefully at this point, as New London becomes increasingly the scene of reference. For, of the three sisters of the brush, one has now returned to join a second that never left, while the third, Eliza, will spend a year at home helping out in 1825–1826, much against her will. Brother William enters the correspondence more frequently, too—he who never left home, just like his mother. The reader of their letters from the twenties thus needs some context in which to understand their gossip and, in later chapters, jobs and politics.

So far as concerns politics, the town looked simple, little changed from the 1790s (above, chapter 1). Obvious as the chief reason for its being was still its great harbor flanked by a great broad street with warehouses and shipyards on the sea-side and a few big houses like the Shaw Mansion (nowadays a museum) on the land side, along with two or three banks, and, up the hill behind, residential housing, churches, and shops. Obvious, too, were all local events of interest: explained by local newspapers, *The Bee* until it moved to New York in 1802, occasional news-sheets, and the *New London Gazette* with its weekly register of what was clearing through the harbor, ads for businesses in these media, and marriages and deaths.[1]

The town had a population of just over three thousand, quite stable not to say stagnant for a quarter-century beginning in the late eighteenth century; there were periodic town meetings for election of town officers; a mayor, recorder, treasurer, clerk, council, four aldermen, sheriff, constable, court system with ad hoc bankruptcy commissioners; assessors and town agent; a U.S. Customs office with its collector; a postmaster with the help of a second postmaster; a three-man health board; two surveyors; and a public grammar school with a supervisory committee. In time, private academies with proprietors or directors were established for both boys and girls, some of whose graduates went on to Yale and Harvard. And of course the banks had their directors.[2]

Let us say, a total town directorate of seventy-five positions? Everything open and above-board, through elections and publications. But at this point in the description what might seem simple becomes in fact knotty. At any given moment in Mary's and Betsey's lifetime a majority of these positions were held by representatives from a dozen families, no more; or three quarters of these positions, by representatives from no more than two dozen. As the three Kin-charts make clear, all of these families naturally intermarried, thus giving to power the shape of the proverbial rat's nest, or Turk's head (knot-metaphors being very suitable to a maritime city). Just as naturally, power came from and gave access to money, so that the political and economic realities were one, and embraced education and religion as well.

In this structure, direct participation by any of the Ways and Champlains was limited to Uncle Ebb. Because of the great antiquity of his line, reaching back to lands held by gift from the Mohican chief Uncas, with himself at the present juncture New London's postmaster (1816–38) while simultaneously town clerk (1817–27), he *belonged*.[3] That his ancestry should count was not unreasonable: for, as in stable societies generally, a strong sense of obligation to the family's good repute was passed along from generation to generation and touched each bearer of a given name. Mary, George, and Sam all speak to that effect expressly; but there was really no need.[4] Everyone understood. In particular, moreover, Ebb was an intelligent, articulate person, his war record as a young man had been quite distinguished; in his middle years he enjoyed enough wealth to entertain in style; owned considerable property; and, once in the post-office, he had his finger on the pulse of the town to a degree enjoyed by no other elected official. That went with the position and the perception of it, witness the various mentions by Eliza of her fear that her mail would be opened; and witness also the less questionable routines of the mail service. How they gave postmasters a hold on the town will be explained later in more detail.[5]

The antiquity of one's line also implied (and didn't count for much unless it included) ties into a wide net of kinship. That might be expected. Take for illustration Jonathan Starr (1742–1838), third of that name (in the fifth generation down from Elder William Brewster of the Mayflower).[6] There is so much evidence of his ubiquity in the various levels and positions of influence in New London, it need only be sampled to give the picture. He had a business selling lumber and many other articles in a store on the harbor-side, Bank Street. His ads appeared regularly in the local paper. He served on the health board, the board of selectmen, the turnpike-company board, the bank board as director and eventually president, and the Episcopalian church board (as warden) from 1783 through its dedication as a newly risen building after Arnold's burning of the town. He was connected with just about everybody: Coits, Deshons, Hempsteads, Tilleys. Like a young Allen and a Seabury, he married a daughter of Pardon Taber, Betsey's grandfather; and there were other Way connections more remote. His own daughter, however, was given more suitably to the mayor, Jirah Isham, while his son Jonathan (1781–1852, Fig. 6) aspired to a great marriage described later on.

Figure 6. Jonathan Starr

Or take the Honorable Elias Perkins (1767–1845), tall and commanding in his portrait by Ralph Earl.[7] The quality of the artist matches that of Perkins' clothes, and the frame, and the grand house in which the painting has hung for a century and a half. It is the Shaw Mansion, already mentioned, home of Nathaniel of that ilk, partner with Perkins in their whaling company and uncle of Perkins' very rich wife. Perkins served as director of the City National Bank, New London's second; but from the start, also as its president. He served in the Connecticut General Assembly and Upper House, the U. S. Congress, and the courts for decades as a judge of increasing eminence; in his home town, as mayor. He had attended Yale, where his son Nathaniel Shaw Perkins studied too before enrolling himself first under New London's eminent doctor North and later under other doctors in Philadelphia, for a medical degree, and, thereafter, himself, going on to join the corporation of New London's third bank (along with Jirah Isham).[8]

When in the summer of 1824 Lafayette revisited America, first to be received ecstatically in New York (**nos. 162** and **164**, below), next brought to New Haven and then to New London, attended at every step by honorific ceremonies, gratulatory speeches, and harried notes behind his back to inform Ebenezer Way, up the line, about the General's progress, New London had ready a committee of welcome chaired by Judge Perkins. Thus the city made clear at that glorious moment which of its citizens it most gloried in. Assisting him were Oliver Champlain besides a half-dozen other worthies, in turn dignified by a company of soldiers and a military band. They conducted the city's great guest to worship in the Perkins pew at the Congregational church (but then of necessity at the Episcopalian as well), before taking him next to a reception at the Judge's house, "famed for hospitality."[9]

At that Episcopalian church, a third illustrative figure in times past: the mighty bishop, Dr. Samuel Seabury (Yale 1748). After fleeing his pulpit in the Revolution to preside as chaplain over prayers for the King in the royal navy and royal regiments, he sought in England the headship of his church in the New World; with difficulty got the needed appointment out of the bishops of Scotland; and, once returned to the land of his birth, was invited to preach to the united Masons of New York in 1782, and in 1787 to receive the new-built Episcopal church of New London from the hands of its senior wardens Jonathan Starr (his brother-in-law) and Roswell Saltonstall (father of his son's wife).[10] No Revolution had disturbed his wealth; no property-owner had more slaves than he in the town of his choice; and there he lived on into his late sixties, long enough to preach a funeral sermon over Jonathan Starr in 1795. The next year his son Charles succeeded him in the pulpit, to 1814. Charles' son in turn, another Reverend Samuel Seabury, continued the family's traditions into the third generation through both his name and his calling. He was a man of books who delighted in showing the contribution made by the classics to Christian right-thinking. In due course he was to apply the Greek and Latin of Homer and Sophocles, Cicero and Augustine, over some hundreds of pages, to the defense of slavery.

Way-Champlain kin-ties included the Starrs, as was just said; included, too, the Seabury family; and touched the edges of the Judge's family.[11] They had long been close with the prominent Dr. Lee: his name, with the names of his wife Eliza and children, recurs often in the letters.[12] A considerable gap can be felt, however, between the uppermost range of New London society and the correspondents in their mentions of it. They indicate a certain ambivalence about the heights of education, perhaps because they were uncertain of their own:[13] Latin they saluted not as a great treasure, bestowed by Yale or Harvard, but with mockery, at one point Betsey's; at another, William's. The Congregational pastor, William writes, "Mr. McEwen, by repeating over certain magical words last night," married a New London couple–"the words I suppose to be *presto sobeeto aquimentum*."[14]

And William goes on to add in a postscript, "Oh Sam, by the way, did I tell you that Joshua Hamilton had been regularly initiated in the Club of Odd Fellows?–because if I did, I told you a damned lie. At any rate he has joined the Lodge of Free-Masonry & is all the time squeezing the fore-finger joint & screwing up his face to make Masonic signs: 'Good morning, Judge Perkins, friend of our trusty & well-beloved brother Rich'd D. Starr.' " The reference to Judge Perkins is explained by his being one of the trustees of New London's Masonic Hall. The Rev. Samuel Seabury's father the bishop, as was mentioned above, greatly favored the Masons; no doubt his son did, too.[15] Masons as such were not much liked.

A sour irreverence toward the Rev. Charles Seabury appears in certain asides from George. Sam's tone is a match: "I met old Parson Seabury," he writes from

New York, "the other day in South Street. I knew him the instant I saw him by that wart on his nose, and introduced myself. He enquired about the family, not forgetting Aunt Hannah, 'I promise ye.' He looks as if he had seen hard times in the face. He was accompanied by one of his sons."[16]

Why this unpleasant characterization? Consider the words of one of those sons, recalling his teenage experience as an apprentice in New York around 1816:[17]

> In the mere matter of being a mechanic there is nothing degrading. They are one of the most useful branches of society . . . [but it was] a most cruel thing to take a boy who has been brought up with some degree of moral delicacy and place him among a set of semi-savages who are utter strangers to the refinemements of social life . . . where, to say nothing of piety or moral deportment, everything bordering on decorum or ordinary good breeding is coarsely ridiculed; where you must be *vulgar* in the lowest degree to escape the imputation of affecting to be *genteel*; obscene and profane, to escape being laughed at as a Quaker or a Methodist; filthy and hoggish in the extreme to avoid being twitted of vainness or pride. A man that looks only at the the manner in which society ought to be framed may advocate his sons going to a trade; but he that sees a society as it actually is may be allowed to shrink from exposing his children to the pollution of vulgarity in its most disgusting forms.

The Champlain brothers, having all three served their own apprenticeships, could not take kindly to such intolerance toward plainer people.

It had for a time been difficult to forget the split down the middle of New London's Episcopalian church, St. James as it was called, between those who supported the Revolution and those others, like the first of the Seabury line just described, who supported the cause of the King. In those days, for their Toryism, Pardon Taber, too, and his son of the same name had been fined in court and the son rejected as a justice of the peace. Their politics were maybe in the blood: they were kin of some sort to Benedict Arnold. But in no long time they changed politics and faith. From Baptists they became Episcopalians, they were very rich, they were forgiven.[18] St. James seemed naturally to draw their sort. It was distinctly upper-class: three out of four of any list of town notables in the period of the correspondence will have worshipped there. On the other hand, there were some Congregationalists of eminence, by name Perkins or Shaw, respectable Baptists like the Tabers (all but Pardon and his like-named son), and certainly respectable Universalists that swung over to their faith in the later eighteenth century: the Ways and Champlains, to name those that are of most interest.

Religion in the letters does not appear as a divisive consideration. Within the Way-Champlain family, the staunchest defender of any sect (his own invention), had been Samuel Taber: ex-Baptist, converted Murray-style Universalist. He published his credo to the world at large in a four-page pamphlet; yet he was in business with a Baptist sprung from a Congregationalist family.[19] That less cantankerous Universalist, Aunt Hannah, enjoyed some intimacy with a certain rector of St. James, while his successor became a dear friend of all the Ways and Champlains and in due course officiated at Eliza's wedding. As there was no Universalist church in town for many years, the Ways and Champlains seem to have attended wherever they felt inclined, generally among the Episcopalians.[20]

A sense of class, however, certainly pervaded Eliza's world. That was indeed divisive. It began in school in children's very textbooks, was reinforced at home, affected church loyalties, marked off certain parts of town, and turns up in all sorts of casual comments in the correspondence.[21] They are especially common in Eliza's letters from New York, drawing attention to the impudence of persons lower than herself on the social scale, pigeon-holing this or that person or occupation, or asserting her own position against encroachment or disregard. The thought of a brother in a low trade is shocking (**no. 237**); Negroes are at the bottom.[22] Her mother, brothers, and circle in general express the same ideas about high and low, though with some difference according to their sex–men establishing their rank more by the work they did and worldly success; women, more by their social accomplishments and decorative talents.

The latter, as was said just above, must include some certain skill in letter-writing. Deficiencies there made one ashamed, even the venerable Aunt Hannah when she writes to young Sam at the start of the new year 1824 (**no. 151**). William who transmits the note adds an amused postscript:

> I received your letter with a great deal of pleasure & was very glad to hear you had so much business. But you don't say what your business is or where. I wish you would, & tell us all about it, & what your prospects are. I am ecceeding glad you go to Mrs. Fitch's–hope you will take their advice in whatever you go about. Give my best love to everyone of Mr. F.'s family. All our family & all your mother's family joins me in love to them.
>
> We are very well at present. Don't let any one see this letter. I grow old & am very feeble & my hand shakes so, I can't write intiegable [=intelligibly]; so you mush write to me as often as you can.
>
> Your afectionate, Aunt H. Way
>
> New London January 1st
> I wish you a happy New Year
> [William's hand:] She has had more fuss about this letter than a little.

Eliza (**no. 152**) on the 11th replies to Mary Way with a report revealing some disenchantment with New York's posturing, amused at those above her but nicely condescending to a mere barber who would challenge them. The moment she describes had involved the sympathies of the city in the Greek revolution, as she explains:[23]

> Well, 'the long, long agony is over–the Bourbons are restored.' I conclude it is impossible that you can any of you be ignorant of the deplorable situation of the 'suffering Greeks'–that in their struggle for freedom from their Turkish opressors they have applied to the United States for assistance, and have not applied in vain.

The Americans, one and all, from having suffer'd in the same cause do sympathize most warmly in their affliction. They have completely enter'd into the spirit of raising supplies for their brethren in affliction, and now no expense is spared to enable them to effect their purpose. You can have no idea of the topsy-turvy state of this renown'd city of Gotham. Everything and everybody is in agitation on their account. Sermons have been preached, theatres and forums opened, balls have been given, and every possible means used to procure them money. But the greatest agony that the inhabitants have yet undergone is in getting dresses splendid enough for the Millitary Ball that has been given in the theatre, as no one was alowed to put their heads inside the house unless in full ball dress. Some of the ladies' dresses I hear cost a thousand dollars and some seven hundred. How true it is, I don't know. A temporary floor was made over the pit, and the first tier of boxes thrown open for the reception of the dancers. Twenty-eight cotillions was chalked on the floor. Nothing could surpass the elegance of the scene, I am told by those who witnessed it–which by the bye was none of us, as Mrs. Fitch did not think it worth-while to attend in full ball dress as a spectator.

But the greatest fun of all was this: one of the most stylish barbers in the city bought a ticket and, shortly after it had been sold to him, the committee of arrangements repented them of the thing that had been done and offer'd him four hundred dollars if he would give them up the ticket. But not so. My gentleman of the strop did not choose to be kicked out of the company quite so easily and, like a good fellow, told them with becoming spirit that he would not take a thousand for it, as he was resolved to go, and swore that if there was the least attempt made to keep him out, as was threaten'd, he would raise a mob that should pull down the theatre. This threat so alarmed the mean-spirited rascals who were concerned in the scrape that they order'd him to be peacably admitted. General Mapes the tailor was at the head of the scrape and took the most active part in keeping out the barber. Even those who felt themselves infinitely above the barber applauded him for his spirit and despised the other for his littleness.

The theatre was splendidly decorated for the Grecian Ball and, as the decorations were to be kept up during the remainder of the week, we all went last evening to see them. The Millitary attended in full uniform, and the ladies of course in full dress. The house was draped with much taste; but as we were obliged to put up with a side box we lost the most beautiful part of the whole, which was a Grecian Cross formed of lamps at the back part of the stage. A full-length portrait of Washington framed with laurel was placed exactly opposite the cross, and the middle shandalier was suspended from a most brilliant star. As I could not see the whole on account of the situation in which we were placed, I shall not give a description of half.

Last week the Batchelors gave a ball at Washington Hall to assist the 'suffering Greeks.' The hall was dressed the day previous to the occasion, and we went to our weekly public on the evening of the same, where we saw the whole without paying for it–which you know was much better. The flags were very tastefully arranged and an iluminated Grecian cross, of course. You know what a set of epicures old batchelors

> are. They thought they would indulge themselves with a pretty stylish supper, with the money that ought to have gone to the suffering Greeks; and, not calculating the cost beforehand, they found when too late the folly in indulging themselves at the rate they did, as it reduced their money to the triffling sum of two hundred and odd dollars. How much this is like the charity of the world, don't you think so? . . .

Replying to this and still others from Eliza (notice the "letters," plural, that are referred to), Mary sends back one of her longest efforts, added to page by page as she waited for an amanuensis (**no. 155** of February, 1824). The Grecian fete receives her comments but also other subjects that have dropped out of the record probably because Eliza later did not like their tone. She was suffering from bouts of depression which she later preferred to hide; but Mary knows of them and attributes them to "love" and its uncertainties; and she takes pains to offer a good deal of fun and diversion, for instance, regarding Jonathan Starr. Reference to his newborn and due payment for that blessed event is explained by, and amplifies, what she has to say about his marriage another day (**no. 166**):

> Your tremendously hum-drum letter, as you modestly call it, was, I assure you, quite a treat to us. We found it very amusing, and would like to receive such a one every day in the week. 'Tis true, I could wish you were in better spirits, but we all have our ups and downs in this world. While we are tossed about upon the ocean of life, we must expect rough weather, and that we should feel a little sea-sick now and then is not a matter of suprize. It is a wholesome disease, and you will be none the worse for it by and by. Therefore, bear it with Christian patience. You will find smooth water yet, I trust, before the voyage is over. However, be that as it may, one thing is sure: we shall arrive at last. Secure in this, well may we brave the furious elements, defy the threatening storm and smile at all its rage. Thus are we armed against a 'sea of troubles,' no matter what they are. This doctrine is the medicine of life, a cure for every ill. For myself, I have neither fears nor cares, for time nor eternity, and I wish I could preach away yours. But you are used to better things and will no doubt set me down and my poor sermon among the trash (you say). . . .
>
> You have done well to take advice and engage to teach in Mr. Glover's school. We must not dispise the day of small things. His school will probably increase, and in that case it will be much better than for you to hire a room to teach in. There is no necessity of your going out in storms when you can make up the time in fair weather. True, it is a long walk, but pleasant and healthy, and habit will render it less fatiguing. It is your duty to make every possible exertion, and if you persevere in well doing, I trust by the goodness and blessing of Providence you will at length be successful.
>
> I am pleased to hear of your improvement in the art, you say, without the help of Neutral-Tint.[24] Better still, I know much may be learnt by study, observation and practice, without the aid of a teacher. Still, however, instruction is important and desirable, and when it can possibly be obtained, ought to be considered indispensible. But, so you improve, I care not by what means.

Mr. R[iley] is very obliging, and you will doubtless profit by the painting he has had the goodness to lend you. As it was done by a pupil Jarvis is proud of, I hope you will make the most of it, and study it night and day. If by this or any other means you could exchange that chaste, labour'd, mincing style of yours for one more easy, bold, and free, it would be the making of you. To copy it would look like a compliment. I suppose you would not for the world, lest Caesar's wife should be suspected; but I should not scruple to do it (were it even the likeness of Halsey, or the black gentleman himself, provided his hoofs and horns were well painted), tho' by doing so I were sure to share the fate of Apelles, and fall in love with the original. Sage advice, truely. I have said it, no matter how it reads. The painting is approved by Jarvis, and we repeat it. This is the least we would do to obtain his masterly style. Now, if you are charitably disposed, in order to save my credit, the following inference may be drawn: first, that I consider excellence in an artist of incalculable importance; secondly, I regard love as a temporary evil, something like the tooth-ach–troublesome enough while it lasts but by no means an incurable malady; thirdly, I think you have not such a gun-powder constitution as to be in danger of taking fire from every spark that flys or falls too near. I trust these considerations are amply sufficient to clear me from the imputation of rashness and extravagance.

Speaking of love, the Devil, and Halsey reminds me of a modest hint I chanced to drop in one of my letters, and your laconic answer: 'I like not mystery'–a mystery which, by the by, you could not fail to understand. But as you require an explanation, here it it. Sally [Way] was in a large circle one evening where this strange animal [John Raymond] appeared with all his originallity about him, holding forth in his usual queer, outlandish way. Eliza was his theme. He related his wonderfull achievements in New York, the dangers and difficulties he overcame visiting and attending you to the theatre, and what he suffered in this terrible encounter, 'with all the pomp and circumstance of war,' till at last he led you off in triumph, in spite of your refusal and obstinate resistance; that to Mrs. Fitch his everlasting gratitude was due for assisting him in the perilous adventure. This is the sum total of the story, and we should have thought no more about it but for your profound silence upon the subject. You see no good comes of keeping secrets (as Aunt Hannah, who wants to hear and tell everything, often says). When people do business with closed doors, suspicion, surmise and conjecture peep into the windows to see what is going forward, which proves fair open dealing is allways best, especially in matters of such vast importance.

Love laughs at human distinctions, and like death brings us all upon a level–this is a self-evident fact. Your story of the miliner is funny enough. Another instance of his arbitary power I will relate. We are inform'd Paulinia is in the broad road to matrimony. John Mason, a grocer, son and hier to a shoe-maker in this city, is the distinguish'd being she has 'stooped to conquer'–a handsome youth on whom she is said for many months to have exercised with full effect the powerfull influence of her attractions. As it is the fashion for lovers to suffer much persecution from the barbarous tyranny of ambitious parents and the cruel freaks and frowns of capricious fortune, that plays malicious tricks and sports with thier distress, poor Paulinia has had her share of tribulation, being obliged to carry on the business by the help of Methodist meetings and moon-light walks, without the knowledge of her father. But (mark this truth) imaginary evils constitute the greatest part of human misery. The fears and sad forebodings of this fond pair prove altogether groundless. By what means he assumed courage to visit her as a suitor does not appear, but we are told he did so, and found plain sailing, a gracious reception, and her father 'willing as the flowers in May.'

Our city you know is famous for the longevity and celibacy of its inhabitants. Nothing here is more infrequent than deaths and mariages. The first is probably the effect of sound constitutions and a healthy climate, but whether the last is owing to our being more wise than our neighbours, or only more difficult to please, is a question the learned must decide. Be the cause what it will, certain it is, old maids and batchelors abound. Jonathan Starr (one of your acquaintance who has entered the blissful state since you was here) has now an hier. The little April fool made its appearance last spring, and soon after thirty thousand dollars arrived from England to crown his felicity. The cash is paid, the price of liberty, the full sum for which he sold himself a willing slave. Alas! for poor Benedeck, she rules him with a rod of iron, plays off her John Bull airs, and treats him like a Jonathan. But there is none to pity. Except his own family, no one has she a single tear on the occasion.

Only two other marriages have taken place here of any note since you left us: General Isham to Eliza Trott, and John Trott to Susan Griffing. Mary Parsons will be married in the spring to Charles Rogers, a commission merchant of New York, where she expects to reside. Also, the two young doctors, H[enry] and S[amuel] Lee's, have taken up thier residence there, to the intent that they may exercise thier professional skill for the benefit of the inhabitants. They board in Chamber Street. I mention this circumstance that, in case you are sick, you may know where to send for a physician.

Mrs. [Samuel H. P.] Lee, who receives weekly intelligence from head-quarters, informs me Ellen [Tooker, now engaged] will remain with Mrs. Tooker. The house is about to undergo some stylish opperations and, when compleated, will be furnish'd by her father in the most superb manner. Of her husband I can hear nothing either good or bad except that he is rich, which is perhaps sufficient. We learn from the same authority that Amelia Laverty has obtained a splendid victory in Albany, but found it less difficult to gain than to secure her conquest. A gentleman (whose name I cannot recollect)[25] but a distinguish'd carracter in high office, a man of large property and great respectability, was so much pleased with her person, he came to New York to see her father and pay his addresses in form. Laverty recieved him with open arms–transported at the idea of becoming 'father-in-law to a three-tail'd bashaw,' is said to have out-done himself on the occasion. The overstrained hospitality, unreserv'd freedom, and social familiarity with which he treated his guest soon discovered the ostentatious and superficial carracter of the man he was about to honour with his alliance, which, togeather with the low breeding and vulgarity of his manners and conversation, compleated the suitor's disgust–who unhappily posess'd a larger share of delicacy and refinement than the case required, regarding riches and beauty (tho' very well in thier place) [as] by no means the only requisites in a matrimonial connexion; and, being heartily sick of the business he entered upon, had nothing to do but back out as well as he could–which was speedily done, and tho' with all possible decency, it is supposed could not fail to produce a feeling not unlike mortification and disappointment.

The brilliant decorations and splendor of the Grecian fete you have described brings to mind the blissfull days of chivalry and romance. Who can say but the spirit of knight-errantry may not again revive. The zeal and enthusiasm display'd on this occasion seems to look a little like it. America could furnish valiant knights, chiefs renown'd in arms allready cock'd and primed for a crusade, and ladies not a few who, like the Princess Matilda of England, would doubtless join the pious enterprise and volunteer thier services to aid the suffering Greeks, could they hope to conquer a graceful infidel like Mallack Adhib. Don't you think so?

Your letters of late (though as amusing and funny as ever) I am sorry to observe all end in a fit of the blues. Duce take this mental malady of yours. Come home and we will laugh you out of it. But you will say, 'The remedy is worse than the disease.' Ah, there's the rub. I wish you had never seen New York. But for that you might be happy here. We are so, business or no business, it is all the same, our spirits never fail. We take it as it comes, fair and easy. Your mother is over head and ears in business and would be glad of your assistance, as in all probability it will continue to increase through the spring and summer. But if you can do better, or be happier there, we are not so selfish as to wish [you] to return merely for our own pleasure and accommodation. To see you happy here would add to our felicity, but if this cannot be, we must do without it and be as happy as we can.

There is nothing I anticipate with more pleasure than the letter I am about to recieve from Mrs. Fitch. I think it will be one after my own heart, should she continue (as I hope and trust she will) to add a few lines to it occasionally when she is perfectly at leisure and feels disposed to write, till it has attain'd its full growth and patience had her perfect work. Far be it from me to hurry the business. You know I have a particular dislike to short letters written in haste; but, lest amidst numerous engagements and more important vocations it should be neglected or forgotten, I will thank you to remind her of it sometimes. Tell her I shall not give it up so easily. I calculate too much upon this letter to relish a disappointment.

Cupid and Hymen, who have been so long out of business here, I thought had took thier flight and left the place to set up thier trade in some happier clime where they may find better encouragement and more liberal patronage. But I understand there are now several matches brewing here. You had better return before the beaus are all married off, and try your luck among them. . . .

The hint at the end here, that Eliza is once more free and her suitor rejected or withdrawn, shows how New London explained her low spirits; and (**no. 157**, dated

March 21) she takes up this very point toward the end of her answer to the two last letters, or more specifically to her mother:

> . . . The evening before your letter arrived I had been to a large party, or rather ball, given by Mrs. Cowdrey and her daughters for a young cousen of thiers who has been lately married. The bride was formerly Eliza Anderson. She is now Mrs. Lord. I think you must have heard of her. She has always been celebrated for her fascinating manners, and for once I think report spoke truth. She is certainly a sweet creature. She and Ellen Tooker were formerly as intimate as Mrs. Fitch and Maria Clinch is, but a quarrel which the two bridegrooms have lately had (and which I am told and believe was entirely owing to Hudson's folly) has entirely destroy'd the intimacy of thier wives.
>
> The ball was open'd by Mrs. Lord and the handsomest man in the room. She danced as gracefully as she does everything else, and was admired by all. After the first cotillion she was call'd upon to play and and sing. She did so. I never heard so plaintive and yet so sweet a voice, and what bewitched me most was the total absence of affectation in whatever she said or did. I never witnessed so splendid a party before. They were all dress'd in such superb style–scarcely anything but silks and sattens with laces over and wreaths of flowers tastefully disposed round the hair or on the bottoms of thier frocks. Short sleeves and long white kid gloves was the order of the night, with jewels not a few. I was so charmed with the scene that I could not for that evening stick to my text, that 'beauty unadorned is adorned the most.' I thought dress became every one, for all looked well. You may think it was a little out of the common style of parties, for tea was discarded. Our only beverage was lemonade which, to the dancers, was peculiarly grateful. We had every delicacy in and out of season–two superb pyramids of ice-cream that looked so beautiful I could not bear to see them cut down. The jellies looked like amber and came round with most amazing velocity; every kind of cake and sweetmeat of course in great plenty. But if I was to enumerate the thousandth part of the good things I should fill my letter and tire your patience.
>
> Elizabeth Cowdrey is quite a genius. She has taken two very accurate miniatures on ivory of her father, with which the family are all highly delighted, particularly the Counsellor himself; for notwithstanding the likenesses are very striking, they both look full as handsome as the original–which, you know, is half the battle in this flattery-loveing world. She is still my pupil, and one that I am quite proud of, as not one before her has ever soar'd so high as miniatures.
>
> The second day after the ball she came laughing to school and told me she did not know that she should have lived through the scrape they had at thier house the evening before. She said her mother had consented that one of her little sisters should have a large party the next night (I suppose for the purpose of disposing of the fragments of thier former scrape), and just as she was about to send tea in, her father who had been that day elected Alderman returned home with all his friends, for his wife to furnish a splendid supper in the twinkling of an eye–which was accordingly

done. As Mr. Fitch was not one of his friends, he was not of course among the number. There was eighty persons invited to the first party, sixty of whom went. A violent thunderstorm of rain comeing just as it was time to go prevented some, as all had to ride that chose to go. At the second party, she said they had one hundred and fifty. I suspect you will laugh at my circumstantial account of so triffling a thing as a party, but it so rarely happens that I am pleased at one, when that is the case I never fail to talk and think much of it, and you know I am very partial to lawyers. Almost all our beaux were limbs of the law or, as some would call them, limbs of Satan.

If you look for delicate shading in my letter, be assured you will not find it; for if I do not plump from one subject to another with the speed of lightning, my paper will be running over before I have said half that is now floating in my brain pan. Your letter as usual was very interesting, particularly your strange account of Paulinia, as I should as soon have expected to hear Aunt Hannah was 'in the broad road to matrimony' as her ladyship. Give my compliments and tell her I wish her all possible success and happiness with the amiable youth she has 'stooped to conquer.' I sincerely hope she will not go barefoot, as they say shoemaker children always do.

As we are spending our time about the Goddards, I have a few words to say about Halsey.[26] In the first place, I am much obliged to you for this explination. I assure you the only reason I did not mention it in my letters was, I did not think it of sufficient importance to pay any-one for the trouble of reading it; and regarding him and the scrape so lightly as I did, it had almost entirely faded from my reccolection. As you have raked his visit here from the jaws of death, I shall mention a circumstance so triffling that it, with every-thing connected with him, has long been buried in oblivion–but, supposing that in some future letter I shall be accused of keeping a secret (a most unusual charge against a woman), I will if I can call it up [and] relate it. You must know that his godship was highly pleased with Mrs. Blauvelt, as all men are. Captain B. often invited him to his house and I believe he invariably accepted his invitations and call'd often without any invitation at all. She was pleased with his originality and amused herself most outragiously with the queer thing. In one of his visits at her house Mr. Riley call'd and was immediately introduced to Halsy by the jade as a beau of mine–or, to use her own words, a rival. This was quite enough to set the fool going. He immediately began about me and belabour'd me well. He threaten'd to fight Riley immediately and harped upon the subject till it was worn threadbare. His rival was at first struck dumb, but, soon perceiving his man and humouring his freaks, they parted without fighting. Next day Riley call'd to see us and asked if I knew how narrowly he had escaped loosing his life on my account the day before. Not dreaming what he meant, I looked up very suddenly and demanded an explanation. He laughed more than I ever saw him before, gave a very unsatisfactory one, and soon after took his leave. The next day I call'd on Mrs. B. who furnished me with the account I have scribbled for your amusement; so if you have heard of it or if you should hear of it from that nincom, don't accuse me any more of doing business with closed doors; for in matters of such vast importance, as you say, secrets ought to be avoided and, unless they are forgotten, generaly are so.

I am inclined to think the story you have heard respecting Amelia Laverty is not correct. It is true she may have made more than one conquest at Albany, but the gentleman to whom she is shortly to be married is a merchant in Albany. His name is Charles King[27] and he is worshipped by her wise father. Ellen [Laverty]'s husband, who I have frequently the honour of seeing, is what I call a pretty man and nothing more or less. As to mind, I think the stand on which I am now writing has as much as he has. Her house is indeed furnished in the most superb style. I have never seen anything surpassing in richness her furniture. She is now finishing the quarter which she commenced just at the time her father died. She still

'Bears about the mockery of woe
To midnight dances and the public show.'

She wishes to have it understood that she refuses all invitations to parties till the term for mourning is expired. She refuses *many* but not *all* the invitations she recieves, and that with the most heartfelt reluctance; and, if not, she has dispatched [?]his cue, for it always rises with the image of its ghostly wearer.

But I must stop my clack about beaux and all other animals to tell you that I have got your frame and hope it will suit, as I had no idea I could get a frame of any kind for a dollar, as I have always given ten shillings for the cheapest frames. This was precisely one dollar. I enclose the shade tint, and am told that it comes now in cakes. It is called neutral-tint. I hope it's not the ashes of the old scamp ground and prepared [see note 41]. He was so fond of the tint, you know, he may have adopted this method to improve mankind in the art in which he took such delight.

Good-bye–

I have folded my letter smaller and again present myself before you. I enclose the Cupids which you requested me to sketch, only, as one of them is Hymen, I had not time to alter the pattern into a Cupid, so you can tell the girl that by leaving out the torch and substituting a bow and arrow and, if she pleases, making the urchin laugh instead of cry, she will have a Cupid in a trice; for the flying one I have nothing to say more than that I wrote its name to let you know what I intended by it. If she alters Hyman into a Cupid, I think the word Love on the alter will be an improvement; but if she intends to let him weep on, she can put what she pleases there.

My paper always gives out before I have half done with it, so you lose much wise and interesting matter on this account. I have not half answer'd your letter, and cannot at this time without I take another sheet. I am happy to hear of the domestic felicity of Cousen Johnathan. So that he is treated like a 'Johnathan,' I am content, and care not who administers the pill. You advise me to return and try my luck amongst the beaux. To tell you the truth, I don't think you have any there that is worth trying one's luck for. . . .

Aunt Hannah also got a thank-you note from Eliza a little later, giving a very light treatment to Halsey Goddard (**no. 158**, April 4):

My dear Aunt,

I have recieved the flower, and if anything could enhance its value it would have been the inimitable bearer, who was no less a personage than the renown'd Halsey Goddard who has just arrived in the city. He said he went on board of Lampheer and found this famous box directed to me, and was glad enough of an excuse to call and see me. It was of course very gracefully presented by his fair paws (I had almost written four paws). He seated himself and gave us an account of a beautiful young widow whom he saw in New London before he left there for this last voyage and who has smitten his heart to the back bone. She is the most 'angelic' of human beings, and if she was only not a widow she should be his wife in the twinkling of an eye. But her having been married before is an insurmountable objection to his making her his wife–a most unfortunate circumstance if she is as deep in the mud as he in the mire. And who could ever see the Belvidere Apollo and not fall in love with so fascinating an object? Alas! for the poor widow, I fear her doom is seal'd.

But to return: I am much obliged to you for the flower. I think it very handsome, tho' the colours are not as good as I have seen of your dying. It looks quite gay and answers my expectations, which is the main chance, you know. I suspect it was somewhat sea-sick on the voyage, as it looked quite mauger or in other words indisposed–tumbling about so much, I suppose it was considerably jam'd, but I soon got it to rights and it now looks as well as ever.

I enclose half-a-dozen watch-papers and need not repeat that I painted them for children. The painting will tell that, but I thought them good enough to be destroy'd–as you like to be giving little trinkumbobs away. If at any time you would like a better one, let me know and you shall have it. I enclose a riband also if you think it worth wearing. It is not very gay but I thought would be more suitable than a gayer one for you. . . .

In the late spring the question of Eliza's visiting New London came up again, this time with Anna Fitch instead of Maria Hayden, and Mary writes her niece to urge the project (**no. 160**):

. . . At present we are pretty comfortable, and shall be very glad to see you. We are all very much pleased and obliged to Mrs. Fitch for proposing this friendly visit and we shall certainly do every-thing in our power to render it agreable. Yesterday Sally and your mother was about to pull caps, contending for the exclusive honour and pleasure of her company. The dispute ran high, and much civil and polite contradiction ensued. Sally insists that Mrs. Fitch shall stay with her, as they have rooms enough and nothing to prevent it, and your mother is determined she shall stay with us, to save herself the trouble of going up there to see her; and besides, we shall be altogeather and take more comfort with her here. This is her opinion. What do you think of it? We can accommodate her very well (if not according to your wishes), far beyond your expectations, I can tell you. We have smarten'd up amazingly since you was here. Not having time at present to relate particulars, I shall only say, thro' much exertion, contrivance, and good management, the house is quite another thing, both in appearance and convenience–improved to a degree that, if your pride is any-where within the bounds of moderation, you will have no reason to be ashamed of your maternal home.

How strange it must appear that you should show such extreme reluctance to visit your friends, and look like a criminal prepared for execution, when it is only hinted at. They must conclude we are a race of savage tigers and beasts of prey, and you expect to be torn in flitters the moment you arrive; for less than this can never justify the expression of that wo-frought, terror-stricken countenance of yours whenever the subject is mentioned.

Now it is my request when you present the enclosed to Mrs. Fitch that you will do it handsomely, and, if you can or ever mean to smile again, let it be on this occasion, lest your ruefull phiz should contradict all I have said in favor of her visit. Brighten up, I say, put on your best and prettiest looks and use your influence to hasten the business. Let it not be put off like the Hayden visit till it is out of season. Spring is a pleasant time, before the weather is too warm. We are prepared to see you, and the soonner you come the better. Please to reccollect what I have said above–the change we have experienced. We are very, very genteel, and live in *style!!!* (comparatively speaking). I add this little word because I know it will have more weight with you than all the persuasions I can use or the most solid arguments drawn from reason and philosophy.

Adieu. . . .

Plans for the visit were interrupted by news from Sam. Back in January and February he had renewed his attempts to get himself a clerkship at the Franklin Bank. His uncles Oliver and Ebenezer had weighed in with the names of rich and respectable sureties such as the position required. They could be counted on for that, as Sam for his part could be counted on to delay and delay in acknowledging their help with thanks, and as his mother was bound to write him in anguish over his bad behavior (**nos. 153** and **156**). He failed in his application, but tried again in June–without success, as it was to turn out. Nevertheless, the usefulness of kin-ties and the shape of power in his home town appear quite clearly in his appeal once more to Oliver Champlain (**no. 161**):

Dear Uncle,

As this business requires despatch I at once enter upon it. In the Franklin Bank in this city there has lately a vacancy occured, and I am advised by my friends (of whom 5 are bank clerks with whom I have been intimate since my arrival here) to make application for the situation which I well know I am competent to fill. They will render me all the assistance in their power. The references I can give here are very good. Mr. Doyle, the man who I am at present with & who is a director in that bank, is one. The rest are equally as good. My wish is that you would endeavor to get the signatures of some of the most respectable men in New London as to my character, family &c–say, Dr. Thompson, Dr. Lee, Anthony Thatcher, Geo. & Rob't Hallam, Stephen Hall, and whoever else you may think fit.[28] I particularly wish you to get the Messrs. Geo & Rob't Hallam's & Mr. Thatcher's signatures, as they are concern'd in the bank in N. London and of course are known here. Mr. Thatcher I am better acquainted with than either of the Hallams, but for that matter they all knew me when I was with Mr. Hall. As I before observed, their names would go farther than any of the rest, as they are known here. Both Hall & Quinby are particularly anxious I should get into the bank, and will do all they can for me. Mr. Hall proposed I should write to you to see these gentlemen and appear to take a very active part in my welfare. A favor of this kind you once did for me & which I have not forgotten. You will confer a lasting obligation by attending to this request as soon as convenient, as in all probability the appointment will be made in all next week. My salary, should I get the situation, would be $500 the first year. I should not forget my relations in Connecticut, should I succeed.

I am, sir, yours respectfully,
S. Champlain

August revived discussion of the Eliza-Fitch visit to New London (**no. 162**) and of Sam's now suddenly improved situation, which he explains later. Eliza writes to her home:

. . . As I told you once or twice before, I tell you again: I had no hand in the letter Mrs. Fitch wrote to you. I have had no hand in her conduct since she wrote it. As you requested, I presented your letter with my best grace and my most smiling face; for the favorable account you gave of the '*style*' in which you lived, together with the quarreling of Mother and Sally about which should entertain Mrs. Fitch during her flying visit, enabled me to hand your letter as you would yourself have done. I presume you do not wish I should *ask* Mrs. Fitch to write to you, and if you do, I am not willing to do so. I sincerely wish she *would* write, as I know no more what her intentions are than you do respecting this New London visit. She is now over head and ears in work preparing for her annual visit to Saratoga Springs, a jaunt which the warmth of the season renders peculiarly delightful, if we may judge from the hosts that are daily and hourly flying to that fashionable resort, or meeting of the waters. Although the city is perfectly healthy at present, they fly for amusement, not for their lives. If Mrs. F. did not detest a question-asker, I should learn all I could respecting this old story of a visit. As it is, I shall let things take their own course and inform you when I am so fortunate as to learn particulars myself. I don't blame any-one for detesting curiosity, for I do it myself, and could knock a person's head off for asking the most trifling questions that I do not choose to answer; and I generally let them know it. But although I do not consider questioning on this subject impertinence or useless curiosity, I still do not choose to question. You know you can if you like. I have seized the pen fifty times to write to you since your last, and as often thrown it aside in disgust, as I knew no more than I do at present what to say on this tormenting subject; so I hope this is a sufficient apology for my long silence and a sufficient excuse for dismissing the subject neck and heels from my paper, and, if possible, my thoughts. It has plagued me enough and you too, I suppose.

We had the honor of a call from Capt. Hayden last week who (if you will believe it) has again moved to New York. He has once more enter'd the army and is order'd to New Orleans. His family are to reside during his absence with Maria's parents, a move which I am pretty confident is not much to her taste, and I should not suppose it would be. Julius Caesar is now four years old. How many more there is, I did not enquire, as the Capt. also detests curiosity. He said at the request of his wife he called to see how we did and when we heard from you; and moreover also he wished to clear himself from the charge of being at the bottom of his wives' silence. He did not hesitate to say that he knew you would think he was to blame for her not writing to you, and on that account he had frequently urged her to despatch a letter; but owing to her extreme aversion to the pen the thing had never been done. So as he and I have both confessed our manifolds I trust we are forgiven. . . .

I suppose you have heard from Mr. Samuel Champlain since his promotion. He is now clerk in the Mechanicks' Bank and has only five hundred dollars a year. He is I assure you a great character and cuts quite a swell at present in this reverend city. I hope it may continue. . . .

Elder Dodge is now cutting up his capers at the New [=Swedenborgian] Church. Brother Ditchett and one or two others are quite in love with him. They think him a deuced smart man and for aught I know prefer him to Mr. Mitchell. It shows what saps they are to be cajoaled by such a jackanapes. I am very glad we have now got a 'second best' church where we can send all our trash and find the worthy pillars of it glad to get them, as I should be as willing to take a horse-whipping each time as to hear the drowsy, dead-and-alive sermons we are obliged to put up with when any other than Mr. Mitchell preaches.

Give my love to the inhabitants of the upper house [=Ways]. I should like much to see them.

Adieu–write soon and knock my head off, as I suppose you feel inclined to do so. Mother, do pray send *Hebe* to me.

For heaven sake commit this letter to the flames the instant you have run it over, for such horrid blots and writing I never beheld in my days. I suppose you have heard what a fuss they are making here to recive LaFayette in style. Mr. Fitch has been purchasing an engraving of him and placed it in an elegant frame. If it is a good likeness I never desire to see him, as so forlorn, so woebegone a countenance I scarce ever beheld in this vale of tears. The proportions are miserable and it has almost as much expression as an oyster, but not quite. There is not an atom of the vivacity of a Frenchman and especially such as he was.

Good-bye.

No more than a week later Eliza again addressed her mother (**no. 163**, dated August 15), making a recent art-exhibition the center of her letter. There, the alarm felt at the possibility of women being affronted by the nakedness of the sculpture was entirely of the time, witness much contemporary report of outrage at indecency in art; but its amusing side is not lost on Eliza:[29]

If you know I'm well, I don't suppose you ever wish to hear from me again; but as I always do everything I like when it's in my power and suits my convenience, I shall now write. Mr. & Mrs. Fitch left here yesterday for the Springs and will probably be gone three weeks. A few days before their departure I accompanied them to the Academy of Fine Arts to see the celebrated bust of Lord Byron that is now there and which I understand was esteemed an excellent likeness of his lordship both by himself and others. I had previously received a very pressing invitation from Riley to go with him and see the image of my 'favorite'–which, tho' dying to see, I had declined, as I did not choose that mode of conveyance. As Riley is an Englishman and a warm admirer of his lordship as a poet, I believe he was not slightly displeased at my refusal, but you know sometimes 'tis delightful to plague a body.

I was prepared on entering the room to see a very masculine as well as a very handsome face, but was disappointed in some measure. Handsome it certainly was, perhaps strikingly so, but my imagination had painted a more perfect head than the sculptor had chisel'd–a trick it is too apt to serve me, as I have seldom if ever found my expectations realized where my imagination has been previously excited. The nose, which is not large, has an inclination upward, which hurt my feelings amazingly; the forhead was fine, tho' almost totaly concealed by the ringlets of his hair which cluster'd thick around it; and in the mouth and chin I could easily trace a resemblance to that bark-paper painting of his lordship by Carter's sweetheart. I have often read of the 'paleness of monumental marble,' but since I was created I never saw anything to equal the deathlike paleness that dwelt upon his brow. There was a sternness in the expression of his face which I liked very much, tho' not enough for those two lines of his beautiful *Corsair* to be applicable to himself.

'For where his frown of hatred darkly fell,
Hope, withering, fled and mercy sighed farewell!'

There was a most inimitable statue of Hebe placed in the centre of the room. I never saw anything equal to the youthful beauty of her countenance. She was stepping with the lightness of a sylph. Her feet scarce touched the earth. As she was the cup-bearer to Jupiter, she held in one hand a goblet and in the other a vessel from which she was pouring his draught in the most graceful attitude you can imagine.

With Inman at thier head the committee have at last muster'd up the delicacy to add a fig-leaf to each statue in the Green Room. Wheather 'tis an improvement or not I leave to you (whose feelings were once so much shocked at their nudity) to judge. Mr. Fitch first took a survey of them and, when he quit the room, we entered, to spy out the nakedness of the land; and I must confess that notwithstanding the aforesaid fig-leaf it was as much as we could do to take a very scrutenizing survey of them all. Do you reccolect those heavenly three Graces? I could have looked at them forever and never tired. And in this delectable room was placed a bust of the angelic (I may well call her so, for she is now dead as a nit) Mrs. Trumbull, wife of the Colonel.

I understand from Riley (whose father's portrait, painted by Inman, was sent for on the occasion, and who is himself intimate with Inman)[30] that the members of the Academy have spared no pains to collect together as many of the first-rate paintings as they possibly could muster for this season's exhibition, and I really think their efforts have been crowned with success, for a more brilliant exhibition I have never witnessed. The paintings are all most splendid [and equa]l, it appears to me, the brightest geniuses of the age in which we live; and one in particular hit my fancy, as I knew the instant I set my eye on it, was done by Inman. I had seen it before and perhaps told you of it before. I have seen and admired softness in painting, but I never saw such feathery softness as this painting exhibited. It was taken for a brother of Inman's. He was enveloped in a fashionable cloak with a profusion of fur about it; the face, beautiful, and spectacles on. On the whole I fell in love with it. That painting as it deserved had the highest seat in the synagogue among the portraits.

Next to that sat Washington Irving, also enveloped in a cloak.[31] He set looking at you as if in deep study, with such a consumptive contemplative and somewhat woe-begone cast of features that I could not help thinking he must have been cogitating, at the time he set, his 'Broken Heart,' for nothing less than that could have produced such a woe-frought countenance. There was the original Cupid, from which Dick[in]son's was painted, painted by Dunlap. What you call elegant rags is nothing more or less than a crimson cushion under his head, with golden tresses and a purple mantle spread or rather thrown in easy confusion under him, to prevent his lying on the ground. The band to which his quiver is attached the artist contrived 'a double debt should pay,' as it serves more purposes than one. Understood? Incense was burning at a little distance in a vase placed on a white marble slab. The Cupid in strong relief. There was a splendid painting of Egypt's queen Cleopatra just landing. You may go to Shakespeare for a description of it. The barge wanted nothing but those fanning Cupids that existed only in the imagination of that immortal.

Well, I have the pleasure at last to announce the arrival of Lafayette. The drums, guns, and bells that are deafening me oblige me to close my account, if my paper said I might go on.

Yours,
Eliza

The arrival of General Lafayette at the Castle Garden to an ecstatic reception by the inevitable committee, bands, speeches, and subsequent extravagant balls, as it was the last item in this last letter, is the first item of importance in Eliza's next. The event had been eagerly awaited by the city, all sorts of plans made, and Lafayette's open-carriage ride up Broadway to City Hall, on August 16th, was a time of civic ecstasy for just about the whole population, including such children as Eliza's future son-in-law; but she knew nothing of that.[32] She writes to Anna and her family in their summer retreat at Saratoga Springs (**no. 164** of August 18), which had displaced the New-London trip:

. . . Lafayette has arrived at last, and not only the city is turned topsy-turvy, but the brains of half its inhabitants, and I have no idea that their senses will be restored untill he quits, which will be this morning. I have not yet seen this god tho' almost all creation flew to meet him on his arrival. I assure you he was received with the 'honors of war.' The Fourth of July I am told was nothing to the fuss made on Monday last to receive as we ought this truly great man. As I was not a spectator I shall not attempt to describe the scene, but I think it must have been highly gratifying to all parties. The newspapers I have long before this told you all. You can't think how sorry I am that you are absent at this time, but hope you will see him on his return.

I received an invitation from a gentleman yesterday to go this morning and see Lafayette, which I intend to accept. The person is *not* R[iley]. . . .

Mary a week later acknowledges the deferral of the visit she so much hoped for from her friend Anna and her niece (**no. 166**). It was a bitter disappointment which she handles in her own way, getting it off her chest. That matter settled, however, she next describes to Eliza and her modern reader how Edward Cort Riley's courtship had begun, back in June of 1822—as close as the correspondence gets to any account of it at all. She offers it in a playful way; but the whole long composition is something she evidently took seriously, asking her sister to copy it out twice and making little improvements in the second version:

Dear Eliza,

Your last letter informs us Mr. and Mrs. Fitch have gone to the Springs. I wish them a pleasant visit. At first I felt disposed to sue her for breach of promise, but second thoughts are best. People have a right to change thier minds, and I have no objection. Upon the whole, I should be very sorry to have any one put themselves out of thier way in the least merely to oblige me. When we confer an obligation, we recieve one. A benefit must be mutual to deserve the name. Also, a visit, unless it gives equal pleasure to both parties, is not to be desired, and the favors of those who do not perfectly understand and approve this mode of reasoning (however highly esteemed or valuable they may appear), when weigh'd in the balance, are found wanting. Look at it, take it home to yourself, apply it to others, analize and examine it critically, you will find this sound doctrine and will bear the strictest scrutiny.

Now to the point. You tell me I must practice patience as well as preach it. I have done this so long and so effectually that I can wait very comfortably to the end of time. When we meet in the 'spirit land' I shall see you both, and no thanks to either of you.

I am thinking how widely doctors differ. My amanuensis will condemn the foregoing and tell me it is better to be silent on the subject than to handle it so roughly, lest it should wound the feelings. Plain English is so old fashion'd, so provokingly intelligable, that I am often reproved for not speaking and writing in a more soft, delicate, and complimentary stile. True, 'tis very pretty, but rather flat and insipid. Soft handling and delicate touches are not exactly to my taste. I like a bold stroke now and then. It gives life and spirit to the piece. Your letters suit me in this particular. I was not born with a smoothing plain in my pocket, and have a natural aversion to all that sort of thing, as you Yorkers have to 'question-askers' and Yanky curiosity.

But with regard to your antipathies, let me tell you, we (of the honourable fraternity of guessers) will not tamely submit to foreign invasions. Like our fathers of glorious memory, we will defend our liberties against English usurpation (mock dignity and reserve), who would impose thier laws upon us, stop the mouths, and tie the tongues of free born Yankys. We are determined to maintain our rights and priviledges by the full and free exercise of our guessing powers. Therefore, take care of your secrets, for our sharp-shooters seldom miss the mark.

Besides, don't you believe in dreams? Of course you do. None but an infidel will doubt thier infallibility. What's the sign to dream of wedding rings, musical instruments tuned by Apollo, and nobody knows what all? I should be sorry to judge rashly in a case of such importance. You may be inocent as the 'flowers in May,' for aught we know to the contrary. Still, however, appearances are dark and doubtful; the fact is, dreams must have a meaning. We repeat it, they must be omenous of something either good or ill, and there are those who by thier faith and skill in this ocult science are forewarn'd of all that is to happen to them and to thier friends through life, and more than all. Now I must rest a while and take a pinch of snuff, as Aunt Hannah says, and then will relate what I saw in a vision of the night, and leave you to judge whether it is not portentious.

I dreamed we was at our residence, the Langly house in Chatham Street, where we sit painting at the window as in days of yore. Mary Ann Mason entered the room and introduced a young gentleman that shall be nameless, who gave us to understand he came for the express purpose of setting to you for his picture. With some difficulty you was prevail'd upon to commence operations, and things went on smooth and regular, with every appearance of a comfortable time. The scene soon changed. Mary Ann vanish'd, beau and all, and we was with Mrs. Fitch at the house where you now reside. I requested her to look at the outline you had drawn and give us her opinion. She said nothing, but after viewing it earnestly some time, with a face full of meaning, handed it to me, and behold, it was a gold ring. Something was written within, and I was about to read, when it changed to a watch-paper of the first order. Delighted with the painting, I exclaimed, 'Is it possible this is Eliza's work? How much she has improved!' In the mean-time it increased in its dimensions to the size of a plate. The ring was now a hoop of gold intwined by a superb wreath, where flowers of every dye, mingling thier rich colours with the brilliant lustre of the gold, reflecting back and forth upon each other, produced a charm far exceeding my descriptive powers or any-thing you can concieve. This resplendant hoop or ring encompass'd a large and elegant assortment of musical instruments. These fancifully interspersed with music books and scrolls bearing suitable inscriptions were tastefully arranged and form'd a compleat circle within. Indeed, there was so much taste and skill display'd in the arrangement and execution of the articles that composed the last circle, as left it doubtful whether (tho' less dazling) it was not more beautifull than the first. But my attention was chiefly attracted to the centre by the figure of Apollo—for there his godship stood portray'd in more than mortal charms. I knew him by his graceful form and the laurel wreath that bound his golden hair. His down-cast eyes were fix'd upon an instrument he had began to tune.

It was now no more a picture—'twas life and motion. The instrument he held resembled my guitar in shape but of a larger size than that, or those which form'd the circle round him. I wish'd it was my own, and thought what heavenly sounds it must produce, tuned by his skillfull hand. He seem'd disposed to raise it to the highest pitch, and as he strained the finer strings, I trembled for thier fate. As he was thus employ'd and we stood looking on, you said to me, 'This piece must have a motto. What shall it be?' 'Harmony,' said I, 'if the strings don't break; but if they do, Arbitrary Power.' Here the scene closed, the curtain fell, I awoke and beheld it was a dream. To you I leave the interpretation thereoff, be it what it may. Only allow it has a meaning, and I am satisfied.

'Tis true, the fag end of this seemingly prophetic dream does not entirely coincide with my waking sentiments, having placed my apprehensions on the wrong side, for who can doubt Apollo's skill divine. Therefore if the riegns of government are over-strain'd it must necessarily be on the other hand, and this would be no less deplorable; for what a pitiful animal is the hen-peck'd husband. We have a sorrowful instance here before out eyes, in the case of Jonathan Morgan, as he is call'd. Poor fellow, every-one allows he has an amiable disposition, many virtues and excellent qualities; but let us not suppose (although we may posess ten thousand virtues) our smallest faults will go unpunished. He had only two (vanity and the love of money), and these have seal'd his doom. Happy in a state of single blessedness, in the bosom of domestick peace, the idol of himself and family (whose study it was to gratify his every wish), surrounded with affluence, a stranger to care and trouble of every kind—but how vain are flattering prospects! The day of adversity will come at last, in one shape or another, and often in the way we least expect it. It was an article of faith with him that a good husband will make a good wife, and, being naturally disposed to make the best of husbands, consequently he had no fears of matrimonial infelicity. However, he bears his disapointment as a Christian ought, with patience and resignation.

Ever since Lady Morgan and her family returned from England they have liberally supplied the inhabitants of Yankey Town with an ample subject for conversation and amusement. Her ladyship soon after her arrival began to play spider, and spread her golden net to entrap the hearts of men (as Shakespeare says). She visited Aunt [Elizabeth Taber] Starr, and there display'd her musty parchments, requesting [Elizabeth Starr's son] Johnathan to look over and arrange her old family papers and documents, whereby he discovered her daughters, on thier marriage, were each intitled to the sum of thirty-five thousand dollars. At that moment no doubt he would gladly have married both, had polygamy been tolerated here. Be this as it may, he did his best to secure the prize now offered him, tho' on hard conditions (as he thought). The old lady was extravagant in her demands, which he refused, and the match was nearly broken off. At length he offered her eight thousand dollars and after some contention she complied, and Lady Ann was placed among the *Stars*–to his eternal woe, as a certain relation of ours would say.[33]

But the old lady was by no means satisfied with her bargain, and determined to dispose of Sarah to more advantage. For this purpose she purchased a house in Federal Street directly opposite Doctor Lee's, and set her trap for [his elder son, Dr.] Henry. The house is fitted up in English stile with a vandangle (as she calls it)[34] at the end, to astonish the natives, where Henry was invited to eat strawberries and cream with Sarah. He swallowed the bait, and here the courtship began, and went on rapidly like a house on fire (as Maria used to say). Nothing was talked of but Lady Morgan's vandangle and the approaching nuptials. Doctor Lee's house was furbish'd up and new painted on the occasion, the wedding garment prepared, the publishment was written and lodged in the hands of Mr. Judd against the next Sabath. The ceremony was to be performed in church and nothing remain'd but to appoint the day. All this time the old lady said nothing to Henry respecting the property, tho', since Ann's marriage, the English funds had risen and Sarah's fortune increased to forty-five thousand dollars. He had promised Sarah he would give her mother ten thousand dollars and settle one half of what remain'd upon herself, the other half to be reserved for thier mutual benifit; and she was perfectly satisfied. They now enjoyed the greatest happiness this world affords, the hope, the anticipation, of future felicity. Alas! never to be realized. Even when we obtain the object most desired, 'our very wishes give us not our wish,' and disappointment is the common lot. Henry was sent for to sign the marriage articles, which were to this effect. He must promise to give Mrs. Morgan fifteen thousand dollars and make over the whole of the remaining property to Sarah, and in case of her death return every cent to the Morgan family. Moreover, he must promise to spend his days in New London and on no account to remove or reside with her in any other place–in consideration of which, he was intitled to the honour of of becoming the husband of Sarah, and the supreme felicity of living with her mother and family, who would generously furnish him with house and home, food and raiment, and all other necessaries and comforts of life. This paper he obstinately refused to sign, tho' Sarah with tears besaught him to do it for her sake, as her mother and sister would consent to the marriage on no other terms. Lady Ann Starr flew into a violent passion and, after treating him in the most scandalous and abusive language, ordered him to leave the house and never enter it again, while Sarah–drown'd in tears, trembling with fright and agitation–beg'd he would not give her up or take a refusal from any one but herself. Thier rage was now increased to ten-fold fury, and they reproved her sharply for her indelicacy in owning her attachment to a man who was about to forsake her and had proved himself unworthy of her love. Amid this whirlwind of contending passions, Henry stood awhile like one planet-struck. At length com[p]ell'd to quit the house, he promised Sarah when she sent for him he would return, and not till then. The poor girl was instantly confined to her room by her avaricious mother and tyrannic sister and treated with much severity.

This affair you may suppose made no small noise in town. Every-one felt interested. Some advised Henry to carry her off by force or stratagem, and offered to assist him in the enterprise; but this, if he had been disposed, the vigilence of her guards rendered [it] impossible. For two long months, Sarah tho' much talked of was never seen, and Henry bore the tortures of suspence. At length he recieved a message from herself, and flew to meet her on the wings of hope. She appeared, and in a few words gave him a formal dismission, in the presence of her brother and Mr. Judd, who had been sent for to witness the ceremony. When it was concluded, she bid Mr. Judd good night and, without speaking to Henry, instantly left the room. Soon after, she appeared in public, gay and smiling as ever, and it is the general opinion that our cousin Johnathan would willingly exchange conditions with Henry and think himself a gainer by the bargain.

By a concatination of ideas I was insensibly led to the story just related, which, had I considered the large space it must necessarily have occupied to the exclusion of matters no less important, would probably have been omited. More remains to be squeezed in than this paper will admit. The letters we recieve from you give us too much pleasure to be forgotten. The three last with the whole of thier valuable contents should be separately considered and answered in due form, did not the limits prescribed forbid this indulgence. I was highly gratified with your account of spring and summer exhibitions. Next to visiting the Academy is the pleasure of reading a discription of the paintings and statuary. The committee have done well to bestow a fig leaf upon the latter, and, I think, to throw a light drapery over some of the figures would be a still further improvement. The head of Byron must have been a treat to you and Mrs. Fitch if it resembles the strange-looking picture you both copied and admired. William read to me a particular discription of his lordship's person and manners, written by an American who had seen and conversed with him in Italy, by which it appears he was very handsome and his style of face strikingly uncommon. But to me Washington Everven's [=Irving's] picture would be a subject of deeper interest. Byron has often charmed my ear with concord of sweet sounds, soothed by turns and harrowed up my soul with his terrific images; but Ervin's is a genius better suited to my taste. His *Broken Heart* contains more of truth and nature than all the poet has express'd.

What will become of poor Sandy [Clarke]? He must surely die in imitation of his lordship, if he is not dead already. I have heard nothing of him for an age. In his *Elixir of Moonshine* you will find 'Lines on a Young Female Artist,' supposed to be that pale sickly-looking girl he took for Mrs. Heyden's sister. You will doubtless recollect the time, place, and circumstance that has rendered her immortal.

Heyden is a pretty fellow to clear himself and throw the blame upon Maria, but it is the trick of husbands. The First Man did the same as soon as honey-moon was over. Maria is a good soul. I can excuse her silence. Aversion to the pen is a general complaint and wives have enough to do to please thier husbands. If they remember

> thier friends, it is all we can reasonably expect. I am very sorry New Orleans is Heyden's place of destination. His health is delicate and his wife will suffer much from apprehension. Your brother George has removed from thence to Nashville. His last two letters you will find with two we have recieved from Mrs. Bryant, in Aunt Hannah's little band-box. That dear old soul cannot write. She has sent you some of her play-things, and they speak volumes. A falling leaf is a lesson to a philosopher. Moral truth may be deduced from the most trifling circumstance. Every-thing is full of it, the trinkumbobs this little box contains 'out-preach the preacher' and show, all is vanity.
>
> The little green plates she made of grass. She says they are better than earthen and not liable to break, and clever to set cups upon at breakfast, and prevent the cloth from being soil'd. The large ones are for coffee and the small ones for tea. She thinks when you are married and keep house they will be usefull. The basket (which contains her picture, and the picture of us all) is to put your thimble in and ball of thread, that it may not roll about the floor. The flowers she says you may wear, give away, or keep to play with, whichever you please. She sends them out of pure love and gratitude for the watch-papers, which she has disposed of to her–

"Satisfaction"? The letter breaks off abruptly, the amanuensis perhaps exhausted or a page lost.

Just a month later, on a date (September 14th) fixed by the fame of the event she laments, Eliza describes what she was at the moment missing: indeed, a famous celebration for a famous benefactor of the young nation (**no. 167**).[35] She also had in mind to answer Mary's many pages (**no. 166**), which, again a few weeks later, still occupy her (**no. 168**–undated, of late September or October). For convenience these two letters of hers may be run together:

> Well, a gay trio have this instant drove from the door dress'd in sattens, silver'd gawze, and feathers for this splendid La Fayette Ball at Castle Garden, while I am left alone to the indulgence of my own reflections. And, faith, I will indulge them with a vengeance–that is, by giving vent to them. 'Tis rarely that I take interest enough in such amusements to honour them with the slightest wish of partaking in what is so falsely termed pleasure; but to this fete I had a most ardent desire to go, as I am told its splendor will far surpass that of the Greek Ball that turn'd topsy-turvy the brains of all New York. But independent of the brilliance of the scene, I should have had the pleasure of seeing La Fayette, a gratification hitherto denied me. I could indeed have gone (for my invitation to go was twice repeated), but then I must have appeared in so plain a dress as to have excited the laughter of many of the sons and daughters of prosperity with whom I knew beforehand I should mingle if I went; and that idea was too insupportable to be borne with any degree of patience. So, suffer what I might, I had the resolution to decide on staying home, even tho' it killed me–and it has almost. If it had not been worse than madness to think of getting a dress suitable for the occasion, I am not sure but I should have done so, for I was most sorely

tempted by Satan. Mrs. Fitch has been a week preparing for it and is now dressed as I believe she never was before. The struggle between poverty and pride has been long and hard on this occasion, but pride came of[f] conqueror as she always does in affairs of this nature; for, although I suffer keenly, it appears to me I had rather obey *her* dictates than those of any other infernal passion with which the worms of the earth are cursed during their crawling time. I am not in sufficient charity with one of the aforesaid worms at this instant to speak with less bitterness–for believe me I hate them all.

Hayden call'd here last week to say they had taken a house in Broad-Way and moved into it. You know a call from him (with his compliments left in the bargain) could not be too promptly attended to, so we determined to call on his wife the next day, to show how highly we esteemed the honor as well as from a desire to see her. The next day it pour'd from morning till night; yet still, so anxious were we to go that, notwithstanding the heavens wept so sore on the occasion, we were almost tempted to 'bide the pelting of the pitiless storm.' But wiser thoughts at least succeeded, and we postponed till a more favorable opportunity the pleasure we promised ourselves. The day after (which happened to be the one Mrs. Fitch had decided on going to the Ball) all nature took to smiling, and except mine I don't know that there was a sad heart in this populous city.

So we sallied forth for this delightful call. After calling at fifty wrong places, we at length, about sundown, found the right one. Maria, Jane and Eliza had all gone out in search of splendid dresses for the approaching fete, as it was Hayden's lorldly pleasure his wife should grace it with her presence and, of course, like or dislike, she must go. We found Hayden, [his brother-in-law Captain] Johnston and Eveleen, with Julius Caesar and Emma, at home. It was long ere the ladies return'd, but we staid to give Hayden and Johnston the trouble of entertaining us during their absence. At length they came and many kisses and compliments and enquiries of course passed between us. They each asked me separately if I was going to the ball, and each time the question went like a dagger through my soul. They all seem'd thunderstruck at my saying no, as they would, I believe, sooner have kill'd themselves than staid home on such an occasion. You know what an unceremonious hoyden Eliza is. She asked me *why* I did not go. This was a question I had anticipated, yet still was as unprepared with an answer (except the one I could not bear to give) as if I had not expected the question from them. If the gentlemen had been there I should have made some other excuse, but as they had quit the room I said, I was not in the habit of attending balls and of course was unprepared with a more splendid dress than I could wear to the theatre or the public places of far less consequence in point of dress than this immortal fete.

Eliza (good soul) was so desirous I should go that she immediately began with, 'Why, my dear girl, I will tell you how you can get a very cheap as well as a very beautiful dress, and go as well as not;' and was proceeding to give me instructions on that head when, for fear she would tempt me beyond what I was able to bear (for I was in an agony) I instantly cut the matter short by saying, 'I have told you my wardrobe will not permit, as it will not furnish even a plain white satin and that without a lace or gauze dress over it would be considered far too mean.'

But she did not seem disposed to give up the matter yet, and I could perceive by the expression of her countenance that she was good-naturedly or good-heartedly–which you please to call it–bent on torturing my soul out, when, casting a look on her that I was determined should silence her–for, if it did not belie my feelings, it said as plain as a look can speak in the words of form, 'Your honour is very good' but for heaven sake hold your tongue–she at length saw that my feelings were getting the mastery; and, apparently feeling hurt that she had said so much without knowing how keenly she had unintentionally made me suffer, she suddenly changed the subject before I was quite dead.

Maria during all this time had not spoken, and on looking to see what had become of her I met her eyes fixed with an expression of the deepest sadness on my face–for, tho' in general what is call'd dead eyes, they can express at her bidding the most soul-searching glance I ever met. And, as Poverty has been the sole cause of all this suffering, and harrow'd up all those devilish feelings in my soul, I again pronounced her the verriest curse that ever was sent to torture man or womankind. This is, as you may perceive, written feelingly, and even while I am smarting under the recent lash she has inflicted. I pray I may one day escape from her clutches, or that my existence may not be prolonged to old age.

In your answer to this part of my letter, speak lightly if you speak at all on the subject of the La Fayette ball, as I am not at all desirous that Mrs. Fitch should know (or indeed anyone except you two) how acutely I have suffer'd; for I acknowledge my folly in feeling so much more than the rotten ball was worthy of. But it is done, and my story with it, thank heaven. Therefore I will thank you to be sure and answer this part in the codecil to your last will and testament, as I fear this letter will never get answered till that time arrives. It is so much longer than the moral law.

Since the foregoing was written–which you will perceive was on the evening of the La Fayette Ball–the angry passions which nerved my hand and gave swiftness to my pen have had time to cool, to subside, and sober reason to resume her hum-drum sway. I had abandon'd the idea altogether of sending it to you and was about to wisp it and commit it to the flames, as a most intemperate piece of folly, when Mrs. Fitch enter'd and, presenting me with a printed account of the ball, desired I would enclose it in my next letter to you. . . .

I think I shall copy 'Mary's Dream' for the good of posterity, for 'tis pity a thing so beautiful should vanish like a dream in empty air–although . . . I shrewdly suspect that this same musical dream was concocted in your pericranium for the express purpose of discovering how matters stood betwixt me and my musical beau. . . .

I have not so strong a predeliction for leading apes [= teaching] that I could not possibly be prevail'd upon to quit the employment for the more popular one of scolding servants and whipping children. Neither have I so great a desire to marry as to put up with a person I don't love, for the sake of becoming a wife, as too many fools have done in the world. Of course, I prefer for the present the life of an ape-leader to becoming the wife of any man I have yet seen, who could not support me in the style I choose to move; for when I marry I must better myself, or at least have that prospect in view. I think a contrary course of conduct would be utter madness in me, tho' it might not in another. For these reasons and these alone I am still in a state of single blessedness. I hope, now, your question-asking 'Dream' is answer'd to your satisfaction, for further on this head, the preacher saith not. Understood!

You tell a deplorable story of the Morgan's family, poor Jonathan Morgan especially–tho' I don't know that anything better could have been expected from her Sapient Leadership or any of her posterity. I heartily congratulate Henry Lee on his escape from Miss Sarah's *vandangle*, as a connexion in that quarter must necessarily have been productive of nothing but misery to him and perchance his family. To me it appears somewhat strange that in the many traps set for Henry Lee, he is not yet caught. . . .

(**No. 168**) I am much obliged to you for the flattery you bestow upon my letters, and suspect that not only the style but the hand-writing of this will provoke a fresh volly of compliments, for I assure you it is a most inimitable epistle in one sense of the word.

I have not been to the Academy of Arts since I went to see the head of Byron. You ask what has become of Sandy, and think he must *die* in imitation of his Lordship. Not so, Sandy. He knows a trick worth two of that. I suspect he approves of the doctrine, 'The coward sneaks to death, the brave live on.' He appears one week in the garb of a prince, the next that of a beggar, and is far too high above this world to notice any of the reptiles he meets as he flashes with the speed of lightning up and down Broadway, millions of times in one day.

The instant I saw those lines you speak of in his *Elixir of Moonshine* on a Female Artist, I took them to myself, as they are the same words he used in prose on the occasion. Don't accuse me of vanity in saying thus much, for, believe me, nothing Sandy could say in my praise would have sufficient influence to arouse even the slightest and most insignificant of all our follies, vanity. I don't respect him. The praise of such a character as Florio [=Brooks] would indeed give me pleasure, as there is something god-like in that poet; and all of which Sandy can boast is his talent for writing. I never mentioned those lines to any one nor ever should have thought of them again, had you not brought them back to my recollection. I can say with Charles Clinch, 'I would give much for his imagination,' and that is all belonging to him for which I would give anything.

And now for Aunt Hannah–was there ever such a good old soul as she is? I thought I should have laughed myself to death at her little housekeeping mats. They are without exception the prettiest little devils I ever saw, and have made me shed quarts of tears over them. But I am heartily sorry she thought I wished more for those little paltry watch-papers than the flower I sent for. I did not even think they paid her for that, and the instant I can collect some more 'Eliza Cast-offs' I shall know how to dispose of them. If I could collect a party of Lilliputians, I could bring those little mats into immediate use, as they appear to be made for such characters; for I fear if they are not used till the time she anticipates they will long remain in a state of inactivity. But I shall never look at them without laughing; so they will not be quite useless, as I prize a harty laugh now-a-days more than I ever did before. For th[e]y are 'like angels' visits–few and far between,' and anything that will produce a good rousing old-fashioned laugh is, I assure you, highly esteemed by me. But I must write her a letter on the occasion and wish I could muster something with enclosings in it. I am very sorry to hear she is failing, and would give more to see her than allmost anybody I know–for she is a dear old soul. . . .

As I was always delighted with Moore's *Temple of Friendship* (Pl. 7.17, 1824), it has ever been my intention to design a piece from it the instant I could attend to it.[36] I have at length completed it and send it to you as a specimen of my improvement. Understand me: I don't say I make you a present of it, for if I should, I know you would lend it to all New London and perhaps at last give it away. Also, I may be under the necessity of sending for it to dispose of, for I would not paint it again for ten dollars, my eyes paid so severely through the nose in doing this. It has been in Mr. Marquand's store a short time and very much admired. I took it thence to send you. I desire you will not lend it out of your desk, as it is highly prized by me. How it will bear examining through your forty pair of spectacles and as many magnifying glasses, I am at a loss to determine, but should suppose it would look rather coarse, as I have had no keener magnifyers than my naked gooseberry orbs, either to paint or view it with. So I won't advise you to throw it aside the first tier, and behold it with the eye of charity through the second, as I am sure it will not bear closer scrutiny than they will afford you.

I had the shadow of a shade to assist me in desining this piece, for all but the figure of Laura; but that was altogether the coinage of my own brain; and I would like to know how you approve of it. The instant I had sketched the figure, its resemblance to Mrs. Fitch struck me, tho' I had not thought of her before. Cornelia looked over my shoulder a few minutes after, and said, Miss Champlain, did you take that for Mamma? No, I said. Well, it looks just like her, said she. I then asked Mrs. Fitch to take it in the office and show Mr. Fitch, and if he thought so, too, there must be some resemblance. She took it and asked if he ever saw any one whom that figure resembled. He said it was an excellent likeness of herself, and almost every-body that has since seen it is of the same opinion–so there must be some likeness. And on that account if no other, I have reason to prize it. So pray be careful of it.

Mr. Mitchell's health is no worse and he now speaks three times a day. Elder Dodge is settled in our second best church[37] and is, I understand, much liked by the congregation. I never have nor never shall take the trouble to walk so far to hear him, as I don't think him worth the trouble. Should you? The church is erected at the corner of Prince and Orange streets, far enough from here. . . .

No. 169 of October 24th supplies the only mention of the epistolary collection which in time grew into this present correspondence. Writing to her mother, Eliza makes clear the high value she set on it, not so much by how she terms it as by the fact that she had wanted it down in New York with her:

On Friday evening, the 15th October, the band-box containing the treasures of the East was delivered to me. I answer'd all your letters immediately, and I trust to your satisfaction; seal'd them *up*, packed them *down* in the box, and directed it to you; dispatched a note to Sam, which has met with just the measure of attention I expected–that is, none at all. Here stands the box by my side, and here I expect it will stand till you send an express for it.

And now I wish you to attend particularly to this passage in my letter. I have sent in the band-box a bundle of old letters for the express purpose of protecting a small piece of painting (which I send to you as a specimen of my improvement), by filling up the chinks of the box and prevent the painting knocking about from side to side, to its utter destruction. 'Now mark me, my boy,' I mention those letters before you get the box to prevent your tearing open the bundle like crazy creatures, and finding nothing for your pains but a packet of old letters that you have read before. They are the same that you sent down in the little gilt trunk that I left home. I have tied and sealed them all in a piece of brown paper, and all I entreat of you is that you will, without opening them, deposite them in a place of safety from the gaze of vulgar curiosity, as nothing ever made me so mad as the unnecessary exposure of my old letters, and, if I could have found anything that would have answer'd the purpose as well, should have sent it in prefference. But they were more compact. Pray do as I ask you, and in your next, tell me you have done so, and I shall be content–and not till then.

I was out when the bearer of the box called and of course could not deliver the ivory according to William's request, tho' it had been seal'd for ages in a letter to you. I lamented to no purpose the lost opportunity, as most probably the last day will arrive before another equally desireable presents itself. The letter in which the ivory is enclosed was of course written before the arrival of the box, and as it contains a request which requires your speedy attention I shall again stick it in this letter, that you may comply with it before the day of doom. I have sent an earnest entreaty for those ear-rings that Aunt Mary recieved from Maria Hayden, of which she made me a present. I want them very much indeed, and that, immediately, and I shall certainly expect them by the first safe conveyance. Do attend to it, will you? Don't fail. . . .

In sending this, as in numberless other occasions for a messenger or escort, Eliza had to do without Sam, despite the notes she had the Fitches' servant deliver to him through the city's post-office. She faithfully complains about him to his mother and aunt and Anna Fitch; New London passes on the complaints with interest–as has been seen in previous letters. Nothing works until Betsey's remonstrance of October. Then from Eliza (**no. 170**):

> 'There is more joy in heaven over one sinner that repenteth
> than ninety and nine just persons that need no repentance.' . . .
>
> Nothing could have been more unexpected than his [= Sam's] sudden appearance last evening, as I had no reason to suppose I should ever again behold him, except by accident, with my bodily eyes; and I assure you it was some time before I could believe them.
>
> When at length I was convinced that they did not deceive me and that it was really himself, I made a violent effort to conquor the rising indignation I could not avoid feeling at his late conduct (as I thought the exhibition of anger would not so well suit my purpose) and enquired in as mild a tone as waring feelings would admit, to what I was indebted for the honour of his visit. He answered by putting your letter into my hand and appearing extremely affected by the reccollection of his late conduct. I asked why he had behaved so for such a length of time, for to me and to all his and my friends his conduct appear'd most mysterious. He said God alone could answer that question–he could not, but that he never should forgive himself for acting as he had toward you, particularly respecting the ivory. His curses were 'not loud but deep,' and (to his honor be it spoken) he vented a round dozen or so of them on himself in true Champlain style; and, as I thought that they never could be bestowed on a more deserving object, I did not attempt to check their fury, but let them exhaust themselves, which after a time they did. But the fun of it is, he says for the soul of him he cannot account for his actions. They were without thought or reason.
>
> I assure you I was not a little pleased to find the fellow 'made of penetrable stuff,' after having for so long a time abandon'd that idea, and, finding him in such excellent trim to work upon, I immediately commenced opperations, and have no doubt but I deliver'd as eloquent an oration on the subject as you could yourself have done, while he walked chafeing about the room with his eyes wide open to the enormity of his offences. I made him promise fifty times over that he never would be guilty of the like again, and, if their is any faith to be put in this spir[i]t of feeling, I think he never will; for I really believe he has suffer'd enough for his sins to avoid committing at least any more of the same kind.
>
> We next proceeded to the discussion of William's affair, and he assured me he would immediately proceed to the business of looking him out a more eligable situation than his present (which is indeed poor enough) as you have represented it.[38] But with what success his efforts will be crown'd, he cannot of course yet tell, as a situation in the post-office here is, I fear, a situation of too great importance to be obtain'd without a more influential applicant than Sam is yet, and for that situation we both thought him much better calculated than any other, as clerks must be as great dabsters at everything they undertake as if they had always served an apprenticeship at the business, be it what it will. But he says he will immediately write and tell you all about it, and, after faithfully promising to

call the instant a packet was about to sail to put the band-box on board, he took his leave.

I retired to bed with a lighter heart than I had before for many weeks; but for the soul of me could not sleep till near morning, when, just as I got in a sound sleep, I was awakened by a loud cry of *Fire*! I started up and found my room brightly illuminated by the flames of the opposite house of our narrow street. Mrs. Fitch at that instant rushed in in her night cloaths, frightened to death and as pale as a sheet. The neighbours, half distracted at the 'thief-in-the-night' style in which it came upon them, were filling our stoop with their goods and chattles and throwing everything that would not break and some things that would out of the windows, just to keep them a few moments longer from blazing before their eyes; for we from the appearance of things had every reason to suppose we should yield up all to the devouring element.

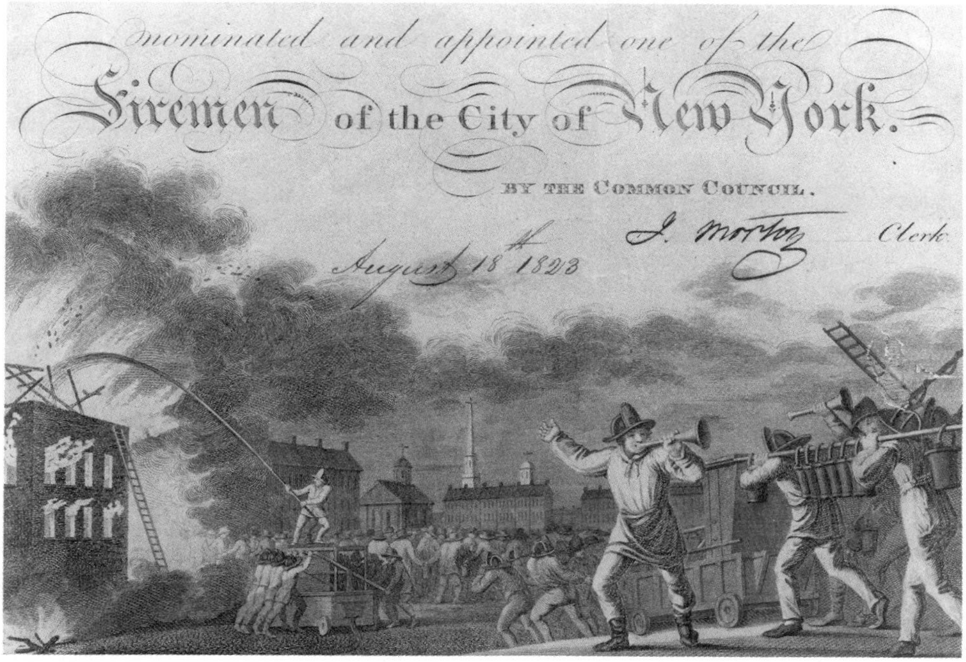

Figure 7. Sam's Certificate

But 'twas order'd otherwise. In the midst of the hurly-burly and confusion, Sam who had just been playing away merrily at an engine before our door enter'd in his fire habiliments which, I assure you, is not the most splendid garb in the world. He was apparently cover'd with sack-cloath and ashes, but in very good case. Mr. & Mrs. Fitch made him drink some brandy and water before he again proceeded to business and then order'd a pail-full of strong coffee to be made (boiling hot) for the company to which he belonged. It is consider'd much more scerviceable for the firemen when they are on duty to swallow hot coffee than spirituous liquors, as the first animates and the last enervates; and for that reason it has become a kind of fashion here with all who have the soul to do it, to open their houses and spread their boards for the relief of those fire-men who are at work nearest their own houses, and towards whom one feels as if they owed something.

Soon after, Sam stopped in again to assure us we need not alarm ourselves, as our house was fire-proof, and if it was not, that they intended to stop it at the corner of Jameses Street. Mrs. Fitch, greatly relieved, after making him swallow a cup of boiling coffee (of which he appear'd to stand in need more from his wet cloaths than from fatigue), dispatched him in quest of Charles Clinch and a Mr. Cook, an acquaintance of ours who, Sam said, were engaged at another engine close beside him. They however could not or would not come, and the pail of coffee was set out on the steps to be swallow'd by Sam's company; and it would have done you good to see them refresh themselves. They gave a great shout at the unexpected treat. One of them who I suppose did not get enough said to Susan, our black girl who waited on them, 'We are already under ten thousand obligations to you, but I wish we had some more.' Mrs. Fitch thought of opening the house and having them in, but Sam begged she would not, as their would three or four hundred rush in at once and with their dirty cloaths ruin the house; so she gave it up.

At sun-rise the engines departed and about an hour after that Sam made us another call, in his brown frock coat, beaver hat, and everything in superb style to match. I scarcely knew him, he was so completely metamorphized. This is the second fire we have had in the course of three or four weeks close under our nose. The first warmed our back as well, and the second warmed our front. I sincerely hope that we shall not be anoy'd again in the same way–and will now bid you adieu. . . .

I am ten thousand times obliged to you for the ear-rings, also for your *Happy Father* with his 'naked-tail'd' offspring. I think with you that a slight covering applied to the parts affected would not only improve the piece amazingly, but would also spare one such an irisistable desire to bestow a spank on the aforesaid parts, as they never fail to feel at beholding them. But the faces are beautiful and would scarcely admit of an improvement. . . .

To the last three of Eliza's letters, Betsey now got around to responding all at once (**no. 172** of November 16th):

My dear Eliza,

We have rec'd your favours at length, and feel a degree of gratitude not easily expressed. We had anticipated the pleasure this box of treasure would afford us, a week or two previous to its arrival, and, had not the variety of pleasing sensations been gracefully interspersed with others more painful, it would have been a perfect jubilee. We smiled through the tears that the tragical subjects had excited, which at first threw a damp upon the spirits, but the cloud soon dispersed that hung over us and a clear sunset followed. Your requests were faithfully attended to, every packet of letters &c were put away in due order, that your mind may feel entirely relieved from any apprehensions.

I have heard it observed that no person can write well with a dog at thier back, to write in thier lap, or to write in a hurry. All these inconveniences I am at present labouring under, and more too, and must leave embellishments to Mary, who likes them. You may be glad to get a hum-drum from me. It is so seldom I find a chance to write in my own name, which by the bye I shall not sign. As your letter is not before me, I must content myself with only speaking upon the subjects most striking, one of which is, the merit you are justly entitled to for the strength of mind you exhibited in withstanding the temptation of attending the [Lafayette] ball. This deserves greater credit than I can give you, particularly when placed under all the above mention'd difficulties; but I have no doubt but you will be amply rewarded for taking up the cross in the course of time. To gain the victory over ourselves is the greatest of all. Self-controul (as in this case) is indeed worthy of the highest praise. When I read this part of your letter, I was in as great an agony (to use a bold expression) for the want of power (in season) to have relieved you, as you could possibly have suffered from absenting yourself; but you acted wisely, and perhaps eventually may have a more salutary effect than if you had gone; for there generally is a succession of mortifications attends such splendid fetes. I am no stranger to similar mortifications, and when they effect me in a much more sensible manner than they could now, still, to know we have acted right is a more refined pleasure, and self-approbation is the highest felicity we can possibly enjoy; and not only this, but be assured there is eternally a draw-back upon every other pleasure on life, from the king to the beggar. I think a girl of your understanding could not have arrived even to your years, and yet be ignorant of this truth.

In the next place (what shall I say), the *Temple of Friendship* exceeds all the painting of any kind I ever saw in my life; but even this pleasure was not without a draw-back. I felt as much pain as pleasure at the sight of it, my fears for your eyes over-balanc'd, and from henceforth and forever, amen, let me entreat you, as you value your sight, never to attempt another of that size, for all the aplause you can possibly gain will never make you amends for the strain of the eye. Just as I decieved myself, in thinking I was a great gainer in time and expence of ivory, when I drew profiles so small, but now (almost too late) I see my error in judgement, and therefore warn you, if in season. Make the most of it. Every person that has seen this piece appears to have a bright sense of its value–in fact, as Doctor North would express it, 'There is but one voice about it.'

If there could be a line drawn amid so many beauties, I think the foliage surpasses. The whole looks to me like enamel more than any kind of painting, and is considered so. I think with Cornelia [Fitch] that the figure resembles Mrs. Fitch's person, and the face, critically examined, is not unlike; but the eyes (as far as the eye can see them) reminded me of Mrs. Northam's–the coulour, at least. It has been greatly admired; but fearing to expose it to vulgar eyes lest they might ask the loan of it, I scarcely dare have a thing of so much worth in my posession. I desire you, however, to draw all your future pieces upon a larger scale, and give up watch-papers and everything of the kind. I trust you will not forget my request.

I will just give you a little sketch of my late paintings and the extreme difficulty I have had with as many as six of my last front-faces; but when I devoted myself to an examination of the case, I found from what it all proceeded: in the first instance, the natural decay of eyes of course requires an enlargement of the size (this matter is settled), for even young girls acknowledge those perfectly accurate, through my magnifying glass, which otherways were thought obscure. How then must it be with older people? Among the number of those sitters that has killed me was Lucretia Thompson. She brought her beau's likeness, taken by Rogers.[39] I have copied from a number of portraits that were said to have been drawn by the greatest artists, and miniatures also, but none of them had so much energy infused into them as three I have seen of Rogers' production. I borrowed the piece in order to copy the head and had put on the boldest shades (I so much admired) and had the likeness so correct as to be drawn by Mrs. Dalrymple and Mrs. Ishum; and they had seen him only passing. I had it in my possession from Monday till Thursday, and only wish a day or two more to have blended the shades a little and to have it exactly like the original; but, recollecting that I could borrow Mr. or Mrs. Whistler's miniatures (when leisure offered), that were taken by the same hand, I gave it up for the present. Not caring for drapery, I took a round plate of ivory just large enough to introduce the head, which was larger than a cent; the collar, that stands up around the face; and a little of the cape of the coat–just to say it is black, is all the drapery that appears. But when I was mentioning my difficulties that attended my mode of painting, [I] forgot to observe that I never had fixed my room properly for the purpose, which was entirely wrong. Why I never found this out before is to me astonishing; but so it was; and better late than never. There was a painter several years ago by the name of Johnson that came to see me. He insisted I should have my room darkened. With much persuasion he prevail'd upon me to consent to have curtains just to show the effect, and with how much ease I might paint. I, not intending to practice in this way (because I thought it needless to adopt a better plan than I had been persuing), paid but little attention to all this wise discourse. Your father was present, who desired to sit, and I must confess I was astonished at the advantage it gives a painter. You see before you what you are to copy, without laying more upon Fancy than she is able to bear or crowding her delicate stomach with too solid food for her digestive properties.

Upon the strength of my late wars, I have been determined to have my room fix'd properly for the express purpose of painting to advantage. We have green blinds to the outside of the windows, and lately I have had, to my two fronts, new blinds that shut or open at pleasure. The others are stationary. Those I obtained by dint of argument, of Uncle Starr, but not without pleading equal to a lawyer. He would not, notwithstanding my eloquence, grant me but two, and without something upon the inside, there is no harmony. I have consequently engaged a joiner to make the three wooden window shutters, to be painted a handsome green upon both sides, to be made of seasoned wood that shall not warp, with brass handles to hold them, with a narrow door to one, to open and or close at will. This door is divided into two–the upper, to admit as much light upon the patient as will produce this rich gold shade I have before mentioned. That advantage, togeather with enlarging my plates of ivory,

I think is all I need, as new eyes must be dispensed with for the present. I have taken the size of the ivory Mr. Whiten's likeness is taken upon, and enclose it, and if you have not already purchas'd the ivory I last sent for (since I rec'd those with the hose), you may buy as large as this paper; but if you have, send them. They will answer by sketching the picture larger upon them. I also, untill this moment, had forgotten to observe to you that I have since written to Sam and enclosed three other dollars for this purpose; but undoubtedly he has informed you of it before this. If you are allowed to pick them, observe those with the least grain, and the thinnest. I don't think I could make use of the ivory if this charge was omited. The plates you last sent is exactly the size I have been wishing for, for profiles, but as fronts are attended with so much greater difficulty, I have given up the idea of ever undertaking another so small, as I am confident that I lose more than I gain.

You are determined, it appears, to keep your love affairs as obscure and inaccessible as the far distant hills on the Isle of Santee, with all thier *nytchnydycal* appendages. I conclude you think that if the nuptials were really celebrated we should know it without a flourish of trumpets. But with all your care, you are in no small degree of danger, as long as dreaming is a common priviledge; and so we will 'maintain our rights,' and no earthly power shall deprive us of the aforesaid priviledges.

But I am glad to find you so well guarded against an invasion. For my own part, I am not seeking any unlawful knowledge upon this head, never expecting greater (till it comes to a close) than I may obtain from dreams. In such a critical case as you are in, it is well to be acquainted with the amazing power and velocity of her [Mary's] blunderbuss, eternally charged with battering rams (for she lies in ambush) ready cocked and primed to blow up your magazine, vandangle and all, or any-one's else that comes within the compass of its devouring muzzle, sky-rockets scaling the moon, sharp-shooting engines of mischief loaded with iron spikes and all manner of fearful combustible–or, in other words, if you breathe awry, you are drown'd in a whirlpool of sarcasm.

I declare, so much hot stuff has set your Speaker into a violent perspiration. I was fearful that her last would give her *dinger* [=heart] a mortal wound, but I am truely clear of the blood of it. I entreated her with tears to permit me to perform the part of a surgeon, and would have applied one of my most effectual and balsamick smoothing-plain plaisters; but she kicked and flounced like a sea serpent, and I was obliged to let the 'wound go undrest.'

One would think to read the above that it was the description of a demon. Not exactly so–for there is no one more sensible of the sublimity of her compositions than myself. In fact, I scarce ever saw her equal either in lofty ideas or in the arrangement of them–sound of judgement and wit in the extreme. But I sincerely think she squeezes to much elixir vitriol or scandal (for the lemon is sweet to it) into all her compositions, and sacrifices too much to humour; but there is not a rose without a thorn upon earth. We must therefore learn to discriminate between the beauties and errors, and profit withall.

I suppose Sam has informed you, we have had news from George, not by letter but some person saw him at Nashville, that he was well and *very steady*, the most so of any young man in the place—the very same news of Sam I have heard, with this addition, that he is the handsomest youth in the place. This last, you must be a judge of the truth of it. But whether or not, it is of little consequence, so that the former is true. And if his reformation is genuine, he will call to see you often, as I have desired him to do, and attend to this business of William's that is of still greater importance. I would thank you to prevail upon him to let no opportunity slip by inatention; for my heart is too much set upon it to hear a disappointment. He either has, or will call, to hand you the money for the ivory. If you will just give me a line after you have purchased it and mention the price of the enclosed size, I will take it as a favour.

I am this moment expecting Mary Perkins to sit, and don't know whether I shall be able to add another word.

We go on pretty much in the old way, and I believe enjoy ourselves as well at least as most couples. We certainly have our proportion of fun, as that is the Ways' inheretance, and no ways deminished by the approach of [?]Whit Leathers. It is, however, a little provoking to be obliged to stop growing handsome, out of pure complaisance to age—that is to say, we grow a little oldish, we don't neither exactly stand still, for we shake a little when we get into one of our high frolicks, and not only so, but shake the house a triffle; and if you was with us (at times), perchance it might rattle down about our ears, which would doubtless spoil our future fun.

Aunt Hannah was tickled to death with your letter, and it was enough to tickle any one. None but *E* could have dwell't so long upon so childish a subject, and at the same time so much to the purpose. I could see her in every line, and laughed till the tears flow all over it. In short, it was the very dandy. I wish you would write her more frequent, instead of sending her more watch-papers, as it will please equally as well and save your eyes. Mary agrees with me that this is the best plan, as she will not keep ever so valuable a trinkumbob one moment longer than she can find any-one that will accept it, however unsuitable the subject. For instance, Henry Lee's Sandy Claws is a sufficient proof of her want of scence to dispose of them. One day she came down to spend with us, and in the course of the time went to the glass to fix her cap that had got a little incomod'd by the wind. Fetching a sight, she exclaimed, 'O dear, I grow so old and homely, nobody loves me.' I screamed at the fun of it—said, I, 'What makes you think so?' 'Do you think I'm a fool?' she replied. Mary says, 'Why, Aunt Hannah, I really believe you want to grow young and handsome.' 'No, I don't,' she says, 'I want to be old and handsome.'

If you could imagine the pleasure your letters afford us, I think it would tempt you to write more frequent. These last seem to stick by the ribs, and we feel as much better for reading them over as an empty stomach does from a 'feast of fat things.' It appears your energies were on tip-toe when you wrote, as I never saw composition that would make one feel so alloverish—that is to say, every kind of sensation the human body is capable, is excited 'with a vengeance.' I am certain that if you feel as strongly as you express, your neck cannot be larger than a pipe-stem.

Mary is about to commence operations, and your epistles will be answred in full tale. She has a peculiar faculty in digging up the frozen entrails of the earth to find matter, and when she has found it, she makes herself tenfold more the child of Satan than before.

I have made both ends meet, and that is as much as can be expected, these hard times.

When she writes her mother in late November,[40] Eliza has more of those endless art-supply errands on her mind, but good news about her reformed brother to add:

. . . Your 'magnanimous' son Samuel (as you style him) has most nobly added three dollars to your three, which has enabled me to procure the quantity I have the pleasure to enclose. I think this is very handsomely done, and have no doubt but you will agree with me, and give him all the praise that is his due, and that we are so apt to think ourselves entitled to whenever we confer a benefit on another. Don't suppose from what I say that the act was ostentatiously done–far from it. 'Twas quite without parade or the slightest sound of trumpet; but still I should like to have it acknowledged by you, as I think the effect will be salutary on a mind like his. But I need not advise, for I am pretty confident you will use your smoothing plane to advantage in the present case. Blow him up to the third heaven and there let him stick; and there I would leave him for the present, had I not something farther to say about him.

So you have heard he is the handsomest youth in the place. I cannot exactly agree with your informant, as I think I have seen a handsomer youth. The moderate share of family vanity with which I am blessed has induced me long since to set myself down (very modestly, I acknowledge) by far the likeliest of my mother's children; and if it was not for myself, I should not hesitate to place him in the top of the list of worthies. But as I am what I am, I shall never knock under to one of my brothers in the slightest article, but fight my way manfully through the world, asserting the 'rights of Woman,' and particularly my own superiority over the rest of your children. . . .

[Anna Fitch's niece] Miss Caroline Northam from Newport is at present on a visit to us. Her standing in society at Newport is exactly what the Perkinses, Larkins', Lees', and Stewarts' is in New London, except that her father is quite as rich as the whole scrape I have mentioned put together. We must of course devote every instant to entertaining her, as she has always been accustomed to the greatest attention from everybody. But she is a sweet girl and an enthusiastic admirer of painting. She paints very elegantly herself, and has never in a single instance betrayed the slightest show of an envious disposition–that most rascally of all littlenesses. I admire her, and we shall be extremely sorry when she goes home, as we paint together.

Good-bye

The correspondence now turns the corner of the year into 1825, with Eliza suffering from periods of depression and disturbed sleep which she is willing, in **no. 173** of January 16th, to attribute to "dissipating": "I have attended many parties of late," she writes, "and sometimes for three nights together have been kept up by them till three o'clock in the morning." But in spite of this apparently gay life her situation was not a happy one. Her twenty-seventh birthday approached. She had not relented toward her suitor, and so had none; her artistic talents did not provide her with an adequate business, a true living, so she had none of that either. Advertising fancy-pieces like the *Temple of Friendship* didn't pay as portraits could; and teaching art had had its day. She was dependent for her food and shelter on the kindness of the Fitches; and it was this family, too, that gave her access to such entertainments as she could afford. In society she had not found anyone to "support me in the style I choose to move" in (**167**); surely she found something humiliating in being shown about to such little effect; yet the thought of returning to her home-town chilled her to the bone. Why should she not be depressed?

But she moves on to an incident flattering to her talents; one of the city's most experienced teachers and demanding judges of art, not to say one of the most acrimonious, John Smith, had sought her out. She refers to him as usual under the nom-de-guerre, "Neutral-Tint" (alias "Natural Squint"!), which he most often assumed in his public statements.[41] What lay behind her evident dislike of him may have been just those statements, attacking the American Academy; for such lights of that institution as Trumbull and Waldo she looked on as the benefactors of herself and Mary:

> . . . One morning last week while a host of the Blue Devils were paying their respects to me, and more than usually ingenious in tormenting me, Mr. Fitch enter'd the keeping-room and said Neutral-Tint was in his office and that if it was agreeable he would introduce him to us. I said not a word but, catching up the piece I was painting, flew like lightning to my bed-room, where I was soon followed by a message from R. Fitch that I would come down. I sent word that I was engaged. At the impudence of that answer he colour'd scarlet, as he brought the cross old 'Natural Squint' (as he is call'd) on purpose to see me; but, as I said before, I was at the time beset with Blue Devils and wanted not a bluer than them all to combat. After he was gone, Mrs. Fitch told me that he admired *Mary Queen of Scots* more than all my pieces, and said as he quit the room that when he left home he did not expect such a treat. He also said that he was very desirous I should attend his lectures on heads; that he thought I had much genius; but that he could improve me. This from him you must think was a compliment indeed. He says he thinks it his duty [to] keep public taste correct, and for that purpose he overhauls all our artists without mercy. The slightest defect in a piece is instantly apparent to his eagle eye and never fails to receive his censure. . . .

Betsey answers promptly toward the end of the month (**no. 154**),[42] trying to pick up her daughter's low spirits by another flattering mention of Eliza's *Fancy* and by turning her mind to her art–to the possibility of lessons with "Neutral-Tint."

> Dear Eliza,
>
> I am only able at this time to write a line, to do my best endeavour to lay your troubled spirits, as I never was in a greater hurry of business than at present. I intended writing immediately upon the receipt of yours, but company prevented.

I was therefore oblig'd to postpone it till now. I am of the opinion that your dreams proceed only from your dissipation, as you term it. Late sitting up has a tendency to weaken the system–undoubtedly often causes unpleasant dreams. This I know from experience, and perhaps there is nothing will make a person grow old faster. Mary bid me say to you, that there is no meaning in any dreams, but hers concerning you and yours apalls, and that you may throw all your Blue-Devil ones to the wind, as for any faith she has in them; that it is nothing but superstition and the eternal round of company that whirls your brain pan about so–and there is too much justice in the observation to doubt of the truth of it. . . .

I have just finished a copy of Mrs. Whistler's picture taken by Rogers, and have been successful in imitating the style, and though like her, is vastly handsomer than the original; but I suspect would not be thought so good a likeness. That, however, to me is of little consequence, as the copy is my own, and probably will be more benefit to me than if less beautiful, among fools particularly, and those fools who have never seen Mrs. Whistler. It is the highest style of shading, and looks as if it would speak. It is for a future model, and think I have gain'd by it more information than from all I have ever seen or copied before. A white merino shawl, shaded to resemble black, and pencil colour'd ermine, the white drapery very dingy, and drawn upon the deepest yellow ivory that can can be, that appears for the harmonizing tints between the light and shade, the hair is slap'd on, and left the naked ivory for the high lights, but as natural as life. The destruction of painting is, to be done too fine and to be too sparing of shade–a fault I have ever commented to the present time, but think this will set me right, and is not one quarter the work, and looks ten thousand times better. It is my particular request, that you will attend Nutral-tint's lectures upon heads, and Mary is also very anxious for it. He would learn you more in an hour than you can gain in ages, and think the mony would be well spent. Mrs. Lee says your *Temple to Friendship 'is painting,'* but I think none has been more struck with it than Doctor Lee. Mary made me send it up to Dr. Swift's, and if there is any blame attached, let it be upon her; but it is as nice as it was when it came, and I have not given it away. They admired it exceedingly, and upon the strength of its beauty, harassed Mr. and Mrs. Whistler's pictures; but, on account of want of time and the shortness of the days, have but just completed it, though I rise at 6 and three times at 5; but it is too great an exertion to be practiced for any length of time. Nothing to me is a substitute for sleep. . . .

Captain Halsey Goddard was married last Monday night, to Miss Sally Fulton, daughter of Mr. John Fulton, both of this city. Nobody knows when or how the courtship commenced or ended. I never was so surprized at a piece of foolish news in my life. So now you see you have not only lost your beau, but 'a barrel of pork, a barrel of beef, and a due bill,' all of which he promised your lady-ship if you would marry him; so you see there is no Jack without a Gill. Yet, after all, I am right to think Halsey will make a pretty good husband, if those that ought, can fancy him. . . .

William, too, in answer to his sister's low spirits now sets himself to write cheerfully (**no. 175**, February 13):

I thought it would not be out of character to give you a letter once in my life. It's my intention to try to write a long and amusing one–that is, as much so as a Natty, Lucy, Phebe & Jerry can make it, of whom you ought not expect much. I shall begin with George. What think you of him? Is he the likeliest, smartest &c of the Champlain family? For yourself, you have pronounced that you ought to be look'd up to as the 'oricle' in wit, wisdom, and beauty. This we do not deny. At least for myself, I do not, for I always had a reverential fear of your dignity which I cannot account for. It might have been fear of your 'ten commandments' [i.e., fingers] & my 'oven-broom' [head] coming in contact that possessed me somewhat with the dread, or your tongue or pen. What it is I cannot [say], but so it is. Of George I do not know what to think. He hardly seems my brother–been so long from home, & no disposition to return, appears to take no interest in our fate, never writes, & the last news we had from him, he was with a company of players. Whether he was one of the company as a player or that he merely fell in with them in his travels, I know not. He mentioned in his last letter to me (it was last May, I think) that he intended to quit New Orleans & visit the western states for his health, which had been upon the wane for some time. I hope he will regain it & visit us.

What for Sam? Is he the handsomest, steadiest youth in New York (as Aunt Hannah tells our neighbours)? He is represented to me as 'quite the dandy' by some of his old school-fellows that have seen him, & that he can hardly speak them. If it is so, I am sorry, for I do abhor to see old friends & school fellows pass each other without giving the time of day. It awakens the worst feelings in the human heart not to be noticed, or look'd at with contempt, merely because one is dress'd better that the other. The one that does it I hate & dispise & wish him nothing but misfortune. Whether Sam does it, I know not, but he is spoken of, as the phrase is, 'verry stiff.' For my part I always think it better to make a friend than an enemy, & win an enemy over when I can, as it is full as easy; and give me one friend to a dozen enemys in time of trouble. Do you know what pay Sam receives for his services? I heard it was $200 per an. If it is so, I should like to know. All is, I wish him well.

For myself, I am yet with 'Uncle Ebb' in the post-office. My pay is rather poor but good living, though he cannot afford much, as his income is small, & if I could better myself I would quit immediately. That is uncertain, & therefore am I forced to stay. I have written Sam upon the subject often, & requested him to look me up a berth in your place if he could. He says he has tried but cannot succeed as yet.

For yourself, how is it? Do you ever intend to get married & add one more to the usefull numbers of society? Or shall it be 'born, live, & die in single blessedness'? For my own part I would rather you adopt the former, provided you find one that answers tolerably well; for one that is difficult to suit generally 'withers & dies upon the virgin thorn.' I was looking over the records of our births the other day and find that Geo. was 29, the 17th of Oct'r & you will be 27 the 29t of this March coming. If you intend to do 'better' than 'well', you must strike very soon or you will be on the wrong side of thirty, which is rather feared by most ladies unmarried. That you would make a good wife I never doubted. I think you are well qualified for transacting all business which requires a man's attention without having any intention of wearing the b[ritche]s, & this ought to be considered by the man who is fortunate enough to have you 'a jewell of inestimable value.' To be sure, he must mind his P's and Q's, but that's neither here nor there, for a good wife who doth not love. If I was to be married I should look the world over to find just such a temperament as yours if it was possible.

Mother & Aunt Mary are both well & enjoy themselves 'exceeding well,' as Aunt H. says. Mother has learn'd more within a year about painting than ever she knew in her life before. She has been copying the miniature of a lady here (Mrs. Whistler) painted by Rogers of New York, & I think she has done it full as well in point of style, but she has not taken so good a likeness–which ought not of course be expected. But had she had the original to set, she would have made one full as good, if not better. I wish it had been in her power to have been instructed by some person like Rogers. At this time she would have been independant. But she labors under a thousand difficulties to prevent her progress in the art which others have not. The first & last I may say is poverty. Could she enjoy the advantages that Rogers & others have, I have the vanity to think she would have excelled some of them. His style you know undoubtedly: boldly shaded & dark back-grounds. At first Mother detested it, but the more she saw it the better she liked it, & now she thinks no style equal to it. Her former style looks flat & unfinished compared with his. But give me deep shades forever–correctly put on. It gives life, ay being, to the peice; it brings it out & makes a living being of it. There is a finish in his style which I never saw in others.

Now I think you ought to improve your time in visiting these geniuses & learn the art of finishing a picture as soon as they do. When Mother will be two weeks in doing a miniature, they can finish it in three days. That's the thing you want, for you are about as long in painting a picture as she is, & that of course is most necessary to make it profitable. You have an opportunity that she never did & one that would benefit you more, could you learn it, than any-thing else. And another thing to be considered is, you would make money & then, you might swear for it, you could have your pick at beaus, & whether you are on the wrong or write side of fifty, it will make no odds; for money you know is much more marketable than beauty. Not but that you have thousands of the latter, yet it wants a little of the former with it by way of an 'anchovy.'

I expect you will answer this.

Ever yours,
W. C.

These thoughts and urgings on getting married, which William pursued with all good will, will not have done much for his sister's depression. It still holds her in her next, written toward the end of February:[43]

Dear Mother & Co.,

I thank you for your letter, and wish it was answer'd. If it is an invariable rule that a bad beginning makes a good ending, the concluding period of this epistle ought to be fine indeed, for I am at this moment labouring under all the dejection of spirits that a recent fit of sickness must naturaly produce–a sickness occasion'd entirely by the evils that hang over me and weigh me to the earth with irresistable force. Nothing would have induced me to write at this time but the certainty that I should never get a better unless I did; and if you don't write something to amuse me before long, I feel as if I should soon be in my grave.

If thou canst 'minister to a mind deseased' without knowing in what way it is suffering, do so, if you love my life. And to think of communicating the will of which I speak by letter would be as much impossible for me, as to exist much longer under the accumulating sufferings to which I allude, without some-thing to arrouse my soul from the deadly lethargy in which it has so long been encrusted. Don't say 'come home,' for from that sad sound I turn with as much disgust as a sick person would who has just swallowed a dose of salts from some good friend who is standing over him with a dose of oil, to see how he likes variety. For at home I only stay, I don't live; and here I live in misery; and, strange as it may seem, of the two evils I think the latter the least. I have tried home and find it too homely to bear the idea of seeing it for any length of time. Solitude that once was my delight would now send me to the shades; and, of all the solitary places, yours is the most so. I no longer blame a person who has it in their power for rushing into dissapation to drown reflection. 'Tis the best cure, and the first plan that I should adopt, did my circumstances permit. I am confidant my mind must be debilitated or it never could be sunk to such a pitch of dejection, so deep that with my utmost exertions I cannot raise it an attom if I might save a world. I have endeavour'd to do so long enough, and shall now give up the chase. If you can, 'tis your duty to do so.

Do you recognise in the foregoing part of my epistle the least trace of a disposition by nature gay and lively? And do you think 'twill ever recover its natural tone? I begin to be completely discouraged at the somber hue it is taking. I never was constructed to exist in a gloomy atmosphere and, unless the clouds and 'darkness visible' in which I am at present enshrouded disperses, I pray that I may myself disperse. I very often think of Mrs. Lee's question to Sarah when she was dying (tho' I laughed when I heard it). I now think it was not so very much out of the way. She asked her as she was suffering 'if she could forgive her for creating her.' I think if the same question was put to me now I should say No with my whole soul, for anihilation is changed of late and, as mind and matter is condemn'd to mingle in this sublunary state, the spirit suffers with its vile associate.

If you think this letter of distress worth answering, and as you boast so much of your skill at guessing, I will be eternaly obliged to you if you will guess at the variety of ills that surround me, and send me a dose that will lay low spirits as deep as their victim. But in your guessing don't miss the mark, and I fear 'twill be impossible to hit it unless I give you some clue. And that is not my intention.

Do you believe it is possible for a person to alter their fate, do you think they have any control over their own destiny?–and that, tho' they appear to have been instrumental to their own unhappiness (blindly so, of course) that they are really to blame for being so? I think the sufferings occasion'd by another is nothing to those we bring on ourselves, or at least think we are the cause of, if we find that, had we acted differently, we should have been much happier and that the cause of actions that we lament (when too late) was in consequence of not having a friend to advise us. But perhaps I should say, one who could but would not advise, would be speaking with more propriety. For I think this is my case at present. Don't suppose that I have been guilty of a crime. I have not. I have only acted in an affair of consequence as I wish I had not, and repentance, as it always does, has arrived too late!

Your account of Halsey's marriage set my risibles in motion. I am sincerely glad that he is at last settled for life, and think with you that if he is properly managed he will make a good clever ourang-outang sort of a husband, and should suppose it would require precious little manneuvering to get along smoothly with such a lover of the fair sex as he is by nature. By the by, I think your New London girls must be pretty hard-run for husbands, to snap so greedily at anything of the masculine gender as they do. I think *I* should prefer more difficult subjects to excersize my matrimonial talents upon than many of your newly made husbands in the Land of Steady Habits. Mary Ann [Mason] told me the last time I call'd there that Halsey call'd on her as he passed through New York, and said he would certainly come and see me, but he knew beforehand I would not *have* him, and to come for no purpose would be folly. I think if his wife gets the right side of him she will soon find out how the *torpedo* is to be managed; and I sincerely wish her success. . . .

Night before last we all attended the theatre for the purpose of seeing the very celebrated play *Cherry and Fair Star*, and the more celebrated actress Miss Kelly, of whom you must have heard before this. She is in truth a most astonishing actress and facinates the attention of the audience to a degree I never saw equal'd. To the greatest versatility of talent is united the utmost ease and grace. Her form is fine and commanding and her dresses always adapted to display its symmetry to the utmost advantage. She is so perfectly concious of her superior talents that she acts as if she scorn'd her spirit that could be moved to act to anything. In *Cherry*, her dress is a very becoming hat, a green velvet frock trimened with gold that stops just above her knees; from them, a flesh colour'd knit pantaloon tighter than the skin, that closes at the ankle and is met by a red morocco shoe. Her legs are so much admired by the gentlemen that it is quite a common saying, 'Have you been to see Miss Kelly's legs?'

The scenery of this play is the most beautiful I ever saw: a splendid car descends from on high in a cloud. It contains the queen of faries, and as soon as it strikes the floor she steps out of it and is instantly surrounded by a train of sylphs with their golden wands, while a beautiful little rascal of a Cupid, instantly catching up her transparent train, supports it while she harangues the sylph-like forms that surround her in true fairy style. Nothing in nature can be more beautiful than the wings of gossamar star'd with gold and the light flaxen and golden ringlets that that float over them, while the beautiful faces of the faries are turn'd toward their queen as she gracefully waves her wand in the air. Miss Brundage, the sister of Sandy's wife, is a *real* fairy, and when she personates one she is something more than mortal. Her star-spangled scarf floated far in the air by a wind that was introduced for the purpose of raising their gauzy tapestries and giving me my death of cold; and it accomplished its purpose to a T. I have scarcely breathed since.

As I am writing about spirits of air I think I must give an account of a sea-serpent I have lately been painting in Miss Northam's album. Although I do not belong to the family of sea- or land-nymphs myself, with my Way & Champlainish-constricted carcase, yet I have been so fortunate as to create a sea-nymph that has astonished myself as well as evry beholder with her surpassing loveliness. She is delicate, even to fragility, and their is a fairy lightness in her appearance as she sails through the air (for you must know I have just brought her up out of her coral caves, glittering with shells, to show herself and make a speech during her aerial tour.) She has coral in one hand and in the other a rozy coloured shell 'which ever and anon is wildly blown.' She has a face of perfect beauty and her light drapery I have tinged over with all the colours of the rain-bow. As I take it for granted her caves are illuminated with all the rain-bow's dies, I have made bold to reflect them on her light and flowing robe. Perhaps you will say that green drapery would have been more in character for a sea-nymph; but 'tis impossible for me to cloath an aerial being in anything but the most transparent gauzes.

I have attended many parties this winter, all of them very splendid indeed, but Mr. Cowdrey's surpassed all the others in point of style, as they always do. I think much of that family, as I have received more delicate attention from them than from any other family in New York except the one I am with, and Mr. Mitchell's—no disparagement to others, either. I have never received a slight from any person to whom I have been introduced by Mr. or Mrs. Fitch. On the contrary I have experienced every attention from them. If that was not the case I should never have troubled them with my presence again, as I never experience the least coolness but once, and that but for an instant. True, there are some poor pitiful pimples on the blotted forehead of creation which death would hardly think worth gathering, as Sandy says; but with reptiles of this description I have little to do, and if I was dying in a ditch and they passing me in a triumphal car I should feel I honor'd them by deigning to cast my eyes on them. As far as mind is above matter, or as far as the heaven's arc above the earth, so far superior do I feel myself to such hogs, and should continue to feel the same, through every change that the fickle fool Fortune should, in the greatness of her folly, compel me to pass through. My soul abhors such vermin, and yet how large a portion of the human race are composed of such base materials.

I cannot avoid smiling at the pevish and irratable manner in which I have expressed myself. It partakes strongly of the disposition of a person who is neither sick nor well, a state in which I have for some time felt myself.

You desire to hear what I have to say respecting Mrs. Hayden. If I can muster life, soul, and memory sufficient I will tell you. She, or rather he, took a house in the upper part of Broad-Way a few weeks previous to the Lafayette ball and Hayden's departure. The family who let the house resided in part of it, and the Haydens had been but a fortnight in the house before Mrs. Proudfoot, their landlady, asked Hayden to advance her twenty-five dollars' rent for the purpose of buying Miss Proudfoot a dress for the La Fayette ball. You know Hayden. Without a moment's hesitation he produced the money (not so, his wife). She was disgusted at the request and perhaps show'd that she was so. I think it's most likely. From the moment this affair took place their was a visible alteration in the manners of the family, tho' nothing was said or done by them before Hayden's departure that was absolutely rude. But the day after that event took place, 'the landlady of France' began to cut up her didos. You know how a person can go to work that is determin'd to quarrel. She let no oppertunity slip of insulting Mrs. Hayden, who was determin'd to take no notice of it unless she was too grossly insulted to avoid it, which was at last the case. The hussey sent her black wench up to Mrs. Hayden's door with mud for her to place it on the sill–which command she faithfully executed, and added to this pretty action the most blackguard language.

It was at this last act that the 'lion was roused.' Maria came out of her room and, catching hold of the beast, she gave her as sound a drubbing as her fair hands could inflict, with a promise of another as soon as she had got over the effects of this. She heard no more from them that day; but the next morning as she sat ruminating on her forlorn situation and thinking how she should ever live without Hayden for three years, Wallace enters. She of course would conceal such a low scrape from every one and accordingly endeavor'd to appear as usual, and endeavor'd to banish the whole affair from her thoughts and face. As she was struggling to regain her composure, a constable enter'd (without even the cerimony of knocking at her door) with a writ to take her to [the city's] Bridewell [jail]. Now of course the affair must be made known to Wallace. She told him and the constable the whole affair and they both said she did perfectly right if she had even kill'd the wench; but still the fellow with the writ must discharge his duty, which was to take her to Bridewell. Wallace, who you know is a limb of the law, instantly rose and said that Mrs. Hayden should not go–that he would see to it and appear for her, and, bidding her good morning, he follow'd the man to Bridewell and settled the affair.

It was now of course necessary for her to move instantly; and the next week she return'd to Bellvill to her parents, and I have never heard a word from her since. This account she left with Mrs. Fitch. I was at my school at the time and never saw Mrs. Hayden except the time I mention'd to you just before the ball. Don't you think it a second Tilyan scrape? I am afraid that woman will get herself hung at last, tho' I have no doubt it will be in a good cause. Yet still, it will be paying rather too dear for her whistle.

This from Eliza, with its detailed and emphatic paragraphs at the commencement which describe her state of mind, produced an instant reaction from both her mother and her aunt, in the same mail and, by a long follow-through, still more after a week. The series are **nos. 176-7-8** of March 10th and 16th. They make plain to its depth the framework of values which gives shape to their lives. Let Betsey speak first:

My dear Eliza,

I felt it my duty to leave every branch of business in which I was engaged, and turn my whole attention to your case, hopeing to work a cure through the divine blessing. I shall not be particular as to the manner in which I express myself. So that it is but understood, I care not, for it is for no eyes but yours. We have rec'd your lamentable letter and note the contents, and have hit upon the only plan that we think can reach your case. 'Tis true, it is possible that the balsam may not prove efficacious enough to produce a perfect cure, when applied, but it is our opinion that it will if you will only suffer yourself to be persuaded to perform your part–without which, nothing can be done in order to accomplish it.

Now I see your potatoe-holes a foot deeper than usual out of pure fear that the dreadful words, 'Come home,' will be the proposition. That it is, and nothing worse. Of whatever nature your present troubles may be, let me inform you that you are sick, and all this hypochondriac gloom and dejection of spirits proceed from a quantity of bile upon your stomach that, exclusively of any other cause, is alone sufficient to give everything in life a sombre shade. This I know from experience and observation; this must be removed before you can be essentially better. I have seen the time that I have felt all that you express and more than any language, tongue, or poet's pen could express, and longed for death more than for any hidden treasure every instant of my life. This was bile upon the stomach that sunk the spirits to the lowest ebb of dejection, that produced all this train of dreadful images, posessing power to make us loath life.

Now the best and surest method of effecting a cure is this: I have inclosed a ten-dollar bill for the purpose of paying your passage to New London, but to stay just as long or as short a time as shall best suit your own feelings, with the belief of a perfect cure being wrought into the bargain. Surely if your natural affections work half as hard as mine, you will be ready to set out in the first packet that offers, and the thing may be put in execution immediately, if you will consent. You say you have lately recovered from a fit of sickness. Then you must of course be in a debilitated state, and as health is the greatest blessing in life, on which the happiness of both body and mind depends, it is highly necessary that you lay aside all business for the present at least, untill you have regain'd your health; and by this means your late trouble will insensibly lose its dominion over you and your spirits will return.

Then it appears you have sent a challenge to our guessing powers, and yet refuse to meet us half way. This is placing us under great disadvantages and imposing as hard a task upon us (without the aid of inspiration) as the King laid upon the Magicians when he commanded them to tell him the dream he had last, and then its interpretation. Could you imagine we were up to it, I should call this 'being Up-to-snuff Miss Way.'

Many things at the commencement appears to us exceeding wrong, and we often repent the steps we have taken (although done for the best); but after a while we are made to see that it was the very best thing that could possibly have happened to us. This too I have proved, and more than once, and have heard others remark the same. If your present affliction proceed from either of the causes I think most probable, you cannot reasonably blame Mrs. Fitch or any other friend for not giving advice, even if solicited, in a matter so important and in which your happiness was so deeply concern'd. I confess I should not have dared to have done it, had my advice been requested ever so ardently. Your letter expresses to my comprehension no other meaning than either consenting to marriage, or having given a final dismission, and all who has offers must do one or the other; and let it be which it may, 'tis right it should be so, perhaps, in the termination. You observe, 'To think of communicating the evils of which I speak by letter would be impossible.' If this is the case, I intreat you to come home for a short season, at least long enough to inform us, since you have excited not an idle but an anxious curiosity that seems to heighten the distress. Change of scene, I should suppose, was indispensible to this crisis, and a sail from New York here, I have no doubt, will have a salutary effect upon your system.

And we are not so coarse as you may immagine. You must not judge by our former appearance and style of living. The house is newly painted inside and out and the floor of our keeping-room painted and carpeted, our manners much improved since you was here. I cannot say quite so much in favor of our youth, beauty, and accomplishments as I wish I could–and keep truth in view. I hope, however, you will have the opportunity of judging for yourself before many days, and I have no doubt but you will like us better upon a more mature acquaintance, as Mary and her beau flattered each other they should; and I have a variety of instruments that sooths many a dull and tedious hour. Perhaps your enthusiasm might be eloquent enough to answer in these words:

> 'What is music to the ear that's deaf
> Or scepters to the dying wretch.'

This language is strong enough to suit your step, and of such was the whole of your letter composed.

'Tis unfortunate for yourself and friends that you are such a sensitive plant. You say, 'At home I only *stay*, and here I live in *misery*.' Which of these two modes of existence seems least wretched to the rational mind? I should not hesitate to say the former. Staying seems merely to express a dormant, humdrum state, which I should suppose any one would prefer to real misery; but I hope yours is but immaginary. I should not be afraid to bet a thousand pounds that we can laugh you out of your spleen and your 'gay and lively disposition shall recover its natural tone.' I have two or three paintings I very much wish you to see: one is my masterpiece and I wish you to bring with you *Mary Queen of Scots* and your *Sea-Nymph*, and as many more as you can conveniently bring.

I understand Mrs. Lee's question to Sarah in a different point of view from you entirely. I receive it in this way: that from Mrs. Lee's knowledge of Sarah's being in a carnal state, or state of nature (that is)–not a believer–[she] thought possibly the darkness of her mind proceeding from ignorance of spiritual things might naturally, from her suffering, produce an effect of this kind; for it is very certain that the stronger our faith is in God, the more we become resign'd to His will, as resignation is the fruit of faith. It is the believer alone that sees, with clearer views than even common reflecting minds, the hand of a higher power acting from motives the most wise, merciful, and benevolent in creating us. The parents ought not to take either blame or praise upon themselves for being instruments in the hands of God to bring others into existence. Marriage is honourable, and was in the first instance a heavenly institution.

[Follows here Cowper's *The Time-Piece* (lines 161–78), as above, **no. 40**]. . . .

This inimitable piece from Cowper is a more appropriate answer than anything I could offer, and speaks my sentiments more fully, which are of the same tenor. Do you reccolect Sarah's answer (to a question never put to any child by a mother but hers), 'No, Mah.' It appears as though she had her reason in full exercise. Though ignorant of religion, she was equally safe in regard to a future state, but could not experience that joy at the approach of death that is enjoy'd by the believer.

You have earthly friends who have the will but not the power to help you, and who are suffering daily for you; and this want of power clearly proves where our help lies (I hope you are not ignorant of this). It is often-times not in an arm of flesh to perform so great a work. There is nothing short of the most poignant distress that will bring us to Him who is all-sufficient to help us. Let the case be ever so deplorable, He is adequate to all our wants, and when that time comes we never petition in vain. 'Ask and ye shall recieve, knock and it shall be opened unto you. Blessed are the poor in spirit, for they shall be comforted.' Believe this and take courage.

Still, it is our duty to do all in our power to produce health, and good spirits will of course follow.

Now let me beg you not to give a refusal to the plan I have proposed. But if you are determined and it as as hard for you as you have signified, and if the nature of your late trouble seem to require your immediate presence there, let me know. I would not for worlds add a new affliction to that I am endeavouring to remove. But keep the enclosed, for, as sure as you return it, I shall have the trouble of sending it back. I only wish it was in my power to send fifty times as much, but alas! 'my arm is hampered,' or I should often have done it before this. I intended filling the sheet but Will'm has called and is waiting. I intend next week to begin another letter and a longer. Come if possible, and let me know immediately your intentions.

E. C.

Mary is writing, but I had not time to copy it. . . .

These last words, in a postscript, lead into the following, of the same date (**no. 177**):

Your letter which we rec'd last night reminds me of a certain king of Babylon who sent for his magicians and commanded them to tell him the dream he had forgotten and make known the interpretation thereof. The task you require of me is no less unreasonable or impossible, and would require a second Daniel to perform. It seems (from what I can gather) that I am to 'administer to a mind diseas'd' without knowing the nature of the disorder; to find out a secret you are determined I shall not discover, and to offer my counsel and advice in a case of which I am wholly ignorant–tho' both would be entirely useless, as you say the deed is done and cannot be recall'd. But these little incoherences no doubt the occasion will justify, neither should I scruple to contend with some few triffling impossibilities, were it probable my exertions would be in the least beneficial. But, according to your statement, this is not to be expected; therefore I shall not at present exercise my guessing talants, as I feel no disposition to pry into your affairs unnecessarily or endeavour from mere curiosity to discover what you are determined to conceal.

With regard to the past, I can only say I am sorry you have made yourself unhappy or done anything you have reason to repent. Had you been scruplous, and advised with your friends, you might perhaps have acted differently. But why waste words in vain regrets? Let us rather modestly enquire what is to be done. Is there no remedy? Would not a different mode of conduct remove the misery you have so much deplored? Or has the decree gone forth, according to the laws of the Medes and Persians, that altereth not? You who know the circumstances can best judge whether it is alterable–whether the nameless deed, whatever it is, may not be undone. This is the question; and you would do well to consider it cooly and dispassionately.

We often say it is impossible to do a thing merely because we are not inclined to do it. It may require some exertion or perhaps some little sacrifice which pride forbids. 'To err is human,' but to confess an error is something more. The pride that objects to it, is meaness, and ought to be dispised and kicked out of company. Have you been guilty of a fault, own it, and it is more than cancell'd. Have you hurt, injured, or rendered any one unhappy (beside yourself), it is both your duty and for your interest to prove that sincerity of your repentance by making reparations to the utmost of your power. If the injured party is not perfectly satisfied with this–nay, if they don't think ten times more highly of you than before–they are not worth a thought, and well deserve the injury they have sustain'd, be it what it may. But on the other hand, your conscience is clear and you have no reason to reproach yourself that you have given unnecessary pain to anyone or disturbed the peace and happiness of others. If the action you lament with its effects is confined to yourself alone, be thankful, and rejoice that you have not a partner in affliction. In this case, 'twill soon blow over. The wound will heal and all will be well again.

You say it is no crime. Then 'tis a matter of but little consequence. Of course your sufferings cannot long continue. Surely you are not so silly as to grieve for triffles, and indulge dejection at such a rate for any length of time. There's pith and marrow in the old saying, Never cry for spill'd milk. Why torment yourself to no purpose? If the thing can be recall'd, set about it at once, and may success attend you. If not, e'en let it go, and make the best of it. Perhaps it should be so. 'Act well your part, and leave the rest to Heaven.' No doubt good will come of it. We are not competent to judge of actions and events, with thier remote and final consequences. We experience trials and misfortunes, but know not the blessings they contain in thier effects and tendencies. The result is in futurity. In short, we see a part and not the whole. 'Tis viewing an infinite picture. Many things seem wrong which, when it is compleated, disappear, and the ignorant unskillful eye that was before offended now is charm'd. Let us wait for the finishing touches–all will come right at last. The Hand that held the Pencil cannot err.

Don't you think I am very good to write so much (and I fear to so little purpose) upon a subject I know nothing about? Take care of your health. This is the best advice I can give at present–when you recover that, your spirits will return. Fear not that I shall offer you a dose of 'castor oil.' Your mother will perform this friendly office, and I wish her arguments may induce you to swallow it like a good Christian.

Will'm has call'd for our letters and I have only time to say adieu.

Mary Way

And last, Betsey's more considered, longer response (**no. 178**):[44]

Dear Eliza,

I should have fill'd my last letter but was prevented by frequent interruption through the day, being determined if possible to dispatch it by the first mail after the receipt of yours. When Will'm came for my letter I could scarcely prevail on him to wait for the finishing touches, as I suppose the mail was to be closed directly.

The more I read over your letter, the more I conceived it my duty (if not to advise) to say what I think I should have done were it my case, yet fearful of the consequences of doing even this. You know it is so handy to have some-one to lay all our errors and misfortunes to; but if you are accommodated, I will endeavour to put myself out of the question. I confess I thought of proposing plans in my other letter that would not (in such an important matter) have wounded my own conscience to have put in execution, and that I am pretty confident is yet practicable; but your unhappy Touch-me-not disposition and railing traits made me abandon the idea altogeather. For instance, 'I have said it.' You must be blind not to be struck with the likeness: these definite decisive determined resolutions and expressions, your manner of pronouncing sentence, partakes somewhat of the spirit of the Medes and Persians in the execution of thier laws, that altereth not–this, and this alone, forbid it.

But after all, I may be as wide from the mark as the poles are asunder, in understanding the nature of your case. Every-thing in nature ought to have a name, or we cannot discourse with ease. By what name will you permit me to give your disorder? Well, since we cannot afford it any, let us for argument sake say it is something of this nature: having consented to marriage, but after that dreadful monosyllable yes was pronounced, there arises doubts and fears or some cause for a change of mind. Ought you not to communicate this circumstance to the one principly concern'd, and not, through a mistaken delicacy, conceal it, and commit a greater error by setting your seal to the destruction of both parties? I think you ought.

On the other hand, to reverse the case, if you have unadvisedly or involuntarily given Mr. Blank (he shall have a name if it is at my own expence) a final dismission–with a well-riveted emphasis, I warrant you, according to your general custom–I should suppose it by no means impossible to revoke the sentence, and think I should not scruple to do it if I considered that my happiness depended upon it. Now comes the Touch-me-not again, flying into one's face and eyes, scratching as it goes (perhaps you are sensible, hope indeed is included in these words). In the first place, does he support a good carracter, is he worthy of a recantation? If so, and your principle motive in giving a dismission was founded on pride in regard to his property being insufficient to support you in stile, I think it was an error, and ought to be revoked.

You certainly must know your own views in discarding him; therefore persue that path that reason points out, nor yield to fancy alone, if in opposition to your better judgement, for it will be found wanting when weighed in the ballance with the cardinal virtues. . . .

It is my opinion that the sentiments here exprest [in a poem by Betsey here omitted] are appropriate to every individual that have arrived to a state of maturity, nor can they be strangers to the truth it contains. Fear is one of the most tormenting passions that ever posessed the human mind; but how to divest ourselves of it, 'there's the rub.' There is, however, one blessed antedote against it: that is, resignation, when we are so happy as to attain it. In fact, that is a cure for every malady both spiritual and material. Indeed, it is a blessing to be desired above all others, for in that, everything is included. It posesses a devine influence to convert every-thing to good, and from reflection we trace its origin. Faith–firm, unshakable faith–conquers our fears and produces resignation. Perhaps (notwithstanding my natural flow of spirits) there never was a person that has suffer'd more from this evil than myself; yet we may in some measure arm ourselves against it by putting our reason into exercise, believing that every-thing is in the hands of a wise and good Creator who will eventually turn all things to our advantage. Nothing contrary to this belief can do justice to a Perfect Being.

If a letter so wrapped in gloom and tenfold darkness could have admited of a smile, I think that part that exhibits Miss Kelly's legs would have excited one, as also the bare idea of such a woman as Mrs. Hayden's being sent to Bridewell. Although there is a little smattering of tragedy about it, I believe she is a 'Truth of a Nag' when engaged in a good cause. I admire her very much; but we must all fight our way through the world as well as Mrs. Hayden.

The *Temple of Friendship* has gain'd you great applause, and 'tis impossible to help laughing to hear the groans re-echoed round the room among the female class gesticulating as expressive of thier admiration and astonishment, as if they were in perfect agonies. It is certainly the most beautiful piece either of your's or any one else I ever saw or ever expect to. Mrs. Parkin, Mrs. Parker and Mary [?Parsons] who senses the fine arts very slightly was enraptured with it and, after one of them had seen it, the others came on purpose. A number has enquired for it; but it never fails to excite a general *groaning*. I show my pity by laughing in thier faces. You say you would not do another for ten dollars. I positively would not, if I could, for a hundred. I took the liberty of sending it up to Sally, and she took a greater, to lend it to Doctor Swift's family for a short time. It however was returned without the slightest injury and has not been out of my desk since but to be admired at home. The Swifts and Whistlers gave it its full share of praise. Mr. Whistler is a complete amateur,[45] and to hear him converse upon the fine arts is meat, drink, and pretty good cloathes, and the greatest performer on the flute I ever heard except John Raimand; but Mary willl not give him up for all she ever heard in New York. Mrs. Adams, Mr. and Mrs. Whistler spent the evening before Thanksgiving with us and he brought his flute and she sung, and of all the soft melody I ever heard it excelled. Mary and myself were invited to spend the following evening with them and in the evening we all went over to the Doctor's, and a very agreable visit we made, I assure you. But Mary will at a future time give you the particulars.

Last week Mary Goddard made her appearance, whom I have not seen before for three years. She enquired affectionately about you and wished very much to see you. I told her I was greatly in hopes of your coming on this spring. She wished she might have the pleasure of seeing you once more as she expected to be in town some time. Mary appears more like her mother or grandmother than like the Mary Goddard we once knew. She has been very much engaged in religion within four years. She tells me she has become a member of the Presbyterian church in Stonington. She has been a private teacher in General Williams' family for the four last years.[46] She is at present at her uncle Hezakiah's, where she expects to remain about six weeks, and then calculates to return to her mother and sister. I forget the place of thier residence. But there is one great objection to her returning: she tells me the principle part of the people are Socinians, and she is under the necessity of renouncing her tenets if she joins them, which is almost an insurmountable bar to her returning. She observed to me at the door that she had a plan in her head, but did not explain anything more. I am of opinion that it is to live with them, if she finds it agreable.

You observe, 'You are sure that you can suffer more exquisitely than almost anybody you are acquainted with.' Too well I know this, and it is to my 'eternal wo,' as our cousin Natty Payne would express it; and as well I know that such a sensitive plant ought to grow in the shade like a toad-stool, obscurity is the only safe soil for an immagination like yours. But it is your opinion after it has once inhaled the sunbeams of prosperity, then to transplant it into its native soil, it could no more take root and flourish but would wither and die. And this your own words prove: 'Solitude that once was my delight would now send me to the shades.' But is there not a degree of enthusiasm in the idea? St. Paul left us an example worthy of imitation, who observes that in whatever situation he was placed, therein he learnt to be content. However, we are not expecting to obtain that victory ourselves. That must nesessarily result from inspiration; but [I] would modestly suggest that it is not putting our reason into action to insist that our stations in life shall bow to our will, or run frantick because they will not be so complaisant.

So in these three long letters the religion, psychology, philosophy, poetry, and medicine of Eliza's mother and aunt, compounded with much tenderness, were applied as balm to her distress. They help to explain something important in the present chapter of her life; but they belong also to her times; for there is more than comfort to be read in what her elders had to say to her. With peculiar candor, because of the circumstances of the moment, they express thoughts of peculiar import in their world–thoughts by which they actually tried to live–and by proofs scattered through the correspondence it can be shown that these were not eccentric; rather, quite representative of their period and place. Sometimes small clear windows give a better view of the past than more historiographically conventional big ones.

Plate 1.1 Polly Carew

Plate 1.2 Baby
(2½ × actual size)

Plate 1.3 Reverse side of *Christ Rejected*

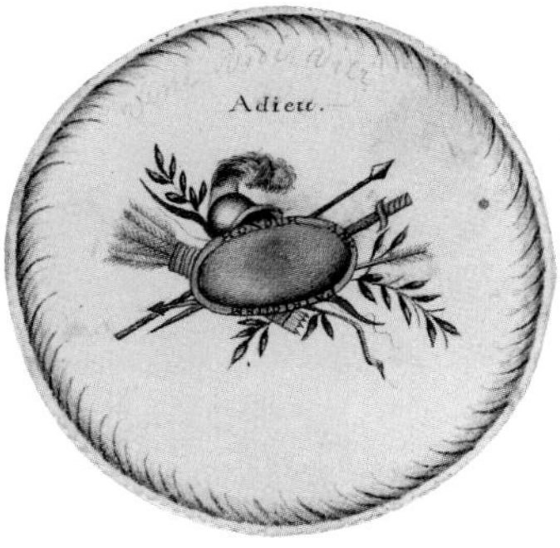

Plate 1.4 Eliza's *Veni, Vidi, Vici*

Plate 1.5 Eliza's *Iris*

Plate 1.6 *Mourning for Washington*

Plate 2.7 Charles Holt

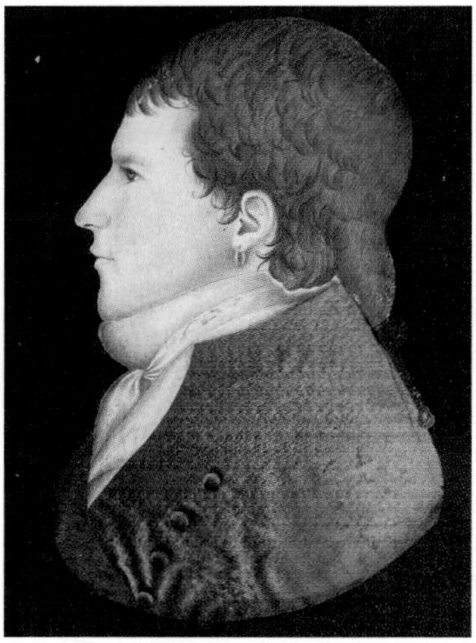

Plate 2.8 Giles Holt

Plate 2.9 Pardon Tillinghast Taber

Plate 3.10 Betsey's Unknown Sitter (2× actual size)

Plate 3.11 Betsey's Self Portrait

Plate 4.12 Betsey's *Christ Rejected*
(2 × actual size)

Plate 4.13 Dunlap's *Christ Rejected* (detail)
(Art Museum, Princeton University)

Plate 5.14 Aunt Hannah (enlarged)

Plate 6.15 Eliza's *Fancy* (reduced)

Plate 7.16 Eliza's *Sterne's Maria* (reduced)

Plate 7.17 *The Temple of Friendship* (enlarged)

Plate 8.18 Edward Cort Riley (26″ × 29½″)

13

Eliza Up, Down, Home, and Engaged

"*The dark hour has pass'd*," Eliza announces to her aunt and mother (**no. 179** of March 21, 1825). Whatever agonizing thoughts had plagued her in the previous months had disappeared–where? She offers no explanation; rather, a note of apology in her description of her despair, of having written as she had, of her decision to put those thoughts in the mail at all:

> . . . So you think that nothing but a beau could have produced such mental suffering as I have endeavoured to describe. This, I alow, might be true if I had ever lov'd; but when indifference was return'd for the aforesaid article, 'I thank you, no sir' twice repeated, you must suppose that our business was settled to a fraction, and not only so, but that it was done in a very business-like style. Not but that I should have said Yes if I had felt that way enclined; for, as I believe I have told you before, it is not my intention to say No! if I had rather say Yes! You know I have all my life been surrounded by 'single blessedness,' or in other words 'blessings in disguise,' and, as the slight shock of one marriage in the family has not given me a very keen relish for matrimony–for if I could have put in my ore[=oar] at the time the publishment was read, I think I should not have hesitated to forbid the bans–so all these things taken into serious consideration, you must alow that I have not had a very fascinating taste of either. If I have an offer that I like, I shall accept it, not else! And thus I close the first lesson. . . .

Here she inserts an elaborate picture of a dream she had had (though Way-Champlain visions generally seem too good to be true) before she reverts to the letters she must answer. They are not much to her taste–her mother's irritating because,

> In the first place, Mother, I don't like to have religion poked into me. I have plagues enough without the plagues of religion, and fear that if I should get that, I should be dished for life. It is, I alow, a very good comfortable kind of thing for a parsle of

> snuff-taking old women to mix up with their tea–and no disparagement to it, either, for I positively have the most profound respect for it. But then, it is our last resource, you know; and when I think I have come to my last prayers I suppose I shall turn to it. But deliver me from gloom, and I am sure that I never could be religious and cheerful, for the idea of the thing always brings up the grave and its frisky worms!

As to her Aunt Mary's sympathies and counsels, she finds them too rational, and "there is no being on earth I hate like Madame Reason."

> But I am much obliged to you for your letter, tho' you have not hit the nail on the head. I only wish 'twas longer and had a little more sugar in it. The cause of all my late sufferings is not removed, and I can no more account for the life with which I answer to your epistles than I can account for many other inconsistances in my character. I feel at this instant in tolerable spirits, without the shadow of a reason for so doing, and in mercy to you both I write before I am visited by another troop of Blue Devils.
>
> If there is two words in creation that I hate, they are 'genius' and 'sensibility'. I have heard them harped upon till the sound sickens me. I think I have enough of the former in my composition to enable me to do great things if I could be seperated from this accursed diffidence; but they are so intimately woven together and measure in such exact proportion, one to the other, that nothing less than the strength of Sampson could seperate them, and *united* they *cannot 'stand'* and accomplish very much, I greatly fear. I have struggled long and hard to seperate the wheat from the chaff, but to no purpose. Sin and misery are not more intimately link'd to them than these two things, or more impossible to seperate. Of sensibility I have not much to boast, for I don't think that acute feeling is always a proof that it exists. If it is, then dumb animals may often be said to possess the spark of devine light, for we often see them lament the death of their companions. But a truce to such dry stuff, or rather wet stuff, for I know not a more moist article than this same thing that is dignified with the name of sensibility.
>
> Speaking of genius and the like reminds me of something I should have forgotten else. Who do you think I saw last Sunday in church? No less a personage than your genius [John Raymond]. He sat opposite to us over Mr. Mitchell's head. He appear'd in all the glory of rags. At first I did not recognize him, but when I found his large dark eyes sparkling from under the 'shaggy pent-house' of his eye-brows, rivetted on my face with a recognizing expression, it instantly flashed upon me that I was undergoing the scrutiny of perpetual motion. 'Lord' can be stamp'd on any clay, but inspiration can only be impressed upon the finest metals. . . .
>
> I got seated next a gentleman the other night at a party whom I have frequently seen in company, and who has made many an unsuccessful attempt to converse with me; but nothing more than a monysyllable could he ever extract, and not always even that. At first he hesitated about talking at all, but at last, seeing the necessity of the case, he made some triffling remark which I answer'd, and made another in return (if you will believe me). Encouraged tho' evidently astonished, he commenced

a conversation which was sustained with considerable spirit till the party broke up, which was two o'clock. But before I proceed, I must tell you that the gentleman in question was a doctor, or he never would have succeeded as he did. You know I am by nature attached to doctors and lawyers. As we walked home together, he told me how agreeably disappointed he was in my character—that he had no idea I had one particle of vivacity in my composition, but from the specimen I had that night given of what I could do, he was perfectly astonished that I hid my light so completely under a bushell. All this was said in the most polite manner, in the most elegant language, and not at all as I have expressed it. I soon found from the run of his conversation that he had always considered me a dull, cold, phlegmatic, indifferent character, and one of all others to which I have least claim, for I detest it.

'But have not learn't the painful art
To smile above a broken heart.'

And the slight flash of animation I that night exhibited was entirely owing to skillful maneuvering on his part to draw me out. As soon as I saw what he was about, I was determined to come out, that he might not this time labour in vain; and accordingly I rallied all my forces, and tho' they have been dreadfully depressed and cut to pieces in my three years' siege in this satirical land, I succeeded much better than I had reason to expect. We both enjoy'd ourselves, I know, more than the dancers. Now, don't suppose I am in love (for I know you will). The gentleman in question has been engaged more than a year to a lady who is celebrated for her wit and beauty. He is about thirty-five, his manners and appearance much in his favor. . . .

Sam re-enters the correspondence at this point in the course of responding to recent bank legislation and advancing himself at the same time through one more appeal to Oliver Champlain:[1]

Dear Uncle,

On the 5th of July last [i.e., 1824] I obtained a situation as clerk in the Mechanics' Bank in this city through the influence of two friends who are clerks there and references which I gave to 2 or 3 gentlemen that are acquainted with me here, as well as the one you had the goodness to send me at the time I endeavoured to get the same place in the Franklin Bank. My situation in the Bank will be a permanent one if I can obtain one thing. You must know that in all the banks in N. York the clerks are obliged to give bond for $5000. It is a new nominal thing but it must be complyed with. My salary at the time I went in was but $400 per year, which is the salary always given to a new (or as the cashier terms it) an *assistant* clerk; but at a meeting of the board of Directors last week I was appointed check-clerk with $600 per year.

Mr. Fleming (the cashier) then asked me if I could give him the names of my bondsmen. I went in the afternoon to Mr. Sam'l M. Fitch (perhaps tho' you don't know him, but Aunt Mary can tell you who he is) knowing him to be a worthy man, and he immediately offered to stand as one of my sureties. Mr. Doyle where I lived last year would have stood as the other if I had been in any other bank in the city, but, having a most bitter enmity to one of the directors (Mr. Allen) for some political reason, he would not. Henry Holt would if the bank would take him but he is a man not sufficiently well known.

Now the object of this letter is to get another bondsman. Don't you think Mr. John Hallum or George Hallum or some gentleman that is known here would lend his name for that purpose? If you would have the goodness to procure (either of them), you would confer a lasting obligation on me. They both know you, they knew my father, they know me, and they know there never was a Champlain or a Way that ever sold himself or forfeited his honour or ever will, I may add.

Adieu. Yours ever truly,

Sam'l Champlain

The bond is $2000 each. Please write me as soon as you can, that, if they neither will, I may get some one else.

P.S. Give my love to Mother and the rest of our family.

A space of some weeks again interrupts the correspondence, and only in May is it taken up, partly by explanations: a run of illness at the New London end. The opening of Mary's note to Anna Fitch (**no. 180**) is lost, and the first full sentence of it is headed in characteristic fashion by lines from Shakespeare (*John* 3.1.74f.):

'Here I and sorrow[s] sit. This is my throne!
Let kings come bow to it!'

–an arm'd-chair by the fire-side which I have not left this winter, obstinately refusing the kind solicitations of my friends. I have not made a single visit or been out of the house except Thanksgiving day (when I was compell'd to go) since last fall. I spent a few weeks with Mrs. Lee, where they treated me with music and read to me night and day. But (as there is allways a draw back on felicity) she has Martha's portion–busy and troubled about many things, her time divided between care and company, works of charity and hospitality, a continual round of company which to me is unpleasant–tho' I had a room to myself, admiting only those I chose to see. Yet Mrs. Lee would not leave me alone even for a moment, to amuse me or to please herself. She and [her daughter] Eliza must be with me continually, and I felt I had no right to deprive others of their company; and those attentions which, while I staid, were paid to me allmost exclusively. So, having promised to consider it one of my homes, and return again when I should feel disposed, I left them, and come to pass the winter here where I can be more retired.

I shrink from observation, and in society my feelings are distress'd. Common-place carracters disgust me. I dread nothing so much as the company of indifferent people, the stare of idle curiosity or the gaping pity of the crowd, which, rather than submit to or endure, I would prefer eternal solitude. A few select friends only are admitted to my presence. Mrs. Lee and Eliza visit us often; the latter reads to me, which is very gratifying; and I regret she has not more time to spare for this purpose as she is an excellent reader–one of the best I ever heard. Her manner is particularly pleasing, which, with the mellow, full yet soft and varied tones of her voice, produce the combined effects of reading and music. Besides this, she is a girl of uncommon sense and acquirements–of course agreeable, as well as useful in the capacity of reading. But bad weather and other engagements prevent her coming as often as I could wish. She call'd here the other day to introduce Miss Perry (sister to the Commodore) who is on a visit to the family, and come to offer her service to read to me. Mrs. Starr also proffered hers, and many others who, tho' they sometimes read a page or two, generally find ample employment for thier tongues without the aid of books. I ought to feel myself obliged to them because they try, and really think they do, amuse me.

Such are my present comforts and such my future prospects! Patience is all I ask–is all I need. And you, my friend, whose condition is far more enviable–even you will surely find (especially when you read this letter) that patience is certainly the most necessary of all Christian virtues.

Adieu! . . .

Similar in its report of illness, this from Betsey (**no. 181** of May 9th):

Dear Eliza,

How are you at this time, and how is your spirits? I could no longer forbear writing, though I have nothing to say, and 'tis painful to write in this case. Mary and myself have been sick, is the principle reason I can give for not writing for such a length of time. Mary has had the influenza all winter, and has not been out of the room since last Christmas. I have been so fortunate as to have escaped that evil but am afflicted with a very weak back which I am confident is the rheumatism, and the jaundice for company. I am taking dandalion tea for one and violet for the other complaint; yet notwithstanding all this, have been getting very fleshy and am in pretty good spirits.

Thus far I conclude I have entertained you to your heart's content, with our own infirmities, and now for my neighbors.[2] Your Grand-Mah S. Way has had a paralytic stroke about three weeks since. She was expected to die immediately, but is like to recover. I suppose Will'm has informed you of the death of your Aunt Prudence Prentice. Mrs. Tracy went to New York last Wednesday to gratify Eliza who had sent for her repeatedly, but much against her consent. She, being determined to compel her to go, wrote her she had taken a house for one quarter. Mrs T. expects to suffer much with home-sickness and to [ret]urn at the expiration of the quarter.

It has for some months been [re]ported that Uncle [Pardon] Taber and family intend returning to New York to settle and keep a boarding house–that is, Uncle [Jonathan] Starr call'd here some time in the forepart of winter and observed that he had rec'd a letter from Brother Taber, which mentioned that Mr. Coit, his new son-in-law, had persuaded him to take this step.[3] This to me would be a very pleasant circumstance, were I an inhabitant of the place. . . .

Betsey closes with some quite forlorn requests for news from both her New York children, who have been silent too long; and William a week later reinforces what she says:[4]

> Mother has been beging me to write you this some time, to know the reason of your silance. When you receive this I hope you will write immediately, as it will be a relief to her. Can you tell me any-thing about Sam? What he is doing &c? I have not received a letter from him these some months nor is there any prospect at present. If you can give me any reason why he behaves so, I should like to have it verry much. I know of no excuse for him after his promise so fairly that he would write Mother regularly, & she has not received one since that. How does he employ his time when he is not in the bank?–which is not a verry small portion, as the bank opens at 10 & closes 3. At these times I should think he could just drop a line to let Mother know how he is.
>
> George is the same. I have not had a letter from him in a year. Where he is or what he is about, I know not–only the last news we heard from him. He was with a company of players, in what capacity I know not. . . .

–and William then closes with some words on the Lyme (Connecticut) and New York Champlin-kin.

These reminders from New London did the job, and Eliza now answers promptly (**no. 184** of May 18th):

> Dear Mother & Company,
>
> Your last letter has arrived and should have been immediately answered according to your request, if it had been possible. Total silence has reigned so long in the East, I began to think 'twas the order of the day, and in compliance with your desires have observed one as profound. I am happy to be undeceived. Nevertheless you have lost very many bright ideas and much good sense and many an edefying epistle by this (apparently) churlish or capricious silence; for you know, on such occasions, I can always 'be Up-to-snuff Miss Way.'
>
> I am very sorry that illness in the family should ever prevent your writing, for I look upon it [as] a most impertinent intruder, an imp that ought to be bastinadoed. Your letter gave me the first information of a death in the family, and if I could with truth say I am sorry, I would say so, as it is the least we can say in a case of the kind; but as a friend to the deceased, I say I am not sorry. Life must have had precious few charms for her and, when that is the case, 'tis of little consequence to us how soon we make our exit. She possess'd a larger share of enthusiasm and was in my opinion by far the best of the bunch. You know I am not much attached to the Champlains. I have too much of their blood in my veins to boast of an extremely affectionate disposition, and there are few out of the pale of 'Aunt Hannah's old church' (that is, out of the Way side of the house) whose death would inflict a very severe pang. This is the language of truth and soberness, tho' it may surprise you. You know I speak

plain English when I talk on this subject, and as 'tis not an agreeable one we will if you please change it.

I have just finished a miniature for ten dollars, and one hundred would not have been any compensation for the martyrdom I have suffered in taking the likeness. 'Twas for Miss [Caroline] Northam, and in the whole course of my life I never met with so hard a face before. I have taken nine different faces and spent two and sometimes three days upon each, and all without the least shadow of success; and on this I am resolved, that if ever I meet with so hard a face again I will instantly abandon it and never murder my eyes and my patience again as I have in this case– no, even tho' I should receive one thousand the instant 'twas completed. I would not attempt it for 'twould be no recompence. I would have given much that this likeness had been good, for I like her and her father more than any two people with whom it has lately been my lot to associate.

I have seldom seen a man in my life who possess'd the talent of inspiring affection in all his friends (without one solitary exception) like Mr. Northam. I think it must be the eloquent manner he has of expressing his love for all in our house that has taken such firm hold of my feelings, and I would bundle the most of my relations in a heap and set them adrift for the sake of having him in their stead. He is, you know, the brother of Mrs. Shearman–many years older than herself and not half so handsome. He is quite grey and rather corpulent, yet notwithstanding all these disadvantages I have taken a monstrous liking to the cut of his jib, and wish with my whole soul that he would move to New York. He did talk of it but is now engaged in building a steam-boat at Newport and will of course abandon that scheme for the present, if he ever should put it in execution at a more remote period. He told me if I would go to Newport and make them a visit I should paint a family piece for him, and should not want opportunities of taking the most elegant views Newport affords. To this tempting offer I could only thank him, as I should never think of accepting it.

As I am speaking of those whom I like, I think I shall go on and give a description of another paragon of perfection of the masculine gender whom I have seen since I had the pleasure of seeing Mr. Northam. This is no less a personage than the former governor of Ohio, Ethan Allen Brown.[5] He has always been intimately acquainted with Mr. Fitches family, and as he passed through New York last week on his way home he was of course invited to dine here. He came, and since my residence in New York I have not been so charmed with the conversation of any gentleman as his. He is a man of very great talents and has the reputation of it. His information on almost evry subject is very correct and extensive and, more than all, he possesses in an eminent degree the happy talent of communicating his knowledge with the utmost eloquence and ease, and in such a way as to banish every other thought from your head while you are listening, tho' the subject may be of the most trifling nature. I have frequently heard of the talents of Brown and was prepared to see a demigod. I am not disappointed. His person is tall and commanding, his face tho' not strikingly beautiful is nevertheless of the first order of fine faces, and there is a fire in the quick facinating rays his fine eyes send forth that would alone class him with a superior order of beings. And this most elegant man is a batchelor! He has too much mind to marry (you will say), and perhaps you are correct. He has studied the female charracter, I could discover, with the persevereance of a person deeply interested in the study to which they applied themselves; and yet he insinuated that woman, lovely woman, was an enigma after all!

His address is very handsome, 'he reads much, he is a great observer, and he looks quite through the deeds of men.' He overhaul'd and critisized all the poets from Homer down to Byron, and you must think he possessed the gift of gab in a wonderful degree to be able to accomplish such an Herculean task in the short space of three hours. He is not quick of speech–on the contrary, slow. But he comprehends much in few words, a gift much envied by your Speaker and possessed by very few.

As I said before, he acknowledged woman was to him a riddle, but however well or ill he may have been treated by that riddle, his admiration of them was evident not so much by the words he uttered as from his manner of uttering them. He pretty quick saw into Mrs. F.'s character and I could discern an ill-suppressed smile in his expressive countenance at the soreness she exhibited on the subject on which she feels most sore, the 'rights and priviledges of woman.' This was a fine field for her to defend their rights, and I assure you she fought like an Amazon–she fought with a zeal worthy of a greater cause, at least. 'Tis strange to me that a woman can have so much of the 'doublet and hoes' in their disposition as to become almost wretched because Dame Nature chose to call them the weaker vessel. I think those two lines of Burns should reconcile them to their lot if nothing else would, when we consider the truth of it–

'Her prentice hand she tried on man,
And then she made the lasses.'

For my part, setting aside some few inconveniences attending my enitiation into the class of weaker but more perfect vessels, I think I prefer the feminine gender. Nature in making me woman has offended me less than in anything else she did when mixing up my composition; for in truth 'tis a queer medley. She intended me to get along through life by my own exertions, and the hussey never threw in one simple ingredient that would enable me to do so, while, to those who are not obliged to fight their way through life, she gives the very talents that are necessary for doing so; and this, to them, is as great a plague as my want of them is to me; for, because there is no necessity of their fighting their way through life, and they possess the aforesaid fighting talent–and as whatever talent we possess must come out–they fight all who come within reach of their tongue, for the exersizing of their otherwise useless talents.

As we all have a sore place somewhere about us, and as this is my sore spot, I was insensibly led from the subject I was upon, to this. If it had been better handled I should pass on without apology. As it is not, I shall say Pardon this digression–'tis not well, 'tis only feelingly done.

To return. The governor was all humility and submission while the storm was venting its rage, and would now and then adroitly draw his smoothing plane gently across the parts most deeply inflamed, by way of an anchova soothing the fretfulness at which he could not but smile. He said that Pope had very clearly pronounced his own sentence in railing at our sex as he had, and that it would have been much wiser at least for him to have held his tongue–that he did not think there was any difference in the capacities of men and women except what was in favor of women. He thought they possessed finer feelings than men, that through life he had observed (and I know he has observed criticaly) that the sensibilities of females were much more exquisite than that of males, and, in short, that they were by half the better part of creation.

This was so well done that the bait took. He perceived it and went on with his birds'-egging. He made angels of light of us, tho' we are sometimes devils incarnate, and that, in such an artful manner that even your friend Anna, renown'd (and justly so) for her acute penetration, did not perceve that he was administering a dose of Congress for the purpose of clearing out a small quantity of bile, at least. I have no doubt but that was his intention, for he seems to have the ultimate good of his fellow creatures at heart and never administers a dose of anything without first tempering it with honey or some sweet-meat so that the patient can seldom discover that they are taking a pill. I should like of all things to take a dose of salts and oil prepared by him, for I need them both, and I know if prepared by his skillful hand that they would set on my stomach.

As I was walking through Broadway last week in quest of a spring hat, with one upon my head which would come under the denomination of shabby-genteel, who should I see comeing towards me but two of the last people on earth I should wish to meet under such circumstances: two dashing officers, Hayden and Johnston. My first thought was to give them the go-bye, but I had unfortunately caught the eye of both before I had presence of mind enough to put this magnanimous act in execution. So, seeing the necessity of the case, I for once in my life resolved to make the best of a bad bargain and carry it off with the best grace I could (not but I should have been glad enough to see them in more stylish garb). Accordingly we marched up front to front and, after a most cordial grasp of the hand on all sides, I rallied my forces and made the necessary enquiries respecting Mrs. H., the children, &c. But not one word of answer do I reccollect, tho' I appear'd to be listening with all the attention in the world; so you will get no information on this head. I knew that Hayden had rather see the devil than an acquaintance who did not look as rakish as *he* always does, and, as I said before, *I* did not.

He was quite friendly and extremely polite–said he was in search of a box, and as soon as he got one should expect me to visit them as usual. I thanked him perhaps somewhat coldly, for at the instant all the Hayden horrors rose in review before [me] and I believe blanched my cheek; for the sensations to which the recollection always gives rise are sufficiently acute. But to conceal that they did so, I threw as much indifference into my countenance as I could assume on the occasion. He seem'd desposed to pay me a compliment, but, as he could not make out without my assistance, I lent him a hand. Why Eliza, said he, you look–you look–. And for fear that another 'You look' would follow on the heels of the two preceeding ones, I hastily added, handsome! and wished them good morning. Thus commenced and thus ended my rencounter with the two most noble Captains, and I have never had the honour and supreme felicity of beholding either of their pretty faces since.

About a fortnight since I receved a summons to Huntington, Long Island, forty miles from here, to teach painting in a school. The terms were liberal and nothing but the paltry engagement I have at present with Glover would have induced me to decline their proposal. Honour not profit obliged me to stick to my text and fulfil an engagement from which I shall reap no benefit in comparison to the other. My disappointment was great but 'twas to be so. Mrs. Fitch transacted all the business and told me that the gentleman said Newtral-Tint sent him for *me*. . . .

At some point late in the same month or early in June Aunt Hannah suffered a fall of some sort or a stroke, unreported in the surviving letters; but her degree of recovery is explained to Eliza by William a few weeks later (**no. 185**). She was now eighty-six:

I received yours this evening. The reason of my not writing before was because there has no material change taken place. She has been rather better for two days past than any time since the accident, even so much so as to hitch along several feet from the bed without assistance. Her senses have also returned, excepting at times she is a little wild. Her speech is not as unintelegible as it has been and upon the whole she appeared more natural, more like herself than any time since the accident. Aunt Mary is constantly with her, proving the friend in need, although Sally and the rest in the house pay all possible attention. We have heretofore had watchers, but she is so much better that she requires none. Aunt M. sleeps with her & that is sufficient for the present. She is verry droll at times. She is much addicted to saying, 'I am a poor miserable kreeter,' and was saying it for the hundredth time at least when she got stuck and could get no further than 'I am a poor.' Sally to help her out adds, 'miserable kreeter.' 'Yes, & so are you,' quick as lightning added Aunt Hannah.

Betsy Allen was here the other afternoon, &, standing by the bedside, Aunt H. was viewing her gown very attentively when Betsy asked her what she thought of it. 'Why, she thought it was a remarkable peaceable looking thing.' She has over-much irrational stuff, proving 'her mind's diseased.' When the accident first happened it was painful to be in the room if she was moved, her screams were so agonizingly piercing. She is a woman that has suffered very little pain during her long life, & to have such acute pain come upon her in her old age is indeed tr^{re}ebly distressing, as she is a mere child & cannot bear it with that firmness & patience she once could. However, she is now so much better that she is moved & can move without any screams, for which I am very thankfull, & probably (from present appearances) she may linger out a month or two. Longer than that I think she cannot, for her advanced age appears almost to preclude the fact that she has lived through what she has. She never could unless her constitution had been of iron, which she used to say was owing to her pruddant treatment thereof–which no doubt was a great assistant.

There is no news worth telling you, here. Anna Starr (she that was Anna Morgan, the English family, and who some time since married cousin Jonathan, Junior) died yesterday. She was worth at her marriage about $20,000 dolls., given her by her deceased uncle & aunt in England. Jonathan Jun. (when they first returned from England, which is three or four years since), hearing of this rich cruizer, determined to make her his prize if possible. This money, it appears, was so willed that she could not possess it untill she married a sound Protestant Episcopalian & also had her mother's approbation. Jonathan Jun., & in fact the whole constellation, is body & soul Episcopalian. This was the verry thing. Well, as they so well mated in religious matters, it would have been truly unfortunate if there had been any disparity in purses, which, 'praise be blest,' was not the case; for cousin Jonathan Junior, you know, was a remarkable economical young bachelor, & he was not the less so as he advanced in years (of which he has seen *41*); so that at his marriage he was worth about the same as his wife, viz., 30,000. They were married, not before, however, old Mrs. Morgan had made cousin Jona. sign some written obligations to liberally educate 2 of her sons (for the old fox was determined to receive some benefit from so large a portion, of which she was in fact the main-spring in procuring it).

Well, the old woman after their marriage completely won Anna to her side–that is, she made Anna forever bore [= nag] Jona. to assist her family more in the luxuries and grandeur of which she had so largely partaken in former years. This was more than our poor cousin could bear. He had performed all he had agreed to, & much more. Things took a sudden turn. He quit & boarded with his father & she quit & boarded with her mother. She soon began to decline &, though he often called to see her, yet she grew worse & worse. There was no visible bodily disease, yet she faded; and, as we have no physicians that can cure 'a mind diseased,' she yesterday was divorced & weded death. Thus the old saying that Mother has so often fastened upon my mind came in play. 'Money is the root of all evil.' Would I could finger the root!

In haste, yours,
W. C.

In **no. 186** of July 20th, from Eliza, paragraphs of news alternate with those declaring her unchangeable character, for better or worse, and her renewed depression:

Dear Mother & Company,

In the hope and, from your silence, the belief that Aunt Hannah is better, I now write. Your letter was a great gratification, and it was my intention to have instantly replied to it; but the unprofitable labour of finishing off my scholars' pieces for them, to go to the country during the month of August, has employ'd every instant since the fourth of July, which was the day on which I received it, and 'twas all the treat I had for the day, for you must know 'tis thought monstrously vulgar for those who call themselves ladies to partake in the slightest degree of the amusements of the day. A short gown and petticoat–and that, dirty, if you please–will be sure to distinguish you from the common herd, who always make it a point to put on their best bib and tucker and sally forth on this joyful occasion.

Now, as I have a warm affection for everything that presents itself in the form of independence, I hold in utter contempt the absurd practice of the genteel part of the community, and tho' I always have and while life remains always will lay claim to the title lady, still, I shall never resort to this method of supporting it, and always think more highly of those who pay the utmost respect to the day than of the others who clothe themselves in filthy rags. So, out of pure spite and malice I always make it a point to dress myself as well as I possibly can on the fourth. A gentleman who knows well my opinion on this subject call'd for me at ten in the morning to go and see the troops. The heat of the day prevented. He then asked if he should have the pleasure of escorting me out in the evening, to which I assented, and after tea we went out as far as the Arsenal to see the rockets and fire works at Vauxhall, which I assure you were splendid indeed. . . .

Mrs. Fitch will once more see you in the flesh. Don't laugh at this fifty-thousandth alarm. I am <u>sure</u> 'tis not a false one. They have long talked of visiting Newport and as New London is in the way, 'tis their intention to honor it with a call. So prepare yourselves to see Mr. & Mrs. Fitch, [her mother] Mrs. Northam, and [her daughter] Cornelia the paragon in the month of August; and for fear you should not know Mrs. F., 'tis necessary to tell you that she has grown twenty-eight years younger than she was when you last saw her, if dress and disappation can effect such a change; for no other measures have been taken, and she is the alter'd woman I tell you from the comparatively humdrum Mrs. F. . . .

I don't know whether I have told you that she has commenced going to riding school. You must know that this [?]*Die Vernian* accomplishment is all the rage. The ladies are all crazy about it. But whether 'tis the beauty of the riding master, the enormous sum which he has for teaching, the desire to display their pretty feet and ankles (and for ought I know their 'agillity' to boot) or what the plague it is, I cannot find out. But they all of them act more like a parcel of fools than like rational creatures about it. Mrs. Corset-Makers & Mrs. Mantua-Makers are going by the dozens, and I expect nothing but Mrs. Tag-rag-and-bob-tail will close the procession; and after all the fuss I don't believe that one of the whole scrape will sit gracefully in their saddles, for I never saw but one lady in my life that did, and I have seen millions ride. This equestrian exercise is so little in accordance with my studious habits and mode of existence that I have never yet honor'd them with my presence at the Circus, tho' I have been repeatedly invited. I cannot boast much of my 'agillity', and as my Way and Champlainish gambadoes would never make any market, I don't think I shall go this trip and twitch. If the sprains with which both of my ancles are now encumber'd should ever go down and I should become independent, I don't know but, for the sake of popularity, I might be induced to get my neck broke. Nothing else would have sufficient weight with me to make me mount a horse.

Have I told you that our [church's] top-not came down some time ago? It happen'd on a week day; for if Mr. Mitchell had been in the pulpet he would have got crushed to atoms. The whole of the ceiling tumbled from over church and injur'd the pews so much that the church was obliged to be closed for six or seven weeks. In the time, the New-Jerusalemites had the politeness to offer us the use of their church which used to be our old one till ours could be repair'd. Mr. Mitchell accepted it with gratitude and prayed most fervently for blessings on their heads; and I believe the trustees made them take all the collections that were taken during the time that we occupied it. [Samuel] Woodworth and Riley's family are the firmest pillars of it. The first Sunday after our church was open'd, it was honor'd with the presence of Mrs. Hudson, Miss Ellen Tooker that was, and I expected nothing but to see our ceiling fall again to pay us for the honour of her company.

The miniature of Charles Clinch has just been brought me to dress the hair in more modern style, and here he lies scowling defiance at me as I write. He looks in the last stage of a severe cholic. I suppose you are yet uninformed that this most eccentric of beings has at length espoused the widow bewitched, Mrs. Allen, alias Mrs. Walters. The last time I heard of their love affair he was breathing anathemas against her ladyship and swearing by all the gods he would as soon marry the devil. If 'age could wither her' or 'custom stale her infinite variety,' of course she would not now be Mrs. Clinch–unless 'twas as his mother, for which her age much better fits her, as she is about forty-five and he about twenty-five. The net her ladyship has spread for him she has been some years weaving and, if the material of which it is composed proves strong enough to hold him to the end, I shall be glad, as the die is cast. But, like old Mother Culberson, 'I have my doubts.' Time which destroys most women's attractions passes without injury by the adamant of hers. How she has contrived to work her card so admirably I know not, but believe it is a talent that lies only in the breeches of widows bewitched.

That most eccentric chap Sandy [Clarke] has at length realized a fortune and of course, tho' his crimes were of crimson and scarlet die, they would become as wool or as snow. His society is not only tolerated but courted by this most vilinous world, or at least that part of it (and they are by much the largest part) that scorn'd him in diversity. If he has two atoms of sense he will now repay their scorn with interest. *I* would.

I am sorry to tell you that I could not get you such a plate of ivory, or even half as big, as the size you sent, if I would give my life for it. If such a thing had been possible I should long since have been in posession of it, as I have wanted it enough to take Cornelia on. I never have seen the painting you describe but have heard from the multitude the highest encomiums on it. Inman however don't approve it, and of his judgement and taste as an artist I have the highest opinion, from what I have heard. I should like much to see it notwithstanding all that he has said.

Your account of Aunt Hannah is a strange one. As to her dislike to be thought old, you know 'tis a family disorder and therefore not so much to be wonder'd at; and in fact they never do think they are out of their teens till they are at least half a hundred. So rapidly does that impolite old gentleman Time fly with them. Now, as 'tis the practice in this family to teach children that they are old people, I begin to think myself in my dotage and feel as if I had number'd Methuselah's years. Tell William to give no more slaps at Aunt Hannah's constitution–'iron constitution,' as he calls it. I think she has naturally a good one and, having good sense, she has neither unnecessaryly abused it by carelessness nor kept eternally swallowing drugs, to the eternal woe of herself and those around her. I think 'tis rather a sign of a delicate constitution to not be able to take so much medicine, than to swallow fifteen thousand drug shops and then live through it all, to all eternity. Such a constitution as this will beat hers all hollow in point of strength, and I would not be obliged to live with such an one for the wealth of Croesus.

I have scarcely room to say that I had a call from Captain Hayden and his wife day before yesterday. They have lived in town since the first of May and, owing to the illness of Emma and her having no help, she has scarcely been out of the house during all that time. She look'd handsomer than I ever saw her in my life and appear'd in better spirits, or else I fancied it, because she looked and talked as if she had a soul in her, which I assure you is now a treat to me. She tried to make me promise I would come and spend three or four weeks with her, but, tho' I should once have jumpt at the invitation, I should not now think of such a thing, after the 'Hayden scrape.' She talked much of you and, after bidding me good-bye and quitting the door, she returned and, grasping my hands with so powerful a hold as mashed my fingers to a mummy, she said, 'I long to see your aunt and the moment my babe is old enough I intend to go.' 'Twas well this speech requir'd no answer, for if it had, devil a bit could I have return'd.

You ask when I have seen Sam. I sent him a note to come and change a check for me, which he instantly obey'd, and that was much more than I expected.[6] To sum up his character in few words, he is a sort of crack-brain'd Champlain (if ever there was one of the name that was not), and therefore we must not be astonished at any caper he may chance to cut up or at anything he may please to do except it should be the slightest exhibition of common sense. That indeed must make us stare!

You ask how are my health and spirits. The last are in that apparently torpid state that feel blunted to all the freaks of fortune (and the imp don't spare me), and the former is keeping them company. 'Tis a morbid and very cross state of health–but of that, you are by this time sufficiently well aware. But before I close, I would once more remind you that it don't take many questions to put Mrs. F. out of tune, so look to yourself and act accordingly. She detests Yankee curiosity as she terms it.

Adieu–adieu–

Eliza C.

At this point, toward the end of June or the first days of July, Aunt Hannah Way died.[7] It is strange that no word of the fact, no word of mourning or shared sadness, survives from the months after her death.

The Eliza-letter of July, at least in its ending, and others that were still earlier, with their complaints, now draw from Mary a protracted fit of impatience, dignified by the verse-quotation with which it begins (**no. 188** of August 18, 1825). At several points words have been lost through damage to the page, and hortatory parts have here been much shortened:

'Methought no living thing could be
So weary of the world as me,
While on my winding path the pale moon shone.'

My dear Eliza,

What's the use of lamentations? I am ten thousand times more tired and sick of the world than you can be, or I express, and have as many reasons why I should more heartily rejoice to leave it. Indeed it is the only thing I can think of with pleasure, and the only pleasure that ends not in disappointment or disgust. For some time, my spirits have been so depress'd as to render me incapable of the least exertion. To write required an effort it seemed impossible to make, a task I had niether inclination or resolution to perform; but your last despairing letter has rous'd me once more to action.

'Misery loves company.' Why do you complain? What is the mighty evil you deplore, that I have not experienced? Nay, countless millions have endured the same before we had existence, as well as at the present day, and will till time shall be no more. From the beginning it was so. Trials and afflictions are the common course of nature. We have a taste of pleasure by way of contrast, that we may realize and feel them still more sensibly. In the morning of life, love and friendship smiles around us and the world appears a paradise; but soon the scene is changed, our increasing knowledge of good and evil by degrees disolves the charm; e'er noon, the vision's fled, our blissful Eden vanishes in air! Like the first parents of mankind, expell'd from this ideal paradice into a world of tumult and disorder where storms assail us from without, and furious passions rage within, more fatal to our peace, like them condemm'd to tread life's rugged flinty path, to till the ground from whence we came, that yields us thorns and thistles–to labour for a scanty pittance to satisfy the stern demand of nature or eat the bitter bread of slavery and dependence–or, if you please, solicit the cold hand of Charity to prop a crumbling clod of earth that soon must mingle with its kindred dust!

This is a true picture drawn by an honest pencil that knows not how to flatter. . . .

Would you be happy, try to make others so, govern your temper, restrain your wishes, limit your desires, say to these restless billows of the mind, 'Thus far shall't thou go, and here shall thy proud waves be stay'd.' Take Young's advice:

'Chain down some passion, do some generous deed,
Teach ignorance to see and grief to smile,
Or with with firm faith and confidence devine
Spring up, and catch fast hold on Him that made thee.' . . .

You don't express even a wish to see us. Absence has wean'd you from your native place; you have, as it were, become a stranger to your family. You say little of your business or prospects, and we know nothing of your affairs except that you are in trouble; but of what sort or kind, we are not even permitted to guess. Is this indeed the self-same being, once so mild and gay and chearful? What has wrought the change? Your letters gives us pain as well as pleasure. They show a mind harrass'd with cares and torn with conflicts, and remind me of Collins' ode to the passions, with Graham's supplement to boot. I hope, however, when they have all played thier parts and had thier frolick out, Dame Reason will resume her sober sway. . . .

Tell my dear Mrs. Fitch I will answer her letter as soon as I can muster spirits sufficient for the purpose. When I stood in need of consolation, while sitting by the death bed of the guardian of my youth (all the mother I ever knew), this kind and friendly letter came. But it is not the first time the writer has given me comfort in affliction.

And now, my dear Eliza, what shall we say–what arguments can I use to prevail on you once more to visit your humble peaceful home? Your case requires change of place and scene. The quiet you may here enjoy would, I think, compose and tranquilize your mind. We will try to please you and make your visit agreable, be it long or short. Did you only know how much we wish to see you, you could not be so obstinate and unpersuadeable. But we will take no refusal. . . .

August 30th   Since this letter was written, we have had the pleasure of a call from Mrs. Northam, Mr. and Mrs. Fitch and Cornelia, unexpected indeed but not the less welcome. Mrs. F. did right to take us by suprize, her reasons were good, lest what should happen, and another disappointment insue–tho', had we rec'd previous notice, anticipation would have lengthened the pleasure and given us time to prepare rooms for thier accommodation, at least more to our satisfaction. But I know thier friendship and goodness will excuse all deficiencies in this respect. It seem'd but a moment, it vanish'd like a dream! I can scarcely realize that I have seen them. Only two days! But were it two months, when past, 'tis all the lost, the shadow still remains, a visionary something. . . .

Once more a letter has been lost, in which William in early October reported on his mother's sudden serious ill-health. Eliza's reaction was panicky, and he tries (**no. 190** of the 14th) to calm her down:

Your letter I have received this evening & shall answer it immediately. Mother has much improved since I last wrote you. Doct'r North has been very attentive & with the attention of all her friends she could not lack for every attention possible. All I ask is that none of the human family when sick may have less, for by such attention she has gained fast. It will be some time, however, before she gains sufficiently to get about again, & I hope if Sam has got any feeling he will (if necessary) send her something, should she want it & he is able.

I wrote Sam a letter by the same mail that I did you, informing him that Mother was sick. But as I don't get an answer in return as soon as yours, I have reason to think that he will treat that with the same regard that he has all my my former letters (viz.) with silance. However, I can better tell by tomorrow's mail. Should I not receive one then, I will write again to him & inclose it to you so that there shall be no mistake; for perhaps I am censuring when I should not. He may have not received my letters & that be the cause of his silance. If he is silant after he hears of her sickness, I would not give one damm for his gratitude, his affection as a son or brother, or his relationship. I would spurn him should I meet him in distress. May my fears be unfounded & may there be one son who has some natural affection.

I will write you every mail-day, which is three times a week (viz.) Tuesday, Thursday, and Saturday, so that you will get them Wednesday, Friday, and Sunday mornings, as that is the time the mail arrives in New York after it leaves here. Should she grow worse, I will give you the earliest notice. But from present appearances she will continue to mend, I humbly trust. You are altogether wrong in letting this alarm you so. She is not verry sick & that, I told you in my first letter. But by the extravagance of your letter one would suppose the person at death's door—a place by the by where we must all go by, and enter, for that matter. But though death should not take her now, die she must & if she is call'd now she has no more deaths to die—a comfortable thought, come to think of it, for I have often envied some of my friends, to think they have gone through with the job & left me (almost alone, as I then felt) to plod in sin & misery how many years God only knows, this miserable life, and then sink lonely to the grave. There is a comfort in being sick at home, for to have our friends & acquaintance about us when we are about to quit this stage, to cheer us to the tomb, is something verry comfortable & something that I most sensibly feel, although I have been but a few miles from her during my life.

However, I must now quit & tell you that I will perform what I have promised in this letter, above. Therefore don't be uneasy, but attend to your affairs as usual. Recollect, she is better.

Good night,
and God bless Mother.
William

This indeed brought his sister's anxiety to a tolerable level, for which she is thankful (**no. 191**):

Dear William,

Your Monday morning's letter restored the senses that your Wednesday morning's put to flight. I never was so frightened in my life; for from your manner of writing I did indeed suppose Mother 'at death's door,' so take care how you scare me so to death again, for I would not suffer again what I did between Monday and Wednesday for the universe. I devoted the time that I speak of to packing up my goods and chattels in the most crazy manner possible, and in such way that if I had gone with them as they were fix'd and as I expected to, I should unquestionably have smashed everything that was smashable and ruined all my paintings to boot. I had

> nothing to do but lock my trunks and step on board the steam-boat, if your last letter had said she was worse.
>
> My affairs here are all at sixes and sevens, of course. I did not write a note to Sam as you requested because he is in ill-health, and I know that the information would do no good. Whether 'tis the confinement in the bank and his not taking proper exercise, I know not, but he is evidently in ill health. He is very thin and very sallow and has a melancholy expression. I met him in Broad-Way last week walking with a young gentleman, and if he had not bow'd I think I should have pass'd without recognizing him. So if you write to him again, take care how you speak. He is not at all communicative, but I know so much as this from what he has said: that he is as far from happy as any of us, and while this is the case you will not expect letters, for *he* don't choose to make a song of it, and *I do*. For I find that setting troubles to music lightens it. Don't let Mother see this, for the world, as I would not let her know what I have said about Sam for a triffle. He told me a great while ago he was going to quit that duce'd engine that will kill him if he don't; but I understand he is still attached to it, and that may be the cause of illness.

Betsey's illness moved rapidly to an end. On October 25th, she died at the age of fifty-four: so says her headstone. In a letter of condolence to William, Anna Fitch excuses Eliza's not returning home now: it could only increase her grief; and in another note, Samuel has heard only that the end is approaching, and deplores his inability to attend his mother's deathbed. William was prompt to supply Sam with the full account of the decease such as people of those times expected and wanted:[8]

> You probably have heard of Mother's death by Mrs. Fitch or Eliza (I wrote the former). She died last Tuesday morning at half past eleven o'clock & Aunt Mary & myself determined to keep her as long as possible, hopeing that you and Eliza would come up before she was buried & you would have the consolation of seeing her (if consolation it is) for the last time. I felt deserted to walk almost alone–that is, the nearest female relation to walk with me was Aunt Dolly Way. She has been a most excellent friend throughout her sickness & so has Aunt Sally Way & Mrs. Lee & Mrs. Jonathan Harris particularly, and Mrs. Charles Culver who has lived with Mother in the same house for two or three years & feels in her death all she could for her nearest friend. In fact, she seemed a universal favorite. Whoever knew her felt a loss in her death, & those particularly acquainted, her old friends, felt more than I should believe any-one but you or me could feel. However, death has removed her to the grave and personally she can be no more any joy or sorrow to any living.
>
> I should not forget to mention that Oliver Champlain has been particularly kind throughout her sickness. He has sent her oranges & chickens &c (things necessary in sickness), often besides attending her as much as once a day regularly, & she was verry fond of him, as he was an old friend and she could converse with him freely. North who attended her while sick said he did not know she had so many friends untill he saw so many and all anxious to wait upon her and assist her.

She would often call me by the bedside & make me sit down & hold her by the hands for hours, with many an endearing expression, though spoken in agony, for the last day & a half she could only speak in whispers & when she spoke it seem'd like seeing a person with an ax pounding at a distance. We see the motion but the sound comes afterwards. All that was agonizing she suffered. I had her by the hand the day before she died &, turning her eyes upon me, she says, 'W'm, do you see how disturbed I am?' It was for breath. Her forehead has been covered with beads of sweat, as cold as death, from difficulty of breathing & the rattling in her throat was most distressing to hear.

Poor soul, how often I think of it. But there is a 'luxury in woe.' I would not but have been where I was and seen what I have seen for worlds. I once thought that if Mother died, I should die. But reason has had its weight–not but I feel a startling loneliness when I think of it, and especially when it comes night, to sit by poor blind Aunt Mary & Nobby Payne (Nat's widow) by the fire-side, and each feeling too bad to speak. It's lonely. But I expect to feel her death more sensibly when I want her help, for she had been a friend indeed to me. Nothing but what she would assist me in, if it were possible. How much she has mourned that you and George would not write her, & write oftener than you did. But she will mourn no more on earth. I have no more time to write at present, but will when I have time give you a full account.

And to his sister William did send a full account (**no. 197**):

Dear Eliza,

Your request for me to give you the particulars of our mother's death I will comply with as well as I can. Two weeks ago yesterday she gave up, although she was verry sick for a week before. Yet, as she never would yield heretofore until she was completely exhausted, it was so in this case. When I went down to see her that evening (as was my custom) I found her sitting in an arm-chair, verry sick and low spirited. She requested me to call upon Mrs. Lee & ask her to come down & advise with her. It was Mother's intention to state her case to Mrs. Lee & she state it to the doctor her husband, and then they were to act according to his prescription. This was because of her dread of a personal interview with a physician, a dread which she and poor old Aunt Hannah had been troubled with from their infancy. I was aware that this was an imperfect way of attempting a cure; yet as she anxiously insisted upon it I intended complying.

When I returned home to tea I mentioned her illness to Aunt Sally and gave her an outline of how sick I thought she was. She determined to have a physician that night, and I was nothing loath. Accordingly after tea we called upon Doct. North and took him along with us, he having always been a favorite of hers, you know? When we arrived (Aunt Sally being call'd by the way) she was still in the arm-chair, without a light, and I, knowing her nervousness and that she would be agitated to see four of us, & among them a doct., spoke as easy as I could–that the doct. was with us. But she was verry much agitated and (as they had procured a light) I saw she changed her colour, while in a rapid and confused manner she was giving him the particulars of her feelings, poor soul. I then almost repented that I had brough him down. But it was so.

He questioned her for some time and examined her anckle which was much swoln, inflamed, and verry painfull. After he had made what enquires as necessary he tried to rally her spirits, but all would not do. She could not be made to smile, which was somthing new with her, especially where there was so many to cheer her. It was what I considered an ill omen, from that time, as I had never seen her so low in spirits before. After a while he bid her good night and went home. When he had gone, she fainted from exhaustion and being somewhat alarmed, though before he left she told him to have a bed brought down the next day and put in the front room (which was accordingly done), as she was going to have a fit of sickness.

That night (before she went to bed) she overhauled all the draws &c, putting things in order for the event (as she thought) but in fact displacing every-thing; for she was then quite delirious and had been for several days before, wherein Aunt Mary could not account for it, as she was not then considered verry sick. That night when she went up the stairs to bed (having Mrs. Payne with her) she took her into both chambers. The first one she went into she complained of 'smoke'–'its being verry smokey'–although there was nothing like it, and when she went into the other, the moment she opened the door she screamed fire with all her strength and alarmed the whole house. Mr. Culver who was in bed sprang up &, running into the entry, asked where it was. She told him, the garret–that it was all of a light blaze, and he went up there as quick as possible. In the mean-time she hobbled down to the front door and stood there some time, screaming fire, & saying it was the strangest thing in the world, the house being all on fire and no one would speak a word. Thus it clearly proved she was delirious; and after some time she was pacified.

She rested poorly that night and in the morning the doct. visited her again; and that day was the first of her confinement to bed. She was verry restless both day and night, especially nights, continually talking, owing to the delirium increasing, being quite wild some of the time, and then again blending rational conversation with the wildness. Her increasing request was that she might have her own way, that she might not be compelled to take any medicine or do any thing particularly disagreeable to her. This request was complied with as far as possible. The doct. particularly was as kind as possible in this respect. He would sit hours by her holding the medicine and gently persuade her to drink it, which was verry painfull to her owing to the sourness of her mouth and throat and a peculiar distress to her stomach. This difficulty of taking the medicine continued through the illness though it was not so bad during the last as at first. Her wildness continued through her sickness, though during the last two days of her sickness there was less of it than any time before.

The morning on which she died, I believe she had her senses perfectly restored. She called for me half an hour before she died. She smiled upon me. She tried to speak but it was in whispers so low that it was imperfectly understood. They were endearing expressions to me–that I could see from her looks. If ever the portals of my ears were open it was then, to catch the last, the dying, whispers of so good, so excellent a mother. She called for Aunt Mary but a few minutes before dying, and then I could see no more. I left the room and did not return untill just as she breathed her last breath.

'Had Socrates, for godlike virtue fam'd
And wisest of the sons of men proclaimed,
Beheld this scene of sorrow & distress,
His soul had sunken to its last recess.'

Doct. North set by her bed side from early in the morning until she died, as he saw it was a gratification to her to be there. Poor soul, she thought to get well until the morning on which she died. Then she was aware she could not live, for she said to Aunt Sally, 'I see by your looks what you think of me.' The day before she died, Aunt Mary and Mrs. Lee were asking the Doct. just what he thought of her. He turned and said, 'Mary!! Your sister is going to die. No power nor medicine on earth can save her' (I was seting close by). His face (which is naturally pale) became flushed and his eye sparkled with a peculiar brightness. It was what I had anticipated, but it was so solumn that the words rung in my ears long after. I had hoped. I thought I could not part with her. It was *Mother*. Words will not express what she was to me, and to you all. But Mother is dead, gone to her death-bed. My consolation is that she is better off then if living, and that I hope to see her again.

The reason why you was not sent for was because it was her earnest request that you should not. 'For worlds (s'd she) I would not have her know that I am sick. It would so trouble her.' I did let you know that she was sick for fear of what has happened, but as it was both Mother's and Aunt Mary's request that you should not know the worst until dire necessity compelled it, I did not write for you to come until North spoke those blighting words, which was the day before she died. Then I wrote you immediately. Aunt Mary and myself kept her as long as possible after her death, hopeing that you would come in time to see her and attend the funeral, and also because it was her request to be kept. She died at noon. We kept her until Friday afternoon although we were strongly opposed by our friends and relations. Yet it was some satisfaction to know that we had done her request. She was, I thought, the most natural looking corpse I ever saw, and so said every-one that saw her. She looked as if in a calm sleep–no contraction of the muscles of the face nor pinching in of the nose, as is generaly the case. All was calm and smooth like a deep sleep. And deep indeed is the sleep. 'We make the grave our own bed and then are gone.'

Eliza! Think of Aunt Mary's situation. With her it is eternal night. She has lost her nearest earthly friend, her supporter, one that she took much comfort with. She is left alone, or depends upon the bounty of that friend who may step forward and offer her a resting place. She has no choice. This or none is the sad alternative. She lived to her mind with Mother, but now, let things be as they may, she must not complain. During the 'aching void' that is to fill the measure of her days, she will have but too much time to sorrow o'er the recent comfort she is so early deprived of. Think of it, and do not you murmur; for there is one poor soul who suffers more than we do by her loss–though she was to us more than an earthly parent. Therefore I beg, when you receive this, you will come immediately and offer consolation to the one most afflicted, besides being here to attend to those things which none but you can attend to.

Mother sleeps by the side of Father, about the center of the burying ground. It is the Champlain family lot. In the center of the lot our grandmother is laid; on her right is Father, and on the right of him, Mother. On her left is Aunt Oliver Champlain,[9] and on the left of her is just space enough for Uncle Oliver, should he die here. I did wish to make one of the group should I die here, but there is not room for me.

Come up. I can tell you more at a glance of an eye than an hour with the pen. Aunt Mary wishes affectionately to be remembered to her true friend and each of the family. I offer the same for myself,

from your brother,

William

On the same day, to William's closing request on Mary's behalf, Mrs. Lee adds her emphasis (**no. 196**):

My dear Eliza,

I have just returned from visiting your dear afflicted aunt, rendered doubly so by the discription given in your letter of your own suffering. The friendship that existed between your much lamented mother and myself autherizes me to write to you at this time. I was with her during her illness much of the time, and her other friends were constant and faithful in there attentions. There was nothing spared that could contribute to her relief or recovery. . . .

Your Aunt Mary is anxious to see you, and I am confident when you reflect on her peculiarly lonly situation, far more distressing than your own, but which has ever distinguished her in all her trials, you will hasten to shew her by your presence that you can feel for her loss as well as your own, and learn from her example to endure those trials of life which are given us in wisdom. The memory of your excellent mother also, who with cheerfulness endured the trials of life, should inspire you to act worthy of such a mother and be resigned to this dispensation of Providence.

Your aunt remains at the house yet with Mrs. James who was your mother's attendant and nurse during the whole of her illness. She wishes to return to her own house but cannot leave your Aunt Mary untill you arrive. Nothing can indeed be done with-out you.

You will find many friends here and I need not add that as one of your mother's earliest *I* shall ever feel interested in your situation and happiness. With feelings of the warmest sympathy,

I remain your sincere friend,

E. S. Lee. . . .

To these appeals if not to her natural affection and pity for her aunt, Eliza responded immediately, and was home in New London within a week (**no. 198**). From there she wrote to Sam:

My dear Brother,

I am passing through this sad, soul-sickening task, and nothing but the certain knowledge that it must be of short duration sustains me. I have done but little yet except parceling out letters to leave. I have not open'd Mother's papers.

If this piece of information can give you the least satisfaction, take it: if Mother had recover'd from this last illness, it is the firm opinion of Dr. North, Mrs. Lee and all her friends that she would have been for the rest of her life insane! So think no more of it. She was taken in the right time. I cannot write you particulars. I must tell them.

All I write at all for is to intreat you, as you value Mother's memory, to write Oliver a letter of thanks for all he has done for yourself that you have not noticed. To be sure, 'tis the eleventh hour, but 'tis not yet too late. Oliver is proud. He has been repeatedly asked by those gentlemen who interested themselves in your behalf since your establishment in the bank, 'Well, Capt. Champlain, how does your nephew suceed?'–and has had the extreme mortification of answering to all their enquiries (and that not without blushing for you), 'I know nothing at all about him. He takes no notice of the affair. I cannot account for his conduct.' Sam, you are the most ungrateful being in existence if you delay writing to him one instant when you receive this. In the name of heaven, excuse yourself to him, and that without a moment's delay, or I will write a letter in your name and have it conveyed to him. If I could convey to you the least idea of his goodness to Mother in her sickness–his constant anxiety about her, his attachment to her, his unwearied attentions to her and the assistance he has afforded on this most distressing occasion–you would write if you loved her as she deserved to be loved.

I never liked Oliver. He knew it. He did not call on me when I arrived till last evening (Sunday). He was much affected, said but little, and never named you. I did not expect he would. I only hoped it, that I might excuse you, which I would have done with my heart and soul. He arose to go, and said he had no home to ask me too, but he would call often to see me. His calling at all was evidently the greatest exertion, for he possesses the most exquisite sensibillity and wishes like yourself to avoid the house. He told me that Dr. Lee had just enquired of him if I had been sea-sick coming up and that he answer'd he did not know. This enquiry Dr. Lee made only to see if he had been to see me, as he came into the Ladies' Cabin on purpose to see if I was sick. I know you will write soon to him, for 'twas Mother's wish.

I have written this letter through much difficulty, and for no other purpose than to urge your speedy attention to my request. Mother set her heart upon Oliver, and since his wife's death the prospect of visiting here was his only consolation. He felt for her, he feels for her children. He is one of the most wretched beings in existence, and soon will be, I think, deposited by the side of his wife. 'Tis all he wishes; for he has never receover'd from her death and never will.

Pray call on Mrs. Fitch often. Do reform and be yourself. You know they are now my best friends on earth, my only disinterested friends, and the only friends on earth that I love altogether. Write soon. I need your letters and those of my friends. . . .

For a time now, since Sam is still silent, New York and New London communicate only through Eliza and Anna. The latter writes in early December, Eliza replies, a third letter follows on New Year's day from Anna. In all of these appears, or half-appears, the younger Edward Riley's name linked with the question, should Eliza take him. Against his suit are his inadequate means and his failure to rouse an answering love. In favor of it are Anna and the lack of any rival–it can even be said, the lack of any other tolerable plan for Eliza's life, given her determination not to spend it in her home town. She must *marry* into New York. But neither correspondent can or will be quite frank. Here, first in the series, is **no. 201**, in which Anna is helping Riley to find employment as a teacher, just as she helped Eliza:

Dear Eliza,

I would have answered your letter the instant I returned home, but waited until I should have something to say which would interest you. I have been anxiously expecting a call from Mr. Riley in the hope that he might be the bearer of favourable news. He was here last evening and had been unsuccessful in his inquiries for a situation. I requested him to call on some other schools, which he promised to do. He is a very clever fellow and I think the best thing you can do is to secure him.

Your brother called here last week & said that he intended writing to you that evening. I requested him to mention to you my reason for not answering your letter. Silence I thought better than an unsatisfactory letter, and yet I have been obliged to write such a one now. I trust, however, my next will be in a different style.

I am glad to hear that your presence has been able in any degree to cheer your aunt [Mary]'s spirits. You surely must consider it a sufficient remuneration for the sacrifice you have made. I should deem it a privilege, were I near, to aid in your affectionate and praiseworthy employment. . . .

And Anna expands a good deal on the subject of self-sacrifice and its rewards.

Then, next, Eliza writes (**no. 202**) in the midst of settling her mother's effects and herself into new lodgings with Ebb (it will be remembered that he had moved himself and his post-office into Hannah's house, years ago):

My dear Mrs. Fitch,

Your long-expected letter caught me at last in the height of moving. I had scarcely time to read it, but 'twas the more acceptable on that account, for it diverted my mind from the cares with which it was oppress'd, and convinced me that I was not forgotten. I was surprised and a little hurt at your silence, for many days had elapsed after I wrote before the answer came; but your excuse for not writing sooner was sufficient. I should have answer'd it immediately after we arrived at the post-office, but for the unfinish'd pictures that I have been under the necessity of retouching. I have devoted every moment to them, and at last the worst is over. I shall not be obliged to hurry so much with those that remain in hand.

About a month after my return, my brother William ruptured a blood vessel. He did not raise much, but he has complain'd ever since of a difficulty in breathing. I feel very anxious about him yet, though I trust he will get entirely over it if we can make him more careful of his health than he has been. His constitution is naturally delicate and he has exerted himself lately more than he ought to have done, and in fact more than was necessary. As Doctor Wright recommends boil'd milk in this case always, I made him drink it for several days, but he has now got tired and won't taste it.

Aunt Mary has been quite sick with the influenza. She is now recovering. Indeed, we have all been ill with it. I hope it has not visited New York or, if it has, that yourself & family have escaped. The typhus fever has been rageing here since my return. It has now, I trust, quit forever. I think I never knew New London so sickly as it has been within the last year. 'Tis thought, however, that a bitter cold winter will once more purefy the air and set the place to rights. New London looks strange and gloomy to me. I perceve a change in every thing, but cannot add I am pleased with any of the changes that have taken place since my departure.

My friends are all very good and do all in their power to make the time pass pleasantly, particularly Uncle [Ebenezer] and Aunt [Sally] Way. I like their conduct both before and since my return. Aunt Way did much for me and mine when I was unable to do without such a friend. I trust I shall ever remember it. She was a second Mrs. Lee. This is saying enough.

There is a young lady spending the winter here that I am much pleased with. She is the daughter of an English gentleman that failures and misfortunes have driven to America. Their estate in England is mortgaged for seven years. At the expiration of that term they expect to return and resume the style to which they have always been accustom'd. Miss Stammers (the young lady in question) has had a very superior education. She has been taught every-thing that possibly can be taught, and in my opinion much more than is necessary for a female. She excells in music, for she is passionately fond of it. She excells also in painting, for she has a fine taste. I don't think that either you or Mr. Fitch would call her handsome. She is not so, otherwise than a very expressive face makes her. She has not even a regular set of features. Her eyes are fine, her hair is beautiful but black as jet, her teeth white and handsome. She has a good English form and dresses in English style. I have seen during my residence in New York many young ladies that have been genteely educated and some that I was very much pleased with, but I never saw one that would bear the least comparison with Miss Stammers. She is without one exception the most genteel young lady I ever met with. She has no little pride in her composition, and I am convinced that in any situation she would never take airs upon herself. You know this of course.

The family came over from England with Capt. Griswold, son to Governor Griswold.[10] He knew they had put aside the luxeries of life till their debts were discharged, and intended to earn their living by the sweat of their brow for the present. He was much interested for them and immediately on his arrival here introduced them to all the first families: the Stuarts, the Winthrops, the Lees and Perkins families. They of course paid them every attention and assisted them in every possible way. It was at a party at Judge Perkins' that Aunt Way first saw Miss Stammers, and was so much pleased with her that (knowing she wished to board in a private family) she offered to take her as a boarder. Miss S. was much pleased with this and came the next week to Aunt Way's. She has a very fine piano that has moved here with her, and, as 'twas her intention to turn this accomplishment to advantage, she immediately commenced teaching music. She has as many scholars as she can attend to, and, as her manner of teaching is much approved, I think she will probably continue a year in this place.[11] She is our organist at church and our favorite at home, and, what is more than all, the better we know her the more we like her. She has a fine disposition and excellent sense. Aunt Mary is extremely pleased with her, as every one must be that knows her. You see I am in love with Miss Stammers. . . .

You know I set my heart (as poor old Aunt Hannah used to say) upon New York. I have had many very warm friends in the place, and it would be strange indeed if I was not attached to it. Pray send me some news that I shall like to hear–in fact, anything in the shape of news will be interesting at this time. Does that strange brother of mine call often to see you? I had a long letter from him about the time I recieved yours, which I have not yet answer'd. Does Riley (how I hate the name) call often? . . .

On New Year's day of 1826 Anna Fitch responds with comments on Eliza's letter and then with her own news (**no. 203**):

. . . Your friends here are all well, at least all that I have seen, for I have been out very seldom since I returned. [Daughter Cornelia =] Corry stays at home this winter & continues her studies under my direction. She has commenced French.

You ask for news that you will like to hear. In such, I am very deficient; but such as I possess you shall have. Poor Mrs. Hayden has met with a sad misfortune: turned out of doors by fire. The day after it happened, I heard that there had been a large fire in Spring Street which had consumed fifty houses. I thought of Mrs. Hayden, and immediately rode to the spot, where we found nothing remaining of her house but the iron railing. After making many fruitless inquiries in the neighbourhood to ascertain where she was, I recollected her Uncle Taylor, & thither we went, & were there directed to Sandford's in Broadway, and there at length we found her, her children (whom I was rejoiced to see safe), & Eliza Sandford. She & [her sister-in-law] Mrs. Johnson were fortunately with her at the time. She had just laid in her winter's provisions & fuel, & had that very evening had a grate fixed in her bedroom. The best of her furniture was saved. In her night-clothes as she sprang from her bed, she ran alone half a mile to her brother to get him to assist in removing–a thing which (she said) she would not have done in her senses on any account. She has had a great deal of trouble since in finding a habitation, but has at length succeeded in getting an uncomfortable one. . . .

Your strange brother, as you call him, has not called since. Mr. Riley has been here several times, but not very lately. He has made all the inquiries I requested but has met with no success. There are so many applicants. Don't you think that a knowledge of music (which you might acquire from Miss Stammers) might prove beneficial? Where painting fails, that might perhaps succeed. It would at least be increasing your resources. But you have a friend near you who is able to advise you. Indeed, I know no one better qualified. Give my love to her. I consider writing to you & her the same thing, therefore I hope she will use her slate & pencil & give you the pleasure of copying a letter for me. . . .

And more New York news from Anna in **no. 204** of February 4, 1826:

Dear Eliza,

Mr. Riley came here on Monday to say that you had sent for your things which remained here. I did not see him, being confined to my room with the most severe turn of influenza I have ever experienced. You will readily believe that it was somewhat serious when you hear that it had the uncommon effect of preventing my coming down-stairs for four or five days. Mr. Fitch is just recovering & Susan is confined to her bed. We have each taken our turn except my mother, who I sincerely hope may continue exempt from this uncomfortable intruder. I have never known the city so universally afflicted by sickness as it is at present.

This morning Mr. R. sent for the articles belonging to you, but I cannot reconcile your last letter with this step. Why in the name of reason did you not leave your things here if you intended returning to the city? And what else can you expect if you change your situation? Surely I cannot have misunderstood your meaning when you say, speaking of the favourable impression made on all by Mr. R., 'I have taken your advice.' My advice, however, on this subject you know was always conditionally: if you think such a course calculated to increase your happiness, neglect not to pursue it. If not, think no more on the subject, be decided–for in amusing yourself, another may be made to suffer. Do explain this mystery soon, as you know I am of the same sex with poor Aunt Charity, and none can tell but her fate may be mine. . . .

Your brother called here the evening that I received your last. He appeared when he first entered in good spirits but soon began to sigh & appear dejected. I tried all in my power to rouse him–talked of every foolish thing I could conceive to endeavour to interest him–but all to no purpose. At length, seeing him rest his head on his hand, I asked if his head ached. He said, No, but that he was the most unfortunate fellow in the world. I was of course not long in inquiring the cause of his misfortunes, & found it to be the same subject which you had mentioned to me: the impossibility of getting another person to sign his bond. I was surprised, as I thought this business was all settled by this time. In this dilemma I called upon Mr. Fitch for advice. He directed Samuel to Charles Holt, & told him if he was unsuccessful there to let him know & he would endeavour to procure one of his own friends to sign it. He again called, had not seen Mr. Holt, & Mr. Fitch in a few days found a gentleman who after some hesitation promised to become security. Sam was in extacies at this news; but, strange & unaccountable as it may seem, he has never called since, to have the business arranged, & a week has now elapsed.

Sunday evening

This afternoon being fine, I ventured out for the first time in nearly a fortnight. After church I called at Mr. Mitchell's, where they are all invalid. They have had ten sick at once. They asked when I had heard from you, & Mr. M. made many enquiries respecting your aunt. He dwelt feelingly on her merits & misfortunes, in his peculiarly energetic manner, & I listened with the pleasure which we always experience at finding another think precisely as we do, & enter into a portion of our enthusiasm, on a subject where the heart is interested.

I have attended but two parties this winter, which is just two more than I had any idea of attending: one at Mrs. Oakley's, the other at Mrs. Innes's. For the last, there were two hundred & fifty invitations given. . . .

P.S. As my letter is still here & unsealed, I must add a few words more. Mr. Riley has just called. I never saw him look handsomer, though he says he has been quite sick. . . .

Most likely at this time,[12] a couple of months after Eliza's return home, Mary writes to Anna to acknowledge Anna's "most kind and most welcome letter with its accompaniments, presents and books." As usual, Mary embroiders her thoughts with much poetry, much scripture, and her own reflections on the state of the world and its inhabitants, herself included:

. . . 'Celestial Happiness when she descends
To visit earth, one shrine the goddess finds,
And one alone to make her sweet amends
For absent Heaven . . . '

. . . When your dear letters are read to me, I feel the truth of this beautiful sentiment in its full force and find 'I have not yet forgot myself to stone.' While I hear the voice of friendship and listen to the works of genius, warmed into life and glowing with Enthusiasm, I am myself again, and not the stupid torpid thing I seem.

Ah! hopeless lasting flame, like those that burn
To light the dead and warm the unfruitful urn.

Useless to *me* indeed–but what is life without it [= enthusiasm]? this soul-intransing power philosophers regard with contempt, as little better than insanity that hurries us away beyond ourselves, beyond the sober medium of truth and reason and all the dull realities of common-place existence, improves our pleasures, brightens our enjoyments, and sheds a lustre o'er the dream of earthly happiness richer, far more bright and vivid than ever hope can give. . . .

Soon after I received your favour, the above was written. Since then, time has lag'd less heavily, or rather slid insensibly away, thanks to your dear letter and books. William reads when business will permit and fortunately my little friend Eliza Lee is now restored to health and again resumed her charitable occupation, so that altogether the two last months has afforded me more pleasure than I've experienced for such a length of time in many years. ' 'Tis vain to seek in man, for more than man.' Sinner that I am! I feel reproved and self-condemned when I consider my ingratitude. The mind sunk in depression and abandoned in sorrow is ill-disposed to realize the goodness of indulgent Heaven. There's a perverse rebellious spirit that mutinies within, and in the paroxism of despair forgets, rejects, and disregards all other blessings but that of which we are deprived. This, alas! has been and is too much my case. We cannot always acquiese in the dark mysterious ways of Providence, even when our better judgement is convinced, 'Whatever is, is right.' . . .

Most heartily I congratulate you, my dear friend, on your hair's-breadth escape from a long sermon. I had begun as you see by the text chosen for the purpose (showing the probable consequence of such an overturn as you sugest), which, together with the foregoing, would have been but a mere preface or introduction to a *Treatise on Practical Philosophy*, dry as the remaining biscuit after a voyage, and so on to the end of the chapter. What might have followed next, I cannot say, but something equally dull and proseing. From all this *gimbletism*, you have been happily rescu'd by the arrival of Eliza,[13] for 'tis quite impossible to write or even to think while her clack goes so merrily. To let you see the danger you were in, you must be inform'd, I've been deliberating for the space of half an hour whether or no 'tis best to wait till after she returns, and finish my letter off in style by adding half a dozen more sheets, or send the fragment as it is. Fortunately for you (as well as for myself), I have determined on the latter, for by this means I may hope to hear from you again sooner than I could otherwise expect.

How delighted I should be to see you here and have a little chat. I am half angry and strongly tempted to call you whimsical, tho' Charity declare 'tis only in appearance, by the way. 'Tis not the first time her Ladyship has interposed in your behalf; and from my knowledge of your character I must of course conclude you have sufficient reason to justify your conduct now, as well as formerly upon a similar occasion.

I am grieved to hear Mr. Mitchell is so low. May Heaven spare his precious life in mercy to the world! Oh! I have much to say–but must not add another line. Eliza goes so soon, my amanuensis I fear will not have time to copy this. When shall we meet to part no more, and real happiness begin–for here 'tis all a sham? Well, it will come at last and will not tarry. Adieu! Write soon. Present my best regards to those most dear to you, and believe me yours.

I am glad to find Eliza's sickness is not unto death, and hope in due time she will be again restored to health and reason for (between ourselves) I think she has been partially deranged for many years. I cannot otherwise [account] for all her queer manners and strange conduct of this [most] singular and finikish of human beings. Still, there is no effect without its cause. Great allowance must be made for the condition in which she has been placed; but I am not at leisure to enlarge upon the subject, and must leave it for a more convenient season, at present. I shall only say her spirits are much better than when we saw her last. I think she grows more rational, is lively and animated, full of fun and nonsense. She keeps us laughing half the time. The boat is going this moment. I must close.

Adieu.

The restoration of Eliza's spirits is best explained by her having settled her relationship with Edward Riley. That cannot have been easily done by letter; but its results show in the next surviving word from her hand, of mid-February (**no. 206**), showing here and there that a correspondence of declared tenderness had been going on between them for some time:

My dear Edward,

I find it difficult to express all the happiness I feel at hearing from your own pen that you are well, quite well, and capable of making any exertion. Believe me, dear, I am incapable of making the least. Even this letter will be written by snatches, and so badly written that I very much fear 'twill be quite unintelligible, even to you. I have not quit my bed-room (scarcely my bed) for six days. What a rascally disorder this influenza is. Don't you think it requires more than the patience of Job to bear it well?

You need not fear a lecture on patience in this scrawl. I have not a sufficient stock to pen it off, if I ever thought it would benefit you. And since you have had the nobleness to acknowledge your error, that alone would prevent my saying more on the subject. I always thought 'twas the strongest proof that we could give of a generous mind, to confess manifolds to any friend who was kind enough to point them out in such a manner as to avoid wounding the feelings. If I am sharply reproved for my faults, my reprover may go whistle for all the thanks they will get at my hands. If 'tis delicately done, it touches me to the quick. I believe I often make you angry without dreaming of such a thing, and think if I was able and disposed to lecture you at the 'present writing' I could put you in a passion instantly, for I am at this moment most gloriously irritable, and 'tis ten chances to one that I won't make you angry before it's over, unintentionally of course.

My spirits have been more depressed with this cold than with any sickness that I ever had in my life. The night that I suffered most I thought I should suffocate for want of air and in exposing myself to the air I encreased my cold. Once I thought I should die. It would have given me much pleasure to have received a letter from you at the time it was at its height but 'twas too soon to expect one and I was obliged to place your old ones in my work basket on a stand at the side of my bed. I could do no more that read them over & over again. If I came across an expression that did not exactly suit my step I was angry enough to box your ears. You cannot think what a child I had become–but 'tis over now. I am quite a lady, & behave charmingly. I am beginning to breathe better, taste & smell (if hartshorn is put to my nose). Aunt Mary is an excellent nurse. But for her, I think I should have made my exit this time. I have grown amazingly delicate. You would scarcely know me. By the bye, I hear from Mrs. Fitch that it has improved your looks. Pray don't expose yourself unnecessarily. You are a careless fellow at all times. Recollect this is a critical time upon earth, and if you don't mind your P's and Q's, you may chance to be sorry.

My affairs have arrived safe. They were just a week on their passage, and from their mauled appearance I strongly suspect they were most miserably sea-sick or have had the influenza–I am quite at a loss to determine which, as they do not complain. I rather think however 'twas sea-sickness as one of the bundles had its mouth wide open.

Pray tell me if you received the answer to your explanatory note. As you do not even mention it, I fear 'tis lost. I enclosed in it a Riddle of Byron's [the pseudonymous *Enigma*], for you to cudgel your brains about, and would like to know its fate.

Your letter that I am now answering has contributed ten thousand times more to my recovery than the rascally drugs that I have been obliged to swallow without the least interruption. It has raised my spirits astonishingly. I feel quite like myself. Don't you think I act so?

I was extremely interested at your account of the interview between yourself & Mrs. Fitch. I saw the prying look of curiosity with which she regarded you, as she discussed an affair in which I know she takes so deep an interest. You ought feel flattered by her good opinion, for she has no common mind. She is far enough superior to the most of her sex. If I had not known this, well, I should never have taken her for my best friend next to my dear mother.

I am sorry, my dear Edward, you think, or appear to think, that I accuse you of timidity & pusillanimity. Believe me dear, I do not, I never could love you as I do, if I could lay such weaknesses to your charge. I have never yet found you destitute of manly firmness in any situation, and I trust and believe I never shall. To be sure, you have never yet been placed before my eyes in any very trying situation, and I am therefore not so capable of judging as your own family would be in this affair. Still I think you will always acquit yourself well in any situation, and I love you accordingly. Will this satisfy you my dear? I know not what more to say to convince you that I do you justice. I could no more love an effeminate man, than you could love a masculine girl. They are both out of character, and of course disgusting. I don't care how much manly tenderness a man displays, provided he chooses his time well. I do not call this effeminacy, on the contrary, it would encrease my love. I think that manly tenderness is as much the glory of your sex as strength, and you know my opinion on this point. I like also to discover in the masculine gender a contempt of danger. It suits their character and sets *well* upon them. Understand me, I do not mean carelessness of health, for I consider this not only foolish, but wicked. I think it shows prudence and judgement to avoid all danger that is possible to avoid. What is not possible to avoid, meet with manly firmness, or if you please it, contempt. Don't, my dear E., accuse me again with accusing you of cowardice. I am only telling you what I like in the male sex. I aim at no one, least of all, you, will you believe this, Sweet?

You wish me to answer you that, should you fail to realize as much as you expected, I will let the ceremony take place notwithstanding. If, dear, you make all the exertion that is in your power and still do not accomplish your purpose–if your happiness depended on our marriage under such discouraging circumstances–I would not postpone it longer though I should think it premature and would rather wait till the prospect brightened. I feel that I can do much more to promote your happiness in case of necessity than I once thought I could. Every day strengthens my attachment. Your recent illness, your absence, your letters, and more than all, your worth (knowing it well) has added fuel to the flickering flame that at the commencement of our acquaintance (and even at a more *advanced* period) played around my heart. The objection of brothers or any of my friends would only make me the more determined to do as I please, for in some things I am very obstinate, and this is one. Nothing but your proving yourself unworthy of my love would now prevent our union, and of this I dare not think. Indeed, I need not, for I think you very honourable.

You gave Mrs. Fitch the right answer when she asked why I sent for my things. I am quite sorry I was under the necessity of sending for them *all* as I did not want them half. I received a long and interesting letter from her, when I was too ill to hold it in my hand. What made it more interesting than anything else, was her praising you. I have not yet answered it, though 'twas received before yours arrived.

I am yours, dear Edward, most affectionately,

Eliza W. C. . . .

Nothing (within the conventions of the day) could be more committedly engaged, even if conspiratorially, than this; and the series of letters to follow only confirms the fact of that commitment.

14

Ending in a Wedding

Once Eliza's decision was made, let us hope not for lack of a better alternative, the news of her engagement to Edward must come out. If Mary had been the first to learn, the rest of the Ways and Champlains hadn't long to wait. Toward mid-January of 1826 he had paid a visit to New London and had been shown around to general approbation. So Eliza had told Anna in a lost letter, "speaking of the favorable impression made on all by Mr. R." (**no. 204**, above). Now Eliza writes again (**no. 207** of February 20th), after an opening page on the winter's ailments, and with disingenuous casualness:

> My dear Mrs. Fitch,
>
> . . . So you think there is danger of your shareing the fate of poor Aunt Charity, who died of a Frenchman, by dying yourself of an Englishman [i.e., Riley, born in London] unless the mystery is explained. Believe me, there is nothing to explain. I meant simply what I said, to take your advice with regard to Riley. By the bye, I thought the business was concluded without an 'if', till you told me in your last letter that it was not.
>
> I don't know how it is that all the petty slights he has ever recieved that has come within the compass of my knowledge enhances his merit and raises him in my estimation ten thousand-fold. This no doubt is entirely owing to the natural obstinacy of my disposition. I hate fools and I think 'tis fools alone that have ever treated him in a slight way. Perhaps you will think this is calling myself a fool. I do not think it is. I treated him at the commencement of our acquaintance in the manner that I did because he did not interest me, not because I thought him unworthy. I thought him even then sensible, amiable, and handsome; but all this was not enough, and I told him so. But 'tis nonsense for me to write what I have said to you before. You surely recollect our conversation respecting him just before I left you. My friends here are very much pleased with him. His visit was altogether unexpected, I believe I told you, and the impression he made on all, very favorable.

> The reason I sent for all my affairs was this: I wished to get at a few of them that I thought was in the small gilt trunk. I did not find them in it and had not the least idea which bundle to send for, as you know I was crazy when I packed them. I did not like to do so, as it would have been quite unnecessary if I had been blessed with Doctor Mitchell's memory. . . .

The man she chose, and her reference to the "slights" he had received, need to be fitted in to New York and her circle there; but it can be said at the start, she had not made a choice she need be ashamed of.

The elder Edward Riley (1769–1829), father to her Edward Cort, was an exact contemporary of Mary Way. From Shrewsbury (Shropshire), his family had moved to London in 1780.[1] There by the early 1790s he had set up shop on the Strand where he engraved and sold music, made and sold instruments, and for a decade gave lessons in the flute. He moved again, this time to the New World in 1805, landing with his second wife and four children "in Perth Amboy and eat oysters for the first time"–so runs the text of a ridiculous family recollection–before he settled in New York. His shop there in various locations lay within the "village" that Mary Way and her circle belonged to (Broadway, Dey Street and, from 1813, Chatham Street).[2]

Here his wife in 1806 opened a school for English, arithmetic, music, and other social skills, while he offered instruction in voice for men and women, in the German flute, flageolet, piano, and guitar himself, and, as he gradually expanded his trade, in other instruments by "proper masters." To audiences that liked infant prodigies, a girl of his teaching gave a piano concert in 1806, and his young daughter Louisa followed in 1810. From 1806, too, until 1823, he offered voice and flute performances in the City Hall and various theatres and "gardens," and undertook libretto- and score-composition for others. A few years after his arrival in the city he also resumed the engraving and publishing of scores. The growing market for music at the amateur level, whether singing or playing, has been suggested in chapter 11, above; and he had brought his up-to-date dies with him from England. By 1812 he decided to set up an independent house with an excellent copper-plate printer, Thomas Adams. It is uncertain how early Riley Sr. began to make, or perhaps only to preside over the manufacture of, musical instruments; but a number of fine flutes with his name on them can be found in the major collections today–Betsey owned such a one (**no. 125**)–and two of his apprentices (later his sons-in-law) joined with a third person to launch a well-known firm for their manufacture (Firth, Hall and Pond, from 1832).

Now, granted, these chosen lines would never make a man a millionaire; and, even so, in the purveying of everything connected with music, there was plenty of competition. It was offered by Philadelphia for a time, until New York established its own ascendancy, and then and always there was competition within the city, too, from the steady inflow of European talent of every sort. However, by the late teens of the century Riley Sr. stood out as preeminent in the work he had made his own through a career that demonstrated quite remarkable talents, energy, application, and business ideas. In these respects he recalls Samuel Woodworth, his neighbor on Chatham Street with whom he collaborated in the publishing of various single songs and collections. Woodworth was librettist for the country's first opera and enjoyed writing for the parlor and concert-hall as well.[3] There was Mrs. Bradish, too, among the song-publishers whose scores Riley engraved, toward the middle of his New York career; various other customers besides her; and his own vocal compositions to be published and sold, the most popular of which celebrated Lafayette's visit in 1824. In 1820 he had brought out in his typical style, that is, on a more ambitious scale than any other music publisher of the city, "Riley's Vocal Melodies, being a collection of American, English, Scotch, Irish, Welch, French, German, Italian, Swiss, Tyrolese, Danish, Swedish, Turkish, Hebrew, and Chinese Airs, adapted to American words and arranged for the piano-forte." What a miracle of multiculturalism!

On the same scale and over the span of the preceding six years, in six volumes, appeared his collection of more than seven hundred melodies for the flute. Though the profits of publishing were easier to find in ephemeral vocal compositions, Riley Sr. throughout his life showed more interest than his competitors in the instrumental. On the other hand, he could not ignore prevailing tastes, and his anthology accordingly drew its tunes from absolutely everywhere. It was uphill work to educate the general public in Haydn, Mozart, and Beethoven, or in any genius above the extraordinarily prolific and popular Ignaz Joseph Pleyel (to be heard in all "garden" programs in New York as elsewhere, though in due course quite forgotten).[4] Riley Sr. could only teach such talented amateurs as turned up, perform chamber pieces himself, and regularly join the small orchestras that supported productions of operatic scenes or tableaux. Nothing more was called for or supported by the city's audiences until his son's lifetime, just about to unfold.

But first: collaboration with Woodworth had involved Riley Sr. in more than music. The two men were the chief pillars of the New York society of Emanuel Swedenborg's New [Jerusalem] Church–Riley in fact its founder. A convert from the 1790s, his efforts from his very first arrival in the city had called it into being.[5] It was he that had discovered what three or four other converts from the previous decade still retained their interest in the faith, gathered them for readings and worship in his home, and by 1811, joined by Woodworth in the next year, rented a room for larger meetings. The two men then undertook the publication of a church periodical, for a time enjoying a subscriber list of three thousand, and then a second periodical when the first died. Later, incorporated in 1816, a New York New-Church missionary society chose Woodworth as one of its officers. By 1821 the congregation was large enough to fill a proper building for worship and bought the old Universalist church on Pearl Street; but shortly thereafter they split very badly and in time had to sell their meeting-place (as Eliza mentions had been done, above in chapter 12, **no. 162**). Riley Sr., emerging as leader of the larger portion, was to serve as its delegate to national meetings. It remained a generally flourishing group.

Of his three sons, all pursued their father's line of business, Henry independently some years before his father's death, Frederick too, but not till long after–both with their separate specialties.[6] Yet the clearest as well as the earliest success was Edward Cort Riley (1799–1871).[7] From 1823 till his death he advertised as a music professor, for a long time was involved in music-engraving and publishing, headed his own separate firm for a half-dozen years (from 1836) at various locations that crept uptown and ended at 149 East 30th Street, Murray Hill, close to the 35th-street Swedenborgian church that still stands; taught, sold, composed for piano, flute, and voice, performed; manufactured, tuned and repaired instruments; did everything his father had done. But he also held patents for improvements in woodwind design and served as a violinist and prominently as one of the conductors of the city's Philharmonic Orchestra in its second brief life (1824–27) and again in its third resurrection in the 1840s. His conducting of various groups had in fact begun back in 1821. Like his father's, his professional life gives proof of a great range of talents and equal energy.

Further, like the elder Riley, he rose to the head of his church while still in his thirties, presiding over its repair after a very difficult time in the 1830s and representing it also to the national convention.[8] His fellow delegate was then the artist mentioned in other contexts above, Samuel Waldo.

But this is to anticipate. For the moment, all that is relevant is how the world, including not least Eliza, might look on this slight, slender, sandy-haired, sober young man. Like her he was inventive, if not in any serious way creative; educated about as far as one could be without college; his life and thoughts engaged in higher culture, as it may be called, though in a different quadrant from Eliza's choice; busy to make his living out of service to that culture; and, so far as people around him would judge him, of a comparable status to hers: far below the great houses that could invite a hundred guests to their receptions, clearly not on a level with those doctors and lawyers for whom Eliza admitted an admiration, of a family no more than respectable yet well above the ordinary merchant or manufacturer ("Mantua-makers," Eliza calls some of them). So, in sum, a "suitable" suitor.

Having decided to accept his offer, Eliza set herself to enjoy it. In the six months and more that were to follow, she settled down to earn what she could with her brush and to look after her aunt with cheerful affection. But she made room for continuing courtship and its attendant rituals, room for love-letters. In this part of the correspondence, as it leads nowhere but to the altar, some heavier editing may be allowed, beginning in February (**no. 208**) with a paragraph on the slowness of the mails, her uncertain health, and a funny story Edward told in his last; then, the question of how he was to make her more nearly perfect–that is, more like himself–as, in other letters, she wants to re-make him in turn:

> . . . I read your lesson to Miss Stammers. She understood it perfectly and as soon as 'tis possible for me to attend again either to playing or singing is going to make me perfectly understand it. I am much obliged to you for it. The lines [of verse] you sent are much admired. *I* think them beautiful. Your miniature is thought a good likeness, only not handsome enough. Don't you think my friends are very partial to

you, my dear? I positively fear you will cut me out, and this I shall certainly resent. So take care.

'Twas Aunt Mary & Aunt Way that grasp'd Byron's *Enigma*. I agree with you, 'tis not as good as the other. When did you see any of Mrs. Fitches family? . . .

You may with propriety accuse me with having a bad memory. I have a most villianous one; but you should recollect that it was very natural for us both to say many things at the moment of parting that upon reflection had better have been left unsaid. The request that you say I made at that never-to-be-forgotten moment, I do not deny, but when your letter arrived, it appears I misunderstood; for from your style of writing I could not for the soul of me make anything else out of it than I did, and commanded, as you say, your absence till the appointed time. I know not what else to do. Understanding, or rather misunderstanding you as I did, I had reason to fear a visit daily, and was astonished and concerned at your apparent want of resolution, and afraid if I did not command you to do your duty, that you would neglect it altogether. You could not suppose that I did not wish to see you till September; but where is the use of wishing what is wrong? And I cannot help thinking it would be wrong for you to neglect business for the sake of seeing me sooner than that time. . . .

Do you know, it is currently reported in this renown'd city of Gotham that I am to be married in the spring to the young Englishman that visited me in January? Uncle Way has been repeatedly asked the question, so has William and Miss Stammers. . . .

And now, my dear Edward, I would ask why you expect so much gratitude for my granting what it would be mean and ungenerous in me to refuse: my love in poverty as in affluence. Can you think so meanly of me as to suppose that your poverty would prevent my loveing you as sincerely as I should if you were rich? You little know me if you think I love money for its own sake. I certainly do not. I don't deny that I value the comforts cash procures, but hoarding it never would give me one moment's pleasure. It appears in many of your letters as if you thought I lov'd money too well. I have given you my reasons for wishing to set out in life with something. 'Tis useless to say more on the subject. Tell me if you have ever been offended at my manner of exposing myself on this point, for if I mistake not you have. At any rate, you have slightly hurt my feelings by what you have said, whether you meant it or not; so if you please, clear up this affair soon. . . .

Adieu, dear. If you think any part of this letter sounds cross, excuse me for it. I feel not yet exactly aright. I am not cross to you, however, and so soon as I get entirely well, shall be very pleasant indeed. Your Eliza. . . .

On the second of March, again, the uncertain mails (**no. 209**):

My dear Edward,

I know not how it is that our letters get so strangely delayed. I never let the New York mail close after recieving a letter from you without my answer. You appear to be equally attentive, and yet the letter don't arrive till long after I have expected it. Explain this in your next if you can. I asked William the meaning of this. He smiled and, screwing up his face with its most quizzical form, said that lovers' letters always got delayed. 'The course of true love never did run smooth.' I gave him a box on the ear for his impertinence, a thing I always do when he don't please me–which is often the case. I do not like to ask Uncle Way about them, as I should mind his quizing much more than William's. So you see how prettily I am fix'd. . . .

I ask your pardon for not answering, in my last, one of your questions that interested me most. 'Twas this: You wish to know if I will accept your offer of composing me a song. Be assured I will do this with the greatest pleasure and shall await its arrival with impatience. So do your prettiest, my love, will you?

Why, my dear Edward, are you so anxious I should learn to play and sing *Home Sweet Home*?[9] Will the home to which you invite me be so very sweet that anything else but this will be proper to sing and play in it after I grace it with my presence? There are many things I fancy more than the thing in question, and consequently should learn with more ease–that is, to play. Pray excuse my singing. You know I cannot sing. Therefore don't urge it. I am in fact quite discouraged about ever playing well. You know I told you I certainly never could learn anything by rule. I was not born by rule and I know I never should have painted decently if the rules of painting had been stuff'd into my skull. Don't you think I express myself in most elegant style?

I would ask you without hesitation any questions in music that I had to ask, but I positively am still such an ignoramus in this delightful art that I know not what to ask. Don't trouble yourself, dear, to send me another lesson by mail till I feel a little more encouraged about playing and singing that I do at present. Miss Stammers has assured me repeatedly that I shall learn, if I will only mind what she says. This I don't feel disposed to do, more than half the time. Do tell me what you think of the Crazy Betty that you and she have so patiently taken in hand. Pray encourage me, or I certainly must throw the whole affair aside. . . .

Do you know I don't think your letters much like love letters? That is, you very frequently stop short, in some very tender scene, to tell me of my faults. Is this pretty, do you think? Is it pardonable? I am obliged just as I have set my mouth for a sugar plum, to swallow a pill. In future, if I must take both, have the goodness to give me the pill first and the sweet-meat after, do you hear?

I believe I must bid you adieu soon, for I find the writing of this letter has not sweeten'd the present temper of my eyes. They are smarting with the unusual exertion.

Before I close, tell me if you seriously think of shewing your pretty face in New London before September, and, if you do, how soon. Recollect, I do not wish it because I think business of more consequence to both of us at present than making love, and if you attempt to carry them both on together, take my word for it, that that is of most consequence will get neglected. Do you believe this? . . .

This letter was written yesterday. This afternoon I have been murdering out a lesson on the piano, and am quite in despair at my bad success. Is not this encouraging?

And once more, those confounded mails (**no. 210**, March 10):

My dear Edward,

As I know not exactly the reason or reasons that our letters are delayed, I shall endeavor to be more guarded in my expressions, till I discover the real cause. 'Tis very mysterious. Surely it cannot be altogether owing to bad roads and careless drivers. Mail robberies are now quite fashionable, and untill the rage for this sport has a little subsided I shall never send a letter off without some anxiety respecting its fate, nor await the arrival of yours, without fear.

As you so very politely request me to prosecute my musical studies under the direction of Miss Stammers, I cannot without rudeness refuse to comply with your request. Be assured, Mr. Riley, Miss Champlain will set about cudgeling her brains at that rascally instrument as soon as Miss S. returns from Black Hall, where she is going today to see her family. Will this promise suffice? . . .

Is it possible you could feel hurt at the nonsense I expressed respecting *Home Sweet Home*? You surely did, or you would not have sent your answer to this part of my letter as the *pill* of yours. It is indeed a pill and a most bitter one that you are eternally mistaking me, and I you. Suppose we both of us in the future put the best possible construction upon whatever either of us says that is at all obscure to the reader of the letter. . . .

I thank you sincerely, my dear Edward, for this one promise: that you will abandon at my request any course of conduct that I might disapprove. Know that this assurance has given me more pleasure than anything you ever said as I think 'tis the strongest proof of love I ever received from you. *I believe you*–and after such a declaration I think I can trust my-self with the fullest confidence to such a man. . . .

I should congratulate you on the increase in business if I did not fear that your health would sustain some injury by such constant confinement to such drudgery as teaching. O how I hate it. I would give much that you could give up this part of the business, for I think 'twill hurt you. But of course 'tis impossible at present. . . .

Yours most affectionately,

Addeliza

how do you like my new name, dearest?

Only three days later, and as usual devoting the opening paragraph to the subject of the mails (**no. 211**), Eliza writes once more about her application to music:

. . . Miss Stammers has returned and I have been bothering her and myself at that plaguy instrument. She encourages me always, but still I don't think much of my natural taste for music. I fear I shall never excell in it, and to attempt anything of this sort and not excell is quite beneath my ambition. I love it very much indeed and, if there is anything on earth that in infancy made me fancy myself in Heaven, 'twas hearing a full band of music. I cannot describe to you the rapture I experienced when listening to it. There is something in a good band that always lifts me from earth and keeps me from it till it ceases. I am an enthusiastic admirer of this delightful art as I believe I told you in a former letter, and if you think my admiration of it will carry me well through the drudgery of learning, I will persevere. . . .

I had an invitation to the last ball and was much urged to go, but had not the slightest inclination. I wish you had been here that you might have seen some of our beauty and fashion that is, I assure, you well worth seeing. I believe you did not see any of our belles the night of the ball. If you had been here last week I don't know but I should have gone to see them dance as it was perhaps the last ball that I should ever have the opportunity of witnessing in N[ew] L[ondon]. . . .

Having in a previous letter asked Edward to address her care of her uncle Ebenezer, "Esq.," for which he teases her about her liking for titles, she now replies (**no. 212**):

So you felt disposed to laugh at me, young gentleman, did you, for wishing you to direct letters properly to my uncle. Don't suppose that he ever said a word about the affair, for he is not at all apt to trouble his noddle about such trifles. I never enquired, but conclude, a Public Office constitutes an Esquire, as that is always their address. He has never received a letter from any quarter since he held this Office without Esquire tacked to it. . . .

You wish to know how I would like the title of Countess O'Riley. I assure you I don't care how many titles you muster, but for heaven sake find a name I like better than the one in question. Do you know that my consenting to take it is no small proof of love? Why can't you muster up Fitz Clarence, Fitz Gerald, or some such sweet name. By the bye I like Fitz-Clarence much the best, and shall have fits if you can't contrive to make me a present of it. . . .

I have read [Mme de Staël's] *Corinna or Italy*, and was delighted with it. 'Tis an elegantly written thing. But it has faded from my memory very much as I was quite a child when 'twas put into my hands. Still I never read of genius even in infancy without being deeply interested. 'Twas sure to arouse and fix my attention when nothing else would. . . .

Do you know I cannot think you are in love unless you can send me some exquisite poetry. 'Tis a fact, I assure you, so you must hammer away at your noddle till it will discourse most excellent music. 'Tis a pretty piece of business truly, to tell a lady you will send her something very fine of this sort and after she has set her mouth for the thing many days, to get instead of it a request that she will save you the trouble by writing it herself. I am quite ashamed of you, Sir, and am sure that Cupid has bid you good-bye. The only thing that you can convince me to the contrary is by sending the most sentimental affair that ever was pen'd by man. So look to it. If 'tis not very good I will certainly send it back again, for it is to pass a critical review. You know I like love amazingly. The subject must of course be love, and I will not limit you to two verses as you do me. . . .

When I see you again, you must recollect your promise to wear such & such articles that I am fond of, to look as handsome as I know you can look if you have a mind, and to sing bass. Will you do all this, my sweet? I know you will, so I shall give myself no more uneasiness about the affair. I have set my heart upon your promise so you *must* perform it.

I am thumping away at this deuced instrument. You can't think how I hate it. . . .

Word now from Anna Fitch in early April (**no. 213**) interrupts the flow from Eliza, answering hers of February. There is a dearth of news in New York: a visit from Edward and a book lent by him, mutual friends seen lately, a project to varnish a map which needs some advice on the finish to be used:

. . . I have met with so many interruptions since the commencement of this letter that I begin to despair of finishing it very soon. The first was the entrance of the ex-governor, Mr. Brown, Dr. Bryant and Mrs. Knapp; & last evening I was again engaged with company among whom were Mr. & Mrs. Oakley. The latter inquired if I thought you had any watch-papers to dispose of, as she knew some persons who wished to purchase some.

Mr. Marquand has disposed of your *Mary* & I shall enclose the money in this letter.[10] He says that another is applied for, which, if you think proper to send, I will hand to him. . . .

Have you heard the news that the Great Unknown is at last discovered, & proves to be no other than Walter Scott, after all the pro's and con's? In consequence of a recent failure he has lost the immense fortune acquired by his works, & in order to substantiate a claim has been obliged to swear that he is the author of Waverly. But don't be alarmed–there is at present no danger of starvation, for his wife has a large fortune & he holds a lucrative office, so according to your criterion his claims are not yet very strong to the character of genius. . . .

Affectionately yours,

Anna

A good quantity of other lovers' correspondence survives from this period with which the present series can be compared; also, of correspondence between a small town and a large, the small town generating complaints of its dullness. Mary Way has been heard excusing New London to Eliza, and Eliza deploring it:[11] nowhere "a more destitute place for news than this same New London of ours. 'Tis its stupidity that has given me such a distaste to it–nothing in the shape of amusement presents itself except a dancing school to which Henry goes, and once in a great while we have a ball. I think there has been three this last winter and they talk of having another this spring. Uncle Way & Charles Lewis (Whiting's pupil) are managers. Aunt Way attended one of the balls this winter and I think she will go to the next. She is extremely fond of dancing. We have deaths but no marriages, no murders, no anything to talk about."

But then after all there might be one marriage. That only produces a joke (**no. 215**): " . . . We have just had a very dashing wedding in our renowned City of Gotham. Uncle & Aunt Way attended, and when they returned, which was of course late at night, Uncle sent me up some of the cake (as I had retired) with a charge to put it under my pillow in order to dream of you. Accordingly I placed it there, and instead of your pretty face presenting itself in my dreams, I was annoy'd all night by no less a personage than our beautiful cat Malt. The next morning when I went down I was obliged to give an account of my dreams. Uncle Way laughed heartily at my beau, but I did not care, and determin'd to dream on the cake again, and again, as the rule is three nights. The next night (which was last night) I made a second attempt to get sight of you, and was prevented exactly as I was the first by that rascally cat's presenting himself and no one else. Tonight is the last, and if I dream of her again I will shoot her tomorrow. The name of the lady that was married was Miss Augusta Saltonstall. The gentleman's name is pronounced Arkelarious.[12] How 'tis spelt I know not, as I have not seen it. He is a very rich merchant in New York. His brother came with him to the wedding and has not returned with him and the bride. 'Tis conjectured he has found 'metal more attractive' here. Do you know anything of them?"

Edward kept Eliza's letters and, whether to quantify her love or their tedium, counted them after a couple of months: there had been eighteen (**no. 216**). "How severely your patience must have suffer'd," she answers. She dreads the coming wedding ceremony, which Sally Way intends to make too grand. But she has her own ambitions: "I have determined on being very particular with my dress, and mention it to you for no other purpose than that you should follow suit–that is, wear a suit that you know will particularly please me. Will you do that, dear?" For a change, she complains not of a lack of news to fill her page but of the distractions (**no. 217** of May 4), "for Whistler's rascally flute, Uncle Way's voice and Miss Stammers' fingers have all been as busy as they could possibly be since I have been writing; so you must take it as you find it, for nothing would tempt me to copy it." Then she acknowledges Edward's project to please his relatives-to-be:

> The book and seeds have arrived at the eleventh hour. Aunt [Sally] Way is very much pleased with her present and insists on my giving you a pressing invitation to come up here when our tulips are in bloom. The garden then looks so elegant. I told her I would not, and that if you came before September we should have a spat.
>
> Why do you call the *Opium Eater* [by DeQuincey] excellent? Is it his character you admire, the style, or the moral tendency it is likely to produce generally? I should like to have your opinion of it, & will then give you mine. Last night after I had retired I was startled by the sudden and violent fireing of guns. I learned this morning at breakfast 'twas for the arrival of the renowned [Captain] Halsey [Goddard]; so you may soon expect to see him. But I know I shall not. How exquisitely happy his wife must be at this circumstance, if she has much mind.
>
> So, dear, you permit me to choose your suit, do you? as the milk-maid said. I think green becomes your complexion best, therefore green it must be; but for Heaven sake don't let the coat be too short, for this would surely be the death of me, as boots of you. If you really think that boots would be the death of you, I suppose I must permit you to wear shoes; but if they only cause you two or three

hours' torture, I cannot possibly have shoes worn. Do you know, I thought I should have laughed myself to death at your declaration. Why, my dear Edward, what is a little torture on such an occasion? Just nothing at all. So I hope I shall see the boots, shan't I?

I wish you to have this famous suit made by the most fashionable tailor in New York, the boots by the most fashionable boot shoe-maker, and then just think what a handsome fellow you will be. But not else. So pray attend to it, dear, and excuse my impertinance in dictating in an affair where you do not presume even to advise. Be assured *I* will consult your taste in my dress. . . .

We have fine music here often, and I assure you your presence would at such time be particularly acceptable, particularly to Aunt Way and Eliza W. Champlain. Did you ever see this lady? Be sure bring your flute when you come up and as many more musical instruments as you can play upon. I am ashamed to tell you how slow I progress in music. . . .

To her inquiry if he often went to the theatre, evidently Edward gave the wrong answer, and she compares her own tastes in amusement (**no. 218**):

. . . I am not a little surprised at finding you do not witness Keen's acting every night that he appears, you are so much in love with him. I should like much to see him and hope I shall before he quits New York. I think *The Voice of Spring* is handsome, but I have seen poetry of Mrs. Heman's that I like much better. I thank you for copying it.

I congratulate you on your success in business and hope it will increase, as money is the one thing needful at this time if we are to believe all we hear about no business and hard times.

Uncle [Oliver] Champlain is very ill with pleurisy. I have not seen him and hope when William returns he will bring better news of him, but I think 'tis doubtful how his disorder will terminate. He has been out of health ever since the death of his wife. She was an uncommonly fine woman. . . .

Will you have the goodness to get me with the enclosed dollar an ebony frame the *exact* size of the oval marked on the bottom of this letter. You will find it at Bailey's fancy store in William Street where I always get my drawing and painting materials. I don't recollect the number of the store but when I left he occupied one between John St. & Maiden Lane on the left hand side going down. I don't think he has moved as he has long had that store. If however he should have quit I will thank you to look at the directory for him. Just see that the frame is not scratched and that the glass is clear white, as the fashion of shopkeepers is to put one off with their worst articles if they can. I have met with an accident in a frame that did not belong to me, and am extremely anxious to replace it before the accident is discovered, which I fear will be before long. This is the reason I am so particular. If there is the least difference in them I shall be sorry. The one I speak of was bought at that store [and] cost exactly a dollar and was very handsome. I must then trouble you to put it on a board Lamphere–but when you will catch him in New York I don't know as he has almost just arrived here and is as slow in his movements as in his speech. I was in hopes I should not be obliged to trouble you again with my affairs, but I am and can't promise but I shall again be guilty of the like. I think you have enough to do to attend to your own affairs, without bothering with mine, but you see I consider you my best friend by my asking all sorts of favors of you. . . .

(**No. 220**): So there is no one at Mr. Fitches now to court. I neither wish nor expect you to visit there as often as you formerly did. I only wish you to call as often on them as your own good sense shall direct without the least regard to inclination, as this article must often be sacrificed to the cold and rigid rules of propriety, and don't suppose, my dear, I wish you to visit there for the purpose of obtaining assistance in your business. This would indeed be selfish enough and one of the last things on earth that I should dream of, for tho' Mr. Fitch is a most excellent man, I know he could not benefit you. He is not at all calculated to aid the aspiring. He is retiring and diffident of his own abilities, consequently he will never be a very popular character, as it takes a vast quantity of assurance, and plenty of cash to become a popular character in New York, and 'tis such and such alone, that can patronize. So clear me from this charge immediately, as you value my favor, do you hear? . . .

Mrs. Fitch determined to see me married, and she will do it in spite of my teeth. Unless I am extremely rude I canot refuse to see her on the occasion and as she is my best friend next to you I don't know that I ought to wish her absence. Still I would from choice have only those present that I cannot possible do without, as the less fuss there is on the occasion the better I shall be pleased. But Mrs. Fitch must come. I find from her letter [**no. 219**] that I cannot refuse her request. So you will have the pleasure of escorting her ladyship when you come up, as Mr. Fitches business will of course prevent his leaving the city in September, even if my churlishness would suffer me to extend my invitation to him. But the company of gentlemen on this occasion is much less desirable than ladies, especially quizzical gentlemen. Promise me in your next that not a soul shall know what I have just told you–least of all Mrs. Fitch.

Uncle Champlain is much the same. Dr. North attended him and after bleeding him profusely he ordered them to give him a large pill of opium. 'Twas done but would not ease his excruciating pain. The doctor then ordered another. Just as he had taken the second, William and I went down to see him. He was very glad to see me, appear'd to be quite rational when we first enter'd but soon grew flighty, and began talking to me of my mother's fondness for music, painting, and poetry, and wished to know if *I* was as fond of them all as she was. I told him *no*, that no being on earth could match her in this. He said he supposed not, and then lay some time in a musing posture. He had several severe turns of pain while I staid, which was not long. He had two watchers that night, and the instant they went away in the morning and he was alone an instant he went immediately to the nearest barber's to get shaved and was so exhausted that he was obliged to be carried home. There is no doubt but the opium lent him strength to do this. He has escaped once since just so, but is now too ill to rise from his bed. William has watched four or five times with him, but 'tis the general opinion that he will recover. I sincerely hope so. . . .

As Anna Fitch had complained gently at having no answer to her last, Eliza defends herself (**no. 221**):

My dear Mrs. Fitch,

You know appearances are often deceitful. As you are willing to hear my defence, here it is. I have been some weeks engaged in painting a family piece. I had just finished it when your last letter was handed me. It has left my eyes in a sad state, as they have never entirely recover'd their strength since I had the influenza last winter. This of course was nothing to the purpose. Paint the piece I must, and in a much shorter time than I ever painted so many faces before, as the instant 'twas finished, it was to be sent away. The vessel sailed, at last, sooner than was expected and I was obliged to part with it before I was quite ready, but it gave great satisfaction to the family 'twas intended for, and that was sufficient. I think I never met with a more difficult set of faces. They all had handsome features but no expression. Of course 'twas impossible to get striking likenesses from faces that would not strike. It has been quite impossible for me to touch pen, book, or needle on the evenings of those days that I devoted so laboriously to painting, so I generally practiced at the piano or retired to rest. You know Riley has heard from me since your letter was received, and can, I suppose, guess the reason. I knew if I did not answer his letters almost the instant they arrived, that the first thing I should know he would be in New London; for nothing that ever happen'd to me was more unexpected than his visit here last winter. You know whatever he does is done in the twinkling of an eye. A flash of lightning is not quicker than all his movements, and, as I do not feel desposed to see him before September, I am obliged to do all in my power to prevent his comeing. So between the settings of my patients I have generally scribbled to him a few lines. I mention this because I know you must have thought it very strange and almost inexcusable in me to write anything in the form of a letter before I answer'd yours. . . .

[I] must decline your offer of desposing of another *Mary*. I think I have forever done with such very fine work. Aunt Mary advises me never to think of it again, as she says I have already done too much of it. I will thank you to tell Mrs. Oakley this, if she has not by this time forgotten the request she made about the watch-papers. I believe I told you I had commenced a miniature for [the Fitches' servant] Susan on ivory before I left, as she never was quite satisfied with the one I took for her on paper. As soon as 'tis finished I shall send it to her, if you will be so good as to mention if she is still with you when you write again. I enquired this just before I was attacked with influenza, intending if she was with you to finish it right off. Of course I was prevented , and the fear that she may yet go before I get it finished fidgets me not a little. I have your and Mr. Fitches miniatures in my possession. You will see them again.

Aunt Mary is quite delighted with the *Opium Eater* (what a horrid title the book has). You would fancy her under the influence of opium while she was listening, she was so completely lost. It quite amused me to see her listen, and I assure you

I was fearful she would become as great an opium sot as the writer. I have read it once to her but this is not enough. Miss Stammers must read it again. Miss Betsey Saltonstall is now reading it. The Miss [Augusta] Saltonstall whose marriage you saw in the paper is a very pretty girl. She had quite a dashing wedding. Uncle & Aunt Way attended. Amelia Allen and a niece of Capt. Lee's are spending a week or two with us, so you must not expect anything but a scrawl, which by the bye is I believe what you always get from me, is it not?

I have been very much engaged with music since I commenced taking lessons. I find it an interesting tho' extremely difficult study. The reason I suppose is because, if I learn it at all, I am determin'd to learn it well. This I understand is not at all the fashion now-a-days. They think to skim over the surface of this art, so as to play off a few airs and graces, is quite sufficient without the least knowledge of the groundwork. I am of a different opinion. I think what is worth learning at all is worth learning well and am therefore desirous of diving to the bottom; and, tho' by the time I expect to quit New London I shall scarcely know anything of music, I shall understand more thoroughly what I learn, Miss Stammers thinks, than any other scholar she has, for they are all crazy to learn the first quarter what will benefit them least. She is quite pleased at my determination and thinks I shall play extremely well when I have learn'd, which she says is more than she can say of any other scholar in the way they will learn. I am going to hammer at the rules as long as I stay here but I shall not attempt a tune till I get in New York. I admire Miss Stammers' manner of teaching. She understands well what she is about. She is now in very ill health. She has raised blood ever since she had the influenza and we are all alarmed about her, but she fears nothing.

William has quite recovered. Uncle Champlain has been and is still dangerously ill with pleurisy. He has been repeatedly bled. Doctor North attends him and is doseing him with opium. This makes him so freakish that he running all over town every other day and has watchers every night; and they can't confine him without chains. . . .

I shall be most happy to see you here at the time appointed, tho' I have not yet determined what time in September it will be. You shall know in due season. Remember me to your family and all enquiring friends, and believe me yours sincerely,

Eliza W. Champlain

You asked in your last letter but one for instruction in varnishing. Desolve a small quantety of isinglass by a slow fire (without boiling). Let it be almost cool before you use it. If strong enough 'twill be a thin jelly. Wash the map with this and let it dry thoroughly before you repeat the dose. Do this three times and then 'tis ready for the varnish, which must be as often repeated. Be sure let it dry well between each coat.

Another slight difficulty had arisen between the lovers to which Eliza now returns more forthrightly (**no. 222**):

. . . I see I cannot make you exactly understand what I would be at except I put down every word in plain English. You are the greatest plague I know. I was very willing to make you take a hint in my last, but you appear resolved to put me to the blush in spite of my teeth. It has been hinted to me since your departure (by one that I think much of) that you appear too cold in your manners (when you visited us) for a lover. I said I did not think so–that more fondness than you display'd would have disgusted me and I liked this trait in your character better than any other. I said this, but do you know I felt mortified at what I heard, and thought I would effect a slight change in your manners when we met again if I could. The remark mortified me not a little because it sounded as if the speaker thought I had been 'won unsought,' and as you know I must always speak plain out my wishes, to you, I thought the sooner 'twas over the better. All I wish when we meet, is, that you will treat me a little different from a common acquaintance, and this would be the last thing I should dream of asking if different manners had not been found fault with by a person that I highly respect, as your manners in company in this respect are very much to my liking, I assure you. So don't accuse me again with resorting to tricks for the purpose of encreasing your love, neither accuse me with indelicacy in saying what I have. . . .

Don't have your hair cut close when you come up, for it looks like a fool if you leave it to the taste of the rascally barber. They never know anything. I think I shall like gaters if I can't have boots, but you do look so plaguy young in shoes that I can't endure them. Miss Saltonstall that was, now Mrs. Arcularius, has written home that she has 'found her little Dutchman everything she could wish'–that is, a great dash of course, as this is her hobby. She will cut a fine dash I have no doubt. I shall not visit her tho' she has urged it so much.

Dr. Henry Lee, second son of H. P. Lee, has just arrived with his bride. New London is turned quite topsy-turvy with the fuss made on the occasion. All the gentlemen in town dined there yesterday. Uncle Way has not quite got over his frolic yet. He does enjoy weddings of all things and promises himself much pleasure from mine. The bride sees company tomorrow evening. About two hundreds is expected to attend. Uncle and Aunt will go, but I shall not. The invitations have been out ever since their arrival. She is worth only twenty-five thousand dollars so I suspect 'twas a love match, particularly as she is not handsome.

I suppose you recollect Eliza, Henry's sister. She will shortly be married to young Radcliffe of New York. A Miss Parkin (niece of Frank Winthrop's who has so many country seats about New York)–do you know him?–was married yesterday morning just as the gentlemen had begun to assemble at Dr. Lee's. She lived next door to Dr. Lee's and the street was thronged with carriages all day. She was married to a gentleman by the name of Saltonstall, tho' no relation to the young lady I have been speaking of, only the same name. They started instantly off as soon as the ceremony was performed. This is now the fashion. I like it very much. Don't you think we are having grand times? I do. . . .

Lamphere is not in yet. Do you know he has taken a might shine to you. Don't you feel flattered. Uncle and William say so–that he thinks you a plaguy likely fellow.

Adieu, dear–yours affectionately,

Eliza excuse bad spelling
worse composition

At last, one of Edward's letters (**no. 223**), a short one:

D'r Eliza,

The little song is the work of a few interrupted moments, and its defects must therefore be excused. The words are a translation from the opera of *Der Freyshutz*. They are only tolerable. I chose them solely for their easy adaptation to music, not for their literary merit. If my hasty attempt should be found to contain some faint breathings of genius, attribute them to the love with which you, my beloved girl, have inspired the bosom of your faithful,

Edward. . . .

Toward the end of June came news from Anna of Hannah Dawson's brother lost at sea and of Maria Hayden's imminent departure with her family for New Orleans (where, unknown to her, her husband had just died); also regarding the Ohio governor's marriage to a New York widow (Mrs. Thayer), governess to his children and occasion for an obvious play on words (about as witty as Anna is likely to get); further, thanks from her Susan for Eliza's portrait of her to send to her beau–"she is much obliged to you, & when you return will settle with you for Julian's picture. She has been at St. Thomas' since last winter" (**no. 224**). But a month later (**no. 225**):

. . . Susan has met with a sad disaster. She was just going to enclose her picture in a letter to Julian, & got a spot on the face which, in endeavouring to remove, the skin came with it. This has been a great disappointment, as the vessel is to sail to-morrow. There is however another to leave this [place?] in about a fortnight & I consoled her by saying that she would be able to send it at that time. Alas! for the fine arts when they fall into such sable clutches! . . .

I had nearly forgotten to mention that Mrs. Floyd called here the beginning of this month to see you, respecting a likeness which she wished you to take of a gentleman (another beau, I suppose). She heard at the door that you were absent & sent up for me. I need not say that I was far from being greatly delighted with the call. It appeared from some of her remarks that she knew you had left the city, although she expressed great surprise when I told her you were gone. I said that you thought of returning in Sept. but did not mention how. She requested that I would then inform you of her residence in Fulton St. where she keeps a boarding house. She had no doubt but it might be of some service to you to call. It certainly could be of no disadvantage. Doctors differ, thinks I to myself. . . .

I must not neglect to tell you of my good fortune. I have seen Percival.[13] We were visiting Prince's Garden at Flushing & there met him. I must confess, though it be to the eternal disgrace of my discernment, had I not been told who was coming, I have no doubt that I should have passed him by as a mere fellow being, without ever taking a second look; but as it was, memory recalled those soft and glowing sketches touched by no vulgar hand, & fancy soon discovered the true stamp of genius.

Susan thought that the right cheek bone was too large, but, having explained to her that it appeared so from the position of the head, she seems quite satisfied. . . .

Eliza replies in August (**no. 226**):

. . . I have been so much harrass'd with painting for the last two months it has been quite impossible for me to answer your letter as soon as I intended. I am still very much hurried with business but my stay here will be so short that I shall soon be obliged to refuse whoever applies. I have not yet done this and 'twill go most terribly cross with me when I do, but necessity knows no law. I must. New London is no more agreeable to me than when I first came home, but I would have endured it longer–much longer–rather than act so very much against my interest as quitting it at this time will be, but I find that all my eloquence has no weight with Riley on this subject. Go I must before the middle of September, ready or not ready. Don't you think this is most abominably provoking? *I* do. If I had known exactly how I should have been situated in New London at this time I never should have come to the conclusion that I have–that is, if we could foresee events we should avoid doing many things that we now do, because we cannot see into futurity, and perhaps it is best that we cannot lift the veil, if we could only think so. Don't suppose from what I say that I repent deciding as I have. I assure you I do not. I only wish I had put off my departure to a later period, and 'tis now too late to repent.

I have just finished a couple of miniatures for the two young Lewis's, sons of a deceased nabob that formerly lived here. I don't know but I mentioned them to you in a former letter. They are highly delighted with them. I am now taking the likeness of Mrs. Ogdens. Do you know her? She is from New York. She was a Seyton, tho' I believe no relation to Catharine. She is English, and her manners are extremely polished. I am quite in love with her. She is not at all handsome. . . .

[Aunt Mary] has requested me to say to you that she shall depend on your bringing with you every-thing that ever you wrote in your life and if you do not she shall never get over the disappointment.

Uncle and Aunt Way are trying to persuade me to go to Pomfret and spend a day or two before I quit New London. Aunt [Amelia] Allen's family[14] are so desirous of seeing me, and Aunt Mary says if I go, as I certainly *must*, that she and you will have a grand time at reading. It really hurts my conscience that I have not been able to read any more to her since my return, but almost every moment has been devoted to necessary business and scarcely one to reading. Miss Stammers & William cannot read on account of their lungs and want of time prevents all the others, so you see she is completely deprived of this greatest of all amusements, and 'twill be quite a deed of charity to bring up everything in the form of your writing when 'twill give so much more pleasure than anything else. She says she shall not be half so glad to see you without your children [=writings], so bring them up I pray you. Eliza Lee generally devotes Sunday afternoon to reading to her but she is supposed by her family to be in consumption and is now travelling for her health. . . .

I am much pleased at Mrs. Thayer's success [in marrying the governor of Ohio], and hope he is as great a man as I believe his predecessor [Ethan Allen Brown] was, and is. Riley don't like her much because she threw the 'husks' in the face of his church when she found there was nothing else to glean. I don't much blame the woman, for really their [Swdenborgian] religion is in my opinion a 'dry morsel in quietness,' and I don't much think I shall ever fumble with it. I have been giving him a lecture for speaking of her with the bitterness he has, since her marriage, but don't tell him what I say. I know he hates her, let him talk as he will.

If I had been urged to go to Portland when I could have accepted the offer I no doubt should have gone, and am glad that I have been prevented as I begin now to think I never was born to succeed to my liking in any undertaking. I am however much obliged to Mrs. Dearing for interesting herself about me. . . .

Well, at last, plans for the wedding got serious; Samuel must be told, and his brother William writes him an affectionate invitation to the affair (**no. 227**):

. . . I have mentioned to you before this, that [their sister] was to be married, and to whom. Eliza thinks you will take no notice of this, or else she would write you herself. Now, Sam, if you can come, it will be really a happiness; for it will be the first time (should you come) since you left home, and in that time you know what a complete revolution has taken place. Did you think, Sam, when you parted with Mother so carelessly, it was the last time you were to set eyes on her in this life? You did not, I know. Yet probably she did, for her spirits were heavy until you were well situated, and then she was forever thinking of you. Life to her was a burthen. Death was kind to her alone. How much I miss her no one knows, for no one was placed as I was. She was a *mother* in the true sense of the word to us all. Poor Father is forgotten when her name is mentioned. Yet may God rest his soul.

We all are well. If you cannot come, will you answer this letter and tell us the reason why?

Ever your brother,

Bill

But Sam explains (**no. 228**):

Your kind letter of the 18th [August] I rec'd yesterday requesting me to come up to N[ew] L[ondon] and be present at Eliza's marriage, (by the way) something entirely unexpected and agreeably suprising, I assure you, for I had no idea that this thing could have been carried on so long, and I heard nothing about it from any quarter, with the exception of your mentioning in one of your letters something about 'Eliza's beau Mr. Riley' &c–but as every girl has her beau I thought (you know) nothing more about the matter.

But Bill (between you and I) I believe him to be a very fine young man, what little acquaintance I have had with him, and certainly very much of the gentleman in his manners; and Eliza used to think so, too, for frequently she would ask me 'what I thought of Mr Riley.' 'Wasent he handsome' &c, & then show me his miniature, & when I'd say, 'O, I don't know,' 'Yes you do, you little fool you' would be the next thing.

But, Bill, about my coming up to New London, I know of nothing 'under heaven' that would gratify me so much as to see Eliza married to the man of her heart; but I am so situated that I could not be gone 6 hours without having some-one of the other clerks to do my work for me & his own too, & at this time 2 of our best are very unwell. I hardly see how it could be possible for me. My situation is 2d bookkeeper (there are 5), and my ledger (A. to E.) the largest in the bank by two folios, having 2752 accounts altogether. There is no putting off until next day all the deposits that are made & all the checks that are drawn. About 250 checks and as many credits or deposits that go into my ledger or are my letters *must* be posted and the accounts examined to see that no man overdraws his account (for in these times of terror the banks are very particular), & that, too, between 10 & 3 o'clock. Since I have been in the bank I have never left it for an hour except on business that concern'd it (& that is more than any other man in it can say), because I knew that every-thing depended upon my good conduct.

So you see how poorly I could leave. Was I any-thing but a bank clerk, I could find time to go out of town, but they poor devils are obliged to be always at the desk.

Give my love to Eliza, tell her God knows I wish her all the happiness that this life can afford, and to Mr. Riley my best wishes & congratulations.

Remember me to Uncles Eb., Oliver & Thomas, and their ladies, not forgetting Aunt Mary, dear soul, & all the rest of the relatives–both houses, 'York & Lancaster.' Tell Uncle Tom that I have not pull'd a trigger in almost 6 years! (It's the first six, faith). How is that little curl'd maple gun of his? Is she as good fire as ever?

Adieu. I am still & ever your brother,

Sam

N.B. I r'c'd 2 letters a few days since from George. He is well and sends his love to you all. Bill, write as soon as you receive this.

On September 10th, in Ebenezer Way's house and by the family's friend, the Rev. Bethel Judd of St. James church, Edward and Eliza were married.[15] Her New London days were over. Off she went to New York, there to take up a married life.

15

Much about the Brothers

Within a few weeks after her arrival in New York, Eliza wrote to William to give him a picture of her new life. She and Edward had rented rooms on James Street two blocks over from the Fitches, one block over from Pearl Street where many of their other friends and acquaintances lived; they enjoyed little excursions in place of what a later generation would call a wedding trip; but she had been working hard, too. Likewise, William: her reference to her brother's "gaugeing instruments" indicates his new job, a subordinate position in the Customs office under Captain Richard Law added to one in the postoffice under Ebenezer Way:[1]

> I have scarcely time to breathe on account of those deuced miniatures that I wish from my soul I had never commenced. I must be every instant jaunting about and can-not possibly give them the finishing touches.
>
> On Sunday we went in a gig to Patterson Falls, and came within an ace of being thrown out. R[iley] got his forehead cut very bad, I had my foot crushed a little. It is now better. As the hotel we stopt at was crowded with company I took a private dinner, and him, half starved to death from riding so far. I did credit to my keepers. We had every delicacy of the season in great abundance. After our meal was concluded we took a guide & proceeded to the Falls which is about a mile from the principle hotel. I was much pleased, for although so far inferior to Niagara they are still sublime. On our return to the house Riley was accosted & congratulated by Baldwin, the first clerk in the Mechanics' Bank, on his marriage. They have always known each other. 'Tis the same fellow that Sam values so highly. He is a very worthy chap I am told.
>
> Early on Tuesday morn Riley called on Sam at the bank to inform him of my arrival. My loving brother was quite delighted to hear it and congratulated him on his marriage & sent me word he should come to my boarding house the moment the bank closed. I awaited his arrival with the greatest impatience as I wished to go out after seeing him. 'Twas a week yesterday since he has known of my being

here & I have not seen him, so when I am honored with a call you will get your gaugeing instruments & and not before. Riley despises his show of affection more than anything else. I am quite indifferent to his capers, for I find him not worth caring for; so he can act as he likes about calling.

Give my love to all our folks. How do you & Miss Stammers come on & Mary & Lewis [Allen]? Tomorrow we go out of town to visit Mr. Doughty, Riley's [Swedenborgian] minister. I should be quite willing to get excused, but there is no come-off–go I must. The devilish musquitoes have bit my soul out since I have been here. I have counted 84 bites on the back of one hand since I commenced this letter. The other hand is an excellent match, so stiff with lumps that I can scarcely guide the pen. I find their bites very poisoning indeed.

Write soon. . . .

In her next (**no. 230**), she straightens out her instructions about having her belongings shipped to her, and touches on New York names of interest to Mary Way: the elder Clinches, Maria Hayden, Anna Fitch, the non-existent Sam; but to this William responds only briefly (**no. 231**, November 12 of 1826):

I have received your letter, and answer it immediately. We are all well, therefore let that give you no uneasiness. Aunt Mary told me to tell you that she was so low-spirited she could not write but beg'd that you would write her–which don't fail to do.

Tell Edward that I am verry much oblig'd indeed for that ale; that it was excellent, but unfortunately 3 bottles got broke on its passage up.

I will not fail to send that chest and trunk by Lampheer his next trip.

Give my love to E[dward] and others in authority. How is Sam? Do you hear from George? Write all particulars. I should have written before but I have been much employed at the Custom House and on board of vessels as Inspector. I am now on board the Sch[oone]r *Mark*, where I shall be detained two or three days at least, and I have been on board of other vessels is the reason I have not written you before. My pay is three dols. per day. I have purchased a second-hand set of gauger instruments for five dollars, therefore shall not want a new set. Tell Riley I am a thousand times obliged to him for his kind attention & inquiries respecting them for me.

Write soon. Ever your brother,

Bill

I wish you to ask Mr. Lee[2] what is the best medicine for bile except mercury, for *that* I will not take, and I think his skill in such things great. I have been under the necessity of consulting a physician on this and my constant medicine, magnesia. Now I have precious little faith in these things because they are both so palatable. Still, I shall follow his prescriptions unless told that they are not good. I have an excellent appetite.

Mary Way is now heard from, writing on Christmas Eve (**no. 232**) but adding one continuation after another to her letter till the end of February, 1827, over the course of a bitter winter–bitter in a double sense. She cannot reconcile herself to her blind state and its consequences, cannot philosophically forgo both painting and writing; so at least she writes, even when there is nothing to say, and suffers from the tedium she inflicts on her reader–eight pages of tedium, of which only parts are given:

My dear Eliza,

. . . 'Welcome kindred glooms, congenial horrors hail!' Poor Maria,[3] I know her character and feelings. Your account of her distress 'accords with my soul's sadness.' From our first acquaintance I marked her as the child of sorrow. I saw too plainly she was born to suffer, and this presentiment awakened then the deepest interests, the most sincere commiseration–not that cold pity the world in general bestows on the unfortunate.

. . . Don't tell me I am less unfortunate. I will not yield the palm of misery to her–no, not to Job himself. I feel my own preeminence in this and will maintain my right. There are afflictions Job never had experienced. 'Could I disclose the secrets of my prison house,' he might have blushed to grieve at such a rate for slighter evils. What is the loss of friends, of health and property (the first may be replaced, the last restored)–'trifles light as air,' mere every-day occurences, transient evils that all must feel and suffer more or less. Common trials require but common fortitude. There is a deeper deadlier woe, if I had words to speak it. Do you meditate among the tombs and fear being buried alive? I am, and can tell you all about it. Does imagination lead you to the prisonhouse, the dungeon's gloom? There you may find a subject worthy of an artist.

. . . So you have left Mr. Mitchell's church, it may be, with as much sang-froid as tenants change their houses for a more convenient place of residence. Tho' I think you must feel some regret, I am not disposed to pity you, for had you known the real worth of such a church and such preaching you would not have renounced it, no, not for fifty husbands were they all made of gold and set with diamonds. I mean no disparagement to the husbands or to New-Jerusalemitish principles, which, tho' less understandable, is no doubt as good as many other doctrines and traditions of men, though to me it appears far more obscure. Some years ago I studied hard to comprehend its incomprehensibilities and tried to dive into the mysterious 'sience of corespondances,' but found less pearls than pebbles there. The former lay too deep for my research. I should be pleased to have been present at the attack made on Mr. Riley by two such redoubted champions as Mr. Dean and Mr. Mitchell. The odds was great–one, I should think, would have been abundantly sufficient. You say he stood his ground like a good fellow. I should like to have seen how he could defend himself against 'the weapons of there warfare, which are mighty, to the pulling down of strong-holds.'

Present my affectionate regards to the Mitchells, Mr. and Mrs. Fitch, and Mrs. Northam, those dear friends I most esteem and value. I long to see them but don't expect to till we meet at that grand feast above–tho' I would like to indulge my appetite and take a luncheon with them here below, just to stay my stomach for the present and give me patience to wait for those more solid and substantial pleasures.

We are glad to hear you think of making us a visit next summer, and hope you will not fail to do so. We are quite anxious you should fulfill your engagements, for, to say nothing of your conscience and its advantages to yourself, your company will be no small gratification to your friends, and beside all this you have gained much credit as an artist and given such general satisfaction here, a visit from your pencil may be esteemed a public benefit and insure you a double welcome, as it is presumed you cannot see youth and beauty fading around you and refuse to stretch forth a friendly hand to save it from oblivion. Therefore, bring——

January 14th 1827

Here Mrs. Lee entered and broke the thread of my discourse, just as I was about [to] say bring plenty of flannel and come prepared to make us a good long visit. 'Tis three weeks to-day since this letter was written. The day before Christmas was Sunday, the family were all at church as usual, and I was left alone to indulge my own sad reflections and pour over the miseries of life; so for want of better business, pour'd them on the slate for your amusement. While I was thus employed, Mrs. Lee came in. She read my letter, exorted, lectured, and reproved me for giving way to moping melancholy and brooding over irremediable misfortunes. Like the friends of Job she talk'd and reason'd wisely on the subject, and like them too she talk'd in vain, for I can say with him, 'miserable comforters are ye all!' How easy to preach to others in affliction, how hard to practice, when it comes home to ourselves. She says if I will spend a week or two with her she will engage to cure me of the blues. The cure is not so easy. When the cause is removed the effect will cease, and not before.

. . . I have the pleasure to inform you that Mrs. Henry Lee [Jr.] has grown quite popular. Our descerning ones have at length discovered something agreeable about her and allow she mends upon acquaintance. The frown that lowers upon her brow is intersected by the smile of good humour; her rough unpolished manner, free, easy, unsophisticated nature–plays and sings divinely, gave a party this winter, appeared to much advantage, and performed to admiration. Your uncle, aunt, and Miss Stammers were there, and all charmed. . . . Feb[ruar]y 22nd 1827

. . . Washington's birth-night that they are now celebrating concludes the balls and terminates their dancing for the winter. Next week is spring! my own delightful season, in days of other years, when 'from the chambers of the fleecy east the very spring look'd out–look'd out and smiled.' With transport I have watch[ed] and welcomed its approach. Could you have known the feeling it inspired, you would have thought I had my share of bliss. Where are those raptures now? Others may see its beauties and pertake its pleasures, but what is it to me? A lesson of instruction, source of consolation, a bright and striking emblem of the Resurrection.

Adieu!

The wintry storms of life will soon be past,
And one unbounded spring encircle all.

Thompson

The months spent on Mary's long lament were punctuated by letters that her niece and nephew exchanged. However, they both had troubles of their own: William on January 10th (**no. 233**) must report their uncle Ebb under attack, but the situation in the Customs office on which he himself now principally depended was even more grave. Unlike Ebb, he had no financial resources to fall back on. Now, the port's activities from the high days of fifteen years prior had fallen off precipitously in the second decade of the century, failed to recover against the competition of New York, and remained sadly diminished:[4]

. . . I inclose you the dollar I have owed you so long, and right glad it's in my power to do so. Commercial business here is at its lowest ebb. I am told by the Collector (Capt. Law) that since he has been in office he has never known so dull times, and I sincerely hope it will grow no worse. I have not had an opportunity of guaging since I have been in office, which to be sure is but one quarter, yet that is uncommon. My receipts for the last quarter was but forty-eight dollars. That, however, was nearely enough to pay all my debts, lawyers and all, which comforts me much.[5] Since you have left here, at a town meeting held in this town, Mr. Way was turned out his office as town clerk and Henry Douglass, a shoe-maker, appointed. This was done by a parcel of young fellows, a few of the leading ones having some enmity to Mr. Way. The fees of this office you know came to me. However, I cared verry little for it as it was worth but 30 or 40 dollars per year and more bother to attend to it than would ballance the income. Before the choice, however, these young men came to me and offered to put me in if I would accept; but I declined, for the reasons stated, and also because Mr. Way might think I was combined with them to deprive him of it. Another thing: should there be any business stirring, I shall have as many offices as I can attend to. I write in the Collector's office evry day and stay at Uncle Ebb's after I get through there, which is from 9 o'clock in the morning until 4 in the afternoon.

I wish you would make Sam write me, for he is too neglectfull of 'his poor relations in Connecticut' entirely. Remember me to Riley and ask him if he will inquire of his father whether he received a letter from me dated the 26th Dec. 1826 enclosing $4.31, which was due him for the music I sold and which I sent by mail, as I feel anxious to know whether he has received it.

All here are well without one exception, and I hope will continue so. I wish you and young a happy new year. Mr. Way has sold Judge Perkins a [lottery] ticket that drew a prize of 1056 dollars. That's a darned pritty kettle of fish, as Joe Strickland says. Write without fail and answer all I have asked you.

Ever yours,

William

Dowe said the other day, when I gave him a new one-dollar bill like the one I enclose, that he had as lief put a tin pan in his pocket, it made so much noise–said in his way.

"Dear William," Eliza replies the next week (**no. 234**):

I should have answered all your last letters with my usual promptness but for a most rascally nervous disorder with which I have lately been attacked. It is entirely owing to the confinement I endured while in New London. If my nerves had been composed of iron they might possibly have stood the racket, but being 'made of penetrable stuff' they are now paying me off in high style. If I had known when I condemn'd myself to the pencil from morning till night, and to the needle from night till morning, how severely I should suffer for it, I would have sent them both to his Satanic Majesty in the twinkling of an eye, spite of its consequences; but I never dreamed of what was to follow. I thought 'twas a momentary inconvenience I suffer'd. I now fear 'twill be lasting as life, for, of all the evils in creation, a nervous attack is the most intolerably tedious. A physician has been applied to. He says the optic nerve is strain'd and that nothing but early rising, frequent walks in the open air and dieting will restore my nerves to their former tone–a total discontinuance (of course) of all my previous habits, for they have been very pernicious. I am not allow'd to paint, to read, to eat or do anything else but walk insessantly and practice the piano. He thinks with our romantic cousin that 'music has charms to soothe the savage breast,' and in fact so do I. I am confidant that I could not have undertaken anything so beneficial as learning music at this time.

As all the evils in Pandora's box attend this vile complaint, one of the greatest is a dimness of sight, apparently occasioned by the sudden and violent rushing of blood to the head, with extreme pain in the eyes at strong or even moderate light–a distress almost producing faintness at bright colours. In consequence of this dislike of light & brightness I am under the necessity of excluding all light except just enough to see my notes as I practice the piano, and when I walk, to guard against it as well as I can. I have had serious thoughts of being cupped, for I know my head is overflowing with blood; but I cannot muster courage, and to be let blood with the lancet is what I can never think of. Mr. Fitch advises me by all means to be cupped for it. He has been attacked by the same complaint in consequence of straining his eyes with poring over law books late at night. He has been cupped and received benefit. But as I look upon bleeding in any shape only as temporary relief & as I have an utter abhorance of this same violent remedy, I shall endeavour to get at some method that will strike at once to the root of the matter. A total suspension for the present of all work that could possibly strain the eyes is the first step; doseing for bile, the next; and so on. . . .

I have never had a glimpse of Sam since the first time I saw him after my arrival, nor has Ann Fitch seen him since long before that time; so whatever message you would convey to him must be through some other channel. Riley has seen him at a distance several times and thinks him very thin in flesh. I think it more than probable that the confinement he endures at the bank will ultimately destroy him.

Tell Miss Stammers that I have not forgotten her miniature. Remember me to Mrs. Culver and tell her that if I do not visit New London during the warm season and fulfil my promise about the miniature of her, that I will make all the reperation in my power, which will be finishing the likeness of her brother that is commenced on ivory, as a substitute for what I was prevented doing. It is probable that I shall at some rate or other see Uncle Ebb & Mary again in the flesh and perform my promise about their profiles. An unperformed promise weighs heavier on my conscience, I believe, than it does on most people's that I have known intimately, for I would rather have taken the likeness of that little Hurlbut without receiving one cent for it than have engaged it and been obliged to abscond as I did. . . .

–and the letter closes with news of Anna Fitch's lace-making and parties and other trifles (or "triffles" as all three sisters of the brush were used to spelling the word).

In Eliza's next (**no. 235** of March 4th) there is more news of ill-health:

. . . Samuel has had a most alarming fit of inflammatory rheumatism. He is now recovering but he has been dreadfully ill. We of course discover'd it by accident. One of his fellow clerks in the bank who is acquainted with Mr. Riley met him and told him of Sam'l's situation. We both of us immediately went to his boarding house and found his disorder at its crisis. If I had unexpectedly met him looking as he then did I certainly should not have known him–so much had pain and sickness alter'd him. At the time we call'd he was in such excruciating pain with his disorder that he did not feel the pain of six blisters that were at that moment drawing on different parts of his pale and emaciated forehead. He could scarcely speak when we address'd him. I told him I was going to write to you and asked if he had any message to send. After a violent effort he told me to tell you that he was going to send you a gun. He has since his disorder taken a more favorable turn–told Mr. Riley who was calling on him that you were as clever a little fellow as ever was *spawn'd*. So don't send him any more of your Champlainish letters, at least till he recovers.

I feel fearful that his sedentary life will either put a period to his existence before many years or else lay a firm foundation of complaints in old age. His constitution is dreadfully impair'd. He did not wish that you should be informed of his illness but I fear'd your letters to him and was determined to tell you his situation. . . .

The family with whom we board expect to move the first of May to a delightful house in Broad-Way. As we like them very much, we calculate on going with them. The house in question is at present occupied by a physician of eminence. The rent is eight hundred dollars a year; but I value it more for its situation than anything else, for I do abominate this part of the town most cordialy. It is too near Cherry Street that I always hated. . . .

We talk some of going to England before long. I don't know how it will terminate. I should be pleased to see England but should not wish to reside there.

How does your weighing & gaugueing business come on? I hope 'tis at least as profitable as ever. I forgot to say that Sam is attended constantly by two of the finest women that ever existed, the lady of the house and her daughter. Sam say'd he should have died but for them. There is nothing that can add to his comfort that it's in their power to bestow but the[y] do so with the greatest cheerfullness. They are Quakeresses.

Since the foregoing was written, Sam'l has almost entirely recovered. He has not yet been to the bank nor will he go for some days. Tell Aunt Mary I want to know why she don't write to me. 'Tis altogether beyond my comprehension.

When I first came here I was introduced to my sister Louisa Riley. I thought her one of the most beautiful creatures I had ever seen. She was universally admired for her beauty. A very few weeks ago she was seized with that most villianous of all bile complaints, the (?)varisloid, and after suffering beyond expression she is at length well, with the total loss for the present at least of her beauty. We hope by August that she will recover her former looks but think it very doubtful.

Mr. Riley has been very happy in meeting of late an old friend that he has not seen in four years. He was Capt. of Marines in the Columbian Navy. He has now gone on to France for the purpose of recovering property left him by his grandfather that will enable him to carry on mercantile operations on a large scale. He is a most interesting youth. I was quite smitten with the melancholy smile that kept its station around his beautious mouth. His nose is 2 sizes larger than Mr. R.–'s, consequently 'tis his most prominent feature. Seriously tho', he is one of the most elegant fellows I have seen for many a long day, and extremely interesting, and if he had not quit this country as he did I certainly think I should have set my cap for him. He is such a Jimmy Boy, as Dow would say. His name is Hyacinth Robert Agnel. He has a sister married in Portugal by the name of Felicity. Did you ever hear such beautiful names in your life? . . .

And from the Hyacinthe Agnel in question next comes the following (**no. 236**) in abbreviated form which preserves only a page with a clever little sketch of Gibraltar. He has recalled the memory of his visit with the young Rileys which made him

. . . as happy as my present fluctuating fortunes would have permitted, & I am allowed to think the sympathy of our tastes have rendered you equally so.

I spent this day on shore, having obtained a permit, for the procuring of which some formality is necessary. The town is prettily built, extremely clean, neatly paved & very thickly populated; pretty women, English & Spanish, whose appearance tended not a little to fortify my prejudice upon a certain point. The troops make a fine appearance–fine manly fellows & officers. There are three regiments here of which one, Highlanders, a novel sight, you may judge, to me. I admire them much.

I have not yet visited the fortifications, practised in the solid rock, which is in a great measure excavated, but will in a few days when I should be able to give you a more circumstantial acc't. From the quarantine ground I took a sketch of the rock & annex the profile. It will give you an idea of the form of this tremendous place. The rock is 1600 feet high, perfectly shelving on the Mediterranean side. The following view was from the bay. . . .

This afternoon I took a walk upon the neutral ground [indicated as such in the sketch] & had a full view of the placid blue waters of the Mediterranean &, beyond the streets as far as the eye can reach, the mountains of Andaluzia with their summits capped with snow. The climate here is delicious, the air is still keen. I feel a certain vivifying something in the atmosphere I never experienced in America. Vegetation in force. Oranges, vegetables &c stock the markets.

I shall probably write you next from Marseilles. I do not write from here to your father but will from M[arseilles]. Tell him the cheese was an excelent relish & the porter proved divinely exquisite after the many repeated Eastward dinners of codfish & potatoes, which made me feel excessive regret at the privation of his favourite bubble-&-squeak, Irish stew, toad-in-a-hole, &c &c. My love to your mother. Tender my sentiments of friendship to Henry, Frederick & Louisa & Albert. Remember me to Mr. Jacobson . . . ,

the last-named being the manager of the Riley store.

Eliza's next (**no. 237**) marks the beginning both of the month of April and of her handsome imported letter-paper, in marked contrast with the odd and sometimes re-used scraps or workaday local manufacture which she had made do with in the past.[6] From this just as well as from other details of the correspondence at this point, the relative prosperity of her husband's business may be guessed. His hard work was paying off:

Dear William,

I was very much surprised a few evenings since by the appearance of Miss Stammers. If I had seen a spectre I should scarcely have been more startled, for notwithstanding what you said in a former letter respecting her visiting me soon I put very little faith in it, as I have known her talk of leaving New London before without doing so, and supposed that this threat would end like the others. But I was hartily glad to see her and was in hopes I could have kept her at least all night; but she had scarcely seated herself before she was seized by half a hundred relations at least, and I was obliged to forego the pleasure that a little conversation of absent friends would have given me. Mary & Martha[7] with their guide instantly laid violent hands upon their victim and, in spite of all my eloquent entreaties, bore her from my sight. She tells me (what by the bye I well knew before) that there is nothing on earth so fickle as the breath of patronage. Faith, 'tis a broken reed to lean on. 'Twill rarely blow us the necessaries of life, setting aside its superflueties. I am sorry New London has not taste enough to encourage such an elegant science as music. 'Twill not tell well in history, I'm thinking.

We endeavoured to persuade Miss S. to accompany me to the Euterpean Concert which was to take place in a few evenings (and if she had consented, *I* would have gone, although I have not ventured at any public place this winter); but she said the illness of her little sister put it out of her power to go at all, so I instantly abandoned the project altogether.

Give our respects to Col.'l Walbank and family, but tell them and all whom it may concern (as politely as you please) that Mr. Riley will have nothing at all to do with the tuning of organs. Upright nor downright pianos, neither stringed nor wind instruments are to be improved by his skill during his stay at New London. This same determination has passed from his lips according to the laws of the Medes & Persians that altereth not; so you can if you please make known this piece of his mind to the Col.'l, Gen'l North & all others in authority. He has said it. Mr. R. wishes all those that would like to employ him in this way to thoroughly understand this determination of his before he visits New London, that he may not be annoy'd when there by requests of this sort. This branch of his business is never attended to by him except with very old and proffitable customers, and will soon be dropped entirely, as it never was an object, and only attended to in certain cases to avoid giving offence; but there is no need of putting it in the paper. Just mention it to any one and 'twill spread east, west, north & south in a twinkling.

By the bye, I don't see the use of a printing office in your good city. Your tongues wag with such extreme nimbleness, taking the paper was always quite an unnecessary expense.

Sam's friend De Angelis informed Mr. Riley the other day that he was at the bank again but still an invalid and rather lame of one leg yet. I am very sorry to hear this as I hoped his disorder would have left him entirely before he was obliged to go again to business. He has had ten blisters and two or three bleedings, poor fellow.

I do not give much credit to the information you have received respecting George, as I do not think it correct. I cannot think him so fallen. When your letter first arrived, thinking your statement might possibly be true, Mr. Riley & myself felt very unpleasantly; but on strict investigations being made by Mr. R. into the affair we give it up as a false report. The information given was to this effect, and given by a manager of the circus, that a person (not answering in one particular to the description of George) had been attached to the circus, by name Daniel C.– that he died about two months ago somewhere amongst his friends. This certainly is more likely to be true than what you heard. For my own part I think I had rather hear of George's death than that he belonged to such a desperate class of villians as they are–even the best of them, low as the dirt. A snuffer of candles at the theatre is in comparison an emperor on the throne.

Remember me to the households of faith & tell Aunt Mary that I have received her welcome letter and will reply to it as soon as I return from Orange Springs, where I am going immediately for the benefit of my health, which strenuously demands this jaunt or some other. If the pressure of business demands it (which I greatly fear it will), Mr. Riley will leave me there for a fortnight, as a shorter stay would not have the desired effect. . . .

On the same elegant letter-paper Edward next month writes to his wife. She is at East Orange recovering, as she said, from her debility (**no. 238**), while he must return to his business:

D'r Eliza,

After a most unpleasant ride through clouds, I might say masses, of dust, we arrived at 296 Broadway, looking like a couple of millers. Dinner was sent up stairs, as we were not fit to go to table. The doctor asked particularly after you. I thought he felt slighted that you had not tried his powders before you went. He says they were prepared by himself, very carefully, expressly for your case. He anticipates great results from them. You are only to take them occasionally. By the bye, I told him a fib: I said you had taken one at Orange and did not experience nausea. I am sorry I did so, but he would have felt so mortified if I had told him you had not. This, Mrs. Opie would call a bit of benevolence.[8]

I left the store at the usual hour last evening, thinking to return home immediately, but when I reached the house I felt so solitarie, so desolate without you, that I wandered about Broadway till a late hour and when I did go to bed my sleep was restless & uneasy. Pray write, dear. Tell me how you feel, wether you exercise much, sleep well, if you find the Kilburns [tavern-keepers] kind & attentive–in short, tell me all about you. Have you seen Father? We get no news of him. He's a strange man. No doubt he's wandering thro' Jersey from Dan to Beersheba, and we are totally without clue as to the direction he has taken. If he is at Orange, tell him Mother is angry with him for leaving her so long in anxiety about him.

I tried to find your boots but cannot, you have packed ev'ry-thing so clos'd. Send [?]Almacks as soon as you have done with it. Tell [niece] Louisa I'll kiss her twice when I return, for forgetting to do so when I left. I hope to bring Wm. when I come for you. Write soon, dear. I am anxious about you.

Edward

William's Customs business sometimes required his attending court sessions in New York, and probably on this account he saw his sister in the city in May of 1827. The visit interrupted their letter-writing; but at the beginning of July after he had returned home, "My dear William" writes Eliza (**no. 239**):

I should have answered your letter before this, as I was very anxious to hear from you (fearing you had gone to Davy Jones on your passage up); but my head won't let me attend to any-thing but itself. It is a most villianously unruly member and exasperates me very often. There is nothing in creation that will benefit it in the slightest degree, and I have therefore given up the use of nostrums.

So you at last know, my dear Billy, how delightful a thing it is to live in New London with your heart in New York. I can tell you, my dear, I have served a faithful apprenticeship to that business in days of yore, and it may be my hapless lot to end my days there, as we know not what a day may bring forth; and the evils we most fear often come upon us. But I can safely say I do not wish such a fate. In any situation, give me New York to New London. I have dragged on many a weary month there in the vain expectation that some propitious turn of fortune would recall me here, but devil a turn in my favor did I ever get from the beast in all my days. I hartily wish you could live in New York, as 'twould make my time pass much more pleasantly as well as your own; but the time is not yet, and till a favorable opportunity presents itself I would by all means advise you to stick close to your business there and do nothing rash. It is much easier to get into a scrape than to get out of it. This I know by experience, when I was in business here three years ago. If your prospect is fair where you are, don't for heaven sake quit it till you are sure that 'tis fairer here, or you may rue it.

I have not seen George or Sam since you left nor do I expect to till you come down again and ferret them out of their holes. R. says I have a precious set of brothers. I cordially agree with him. Except you, I have not one an atom like a human being. I think you are much more like folks than could have been expected on the occasion. I wish you could be here on the fourth [of July]. I would give all my old shoes to see you on this great day, as there is more fuss making than usual and we have such a glorious prospect from our situation.

Miss Stammers call'd on the next afternoon of the one you left. I was provoked beyond measure that it happen'd so, but you know 'the course of true love never did run smooth.' It seems she call'd at my papa[-in-law]'s store on the evening of the day that you left here. Mr. R[iley Sr]. was in and informed her that you had been here on a visit and had just call'd on him for the purpose of taking leave. You was of course then on board and off, for 'twas late when she call'd. I asked him how she stood affected at this intelligence, for I thought, if she had any-thing of the heroine (as 'tis miscall'd) about her, that she either fainted on the spot or exhibited the most unheard of fortitude–as you know, 'tis said of the ladies that they always do one or the other of those things on those occasions. But I was a little startled on hearing that she show'd the utmost indifference, and did not even require the slightest assistance from a brandy, rum or gin sling, salts, hartshorn, or aromatic vinegar. Yes, strange as it may strike you, she stood her ground most manfully. She neither sank upon a seat with the paleness of monumental marble overspreading her lovely features nor did the truant blush rush to the aforesaid features and betray her secret, spite of her teeth. No, she stood the shock with most surprising firmness.

When I heard this account, thinks I to myself, Billy, Billy, this looks rather squally. But I said nothing, thinking it best to make my own observations before expressing an opinion on the subject. I had not long to wait. The following afternoon brought her ladyship to my residence. After she had been in a short time, I carelessly said, So William has been here on a visit. She said, Yes, so she understood; and she was not a little surprized at his not calling on her. I told her I understood Mr. R[iley Sr]. that she was not surprized at all at the seeming inattention on your part, and instantly explained how it happened that you did not call. She said that where she felt most, she ever express'd least. So you may make your account of it, for now my story's done. I know nothing of her family at all.

Love to Aunt Mary and the family. I know not how my intended visit to New London will terminate, but, however it may be, I can assure you 'twill not be from freakishness if I don't come, as I have thought much about it and calculated much on it. Mr. Riley's business increases so fast that he can scarce get time to eat and I'm doubtful if it would be possible for him either to come with me or for me, situated as he is at present. Mrs. Fitch has no idea of coming after all the talk, and to go alone would be rather disagreeable to one constructed as I am. Mr. R. is rather of opinion that a jaunt in that direction would not be so beneficial as somewhere else he has in view; but I'm of a different one, as New London air always did agree with me. If we come on to see you, we shall go on to Boston, as R. is desirous I should jaunt if it be possible this summer, and if he does break up his business by going out of town at all, he is determin'd it shall be for somthing. If I could enjoy anything in my present shattered state of health it certainly would be traveling, but I anticipate it with little or no pleasure, and on that account have done with theatres and every public place. . . .

Adieu. Write soon, and particular your opinion of affairs in general or your 'private opinion of *rats*.' . . .

On his return home, William had resumed his Customs duties (**no. 240**):

I received your letter while engaged on board of the brig *Roland* from Curracao with a cargo of salt, and remained on board nine days in all. Therefore I may be excused for not writing you before this, as it was out of my power so to do while on board. The same day I received your letter, I also received one from George, who informed me he has not given up his Quixotic notions of returning to the South and commencing the Green Room again, but has engaged with Geo. Phelps Esq., merchant, corner of Cliff & Fulton Streets, in the capacity of book-keeper. He speaks of him as a verry fine fellow and one of the first acquaintances which he formed upon his arrival there; and I hope it may be the making of him, for he is as well calculated for business as any young man I know of.

From Sam I have not received a line since I left New York. Nothing verry strange, to be sure, yet I thought he would write me. I wish I could have accepted your invitation of going down and spending the 4t [of July] with you but it was out of my power entirely. I should like'd to have look'd out of your window into Broadway and seen its tide of human beings, but it must have been intolerably hot on that day–so much so that I should have been afraid of broiling had I went into the streets, as the heat was overpowering while I was there in May, and that was nothing, I suppose, to what it now is.

I am much obliged for the information respecting Miss Stammers, but I had received a few lines from her requesting me to deliver a letter to Mr. Prentice, the inventor of a mowing machine, one of which her father was verry much in want of–which I did, and answered her letter. She did not mention one word about her family, but mentioned being in New York and calling upon you, which I mentioned in a former letter to you, I believe. You think 'the course of true love never did run smooth.' I'll swear to you, mine shall when I do love, which won't be for some years yet. The misfortune I should most fear would be its not running smooth after marriage. That's the rub, after all. For if in a sentimental or romantic mood your loving lord should ding a lamp of oil or a pair of bellows at your head with an oath, you would be inclined to think the course of love not to be so verry smooth, and most devilish sorry that the knot was tied–tho' Miss Stammers is as kind-hearted a girl as ever I knew, and whoever gets her will get a good wife. She was as kind to me as a sister when here, and I shall always respect and esteem her.

Aunt Mary would be verry glad to see you. She beg'd me to insist upon your coming up here and making a visit. She is in excellent health and spirits. She does not appear to have any Blue-Devil hours such as she used to, for which I am glad, as she used to suffer much from those turns.

I should verry much like to have some chat with George, for he is full of humor. He brings up old times and acquaintances so accurately that while in New York I was carried back by him to scenes which time had crusted over, and I had partially forgotten. For instance, Bets Harris he introduced flaunting in white robes with all the gayetee & grandure of the world, her neck the colour of a tann'd hide, having last been scoured with some of the coarsest white beach sand well mixed with soap of the softest kind; and then, he says, that indiscribable wretched & crazy look which he has often fled from when he has seen her coming towards him in the street, and dart into the first hiding place to escape being spoken to by her, while the eyes of all those in the streets were upon her. If you once get him in the habit of visiting you, he [=you] would find him more entertaining than any of your brothers, I assure you.

I wish you could decide some plan to get him and Sam in the habit of visiting you. It is not coldness on their part, I know, for it was fear of company that made them both so loth to go up with. Two or three genteel ladies to catch Sam alone in a room where he could not get away would just as surely kill the old batchelor as poison, and all George appeared to dread was company. Old acquaintances with whom he thought he might be called to an account with respect to his past life and his dress was not such as to suit him at the time of his visit.

Remember me to Edward and all his family. Possibly I may be able to come down in Oct. next and stay a few days. Should I not, why, I shall come the first opportunity after that, for I do not intend to let such a lapse of time escape as before my first visit, I assure you. Write soon, I pray you, and believe me,

Ever your brother,

William

The description of George Oliver Champlain, in William's sensitive fraternal style, reintroduces this lost actor in the correspondence. Two years earlier, word had passed around of his joining "with a company of players" in journeys and places unknown. His fondness for the theatre his mother had recognized when he was still young, just twenty, and his especial love for Shakespeare shows in all his quotations.

Then he wrote in November 1825 from Montgomery, Alabama, about to leave for Cahaba and next, Mobile; and he wrote twice more, to Sam in August of 1826 from points unspecified. At last he turned up in New York in May of the present year, 1827. From some lodging, certainly of the cheapest–but he had at least found a lowly law job which would allow the employment of his characteristic and at moments even melodramatic hand–he communicates quite regularly with William. The series of his letters extends over six months, beginning now at the end of July (**no. 241**). It provides almost the only information for the period that can be extracted from the correspondence:[9]

My dear boy,

Your note of 23d current has just come to hand, enclosing 2 letters superscribed 'Mrs. Edward C. Riley.' It was left at the office during my absence to dinner, the clerk not knowing the individual who bore it. You express a wish that I should deliver the enclosed 2 letters to Eliza, and 'make Sam go along with me.' With regard to the first request, it will be complied with this evening in 'propria persona.' As to the accompaniment of 'Boreas' [=Sam], I can, to be sure, equal Owen Glendower so far as relates to the calling 'of spirits from the vasty deep,' but the divil of it is, 'will they come when you call them?' In this instance, I am induced to anticipate a flat negative from that incorrigible 'spirit' Sam, knowing his eccentric humour. However, I shall, agreeably to your wish, notify him of the case and if possible prevail upon him to accompany me.

Eliza's well, so is Sam, so is Edward C. (I believe), and so is your humble 'serviteur,' thanks to the Fates, my old friend Atropos in particular, who has so far kindly withheld his 'damn'd shears' from my 'thread' and who (I'm in hopes) may still be induced from applying them for some 10 or 15 years to come.

I can add nothing more at the moment, other than to promise you, shortly, a more lengthy epistle. I trust you will remember me to those choice spirits who 'are still afloat on the tide of time' that may have the kindness to enquire about me.

Unalterably yours,

GEORGE. O.

N.B.} I must insist upon your writing once if not twice per month. Remember! GOC

And again, **no. 242**, in late September:

My dear Bill,

I received yours of 15 some few days back, but have not had leisure to attend to my duty in the shape of an answer 'till now. The letter's bracelet was duly rec'd per hand of Mr. Allen, formerly a clerck for some-one in N[ew] London, I believe, and was immediately put into the hands of Eliza, for which trifle she was much obliged, and all that sort of thing. I must be brief: I regret your inability to come down this fall, agreeable to your promise which you made me last summer, but circumstances are in all cases imperious. Of course I must excuse you. I hope you are all well in N. L. and shall particularly esteem it a favor to have advices from you at least once per month. I am in good health, so is Eliza & Sam & Edward. I shall give you a more lengthy letter in my next. We live in a most unstable, fluctuating mundane sphere, Billy, and I am 'ill at ease.' But damn the odds!

'The mind I sway by and the heart I bear
Shall never sagg with doubt or taint with fear!'
'Hyperion, to a Sayter'

I shall not write you again in all probability until the next month, being too much employed.

Give my respects (I would say love, were it not an obsolete term, or improper at least when applied to men) to all hands, and when I can I will call and see them &c.

After all, Bill, I think with Shakespeare,

'Life's but a walking shadow,
A poor player that struts and frets his
Hour upon the stage, and then is heard no more.'

'Out! Out! brief candle!'–I am almost tempted sometimes to exclaim with all the stern reality of Macbeth's wife.

But more of this anon.

Adieu, my dear boy,
GEORGE O.

No. 244 of October 12:

Dear Bill,

I wish you to inform me if there will be any prospect of you coming down to the city in all the course of the ensuing season. If you reply in the negative, it will be a source of great regret to me, I assure you. But 'business before all' is, no doubt, your governing rule. Consequently I must meet the disappointment as best I may. I shall nevertheless give you credit for adopting the correct course, in the pursuit of future advancement, on which no doubt your eyes is fixed. Well! you are right.

Our old friend and distant relative (aye! some 54th 'cousen german'), Peter Douglass, done me the favor to call upon me at my boarding house (same as formerly), for which I really feel a species of friendship for Peet which I never anticipated I should feel either for him or any of that branch of the original ancestry.

But, 'Holy clerk of Copmanhurst'! with what different eyes do I look upon such 'ephemera'–things of mushroom growth! Aye! However, fortune (forgive the libel, my blind dame!)–Oh! tempora! O! mores!–may in her caprice bestow a temporary supremacy in 'temporal' rank among the devotees who sacrifice at her shrine from 'the cradle to the tomb'! However, I am sometimes induced to think with John Palmer (of the British stage), who, perhaps from the misfortune of possessing a too exquisite sensibility (and over mental excitement) fell and expired upon the stage as he was giving utterance to that passage in the play called *The Stranger*, to wit,

'There is another and a better world!'

I am almost a misanthrope. No matter, you may depend upon one fact: that (compell'd as I am) in my adversity and in my struggle to think and act as 'common men,' I will (par necessity) so far as in me lies conform to the 'existing custom'

'of shouting when the rabble shout!'

But if, 'driven to extremity,' I should not be able to 'stem the torrent' of protracted adversity, 'by the soul of my ancestors!' but I will make 'a last stand' and sing out with Macbeth,

'They have tied me to a stake
And, bear-like, I must fight it out!
Ring the alar'um bell! Blow wind! Come wrack!
At least we'll die with harness on our back!'

God dam'n the whole 'possie comittatus' of the human family (I was a-going to say). But I recall the expression. 'Twas made under high excitement, and sober reason disaproves it. No more!

Eliza is well, as likewise Edward and, I believe, Sam, tho' I have not seen him for some weeks. He is entirely a different being from what he appear'd when I first landed in N[ew] York. But (God bless us all!) he's not to blame, nor have I ought against him–only, I have proved that their may exist even among a 'band of brothers' an order of intellect of different 'calibre.'

'Fidus et audax.'

Ever yours, my faithful Achates,

GEORGE O.

No. 245 of October 20th:

Dear Bill,

I have just been handed yours, under date of 12 current, by Uncle Ebb. The surprise and astonishment of seeing him you may imagine, on my part. I was (from a slight head-ache) in bed when the servant arroused me and announced 'two gentlemen' below. I was 'par necessity' compelled to quit my lair and descend to meet them. Edward I immediately reccognised (altho' 'twas twilight), but I could not E[benezer Way] until I heard his voice, which acted like a talisman upon my half-awake perceptions. I was pleased to see him look so young and well. I felt (comparatively) old in his presence. Our interview was but of a few minutes' duration, when we left my boarding house and walked up in company to Ebb's in Pearl Street, where we parted company for the night after he had announced his intention of giving me an early call on the following morning.

Accordingly, next morning he presented himself and I (of course) was punctually on the ground, and rec'd him at the door. The motion which he made was to pay an immediate visit to Sam (whom he had not seen yet) at the bank. We started directly for his 'shaving domicile' in Wall St. Upon our entrance, I requested one of the clercks to call Mr. Champlain. So soon as that facsimile (Sam) of the sect y'clep'd 'Round Heads' (who flourished under the first Charles of England, and Oliver the

'Protector') heard himself called upon, he wheeled himself around on his seat at the desk and at the first glance recognised Ebb! You should have been here to have seen and enjoyed the brief interview–the rush & retreat alternately of the blood of Boreas too and from his face was truly amusing, for the space of 2 or 3 minutes. However, he soon got the better of his momentary embarrassment and promised to meet us at 4 p.m. that afternoon at Eliza's. We did accordingly assemble at the appointed hour (to wit, Uncle E., myself, Eliza, Sam, & Edward). She (Eliza) told me that she had not seen Sam for better than one year before! We passed an hour or two very pleasantly in conversation and, as it was near 6 o'clock, Edward insisted upon our accompanying him to the theatre (we all having declined his invitation to tea). Sam, however, expressed a mortal aversion to theatres and peremptorily at last declined going with us. Of course, we had to go without him, and Ebb, Edward, old Mr. Riley & myself went to the Park Theatre, where we were all highly gratified with the entertainment of the night. After its termination, I accompanied Uncle E. to his boarding house, where we parted for the night. He proposed for me to call upon him the next morning, which I agreed to do; but unfortunately have not seen him since, in consequence of having rec'd a subpena to attend a cause now pending in the marine court of this city, as an evidence in the case between Grant and the underwriters relative to the state of some damaged cotton, part of his cargo. It has detained me for the last 2 days. I shall be at liberty to-day, however, and will devote the time to Ebb, to whom I must apologize for my seeming neglect. He purposes returning to-morrow, he says.

You have rejoiced me very much by the letter per Ebb., agreeing to come down here this fall, altho' you say such a step might militate against your interests and all 'that sort o' thing.' Come! if you don't stay 48 hours, for I am lonely, dejected, a 'solitary' amid all the deafening clang and confusion around me in such a modern Babylon as N. Y. I cannot, for all that, divest myself of periodical depression in my spirits. Perhaps it is a constitutional failing. Be that as it may, I know not. It exists nevertheless. Your presence may tend to disapate the incubus which sits so heavily upon me at times. . . .

A few days before Christmas, George writes again (**no. 246**) to acknowledge what is evidently a check to be cashed by S[am]. His circumstances have been reduced to this, and lower still. He is ailing, alone, broke, borrowing his brother's shirts, but still himself–an ever indomitable oddity:

Yours of 14th inst. I received yesterday. Your punctuality as a correspondent I must applaud, for it deserves credit and, indeed, is a powerful incentive for me to be prompt in acknowledging your favours, and if possible to prevent the charge of neglect or 'defalcation' (as our classical cousin, Peter Douglass, would say) from being laid at my door. I am gratified to learn that your 'quarter' has been 'better than you anticipated,' and again, on the other hand, sorry the next (in perspective) presents to your view so cheerless a prospect. However, 'nil desperandum' has long since been adopted by me as a motto and, without wishing to intrude, will take the liberty of respectfully suggesting the same to you as worthy of your adoption. Be assured, if, in the course of the winter, I should hear of a vacancy occuring in any of the institutions either public or private which is analogous to your line of business, I shall apprize you of it instantur.

In relation to my prospects, they are much about the same. I have made 4 different applications since you left here for a 'birth' but without success. The clerkship in the 'Temple of Melpomene,' which I had in 'my mind's eye,' that I hinted to you my intention of applying for, has unfortunatly been secured by another, during my confinement to the house by my rheumatic ancle. I am, however, much better than I was, being able to limp as far as H. P. Downs & Co. store occasionally in pleasant weather. But my philosophy and patience have been severely taxed, I assure you, during my late indisposition. I have not seen Sam for many weeks, nor Eliza or Edward since I called for your letter, and I must be in better travelling plight than at present before I shall undertake so formidable a journey as 296 B'-Way again.

Your kind offer is duly appreciated, for which I return you my grateful acknowledgements. I notwithstanding feel a reluctance which I cannot overcome to present yours to S. The truth is that he has already been used by me (relative to fiscal operations), to an extent which is both revolting to my feelings of independence and my pride. True, the am't is nothing (or would be considered as such) to any one in business, but to me, out of business, 'tis formidable enough so as to deter me from further levies of a pecuniary nature. Perchance time may cause the 'tables to be turned' (for all things are mutable in this mundane sphere) and my star may possibly become once more 'lord of the ascendant.'

As for you [?](Lilliputian Labo), I fear your generosity has 'worked windward' of your ability in that last stretch (to finish the nautical phrase) which you made me. Therefore, my dear Bill, I shall rest fully content with the expression of your good will and accept that as an equivalent for the deed. I am well aware of the sincerity of your offer, but when I consider your limited means and your precarious chance of the future, to ask or expect it is more than I would consent to.

I sincerely regret to learn the declining health of Uncle Oliver. He must have suffer'd both mentally & physically in the extreme, when such a change is wrought in such a man as he was. For if I have a correct idea of him, he belongs to a race and is the descendant of a line of ancestry who were never known to yield to trifles. No! Never have I heard that any of that name was ever guilty of 'blenching from the helm when the wind blew highest.' But one ! But time and the infirmities that 'flesh is heir to' are all potent, and we all know that pain is a general leveller, and that the prince equally with the peasant must bow to its supremacy. I hope to see him e're he is 'gather'd to his fathers;' but the Deity alone knows whether that shall be.

You will please remember me to him, for he is the last scion of the 'House of Lancaster' [=Champlain] afloat on the tide of time. I should write him but, alass!,

I know not how to address him–so long a time has elapsed since 'twas my duty to do so.

Fail not to answer this immediately, for it is my only consolation to hear from you frequently now that I am 'in my extremity.'

My business is not worth 5 dollars p'r week. The best workmen cannot realize more. Therefore, 'come fate itself into the lists, and champion me to the uttermost'– e're I will have ought to do with a worthless profession which at best is but 'leather and prunella,' and be dam'd to it.

Fail me not an instant in writing me upon its receipt, for my spirits are at a low ebb, I assure you.

No. 247 of January 4, 1828, once more from George to William, launches the correspondence upon the New Year very low in the water:

Yours of the 29th current is rec'd. I am glad to hear that you purpose visiting us the ensuing spring. My prospects are the same as p'r last advices. I know not how the sequel of such a situation as I am in may prove. I have not seen Eliza or Edward since I went for your letter. My ancle is nearly well, thank God, and I intend, the first fair day, to take a trip up there. I am glad that Uncle Oliver is on the recovery, and likewise that you have been so attentive to him during his confinement. I am not in spirits at the moment to prolong this brief note but will endeavour to make amends for its brevity in my next. Nothing new to give you, either of a local or a personal nature.

There is a respectable number of the youth of this goodly city of Gotham who come under the denomination of that class of our species y'clept 'Miss Nancy's'. In my 'misanthropic mood' I some-times burst into an involuntary fit of hearty laughter at the 'fantastic tricks' which I sometimes see acted 'before high Heaven' by some of the self-elected 'Lords of the Creation.'

'God help us all! God help me too! I am,
God knows, as helpless as the devil can wish,'

&c of my Lord Byron is frequently in my mouth.

However, I am amused often at the recollection of a droll expression of my nautical friend, Bill Grant, on the passage. In a severe squall one night while giving some orders on the forecastle, as the men were in the act of letting go the foretopsail halyards, Bill's leg accidentally got caught in the coil of the halyards and it jerked him half-way up to the 'cat-harpins.' So soon as he recover'd his pins, however, he with great 'nonchalance' sings out to me who was near, 'George?

"The midwife hauls us in, and the Devil hauls us out.
O! good God! how are we haul'd about." '

Adieu! 'mon ami.' Answer this without fail forthwith.

Yours to the Antipodes,
G. O. Champlain

Last in the New York series from George, a letter of April 17th of 1828 (**no. 249**), referring to a previous expostulation–where are the articles requested?–that has been lost:

I must apologize to you for being somewhat precipitate in sending that last note, under date of 15th current. I was excited in feelings when I framed it. Yet I had cause. 'Tis strange to think how human matters are regulated and 'the electric chain by which we are darkly bound' becomes more apparent to me every day. Bonaparte said (& very justly) that ' 'twas not every man that could be an atheist.' I am of his opinion. Now there is nothing here or hereafter which I *fear*, that being a term which I have not in my vocabulary. Still, I must bow me to the supremacy of nature. 'I am but man, and fate, do thou dispose me.' I have been through a great deal, have suffered much both mentally & physically in this world. Notwithstanding the fiery ordeal that I have passed, I still think myself solid in all senses. I am in unison with Byron:

'Yet, though I hope not hence unscathed to go,
Who conquers me shall find a stubborn foe.'

But this is idle talk–doubtless you have so concluded. I therefore close it as well as the letter, by saying that I had not mailed the last note to you more than 15 minutes before your letter & bundle was presented to me. It was, however, too late to withdraw my letter, the mail having been closed. You may perceive in this small matter a singular fact. I went down to the P[ost] Office for the express purpose of withdrawing my note, but it had been disposed of.

I sincerely thank you for the $5. and the accompanying documents in the paper case (i.e. *shirts*). I most confidently trust that the tables will yet be turned, and that my star will become 'lord of the ascendant.' By God! 'tho' Burnam wood be come to Dunsinane, yet will I try the last'! I am in negociation for a situation at the Park Theatre. When it is concluded, I will early advise you of the result. 'Till then believe me,

Ever yours,
G. O. C.

Sam. & Eliza I believe are well. I should be happy to see you in 'propria persona' if it might be. There is a crisis approaching in my fate. I feel it. Whether for weal or woe I know not, and almost would say care not.

'The hull drives on, tho' mast and sails be gone.'

The correspondence may now be picked up from the New-London end with William's letter of the earlier spring to Eliza, acknowledging a mighty event: the birth of Ted, that is, Edward Champlain Riley (**no. 248**, February 2):

I heard accidently the other day that I was an uncle, being down at Mrs. Harrises: she told me that Uncle Oliver had had a letter from Mrs. Tracy some time since, informing him you had given birth to a fine boy and was doing well &c. I asked him why he did not tell me of it. He said the[y] thought certainly I had heard of it long before, & gave some compliments upon my being an uncle &c. Why I have not heard from you upon the subject I am puzzled to know, for it is considerable of an affair to happen in our family, you know; and when you receive this I shall expect an immediate answer respecting its name & whether it looks most like its Ma or Pa, for these are very serious questions for an uncle to have answered. Aunt Mary is quite mortified to think she is a great aunt at her age, as it puts her upon a footing with a grandmother, which is not verry palatable to females generally.

I was told the other day by Lewis Allen that if I did not get married the family name would run out. I told him I thought George & Sam ought to set me an example, but he thought it would not do to wait for them as they had almost pass'd the Rubicon. However, I do not know how it may be, for I have not pick'd out my girl yet, & if I have, 'tis doubtful whether she would accept. But if she should, another difficulty arrises: there is nothing to make the pot boil, which is a verry material article in small families, you know. I suppose you would wish the name to run to the devil, so that you heard no more of it, as it never was a favorite of yours. But I should endeavour to keep it afloat upon the tide of time if I could scrape enough of filthy lucre to support a crooked rib–the which is altogether doubtful.

You have not heard of the death of Mrs. Judd yet, I suppose. She died last Tuesday night and was burried yesterday (Friday). [Her children] Gloriana, Frederick & myself watched the corpse the first night. She has been sick & suffered much for some months. She died of consumption. Mr. Judd [the Episcopalian minister] was verry earnest in his wishes to have a likeness of some kind of her, and wished me to ask you if you thought you could sketch a profile of her from recollection, or if a profile cut for her which he has in the house would be of any service to you if you attempt it. I told him I would ask you but I did not think you would be able. Your acquaintance with her was slight and you was not good at recollection pieces. He seemed to think because Mother was, that you must be of course.

I pity the man, for he has suffered every-thing, being poor, a member in his family, and in miserable health, employed every moment of his time in-doors or out-doors, and his pay not more than five or six hundred dollars per year. He told me, the night I watched, he had not pulled off his cloaths for the last fifteen days of her sickness, but had slept upon a sofa in the room with her because she desired it. Mrs. Smith (Fanny Allen that was) has been there for about a month and has had her hands full, tho' all the neighbours have been verry kind and attentive. 'Settings,' Mrs. Smith says, is but miserable assistance in the family & in her work is more trouble than profit.

Mr. Judd had to marry a couple the day before the death of his wife. He married them on Monday night and she died on Tuesday. The couple were Miss Lucretia Thatcher, daughter of Anthony Thatcher Esq., & Nathaniel H. Perry Esq., Purser U. S. Navy & brother of Mrs. Rogers. Mr. Judd was hurried from the house by the physicians, as they expected her death momently and were fearfull she would die before he could marry them, which would have been a great disappointment, as the arrangements had been some time makeing, and they would have been obliged to get a Presbyterian parson.

Mr. Thomas Pool died in Colchester the other day and was brought down here and buried from where Col. Green lives, his son-in-law. You did not know much about him, I believe, tho' George did, for when he was learning his trade of John Green he were to board with him, and has often of an evening read to Mrs. Pool. Mr. Isaac Rogers, the confectioner, is dead–he that left two minatures of his young sootheads with Mother to have some alteration made.

You have heard long since of the death of Mrs. Whistler, for it was in your city that she died. I felt as much grieved for the death of that woman as I ever did for any person with whom I was no better acquainted. She was as handsome a woman as I ever saw when she first came here, tho' I think she faded considerable before her death; but her manners was so pleasing that if she had been as ugly as the devil they would have made up for it. Poor Whistler must have suffered all that we read in romance, for he was soul and body attached to her. It was a run-away love match in the first place, and it was impossible for any-one to love a wife better than he did her. By the way, I was requested to write you and ascertain if you were willing to part with that minature of hers that Mother copyed, as Whistler intended to to make a present of it to Mrs. Adams if you would, and she requested Mrs. Way to write, and Mrs. Way requested me to, if you will just mention the price and I will inform her.

Now I have written so long a letter, be sure you give me as good an answer; and Mary must be remembered, although she nor any of the others know I am going to write. And, Sir Edward, let me congratulate you upon being a father and I an uncle. Remember me to all your family and believe me ever yours.

& now I 'give it up'

W. C.

The same birth of a Riley child that William was late to acknowledge, because he hadn't been informed, Mary Way was even slower in saluting, if only because her salutes had necessarily to wait for some second person to deliver; so her congratulations are sent only at the end of April (**no. 250**):

My dear Eliza,

How is the little boy? I am more dead than alive or I should have offered long ago my compliments of congratulation upon this joyful occasion. But tho' I can never see the young stranger, he has my best wishes. May prosperity & success attend him in his career through life, may he enjoy all the happiness this world affords & fight his way manfully through the trials & tribulations that sooner or later is the lot and portion of every son and daughter of Adam.

Let me tell you, however, in spite of my good wishes I shall be strongly tempted to quarrell with the new-commer if he should still continue to engross your attention so wholly as to prevent you from ever writing your friends again. Mr. Riley's letter to William gave us much pleasure; from you we have not had a single line for more than six months! This is too bad. Mary P[rescott] wrote the first of January & sent you a cap worked with her own fair hands–would like to know if it is received & suits your taste. Here, it was much admired. My dear Eliza, write soon. Miss Shannon [Ebb's sister-in-law?] has express'd a wish to hear from you before she leaves town, which I am sorry to say will be the last of May. I have enjoyed much pleasure in her society and shall deeply feel her loss. Were she twenty times my sister I could not possibly receive from her more kindness and attention. Heaven reward her goodness & shed its choisest blessings on her head. She is the best of human beings & I should be ungrateful to the last degree did I not love her as I do with most sincere affection.

I shall miss Mary [Prescott] very much. She goes with her aunt to Portsmouth to visit her mother, & will probably spend the summer. Therefore it will not be in my power to write again as I can do nothing in this way without her assistance. . . .

In the fall of this year 1828, George was heard from once more, having left New York at the end of August in service to Junius Brutus Booth's travelling troupe of actors. The period was the absolute apogee of this great talent, "his best days," declared a friend and fellow-actor, in retrospect; and he was appearing with Edwin Forrest, too, who was himself a fine actor.[10] The *Boston Statesman* of September 2nd advertised the great man appearing at the Tremont Theatre, where "the establishment will be opened to-night under the management of Mr Booth–a tragedian whose reputation is too brilliant to require the language of adulation." And in due course it was further advertised (on the ninth of the month) that he "will soon appear in the character of Richard III," by far his strongest role. The privilege that George thus enjoyed in his associations he must certainly have relished, whatever the drawbacks to such a (temporary) choice of life. Still, he writes from Boston in an indirect, offhand style (**no. 251**):

Dear Bill,

As I am not as yet wholly callous to the calls of conscience, I obey her mandate (just given) to drop a line to you, for the charge of ingratitude would be at my door did I not.

To be brief, then, I left N[ew] York on 31st ult. and arrived in the 'literary (Yankee) Emporium' of these United States on the evening of the 1st inst. in 'purty good health and sperrets.' I have enter'd upon the duties of 'mine office' (i.e., clerk, for the time being), for I told Mr. Booth (the tragedian and our stage manager) to allow me sufficient time to recruit myself and restore a partially deranged state of the nerves. He acquiesced, and I shall in consequence not appear before the Yankee audience for some time–say 2 or 3 weeks. I am comparatively happy to what I was, but alass!,

'The wealth of the worlds were heaped on me in vain.'

The result of my first appearance I shall forward you as early as practicable, together with some 'change', if 'tis possible. I can-not tell or guess, even, how I shall 'get on.' Still, if they fool me 'with their corn-cake,' I must have only dreamed of being in the Massissippi country, and not so in reality.

'Something too much of this.'

I was told by a member of our corps, Mr. Jones, that Uncle Ebb was here only 2 days before I arrived. I regretted much his leaving before I had an opportunity of seeing him. Jones appear'd to be much pleased with him &c.

I shall write Eliza and Edward tomorrow and, when more at leisure, will drop you a longer epistle. I start for Salem in the morning (to be absent 2 or 3 days) with Wilson to assist him in preparing the theatre in that place for opening by the 25 current. . . .

To return the scene to New York: now two years married, Eliza was still not prepared to find out how much work it was, and unburdens herself on the subject of servants. With these, Mary Way from her experience as a lodger in the past was familiar, since in boarding houses it was common to buy some housekeeping from whatever girl or woman could be hired in the neighborhood; and Eliza was familiar with them from the Fitch household, as the correspondence shows; but her present troubles involved her in a more difficult situation (**no. 252** of September 26th, 1828):

Dear William,

. . . Tell her [Aunt Mary] if she knew the ten thousand miseries that keeping house in New York brings upon one she would never congratulate me upon bringing my pigs this way to market–amongst which, help is not the least. If they are passing honest, content with a pint of rum a day and don't set the house on fire over your head, you must think yourself highly favored and return thanks ten times a day on your knees for the blessing you enjoy. Notwithstanding this, I should be right glad to see her and all of you down, after I get a-going. But we are still cutting up sundry droll capers in the way of housekeeping that I should not alltogether like to have witness'd, even by relations who are bound to excuse all sorts of distresses of this kind. . . .

I have never had time to give you a description of our 'Tour to the Lakes,' and if 'twould not be too stale and time would serve, I think I could raise a laugh at this late period with our jaunt; but I must scratch pretty fast or your young nephew will open his peepers and then good-bye to pens, paper, ink, writing desk and every thing else that he can lay his claws on. Such another *roarer* (as you say) you never saw in your days. It won't do for you to set and watch him. You must keep both hands fast hold of him all the time or the devil would be to pay. This, you must think, will employ every moment of my time now Jane is dismissed. She enquires very affectionately after you whenever I see her and is going to keep the two-shilling piece you gave her till time shall be no more. I think 'tis a great pity that those carroty locks (or as Riley says, 'fire-brand ringlets') fail'd in warming that flinty heart of yours. I should have taken great pride in my red-headed sister. . . .

Sam was to see me day before yesterday. 'Twas a fetch-fire call, but I was glad to see him. He enquired particularly about you and George, whom I have not heard from yet, except through your letter. He was much pleased with my situation, which is a delightful one from its facing Chamber Street that is improving so fast. My front room is the pleasantest I ever was in. I cannot say so much for the rest of the house, as it is rather out of repair, and we have a surly dog of a landlord to deal with who won't do the least thing under heaven, but makes us go to all the expence. Oh how I could tweak his nose for him at this moment. . . .

From New York to New London at about the same time as this letter, a present was despatched by Edward Riley for Mary Way. As appears from previous mentions, he liked to make gifts, and this, a music box, was an especially well-chosen, generous, and successful one. Mary offers him her full-dress thanks (**no. 253**, November 6):

My dear Eliza,

I've a mighty secret to disclose. You will doubtless be surprized that I should fall in love over head and ears at this time of life, and with your husband too! Yet however it may appear to you, I see nothing so very strange in the affair. 'Tis but the natural effect of of an obvious cause. His goodness and my own susceptibility considered, where's the wonder if I should feel some thing more than simple admiration? 'Tis useless to be jealous now; but let me tell you, had I been young and handsome and as sensible of his merits as at this present writing, before it was too late, we should certainly have pulled caps.

. . . Tell him he is the best of men; his goodness when he was here is not forgotten. The pleasure I enjoyed in hearing him play and the many hours he spent in reading to amuse me don't go for nothing, I assure you; but this last generous deed, this most splendid present, has finished the business, and convinced me there never was his equal. Had he searched the spacious earth he could have found nothing that would have pleased me so well, so acceptable or so exactly suited to my case, unless he had sent me a pair of eyes. . . .

The whole family–uncle, aunt, brother, cousins and all–sends oceans of love. They seem as much delighted with my present as if it was their own. Poor [family cats and kittens] Malt and Goodins are quite chop-fallen, both their noses out of joint. Even Blackey and her two young ones (beautyful as they were said to be) appear only in the back-ground and are scarcely noticed since this new favorite has arrived. It has so much life and animation–so interesting and intelligent, it must have sense as well as sound and motion. You would laugh to hear us talk baby to it. We call it all the dear little names you can imagine (some that will hardly do to mention), but its real name is Edward Fitch Riley, though for shortness we call it little Ned.[11] Now I suppose you would not be willing to exchange bantlings with me, nor do I wish it, notwithstanding all I have heard of yours and of his manifold perfections. It is said children are troublesome comforts at the best. Mine is clear comfort without the trouble. Of course I prise it highly.

William talks much of his nephew and thinks he is a wonder. I have drawn his likeness from description in my best style, but it is necessary he should be here for me to give it the finishing touches. You must bring him next summer to visit his name-sake ["Ned," the music-box]. I should admire to see the little villains play together & amuse each other. I think it would amuse us all. 'We are but children of a larger groath.' Surely no child was ever more pleased with a rattle than I am with mine. I set it on the sideboard and it sounds loud as a piano & far more sweet. Upstairs, I put a tumbler on my table & place it there–it goes equally well. Both tunes are beautiful but when it plays the *Invincible* I am intransed, transported streight to paradise. I hear the musick of the groves, the wild warblings of ten thousand birds, sweet & melodious as the tuneful spheres. 'Tis more than half-divine, and all we can imagine here below, of harmony & Heaven! I find it charms the most fastidious ear, no-one can listen to this instrument and say they are not pleased with concord of sweet sounds.

But I forget, musick is not your passions. I talk of what runs in my head. Your thoughts are full of other matters: domestic pleasures, family affairs, comforts & cares, husband, child, servants, plagues, devil-to-pays and the like. Well, they are all necessary in housekeeping. Good and ill (judicily arranged) like light & shade in painting constitutes vareity & beauty. A due degree of each is requisite 'to keep the balance true.' And both, combined with skill, produce a soft & mellow tint, to harmonise the whole & finish off the picture. You are now mistress of a family. Housekeeping is a science you have yet to learn. Time & application will instruct you in the business & render it 'familiar as your garter.'

But still, I think a word's advice or useful hint would not be much amiss. First, with respect to servants, you may wash & black, scrape, scrub & scour, 'tis labour lost. Nay, even scald or boil them out in lye, it's all in vain. You never will find one nice enough to suit your purpose. Poor help is better than none at all. Be less particular, less difficult to please, my dear, for fear of consequences, broken wrists and so forth. Procure an honest servant & you may well dispense with nonessentials. Excuse & overlook a hundred faults as others are obliged to do. Such servants I consider necessary evils. Unless you are a slave yourself, you cannot do without them. These may answer for present use. But I should rather choose to raise my own servants and 'teach young turnips how to shoot' their (dingers) while they are pliant & manageable. Take one before her faults are fix'd & rooted into habits, weed them out & mould her as you please. Do as you would be done by were you in her condition, treat her well, be not too severe, teach her to love as well as fear you. Then you will be sure of a good servant. People often complain and blame their servants when the fault is in themselves. 'Tis natural to hate a tyrant, & those we hate we seldom try to please. Harsh & ill treatment will spoil the best dispositions &

kindness mend the worst. None can resist its influence. It softens & subdues the most obdurate heart (if it is made of penetrable stuff). We overcome our enemies heaping coals of fire upon their heads. Who can withstand its mighty power when it goes forth conquering & to conquer? . . .

Toward the end of January in another year, 1829, Samuel appears to have earned a raise, or at least he can sign himself "cashier" not simply "clerk" of the Mechanics' Bank where he works. As to William, however, there seems to be little to write about, and he would rather recall his summer's visit to New York:[12]

Dear Edward,

I received your letter of the 11th but, being employed on board of a vessel at the time, could not conveniently answer it. I am sorry to hear of your father's severe illness but I hope he will recover entirely. You must have had a trying time of it in sitting up nights, for I have had some experience at that in my life. It [is] verry trying to my constitution and I should think it would be to yours.

The violin I believe pleases Col. Lindsey, as I saw him a few days after he had received [it], and asked him how he liked it. He said he had not yet given it a fair trial, but he thought it would suit him. The fact is, he is not rich, and therefore is waiting for pay-day to come around before he can settle for it, and I have no doubt will pay as soon as he receives his quarterly payment. As soon as he does, I will remit it immediately by some safe conveyance.

How much I should delight to be in New York at this season of the year. It would be so far preferable to the time I was there before, for then I thought I should roast alive, the weather was so intolerably hot. To go down to that porter house on the North River side and drink some of that excellent old beer–it makes my mouth water to think of it; or to go a jaunt to some such place as Orange Springs would be delightful, and have some old lady, like the one where we boarded, give us some tea such as we had there, with her excellent bread and new butter and shaved beef. Everything is fresh in my my memory as if it was but yesterday–particularly Eliza's wry faces at drinking the Spring water, for which she went the jaunt, & then could be hired to taste it.

Also my rambling in the [vacant] lots with Louisa [Riley]. I attempted to find a shorter way home to the house than going the road, & acted as her pilot across a piece of swampy ground, and had the mortification to get her shoes & stockings well muded, as well as my own.

I think my time was passed as pleasantly there as I ever passed it any-where–though I used to enjoy myself in taking a walk with George down to the Battery of a sunny afternoon, and sit there in the shade and hear him chat till sundown. It was so delightfully cool and the scene of the Jersey Shore about sunset was beautiful, and George had a small spice of romance in his composition of which I am verry fond.

Sam is as differant as can be–he being a real matter-of-fact body, or if he has any romance in him, he hides it all. He may, however, let it out to Espeth the daughter of

Mrs. Macy, with whom he boards. I used to joke him considerably about her until he would get snapping mad; but when I came to see her, I thought he had good reason to swear a little.

How is Frederick [Riley]? I hope he is well, and your mother and all hands. Remember me to all, as well as Hill when you see him. And if you should see that that old flame of mine, Posy-Head Jane, give her my love.

Believe me ever yours,

Wm.

P.S. Since the above was written, Col. Lindsey has paid the bill to Mr. Way, who has just handed it me. $18.

The same January of 1829 revived the troubles that William had alluded to before, afflicting Ebenezer Way (**no. 233**, above): troubles in the form of democracy, by the action of which a mere shoe-maker had turfed him out of his town-clerkship. But the story was not done. Two years later, now, William explains to Eliza what he had only touched on in some recent, not surviving letter, and which, as a Way-Champlain problem, he preferred not to share with Edward: a much more serious move was now on foot against Ebb. It was part of a general phenomenon, on that account especially threatening. The whole country had changed, or so it seemed: Andrew Jackson had been elected. Here was a man willing to announce in his first annual message "that more is lost by the long continuance of men in office than is generally gained by their experience." He could have been thinking precisely of Uncle Ebb, not only town clerk for a full decade (now ended) but holder of a Federal appointment, the postmastership, for thirteen years, and disgracefully acceptable among the New London Establishment, witness his various other offices, his brother Thomas elected beside him, and his presence as a guest in the most fashionable weddings.[13] To displace him at this time of change, behold that entirely suitable newcomer in the town, by name Mussey, only settled in since1816, who had assiduously worked his way up to the level of Ebb's desirable job.

Desirable, it should be explained, because of its centrality in the everyday life of any city of the day, large or especially small. In the days before and during Ebb's postmastership, Connecticut had been suffering a very considerable loss of population to points south and west, to open lands or to New York or Charleston or New Orleans; and the participants in this exodus, leaving parents and other family behind, must often rely on the postmaster to alert them to bad news and the need for their help.[14] In addition to a role that was or might thus be almost pastoral, the postmaster saw people of the community constantly and individually. Absent any regular deliveries of mail, he must publish the names of addressees in the local newspaper where, for example, all of the Way-Champlain writers turn up sooner or later, along with a great number of the persons they mention; and in response to such notification or simply in random hopefulness, these fellow citizens would stop by his shop and incidentally hear or tell the day's news. A likable, interested man could turn such contacts into politics; and the job itself was an unashamedly political appointment, even if its partisan nature was a point of public debate. Very naturally it was sought out and competed for, then, for these general reasons (not for its high profits). But postmasterships by 1828 had increased in number–eight thousand of them in all–so as to make up some three quarters of all Federal posts. The opportunity they offered in every state for partisan reward proved quite irresistible. Which explains the significance of President Jackson's view announced in his annual message, and its bearing on Ebenezer Way and Thomas Mussey.

This much is needed as background to parts of William's letter written to his sister in early February of 1829 (**no. 256**). It should only be added that the actions he describes in defense of his uncle followed lines evident in many similar cases throughout his own and other regions:

> I have not had time to answer your two letters by Lamphere before this. In reply to your enquiries about Uncle Ebb, I must be brief. He has been attacked by a number of discontent men in this place, with Thomas Mussey at their head, to remove him from the office he now holds. They are properly named office-seekers. You have heard of such a political class before this, I doubt not. Their endeavors have been to make it appear that he is uncivil, overbearing & tyranical in his office, and they have made statements, & sworn to them in some instances before a Justice, that he is a peculator and has taken unlawfull postages in some instances, &c. These with many other lies have been sent to Washington, and what 'tis possible they may bring about, I cannot say.
>
> I have lately been circulating a paper contradicting these charges and obtained about sixty names of the most respectable citizens here. The opposition party have a paper for his removal to which they have two or three hundred names; but as Fallstaff says, 'No eye hath seen such scarecrows'–they are tagrag and bobtail, a great part of them are from the neighboring towns, and I presume never saw Mr. Way. To which may be added all the blacksmiths, journeymen, ropemakers, &c. such as are not natives of the town & the greater part have had but a short residence here–therefore not such a class as should have the sway here. I do not think it probable that he will be removed, but 'tis possible; for these fellows have the virtues of patience and perseverance which will effect almost anything. Should it so happen, I do not know what he would he would turn his hand to. However, I doubt not there would be some opening for him.
>
> At some future day I will give you my reasons for boardeing at Allen's. This paper that I have been circulating was forwarded to Washington Monday. The other party have not sent theirs yet, I believe. Whenever there is anything new takes place, I will write you immediately. . . .

William as the stay-at-home, William as the confidant of his mother and the companion of her sister–interpreter of them both when they could not speak for themselves–has in this juncture risen to be head of the family, if one can distinguish that position; and his next letter shows him in that role toward his considerably older brother George (**no. 257**, March 5):

> Dear George,
>
> I cannot account for your long silence. Affairs, I am afraid, are going ill with you, or I think you would have written before this; for you promised to give me an account of your debut on the Boston boards. Last night I dreamed I was in Boston, and after crewying about some time, I met with an acquaintance of whom I made enquiries after you. He first stated that you had gone to Europe & that you had been gone some time; but after hesitating some time he says, 'The fact must be known: George put an end to himself by drowning. His body was pick'd up upon some neighboring shore and was buried.' Now if this is the fact, why, I shall not have an answer to this letter from you. If it is not so, then I shall be in daily expectation of the answer. Therefore if you are alive, think of the state of my feelings that are awaiting the issue of a case of life and death, and be merciful accordingly.
>
> I heard from Eliza some two or three weeks since. She is well as also is her husband and our grand-nephew Edward the 2nd. Old Mr. Riley has had a shock of the palsy of which he will probably never recover. Sam I hear nothing from, except occasionally a friend meets him in the street and tells me he is well. Aunt Mary holds her own like a true Way—they never die till they are upwards of a hundred, which will be her case.
>
> I am now on the list of promotions, whereby I have the honor and not the profit. Old Mr. Nath'l Richards, who has acted in the Custom House as Deputy Collector for the last thirty years, is dangerously ill, and will never probably get out of his house alive again, & I fill his place for the present without yet being appointed to the vacancy, tho' I have the promise of it at a future day; but the pay that was allowed him is not equal'd with what I have been making heretofore while in the Custom House. However, if I outlive a man of 64, I shall probably get his office, which is worth $840 per annum; but I am waiting for dead men's shoes—

in fact William was sworn in within a week and his appointment confirmed by note of hand from the Secretary of the Treasury, S. D. Ingham.[15]

Mary some weeks later, determined to be cheerful despite her spring cold and the most deceitful of spring weather, writes to Eliza in her characteristic style (**no. 260**):

> 'Sweet music wakes the May-day morn
> And charms the ravish'd ear.'
>
> Sweet indeed—not that Petrach's beautiful sonnet is altogether applicable on the present occasion, as it happens to be 'an April morn wrapt in a winter cloud, and clay-cold is the lilly hand' employed in your service. . . .
>
> Miseries love company: if here is not enough, more still remain untold—you may be furnished to your heart's content. But the birds determine to make the best of

the matter (as if ashamed to be outdone by little Ned [the music box], who is going at full speed)–pour forth their souls in liquid melody to comfort and convince us that winter is past, the rain is over & gone! 'The time of their singing has come, the voice of the turtle (and sweeter still the peeping of the frogs) is heard in our land'.

Now what do you suppose induce these little animals to be so cheerful, & rejoice as it were in the midst of tribulation, while Christians murmer & repine at temporary evils, the common ills and accidents of life? Go–mock majesty! 'Go, man (with all thy boasted reason and philosophy) & bow to thy superiors,' the frogs & birds, more wise & happy far, by faithful instinct taught, regardles of the present dreary scene, with grateful songs anticipate the pleasures they are destined to enjoy. What a lesson, this, for Christians–but alas! they are dull scholars, unmindful of their promised happiness, nor cast one thought beyond the dirt they tread on!

I am sorry, my dear Eliza (tho' not surprised) to hear your spirits are depress'd & health impaired–'tis what your friends foresaw would be the consequence of your seclusion from the first. You were never made for a recluse. With all your exentricities, you love society, & might enjoy it with convenience, at least in some degree. Why then renounce all social intercourse, refuse the benefits of air & exercise so necessary to health & comfort, & stay shut up–confined at home, buried alive!–without just cause or reason? If you were to persist in such strange conduct, it's well you are in New York. There you may live or die in peace, unnoticed & unknown! Here we don't allow our friends the precious privilidge. You would have the whole town upon your back at once, a Committee from the Board of Health would be dispatch'd, with a certain General [=Isham] at their head, to pry into the premiss, the why & wherefore, know what you have got in your pocket & drag it forth to public notice. . . .

The books you and Mr. Riley were so good to mention to William for my benefit, [Bulwer-Lytton's] *Pelham* & *The Disowned*, have both been here here & read, I suppose, but not to me. Charity begins & ends at home, my friends (kind souls) make shift to do their own reading, & I may do without. Lungs, time, & inclination are require[d] in order to amuse me, and these are wanting for the charitable purpose. I ask no favors & expect none, unless you could bring a reader with you, a pleasure most devoutly to be wished, yet scarcely to be hoped while you continue in your present mood. I can only say Gran Harris longs to see you all. Adieu!

–to which there is a very disgruntled afterthought added a month later, protesting against word received in the meantime from Eliza that she will defer a visit to New London; so Mary goes on (on May 15th):

. . . So you propose a trip to Orange, & despise your poor relations in Connecticut. What a strange set are the Champlains! You need say nothing of Don Quixot, or Touch-me-not. William is the only natural one of the name–civil, social, and accommodating, willing to 'become all things to all men' and glide smoothly through the world. Were you blest with such a disposition, it would be happy for yourself & friends. This Orange trip of yours makes me heartsick. I calculated too much on seeing you here this summer, tho' I tried not to do so, knowing expected pleasure ends in disappointment. William is one of Job's comforters. He says 'let her go to Orange–she has too much gemusical originality about her for New London. I don't wish her here unless she would do as the Romans do: treat people civily, receive & return their calls & visits & conduct [herself] with propriety, like a reasonable creature. But I know she would not, & would rather she would go to Orange.' So much for Master Billy.

Gladly would I put up with the whims & frieks for the sake of your good company, & so would he, but is unwilling they should be exposed to others. My gentleman [William] will visit you as often as he likes & graciously permit you to return his visits if you will promise to be perfectly gentle & submit to all the forms of fashion–for you must know he has become a votive at her shrine, attends balls & parties & is quite the *Ton*! But he is a good soul for all that, & I've reason to speak well of him. . . .

William's concern for George was not allayed for nearly four months, when his brother at last wrote back from Salem, Massachusetts (**no. 261**, July 15):

My dear Bill,

I have no apology to offer you for my long silence, since reciving your *2* letters, but sickness. I have been for some months in very bad health–disease of a pulmonary character. Thank God, however, I am now nearly restored, and hasten to say a word to you related to past & present operations. I was in Boston 6 weeks only, upon my arrival, in the capacity of private secretary to the manager Mr. Booth. I played but once during that period, and that was the part of Catesby in tragedy of *Richard 3*. (Booth played Richard) and he complimented me on the personation of the character. I was likewise noticed in some of the daily journals in Boston.

The reason of my not playing often was in consequence of the comp'y being a very full one and their was no lack of members–but principally because the manager wanted a private clerk and I was appointed to that station, being better qualified in many respects &c. To tell you the [truth] I prefer being behind the scenes to being before them, and there are many of the actors that would gladly change situations with me. My office is worth $14 per week.

After quitting Boston in October last, we went to Salem, where we remain'd until the middle of January; from thence, to Providence, R. I., where we were 2 months; then return'd to Boston until the theatre closed, which was on the 4th of July. We then, with a part of the company, came down to Salem to spend the summer, among whom is that elegant woman and accomplished actress, Mrs. Duff.[16]

I am at present clerk & treasurer of the company. The Tremont [Theatre in Boston] will open the first week in September and I shall take my old station if I don't go to the South with Booth.

I understand by the appointments lately made that U[ncle] Oliver is promoted to the Collectorship of N[ew] London. I am glad to learn it. Hope you are in the line of promotion.

Write soon, and tell me all the domestic news. I shall drop you another in a few days.

In full summer now, but still in the grip of the bleak winter of her life, past sixty years of age and not in good health, Mary writes again (**no. 262**), to Anna Fitch. She refers to a "beau" of Anna's acquaintance who was to visit and then did visit New London; but he is not named, as Mary explains, because he had no existence for her: she wouldn't meet him when he called at the Way house! In her explanation she sounds quite as contrary as she accuses Eliza of being:

My ever dear friend,

. . . More than two years has now elapsed since Eliza handed you my last unfinished letter, for half was left upon the slate for want of time to copy. Enough was there to prove I answered yours without delay. For this I claim no merit. I found pleasure in so doing. . . . [But] I, alas! fettered & cramped, grope my way & blunder on in darkness. And what is worse, it must be copy'd, no small drawback, this, upon the pleasure that remains. It operates as a damper. I dread to commence what will necessarily give trouble. Beside the delay occasioned by the process, I must of course wait the pleasure of those who have the goodness to write for me, & 'tis often many weeks & some-times months before my letters reach the place of destination. So circumscribed, I cannot please myself. . . .

'Tis time to thank you for my beau, as they call him, tho' we have never met, & perhaps never may. Pleas'd with the portrait you have drawn, I thought him interesting, a man after my own heart, & was impatient to be introduced. Soon after he arrived, my brother called, found him sick & out of spirits. He promised to visit us as soon as his health would permit. Many weeks pass'd by & he did not appear. Were I but young & handsome (thought I) I would besiege the garrison at once & take the man by storm. My courage seldom fails on great occasions, & vanity of course would not be wanting for the daring enterprise. As this was not the case, I was compell'd to wait his motion. At length he came with other officers, & company I don't choose to see. This he has done repeatedly, & I have not appeared. He is here this morning with other company, a small party, tho' much too large for me to join–twenty or more in number, officers, their wives & other gentry. I avoid company as much as possible, I've sought in vain for pleasure there. Why should I appear, to be stared at by those who care not for me, & for whom I feel no particular interest. They have my good wishes, & must excuse me if I prefer solitude to such society. Indeed, I find few with whom I can associate. 'I return to my native place, but my friends, alas! where are they? And Echo answered where are they!' The scene has changed. Other Pharaohs have arisen up that knew not Joseph. I find myself in a land of strangers, and feel like one that treads alone some banquet hall deserted, whose lights have fled, the garlands dead, & all but me departed. I miss my friends–alas! I have outstayed them all. Those that remain are far beyond my reach; but they are not lost, & soon will be restored. . . .

I have long wished to see the books you mentioned–when I receiv'd your letter, was still more anxious, & have at length had the pleasure of hearing [Lord Lytton's 1828 novel] *The Disowned*. I was chiefly interested in the sufferings of Mordaunt & charmed with his character. The sentiments & opinions there displayed perfectly coinside with reason & scripture, & contain the total sum of moral truth & sound philosophy. That knowledge & virtue are cause & consequence, and vice the effect of ignorance, is fully evident to me; & I as readily agree that happiness is not a selfish but a social feeling, & to be perfect must be universal. True happiness is never found alone, when shared is most enjoyed, & ever in proportion with our exertions to benefit & promote the happiness of others. A useless being can never be happy (alas, I know by sad experience). Would not these truths believed & practiced make a Heaven below? . . .

Later in the same month of August Riley Sr. died, as Eliza tells William (**no. 263**):

We are again at home and recall'd by most distressing news that Edward's father was on the point of death. We made all the haste we could but reached here many days after his interment. He died at Yonkers where he was taken the week we left–this, for more reviving air. It has been a dreadful blow to E[dward], notwithstanding 'twas a thing so long expected. He died with great calmness of mind with regard to a future state. His spirit was rather restive at being so long clogged with mortality when the time of separation drew near. I was of course not present, but from what I heard he died precisely as Grandfather left his world of woes, rejoicing to escape.

He was brought home and buried from his own residence, and a melancholy scene it was. The carriages stop't at his own door at three in the morning, that most dreadfully still and solemn hour.

We had a very unpleasant jaunt to the [Saratoga] Springs, and, except I think 'twas the means of saving Ted's life, it would not have been attended with one pleasant event. We met a physician in Albany who gave him a bracing bitter that instantly restored the tone of his stomach, which we feared was gone forever. In three or four days after he took it you would scarcely have known him, it had such a wonderful effect.

Our ride for nearly forty miles was over a road that was making, or on the side of steep hills–either of them you may imagine sufficiently agonizing to me. If pride had been my motive for going, I assure you it would have been sufficiently humbled when I saw that diverging an inch from several miles of road would have precipitated us headlong down allmost perpendicular hills, and crushed us out of the form of humanity. But pride was not my motive and I do not therefore see why the punishment was sent.

We found the Springs crowded to suffocation. Money would neither obtain you necessaries, comforts, nor luxuries; you could only get insolence for your cash and not always even that could be vouchsafed, such miserable hireling slaves compose the tavern-keepers at the Springs; and my opinion free and unreserved I shall give to my friend Mrs. Fitch when she returns from the same tour.

As we were going, we were hailed by the upset passengers of a stage which had taken the same rout four hours before us, the very stage by the by to which we applied ourselves and were refused, because it was already crowded. I assure you I did not feel any more comfortable when we took these quaking Jonahs in; but necessity has no law and I held my peace.

This was going. On our return we found, in a savage part of the road, that a stage had just been upset and a lady's arm broken. The same stage endeavored to go on and, from one of the shafts being broken, the vehicle turned over and a gentleman was severely hurt. So you see I have not exaggerated my suffering; and if ever you go in quest of health, choose a different course from the Springs. . . .

In commiseration, William replies (**no. 264**):

I received your letter some days since, and learn with regret of the death of Mr. Riley. Yet I have thought it probable–but death, come when it will, is shocking. To him, though, it was a release from miseries he wished to escape. He had lingered in miserable health for some years past, and when health, that great blessing, is taken from us there is little in life that gives us even patience. Mr. Riley was a man, and a Christian one, that I esteem'd highly and do not believe he has exchanged this world for a worse even if our sleep is eternal–which to some is horrible even to doubt upon a subject so momentous, although we are all as ignorant about it as when our life shall end, or what may happen centuries to come.

You wish to know when I left and when I got home. I left the next morning early, in the cutter, and that day stopped at New Haven about four o'clock in the afternoon, where we lay until the next morning, 10 o'clock. In that time I had an opportunity to see some parts of New Haven, which is a beautifull place. The college & college green in front is beautifull; and they are now erecting a State House of free-stone which, for dimensions and beauty, far exceeds any-thing in this state and will vie with any building in New England. There is an Episcopal church built in the Gothic style of free stone, which for beauty surpasses any-thing of the kind I have ever seen, not excepting any in your renowned city.

Mary Prescott visited that place a year or two since and has some cousins there, but I did not wish to make acquaintances with any of them, having a superabundance of happiness in the acquaintance of ONE relation of hers. Sophia [Shannon] is a most excellent woman & that, for her kindness of heart, I admire greatly; and, but for her sake, would delight in having her with us; but that, I am inclined to believe, never will take place while she can call another place her home.

To continue: we left there at 10 a.m. and arrived at anchor about 2 o'clock in the next morning, off the town, when we had a tremendous thunder-storm accompanied with the most vivid & incessant lightning. It struck in two or three places in the vicinity of New London, but no lives were lost. The floodgates of the skies were raised to the highest notch, for it was slapped down by the hogshead. However, we were all snug and lay quietly until morning.

The next day I disembarked and commenced my dull round of duty. However, I was pleased with the jaunt, though it was a drawback to be so short a time with you. Yet, even if I had been prepared for a longer visit, your journey to the Springs at that time would have made it more to be regreted. I am sincerely glad that little Ned is upon the mending hand so much. I don't know why, but I take a greater interest in that youngster's fate that I am willing to acknowledge. I am fearful that you will spoil him, some way or other. You must leave the management of him to Riley, for upon him I can depend (with due respect) more satisfactorily than upon you. Three things I beg that he may have: air, exercise, and a good education.

I never saw Sam, when he appeared, to show so much brotherly affection as he did during the time I stayed there. The night of the day on which I left you, I was anxious to get on board the cutter, which lay over at the Navy Yard at anchor. I went down to the docks to find a boat to put me on board, but I could not find one readily, to my surprize. The tide run so strong that they charged too high for my purse. So I thought I would cross to Brooklyn and walk to the upper ferry and get a boat there, as the cutter lay but about 50 or 100 rods above. Well, Sam insisted upon going over with me about 10 o'clock at night, which he did, and paid my passage into the bargain. When we were over, we went to a small grocery, to make some enquiries about the road to the ferry, and found a light waggon or buggie, the owner of which offered to take me to the ferry for two shillings–which Sam insisted upon paying also, and with difficulty [I] succeeded in preventing him. So I bid him goodnight and good-bye, & he insisted upon my writing him whether he wrote in return or not. So he says good-bye, you little fool, you. Take care of yourself–which I considered a tough stretch of brotherly affection.

George I have not heard from since I saw you. He is yet at Boston, upon the boards, I believe. Aunt Mary is in good health, but not so good spirits, which is not strange, all things considered, you know.

I hope Mrs. Riley and Louisa are well. Poor woman, she has had that most cutting of trials, of which those that have not passed it cannot sense it as it is–I mean the separation from a husband by death with whom she had lived in happiness so many years.

This place I am disgusted with: so much fashionable visiting, to make and receive calls (for there are a great many officers with their wives here now). The calls must invariably be returned or you are cut at once–the heartless nonsense! That is the order of the day: the moment your back is turned–slandered, vilified, and abused. Forms an outline sufficient to make me misanthropical and wish to have a place affording no greater entertainment for me.

I hope you will write soon and often. Remember me to Edward.

Ever yours,

W. C.

That unusual warmth in Samuel, just described, brought William's answer a month later (October 12th, **no. 266**). He passes on word that George was "acting as clerk & treasurer to the Tremont Theatre, but that he should shortly commence duty as an actor." He adds news already exchanged with Eliza in the two previous letters, and a genial mention of his uncle Tom Way with whom he "had a long confab about olden times, our gunning scrapes &c."

Mary Elizabeth Prescott, long settled in as a dependent female who made herself useful in exchange, apparently, for board and lodging at the Way house, keeps Eliza up to date in **no. 265**. She writes about the same time as William's letter to Sam. She earned some money by her talents and hard work: "I practice every day, some days more than others. I can't remember the day that I have not touch'd the instrument. By the way, I have two now, organ and piano, so that when I get tired of one I can go to the other; but the organ is my delight. Do you practice at all? I should like to see you at the piano. Don't talk to me about getting married. I would not give up my music for all the husbands in creation." She praises her singing-teacher, thanks Edward and Eliza for the bound scores they sent, comments on clothes-making, and goes on to the items of town events: fashionable marriages, Starrs, Perry's, Allens. And a postscript: "Aunt Mary is dying with low spirits, but will write as soon as I have time to copy it."

To close the year, William issues a mysterious warning to Eliza in December (**no. 268**), against addressing him any longer at the post-office rather than "simply my name & New London–likewise, all letters that you intend to write Aunt Mary. Address them enclosed to me, for whatever goes to the post office here for Aunt Mary will be thoroughly sifted unless I handle it first. I would advise you to send what letters you can by the packets. At a future day I will give you the particular reasons for my quitting the Post Office establishment, provided you will write me often." To dramatize his secret, he adds at the end, "Remember, you write soon or not a word of explanation do you have for love nor money, I assure you."

16

Farewell to New London

The period of the next three years, ending so sadly and abruptly for the family, carries forward certain continuing stories: of Ebenezer Way's embattled situation, Eliza's growing family, the changes in her New London brother. William Champlain had entered his twenty-ninth year better employed if hardly better paid than he had been a few years earlier, and better traveled (at least so far as New York on several trips). He had discovered himself to be something of a force in his own town through his championing of his uncle Ebb; he mixes with more confidence in fashionable society; has an eye for the ladies as he never did, or at least never allowed himself to confess, in earlier years. And he has a little distanced himself from too much family, by exchanging his room in the Way house for one with the Lewis Allens.[1] In a lost letter, he explains his move and what lay behind it. His sister deplores it, in her answer of January 4th, 1830 (**no. 269**):

> . . . This morning your epistle was handed me and I was not a little surprised and grieved at its contents; for, of all things, family jars (tho' they are sometimes unavoidable) are certainly the most disagreeable things in creation. I have had sufficient touch of them since my marriage to be convinced of this truth, tho' thank heaven it is not with any member of the family whom it is either my duty or inclination to respect. But the disagreement you allude to I am utterly at a loss to divine. I am, however, on many accounts sorry it has come to an open rupture, as a quarrel is always apt to leave both sides in fault. But I must say my curiosity is on the rack, to learn the particulars of this rumpuss.
>
> Mrs. Fitch was to see me a few evenings since, and said that [her father] Mr. Northam had been lately on to Washington, where he learn'd that Uncle Ebb came near being turned out of office. I said 'twas impossible because Uncle Ebb was a Jackson man and therefore no fault could possibly be found in him, as that circumstance coverered a multitude of sins. She seem'd however not convinceable and said further she understood that his office was in jeoperdy, and that Mrs. Perry

[the Commodore's elderly widow and family friend][2] wrote to a gentleman at Washington begging him to interceed with the Post Master in Uncle Ebb's behalf. The letter was so abely written (for it appears she is a woman of talent) that the gentleman instead of saying a word himself presented the letter to the Post Master and her eloquence prevailed. This is as the story goes, and you have it as cheap as I. I should be very sorry to have him lose his office, very sorry indeed, on every account that can be named, and I do not yet believe that he will. But don't fail to write me the particulars right speedily, as I am of course anxious to know them.

You ask after Sam & George. You might as well go to the grave-yard and call upon the dead for information, and you would get as much as from me; for I am totally ignorant of the fate of either–except that I hear the Tremont Theatre is going down for want of encouragement, these hard times. Of Sam I don't know as much as *this*. I am glad to hear Aunt Mary is well.

In looking over your last letter that mentions the death of Mr. Riley, I could not help smiling at those senseless calls of ceremony that you so heartily bemoan. They have ever provoked my strongest disgust. I would not give the flip of my finger to another, and I can never think highly of those whose beings' end and sum is a call from people who should, every one, fly from them in distress as we fly from plague, pestilence, and famine. No, I cannot stoop to appear to respect such people, and what's more, I *won't* stoop to it; and as the world is generally composed of such worthless trash I am a recluse for life–unless times should mend. What you say on this subject furnishes me at your hands with stronger weapons against yourself than I think you are aware of.

Do write soon and particular. . . .

Her brother had already complied with that last request, giving a description of the sale of those of his belongings that wouldn't fit into his new lodgings–so it may be guessed. He had been in a cheerful mood, and sent her a present. She replies now, only two days after her previous letter (**no. 270** of January 6th, 1830):

. . . I don't know when I ever laughed so heartily as I did over the letter that accompanied it, and am pretty certain that you was under the influence of your eating table when 'twas written.

I am quite fortunate this New Year. I have recieved a present from R. of a superb portable writing desk with my entire name cut on the centre plate. 'Tis a splendid piece of mechanisam and I value it very much.[3] 'Twas I suppose to recover my lost taste for letters. The articles sold at your fair went enormously high. I think they must have sold for twice their value, but I believe they always do that for the love of God. 'Twas not attended much, like our auction when we sold off for the love of money. I am not friendly to such concerns, notwithstanding I have been benefited by one. I think if each individual had contributed their mite, without blowing a trumpet, it would have been more acceptable in the sight of God, at any rate. I don't believe in such a top-of-the-house and market-place business as this same fair, and I think, verily they have their reward. Bigotry and ostentation are the leading features of the whole transaction, and if I was disposed to assist the poor devils, it should not be in this way. I don't believe in chareties where the giver's name is branded on the gift, but I suppose you will call me uncharitable. It has ever been my maxim to conceal from the left hand the deeds of the right, and my opinion, that an obligation hinted at (however large it may be) is already cancelled. So these good Calvinists that get up their parade may rest contented with their self-satisfying consciences and the homage they get in consequence from their fellows; for they may take my word for it, their reward ceases here instead of being an earnest of what they are to recieve hereafter. I think if I had been present I should have turned my attention to 'My-husband-my-dears' wooden tools, for our kitchen is badly stocked with such articles, and admitting they never came in play, they would have served for a laughing stock.

I have been highly amused with your whole letter but particularly this part that brought those drumstick legs with blue- or mixed-yarn stockings so directly before me. I think Capt. Law about the wisest of the whole concern. I think I should have partaken of your eating table with considerable zest, for one's stomach is apt to grind confounded empty during such a long campaign. I have been ready to eat my fingers at an auction, and this was much the same thing. . . .

In the course of his [=Edward's] rounds this morning he learned that there was a cabal against Uncle Ebb in New London, but to what extent it had gone he could not ascertain. You surely will not leave us in ignorance on a subject where we feel so deeply interested, any longer than till you get this letter. . . .

Ted is seized with another bout of teething and is considerably under the weather. I expect he will be an hundred before he gets them all through. R. is well. Mrs. Riley & Louisa are both well tho' the former has much care on her mind from the arduous situation she is now call'd to.[4]

Not in response to this or to anything in particular, Mary Way puts her thoughts on her slate a couple of months later (**no. 271** of March 28th). She begins as she likes to do with lines of verse, "When all the blandishments of life are gone,/ The coward sneaks to death–the brave live on!" and, with some intervening thoughts on gloomy subjects, comes to the conclusion about life as a whole, that "knowledge of its manifold deceptions is reserved for riper years–the result of deep study, nice observation and long experience, and to acquire it fully an age is requisite, and then alas! it comes too late–we are about to quit the stage." She gives a page to the illusions of the world and its rewards, written against a background of church bells tolling the death of Judge Perkins' wife; speaks bitterly of pretty much all the people now about her, whom she ignores or who ignore her, and goes on:

> . . . William is gone and boards at Mr. Allen's. He was the life and spirit of the house, 'tis now a tomb to me. I calculated much upon your visits here–that you and Mr. Riley would come and see us every summer–and promised myself no small degree of pleasure from this arrangement. Oh how vain are human calculations! Castlebuilding, hopes and expectations, all are blasted, fate has decreed it otherwise.

There is, as you are circumstanced and I am situated, but little probability that we shall ever meet again on earth. Still it's right it should be wrong; and thus we make a virtue of necesity and call it resignation.

April 22nd 1830

Another boy [=George Fredrick Riley]! Last night William received the news. Except our warm congratulations, on the increase of your domestic comforts. But don't suppose he took us by supprize. Free-Masonry is out of date you know, and secrets are no more. A stranger was expected to arrive about these days and make his first appearance on the stage, mewling and so forth in his nurse's armes–a very prodigy it is presumed. Talent in every motion! Suits the action to the word and acts his little part to admiration. He has broke Ted's nose, it seems. The first go off a pretty caper to be sure and natural as life; the last is always best.

But Ted is good enough for me. Miss Shannon said he was the handsomest child she ever saw. I admire her taste and agree with her in every thing. Of course he is my favorite. She told me much about his beauty, and I think you have done well to fix it to the canvas, and secure a copy. After all, nothing pleases my fancy more than peaces of this kind: so beautiful and interesting. I think from your description Ted's [portrait] must be a splendid ornament. I have derived much pleasure and improvement from seeing paintings of this sort. Three in particular are before me in all their glowing colours, rich and bright as when I first beheld them: *Twin Cupids*, a painting most superb by an Italian artist, a child by Jarvis, looking up earnestly at a bird that had just escaped from his hand–part of the string he still retains, the other part, floating in air, the liberated bird appears to carry off in triumph–his face full of expression, more than the soul was there. The last that I shall mention, and far the best I ever saw, was the *Infant Saviour* painted by [John] Trumble.[5] I never shall forget the feeling & sensations the sight of this inspired. Here was flesh and colouring that cannot be described. My first thought was, So children look in Heaven. I never much admired the works of Trumble–rather tame, I think, in general, tho' now and then his pencil made a dash. This was his masterpiece, perfect in face and form. One fault alone I could discern, and that might well be overlooked, and lost amid the dazzling splendor of ten thousand beauties.

I am very glad indeed to hear you are so comfortable, that Master George Frederic is a fine promising child, and his superior qualities noted and considered; but don't be in haste to have his picture drawn. Wait awhile, my dear, for half a dozen more, and better still, then let it be a family affair: yourself the centre-piece like smiling Charity encircled by her ofspring–a charming groupe–domestic happiness! May it ever be yours, whether displayed upon canvas or concealed from public view. May you enjoy it in its full extent and measure, pressed down and running over. . . .

Sunday June 6th

'Flat, stale & unprofitable you will say' [=the present letter]. 'Tis done at last, however, & much sooner than I had reason to expect. Mary [Prescott] staid home from church to-day for the purpose of writing my letter or you would not have received it this summer, we are so full of business. Mr. & Mrs. Shannon are here from Halifax. Mr. Starr and his sister came with them, a cousin of theirs Miss Starr from Norwich, & a young lady from Stonington who is learning music. You recollect Leander Starr, you saw here some eight or nine years ago with the Miss Shannons and Deans. The same animals. He is now a brisk widower, only six months since he lost his wife and already supposed with a marrying spirit. 'Tis doubtful whether sister Julia will hold out to the year's end. So soon are the dead forgotten! None the worse for them & perhaps better for the living. All is right.

William admires Leander's sister, Susan Starr. They say she's very handsome. I wish this same brother of yours was well married & settled here. In that case I think you would be induced to visit more frequently. You don't know how much I want to see you. Adieu.

On the Monday following, to go in the same mail when he went down to the harbor, William took the time to write (**no. 272**):

Dear Eliza,

I suppose it is needless to expect any more letters from you, now that you have two brats to dandle. How can you find ways and means to devote all your time to them? If you was what is called a smart wife, you could so divide your time as to consider that you give to the young ones a play-spell, but, with your habits & disposition (as you have the greatest faculty to heap up troubles of all hues and descriptions), I suppose every instant is devoted to the little fools, in sighs, groans, and tears, early & late–to use a Scripture phrase that I pick'd up, 'watched by one that eateth the bread of carefullness' &c. I wish you would turn over a new leaf and write me twice a week, for if you will adopt the plan you will find it the easiest thing in nature. Habit is second nature, you know! So be persuaded and do a[s] I request.

Mr. James Shannon from Halifax was here on Saturday, but left that day in the steam-boat for New York, bound up the Hudson to see Niagara Falls. He will probably be gone 10 or 12 days. In the mean-time, his wife is staying at Ebb's, she having taken the journey for her hea[l]th, but not being over-strong, thought she would remain here while her husband made the tour. She was here last summer with Sophia [Shannon], and stay'd some time. Sophia she left well, in Halifax, about a fortnight since. Mr. Leander Starr from Halifax likewise stopped at Ebb's with his sister Miss Susan Starr, a very beautiful girl about 20 or 21. He enquired after you and mentioned a watch-paper you painted for him when here before. I should have written by him if I had thought you would like to have seen him, but they were extremely fashionable and I think you are not over-fond of ceremonious calls from extremely fashionable people–tho' Miss Susan I liked much better than her brother. That may be, however, on account of the affection I bear to your sex generally. Her brother is a widower, having buried his wife last winter some-where in the West Indies, and he has gone with his sister also to view Niagara and the Canadas.

How is Sam? I hear nothing from him and I suppose it's the same with you. He is a very strange fellow, and ought to be punished for silence. I believe I mentioned in my last that George has left Boston and gone southward somewhere, but to what spot it would be difficult to tell. Uncle Ebb remains firm in his office yet, and I think will continue to do so. Aunt Mary is very well, and, if we except some trials, gets along comfortably. She wrote a letter to you as long as the moral law, which Mary [Prescott] copied; but it was so badly done that when she undertook to read it over, Meg [=Mary Way] was so mad she declared it should not go, and therefore you must wait until Mary [Prescott] finds time to copy it anew–which may be some time yet, as she is employed in lessons of different kinds.

Our harbour looks quite lively just at this time, there being thirteen ships now in it besides one that sail'd on Saturday upon a whaling voyage. They are all whalemen and pay but little money into the Custom House here. It benefits me next to nothing, there being no duty upon oil; yet it seems to make this place very lively when they arrive.

The clock has struck nine. I must quit & go to the office. I wish you would answer this.

And the next day, Tuesday, William sends yet another letter with gifts to Eliza, the gifts originating in his business contacts with the whaling captains who in recent years had appeared on the scene. Captains, ships and crew are described a little further along in the correspondence. As to the South-Seas articles they now produce–a toy kayak, a genuine heathen idol, and so forth–these had begun to reach New England only since the 1820s. Whalers, mostly from Massachusetts ports, were venturing east and south to Polynesian and Melanesian waters, that is, to Tahiti, Oahu, Hawaii and suchlike points that William spells any way he can, and on their return they brought curios to show around (**no. 273**):[6]

I send you by Capt. Lamphere a small basket secured with purple tape and that sealed; a few small shells brought home here in the whaling ships from the South Pacific Ocean; also, a piece of cloth made from the bark of trees by the natives of islands in the Pacific. These shells are picked up from the beach on the islands with the same high polish they now possess, and brought on board by the natives who sell them to the crews for mere trifles, such as a string of glass beads will purchase a bushel; also, jack-knives, hatchets, &c are quickly traded by the natives for shells. But when they arrive here, they bear a higher value, as every-one is anxious to obtain some, tho' all are not equally fortunate.

The ships that bring these are gone from here from thirty months to three years, upon the Japan coast, Asia, whaling. These shells, however, are obtained at the Sandwich Islands in the Pacific. The name of the island where they generally obtain them is Wahoo, tho' I believe likewise at Otahitie, Owyhee &c. The majority of these shells was given me by Capt. Chester of the ship *Friends*, in whose ship came a large box of curiosities from the missionaries at those Islands, to the 'missionary rooms at Boston.'

As it was necessary to know what the box contained, Uncle Oliver and myself opened and examined it. There were masks made of wood with painted cheeks, eyes, and eyebrows, teeth cut, the underlip projecting about 1/2 or 3/4 of an inch, oval & scooped out like the bowl of a spoon, for what purpose the natives only know. There was a female figure about twelve or fifteen inches high, of wood, with painted face &c, dressed in calico, head covered with coarse black Indian hair. There was a little wooden fellow about 8 inches long who looked the worse for wear, he had been so much handled (we were told why by a whaleman who stood by) by the natives, it being a household gods, and taken upon all expeditions with them &c. There were fish-hooks made of bone, large and small, roughly made, there was the skins of one or two animals stuffed; also, two or three different coloured cloths, the article the same style I have sent you; several specimens of mineralogy; several modles of canoes used by the natives; also one Greenland modle covered with skin with the round opening in the deck (which is of skin) where the rowers or padlers sit, and the opening is so secured by a shirt worn by the rowers that fastens to the deck of skin, that no water can be admitted into the boat if the weather is ever so rough. They have also the faculty of using the paddle so dexterously that they can bring her upright again in the twinkling of an eye after she upsets in the rough gales of wind, &c.

By the way, in the basket I have sent you there are the gatherings of rattling-traps [=odds and ends] for the last fourteen years, as I am now boarding at Allen's and have but one room. I thought if I could get rid of that basket without burning it, I should do well, and after considering what I should send my shells in, concluded you should take some bitter with the sweet, and have accordingly packed them off upon you; so you may do what you please with them–only don't send them back to me. . . .

Eliza thanks William for all this (**no. 274**, still in the month of June, 1830):

My dear William,

The contents of your basket afforded me a great deal of merriment as well as pleasure at receiving so elegant a present as the shells. While I was running over the letters and picking out the shells, a parcel of rattle-traps fell upon the floor and in a pig's whisper Ted had feathered his nest with a razor strop, a black stock, and a pencil–which, by the bye, he calls a peedle–and was vehemently calling out for more 'dies'–a name our Irish girl has given his playthings. The deeper I went, the more I found; and, except a mighty ancient and fishlike smell–'none of the newest, poor John'–throughout the assortment, I should have been well paid for my trouble. But to tell you the honest truth, it was so rascally unsavory as to cost me my dinner.

I was much obliged for your spools of cotton. They were the very number I wanted. The Indian cloth I have before had a specimen of. I recollected the article instantly. R. is delighted with the shells. He thinks them very superb indeed. He lifts his hands in astonishment whenever I am recollected in any shape by a *brother*, although I am an only sister, though of you he has had no cause and therefore does not complain. But I can tell you he has not the most exalted opinion of the other male relations with which it has pleased God to bless me withall. . . .

My reasons for calling your youngest nephew George Frederick were these: first, George is a name that cannot be nickt. Ted's is established for life. There are

> thousands of names I prefer to George, but this one objection holds good with them *all*: a nick-name is eternally attached to almost every one that we could think of, and so, without one thought of family name in the business, I decided on calling him after the best-wearing name. So you must not set up your Ebenezer about it, as no offence was meant.
>
> I sat up last night till one o'clock and my eyes are now absolutely closing over this letter, so you must excuse its *hum-drumety*. . . .

But because of "a houseful of company," a concert to attend and the fireworks of the Glorious Fourth to walk out to, another two weeks were to pass before the letter was actually in the mail.

In August, while Edward, Eliza, and some parts of the Riley family were absent from New York on their now-usual summer holiday, business brought William down to that city. By ill-luck they missed each other but, when they all got home, on almost the same day they exchanged letters of regret and news. First, this from Eliza (**no. 275**, September 2):

> I was surprised and disappointed to learn on our way from the boat to our dwelling that we had arrived home just in time to miss seeing you. How do you always contrive to cross our paths when we are on the wing and at no other time. 'Twas so on our departure for Saratoga, 'tis so on our arrival from Saw Pits (what an elegant name). We find left in your place a couple of beautifully wrought flower-pots from the fair, we suppose, with a letter containing one line from you not at all explainatory of your intention respecting the jars; but we laid violent hands upon them from their being directed to E. C. R. If they have not reached their place of destination, you will have the goodness to let us know and they shall forthwith depart.
>
> It was our intention to have gone to Shrewsbury this season, but on learning the price of board was five dollars per week we relinquished the idea as our party consisted of 8 persons in the whole, and the price did not suit our convenience. On hearing Saw Pits well spoken of we sought it and staid 17 days. We met very good society at the house where we put up. Amongst them was a Capt. Lee & lady &c— 4 children, the youngest, three months old, was call'd George Frederick Augustus after his late Majesty (not so, ours). Capt. Lee is a very handsome English-man who sails in a Liverpool vessel. Perhaps you may know him. We were all much pleased with himself and family.
>
> Nothing occur'd worthy of note during our stay, and the place tho' well enough is not worthy of particular description. On the whole, however, I enjoy'd myself much more than at Saratoga, for Mrs. Riley & Louisa were along and contributed much toward rendering our jaunt pleasant. Ted was the happiest little dog alive. He was always surrounded by a host of children and was generally their ring leader. One of the fair small fry he singled out and designated by the tittle of his wee wife. Her name was Eliza Theressa and after we were seated in the stage to depart, he calls out to her as she stood on the stoop, Good bye Eliza Theressa, I will come back again. So you see he is a chip of your block.

Saratoga is a much more healthy place. Setting aside its waters, we have none of us been particularly benefited by the place. R. does not enjoy robust health at all and thinks he never shall unless Dame Fortune should shower sufficient of her yellow boys to enable him to spend the remainder of his days in England. I do not think with him, for I am certain if he could get out of the intolerable drudgery of teaching he would soon be well enough. But this is such a nerve-destroyer. No one can teach and be well. This I am sure of by sad experience.

Tell Aunt Mary 'twas my firm intention to have written her before I left New York, but 'twas frustrated for lack of time, and I cannot now put it in execution, for the same reason.

Mrs. Fitch call'd to say good-bye about a week before we left, and charged me when I wrote to give her love and say that she had been long intending to write, but her everlasting round of company prevented. She was going from my door then to call on Mrs. Hayden who I lament to say has been obliged to sell all off and doubtless remains in debt.[7] Her house in Broadway is shut. Where she and her children now are I cannot say. If 'twas in my power to aid her I would soon see, but 'tis not, and I keep aloof; for empty condolence does but little good. Some people, however, think it's like poor company, better than nothing.

I have something remarkable to say of Mr. Mitchell.[8] He is on the recovery. All his physicians say he is a miracle, but Cornelia his third daughter is on the point of death with consumption. She is removed to West Chester County and 'tis supposed will be brought home a corpse.

George is well. We had him weigh'd at Saw Pits. He weighed 18 & a half, R. 136, *I* 110, Ted 26. Do write soon or show yourself in person.

Yours in dreadful haste,
Eliza

And from William, *his* regrets (**no. 276**):

Dear E.,

I am sorry I could not see you while in New York, but probably may come again before long. I should not have been at New York at all had it not been upon business. I was summonsed at a trial of the schooner *Marion* seized in this district for smuggling. My testimony was wanted relative to the necessary papers made out by me. The court was held at New Haven and the only way to get there was via Hartford or New York. I went by the way of Hartford and returned via New York. I should have waited a day or two longer but my money was about gone–besides, very urgent business here. I saw Henry Riley and Mr. Jacobson who told me you had left. I also saw Aunt Tracy and our cousins Eliza & Caroline [Tracy]. The latter is married to a very good-looking and acting young man whose name I have forgotten, a carpenter by trade. I drank tea there last Sunday evening. Before I left I saw Mr. and Mrs. Fitch, who had just returned from a jaunt to the Springs. She was rather unwell. Mrs. Northam I did not see or Cornelia but they are well. Mrs. Fitch sent Aunt Mary a book for me to read which I shall do.

I arrived in New York on Saturday morning and left there on Monday at 3 p.m. I saw Sam Saturday after the bank had closed and we took a walk down to the Battery and a long walk up Broadway and back to the Bowery again. Then we got a bite of something to eat, and I proposed walking. We went up as far as Warren Street, when we turned down, it being my intention to take him to see Charles Douglass M.D., a cousin of ours from New London, brother of Peter–of the same family, but much the likeliest of the family. He has located himself as a small druggist in that street. Well, I had asked Sam if he had ever seen his cousin Douglass. 'Cousin Charles Douglass–who the hell is he?' Why, a brother of Peet's. No, he had not, 'nor did he wish to see the d . . . d infernal fool, none of the d . . . d Douglasses.' However, he was not aware he was in the neighborhood of his cousin. I observed I was passing a drug-store–I would step in and get some medicine I wanted, and asked him to go in with me, at the same time stepping in, myself. 'What the hell do you want of medicine. Ah, I understand you. This is that Cousin Charles Douglasses. No, I'll be d . . . d if I goes in.' All my persuasions were useless and I had spoken to Douglass when I was in.

I bid Sam good night, and spent the remainder of the evening with Charles. The next morning, Sunday, Sam persuaded me to take a jaunt over to Hoboken and we spent the forenoon there. In the afternoon we took a stroll in the upper part of the city. In the evening I went with Douglass to see Aunt Tracy and took tea there. The next morning I saw Sam a short time before he went to the bank, and again just as the steam-boat was starting. I think he has got the blues upon him to a most alarming degree. If I lived in the city I should try to get him off from the habit he is in of never visiting. He appears to have no disposition for company, owing I believe to his tenacity in never seeing it.

Aunt Mary is very well but wants you should invite her, for you are the only absent friend she ever expects to hear from by writing.

I have *laid in* with the captains of the whaling ships to procure me some shells when they return (if ever they do) but do not expect them for about thirty months from this. They are Capt. Smith of the ship *Phoenix* and Capt. Fitch of the ship *Superior*. I wish to get enough for you and some other friends, say Mrs. Fitch, and Mrs. Lee, who had asked me to procure some for her if I can–which I promised to.

I was quite disappointed in not seeing my last nephew, who from what I heard is a paragon, an immaculate, a nonesuch! We have the scarlet fever prevailing here very much among children. There are some dozens down with it, and it is also prevalent in your city. Mrs. Rice of this town who was at New York upon a visit lost a little girl about 3 years old and brought her corpse up here for burial in the steam-boat this morning. Gen'l Isham has a son here about 3 years old at the point of death with it. He probably will not recover, and at the lower part of the town the children generally are down with it, besides a number of typhus.

Did you know that John Dickinson was married to Mary Isham and has a son? Also Marcus Starr, a grandson of old John Way's married to Elizabeth Griffing & has a son.[9] Also, that Lieut. Fetterman of the army is to be married to Ann Maria Judd, alias Sittings?

I should admire to have what for a jaunt you have had, with your description of hair-breadth scapes &c. By the way, there was sent you by Lamphere a couple of vases (pieces of calico upon glass tumblers), a present from Mary Prescott. They are in the possession of Mr. Jacobson and there was a note sent by me with directions to leave it, but I forgot. You will ere long I presume have a letter respecting them from her.

Do write soon. Love to all.

Ever yours, W. C.

William's next presents were not so likely to please as the Hawaiian and Tahitian articles (**no. 277** of October):

Dear E.,

Accompanying this, I send you some old cloaths, such as I have outgrown or at any rate given up. But I beg of you for the love of God not to waste as much time in trying to make something of them as Mother would. If you do, I shall hear of it and shall never do the like again.

Why do you not write to at least thank the giver of those vases to you? When I go up there it is always enquired if I have heard from you.

When I was in New York, I saw Mr. & Mrs. Fitch, both well, and had just returned from the Springs. Mrs. F. mentioned she had seen you before starting on your jaunt. She talked of coming up here to make a visit to see Aunt Mary. I told her we should be happy to see her & that I wished I was married and at house-keeping, that I might have the pleasure of her company during her stay. By that I meant it was doubtful whether she would get an invitation to stay at Ebb's–which she readily understood, for she observed there were more houses than our house. However, she has not made her appearance, and from the lateness of the season I presume will not this year, tho' for my own part I should admire to have her come.

Aunt Mary is the same old kritter she ever was, being spunk to the brim. There is the most delicate compliment passed between her and another person occasionally–in a private, family way, I mean–that would make you roar with laughter to hear Meg [=Mary Way] repeat them. As I am clear of the whole affairs now-a-days, I enjoy a recitiation from her of a dialogue which occassionally takes place between them; and God knows I ought to enjoy it, now if ever; for if a thirteen years' tuition under such an instructress is not enough to give me the right of criticism, it at least bestows the right of my turn in laughing.

Tell Riley the Groton Monument is nearly compleated, the whole stone work being finished, which is 116 feet in height and will have an iron railing around the top to be four feet high, which will mean the total height 120 feet.[10] This stands upon the hill a few rods north of Groton Fort, which is 120 feet above the level of the water, making a total height of 250 feet from the top of the monument. You have a good view of Long Island sound, as you can see the eastern extremity of the Island with Montauk Light House upon it. . . .

My business in the Custom House is verry dull indeed–nothing doing at all, tho' I hope some benefit will result from the West India ports being open, which I see is a fact by the papers yesterday. . . .

"My dear brother Billy," Eliza replies, not to the preceding but to some lost letter from William which in turn irritably commented on a lost letter of hers–and so there is a gap in the correspondence until this one, of about late November:[11]

I was quite grieved at finding you in such a devil of a huff at supposing my natural affections could not work without a pair of breeches to set them in motion. Be assured, my dear brother, you were never more mistaken in your life than you are in your present opinion of the state of affairs. My reply to the letter that accompanied the present was written with the din of both children in my ears and for the soul of me I could not tell what I had written after the letter was dispatched. Supposing your Champlain temper would take fire at my apparent slight of your courtesy as it did at the news-paper scrape, I thought it best to leave all things hanging at loose ends and write again if the devil stood in the door. This and this only is the witchcraft that lies in your old breeches. Now are you satisfied?

There was a young lady of great beauty and accomplishments happen'd to be in when your articles were received. She heard me say I should make a suit for Ted out of the pantaloons and to my great astonishment observed she would take off her things and spend the day for the purpose of ripping them for me. I was completely taken by surprise, without the power of extricating myself from the dilemma. I was however obliged to make the best of a bad bargain supposing it arose from pure friendship for me when in fact that had nothing to do with it. The magic lay in the breeches and I was a cypher. I however produced my smoothing plane for once, as the person was my guest, and with as much pleasure as I could muster into my countenance expressed great delight at her determination. I found she had received a pretty good account of you from some quarters (tho' I can swear it was not my quarter) and was resolved by ripping the breeches to get a further insight into your character through them if possible. The dust that arose allmost choaked her, but nothing daunted she pushed on till she came to the inside of the pockets, those common receptacles for all that is filthy in creation. Somewhat daunted at the spectacle she made a pause, an awful pause, prophetic of the speech that followed. My dear Mrs. Riley, your brother must have been hard on his pantaloons, and uttering a Pah, as Hamlet does on noting Yorick's skull, she proceeded with her penknife to scrape the first layer off.

I was having inward fits at the job she had saved me but I put on my long metre and observed these were by no means your roast meats–that you laid them off in lavender. This somewhat restored her waning courage to proceed and she finally made a finish to the business, to my great joy. I think she is in a bad way about you. I encourage her with hopes that business may bring you down in the (?)maning season, and on those she lives. So if you don't pay us a fetch-fire call I'm afraid her case is desperate. One thing I know. She'd let concealment like a worm in the bud prey on her damask cheek, before she'd blow her love. So you must be sensible what a frail and delicate subject you have to deal with. Pray be mercifull.

I hope you have spewed out all your influenza, indigestion and everything else that overloaded your stomach in your last letter. You have quite a salmagundy of a mess pour'd out on my devoted head and I have no doubt but you feel much relieved by having emptied your budget.

Have you heard the awful stories now afloat here respecting the young students? I suppose you recollect a few years ago the public were very much anoy'd by the disturbance of the dead for the purpose of disection. They have now changed their tune. Nothing but the living will satisfy them. They must be taken alive that they may be disected while warm. These monsters have employed a band of villians that no name is bad enough for, to station themselves in the different dark streets of the city and, with a noose that is invisible to the passers, choke them instantly. Another method is meeting suddenly any persons passing, and clapping on their mouths a pitch-plaister to prevent screaming. I suppose you disbelieve what I say but two cases have happen'd directly under my nose, and I know every particular. A young lady had been to a party and was returning late home with five or six companions. She was very cold and said if they did not hurry she should freeze; but they were not disposed to accomodate her (for her brother was her beau) and she advanced ahead some yards. Suddenly she was noosed. Her fright gave her ready wit. She shuffled it off in an instant and screeched for one of the gentlemen behind. They all flew to her assistance and carried her almost lifeless home. She was recover'd but her fright had been too much. She continued at intervals to have nervous fits till the fifth day after when she died raving.

Another case is this. A little child about four years old about a week ago was missing. The mother, a poor woman, was distracted and seeking it in all directions. She was advised by a friend to go to a certain medical concern. She went and was refused admittance. She said with forced calmness she wished to get some medicine. Not suspecting her they let her in, when horrible to relate she found the poor little soul with its feet in warm water that it might not know it was bleeding to death. They had open'd the veins in both its ankles and fixed its feet so that it might not feel the blood trickle. The poor distracted Mother caught it up and ran home with it but she could not stop the bleeding. The child died and she is almost mad.

Don't you read this part of my letter to Aunt Mary, I charge you. It has made me sick at my stomach to write it. I'm braver than I was or I could not have heard it, much more wrote it. I wish the invention of a Hell for the punishment of crimes such as these were left to me. They would find me screw my courage a little beyond the sticking place. I should not give you these as facts did I not know them to be such. The first night I heard the story of the child I could not sleep and it has haunted me ever since. . . .

Your watch would have been home long before this but the person who has alter'd it could not satisfy himself and was obliged to retain it for the purpose of watching its movements. His charge is three dollars. Mine has now gone on the same business and I expect will be detained as long. Do for Heaven sake write soon and let us know the upshot of your [Richard] Law and [Thomas] Muzzy scrape. We are very anxious to know the result. I can tell you in the interim, good-bye, I wish you success.

She followed this up within a few days with her apologies for its tone (**no. 280**).[12] How big George Frederick grows, how great a favorite Ted is with the shop-manager, Mr. Jacobson, and how welcome cast-offs are from any direction, fills up the rest of the letter, along with Ted's cold:

> . . . This climate is killing me by inches with its freaks. In the morning we get up froze to death, before noon all the doors and windows must be set wide, and by night there is danger of yellow fever from heat. Hang such a climate, say I! R. talks of ending his days in England for he can't stand it as well as me.
>
> He has gone to a double-refined concert tonight–that is, the tickets are two dollars a'piece. I did not choose to take the trouble to dress enough for the occasion and I would not go without, so the tickets have gone to the family. . . .
>
> R. saw in the papers the name of De Angelis out in full as an actor on the boards of New York.[13] As there is only one in the place, we are much afraid that our well-beloved brother in the Lord, Sam, has had an additional *stab* under the fifth rib. Your Speaker thinks it quite doubtful if His Highness survives this last haul on his dignity. 'Tis however possible. While there is life there is hope, you know. But 'twill be a tight match.
>
> I wish you had been here on the 26th of the last month [when the city welcomed former President Monroe]. New York never had such a tremendous evacuation before, as Aunt Mary says. 'Twas really a scene well worth witnessing. Fourth of July was a fool to it. I never was more pleased at any exhibition than that. . . .

William is likewise reduced to the weather and comment on the family items his sister had retailed, to fill his first page (**no. 282**, December 17). Then:

> . . . [William's superior in the Customs Office] Capt. [Richard] Law is now away and has been four weeks today, and how much longer he may remain is uncertain. Therefore I have just at this time sufficient to keep me employed all the time, and I ought leave this letter and go about something else. But I believe I will not, but try to make a finish of it for you.
>
> You mention that Riley saw in the newspaper 'the name of De Angelis out in full as an actor.' Who the devil is De Angelis and why should it stab our brother Sam under the fifth rib? It's a riddle to me. Explain yourself.[14]
>
> I must beg of you to present your respects, compliments, or what you will to your beloved Aunt Sally Way, when you write me . . . the lady in question and myself are upon verry fair terms at this present, which I find is necessary for the more especial comfort of a certain Aunt [Mary] of ours. Therefore, mind your P's and Q's. . . .

A few pieces of William's business correspondence survive from this time, running between him and New London's Collector of customs, Captain Richard Law.

There is enough to show what sort of things he had to take care of and what extraneous problems were likely to intrude on the Customs office as on Ebb's Postmastership. Law while in Washington, though he had his own very serious problems, was active on Ebb's behalf, who should really have been there fighting his battles for himself. For Law, advocacy was evidently a matter of personal friendship, a feeling that can be sensed in the way young William speaks of him. Friendship governed, not party. As to political loyalties even in these charged times, though Ebb can be described as a clear Jacksonian, nothing in the correspondence indicates Oliver's or William's sympathies, or the party of anyone else in their circle. Politics, "this high-seasoned mess" that Betsey avoided by silence when she could, were a man's preserve, while the correspondence is dominated by women; so the reader has trouble getting into the subject very far.[15]

But to return to William's report of Customs-office business for the information of his supervisor:

> In your last communication, I was sorry to see your prospects so suddenly changed; but I still hope for better things. This evening before I commenced this letter I went to the Post Office with the expectation of finding some instructions relative to the schooner *Sarah* and cargo; but not a word from any quarter respecting her. How to account for this I know not. I suppose the instructions for admiting her to an entry will come directly from Washington to me. Should this reach you while in Washington, I wish you would make the enquiry whether the papers have ever left there. Neither has there been any-thing received relating to the salmon. Capt. Pendleton came down to see me about selling them. He was perfectly willing, and thought in fact it would be the best plan. Accordingly, I gave him a letter to Mr. Denison who had notice given before the State of them, and I presume has deposited the proceeds of them in the bank at Stonington.
>
> I fortunately have had few interruptions since you left, to prevent my bringing forward the quarterly abstracts. I shall, however, continue to advance them as much as they will admit of it.
>
> I have seen Mr. Way's letter from Mr. Barber and regret to note its contents. He says it is out of his power to leave here at this time, as the quarter is nearly out and the amount due the U[nited] States must be collected and deposited within ten days after the expiration of the quarter. Besides other well grounded reasons for not going, he has written Maj. Barber by this mail. . . .
>
> Ever your friend,
>
> Wm. Champlain
>
> P.S. Capt. Sherman or Sherburn called to see you day before yesterday. He was passing through the town on his way to New York and was sorry he had not the pleasure of seeing you, and desired to be remembered. He was with you in Copenhagen.

A week or so later William heard that his friend had been discharged after eight years as Collector for New London. Mussey had gone after him when he began to sense the Postmastership might lie beyond his reach. The outcome threw William's own subordinate job into doubt; for loyalty to Richard Law and Ebenezer Way were in his eyes connected, and the threats to their tenure of office certainly struck very close to home. He explains to his brother-in-law (**no. 283** of December 29th) what forces had been mustered on behalf of Law, though they still could not prevail: among those forces, a prominent Connecticutter known to be in the President's good graces, although as a Supreme Court judge somewhat removed from politics (Baldwin); also, a couple of party-active New Yorkers, but of no very great influence (Bailey and Swartwout):[16]

D'r E[ward],

Yours of 19t recived day before yesterday. I am glad you have not been able to procure the ebony, upon the whole, for I wanted it for a purpose which was altogether an useless expense. Rose-wood I can procure in abundance at this place, therefore I thank [you] for your kind offer but I think I will give up the idea of making a box, which was my intention, and keep my money against time of need comes along–he [=it] being near at hand, I believe, as Capt. Law the Collector has lost his office and I am now making up his accounts to the date of the expiration of his commission, which was the 24th inst.

What I shall do when he leaves the office I cannot say at this time, but if Mussey obtains the appointment I shall quit, and think it probable [I] shall go down to New York to see if I can obtain employment there. Mussey has been nominated by the President and, although it may meet with some opposition in the Senate, yet I doubt not it will pass. Should he not be appointed but some-one other than Capt. Law, I think I shall remain, as I undoubtedly would be acceptable to whoever is appointed to make him acquainted with his duty, tho' the prospect of any other than Mussey being appointed is very slight.

Capt. Law returned last week after being absent about five weeks. He had every-one of the Cabinet in his favor except Van Buren & he [=Van Buren] influenced the President to nominate Mussey, whom he represented as being very active in behalf of the administration, and Capt. Law not enough so–although he (Law) voted for the Jackson ticket at his election; yet he was lukewarm and would not answer because he did not make noise enough as a Jackson man. He (Law) had the strongest recommendations from some [of] the most influential Jackson men in your city. One of the warmest letters I think I ever saw was from Mr. Swart-wout to the President; another from Benjamin Bailey; another from Judge Bald-win; & in fact he not only [had] letters but the whole of this State delegation go forward, to a man, in his behalf, besides a great number of Senators and Rep-resentatives of other States–Com[modore] Barrow, Rodgers, & other naval men, Mr. Ewing who has formerly been a Minister to France, Spain, and elsewhere, be-sides the strongest recommendations from the whole of this district, Stonington, Norwich, Mystic, Groton, Lyme and this place, requesting that he might be ap-pointed. But all would not do. His enemies represented him as a Federalist in his politics and that he stopped a paper that changed from Adams to Jackson, unfortunately, just as it changed, the year happening to be up and the editors leaving at the same time.

I wish you would send the watch the first opportunity after it is done, with the cost, and in the mean time say nothing abroad [about] what I have written respecting this affair at present; and I will give you further information as I recive it; and never pay the postage of a letter to me and any other person that is upon this business. . . .

This account that William gives had its sequel a fortnight later, in the New Year (**no. 284** of January 12th, 1831):

Dear Edward,

I mentioned to you that I would give you any further information respecting the appointment of Collector at this port as soon as secured. There has nothing decisive been secured as yet. The nomination of Mr. Mussey by the President to the Senate has been made, and it has not been acted upon yet by request of Mr. Foot of the State. I believe however it has been given to a committee to make enquiries relative to the characters of Mr. Mussey & the late incumbent Capt. Law, and furthermore, the most weighty reason advanced by Mr. Foot for its present arrest was the unheard-of act of one State interfering in the appointments to be made in another, as the delegation of New Hampshire have come forward in a body by the influance of Isaac Hill, to make the appointment of Collector for the Port of New London in Conn't. There has been a number of letters & some certificates sent from this and other places which I think will have great influence in preventing Mr. Mussey from obtaining the office, and will have a very beneficial effect upon Capt. Law's prospects. In the event of Mussey's obtaining it, however, I shall leave immediately, as I before mentioned, I think; but of this fact I wish you to be totally dumb, as well as whatever else I may write; for there is no kind of news which is received here which is not out in five minutes after its arrival, if its secrecy is of ever so much importance, and it would surely be here in twelve hours from New York were you to hint it.

My watch I shall expect up by Lamphere's sloop. There is a new captain who is a clever fellow and if you give it him will take particular care of it. His name is Henry.

We are all well here. This d . . . d Jackson party has commenced a new attack upon Mr. Way, but I firmly believe it will have no kind of effect in the way of his removal, for he stands very high at Washington as a Jackson man. There is a great number of two-faced sons-of-bitches in this town who ought to have the bowstring applied to them.

If you ever hear anything from Sam or George let me know, and make Eliza write. Capt. Law is now *acting* Collector, his commission having expired the 24th of last month, and letters addressed to him from the different departments at Washington are to R. L. *late collector* &c &c. This is of course, tho', as when his commission is out, he is no longer such &c.

In haste, yours &c,

W. Champlain

In **no. 285**, William again addresses Edward on February 17:

> I have but a few minutes to inform you that it is probable Uncle Ebb will lose his office through the influence of that friend Mr. Mussey. The President has taken certain papers into his possession which have been in the hands of the Post Master Gen'l and who is the decided friend of Mr. Way, but his calling for these papers, which are charges that have been brought against him by his enemies in this place, leaves but little chance for him to escape the fall of the axe. The first news I receive relative to this affair, I will let you know. In the mean-time, yours as usual.

Still on the doings in Washington, William writes again, but this time to Eliza, on March 3rd. It emerges that Mussey did not get the Customs-Collector job, leaving it to Ingolsby W. Crawford (**no. 286**):

> Since my last, there has been some stir in town. Mr. Way had a letter from Washington a few days since, saying that the papers relative to this Post Office had been returned without any comment as to the President's decision. However, the fact that they have been returned again to the General Post Office I think is much in Mr. Way's favor. In the mean-time, Mussey has returned here and his friends (who by the way are very few in number in this town) have been circulating a paper in favor of him as Post Master here in place of Mr. Way but, from all I can learn, have not done much as yet in procuring names. There was immediately another paper drawn up by Way's friends speaking in the highest terms of him as a public officer and also seting forth Mussey's character as he stood here–without oversteping what is actually felt by a majority of the citizens. To this instrument, John Dickinson and myself obtained about eighty-five of our most respectable citizens' names, and it went in the mail last night to the Post-Master General. From this paper I look forward to a happy result. If he is removed now, why, it is his fate. 'Burnt brandy would not save him.'
>
> And amidst all this political clash, the new Collector has not yet arrived, although he has been appointed nearly, or quite, a month; and what is more strange, we have never had a line from him to know what his determination is whether to accept or not. It has been suggested here that there is an understanding between this Mr. Crawford & Mussey, and that Crawford is to absent himself from this place until after the rising of Congress–then forward his resignation, and the President appoint Mussey to the vacancy until the meeting of the next Congress, when he hopes to have a majority of his own in the Senate to confirm the appointment. And in case this should take place, as I hold to my former resolution, you will have a chance of seeing me in your good city of Gotham. This, however, is but surmise. I am told Mr. Crawford is a poor man living upon a verry poor farm in a town called Union in this state, and I think he has a family of nine or ten children; that he is a worthy, honest fellow, plain in his manners but of good sound sense, having filled high offices in this State, and well liked by those who know him. If therefore he should come in & accept, I should have no objection to remain with him, provided we could agree

upon my compensation, which would not be much, as the office would not afford it. In the mean time, the duties of the office fall upon Uncle [Oliver] Champlain, who is Surveyor, the next highest officer to the Collector at this port, being assisted by me, he knowing but very little of the duties of this office, there being a provission in the law that, in case of the death or disability of a Collector, the duty devolves upon a Naval Officer where there is one; & if none, upon the Surveyor. So that we are in a state of suspense as yet–and where I have been all the winter, for they were forever appointing a Collector, and when appointed he will not come.

There is the deepest regret felt for Capt. Law here on acc't of the loss of his office, he being so much loved by every-one who had any business to transact at the office or who indeed was ever acquainted with him; and as there is always some good to be extracted from evil, according to the old adage, that good worked marvelously to the advantage of Mr. Way, in procuring him many signatures which he would not otherwise have obtained (for you must know he has a great many acquaintances who feel ill-disposed towards him from different causes, but principally arising from envy, he moving in a higher circle than he was wont in his younger days; and they not being able, or not feeling disposed, to keep pace with him, feel heartburnings, which I believe is natural to the human race, & shoot envenomed darts whenever opportunity presents). But in this affair the fear of that man's gaining his point, as he had succeeded in removing Capt. Law, caused them to give their names–when, under other circumstances, they would never have done it.

And for myself, I have supported him willingly as well as I was able through this strife & shall continue to do so while it is necessary, though I sometimes look back to former years without exactly being able to find an adequate cause for so doing.

Now I have given you all the particulars relative to our situation politically, I must also tell how we are bodily. In the first place, Aunt Mary is tolerably well. She had a slight cold but is geting better. She is always wanting you'd to write; her friends call to see her occasionally, and enquire after you. Mr. & Mrs. Way are very well & Mary Prescott. They have [all gone] to a large party at Mrs. Winthrop's to-night, where your humble servant had no invitation, which I do not mind as much as if I was a fashionable–for in that case I presume I should have felt it keenly. But my having no invitation has been the means of my writing you this letter, for which you may thank Mrs. Winthrop, if worth the trouble. Uncle Thos. & Aunt Dolly & family are very well. She always enquires after you as if it gave her pleasure to hear from you. I have had always a kind feeling towards her for her kind attention to Mother in her last sickness, and also as she was the one that walked as chief mourner to the funeral with me, Aunt Mary not being able to go. There are many who ought never to be forgotten by us: Mrs. Harris, Mrs. Lee, Mrs. Culver, the Miss Crannells, Mrs. Way and some others who attended as watchers occasionally. It is a family misfortune, I know, but nevertheless true, that I scarcely ever go to see these people, particularly Mrs. Culver. I think, tho', sometimes it arrises from idleness and lazy habits more than anything else, for I do esteem them all highly–as well as Mr. & Mrs. Fitch for their [kindne]ss to you. She (Mrs. M[= F].) sent a book to Aunt Mary for me to read which I have had a great while and which, if you see her soon, say I shall return the first opportunity, for I have had it ever since last Sept. when I was in New York and, owing to one of the worst habits that ever cursed mankind (procrastination), have not yet returned. . . .

In consequence of the changes in office that he described, William has more work and more news than usual, as he tells his sister (**no. 287** of March 30th):

Dear Eliza,

I have now leisure to drop you a line. For the last three weeks past I have been as busey as the devil in a gale of wind, the office having been removed from Capt. Law's house to the brick building nearly oposite where Doct. Sam Lee once lived—kept since by A. Shepard as a public house. Mr. Crawford was very glad to find that I would stay with him and gave me rather more than I received of Capt. Law as a salary, and am to retain the same office that I held under him of Inspector Gauger Weigher & Measurer; but from Mr. Crawford's ignorance of the duties of the office, my time is entirely taken up with the whole business of the office, so that if fifty vessels were to arrive in a day I could do nothing towards securing the pay arising from my offices of Inspector &c, so that I [am] actually about as well off as when with Capt. Law. Mr. Crawford left here more than a fortnigh[t] ago to visit his family after appointing me his deputy, where he will remain until about the 8t of April and then return alone, as he will not bring his family down this spring.

I have been very much crowded since my appointment under him as it all devolvs upon me, he being totally out of the question, and there are many things with which I am unacquainted, as Capt. Law used to attend to the laws respecting the Revenue and I had the writing and making of abstracts to do. Now, however, I am obliged to read, learn and inwardly digest, which is done in fear and trembling for fear of some error in my duty.

With this letter I shall send a book called *The Critic* loan'd by Mrs. Fitch for Aunt Mary to hear read last summer and which I find is rather the worse for wear.[17] I wish you would appologize for my keeping it so long and also for its appearance, for it is not in as good order as when I borrowed it. However, I believe it is not materially worse, it being only soiled. Use your smoothing plane and tell her I will not forget those shells (when the ships return) I promised. Also let me know [how] she is and Mr. Fitch, Cornelia, and Mrs. Northam. I always enquire of you how they are but never get an answer.

Mr. Way is still in hot water. They are makeing all exertions they can to remove him, but whether they will succeed is doubtfull. Time alone can determine it. Since my last, the Post-Master General has written him making enquiries relative to two affidavits made by persons in this town charging him with neglect and malpractices in his duties as postmaster. He has answered it within a few days & since that I have heard nothing. In fact it is not time yet. . . .

> The whaling business is increasing in this place very much. Our ships have been very successfull this year–all that have arrived–and we hope to hear as good news from those that are to come. . . .

In April Edward brought William up to date on the New York family's health, a young nephew's death, a recent scare over Ted, his mother's extravagant panic at that, and plans to move a good stretch up Manhattan Island to 264 Bowery Road (the continuation of Chatham Street). In mid-month, William replies, though to Eliza.

Whaling occupies him, most obviously in the vignette he gives of the sad, jolly, drunken moment when a ship's crew must sunder themselves from all their land-lives for a year or two or three. Others of his letters of this period likewise reflect a larger picture of developments in the port and its economy. Whaling had been a minor business for New London involving only two or three vessels in the early century, and was rendered inactive for a time by the Embargo and the War of 1812; but it had taken on a new life thereafter. It had helped to support the establishing of a third bank (1827) and gave a name to still a fourth (The Whaling Bank in 1832). While at first, before 1820, it had sent out only a little handful of ships, thereafter as many as eleven whalers cleared out of New London in one year (1829), fifteen the next, and a slowly increasing number of them up to thirty-plus by mid-century. Meanwhile other tonnage remained distressingly low. What William saw and describes, then, on a sunny spring afternoon before his office window, was the remaking of the city's economy (**no. 289**):[18]

> I am now siting in the new [Customs] office looking out upon the [Thames] river (of which I have a fine view), except while I am not writing, for I wish to state the truth, therefore I am thus particular, and behold there is the ship *Flora* bound on a whaleing voyage, lying at anchor and will sail probably to-night or in the morning. She has a crew of 34 men, who are all dancing at this time like devils. They have had a present from the owner of the ship to induce them to go on board and they have bought 'Old Jemecka' [rum] sufficient to make them the merriest group that ever kick'd a fore-and-after. Their heads are bobing up like puppets from this distance, and occasionally I twig their feet where their heads shoud be, from their 'mad bounds' and deer-like leaps to shew off the beauties of a 'real stag dance.' Yesterday they were all over the rigging of the ship in their red shirts, cheering, and scrambling over every part of the spars. The minstrel (a drunken Indian) is seated upon the heel of the bowsprit with his head lapp'd down upon 'his old lady,' eyes shut, apparantly in an extacy at the melting strains which is occasionally intarrupted by a spasmodic jerk towards an upright position of the body and head, the right foot brought down with a thunder-thump upon deck, accompanied at the same time with a convulsive groan, it being a short-hand manner of 'counting time' in the music. They have also suspended from the mizen top-sail yard-arm the effigy of someone whom they honor and have the fearlessness to make it manifest. Well, I wish them all the happiness this life affords: a successful voyage and a speedy return to kiss their 'Molly.'

Now to buisness. I received Riley's letter a day or two since, saying there was 'an emigration of the Indian tribes' 'into different lands.' I highly approve of the movement as it is to prevent the expense of a journey during summer from the city for fresh air, which I believe must be a considerable drawback to his income and which I hope you will find is remedyed in this move. I find that the most economical method of living is much for the interest of our mental and physical capacities, seting aside the accumulation of 'filthy lucre' which is the great omnipotent of the better portion of this world.

Secondly–I mean thirdly: Miss Lucretia Brainard is dead. A sister of John the poet, she died of consumption which is hereditary in the family. I also wish to mention the death of Aunt Starr [=Elizabeth Taber Starr] wife of Jonathan, aged 83. Her death had been long looked for, she having been sick some time. I had not seen her since some time last summer, when I went down with Aunt Mary and she was then very feeble, but so she could creep about. I went to her funeral but did not walk as a mourner, because I was not asked to go into the room where they were, and my pride (of which unfortunately I find some 'small bits' hanging about me) sternly forbade me. I always loved the old mother for her goodness of heart and for her kindness (as far as she could act) towards our mother. In fact, any of that Taber family from which we sprang I always liked, and Aunt Allen I really love. Old Mr. John Way whom you must know–he lives nearly opposite Jonathan Starr's house–went to the funeral and as it rained we walked rather quick, which was unusual for him, he being very moderate in his movements generally (there comes three cheers from the *Flora* again) but feeling ambitious to continue (I am interrupted: Maj. Williams just called to clear the ship *Neptune* for a whaling voyage–she now laying in the stream, and as I am alone shall be obliged to quit here and fall too upon that, there being considerable waiting and I alone to do it. Well, I have finished for him). He–old Mr. Way–continued to walk in the procession up to the ground where the service was rather short on account of the rain, and immediately after the old fellow started, with his daughter Mary Way [= not the Mary of this correspondence], the short-cut across the burying ground for his house where he was going. I was walking with his grandson Courtland Starr, and we soon overtook him and Miss Way, and I offered him my umbrella but he told us to walk a-head and he would come along after with his daughter Mary, so we did, and I came immediately down to the office to write, where I had not been more than ten minutes before Uncle Oliver came in and asked me if I had been to the funeral. I told [him] yes. Well, he says you will have another to attend, for old Mr. Way in coming home, when he had got down opposite the rope-walk (nearly home), fell down dead and was taken a corpse to his house.

You may well suppose I was startled at the suddenness of it for I had left him so few minutes before perfectly well and full of chat. It was probably owing to the rapidity with which he walked to the burying ground and back to get out of the rain and keep up with the rest that caused his death. He was *93* years old, and one of the most respectable old men this town ever produced. He was very fond of Aunt Starr, having been in the habit of going to see her every evening for the last fifty or sixty years. It was probably his attachment to her that caused him to insist upon going to her funeral which he, his daughter told me, appeared to be more determined to to do than anything she ever knew him to set about, although every-one try'd to disuade him from it. He was the oldest man in this town and and never in his life experienced one day's sickness, which is stated in this week's paper. So Elizabeth Griffing who married Marcus Starr, grandson of old Capt. Way, will hear of the death of both grandparents in the same letter. She is at Savanah.

Fourthly, I was last night up at Mr. [Bethel] Judd's to make a wedding call upon Lieut. Fetterman of the army stationed at this port, and Miss Anna Maria Chandler Judd, daughter of Bethie [=Bethel Judd]–they were married at seven o'clock and received calls the same evening at eight. Mr. and Mrs. Way were invited to the wedding, also Mrs. Fanny Smith, all the officers stationed at this port likewise. The groomsman was a classmate of Fetterman's at West Point stationed at Portland, Maine, whom he sent for on the occasion. His name is Napoleon Bonaparte Beauford, Lieut. in Artillery. The bridesmaids ware Miss Maria Lee and Margaret Judd, sister of Ann Maria. The other groomsman was Lieut. White stationed at this port, said to be the smallest man in the army, being not so large as I am, so you may judge. The bride was dressed in white satten with a bunch of white flowers in her hair, looking better than ever I saw her before, but as pale as death, for she was all but frightned there. She was published and married by her father. There was a great many called to see her while I was there, which was not long. Miss Charles Denis of whom I spoke in my last letter to you, and who boards with Mr. [Ebenezer] Way, went over with her husband and Mary Prescott and was introduced. Miss Denis has but a short time returned from Paris where she has been some time with her husband. She is a fine looking woman. The officers at the wedding were most of them dressed in uniform. Fetterman was. All the old and young galls in the villiage were there: the Northrops, Parkins, Stewarts, Thompsons, Trotts, Brubecks &c were there in great abundance.

Lastly, it is night and I want you to write soon. . . .

There have been no further attempts to remove Mr. Way lately and I begin to think he will remain. . . .

In May he writes again to his sister (**no. 290**):

For your long silance I cannot account unless it is to try to catch Ted in another fit. As Riley wrote me, it was rather accidental that you found him in it. You undoubtedly now watch night and day for fear of a similar occurrance, and I may as well give up hoping to hear from you again until he has had enough to make you familiar with them.

George I had a letter from, about a week since. He was then in Portland, Maine. It was dated the 2nd inst. He states that he has been attached to theatres in Massachusetts & Maine for the last two years in the capacity of treasurer. He is anxious to quit the business and procure a situation in a Revenue or Post Office, and asks me if there is no chance here; for his trade, he will never work at again, he says. But there is no chance here, I can assure him; and if he wishes to obtain a situation in an office, he must quit New England. There is too much competition to obtain one whenever we fancy it would suit, in these parts. He enquires after you and Sam.

Aunt Mary is very well except a cold. She had a letter from Mrs. Fitch a few days since who complains of a pain in her side and cough-symptoms. I should fear of consumption. I hope she may not die, for I love her about as well if not better than any of my relations living, and simply for her kindness to you and Sam, for which you both ought to be more attentive than you are to her.

Whether I shall ever be fortunate enough to obtain those shells I promised to send her is uncertain, as the ship I expect them by will not return under two & a half or three years. Should I however get any, I will not forget her. Whenever you see her, remember me to her and her family.

Sally Fulton that married Halsey Goddard died last week and was buried. Her complaint was dropsy. Halsey is in France now or on his way home. It will be a severe blow to him, poor fellow, as he left her well. . . .

Since Ann Maria Judd's marriage, there has been quite a number of parties given in honor thereof. The first was at Doctor Lee's, which I did not attend; the second was at the Fort, Mrs. Thruston's, which was quite a brilliant one, there being about forty ladies and gentlemen. The third and handsomest was here at Allen's, given by Mrs. Garner, wife of Lieut. Garner, who boards here. It was in the hall, which was decorated with evergreens, roses, lilacs, flags, &c&c, too numerous to mention. There were about sixty present and the refreshments were very delicious, besides plenty of dancing, which is something I have become attached to of late.

There is a most wonderful stir among the Presbyterians at this time here–nothing but meetings, mornings, afternoons and evenings. The bell is going continually. There is an effort made for a revival here, but whether they will succeed I think is doubtfull. It would seem this drilling was in consequence of the sentiments of Miss Fanny Wright[19] becoming more popular than is consistant with the temporal welfare of the clergy and others who 'fight to the death' against inovations coming from her, owing undoubtedly to their belief of the bad tendency they would have upon the community–although it may not be denied, there is much in her sentiments which, if seperated from the more repugnant part of her doctrine, would seccure a hearing.

I am at present as busily employed as ever I have been in my life. Mr. Crawford is away most of his time, which leaves all the business with me; and for one to do, it's too much. If I was Collector I should have certainly one if not two assistants, and if he does not take hold and give me a lift, I shall ask more salary–which, if not allowed, I shall quit. . . .

Brother George now floats back into the picture, hurt by William's failure to answer his letter of about May 2–and now the end of the month has come. Just as William says in the preceding letter, George is in Portland, about to head for Boston. He is "heartily tired of being a 'citizen of the world' " and needs help finding other employment. And then once more he writes to William, still neglected, still in Portland (**no. 292** of June 7th):

> This is the *third* letter that I have addressed to you, directed to the care of 'Eben'r Way Esq.,' without receiving one line in exchange, consequently leaving me ignorant respecting their fate, if coming to hand or not. Now, you must be aware that suspense of all other sensations to which poor human nature is liable is most irksome and galling. If you are not in N[ew] London (and I begin to think you are not), I would have supposed that Uncle Ebb. might have forwarded my letters to the place you were in, as they were addressed to his care; and upon the receipt of either of them you would have condescended to acknowledge it. But as I have heard nothing from you pro or con I hardly know what to think.
>
> I am anxious to see you before the summer closes, as I think I shall proceed to the South for good and aye in case I should not succeed in N[ew] London to obtain a situation of some kind that will enable me to live barely. For, as I before have stated, I am heartily tired of roaming the world and am anxious to find a home before I die, however brief the period allotted me to remain there may be. I pray you to answer me (if only a 1/2 doz. lines) upon receipt of this, and give a summary of domestic news, viz. Eliza, Sam'l, yourself & E. C. Riley, Uncle O. & C.
>
> Yours ever, *Geo. O. Champlain*

Then, rather a bombshell from the Ebenezer Ways (**no. 293** of June 21st). It is Aunt Sally who is given or who takes the responsibility of dispatching it. The explosive part of it is preceded and followed by little conventional greetings:

> Dear Eliza,
>
> It is a long time since we have heard from you. Why are you so silent? We heard you had moved to the Bowery which I think you must find more pleasant. We are all in usual health. I am a little lame in consequence of a fall I had from a chair which upset in attempting to stand in it, and the sharp edge of it struck my shin, if a lady may be allowed to have one.
>
> And now, my dear Eliza, I have a request to make, and that is, that you will take your Aunt Mary. We have boarders, I expect to have more, and to continue to have them. We want the room she occupies very much, and she is necessarily very much secluded, which probably would not be the case with you. When Mrs. Lee came to solicit us to take her, she said you engaged to take her as soon as you were married. Our family is large and we feel as if we had done our part, and we now think that it is quite time for some one else to take her. We have an aged mother to provide for and we are obliged to hire a nurse for her, the most of the time–which is a great expense for us with our little income.
>
> And how long your uncle will hold his office is uncertain, these hard times. We have always had a great change ever since we have been housekeeping, which you well know. This is an unpleasant thing to me to perform, but it is necessary.

We should all of us be very glad to see you & your good husband and the little boys. The eldest–we have heard much of his beauty from my sister & his Uncle William, who is very much occupied, having a Collector that knows nothing of his duty.

Mr. Way and Mary join me in love to you & your husband.

Yours affectionately,

S. S. Way

Receiving this, Eliza answers in two directions, on the same day of late June. First, to William (**no. 294**) on the subject of the bombshell, then at a later point her thanks for a present from him. She has before her his package of March 30th, **no. 287**, in which he had "sent Ted & Geo. a fiddling devil"–some sort of toy:

My dear William,

Supposing and hopeing that Aunt Mary is ignorant how delicately she has been handled in a certain quarter, if time lasts I shall write to her by this conveyance without aluding to my having written in any other direction. R. is thunderstruck. I was equally so till I thought; and then I wonder'd I could be surprized at any-thing of this nature that might turn up in that quarter.

A fear of accident prevented my enclosing you a copy of the letter we both have answer'd, which letters we send to you unseal'd to read, comment on, and then seal and deliver with all the ignorance and innocence usually exhibited in an underhand piece of work. As R. says, I repeat, use your own discretion about reading those letters to the unhappy object of them. If 'tis not done with perfect safty, don't think of it, I entreat you, as an increase to her misery I do not desire.

Food to the hungry nor drink to the thirsty was never more grateful than the feeling I experienced on writing a few broad truths in the letter I send for your perusal. If almost five years of kind treatment had not in a great degree crucified the devil that lurked in my veins at the time of my marriage, I should have sent forth what they would have found sharper than a two-edged sword. But thanks to God the fates have given me a respite. I can now think and act reasonably on almost all occasions.

The first unanswer'd letter of yours that at present strikes my recollection is the one you write on not being invited to a party of Mrs. Winthrop's, when the rest of our good friends met this great and glorious distinction. I could not avoid smiling at the idea that so triffling a circumstance could have depressed your spirits for an instant. If I had not early learn'd to cast off such wet blankets as these were once to me, I should have had a sorry sojourn on this earth, for during my residence in New London you know the cause of those slights from reptiles of this description, and during my residence in New York when-ever I have met vermin like those I have received the same treatment, for lack of money. In New London I gave them my hatred, but getting wiser in New York I gave them my most heartfelt pity, and still do the same. So take a lesson from me and rest assured all such people want is to witness that they have distress'd you.

I have this instant been interrupted by the arrival of Mrs. Fitches basket: shells–& my cocoanut shell which by the by is worth them all. It is really beautiful and so handsome a present that I wonder you would part with it. I am much obliged, I can assure you, but much more for those things to her, as I told you in a former letter I valued attentions to her more than to myself. Accept my thanks also for that beautiful dancing devil to Edward and George–which by the by instead of its entering their clutches entered my roast meat drawer with my butterfly needle case and sundry and divers choice trinkumbobs recieved at different times from R. When we are rich we won't forget you, but our tickets never even pay their way.

Any notice of your balls & parties shall be in some future number when I feel more in trim for high flyers. At present the order of the day is il pensiero, for my nerves have recently been shaken to their very foundations and 'twill be long indeed ere they recover their tone.

You spoke so discouraging in a former letter of your prospects in business, that I began to fear you too was about to taste of the cup of misery of which we *three* have all partaken during our sojourn in this city of Gotham; but I sincerely congratulate you that the storm passes over–rolls on–and is no more seen. . . .

According to R.'s belief, as soon as we enter the other world the reasons for all that happens us here are made clear to us as the sun at noon-day; and perhaps you will call me a turn-coat for what I have said, but be assured I do not thoroughly believe in any doctrine, not even my own. I care for no religion. Conscience in my opinion is all that we need attend to. Keep that clear and all will go smooth. And I am happy to add that before God I stand not accused for any event of my life. My intention as far as I know my self has ever been pure. . . .

Mrs. Fitch has been the only being in existence who has seen me through all my rubbish. The others have all seen the rubbish and not me, and for this I feel more grateful to her than for anything else she ever did for me, and for this I think more of her than of any of the rest of them–as I told her the last time she call'd to see me.

R. met Sam at a garden in Broadway yesterday where he is in the habit of lounging after business hours. They entered into conversation, and the poor hipped and bilious fellow, after saying much in the same strain, observed, all that puzzled him was to find out what he lived for. If he could only know this he should be easy. I have my doubts if he finds out soon. From all accounts (for I have not seen him for nearly two years) he has all of Father's gloom deepen'd with a bilious temperament. If I should hear of his cutting his throat soon, I should not be much surprized. In any letters you may send him don't hint at what I have said. . . .

Eliza's direct reaction to the bombshell she expressed to Aunt Sally herself (**no. 295**):[20]

My dear Mrs. Way,

My memory needed not the quickening of your letter to remind me of the most wretched existence of my aunt. She is seldom out of my thoughts, strange as this may sound to you. But as thinking is all that is permitted me to do, I have discontinued writing altogether.

As R. chose to reply to your letter, and that, without loss of time, it has left me but little to say. In justice to myself, however, I shall say that I married him unconditionally, as I esteem a conditional marriage no better than prostitution. He knows the anxiety I have ever felt to have her with me on every account, and I know that every wish I could form would be gratified if 'twas in his power to do so. Mrs. Lee was a good friend to my mother during her life, and at her death she also befriended me when I stood alone in this selfish world; and for the favors she rendered me I shall ever be grateful; but the wording of her speech was slightly wrested from the wording of mine: I said to her as soon as I had a home to offer Aunt Mary, I should not be slow to do so. This I repeat; for a thought of any inconvenience she might be to me I should despise myself for entertaining. Knowing my inability to do as I wished, and knowing my aunt was in a home that of right belonged to her (for this is R.'s opinion–'tis mine and 'tis the world's), I have endeavored since I could not control circumstances to submit patiently to whatever takes place, as any-one who knows what is best for themselves always do, since 'tis no use kicking against the pricks. If 'tis ever in my power to have her with me, without looking to the right or the wrong of it, I shall most unquestionably do so.

I am certain if Aunt Hannah could have foreseen my mother's speedy disolution and have dreamt that the miserable pittance my aunt now recieves would not have been accorded her family–old and childish as you may have thought her–her strong sense of justice would have made her dispose of her property far differently. It would have triumphed over the infirmities of age and made her give conditionally what, in the goodness and simplicity of her heart, she gave as she did; for in the letter of her bequest Aunt Mary was not forgotten. How often have I heard her say, this property of mine I shall divide between Mary, Betsy, & Eliza–of course not dreaming of her last necessities. Her good intentions with regard to Mother, my mother most disinterestedly put down by urging her to the step she was obliged to take. Aunt Mary unhappily has been obliged to call for her due, and, although I have seen the day that I have wanted a home, I sincerely thank God it is not now; nor since I left Aunt Hannah, last, have I ever felt any claim on her estate. These (perhaps you may think them indelicate disclosures) truths and these sentiments have been dragged from me by your letter, or I never should have given them utterance to any living being. I do not wish to anger you now, but your plain dealing demands mine, and you have it–as in the end plain dealing is always best.

And now, since R. would not condescend to any explanations, I will. Our circumstances have not as yet, in a large city, warranted any expense that we could avoid incuring, or I should have remembered Aunt Mary before this. The person who supports me and mine, is not to be (and will not be) dictated too by a wife who brought him nothing, but, on the contrary, has always clogged him heavily with unavoidable expenses since her marriage. My eyesight will never again admit of miniature painting, or I should have resumed it, for fine sewing threatens me too much; and for portrait painting I must go to the school. This is equally out of the question, as you may think. On this account I have uniformly avoided returning calls of all descriptions and I have received many from persons whose society would have been a pleasure and an honor to me. For this reason I have not invited Mary Prescott to make us a visit, as I could not ask company to see her; and it would be amazingly dull, as we live at present.

I should not trouble you thus with my concerns but from a desire to do away any wrong impressions that my silence and my conduct might possibly make on you.

And now, hoping that your ankle is much better, I remain yours truly,

Eliza

Mary Way, at the center of this controversy but kept in ignorance of how little she was wanted in the Way house, now takes William's pen in hand, so to speak, for one of her late, long letters. She is discharging her debt for three of her niece's, and in exchange can offer only a quantity of random sermonizing wrapped around the very little of event that marked her life (**no. 297** of September 9th):

. . . I peep into the the book of nature, find each page replete with interest, trace effects back to their cause, and mark their opperations on the mind. Even the most trivial events and incidents, the situation in which we are placed, and every object around us–all conspire, unite their force and influence to shape our destinies & make us what we are.

I should not be surprized if you were to become a New-Church woman. That Mrs. Clinch should prefer it to any other church, her own excepted, is saying much in its favor and proves moreover Mr. Fitch was quite correct in his opinion of her understanding. I should say it required a head no less than hers to comprehend a subject so mysterious, full of ambiguity, intricate and deep–far too deep for me to fathom. Their tenets and principals I try'd in vain to understand. The works I read appeared calculated more to puzzle than to convince; but I bow to her superior judgement, and hope when you join the Church and are initiated into all its mysteries, you will be able to explain them more fully to my satisfaction.

You say you could preach to grey hairs if they would only listen to you. Preach to me. I will hear & thank you too: 'five years of sober thought have not been lost.' I am glad you have returned to reason, your sermon I approve. Think not, however, the truths it contains belong exclusively to your New Church. They are not new to me. We may doubt the testimony of Scripture, but what we see and feel, we must believe; and that is quite enought to prove its truth. Long have I known our suffering here is at once a consequence and punishment of sin–sufferings suited to the case & for the benefit of each patient, to correct our errors, & convince us that virtue only is the way to peace. . . .

Three weeks since the above was written, Mary Prescott who is now in Portsmouth wished me to give her love to you and say she would have wrote for me, and for herself, had not her time and thoughts been wholly occupied in preparing for her journey. Of course, the task devolves on William. I hope his patience will endure the trial, for he is everything to me. But not another word, lest modesty should take offence and leave it out.

You ask for news. What I can tell, you probably have heard before. In that case, you know, my letter is good for nothing. You heard Mrs. Fitch had wrote to me &, concluding she had told me all the news, destroyed your letter. This was a pretty caper. Suppose she had–from your pen it would not have been the less acceptable. You are not more different from Mrs. Fitch in looks and manners than you are in sentiments and style of writing. I like variety in every form. The same thing placed in different points of sun has all the charm of novelty. One more error of yours I wish to mention (as I feel disposed to quarrel). You think me too particular, and say I consider a poor letter as I do poor company–worse than none. I never thought your letters poor. If that was your opinion, you could not have chosen a more effectual way to punish me than by your silence. Famine is a sure remedy for the over-nicety of an epicure: in such a case, give him plain wholesome food. He will no longer think a first-rate cook indispensable, or that it must be served on plate or china.

A truce with your digressions! Strait-forward business brings us to the point at once. Now for news–deaths, marriages, &c. I will begin with death, the end of sin and sorrow. In the course of a few months, three of our near relations have departed: Aunt Parsons, Aunt [Elizabeth Taber] Starr, and Uncle [Pardon Tillinghast] Taber. For two years past his health has been impaired. The family have known much tribulation since they left this place & still more since their return to N[ew] York. Francis has lost her husband and her property & is now teaching an accademy to support herself & child (mark the ups & downs of life!). Jane, who assisted her in the business, is lately married and gone to the South. Elizabeth teaches music & Charlotte alone remains with her mother. Poor Amy, naturally aspiring, could not be satisfied with mediocrity. Ambition led her on in quest for fortune, & paid her off in the old coin, mortification and disappointment. Aunt [Frances Taber] Seabury read to me a most affecting letter giving an account of her husband's last sickness & her own declining health, with all their sufferings and afflictions–the picture of a broken heart. But where was Amy! You never would have dreamed it came from her. She has joined a church and become truly pious. Ah! how unlike the gay volatile being that once we knew! But there must be something to wean us from the world and teach us where to look for happiness which here we seek in vain.

Our friends go home and like a dream they fade from our remembrance. Capt.s Lee, Cahoone, and many others I have forgot to mention. But enough! You have often told me I was fond of gloom, delight to dwell on death and all its horrors. I see no horrors there. I love to dwell on that state where happiness unmixed is permanent, where they neither marry nor are given in marriage, but are as the angels in heaven. You are for present felicity, transient as it is–so I will mention a few marriages that have taken place, and leave you to decide how large a share they may expect of this same article: Nancy Christopher's, to Mr. Jones of Boston.

This gentleman was an acquaintance of Doct. Thompson's & having just lost his wife was in distress for another. In this dilemma he applied to the Doctor requesting him to recommend some lady calculated to supply his loss and restore his peace. Nancy was mentioned as suitable for the occasion. He 'came, saw, and conquered,' and in less than three weeks had carried her off in triumph. An affair so sudden and unexpected made no small stir among the people. The girls began to look about them, not knowing whose turn would come next, for the doctor promised, in case of future applications, they should not be forgotten. Thus expectations, raised on tip-toe, furnished conversation in abundance until the public attention was called to another quarter by an event still more surprizing–no less than Major Williams, to Miss Nancy Allen. There was, wonder upon wonder, a man for whom any of the girls would have jumped over the moon–Miss Allen too. Neither youth, beauty, nor riches; but she has that which, in the eye of fartherly affection, outweighs them all: sterling merit. She will make an excellent mother to his children & train them up in the way they should go, & he has gained much credit by his choice. . . .

The Lees are all alive and well, still friendly and and affectionate, make many enquiries after you and your family. They are engaged in the cotton manufacturing business & doing very well. [Their elder son] Henry has two sons about the age of your children. Eliza enjoys her estate of single blessedness. Sam is still a bacheldor. Maria is content with hers and in no haste to change it.

This place has much improved within a few years. House-building and repairing, strangers moving in–altogether producing a sort of bustle & noise that appears like life & animation. Even the old mansion house is enlarged & undergoing all the miseries of alterations & improvements. In these affairs I take no interest or pleasure, & gladly leave such subjects for those far more congenial to my taste and feelings. . . .

When you write to Mrs. Sanford (alias Miss Stammers) present my love & compliments of congratulations. I am glad to hear she is well married. I say *well*–what change may have taken place in the course of time, I cannot tell. But I once thought William Sanford bid fair to make a decent husband. Mary Prescott has received only one letter from her & would have answered it had not her aunt failed, who cannot tolerate any thing short of perfection.

Give my love to Samuel, should a chance offer for the purpose. He is still remembered, tho' I suppose he has forgot there is such a being in existance. Poor George, too. I often think of him & feel for his condition. Tho' he may have wandered from the right way, the path of rectitude, he cannot stray so far but love, eternal love, will find him. There is a friend that sticketh closer than a brother, the friend of sinners, who never will forsake him & finally restore him to himself, to happiness & virtue. Being a firm believer in the restoration of all things, I rejoice on all occasions, fully enjoying the unbounded comfort and consolation it affords. Shall I go on? No, it is time to stop.

Adieu.

I have no time to copy this, but give it just as I took it from the slate.

W. C.

In April of 1832 old Uncle Oliver Champlain died.[21] His will, witnessed by Ingolsby W. Crawford among others and communicated to the legatees by Jirah Isham, had been drafted when Betsey was still alive and, after her death, passes her house to Eliza along with $800 and whatever else might be left (some $2300) when various special bequests had been paid: among them, $200 to George; $100 to Mary Way "in consequence of her being blind"; $100 to Samuel; but not even a mention to William. The family could not account for this oversight, or whatever it was. Edward Riley wrote away for a copy of the document, which survives; and his wife notified Samuel of his legacy, adding in the form of a mere postscript a fact of very considerable importance in her own world: Samuel Fitch, Anna's husband the lawyer, had just died. Her bitterness towards Sam, seen in her most recent mention of him as so often in the past, prevented her addressing him in a natural tone. She must even do a preliminary draft of this present notification.[22]

To Anna Fitch Eliza writes also in carefully considered words, but with true warmth (**no. 300**). Here too, but for no reason of cold constraint, she mentions only by afterthought a major matter on top of a still more grave event:

> I was not a little shocked on learning through the medium of the papers your great bereavement. You will believe I most sincerely sympathize with you on this afflicting dispensation of Providence. As you have felt for me on a similar occasion, even so can I, and do I, feel for you. . . . Strange as it may sound, I was informed in a dream what was about to befall you, but had no idea it would be so speedy. As I know you I know also that this and all other afflictions will be viewed in the right light, and am rejoiced that it is so. The certainty that whatever is hardest upon us, however dreadful it may appear, is from an all-wise, unerring and just God is surely a mighty source of consolation, and one which I know is open to you, tho' not to all. I was once blind to this truth, but now my eyes are open'd. It has taught me to look into myself and there do I find most black and grievous spots which has and will take fierce afflictions to work out.
>
> If, my dear Mrs. Fitch, there is any way in which I can render you service, you of all beings on the face of the earth have a right to command it, and I hope you will not fail to do so. My absence from your house at this time will not surprise you when I tell you I have had a dangerous confinement with the loss of the infant–a fine daughter. Since then, I have been troubled with eruptions which have now settled in my feet and incapacitated me for walking.
>
> We have had no news from my poor brother William and are now beginning to fear the worst. My love to your mother and Cornelia.
>
> Believe me your most affectionate Eliza

At the end, here, Eliza's anxious surmise regarding William can only be explained by a much later passage in the correspondence, "William was lost at sea on a trip to New Orleans in 1832."[23] His work in New London–too much or too little–and his pay, always too little, had driven him from his home. Or one could say, he had slowly matured to the point of adventure. He left and died at some point in April or May. Mary speaks of his death as certain in mid-June (**no. 301**):

My dear Eliza,

I am thankful to hear from you at last. Long have I felt like one who has lost every friend on earth. William, our dear William, returns no more! This solemn truth weighs heavy on my heart, employs my thoughts by day and every night it haunts my dreams. Loved and mourned by all that knew him–but he was every-thing to me, and his loss, tongue cannot tell how much I feel, how deeply I deplore! And yet, knowing the miseries of life, how few and how contemptible are its enjoyments, and what the best and happiest must endure, reason condemns my selfish sorrow and says with the prophet, 'blessed are the dead.' True, he was all and more than all to me, and now I should rejoice that he is blest and past the reach of evil. And so I do rejoice in spirit; but Oh! the flesh is weak.

In your sketch of family traits you say William is like other folks. If this is your opinion, you know not his merits. Were other folks like him, the world would be a paradise. William was no common character. He had the sense of feeling which few posses–free from all that's base and selfish. The highest virtues were his own. For goodness of heart, correct moral principals and conduct, true philanthropy, generosity and benevolence, I have rarely seen his equal. 'A hand open as day to melting charity,' that waited not to be solicited when he thought 'twas needed and would be acceptable, he was liberal even to a fault. Small were his means, but all around him shared the benefit. Many have cause to bless him who had no claims upon his bounty but those of mere humanity. Those we have claims upon can do no less–if they could, they would, is sometimes pretty evident. Where is the mighty merit of twenty thousand favours screwed from the unwilling hand by strong compulsion? In my opinion (from a real friend) one simple generous act of voluntary kindness and affection is worth the whole.

Such was our dear William, whose unremitted kindness merit the warmest gratitude. He seemed to realize my sad condition. Nothing in his power was remited to render it comfortable and pleasant as circumstances would permit. Could any-one be happy in the situation I am placed, he would have made me so. I set my heart too much upon him. He was the last remaining hope and consolation for the loss of all my other friends. Now he is snatched away. But it is right, we are too apt to 'lean on earth'–to place our affections on things below.

Through the whole course of my own life, I ever have remarked what I loved best, and valued most, was always sure the first to be removed. 'Heaven gives us friends to bless the present scene–recalls them to prepare us for the next.' They are not lost–when that bright scene unfolds, we meet again. Welcome the blessed hour! It cannot come too soon. Thus in the firm full exercise of faith, I do and will rejoice in the midst of tribulation. . . .

I never experienced such a winter as the past for sickness and sorrow, nor such a spring and summer as the present. Soon after William left us, I was sick with the influenza, which lasted for months, violent to the last degree, tore my nerves to flitters, and reduced me to the state you see. I have not had a well day or hour since last October, and little reason to expect I ever shall again–yet no prospect of a speedy removal, for I am told (by way of consolation) nervous folks live forever. . . .

This moment Mary [Prescott] has informed me Mr. Fitch is dead! Poor Anna! Support her, Heaven, in this severe affliction. Adieu!

A long gap now occurs in the correspondence extending from mid-year to almost the end. At some point in this interval, George returned to New London and for a while stayed with his aunt. He eventually found no better prospects than William, and so moved on; but before he did so he wrote to his brother-in-law, who replies in mid-December (**no. 304**):

D'r George,

For what in the name of wonder did you send that $5? I told you Eliza would not take the three dollars you wot of and, as for the other, as you don't owe it, I shall send it back to you with an injunction that it quits your pocket no more except for your own benefit.

I do not wonder at your agitation on seeing your aunt. After so long an absence, your mind must have been carried back to the days of other years when you were a boy, your parents living, your aunt in the enjoyment of sight, energy and activity, the town of New London your little world. Perhaps you reply, Would I had never enlarg'd it. So, many a wanderer has said; and all, I believe, might say it with truth; for what can supply equivalents to the broken bonds of the heart so well as being in daily association with those who knew and lov'd in common with ourselves. The little span of our early years in after life seems to have been pass'd on some enchanted island. The moment we depart from it, no matter in what direction we steer our course, our voyage is over a sea of troubles, with but one haven of rest. Should chance bring us, no later than even midway of our pilgrimage, back to the once-lov'd spot, how the change comes over us. Death has snatch'd, some decrepitude seiz'd on others, and many are morally dead–dead to us. And were they living? Where is the innocence, the thoughtless gaiety that was the soul of our enjoyments? Alas, gone! The illusion is dispell'd. How emphatically is the future, the all of your aunt's moral existence. And is it wonderful that her reliance is placed on Holy writ?–since she is taught there that, as soon as the spirit has cast the slough that fetter'd it, it wings it's eager way to those mansions of rest where it enjoys a meridian of youth and happiness. What would that prince of doubters, Hume, have given had he never dispell'd the delirium (as he thought it) of his mother's mind. Her deathbed was render'd horrible, for there was no hope. He was present and never ceas'd from that moment to feel remorse.

Excuse the low tone of my letter, some expressions in yours led me into it. Touching your aunt's lameness and swelled feet, it arises solely from want of out-of-door exercise. Do take her daily to see her friends. 'Twill be an action of true charity and the reward goes with it.

If I make any progress towards the completion of my Harlem project, I shall inform you of it, but till something definite is known, mum's the word on your part, you know.

I am sorry your prospects are so poor in N. L. and if I could say anything promising about the printing concern, I would; but I fear nothing can come of it, as the person engag'd in it has chang'd his course of conduct entirely.

Anna Fitch's widowhood left her with no money, for the moment at least. The fact is surprising, against the background of her previous household and parents' wealth. Notwithstanding all that, she is obliged to think about how she may earn money, and in the near term must apply to Eliza for help. She gets it, pays her thanks, and receives from Eliza the next number in the correspondence, in December (**305**):

> It is astonishing how you can view any little service that it may be in our power to render you, in the light of a favour on your side. A favour it certainly is, but done to us; and be assured we both consider it so. Therefore set your heart at rest, for an obligation from this quarter can never be confer'd on you. If ample remuneration had ever been made to you and yours for the manifold obligations once shower'd on me, I should still feel the debt undischarged; for I am so peculiarly constructed as to look upon such debts utterly unpayable, except in the same manner and to the same extent, and scarcely even then are they cancell'd. So at present, you see, you are pretty safe.
>
> Though I lament the cause, I am notwithstanding glad you have undertaken music, as it must necessarily turn the current of your thoughts in some degree–a thing greatly to be desired at this time.
>
> For your prayer, my dear Mrs. Fitch, accept my warmest thanks; but rest assured that as soon as 'it suits my state' (technically speaking) all the horrors of struggling again without capacity must come upon me. To be sure, this may never be, and God grant it; but we know not what fate has in store. The bitter lesson I had to learn at your house has done me good. The hand of God was in it, though I thought and acted as if the infernal powers alone directed my concerns. But if ever similar trials should again, like a firey furnace, be laid before me to pass through, far different would be my feelings and far different my actions. Just so much we must go through if our sensitiveness is like that of the plant. Depend upon it, this will be the first point assailed, and we shall not be let off till it has had a comfortable drubbing. I suppose you will scarcely credit me when I tell you there was once a time when I could not endure even the shadow of an obligation; but circumstances bent me bravely over this, and it has appeared to me as if I should yet have to thank my fellow beings for the breath I draw, for my eyesight, for the power of thinking, and from the highest to the lowest privilidge I enjoyed (or rather, endured) in life. Under this torture I simply had to writhe, and what did that effect? Nothing. I think with our trust placed firmly where it ought to be, we can be brought soon and safe out of almost any state of wretchedness. Would I had been of this opinion when I was with you. But no, I had then a double and twisted bandage before my eyes. . . .

In September of 1831 (**no. 297**) Mary Way had talked about her long spell of bad health and being "reduced to a mere skeleton"; followed by more sickness and debility throughout the whole of the next winter (**301**), with a bad spell in the summer of 1832; so her weakened condition as she starts another year comes as no surprise. She writes (**no. 307** of January 21st, 1833):

My dear Eliza,

I am very sick and very indolent–too indolent to move or make the least exertion. I wish to know how it fares with you & hear from my dear friend & sister in affliction, now dearer to my heart than ever. The attempt to write requires a mighty effort that nothing less would have produced. I feel extremely anxious for Mrs. Fitch. Oh! may she never know, like me, the most severe of all misfortunes–the worst of human evils: total loss of sight. Gracious Heaven! all other sorrows vanish before it, hide their diminished heads and dwindle into nothing. I hope, however, the Eye Infirmary, so famed for skill, may save her from this dreadful fate, or at least in some degree prevent the consequence that naturally attend it–loss of health, friends, & every earthly pleasure.

To preserve health, exercise & air is indispensable. I should have walked out every day. 'Tis now too late. My health is gone forever. Friends the world bestows leave us (nothing loth) when we no longer serve their purpose or contribute to their amusement. This loss is less to be deplored. Heaven grant that Mrs. Fitch may find a friend indeed, as she has proved to me. I was alone and in distress & Providence sent her to my relief. She has a mother and a daughter. Her kind attention will be repaid by those most dear to her.

Here, by infinite goodness that supplies all my wants, I find in my dear friend Mrs. Lee, who is everything I can desire, mother, sister, daughter, nurse & doctor. However, she tho't expedient to send for Dr. North & found his opinion coincide exactly with her own: mine is a case of general debility for which there is no remedy. So says my candid doctor. Want of sufficient exercise and air sooner or later will destroy the best constitution. I shall be well no more. We might as well restore my sight as health. 'Tis past the power of man. Strengthening medicine may perhaps relieve me for the present, so I may be a little more comfortable–which is the utmost skill can do.

I heard my doom unmoved–approved the honest candor that pronounced it, with all the calm indifference justly due to sublunary things. But as I have no objection to be a little more comfortable, I am taking medicine to strengthen and create an appetite, for I had none before. Now my appetite is very good, and that is all the benefit I perceive. I gain no strength. 'Tis more than three months since I left my room. I probably shall no more, until I leave forever.

So much for affairs in general. I've no time to state particulars: the boat goes at six, George has promised to copy this and take it with him. I hope & pray he will find business. God bless him, prosper him and make him all we wish. Adieu

And she goes on in a somewhat scratched-up, re-done continuation a fortnight later to tell about her parting with "poor George":

> . . . after ten thousand thanks and benedictions, for good wishes and advice, and as many promises, we parted, to meet no more on earth. He may now be on his way to England–told me he should like to visit that quarter of the globe. He had seen enough of America &, if he could obtain no business in New York & found a vesell bound to Europe, he should not miss the opportunity. I am surprised he did not mention his design to Mr. Riley, of whom he thinks & speaks so highly; . . . I need not say I feel for his distress. He suffers much–is greatly to be pitied. God help the poor soul, for He alone can do it. We may safely trust him in the hands of his Creator who has promised he will not cast off forever, neither suffer his faithfulness to fail.
>
> I rejoice to hear Mrs. Fitch is taking lessons in order to teach music. If she does not regard every other loss as trivial, 'tis because she knows not how to prize the blessings she enjoys. What profit would it be to gain the whole world and lose our sight?–when we would give ten thousand worlds that it could be restored, and think the purchase cheap.
>
> Here I must stop and leave the rest unsaid, in compassion to Mary [Prescott], who is much occupied. She has not time to breathe. If you know all, you would not wonder she has not answered your letter & writes for me so seldom. In May she visits her parents–will stay there three months. In her absence I must of course be silent. But let not this deprive me of your letters. From you I wish to hear as soon & often as possible, and when I can I will pay the debt. You would have received this letter long ago & twenty more, but I am blind, alas! What depth of misery, how many sufferings & depressions that little word contains. Adieu!
>
> Will you, my dear Eliza, send Mrs. Lee the picture of her child? She says the drapery that was slightly injured required a few touches of the pencil. Requested I would mention to you when it was convenient. She would be glad to receive it and satisfy you for the trouble. She makes frequent inquiries after your welfare. I depend upon your letters and take interest in nothing else on earth but what I hear from you. Tell me when the *stranger* is expected and all about it! Once more,
>
> Adieu.

With this "adieu," Mary Way is heard from no more (she died in this year).[24] All other links to and from New London were now snapped, too. George was abroad, never heard from again. Nothing more is heard of Aunt Sally, though she and Ebb had much of their lives still to live. It was surprising how great a change had been wrought in the space of only a twelvemonth, 1832–1833.

17

Afterwords

The correspondence later collected by Eliza did not end when her aunt died. That event certainly took the pleasure out of it for a time: "so much did I value her letters," she recalls (**no. 324**), "that, after her death, I thought I should never again put pen to paper." But even to New London there is one more Eliza-letter surviving (**no. 310** of 1835), to a member of the Lee family. This indeed seems to write *finis* to the last of the sisters of the brush: that is, Eliza renounces her career as an artist. She explains the fact by "the cares of a young family, [myself] with very indifferent health. . . . I have become quite a heathen–have abandoned painting entirely."

Yet a decade later, moved now from New York to New Brunswick, she confides to Anna Fitch:[1]

> . . . You know I have resumed the pencil since our residence here–not for profit but to contribute my mite toward the discharge of sundry and divers obligations which circumstances have placed us under, to [brother-in-law] Albert [Riley] and one or two other individuals. As you well know, I have little control over the 'mammon of unrighteousness.' I forthwith took
>
> '. . . . . . such materials as around
> The workman's hand had readiest found'
>
> and out of these I have manufactured three heads, and am now engaged on the fourth. I have much more leisure than when I was in New York, in consequence of finding a sempstress who was disposed to take pay in music. But for this, I could not have painted at all, and even now I feel as if I was stealing sheep; for, although I have encountered the aforesaid sempstress, the duties of my large family are still very numerous, independent of sewing, and by no means as faithfully discharged as when I was exclusively devoted to them.
>
> Oh how dearly I love painting, how cheerfully could I give up almost all other enjoyments for the delightful privilidge of painting what I liked as I liked it! In order

> to accomplish the amount of work which I have this summer, in this line, I found it necessary to dig to the bottom of my *antidiluvians*, which I found in a state of high preservation, although they have been buried so deep, so long, that it reminded me of the exhumation of Bonaparte. The sight of them brought vividly to my recollection the days of 'Auld lang syne,' for tis now eighteen years since I have seen them all. I intend to place them down according to their rank in the different drawrs of my mother's paint desk, and cover each drawr with a pane of crown glass, as light and air are bad for them; and my mother's particularly I value as the apple of my eye. *Christ Rejected* [Pl. 4.12] shows great genius and is by far her best piece. What a pity that her talents were cramped in so small a compass. Yet perhaps, if she could have had a wider field of action, the consequences would have been still more lamentable than they have been. I try to console myself with this reflection, be it right or be it wrong. *My* best piece is *Mary Queen of Scots*, which you doubtless recollect. I find my pencil much more free than when I painted in former days–but of course very faulty.

Later still (**no. 324**) she recalls certain landmarks around the Arsenal where she used to walk with the Haydens and which she had recently revisited (the date is 1855): "two or three beautiful old trees which you doubtless recollect as well as myself. They are very handsome willows (my favorite tree), from which I have often sketched branches to assist me in drawing–that delightful amusement which I am now obliged to abandon for the less interesting though more useful occupation of housekeeping."

It must have given her the greatest pleasure by this date that her daughter enjoyed as brother-in-law one of those extraordinary Peales. The connection thus formed was only indirect: her son-in-law's sister, Lucinda MacMullen, had married Titian Ramsay Peale; but family photographs taken by the artist suggest that the connection was a genuine friendly one.[2]

As to Sam, he appears in letters of the early 1830s at the opera or at the posh restaurant Delmonico's, and again in 1836 on an extended leave of absence for his health.[3] Relief from work was much needed. As he confesses at the time, "The last two years and a half has been a living death." He took off for Oysterpond, spent all his time outdoors, and in a month pronounced himself "nearly well–at all events I am the blackest white man in Long Island" (**no. 312**). He returned then to his bank and lived on until–only 1844.

Anna Fitch lived alone with her daughter in something approaching poverty, teaching school, accumulating small debts, careful of the cost of postage; but she kept up with visits from old acquaintances–Lagnels, Johnsons, Maria Hayden, and naturally Edward and Eliza when they were in town.[4] She lent their young Ted an edifying book *On the Human Constitution*, "from which," he assures his parents, "I have derived a great deal of instruction." He was at the time seventeen, very young, very sweet and dutiful, to judge from his letters. A year later he was dead.[5]

A reader of the letters who has taken them to heart must wish to leave their writers at the end happy, if it were possible. But was it?–when so many not yet past their forties, their thirties, or still younger have disappeared. Was it possible for those who were left? At the very center among them, the mercurial, up-and-down Eliza: so vulnerable to the shocks of life, survivor of so many deaths within her New London family, survivor of a still-born daughter, too, and of her first-born Edward while still no more than a child. Remarking on yet another child gone, a niece to Anna Fitch, she says (**no. 320**), "how far preferable its state now is, to when it was on earth. I have thousands of times lamented that I had not been summon'd hence at that early period, and I believe that all who have ever reached my age can say the same, although I know that some are capable of suffering much more than others, in this motley world of ours." She had of course heard the same thought often expressed by Mary Way, often echoed in letters from Anna and from her mother too. There is no saying whether, here, it was mere cant–simply the way the world talked–or whether it was more deeply felt.

For on the next page she continues most cheerfully,

> You will laugh when I tell you that Mr. Riley is moving Heaven and earth to get up a concert in this dried-up place [New Brunswick]. It was proposed to him last summer to endevour to break up the monotony of this abominable place by music in any shape this winter, and now, thinking that he can make money by it from there being such a plentiful lack of amusement, he has directed all his energies to this point. I am only fearfull that the mountain will but bring forth a mouse–although such a vast amount of talent both foreign and domestic is enlisted in the great cause as would astound your ears for me to enumerate. You must know Mr. R. will be the principal performer himself. Seriously, though–we expect it will go off very well. Albert's wife has a superb voice and it has been carefully drill'd for the last three months with a view to this concert. She sings elegantly now, and has three pieces assigned her which 'tis expected will be very satisfactorily executed. Alice [Fitch Riley, aged eleven] has improved very much since you heard her, and will play two pieces which, as she is such a youthful performer, will of course astonish the natives. A couple of young ladies–pupils of Mr. R.–will sing two or three things which he has prepared for them, Albert will play the violoncello, Mr. Montalvo will sing a song, and Mr. Loyd (a student) will sing another; and several other assistents too numerous to mention. As my forte is scolding, if they cannot get up a scolding scene, I shall be necessarily left out; and as this would be the best part of the whole, I think 'twill be a great pity–what say you? Don't be surprised if this same concert puts New York in a great ferment, for I assure you I expect as much. By the way, I had forgotten Frederick, who will grace the concert by his presence and assistance.
>
> Mr. R. is told he will make 100 dolars, but I very much doubt if he makes [?]60, as tickets must necesseseryly be low. He has three or four singing schools which all yield him a small profit. I think 'tis very doubtful if we return [to New York] in the spring, as our prospects here are much better, I think, than there.

And in 1855, when the correspondence truly ends, she writes to Maria Hayden (**no. 324**) in the same up-and-down terms–"The largest portion of my life, as you know, has been spent in extremely straitened circumstances," with all their ill-effects; yet also, "We had a few musical amateurs assembled at our house last week."

A friend in the New Church later recalled all of the Edward Rileys together: a "warm-hearted family, our near neighbors, [they] represented home and instrumental harmony with their piano, cello, and violin."[6] A happy scene. Yet that friend might have noted what was missing amid the sounds of music: the silent art of Eliza's *Fancy*.

Concerning the Kin-charts

The object in these depictions of New London society is to make plain the degree of endogamy in its upper and upper-middle classes, giving it a quality of cohesiveness, often of oppressive coziness, that appears in the Letters; also, to explain a number of details–how the artists found their sitters (Daniel Truman in A, Abby Mercer, Jared Starr, or his brother-in-law Francis Hazard in B, Nathaniel Perry and Kimball Prince in C), by what line of descent the surviving portraits have come down (in A, for example, to Frances Hannah or to the Dummers, cf. **no. 129**), how the New York music firm of Firth and Hall was formed (in B), or how it happened that Grace MacMullen wrote to John Champlin in 1898 on genealogical matters (in C).

It may appear, too, how extraordinary our documentation on these classes really is. Within a generation–say, by 1665–the early settlers of New London, amounting to no more than a couple of dozen families, had established their dominance. They multiplied, becoming a group of some hundreds of persons. Of this group, over the period 1700–1835, we know the names, dates and relationships of well over half at any given moment. In contrast, over the same period, the corresponding classes of Norwich and Newport, for example, with which New London exchanged its sons and daughters in marriage, are much less well known, while in larger towns like Boston they are too numerous to keep track of in equal detail.

From all the New London evidence I have naturally presented only a tiny selection of what might easily be recovered concerning the Mercers, Holts, Dennises, Rogers, Harrises, Saltonstalls, and a dozen other families. But, in view of the Laocoon-twistings of their marriage ties and descent, all too confusing, readers will thank me for attempting no more. References leading to the evidence will be found after the Notes, in a separate block.

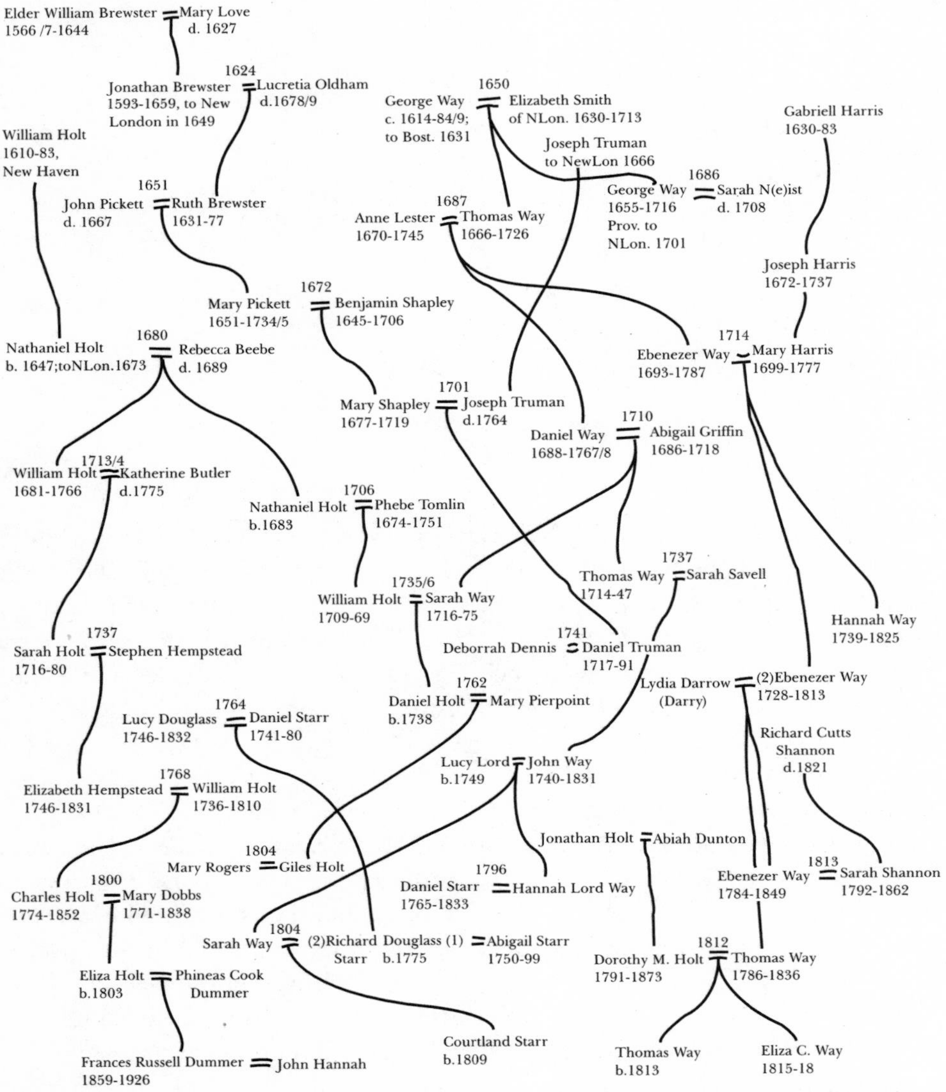

Chart A Tabers, Ways, and Holts

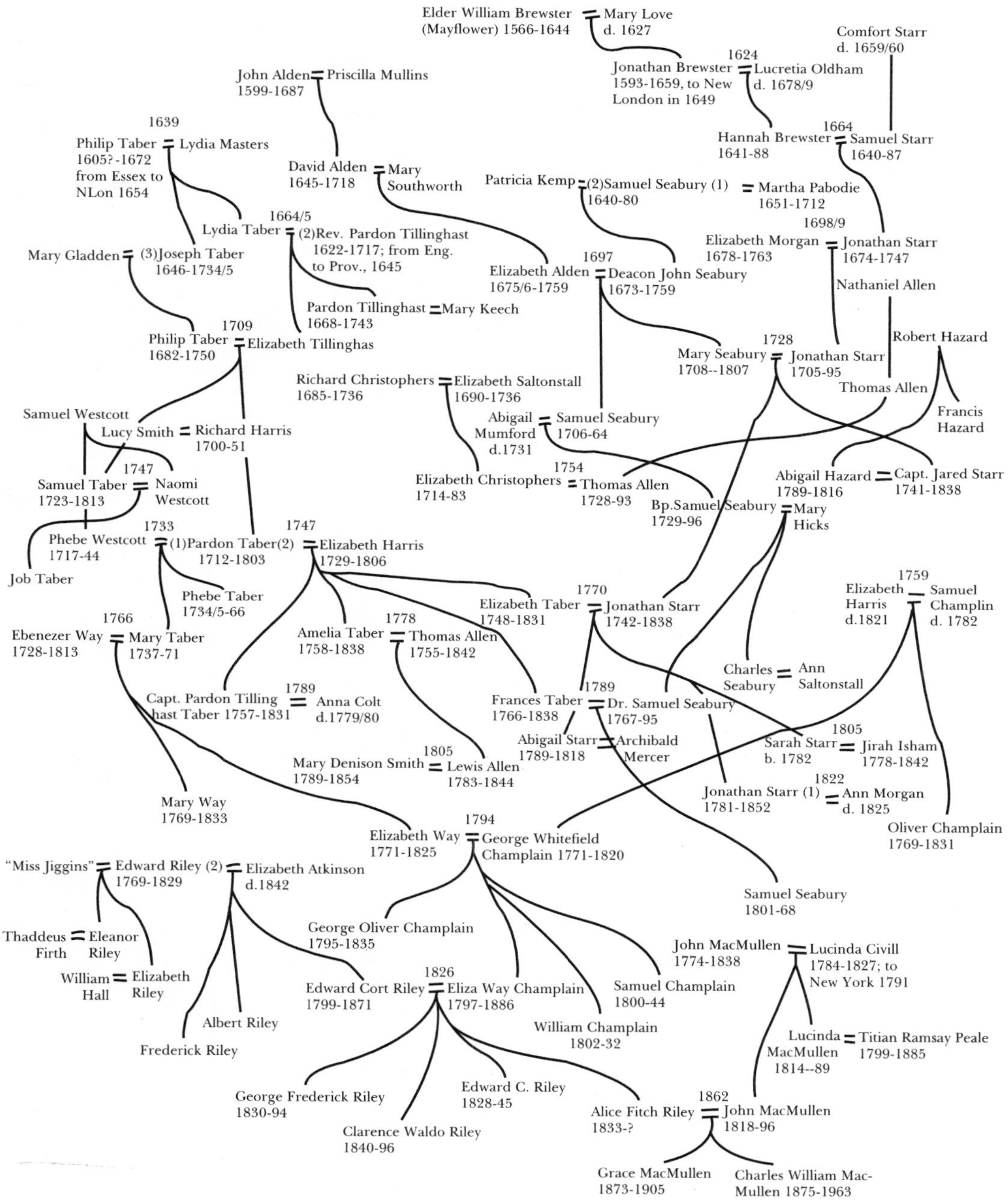

Chart B Tabers, Champlains, Ways, Rileys, Seaburys, and Starrs

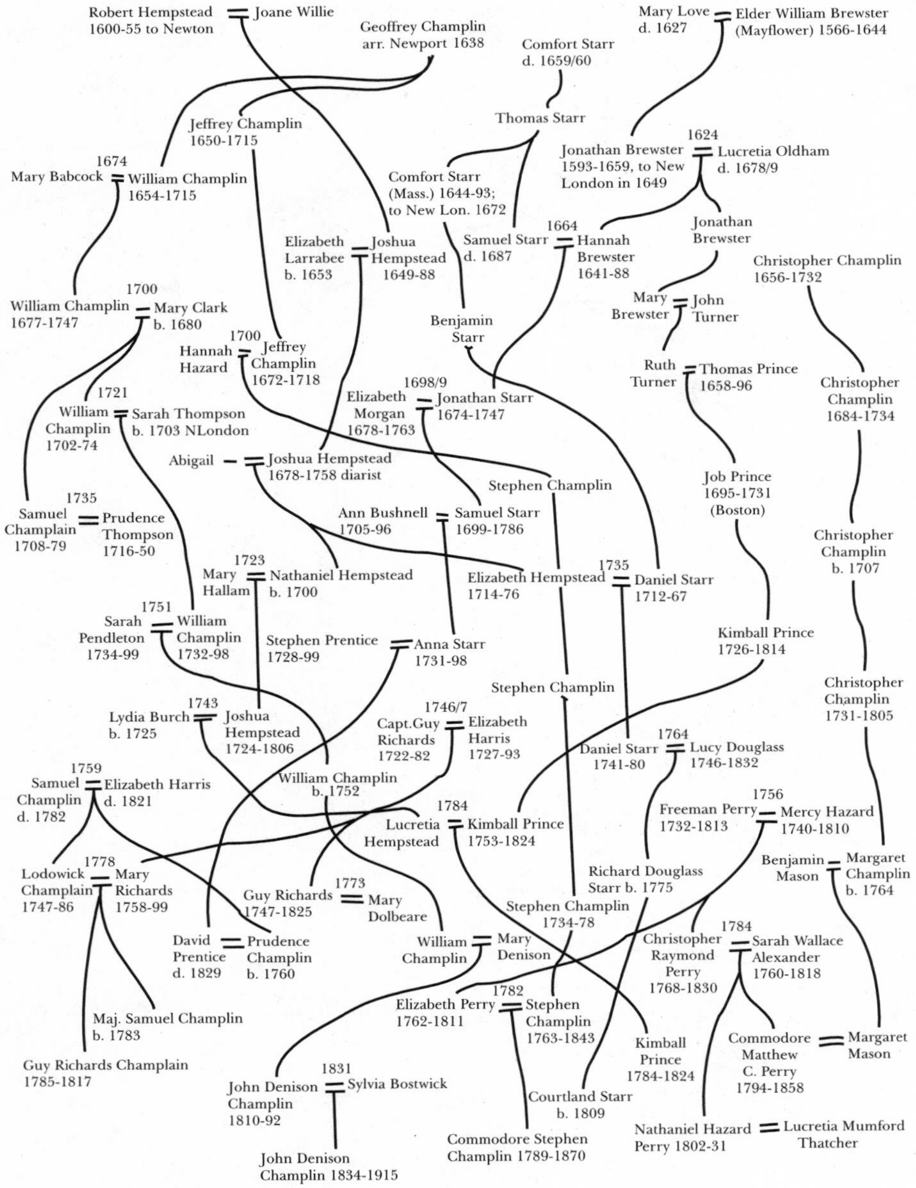

Chart C Champlains, Starrs, and (Newport) Champlins and Perrys

Notes

Notes to the Preface

1. I offer a breezy account of my scholarly efforts in *Documentary Editing*, March 1995; but Michigan State University Press, which I indicate there as the publisher, proved, on experiment, impossible.
2. Robert M. Myers, *The Children of Pride. A True Story of Georgia and the Civil War*, New Haven, Yale Press, 1972, pp. xxif., a model I choose because it represents the practises of the university press I am most familiar with, and because of a similarity of aims: "to produce a story that is at once readable, informative, and moving." I may also claim that "whatever appears on the[se] pages . . . I have reproduced with painstaking fidelity to the manuscript text." For another similar text similarly edited by the same press, see *The Diaries of Julia Cowles* (1931) p. xi.
3. "Staid" for "stayed" or "surprized" for "surprised," both in Milton, "stile" for "style" in Young's "Night Thoughts," "least" for "lest" in Richardson's *Pamela*; and so forth.
4. Though Elizabeth Champlain received her mail under her full name, both her husband and her kinsman Pardon Taber in a legal document (his will) called her Betsey. For the will see F. M. Caulkins, *Manuscript Copy. Green Oblong No. 6 S. T. U. V.* (in the New London County Historical Museum), p. 76.

Notes to Chapter 1

1. For my editorial practises, see the Preface.
2. Eliza Champlain contributes 101 letters; her unmarried aunt Mary Way, 46; Elizabeth = Betsey Champlain, 30; her sons, Eliza's brothers, 35 (William) and 31 (George); Anna Fitch, 15; Betsey's husband who is Eliza's father, George Whitefield Champlain, 7; other persons, still fewer. After her brothers' and aunt's deaths (William, 1832; Mary Way, 1833; George, 1835; Samuel in 1844), only one letter survives *from* Eliza (**no. 324**), indicating she took over the effects of family members at their decease and added them to what they had sent *to* her. Her daughter Alice Fitch Riley passed on the habit of preservation and the family collection to her daughter in turn, Grace MacMullen, who

in 1898 (**no. 329**, **I**) speaks of "our box of letters, ranging from 1786 to 1855." Grace MacMullen's interest also produced a quantity of genealogical material; and it may be guessed that she and her mother were the ones who added certain ink or pencil notes to items and tried to reduce the collection to chronological order; but the attempt was not a very serious one. At some point the earliest document(s) disappeared, since the series now begins only in 1792. It does, however, still end in 1855. When Grace died in 1905 her brother Charles inherited the letters, and they passed in time to his son, always in Manhattan.

3. J. de Laet, *Novus orbis seu descriptionis Indiae Occidentalis libri XVIII* (Leiden 1633) p. 71, slightly different from the Dutch text of 1625; F. M. Caulkins, *History of New London, Connecticut* (New London 1895–unchanged text of 2nd ed. of 1866) p. 22, on the report of Adrian Block in 1614.

4. Ibid. pp. 36ff. (the male captives disposed of from on board vessels in the harbor); the tribe's remnants in the eighteenth and nineteenth centuries, pp. 604f. On their virtual disappearance, see N. Salisbury, *Manitou and Providence Indians, Europeans, and the Making of New England, 1500–1643* (New York 1982) p. 222; they are now "nearly extinct" (*New York Times* Feb. 27, 1994, magazine section, p. 49).

5. On these early names, see Caulkins pp. 57 (Hempstead), 60 and 65f. (Brewster), 70, 77f., 83, and 145f.; add the Reverend Nathaniel Saltonstall in 1691, p. 197. On the early name of New London itself, ibid. pp. 45, 59, and 119; and on Uncas, pp. 21, 54f. On Hannah Way, daughter of Ebenezer, see the *Diary of Joshua Hempstead* (New London 1901) p. 354. Her line went back to Thomas Way in New London from about 1687 (Caulkins p. 266).

6. Caulkins pp. iii and 67 on Hugh Cauken; p. viii on Manwaring. Her book gives the city's story up through the period of this correspondence, i.e. to the mid-nineteenth century; but in a larger sense her work included the salvaging and ordering of a huge quantity of information from manuscript sources, now accessible to inquiry in the New London County Historical Society (her so-called "Manuscript Copy" note-books, along with other materials). For a survey of sources beyond those accessible to her, see R. O. Decker, *The New London Merchants* (New York 1986) pp. 341ff.

7. Caulkins p. 235; further on the city's pre-Revolutionary growth, pp. 483ff. and 501f. ("New London had nothing but her commerce; this was her life, her all"); and Decker, *Merchants* pp. 21–58, and idem, *The Whaling City. A History of New London* (Chester 1976) p. 338, with attention drawn to horses for sale in Barbados, Jamaica, St. Kitts, and nearby–still a major article of trade after the Revolution, cf. the 7,403 horses clearing through the New London Customs in 1791.

8. Caulkins pp. 578f., on Allen's list, immigration and marriage in 1754 to Elizabeth Christophers.

9. See "Fort Griswold, Sept. 6, 1781," in J. G. Whittier, *The Literary Remains of John G. C. Brainard* (Hartford 1932) pp. 73–6, and on the poet, below, chapter 9, note 14; on the total loss suffered by the city, "near a million of dollars' worth of property was destroyed," see pp. 164f. of Prince's *Autobiography* (below, note 11).

10. On Guy Richards' house being spared, though he was a captain and otherwise prominent in the Revolutionary forces, see Caulkins p. 552; Richards' aunt Mary married Lodowick Champlain (brother to George Whitefield Champlain, related to the Lodowick family of

New London), who with his brother Samuel had been prominent as privateer captains during the Revolution (Caulkins p. 537). On these relations, see Kin-chart C; on the burning of Ebenezer Way's store, see **no. 329 G** and **N**.

11. Christopher Prince (1751–1832) of Boston had a descendant who in 1900 copied out, with the original pagination, what he terms his ancestor's *Autobiography*. The original has disappeared. The copy is in the hands of Mr. Richard E. Harding of Weston, Massachusetts, who kindly allows me to cite the work. Its detail on New London suffices in my opinion to authenticate the whole: the age giving the birth-date of "Captain George Colfax" (1727–66), as the genealogies call him, compare the *Autobiography* p. 108; Captain [William] Coit of the *Oliver Cromwell*, ibid. pp. 95, 98; Captain Oliver Champlain of the *American Revenue*, pp. 117–20, 150; Captain [Peter] Richards of the *Marquis De Lafayette*, p. 161, and of the *Hancock*, pp. 151, 154, with Joseph Champlin as lieutenant; the kinship between Captain Lamphere and a Deshon, pp. 100, 109; the great relative wealth of Nathaniel Shaw, p. 117; the $200,000 prize taken by Oliver Champlain in 1777, p. 120; and much else besides. The various captains and vessels can be checked out in the Blunt White Library of Mystic Seaport; but on Samuel Champlain, father of Oliver and George Whitefield and commander of the *American Revenue*, there are additional mentions in Nathaniel Shaw's letters, cf. E. E. Rogers, *Connecticut's Naval Office at New London* (New London 1933) pp. 298, 309.

12. Caulkins pp. 436f. on the Baptists (the incident, of date 1772; and the principal actor had shown his spirit forty years earlier, fathering an illegitimate child, cf. A. A. and A. H. Wright, *Descendants of Joseph and Philip Taber* [Ithaca 1952] p. 23); on Methodists, pp. 595ff.; on John Murray and Universalism, pp. 586 and 599f., and better in his autobiography (rev. ed. Boston 1870, p. 292, quoted); Aunt Hannah's boast, **no. 79**, with a confirmation in **no. 14** of 1811, where, from some years previous, "Mr. [Hosea] Ballou the Universal minister . . . recalled [Mary Way] perfectly and all our family" from his preaching-visit to New London.

13. Caulkins pp. 619 and 633 (Isham as Brig.-Gen. of the city's forces in the War of 1812); **no. 316**, for the city seal; and Caulkins p. 577 for Huntington as Collector (a war hero like Guy Richards, Jirah Isham, and Richard Douglas, later the Second Postmaster, cf. B. P. Starr, *History of the Starr Family* [Hartford 1979] p. 250, and the *Connecticut Gazette* of July 11, 1798 and elsewhere).

14. Caulkins p. 459 (1745, and twice in 1763).

15. Decker, *New London Merchants* p. 269, App. XIII, showing a high of 246 registered seamen in a total population of 3000.

16. Ibid. p. 262, on Lodovick (or "Lodowick") commanding the *Hancock* in the 1770s and 1781; *Connecticut Gazette* January 3, 1798 p.3, naming him a proprietor of western lands in the company of a Christophers, Hurlbut, Griffin, Holt, Harris, Saltonstall, and the like substantial folk. He appears as a recipient of mail repeatedly in the postmaster's lists, e.g. January 8 and 22, 1800.

17. In the New London Customs House Records, listed under the names of the vessels and handy in the Blunt White Library at Mystic Seaport.

18. Customs House Records, showing the tonnage of the vessels, 45 to 81 (the *Juno*).

19. Alexander Allyn master of the *Thomas Pinckney*, *Nancy*, *Olive Branch* (also commanded by his brother Christopher), and *Sally* (also commanded by John Deshon and George Chapman)–as Deshon commanded at one time the *Polly* (also commanded by James Deshon and Chapman).

20. **No. 2**, the tone of longing for family easily matched in other sailors' letters home, e.g. D. Williams' (in the Blunt White Library at Mystic Seaport), September 17, 1797, "Kiss little Maggy for me."

21. Quoted, Timothy Pickering in *Naval Documents Related to the Quasi-War Between the U.S. and France*, pp. 1ff., with material on 1793–5; *American State Papers, Foreign Relations* (4th Congress, Doc. No.119), esp. 119D, pp. 753ff.; H. B. Cox, *The Parisian American: Fulwar Skipwith* (Washington 1964), passim, esp. pp. 47f., 51f., 58f., and 63; A. C. Clauder, *American Commerce as Affected by the Wars of the Revolution and Napoleon* (Philadelphia 1932) pp. 38ff. and 44ff.; M. A Palmer, *Stoddert's War: Naval Operations During the Quasi-War with France* (Columbia 1987) pp. 4ff.; indications of the sort of publicity given to the Quasi-War in *Connecticut Gazette* April 25 and August 1, 1798, or by report from personal experience, as in the D. Williams letters, August 18, 1798 (cit. above, note 20); and, on the consul at Bordeaux whom George Whitefield Champlain mentions, Joseph Fenwick, see Cox, *The Parisian American* pp. 36 and 58. Some of G. W. Champlain's shipping-investment pals, namely Samuel Hurlbut and Joseph and Samuel Tabor, lost a ship–in 1798, cf. Decker, *New London Merchants* p. 117.

22. G. W. Champlain's cane and whistling, **no. 57** (mid-1819), below; his son George's letter **no. 44** of July 16, 1818.

23. The letter, **no. 58** of July 1, 1819, is from Asa Spencer in Liverpool. As to the "instrument" George Champlain played at home-concerts, a possible explanation is that he "played" nothing but his cane, as a conductor–like Moses' rod. "Pulling caps" is in reference to George Champlain's difficult times with Betsey to which she refers also, above, toward the end of **no. 42**.

24. Elizabeth Champlain in debt at her husband's death, **no. 75** (July 1820), after his final illness of late 1819 (**no. 67** of January 27, 1820) and death in about April of the next year. On the writer of the last letter here, Asa Spencer, see below, chapter 11 note 19.

Notes to Chapter 2

1. For the lines of the family see Kin-chart B: by the first marriage, only Mary Way (1769–1833) and Elizabeth Champlain (1771–1825). For the wife Mary of Ebenezer Way, Senior, d. 1771, see Kin-charts A–B; for foster care of the child Mary Way, see **no. 188**, where she refers to the recent death (summer of 1825) "of the guardian of my youth (all the mother I ever knew)," doubtless "Grand-Mah S[arah] Way" of **nos. 181** and **184**. For the memory of Lydia Darrow, see **no. 66**; and for singing in school, **no. 16**. Musical instruction was common in New England schools, cf. D. T. Deutsch, "The polite lady," *Antiques* 135 (1989) pp. 746–48.

2. Twelve of the thirty-seven known dressed miniatures are published by W. L. Warren, "Mary Way's dressed miniatures," *Antiques* 142 (1992) pp. 540–49. He chooses examples in which sitters are identifiable, with correction to be made about the Trumans (pp. 548f.), through a descendant, D. W. Ahern, pointing out in a letter of 1992 to W. L. Warren that

the proposed Daniel and Mary Way Truman can be ruled out in favor of Daniel Jr. and his second wife Deborrah Dennis. See Kin-chart A.

Eight further examples with unidentifiable sitters have been brought out directly or indirectly by Warren's research: five given by the Misses Grosvenor to the Lyman Allyn Museum in New London and attributed to Mary Way by Warren and the museum; one of a girl owned by Mrs. Samuel Schwartz; one of a young man owned by Bert Flaum; and one appearing in a Northeast Auction of 1994 (catalogue of the Center of New Hampshire, August 7, no. 894, R. Bourgeault auctioneer), said in the catalogue to be Mary Way's aunt of the same name, for no other reason than that the dates fit, as given by Warren, p. 548. A ninth unidentifiable belongs to the Morgan collection in the Yale University Art Gallery; a tenth, in private hands in Rhode Island.

Fifteen dressed miniatures, still further, with identifiable subjects are "Captain and Mrs. Huntington of Norwich or New London," according to B. K. and N. F. Little, the work sold at the Sotheby's Sale 6526 of 1994, no. 328 (with errors in the catalogue description), the most likely sitters being Eleazer, Simeon, or Elisha Huntington, all called "Captain," all of Norwich, all born between 1734 and 1745, see *The Huntington Family in America. A Genealogical Memoir* (Hartford 1915) pp. 326, 986, 992; then, one of Peter Thacher of Lebanon, Conn., identified by the Littles and sold as no. 699 to Mr. and Mrs. E. K. Liverant through the above Sotheby's sale; the now "unlocated" pair of Pardon Taber the elder (1711–1803) and his wife Elizabeth Harris identified as Way's work by Warren, p. 548, only through their publication (in F. M. Stoddard, *Genealogical History of the Allen Family* [Boston 1891], facing p. 34); another pair, of Frederick and Prudence Seymour, owned by P. F. Maxson; one of Giles Holt, in the Shaw Mansion at New London; one of the girl Mary House, later married to Gilmer, in the New York Metropolitan Museum; four, of Col. and Mrs. Ebenezer Sage and their son, plus one of Mrs. Burr, owned by Mrs. Schwartz; one of Elizabeth Champlain owned by myself, see below, note 5; and one of Diah Manning (1760–1815) given to the Connecticut Historical Society, brought to attention in 1967 by the Society's editrix P. Kihn, who first noticed that dressed miniatures constituted a cohesive group of portraits, with an identifiable point of origin, "the Norwich-New London area." See her letter of March 9, 1967 to the New London County Historical Society's curator, E. Knox; on the sitter, with a reproduction of the miniature, see M. E. Perkins, *Old Houses of the Antient Town of Norwich 1660–1800* (Norwich 1895) pp. 92f.; and, as an example of the Norwich-connection, the miniature of Jonathan Devotion shown not only in W. L. Warren's article but earlier in J. O. and J. C. Robertson, "The Devotion family," in *The Devotion Family*, eds. L. Mayer and G. Myers (New London 1991) p. 40 and Fig. 14 (datable to 1790–93). The painting was given by a descendant Harriet Devotion Terry to the Brookline, Mass., Hist. Soc in 1949; the sitter can be traced through the Robertson article and *The Huntington Family* p. 627.

Among the above fifteen, the attribution to Mary Way of the Metropolitan-Museum miniature is by the curator Dale Johnson (my thanks to her for her letter); that of the Little and New Hampshire Auctions by the auctioneers; that of Diah Manning, by myself; the Yale example, by R. J. Frank and myself; the rest except for my own painting, by W. L. Warren. He had the remarkable generosity to make over his Mary Way files to me, and I have naturally profited very greatly from them.

3. The dressed profile of a girl, Warren's Pl. II p. 542, born 1771 or 1772, here in her mid-teens, as it seems, therefore painted in the later 1780s. There exist confusions about her

dates and name on the liner of the miniature and in the letter sent to Warren by her descendant W. Lyman, in 1993.

4. New London sitters: in Warren's article, the Colfaxes (Pl.III), perhaps Hazards (Pl.VIII–IX), and the Trumans (Pl.Xa–b); Mrs. Truman's relatives, above, note 2; further, "Mary House/afterwards/ Mary Peachy Gilmer," written in pencil on the back and shown me by C. Rebora of the Metropolitan Musum who helped me decipher the writing; the name and dates are supplied also by letter to the museum from a descendant. Compare a portrait of Prudence Miner of New London (her husband from Hartford), placed by the owner and descendant P. F. Maxson; also Giles Holt (b. 1783, son of Daniel, son of William, son of William who married Sarah Way, all of New London, the sitter identified by the donor to the New London County Historical Society, at the Shaw Mansion). In **nos. 16–17** we have reference to "N. Payne" 's picture, whether one shown in John Payne's book (below, note 33), the initial in error, or a portrait by Mary Way of her "cousin" Nathaniel Payne, see **nos. 178** and **195**.

5. The dressed miniature come down to me has a built-up backing of scraps of paper, hard to write on, with "Miss Way" legible, and "E Champ" and "Mrs Lizy," "By Miss," and "Miss." The dating of the costume is thanks to L. Thrift of the National Portrait Gallery. Another dressed miniature most strikingly similar is in the Lyman Allyn Museum, unidentified (gift of G. and U. Grosvenor 1949); still closer, the similarity with Warren's Pl. Xb, Mrs. Truman.

6. The present owners are Mr. and Mrs. Ezekiel Israel Liverant, by whose kindness I examined the work; excellent photos in Warren pp. 540f., along with correspondence from the New London County Historical Society curator E. Knox, of 1979, the ultimate source for Charles Holt's identity being an essay in a family notebook. On Holt himself, see below, chapter 12 at note 4. Identification of the artist by a business card as backing was not uncommon. For an example, see M. L. Dearborn, *Anson Dickinson, the Celebrated Miniature Painter* (Hartford 1983) p. 64, or A. Winchester, "The editor's attic," *Antiques* 40 (1941) p. 375, on Augustus Burr's card, in which places are left blank to be filled in with his changing city and street address.

7. The unsigned dressed portrait of Giles Holt (1783–1824) is here shown with thanks to the New London County Historical Society. I agree with W. L. Warren in believing it certainly by Mary Way. About the subject, I find nothing beyond what is in F. M. Caulkins, *Manuscript Copy: 2d Oblong. H. I. J. K. L.* (n.d.) pp. 68, 71, that Giles (1781–1864) was descended of Daniel Holt (b. 1738), married Mary Rogers, and "kept the lighthouse on Gull Island."

8. N. Druckman of the auction-house Sotheby's attributes the portraits to Mary Way by comparing them with another Way-pair also auctioned (above) in 1994, plus the Thacher portrait, plus those shown in the Warren article; and the treatment of the eyes of Bethiah Perkins is a good index for the attribution. On the back almost illegibly, "John T[racy] Perkins" and "My grandmother Bethiah Baker . . . Kingsley . . . Perkins," the individuals being John Perkins of Norwich (1736–1800) and his wife (1737–1820). See G. A. Perkins, *The Family of John Perkins of Ipswich* III (Salem 1889) pp. 32f., and *Vital Records of Norwich 1659–1848* (1913) pp. 147, 393. To John Perkins, as it is written on his portrait, was presented "the old clock made for him by Nath'l Shipman about 1790,"

Nathaniel Shipman (d.1805) being a deacon and pew-holder in the same church with Jabez Perkins, John Tracy, Simeon Carew, and Benjamin Huntington–all, family names recurring among Way's sitters. See above, note 2; F. M. Caulkins, *History of Norwich* (Hartford 1866) p. 463; and *V. R. Norwich* pp. 263, 527.

9. Mary Way's ad appeared in the *New London Gazette* of March 21 and April 5 and 12 of 1809. The school was on Main Street, "two doors south of St. James' [Episcopal] Church," where Dr. Seabury held forth. Frances Taber Seabury is reported in 1818 "about breaking up her school," cf. R. B. Mullin, ed., *Moneygripe's Apprentice* (New Haven 1989) p. 116. An exactly comparable one was opened by the minister's wife in East Hampton toward the same time, see *The Autobiography of Lyman Beecher*, ed. B. M. Cross (Cambridge 1961) 1 p. 98. On Mary's competitors, see the *Connecticut Gazette* for January 1, 1800, at next-door Norwich, a "ladies' boarding school . . . tambour, embroidery, & Dresden . . . drawing;" in New London itself, April 6 and 13, 1808, all the same; April 5, 1809, still a third school, "drawing, painting, filigree, braiding," etc., in the very same issue as Mary's advertisement.

10. On Dickinson, see H. B. Wehle, *American Miniatures 1730–1850* (New York 1927) pp. 53f.; R. Bolton-Smith and D. T. Johnson, "The miniature in America,"*Antiques* 138 (1940) pp. 1048 and passim; F. F. Sherman, "The attribution of unsigned American miniatures," *Art in America* 28 (1940) p. 120; and Dearborn, *Anson Dickinson* pp. 1–17. Compare with Mary Way's work Dickinson's Nos. 51 and 72, in D. T. Johnson, *American Portrait Miniatures in the Manney Collection* (New York 1990) pp. 104 (an elderly woman) and 115 (Eliza Champlin of Newport, ca. 1791, a distant relative of the New London Champlains). See also a comparable piece by the French immigrant Louis-Antoine Collas, ibid. pp. 97f., no. 40, of 1816.

11. **No. 14** of February 15, 1811 finds her living with her step-brother Thomas in New London; her New York ad appears in December of the year. In New York, her first lodging may have been in "the Thomas house," cf. **no. 99**.

12. For the New London lodger, Mr. Pages, see the *Connecticut Gazette* for September 13 and 27 of 1797. For Dickinson in 1811, G. C. Groce and D. H. Wallace, *The New-York Historical Society's Dictionary of Artists in America 1564–1860* (New Haven 1957) pp. 43, 47, and 49, with W. Kelby, *Notes on American Artists, 1754–1820* (New York 1922) pp. 34, 43, and 47, on Philip Parisen's ads in the *Commercial Advertiser* of 1802, the ad renewed a month later, and then similarly in 1806 (the portrait of E. C. Riley by this man or his brother is in the editor's possession). For itinerancy among the painting profession in the late 18th and earlier 19th centuries, cf. *Autobiography of Lyman Beecher* 1 p. 93, of 1803; Wehle, *American Miniatures* pp. 39, 46f. (on Malbone and others); F. F. Sherman, "American miniaturists of the early nineteenth century," *Art in America* 24 (1936) pp. 76f. (Samuel Morse); Bolton-Smith, *Portrait Miniatures* p. 4; O. S. Coad, *William Dunlap* (New York 1962) p. 101; W. Keyes, *George Freeman, Miniaturist 1789–1869* (Storrs 1980) pp. 13ff.; J. Hill, "New England itinerant portraitists," *Itinerancy in New England and New York* (Boston 1986) pp. 151–6, E. M. Kornhauser, "Ralph Earl as an itinerant artist," ibid. p. 172, and M. E. Fouratt, "Ruth Henshaw Bascom, itinerant portraitist," ibid. pp. 190–200.

13. That this tiny portrait was passed down to me among Eliza's collection of unfinished, unframed art-work, which includes pieces demonstrably by her mother but none of that

sort by Mary, suggests it is by Betsey; but note the showing of "A Child. Miniature" by Mary Way in the Academy of Fine Art's exhibition of 1818, cf. M. B. Cowdrey, *American Academy of Fine Arts and American Art-Union: Exhibition Record* (New York 1953) 2 p. 385.

14. Surviving miniatures of dead subjects: *The Tannenbaum Collection of Miniatures* (West Palm Beach 1982) pp. 8f.; Johnson, *American Portrait Miniatures* pp. 101f. On mentions of such commissions, see L. B. Miller, ed., *The Selected Papers of Charles Willson Peale and His Family* vol. 3 (New Haven 1991) p. 496, a miniature from a corpse by Waldo exhibited at the Academy in 1817, and admired by CWP; Fouratt, "Ruth Henshaw Bascom," p. 200; G. B. Barnhill, " 'Extracts from the Journals of Ethan A. Greenwood'," *Proc. Am. Antiquarian Soc.* 103 (1993) pp. 94, 142, and in his own portrait-list under 1819, with Bumgardner, "Ethan Allen Greenwood," p. 220; and Groce and Wallace, *New-York Historical Society's Dictionary of Artists in America* p. 48, John Jarvis' ads in 1809, with similar ads by Henry Williams, in M. Fielding, *Dictionary of American Painters* (Philadelphia 1926) p. 411; for a slightly later period, T. Knoles, *The Notebook of Bass Otis, Philadelphia Portrait Painter* (Worcester 1993) pp. 209f., 212ff.

15. Young lovers' fondness for miniatures appears not only in various mentions of the correspondence but in the frontispiece to the popular novel by Isaac Mitchell, *The Asylum* ("he took her miniature from his bosom, and earnestly viewed it by the moon's pale ray"), or again in the poem "To Eliza's Miniature" (the portrait apostrophized by the distraught lover after the lady's death), in *The Ladies' Literary Cabinet* 1 (1819) p. 135.

16. On photography and daguerreotypes (from 1843 on), see Bolton-Smith and Johnson, "The miniature in America," p. 1051.

17. Two portraits on ivory, of the Woodward couple ca. 1800 at the Lyman Allyn Museum in New London, have been identified as Mary Way's, in its records as by its director E. N. Mayhew in a letter of 1978 to W. L. Warren; but I disagree with the attribution, on the sole grounds available, stylistic. I am not persuaded, either, by the latter's attribution to Way of a portrait on ivory of an unidentified young man, gift (1949.121b) to the same museum by the Misses Grosvenor.

18. Quoted, V. J. Murrell in Bolton-Smith, *Portrait Miniatures* p. 2, with explanation, 3ff.; further, B. S. Long, "Miniaturists, their desks and boxes," *The Connoisseur* 83 (1929) 327f.; T. H. Colding, *Aspects of Miniature Painting* (Copenhagen 1953) pp. 156f., 163f.; R. Bolton-Smith, in Dearborn, *Anson Dickinson* p. xxiii; Johnson, *Manney Collection* pp. 15f.; and especially C. Aiken, "Materials and techniques of the American portrait artists," ibid. pp. 27–30. The first serious treatment was written for his brother by Archibald Robertson still in Scotland in 1800. For the initial text, see *Letters and Papers of Andrew Robertson* 2 (London 1887) pp. 21–36, with additions in the next year, also by letter to his brother Andrew, pp. 37–40. Note (p. 157) that it was "sent my brother at New York in 1808; shown by him to miniature painters there, and studied by them; referred to by Mr. Cuming [Thomas Seir Cummings, 1804–1884], the principal miniaturist there, in his public lectures on art about 1830."

19. The portrait in question has come down in pair with that of a bespectacled man of about the same age, that is, his fifties, possibly early sixties. They are best identified as "Uncle" Pardon Taber (1756–c. 1830) and "Aunt" Amy, since we would expect the family to keep portraits only of a family member or very close friend, and Mary Way is known to have

done one of "Uncle Taber" (**no. 96**f.) which she had with her in New York. Her address on the trade card that serves as backing to the male portrait belongs only to the years 1817–19, a period during which the pair passed through the city (cf. **nos. 31**f. and **47**). Aunt Taber is alive in 1822 (**no. 128**), perhaps later; her husband, to ca. 1830 (**no. 297**).

20. See E. F. Ellet, *Women Artists in All Ages and Countries* (New York 1859) 290f.; A. S. Hirshorn, "Legacy of ivory: Anna Claypoole Peale's portrait miniatures," *Bulletin of the Detroit Institute of Art* 64, 4 (1989) pp. 19ff. Anna Peale's father was a miniaturist and taught her as well as her sister Sarah, the first two women members of the Pennsylvania Academy of Fine Arts. Their cousin Rosalba, daughter of Rembrandt Peale, was another painter, like Titian Ramsay Peale II, and so forth, throughout the family. Anna in turn taught her niece Mary Jane Simes (p. 26 n. 6). Further, on women miniaturists of Mary Way's lifetime learning under professional guidance, see C. H. Heslip and H. Kellogg, "The Beardsley Limner identified as Sarah Perkins," *Antiques* 126 (1984) pp. 550ff., the artist in question being only slightly younger than Mary Way, beginning her pastels likewise in her late teens, but related to John Trumbull and Winthrop Chandler and reared with every encouragement of her talents, and never a professional; further on women artists, E. M. Kornhauser and C. S. Schloss, "Paintings and other pictorial arts," *The Great River: Art and Society in the Connecticut Valley* (Hartford 1985) pp. 172f., Lydia Royse in ca. 1810–20 perhaps a pupil of Trumbull; Wehle, *American Miniatures* pp. 62f. (Ann Hall); Sara Frothingham (1821–1861), taught by her father, the artist James, cf. Ellet pp. 291, 299f., 318, 341, &c; and D. O'Brien, *Miniatures in the XVIIIth and XIXth Centuries* (London 1951) p. 55 on the Europeans Mary Cosway, Emma Kendrick (p. 90), Anne Mee (p. 100), Mary Palmer (p. 107), Eliza Sharpe (p. 127), and Emily Weigall (p. 147). A certain Mary Wrench is mentioned by C. W. Peale in his autobiography (transcribed, unpublished, by H. W. Sellers, pp. 100f.): a miniaturist in Philadelphia in ?ca 1770, sister-in-law to an artist, her work "good for a young artist," who then married and was lost to Peale's knowledge–as also to that of modern dictionaries of women artists. Apprenticeships of men are more fully known and documented; but there are self-taught exceptions, including Anson Dickinson himself, see Dearborn p. 3, and Freeman, see W. Keyes, *George Freeman, Miniaturist* (Storrs 1980) pp. 12ff.

21. On Archibald Robertson's treatise, see above, note 18, and A. H. Wharton, *Heirlooms in Miniatures* (Philadelphia 1898) pp. 132f., along with C. W. Drepperd, *American Drawing Books* (New York 1946) pp. 4ff., placing this book within the competition, which only becomes serious in subsequent years. On Alexander's pupils, see Cowdrey, *American Academy* 2 pp. 305f., and the "A. Robertson" who advertises his "class for Ladies" in oil and water-color painting at the New York Institution (e.g. *Republican Sentinel* December 12 and 17 of 1822). The texts of a quantity of ads by both Archibald and Alexander are collected in R. S. Gottesman, *The Arts and Crafts in New York 1800–1804* (New York 1965) pp. 9–14. Other painters exhibited along with their pupils, ibid. pp. 130, 132, 169, 252, and passim. For Ellen Tooker, see **no. 97**–another Robertson pupil known by name was Ann Hall, cf. Ellet, *Women Artists* p. 300. For a Ruysdael owned by Alex. Robertson, see Cowdrey 2 p. 319. And, on other venues in which exemplary art could be seen by New Yorkers, see below, chapter 4 notes 8–10.

22. The opinion about "young ladies" quoted from Barnhill, " 'Extracts' " (cit. above, n. 14) pp. 93f.; also Susanna Page in 1826, quoted from J. Hill, "New England itinerant

portraitists," p. 156. On other women successful, see above, n. 20; but note that American women artists such as Page, unlike the European, come into view at a later date: e.g. Mary Weston (1817–1894), Lily Spencer (1822–1902), Ruth Bascom (from ca. 1820), and Anne Hall (1792–1863). N. F. Little, "Little-known Connecticut artists, 1790–1810," *Bulletin, Connecticut Historical Society* 22 (1957) p. 97, was not aware of any American female artists in the quarter-century after the Revolution. The earliest non-Peale women painters I can instance are the Colonial pastelist Henrietta Johnson (?–1728/9) of Charleston, in Groce and Wallace, *New-York Historical Society's Dictionary* (cit. above, n. 12) p. 355, Sarah Perkins (1771–1831, cit. above, n. 20), and Sarah Goodridge (1788–1853), a generation younger than Mary Way. She began miniature painting in Boston ca. 1812, and opened a studio in 1820. I exclude women painters who would be called primitive or naive, like Eunice Phinney, active 1805 (or 1809) to 1825. See Groce and Wallace, *New-York Historical Society's Dictionary of Artists in America* p. 507, and B. T. Rumford and C. J. Weekley, *Treasures of American Folk Art* (Boston 1989) p. 174.

23. The subject of America's cultural dependence on Europe may be left to many big books, well known; but just as an illustration of the alleged fact of the vacuum of talent to be filled, and the prickly denial of the fact, see the anonymous "Communication" in the *Republican Sentinel* of July 22, 1822. On West's ambitions, see R. C. Alberts, *Benjamin West. A Biography* (Boston 1978) p. 180: West was so obviously a candidate for honors "that in time–as early as 1792–'Sir' was sometimes put before his name on the assumption that he must have been made a knight."

24. Cowdrey, *American Academy* 2 p. 385. Mary Way lived in rented lodging by herself in 1816 (**nos. 20–21**), perhaps briefly in a house to be hired by Charles Holt, spoken of as a project for 1817 (**no. 21**), at 98 Chatham St. in 1817 to the fall of 1818 (**nos. 27**, **43**, and **46**), and apparently with the Dawsons by December 1818.

25. A new pupil, **no. 65** of November, 1819.

26. An excellent photo in Warren, "Mary Way" p. 546; but I have difficulties with Warren's dating and question-marks, having examined the painting thanks to the owners' kindness, and having compared it with that of the woman paired with my Pl. 2.9–though the latter is older. Mary (Dobbs) Holt was born in 1771, and might well appear as she does in the portrait that the Holt descendants believed was Charles' wife, around 1815–18.

27. Barnhill, " 'Extracts' " (cit., above note 14) p. 133. John Vanderlyn (1775–1852) was by 1817 a member of the Academy, "an artist of considerable merit" who was at the time exhibiting a collection of his works seen by an English traveler, Henry Fearon, cf. B. Still, *Mirror for Gotham. New York as Seen by Contemporaries* (New York 1956) p. 102. Jarvis and Dickinson were even better known.

28. On prices for a standard oil portrait, see Groce and Wallace, *Dictionary of Artists* pp. 45, 47 (Parisen), and 48 ($300 for a full-length by Jarvis, otherwise $60 or less); Knoles, *Notebook of Bass Otis* p. 189 ($20–30); for miniatures by Bass Otis, ibid. 208 ($10); by Malbone and Raphaelle Peale ($20–50), Dearborn, "Anson Dickinson" p. 1004; Bolton-Smith and Johnson, "The miniature in America" pp. 1047f.; as high as $15 in Middletown charged by a known artist, in 1835, see D. Bolger, "Ambrose Andrews and his masterpiece," *American Art Journal* 22, 1 (1990) p. 10; and the Sotheby's catalogue #6612, the B. K. and N. F. Little Collection item no. 700, John Brewster's miniature portraits of the early

1800s at $5. For Mary Way's charges, **no. 20** and, for watch-papers ($2–4), **no. 21**; for Elizabeth Champlain's charges, **nos. 32**, **57**, and **67**; for her daughter Eliza's charges in New York, **nos. 130**, **184**, and **219** and **221**; in New London, **nos. 95** and **125** (but for watch-papers, 75 cents, **no. 109**).

29. **No. 175**, Betsey "two weeks in doing a miniature;" Eliza's repeated attempts to get a given sitter just right, **nos. 19** and **94** (the elder Northams), **184** (their daughter Caroline, nine times attempted), **38**, **71**, **83**, and **93** (Dr. Wright), or **21**, **86**, **139**, and **224** (Anna Fitch)–but also duplicates painted for profit by Betsey, **nos. 57** and **59**.

30. "Re-touching for nothing" (**nos. 34** and **249**, by Betsey); updating and repairs by Eliza, **nos. 103**, **145**, and **186**; compare Greenwood's repainting of a portrait to reflect the sitter's loss of weight, in Barnhill, " 'Extracts' " (cit. above, note 14) p. 121.

31. "Crab" is a young male friend of Mary's and Eliza's (**no. 20**), Tabers like Holts (**no. 16**, with N. Payne) are relatives; Mrs. Northam and Anna Fitch are her dear friends (**nos. 94** and **46**); but the rest of Mary's sitters hardly explain themselves: unnamed (**nos. 23**, **27**, **33**, **38**) or unknown (Woodward, **no. 49**, Church **52**, Williamson and wife and John Sistare **65**, "the beautiful Mrs. Crocker" **99**, and **147**, Jane Johnston).

32. Fouratt, "Ruth Henshaw Bascom" p. 190, from 1819 to 1846 in Massachusetts, New Hampshire, and Maine; on Anna Peale, see Hirshorn, "Legacy of ivory" p. 19.

33. See his brief biography in Groce and Wallace, *Dictionary of Artists* p. 691.

34. Miller, ed., *Selected Papers of Peale* vol. 3 pp. 494f., 498; further on this artist, W. Dunlap, *A History of the Rise and Progress of the Arts of Design* 2 (Boston 1918) 2 pp. 356ff.

35. The text (now of great rarity) was identified by Dr. John S. Gage in Cambridge University, who has my cordial thanks. Identification should have been easy, given Drepperd (cit. above, n. 21); but in fact this author offers no help, there is a false clue in the "N. Payne" mentioned (above, n. 4), and a half-a-dozen scholars in New York, Washington, and New Haven (who may not wished to be named!) could offer no help–not even the Library of Congress. Yet John Payne's work in England went through repeated, slightly changing editions. Of these, in the U. S. and England, apparently only those of 1798, 1812, and 1820 survive, and do not contain all that Mary quotes. I have indicated within quotation marks the pages she does quote, i.e. pp. 15f. of the 1812 edition (unchanged in 1820), but do not find the latter half of the quotations in that edition, nor are they in that of 1798.

36. My attempts to identify these three paintings have been vain, except in establishing that they cannot have been by Rubens, though possibly by the younger Jan Brueghel (compare his works on biblical scenes and on copper, none of the size required, but up to 105 X 70 cm, in K. Ertz, *Jan Breughel der Jüngere* [Freren 1984] pp. 294, 296f., 326, 341, 376, and the largest on p. 386). The author by letter most kindly confirms this likelihood and the silence of all art-historical sources on any Saltonstall owner. The Brueghels' work, elder or younger, were at this period in America often confused with Rubens', and of course might originate in the same workroom. Jeremy West's praise had given a particular lustre to Rubens, which might account for the gravitation of the unsigned to his name. For his place in New York of the period, see W. R. Valentiner, "Rubens' paintings in America," *Art Quarterly* 9 (1946) p. 153, and J.-A. Goris and J. S. Held, *Rubens in America* (New York 1947) pp. 15f. The owner of Mary Way's "Rubens" paintings, William Saltonstall (1780–

1823), can be identified in L. Saltonstall's *Ancestry and Descendants of Sir Richard Saltonstall* (New York 1897) p. 234, as married to Sarah Taber. He was a "painter" (**no. 132**, January 13, 1823) who died in Pensacola. His sister Betsey then living in New York returned to her kin through marriage, the Starrs of New London. She was a friend of Mary Way and her sister (**nos. 59** and **221**).

Notes to Chapter 3

1. **No. 10** of Feb. 18, 1799.
2. Hosea Ballou's controversy with John Murray ended in the isolation and defeat of the latter. See, e.g. E. Cassara, *Hosea Ballou* (Boston 1961) p. 31, or, for the flavor of the disagreement, the intemperate J. H. Allen and R. Eddy, *A History of the Unitarians and the Universalists in the United State* (New York 1894) pp. 391, 394f., 398f.
3. **No. 12** of May 26, 1799.
4. Painted in 1815 by Ethan Allen Greenwood, cf. G. B. Barnhill, " 'Extracts from the Journal of Ethan Allen Greenwood'," *Proc. Am. Antiquarian Soc.* 103 (1993) p. 127.
5. **No. 328**, quoted from *Harper's Monthly* 60 (1879) p. 62, the reference thanks to Alice MacMullen's notes.
6. Examination of F. W. Chapman, *The Coit Family* (Hartford 1874), discovers only one possibility for "the Coit sisters," namely (p. 115) Mary, Augusta, and Elisabeth, daughters of Dr. Thomas and Mary Gardiner Coit, all girls of an age for portraits between 1810 and 1820 and kin to the families Prentiss, Richards, and Christophers.
7. For the 1811 portrait of Capt. Jared Starr (1741–1838), see **nos. 59** and **63**; for that of Mr. "Cotes or Coats," see **no. 21**; and for the lines of kinship with the Starrs, see F. M. Caulkins, *A History of New London, Connecticut* (New London 1895) pp. 319f., and Kin-chart B, showing Jared Starr the brother of that Jonathan whose son married Elizabeth Taber and whose grandson Jonathan (1781–1842) first married the heiress Anna Morgan. On the portraits of Jonathan Starr and his future wife in 1822, see below, chapter 12 n. 6.
8. **No. 18** of June or July, 1816.
9. Jesse Denison Smith had married Frances Taber Allen, grand-daughter of Pardon Tillinghast Taber (above, chapter 1).
10. G. C. Mason, *Reminiscences of Newport* (Newport 1884) p. 220, speaking of the city and the ladies of the Champlin clan (so spelt) there.
11. **No. 55** of January, 1819 (just the first dozen lines), the whole of it in **no. 59** six months later, and a fair copy later still, **no. 327**.
12. Nathaniel Perry appears as a sitter in **no. 131** of 1822, as in **nos. 248** (marrying Lucretia Thatcher of New London in 1828) and **265** (the pair, giving a party for Marcus Starr and his bride in 1829). His sister had friends in the city, **no. 180** of 1825, and his sister-in-law in the end (1830) intervened to help Ebb. (chapter 5 note 7 and **269**).
13. The recoverable list of her sitters includes the six in **no. 172** (one named: Lucretia Thompson); other sitters in **42**, **55**, **57**, **121**, **139** (three), **142**, **147**, and **172** (two); but some of her sitters paid nothing: herself (as mentioned in **nos. 38**f. of 1818) and her

husband (**no. 172**). Her only completed portrait, on ivory (Pl. 3.10). arrives to the present in a frame of post-1840, the painting itself dated to ca. 1815 or 1820 by L. Thrift and E. Miles, both experts at the National Portrait Gallery, while the attribution was made by C. Rebora at the Metropolitan Museum in New York, comparing the work to Pl. 4.12. Six miniatures on paper, shown to me as possibly Betsey's or Mary's or even Eliza's work–six members of the King family of Rutland, Vermont–cannot be by any of the "sisters," to judge both by technique and by dating.

14. **Nos. 63**, **162**, and **170**.

15. Photo courtesy The Art Museum, Princeton University, Museum purchase, Caroline G. Mather Fund. As hardly needs pointing out, in the central figure the hand that rests on Jesus' right shoulder, his cloak, and his neck and head have been added by afterthought, and several inches too high, atop the uncloaked torso.

16. Cf. **no. 172**, the painter "Johnson"; tips from "Palmer," **nos. 16–17**; and perhaps tips shared with the less expert Mrs. Bryant of New London, for whom Betsey ordered supplies from New York and whose miniatures Eliza used as models to copy, **nos. 139–40**.

17. C. W. Drepperd, *American Drawing Books* (New York 1946) passim, e.g. pp. 5f. For engravings used as models, see **nos. 19**, **33**, **57**, and **59**; and compare Roxana Beecher's paintings of birds from engravings, in Lyman Beecher's *Autobiography*, ed. B. M. Cross (Cambridge 1961) p. 98.

18. **No. 131**, of October, 1822, with Betsey's request there also for "any you think will answer as a model for a painter"; **138** of the next March, with the news that the boxes in New York were a little different, and much too expensive; and **139** of April, with Betsey's regretful recall of "the kings and queens I have heard so much about."

19. Nathaniel Rogers (1788–1844), frequent exhibitor and Member of the New York Academy. See M. B. Cowdrey, *American Academy of Fine Arts and American Art Union: Exhibition Record* 2 (New York 1953) pp. 309f.; G. C. Groce and D. H. Wallace, *The New-York Historical Society's Dictionary of Artists in America* (New Haven 1957) pp. 544f., according to whom Rogers, a founding member of the National Academy, "was painting miniatures in Connecticut probably before he went to New York city in 1811 to take lessons from Joseph Wood." More precisely: Rogers painted in Connecticut, when presumably the miniatures were made, only circa 1808–1811, cf. F. F. Sherman, "Nathaniel Rogers and his miniatures," *Art in America* 23 (1935) pp. 159f. Betsey's copies are mentioned in **nos. 154** and **172** of 1824 and **175** of 1825, her copy of *Mrs. Whistler* recalled in **248** of 1828.

20. Betsey very busy, **no. 155** (February 1824); once taught school, **no. 121**.

21. Edward Malbone is pretty unanimously rated at the top in American miniature portraiture. See for example his obituary, in W. Kelby, *Notes on American Artists, 1754–1820* (New York 1922) p. 54; among modern judges, M. L. Dearborn, "Anson Dickinson," *Antiques* 124 (1983) p. 1004, or R. Bolton-Smith and D. T. Johnson, " 'The miniature in America," ibid. 138 (1990) p. 1046; and for comparison with Betsey's *Christ*, see Malbone's portrait of Anna Maria Hampton, in D. T. Johnson, *American Portrait Miniatures in the Manney Collection* (New York 1990) p. 150 no. 125.

Notes to Chapter 4

1. **No. 38**, below: *Cupid and the Graces*, exhibited in 1816, cf. M. B. Cowdrey, *American Academy of Fine Arts and American Art-Union: Exhibition Record* 2 (New York 1953) p. 108.

2. See **nos. 66**, **76**, and **83**. Elisha North (1771–1843) was the author of a dozen works and more on medical subjects (1811–1838), settling in New London (from elsewhere in Connecticut) in 1812 and establishing his eye-clinic in 1817. In **no. 66**, young George O. Champlain extols North for his *Treatise on the Eye* and as "that celebrated oculist . . . in the first rank of his profession," amply confirmed by W. R. Steiner, "Dr. Elisha North, of New London, Connecticut," *Transactions American Ophthalmological Soc.* (1932) pp. 1ff., with a miniature portrait of him, p. 2, and the text of his praises in the *Connecticut Gazette* August 17, 1817; and S. R. Italia, "Elisha North," *Bulletin of the History of Medicine* 31 (1957) pp. 503ff., with bibliography.

3. "And the blind and the lame came to Him" (Mt 21.14f.) was transformed into "West's major success in 1811–indeed, one of the greatest of his career," under the title *Christ Healing the Sick*, of which the first version drew great crowds and prompt reproduction in engravings in London, the second in Philadelphia in 1817. See A. U. Abrams, *The Valiant Hero. Benjamin West and Grand-Style Historical Painting* (Washington D.C. 1985) p. 201; R. C. Alberts, *Benjamin West. A Biography* (Boston 1978) p. 348 (quoted); and H. von Erffa and A. Staley, *The Paintings of Benjamin West* (New Haven 1986) pp. 346ff.

4. Notice the verbatim quotation (though from memory) of Jarvis' advice, near the end (the fifth page) of **no. 16–17**.

5. On Dr. North's impatience with female prudery, see Italia, "Elisha North" p. 532. On the Baxters, see **nos. 48** (where the son Tholl can be indentified as 'Lobster'); **20**, below, where reference is made to the 1816 portrait of him; **59**, where Eliza does a portrait of Mrs. Baxter for a New London friend; and **237** for Baxter ties to the New London Sistares.

6. On Sam's apprenticeship, see above, **no. 16–17**; on George's apprenticeship, below, chapter 5, note 4, at a shop from which the son of the master, John W. Green, himself left the city to seek his fortune elsewhere, **no. 18**; and more generally, S. Wilentz, *Chants Democratic* (New York 1984) p. 28, "Apprenticeship remained a standard arrangement in 1820." On George's trip to France, see below, **no. 37**, where he mentions a voyage to France, and **19**, where in July of 1816 Mary speaks of his going to sea as a plan foregone.

7. Waldo helps, usually at his studio, **nos. 19**, **21**, **133**, and **139**; even a tip from Trumbull, **no. 71**.

8. Engravings, **nos. 19**, above, **33** and **59**; a bust as a model, **no. 163**; a painting evidently in public, **no. 85**, "the King and Queen of France;" exhibitions of paintings in the city's places of entertainment, the Vauxhall Gardens, e.g. *The Albion* of July 20, 1822, p. 40; and commercial exhibitions, in City Hall or in great abundance for auction in city hotels, **nos. 19**, **27**, and **33**, or e.g. of his three best works by the young Robert Street (1796–1865), to bad reviews, cf. *Republican Sentinel* July 22, 1822, with Cowdrey, 2 p. 340.

9. Miniatures and paintings by others, **no. 30** of 1817; copies taken of Mary Way's work, **20**, **33**, and **94**, and of her amateur friends', **19** and **21**, as they copy also from better models (**no. 27**); from Mrs. Bryant, a painter in New London, **139–40** and **142**.

10. **No. 133** (miniatures in a private collection), **155** (a portrait), and **163** (loan of works by Inman et al.).

11. T. Sizer in Cowdrey, *American Academy* 1 pp. 3–26.

12. Henry Fearon quoted in B. Still, *Mirror for Gotham: New York as Seen by Contemporaries* (New York 1956) p. 102; but an American visitor (Cowdrey, vol. 1 p. 24) found the collection equally disappointing.

13. Cowdrey's second volume supplies the materials for the listing, including (pp. 227 and 304, 251, 307) the paintings with titles cited, and others to give the flavor, e.g. (p. 229) *Omnia vincit amor* copied from West.

14. Mention of bark paper in the present letter as in **nos. 21**, **87**, **94**, and **163**; use of pith, **nos. 141–3**, and in three surviving examples.

15. These titles for "fancy" or emblematic pieces occur, respectively, in **nos. 19** (**20**, **21**, **27**, and **86**), **138**, **43** (**46** and **124**), **157** (*Hymen*), and **38**. Other subjects or titles are *Harp of Erin* (**138**), *Sea serpent* (**174**), Spenser's *Faery Queen* (**182**), memorial to Commodore Perry, *Silent Eloquence*, and *Sleeping Cupid* (all, **86**), mourning piece (**19**), *Mary Queen of Scots* (**173**, **201**, **213**, **219**, and **320**), and "a fancy figure" (**21**). Eliza's *Fancy* survives, also mentioned in **nos. 21**, **33**, **38**, **75**, and **97**. With the winged figure in Pl. 1.5, compare Pl. 2/48 of S. Schorsch, *Mourning Becomes America* (Albany 1976) and the mention of a "winged victory" or "small angel" in other Washington-mourning pieces (14–15th pages of ibid., unpaginated). They were highly popular and, in various forms and media, innumerable over the period 1800–40; see further, B. T. Rumford, *Treasures of American Folk Art* (Boston 1989) pp. 176f., and D. T. Deutsch and B. Ring, "Homage to Washington in needlework and prints," *Antiques* 119 (1981) pp. 406–17.

16. Ten-minute watch-papers, **no. 137**; as presents or payment, in **nos. 43**, **60** (intended, in payment to Capt. Lamphere), **158**, or **170**.

17. *Quarter-day, or The Horrors of the First of May. A Poem . . .* (New York 1812), 550 lines of it by Woodworth; and the entry on Clinch in the *National Cyclopedia of American Biography* 22 (New York 1932) p. 211.

18. **No. 48**, undated, and out of sequence in my *Transcription* (properly, it should follow **no. 20**). The best clue to its time of composition lies in the greetings offered by Mary to the Taber family in New London ("Aunt Taber, Emma, . . . Caroline"); but (**no. 36**, confirmed by **no. 47**) the Tabers had moved to North Carolina in April of 1818. Further, in the second paragraph, there is reference to Eliza's "visit," singular; and the implication is that the New York friends knew no Champlains or Ways except Mary and Eliza; but by Eliza's second visit they would have known the Ways. Therefore the date must be early winter of 1816.

19. N. W. Chavalier of **nos. 20–21**, **49**, **100**, and **138** (of 1823) advertises as a surgeon dentist in the *Republican Sentinel* of e.g. June 1, 1822 and regularly thereafter, at No. 14 Chatham Street. As he is a Universalist lay preacher, the presumption is that he met Mary and Eliza through their church. He also tried his hand at poetry: "Lucy Ann–A Song in the manner of Lord Byron," in *The Ladies' Literary Cabinet* of July 3, 1819.

Notes to Chapter 5

1. **Nos. 10** and **12** (Murray to Eliza) and **16–17**, Uncle Taber in New York, he of the many children, Jane, Emma, Frances, Elizabeth, Charlotte, and Henry, and many plans (see esp. **nos. 36**, **47**, **297**); and search for gold, **no. 20**, by Captain French, others like him being mentioned in later letters, e.g. **no. 62** (to New Orleans, as Eliza thought of trying, **no. 83**, and William Champlain did try, **no. 329 I**). In **no. 49** Mary Way considers moving to Richmond, as Betsey was invited to settle in Newport, **no. 184**.
2. In **no. 63** it can be seen that George was in New Orleans by July of 1818; the present letter is **no. 22** of January 23, 1817. On Marschalk, see J. D. Shields, *Natchez, its Early History* (Louisville 1930) pp. 40, 235, 244, and 254.
3. On Dr. Ulysses Dow, for decades the master of New London's grammar-school, see F. M. Caulkins, *History of New London* (New London 1895) p. 622.
4. **No. 25** of March 17, 1817; for a little background to his apprenticeship in the business to Colonel Green in New London, see **nos. 25**, **78**, **248**, and below, chapter 12 note 1; the memorial to Samuel Green and his forebears and business in Cedar Grove Cemetery (New London) vol. 1, 2 (1941) pp. 178–88; also, John Bradford, *The Poetical Vagaries of a Knight of the Folding-Stick of Paste Castle* (New York 1815), pp. 9ff., the poem "Description of a Bindery," 50f., "Song for the Tenth of March, the Night on which Journeymen Mechanics Cease Working by Candle-light," etc.; and H. D. French, "Early American bookbinding by hand, 1636–1820," *Bookbinding in America*, ed. H. Lehmann-Haupt (Portland 1941) pp. 90–94. On George's experience in learning his trade, compare the worm's-eye account from a Hartford bindery of the 1830s amusingly written by an irreverent unknown, in *The Andrus Bindery*, ed. N. C. Brainard (Hartford 1940).
5. On the newspaper arguments about the healthiness of the city, see E. C. Pennington, "The aesthetics of everyday life in Old Natchez," *Natchez Before 1830*, ed. N. Polk (Jackson 1989) p. 114; for yellow fever as the scourge of New Orleans, see J. S. Kendall, *History of New Orleans* (Chicago 1922) pp. 132f., noting the particular severity of the disease in 1818 as again in 1822; further, J. Larkin, *The Reshaping of Everyday Life, 1790–1840* (New York 1988) p. 81, New Orleans "very likely the most dangerous place in the United States," by reason of its climate, swampy setting, constant influx of foreigners, and primitive sanitation. Reports of its dangers were well known to the north, see e.g. New York *Ladies' Literary Cabinet* of October 19, 1819, the fever "felt with a fatality never before experienced," or *The Albion* of October 1822, pp. 127, 135, 150, and 167.
6. F. M. Caulkins, *Manuscript Copy: Blue Book, B. C.* pp. 51, 54f., 58f., and eadem, *History of New London* (New London 1895) p. 370, gives the background of the Richards family; on Guy Richards Champlain, see first *The War, being a Faithful Record* . . . vol. 1 no. 44, of April 20, 1813, pp. 116 and 186, and vol. 2, 1814, p. 127, published by Samuel Woodworth, that staunch Swedenborgian and friend of the Rileys, neighbor of Anna Fitch (who presented young G. F. Riley with still-surviving copies of the first two volumes in question); also, G. Coggeshall, *History of the American Privateers, and Letters-of-Marque* (New York 1856) pp. 4, 99, and 105–09; J. R. Jacobs and G. Tucker, *The War of 1812* (New York 1969) pp. 172f.; and, on the *General Armstrong*, R. R. Wilson, New York: *Old and New*[2] (Philadelphia 1903) 1 pp. 306f.; Guy R. Champlain's succession and estate record is dated in New Orleans to 1819. On Oliver Champlain, addressed in New London as "Captain"

(**no. 198**), see *The War* 1 p. 198, quoting the *Connecticut Gazette* of May 5, 1813; and on Captain Lodowick Champlin, the characterization quoted, with other war-stories, from [J. D. Champlin's] "*Champlin Memorial . . .* " (n.d. 1903) pp. (87)-2-3, including his part in an engagement with two British naval vessels and a letter-of-marque; further, R. O. Decker, *The New London Merchants* (New York 1986) p. 262.

7. On the relationships, see Kin-chart C; on Peggy Champlin (wife of Dr. Benjamin Mason), see A. H. Wharton, *Heirlooms in Miniature* (Philadelphia 1898) pp. xiii, 26, 57, and 175; on Betsey's portrait of Nathaniel, **no. 131**; and on the Commodore's mother resident in New London in 1824 (presumably, earlier too), see E. E. Rogers, *Connecticut's Naval Office at New London* (New London 1933) p. 135. Oliver Hazard Perry, son of the Commodore's brother Oliver, was to serve as shipmate with Titian Ramsay Peale in 1838–41 on the Wilkes Expedition; see *Voyage to the Southern Ocean. The Letters of Lieutenant William Reynolds*, eds. A. H. Cleaver and E. J. Stann (Annapolis 1988) p. 169, and J. Poesch, *Titian Ramsay Peale 1799–1885 and his Journals of the Wilkes Expedition* (Philadelphia 1961), passim.
8. *The History of America* by William Robertson (1721–93) went through many editions, the first of London 1777; but it dealt only with the Spanish in the New World, and George Champlain may claim a merely wished-for familiarity with the work.
9. Nathan Daboll (1750–1818) of a numerous New London family taught mathematics for surveying, navigation, and general use in his school, cf. e.g. the *Connecticut Gazette* of December 8, 1807 or March 16, 1808, and also wrote a *Schoolmaster's Assistant* in mathematics which became America's favorite, with 68 editions dominating the schools for half a century from 1800, and which established the $ symbol through its frequent use in set problems posed in money terms. See J. A. Nietz, *Old Textbooks* (Pittsburgh 1961) pp. 138ff., and C. Carpenter, *History of American Schoolbooks* (Philadelphia 1963) pp. 161f. On the Holts' store, see e.g. the ads in the *Connecticut Gazette* of May 22, 1805.
10. The succession and estate records of George Janson (note the spelling) date to 1820.
11. A position as a riverboat captain might have come to George Colfax through the captain of the *Alabama* plying the river in 1819, one Robert Colfax–if a relative.
12. **No. 102** September 25, 1821, with news explained by the address of George to Samuel in **no. 111**, care of Holt & Quinby, who appear as flour merchants in *Longworth's American Almanac, New-York Register, and City Directory* (New York) for 1819–20.
13. In J. A. Paxton's *New-Orleans Directory and Register* (New Orleans), which begins in 1822, George appears in the first three years at nos. 36, 72, and 41 Royal Street.
14. By August of 1824 (**no. 166**) and October (**no. 168**) George's New London family had heard that he had left New Orleans and, by November, that he had reached Nashville (**no. 172**).

Notes to Chapter 6

1. In combination, B. Still, *Mirror for Gotham. New York as Seen by Contemporaries* (New York 1956) pp. 57–124, and I. N. P. Stokes, *The Iconography of Manhattan Island, 1498–1909* vol. 3 (New York 1918) pp. 507ff. and passim, give a very full picture of the city. Among primary sources, [Eliza Southgate's] *A Girl's Life Eighty Years Ago* (New York 1887) pp. 150ff. is useful. Add, the realistic fiction of G. G. Foster, *Celio* (New York 1850), and his journalistic

essays, *New York by Gas-light* (New York 1850) and *New York in Slices* (New York 1849); R. R. Wilson, *New York: Old and New*[2] (New York 1903) pp. 325ff.; and R. A. Mohl, *Poverty in New York 1783–1825* (New York 1971) pp. 6f., 23f.

2. Mary Way in 1811 advertised her studio on Greenwich (above, chapter 2), which incidentally allowed her some "style" in her lodging in 1821 (**no. 99**); to William Street, 1814–15 (**no. 19** and *Longworth's American Almanac, New-York Register, & City Directory* 1814–15) and then to Chambers Street (**no. 19**, 1816); but she moved to Chatham in that same year (*Longworth's*, cit., 1816–20, and **no. 27**, "still" there in 1817), thereafter remaining in the area (**no. 67** and above, chapter 2 n. 24). Her Universalist church was originally (1796) near Pearl Street, in a few years' time moved to Duane near City Hall Park (by 1800), but was on Chatham Street near Pearl by 1817 (**no. 27**)–see Stokes, *Iconography* p. 937, and R. E. Miller, *The Larger Hope* (Boston 1979) p. 682, with **no. 27** of 1816. It was on Chatham Street that Charles Holt resided (**no. 67**–earlier, Pine Street, cf. *Longworth's* for 1814–17) and Samuel Fitch for a time (Longworth's, cit., 1813–15); where Mrs. Hayden boarded (1822, **no. 114**), Mary Ann Dawson Mason began housekeeping (**no. 114**), and the Rileys (**no. 207**, 1821; *Longworth's* for 1813–25) and Samuel Woodworth (from 1815, date of the second volume of *The War*, but on Pearl Street 1826–30, cf. *Longworth's*) had their places of business. The nearby James Street was chosen by the newly married Eliza and Edward Riley to live in (**no. 230**); Pearl Street, also adjoining, was where Mrs. Jiggins walked (**no. 48**, 1818) and Ebenezer Way boarded on a visit (**no. 245**, 1827); but Chambers Street, across Broadway, was where the elder Riley began (**no. 329 R**, 1805) and where Dr. Lee (**no. 155**, 1824), Eliza (**no. 252**, 1828), Charles Clinch (*Longworth's* 1828–29), and the widowed Anna Fitch (**no. 305**, 1832) all lived for a time. Before Samuel Fitch died, he and his family lived for many years on Cherry Street (**no. 7**, 1820, and earlier in *Longworth's* 1817–25). It was that address that he gives when he advertised real estate for sale, e.g. in the *Republican Sentinel* of September 7, 1822, though in October he moves from Cherry St. to the corner of Bowery and Stanton, October 5, 1822. As to the merchant-firm of Titus, Avery & Weeks and its Universalist connections, see below, chapter 7 note 9.

3. Amy Northam married John R. Shearman of Newport in 1802 (*Mercury* July 6, 1802; *Rhode Island Republican* July 3, 1802), explaining the relationship in the mention that, "in Newport," a family friend "dined with Mrs. Shearman at her brother Northam's" (**no. 107**; he, "many years older" than she, **no. 184**); helping also to explain the friendship of Anna Fitch with that same "Mrs. Shearman" (**no. 97** of 1821, and later mentions). Anna was the daughter of Mr. Northam, Amy's brother (**no. 20**), another of whose daughters was of Newport (**no. 117**) and often visited them; also other Northams, of wealth and standing there (**no. 171**). Anna's parents had traveled in Europe (**no. 19**) and made trips to Washington, Baltimore, and Philadelphia as well (**nos. 103** and **269**).

4. On Eliza's beaux, see especially **nos. 20**, **21** (Fenno and White), and **48**; among many other indications of church-related friendships, notice **nos. 49**, **50**, and **97**.

5. On the ubiquity of boarding houses and the prevalence of their use, see sources in n. 1, above; on the prices in particular, Still, *Mirror for Gotham* pp. 66 (at least $6–7 per week in 1797), 90f., and 100 ($18 for two rooms plus meals in 1817); but a bit less in the experience (1813) of young Halleck, cf. his full description in J. G. Wilson, *The Life and Letters of Fitz-Green Halleck* (New York 1869) pp. 132f.

6. On Broadway, see *New York Mirror and Ladies' Literary Gazette* October 18, 1823, p. 93; Foster, *New York by Gaslight*, chap. 1, and *New York in Slices*, chap. 1; Wilson, *New York* 325f.; Stokes, *Iconography*, Plates 81a and 85 with pp. 549 and 563f.; and Still, *Mirror for Gotham* pp. 57ff., 70, 80ff., 86f., 101, 115, 123. On mud in the streets encountered by Anna Fitch on her way to church, see **no. 103**, also *New-York Spectator* March 8, 1822 p. 2; and frequent remarks by travellers.
7. See Stokes, *Iconography*, pp. 976, 981–85: Park Theater and the Atlantic, Castle, Vauxhall, and Niblo's Gardens.
8. The original was most likely one of the lost paintings by John Vanderlyn, depicting the falls from various angles. They were the first of a high artistry to include Indians in the foreground. For Vanderlyn's studies, their inclusion of Indians, and their disappearance, see J. E. Adamson, *Niagara: Two Centuries of Changing Attitudes* (Washington D.C. 1985) pp. 25ff., Fig. 12 on p. 26, and p. 35; J. D. Hatch, "John Vander Lyn's prints of Niagara Falls," *Antiques* 138 (1990) pp. 1253ff. The subject was extremely popular, cf. for example the work by Robertson mentioned above, in chapter 2, with n. 27 on Vanderlyn.
9. A minor point: in this letter's postscript Eliza speaks to her uncle Way, so he is in New London while his wife is in New York; but in **no. 43**, he speaks of attending his wife on the New York visit; so the two must have returned home separately.
10. Omitted are mentions of her own and husband's ill health; Captain Pardon Tillinghast Taber's intended move with his family via New York to Fayetteville, N.C.–this, the Uncle Taber whose portrait Mary Way painted (**no. 96**); further, news of unexpected pregnancies in town, including Mrs. Oliver Champlain's, and the impending marriage of men of the Perkins family, of New London's High Society; finally, the death by scalding of Thomas and Dolly Way's little daughter Eliza, recorded also in the press and in F. M. Caulkins, *Manuscript Copy. Green Oblong No. 6 S. T. U. V.* (in the New London County Historical Society) p. 170.
11. Below, chapter 9 note 33.

Notes to Chapter 7

1. The watercolor on paper, with "Eliza" in pencil on the back, was later mounted in a case for a photograph. Hannah Way is shown reading a book, Jonathan M. Scott's *Blue Lights, A Poem in Four Cantos* (New York 1817). This dates the work to post-1817–probably a year or two later, as new publications took their time getting to New London. Above the sitter's head is written in pencil "Dear old Aunt Hannah" in a very elderly hand.
2. On these songs, see *Love's Young Dream* sung also in London, *The Albion* June 29, 1822 p. 16; its Drury-Lane popularity, the ultimate accolade; and on this and *Jesse the Flower of Dumblane* (written ca. 1817) and (in **no. 45**) *Kate Kearney* (of ca. 1807), see N. E. Tawa, *Sweet Songs for Gentle Americans* (Bowling Green 1980) pp. 200f., attesting to their particular popularity. The author of *Jessie*, Robert Tannahill, was specified as such for the selling of his subsequent songs, indicating the fame of this best from his pen, cf. *Ladies' Literary Cabinet* of December 9, 1820. It was to this tune that Samuel Woodworth set his poem "The [Oaken] Bucket." As to *Robin Adair*, it achieved the ultimate tribute of being taught, words and tune alike, to two Philadelphia nightingales, cf. *The Minerva* I p. 31 of May 4, 1822.

3. Mary's business card and **nos. 27** and **43** show her still on Chatham Street; and see below, note 4.

4. The poem "The Bucket," later with "Oaken" added to the title from the first line, appeared next under the author's name, *The Poetical Works of Samuel Woodworth* (New York 1831) 1 pp. 31f.; the surrebutter to "Agnes" is referred to in **no. 49**, below.

5. **No. 49** is undated, but, aside from looser chronological indications, her saying she "saw the fountain play for the last, last time this year" should be about the beginning of October, when the gardens generally closed. Cf. T. M. Garrett, "A History of Pleasure Gardens in New York City, 1700–1865" (Diss. New York University 1977) pp. 308, 343, 359, and 376. The Garden in question is best identified as the most famous, Vauxhall.

6. The so-called Congress Spring was in Saratoga Springs and it water was taken medicinally–certainly not for its good taste. It also served in the family as nickname for Hannah Way.

7. Here, as above in the report, "I dined with sister Fitch (by special invitation)," Mary adds a little to the picture of the constant visiting between her home and Anna's.

8. My thanks to Dr. Susan Forster, my friend and specialist, for a diagnosis of chronic acute-angle closure glaucoma (the patient being otherwise healthy, the disorder very painful and slow to do its work, and its onset asymmetrical).

9. On New York's asylums see D. Rothman, *The Discovery of the Asylum* (Boston 1971) pp. 158–65; S. Wilentz, *Chants Democratic* (New York 1984) p. 26; and especially R. A. Mohl, *Poverty in New York 1783–1825* (New York 1971) pp. 23ff., instancing the care of the blind *inter alia*, and 75ff. on the administration of almshouses, including the regime of Philip Arcularius as commissioner, "a tanner by trade and a local Republican leader," described in the *Evening Post* as "a man respected by no one, . . . hated by many, despised by most, ridiculed by all, . . . a Hessian sutler." Such were the politics and perceptions of the "assilum" to which Mary saw herself sentenced.

10. This **no. 50** was begun on December 3rd but delayed in the completion, cf. the postscript. Notice in it the reference to a letter by Mary that has not survived–one more reminder that the correspondence is not now complete, by any means; and note also the connection of the Titus family with the local church and (**no. 82**) with the merchant-firm of Walter Titus, John S. Avery, & Robert Weeks, which was also "Wixey" 's firm (so he was "Weeksie"?). The Avery's also were of the church (**no. 87**). The three men had their business together on Pearl Street from 1819 to 1827, dropping Weeks, and the remaining pair split up two years later. See *Longworth's Directory*.

11. On Charles Clinch (1797–1842) as a playwright, see **nos. 114**, **119**, and **123** and *The Minerva* of February 22, 1823, p. 367, announcing the imminent publication of *The Pilot* by the author of *The Spy*; also **186**, on Eliza's retouching of his portrait; and the entry in the *National Cyclopedia of American Biography* 22 (1932) p. 211.

12. The Military Reference Branch quotes F. B. Heitman's *Historical Register of the U. S. Army* (Washington D.C. 1903), to show Hayden starting as a lieutenant of infantry in 1812, discharged honorably as a captain the next year, reinstated in the artillery in 1815, later in ordnance (January 1, 1816), back to artillery in 1821, resigned 1822, and re-joined as Major Paymaster in 1824 till his death on June 10, 1826.

13. Obscurities in this letter, the undated **no. 56**: there is a Samuel Westcot(e) three generations up the family tree, but not known as a deacon; "sister Lydia" (**nos. 4** and **65**) must be the elderly Lydia Way, wife to the elder Ebenezer (1728–1813), a chatterer (above, chapter 2 note 1); Mary's saying "philosophy fails here" seems to be a recollection of the essay she had started to compose in **no. 43**; and the postscript seems to imply Eliza is already with Mary in New York–"Eliza, don't fail to tell Mary to take salts for her eye. It is the most soverign remydy on earth. Enforce it with all your power." But the explanation lies in the fact that Betsey received the letter first in New London and then, passing it on to Eliza at Eb. Way's, added the note on the outside as instruction for Eliza's next letter to Mary (Betsey's hand can be identified).

14. In the opening sentence of **no. 59**, Betsey reproaches Eliza for a long delay (prior to the date of the letter, July 22) in answering a certain request; so Eliza had by then been at least a month or two in New York–actually, since May (**no. 65**).

15. By error, Eliza calls the shop where she got ivory "Tyson's," but cf. "Tryon" in **no. 56** and *Longworth's Register* for 1819–20, "Tryon, Kimberly, combmaker 222 Greenwich."

16. **No. 60** of August 2, 1819. Capt. Lamphere (with *many* spellings of the family name by its various branches in Rhode Island, Massachusetts, and coastal Connecticut) was a friend of the Way-Champlain clan. Perhaps the man in question is Elisha Lanphear of Westerly, whose daughter in 1819 married Albertus Starr, grandson of that Jonathan (1673/4–1747) whose son and grandson are mentioned in chapter 3 note 7, above; but a better candidate may be Capt. James Lamphere (variously spelled) of the *Franklin* and other vessels whose movements between New London and New York are often noted in the *New London Gazette*, e.g. May 1, 1818, September 2, 1825, or March 1, 1826, and who with his son James over many years appears also in the *Transcript of WPA Records, Blunt White Library* of Mystic Seaport, s.v. Lamphear.

17. On the routine use of leeches as well as blistering, see J. Larkin, *The Reshaping of Everyday Life, 1790–1840* (New York 1988) 85–91.

18. This **no. 57** must pre-date Aunt Hannah's selling of her house to Eb. Way (which was news, but a settled fact, on November 24th, **no. 65**); but the reference to "settled in the country" fits with the emptying of New York in response to the outbreak of yellow fever in September (**no. 62**), and the reproach that Eliza "drop'd the correspondance" (here in **57**) fits with her confession of her "long silence" (**62**); so this **no. 57** must belong to about September 25th.

19. **No. 64**, of Oct. 25, 1819. The Frenchman M. Guille was the first on this side of the Atlantic to ascend in a balloon, which he did from Vauxhall Garden on October 19, with a second attempt a little later in the month in which somehow the machine got away from him, and drifted off empty, to a point twenty-two miles north of New London. See T. M. Garrett, "A History of Pleasure Gardens in New York City, 1700–1865" (Diss. New York University 1977) pp. 315ff. (with a third trip in 1820, p. 325); J. O. and J. C. Robertson, *All Our Yesterdays* (New York 1993) p. 89, on New Haven and Boston sightings of balloons in October 1819; F. M. Caulkins, *History of Norwich, Connecticut* (Hartford 1866) pp. 516f., on the Norwich newspapers reporting the first successful ascents in Paris in 1783. Guille in New York advertised his feat in advance, in the *Ladies' Literary Cabinet* vol. 1 (1819) pp. 56, 96, 104, and *National Advocate* August 3, 1819; and later he ascended often, e.g.

in Boston and Camden, as local sources report: *The Columbia* July 1, 1820 and *New York Evening Post* May 2, 1821; at Boston, *New York Daily Advertiser* September 7, 1821, and G. B. Barnhill, "Extracts from the Journals of Ethan A. Greenwood," *Proc. American Antiquarian Society* 103 (1993) 151.

20. The "certain stepmother" must be Eb.'s own, the not very well-spoken-of Lydia, cf. above, note 9.

21. She refers to the portrait of Jared Starr, cf. above, **no. 59**.

22. On portrait-making by machine, see E. Miles, "1803–the year of the physiognotrace," *Annual of the Dublin Seminar for New England Folklife* 19 (1994).

23. For Mary Way's portraits of "the Holt family" see **no. 16–17**; of Charles and Giles, chap. 2; proposal that Mary lodge with the family, **no. 21**; hospitality to the Ways in 1817, **no. 36**; strolls, too long for Eliza, **no. 93**; visits to Mary by Eliza, **no. 52**, whose name appears often elsewhere in this chapter. Dolly Holt (1791–1873) had married Thomas Way (1786–1836), Ebb.'s brother, and Charles Holt's grandmother was a Way (Sarah, 1716–75). See Kin-chart A. There were perhaps other ties with the Ways and Champlains.

24. "Aunt Parsons" will be the daughter of Samuel Taber (1723–1813), sister-in-law (**no. 329 K**) to Ebenezer Way Senior (1728–1813) who was Mary's and Betsey's father and mother-in-law to Aunt Sally. Aunt Parsons died in 1831 (**no. 297**).

25. Eliza Goddard of New London had sent Betsey a customer much earlier, pre-1812 (**no. 21**); so, a very old friend.

Notes to Chapter 8

1. M. B. Cowdrey, *American Academy of Fine Arts and American Art-Union* 1 (New York 1953) p. 30, notes that "the Board voted that the receipts for one day, Saturday, June 17, 1829 [!] 'be appropriated to the relief of Miss Way, an infirm and blind female artist,' and on that day the receipts amounted to $141.35, to which a further sum of $15 was also 'given by some benevolent person whose name is unknown.' " **No. 73** is the list of contributions according to size, eight of $5, etc.

2. **No. 72**, the copy with draft of reply, **no. 73**.

3. *Ladies' Literary Cabinet* New Series 2 pp. 72 and 80 (July 8 and 15 of 1820).

4. **No. 76**; and on Dr. North, see above, chapter 4 note 2.

5. These sentences can apply only to Cornelia Fitch, born January 28, 1817 (**no. 109**). The picture in **no. 85** of her and her mother leaves no room for a foster-child or anything else of the sort, and mention there of Mary's having asked for a description of Cornelia, with the phrase "our little favorite" in **87**, fit the present context; but it is certainly strange that Mary should ask about the *age* of a daughter born almost under her eyes, to her dearest friend.

6. The child's death on August 1, 1820 is recorded in the *New-York Evening Post*.

7. On February 12, 1813 (so says the *New-York Evening Post*) the Rev. Mr. Mitchell had presided over the marriage of John S. Avery, merchant, to Amelia Titus, both of New York: a close and natural connection.

8. There is no death in the family of the right date to explain this reference, which can only be the decisive news of Mary's blindness just described.

9. This debt, whatever it was, was never paid. It ended the friendship with Mrs. Dawson, and made relations awkward with her children Hannah and Thomas (**nos. 86**, **87** in the postscript, and **124**).

10. On *The Court of Death* of 1820 and its models, see D. Evans, *Benjamin West and His American Students* (Washington D.C. 1980) p. 184; H. von Erffa and A. Staley, *The Paintings of Benjamin West* (New Haven 1986) pp. 142ff.; Fitz-Green Halleck's poem of December, 1820, "The Great Moral Picture," in his *Poetical Works*, ed. J. G. Wilson (New York 1869) pp. 359ff., where the poet makes fun of the display as ineffectual though "aided by martial music once a week;" and the notice taken in *The Minerva* of July 12, 1823, pp. 109f., and July 19, 1823, the poem "On Peale's Picture of 'The Court of Death' " by J[ohn] D. G[odman]. I owe the identification of the poet (and my thanks) to E. H. Grayson, with further particulars about the painting in her dissertation of 1995 (George Washington University), "Art, Audiences and the Aesthetics of Social Order in Antebellum America: Rembrandt Peale's *Court of Death*."

11. A "Hinkley" (and so spelt in **no. 184**) submitted a painting to the Academy's exhibition of 1833, cf. Cowdrey (cit. above, note 1) 2 p. 187.

12. As I explain in my Transcription of **no. 89**, the first four pages of **no. 89** appear to be missing, and fifteen lines of the four pages that remain have been obliterated. Whoever wrote the numeral "5" on the first surviving page had the previous four before her; but it is not clear when the censoring was done or by whom.

Notes to Chapter 9

1. On his desire to write, see **no. 42** of July 13, 1818; on his literary tastes, see **no. 58**.

2. I depend on the resources of the Blunt White Library at Mystic Seaport, where in the catalogue s.v. "Verse" will be found dozens of entries of the 1770's–1820's out of Sag Harbor, Newburyport, New London and New York, from logs, journals, accounts, etc., e.g. the verses I quote from Isaiah Burdick's account-books of 1812–13, and the log of Henry Bowers of March 23-July 8, 1812, entering quotations at the bottom of the page from Mrs. [Amelia] Opie, Warren's *Ladies of Castile* (twice), Charlotte's *Letters*, [Robert] Blair's "[The] Grave" (1728), [Thomas] Campbell's "Pleasures of Hope" (1799), etc.

3. Yes, but what *is* the verse? It is not to be found in the *English Poetry Data Base*. Byronic but American?

4. Betsey quotes or refers to Edward Young in **nos. 35**, **42**, **43**, **55**, and **75**; refers to Pope (**55** and **59**) and Spenser (**182**); quotes Chesterfield's *Letters to His Son* of September 5, 1748, "women are only children of a larger growth" (in **76**), Cowper (**176**, the same eighteen lines quoted earlier by Mary in **40**) and *King Lear* 3.14.29 (**167**, the same line quoted by Mary, William, and Eliza); and from the Bible, Jn 16.24.1 (**176**), "St. Paul" (**178**), Ps 37.25.1f. (**188**), and Dan 6.12.4 (**121** and **178**, again a line that runs in the family).

5. In Susanna Rowson's *Miscellaneous Poems* (Boston 1804) pp. 105–15, compare the satirical-moral style with Betsey's "Flattery"-poem, especially in the use of conversation; also, Rowson's "Hymn to the Deity" of pp. 55–58 resembling Betsey's "The dew-bespangled

verdure . . . " in **no. 327**, and Rowson's "Affection" of pp. 79–81 resembling Betsey's "On Parting with Friends," ibid.

6. Mary quotes Job (16.2, in **no. 207**; 3.17, in **140**); Psalms (23, in **91**; 30.5 in **79**; and 37.25.1f., in **67**); Proverbs (4.23 in **85**); Ecclesiastes (3.2f., in **91**, and 7.1, in **271**); Isaiah (2.20.2, in **120**, and 48.22.1, in **92**); Jeremiah (9.4.2, in **271**; 10.23.1f., in **50**; and 23.1f., in **19**); Daniel (3ff., in **177**; 6.12.4, in **177**–"law of the Medes and Persians," favorite with Betsey and Eliza); Jonah (4.11, in **205**); Micah (7.4.2, in **271**); Matthew (7.25, in **79**; 12.34, in **232**; 15.27, in **91**; 20.1, in **40**; and 30.1, in **297**); Luke (10.42, in **180**, and 20.34, in **297**); John (3.1.74, in **180**; 16.33, in **271**); I Corinthians (8.1 and 15.1, in **205**); I Timothy 1.1.5, in **297**; Colossians (3.2, in **30**); I John (2.15.1, in **85**); and the Book of Common Prayer (in **144**).

7. *Hamlet* (1.2.133, in **43**; 1.5.16, in **21**; 2.5.4, in **132**; 3.1.58, in **155**; and 3.2.70, in **85**); *Macbeth* (1.5.25, in **188**; 1.7.60, in **120**; 5.3.40, in **177**; and 5.5.26, in **127**); *King John* (3.1.74, in **180**; 3.4.108, in **232**); *The Tempest* (4.1.151, in **50**); *Romeo and Juliet* (3.3.55, in **232**); *Troilus and Cressida* (1.2.255, in **21**); *Julius Caesar* (3.11.22, in **92**); *As You Like It* (2.1.10f., in **91**; 2.7.139, in **91**; 2.7.144, in **271**); *The Merchant of Venice* (2.7.139, in **21**; 3.3.4ff., in **21**); *Othello* (3.3.355, in **155**); *A Winter's Tale* (3.3.92, in **132**); 2 *Henry IV* 4.4.32, in **30**; and *King Lear* (3.4.107 and 108, in **188**; 3.14.29, in **43**; and 4.6.133, in **50**).

8. Passages from the first book of Young's "Night Thoughts" are quoted in **nos. 205** and **49**; Thomson's "Seasons: Winter" 5f., 15f., and 1078f., in **232**, "Spring" 1142ff., in **250**, and lines I can't identify in **188**; John Wilmot (1647–80), lines 40ff. of "A letter from Artemiza," in *The Poems of John Wilmot: Earl of Rochester*, ed. K. Walker (Oxford 1984), in **91**; John Gay's "The Painter who Pleased No body and Every body," lines 17ff., in **127**; Milton's "Paradise Lost" 3. 50, in **205**; Cowper's "Time-piece" 161ff., in **40**, cf. Betsey in **176**; Gray's "Elegy" 88, in **271**; Collins' "Ode to the Passions" in **188**; Byron's "Corsair" 1.225f. (published in Philadelphia in 1814), in **208**, which Eliza quotes in **165**, and "Bride of Abydos" 27, in **262**; "Byron," "The Enigma" 1ff., which I find in *The Works of Byron Complete in One Volume*[2] (Francfort o. M. 1829) p. 801, among the "Attributed Poems," in **208**; Isaac Watts' "To the Discontented and Unquiet" 60ff., in his *Horae Lyricae*[12] (1770) p. 222, in **181**; James Montgomery (1771–1854), of whose style Mary is reminded by the New York poetaster James G. Brooks, in **123** and the lines 95f. she remembers from his "The Wild Rose . . . " (1796); and Pope's "Essay on Man" 1.121, in **205**; 1.294, in **40** and **205**, which she calls her "motto"; 4.145, in **205**; 4.194, in **177**; "Essay on Criticism" 525, in **177**; "Eloise" 24, 261f., and 366f., in **205**; "Elegy to the Memory of an Unfortunate Lady" 6, in **85**; and "Letter to Dr. Arbuthnot" 132, in **271**. For the quoting of "Whatever is, is right," by Aunt Hannah, see **no. 53**; by Eliza, **nos. 53**, **62**, **100**, and **217**. Notice how it is dropped piously into a letter by the fifteen-year old Eliza Southgate in her letter to her "Honored Father" in 1797, a part of her moral education (in *A Girl's Life Eighty Years Ago* [New York 1887] p. 18).

9. Goldsmith's *She Stoops to Conquer* in **155**; Sheridan, in **287**; Congreve's *The Mourning Bride* 1.1 in **188** and **234**.

10. Sterne's *Sentimental Journey* (Chapter, "Nampont, The Dead Ass") in **56**, Scott's *The Pirate* in **123**, Cooper's *The Spy* in **123**, Bulwer-Lytton's *The Disowned* in **262**, the obscure *Recluse of Norway* of A. M. Porter (London 1814; Philadelphia 1815) in **123**, appearing in Paris in

the same year in the French translation of Mme de B[ons], and *Le solitaire* of C. V. Prévôt, Vicomte d'Arlincourt, translated as *The Recluse* by Miss Lascallas (**nos. 120** and **122**) for the *Ladies' Literary Cabinet* of January to April 1822, after the original had run through twelve Paris editions in its first year, 1821, and provoked 14 plays, three operas, etc., "vogue extraordinaire, colossale;" also ridiculed by Balzac in critical essays, e.g. "Effet du *Solitaire* sur les domestiques animaux," "Lu à l'invers, surprend le *Solitaire* les académiciens par des beautés supérieures." See A. Marquiset, *Le Vicomte d'Arlincourt, prince des romantiques* (Paris 1909) pp. 87, 100, 104f. Two English translations were published as books in 1822 in New York.

11. John Murray's *Life* in **no. 19**; *Gospel Herald* in **124**, **144**, and **147**; Voltaire, in **21**, no doubt in the 1761–1770 translation of his works, or of *Candide* alone (1761, 1771, etc.); in **132**, William Berrian, *Travels Through France and Italy in 1817 and 1818* (New York, 1821); Washington Irving, in **166**; DeQuincy's *Opium Eater* in **218** and **219**; and B. Le B. de Fontenelle's *Conversation on the Plurality of Worlds*, most likely the 1783 translation, in **107**.

12. On public libraries widely spread, see J. D. Hart, *The Popular Book. A History of America's Literary Taste* (Oxford 1950) pp. 67f. Besides the loan of a book just mentioned, from Anna Fitch to Mary (**no. 262**, cf. also **276**, **287**), others are mentioned: from Mary to Aunt Hannah (**19**), Eliza to William (**274**), and Edward Riley to Eliza (**212**, **215**, and **218**). A confirmation of the routine of book-supply lies in the continual packages sent to his sister in Guilford in the decade after he moved to New York (1813) by young Halleck, cf. his letters in J. G. Wilson, *The Life and Letters of Fitz-Greene Halleck* (New York 1869) pp. 143f., 161, 235, etc.

13. See the verse copied into **nos. 116** (including Moore's "Believe me, if all those endearing young charms . . . ") and **122** (including verse by James Brooks) and **143**; and serialized novels, easily found in New York periodicals, and eagerly awaited by Eliza and her friends in **122** (*The Recluse*, above, note 10).

14. **Nos. 120** and **122** (Lascallas); above, note 10; and references in **nos. 50** and **103** to Job Taber, praised for his "Progress of Society: a Poem" (published anonymously in New York, 1815 and 1817, Shaw-Shoemaker nos. 35715, 41891), and Oliver Waite. I find nothing on these two New Londoners, not even among C. W. Everest's forty-two *Poets of Connecticut* (Hartford 1844); but the third, Brainard (1790–1828), is better known. See reff. to him in **no. 289** and to his father and sister, ibid. and **131**, and J. G. Whittier, *The Literary Remains of John G. C. Brainard* (Hartford 1832), and Everest pp. 259–76. Born in New London, Brainard in the 1820s published in the Hartford *Mirror*, both from and about his native city: Whittier pp. 25, 66–70, 73–6, and 79–80.

15. On the bible, ordinarily specified as the New Testament and always read daily, see e.g. W. Burton, *The District School as it Was* (Boston 1897) pp. vii and 55, on Wilton, New Hampshire, schools ca. 1810; W. Ward, *The Early Schools of Naugatuck* (Naugatuck 1906) p. 71, on practices in 1802; C. Carroll, *Public Education in Rhode Island* (Providence 1918) pp. 62, 65, Providence's schools in 1800–04; O. B. Griffin, *The Evolution of the Connecticut State School System* (New York 1928) pp. 18f., on that state and the country generally; and W. Alcott, *Confessions of a School Master* (Andover 1839) p. 130, Massachusetts schools in the 1820s.

16. Caleb Bingham, *The American Preceptor*[4] (Boston 1797) includes snippets of Brooke, Pope, Gay, Cowper, Addison, and Moore; Alexander Thomas, *The Orator's Assistant* (Worcester 1797), includes bits of Shakespeare's *Julius Caesar*, I *Henry IV* 2.4.138ff., and *King John*, with Goldsmith's "Forgotten Village" and *She Stoops to Conquer*, Sterne's *Tristram Shandy*, and Watts' *Hymns* (p. 199, "Virtue that never loves to roam . . . "); Ward, *Early Schools* p. 71 also includes Watts, "Paradise Lost," and Young's "Night Thoughts"; and the anonymous *Essays on School Keeping* (Philadelphia 1831) recommends school libraries to have their copies of most of the English authors of this and the preceding note, along with Campbell, Montgomery, Thomson, Collins, and lesser names.

17. Murray's *Sequel to the English Reader* (1809; cited from the 4th ed. of New York, 1811) pp. 192ff. gives much poetry, all of Gray's "Ode on the Spring" and his "Elegy," some Milton, but Young most generously of all, including the line "An awful pause, . . . " p. 220. On the *Reader* itself and its popularity, with a great many subsequent editions up to the appearance of McGuffey's *Reader* in 1849, see Ward, *Early Schools* p. 74, C. Carpenter's *History of American Schoolbooks* (Philadelphia 1963) pp. 63ff., and J. A. Nietz, *Old Textbooks* (Pittsburgh 1961) pp. 66f.

18. William Scott's Reader, *Lessons in Elocution* (Hartford 1795), was more comprehensive, and must be intended under the mistaken title, "Scott's Beauties of Eminent Writers," which is one of the three texts named as the most popular by T. Dick; similarly comprehensive were the anonymous *Essays on School Keeping* and the practices of his own day that T. Dick reports in *On the Mental Illumination and Moral Improvement of Mankind* (Philadelphia 1836) pp. 47f. These authors represent the 1820s and 1830s.

19. Sam quotes "Believe me, if all those endearing young charms" (**no. 116**), plays with long words (**134**, with William's reply, **136**), and is thought by a friend to be an intelligent audience for a quotation from Addison (*Spectator* 68) and some French (**306**).

20. William quotes I *Henry IV* 4.2.38, in **no. 260**; *King Lear* 3.14.29, in **266**; *A Midsummer Night's Dream* 1.1.85f., in **175**; and *Macbeth* 5.3.40, in **185**; also several lines with small (reasonable) misquotations from William Falconer (1732–69).

21. George's fondness for Byron, in **no. 322**; quotes "The Corsair" 2.1.33f., in **24**; "English Bards and Scottish Reviewers" 1051f., in **249**; "Childe Harold" 3.282 and 1546, in **249**; and "Vision of Judgement" 114, in **247**.

22. George refers to Scott's *Castle Dangerous* and *Ivanhoe* (just published) in **66** and **78**; confesses to a lot of boyhood reading in light fiction as well as European history and a work on American (above, chapter 5 note 8), in **78**; quotes Gray's "Elegy" 17f. and 49f., in **102** and **160**, and Goldsmith's "Forgotten Village," in **66**; but from Shakespeare recalls *Hamlet* 1.2.140, in **242**; 3.1.62, in **246**; 3.1.79f., in **23** and **25**; *King Richard III* 4.4.196f., in **66**; *Macbeth* 3.1.71, in **246**; 5.3.6–14, in **41**; 5.3.40, in **185**; 5.5.24, in **242**; 5.7.1, in **244**; 5.8.30, in **249**; *Julius Caesar* 4.3.218, in **111** and **150**; *King John* 2.1.463, in **66**; I *Henry IV* 2.4.245f., in **44**; 3.1.52, in **241**; and *Romeo and Juliet* 3.1.106, in **37**.

23. Eliza quotes Lk 15.7.1, in **170**; Dan 6.12.4, in **237**; *Hamlet* 1.2.3, in **207**; 1.2.133, in **43** and **207**; 1.4.90, in **173**; 3.1.78, in **145** and **207**; 3.2.388, in **82**; 4.7.200, in **279**; 5.1.221, in **279**; *Macbeth* 1.7.60, in **279**; 5.3.40, in **174**; 5.8.34, in **279**; *King Lear* 3.14.29, in **97** and **137**; 4.6.133, in **43** and **50**; *Twelfth Night* 2.4.113f., in **279**; *Antony and Cleopatra* in **33**; 2.2.191, in **163**; and *King Richard III* 1.4.8f., in **218**. Pope's "Essay on Man" 1.294, is quoted by her

in **118**, **133**, **267**, and **286**; 4.203 and 247f., in **217**; *Imitations of Horace*, Sat. 1.2.127, in **171**; and "Elegy to the Memory of an Unfortunate Lady" 57, in **157**; Goldsmith's "Edwina and Angelina" 57, in **202**; Moore's *National Airs* in **168**; and Byron thrice, "The Corsair" 1.225f., in **163**, in **296** for a joke, and more generally for admiration in **50**. For Congreve, see **no. 234**; Porter's *Recluse* in **120**; and DeQuincy, in **217**f.

24. Milton's "Penseroso" in **294**; Blair's "Grave" 590, in **168**; Burns' "Green Grow the Rashes" 23f., where the poet sees the creation of Adam as mere practice for better work on Eve in **22**; Sterne, in her painting (below, at note 58); Cervantes, in **38**; and Mme de Staël's *Corinna or Italy*, doubtless in the English (New York) edition of 1808, in **212**.

25. **No. 218**, Felicia Dorothea Browne Hemans' poems published first in 1812; in **107**, *St. Clair* by Lady Morgan (1783–1859); Irving, in **163**, a work she knew her aunt loved; Scott, in **148**; and Cuthbertson in **45**.

26. Anna Fitch had Sheridan's *Critic* (**287**), Pope's "Essay on Man" (**87**), and *Werter and Charlotte. The Sorrows of Werter. A German Story to which is Annexed the Letters* . . . (Boston 1798), in **103**. On the type of this novel see Hart, *The Popular Book* pp. 61f. In the same letter, too, Anna counts her novels read in recent days, three and a fourth on the way, with Brown her favorite (**107**); lends Mary Bulwer-Lytton's *The Disowned*, in **262**; at other times, DeQuincy (**218**) and a recent play (**87**).

27. **Nos. 107** and **129** indicate Eliza's enjoyment; and for background, such works as R. R. Wilson, *New York: Old and New*[2] (Philadelphia 1903) 1 pp. 287f., and D. L. Clark, *Charles Brockden Brown* (Durham 1952) p. 113, repeating that Brown was the country's first professional author and discussing (pp. 137f.) his insistence that America could indeed supply its own writers (cf. quotations from the *Monthly Magazine* of 1799–1800).

28. On James G. Brooks (1801–41), see brief biographies in E. A. and G. L. Duyckinck, *Cyclopedia of American Literature* (Detroit 1875) 2 pp. 130f., and S. J. Kunitz and H. Haycraft, *American Authors 1600–1900* (New York 1938) p. 102; further, the elder Mrs. Henry Lee of New London on this poet, in **122**, and Eliza's comments in **122** and **168**.

29. William's jokes at the expense of the Gothic, in **no. 115**; Eliza's, **45**; and the *Connecticut Gazette* of September 26, 1798, "A romance is at present in the press in which there are thirty-six *ghosts*, two dozen *hobgoblins*, eighteen *witches*, . . . and one *probability*."

30. For Mary's essay, barely begun, see **no. 51**; for the account of the fever-struck George's vision of a trip to heaven, see **no. 169**. This little piece of fiction, unsigned, depicts George nearly on his deathbed visited by a certain "Edward," who writes up a report of the patient's delirious vision; but the hand is certainly not Edward Riley's, George's own, or William's, while being almost as certainly Sam's. Among the "dreams," see **nos. 130** (with **131**) and **165** (with **167**).

31. "One way to conceive of the influence of fiction is to recognize that people thought of their own lives as stories, following narrative lines like the ones they so frequently read. They intermingled literature and life. Diarists, letter writers, and memoir writers, in describing their expriences, lapsed into prose that seemed to be taken from books. They would sketch scenes that could easily have taken place in stories"–so, R. L. Bushman, *The Refinement of American Persons, Houses, Cities* (New York 1992) p. 288.

32. **No. 122** of May 15, 1822, Eliza quoted. Cf. *The Ladies' Literary Cabinet* of July 10, 1819, p. 72, replying to Anna in its columns, "*Agnes* is greeted with hearty welcome, & we only regret that a previous arrangement will keep her effusion from the public eye another week." She appeared in **nos. 49** (October 1818) and **122** (1822, her parody of "The Oaken Bucket"); also on September 11, 1819, April 19, 1820 (a piece of prose moralizing in *Rasselas*-fashion), and again in August of the same year; in *Albion & Ladies' Literary Gazette* of April 26 and June 7, 1826 and March 21, 1827; *United States Literary Gazette* of 1824 and 1828; *Atkinsons's Casket* of 1829, 1830, and 1835; and *Minerva* of June 22, 1822 and March 23, 1824, p. 408, "To Florio": "I listen'd, for methought the strain/ Was sweet as angel's minstrelsy. . . . "

33. Alexander M'Donald Clarke (1798–1842) appears above in chapter 6 at note 11, where his extreme eccentricity is emphasized; cf. a friend recalling that "something that was not quite insanity, but was nigh akin to it, marked his very boyhood" (N. F. Adkins, *Fitz-Greene Halleck* [New Haven 1930] p. 242). He may be here introduced through an advertisement in the *New-York Mirror, and Ladies' Literary Gazette* of October 25, 1823, p. 103: "soon to be published by M'Donald Clarke, a collection of poems, some satirical, . . . " testifying to his frequent appearance in the poetry columns of New York publications in the preceding years, e.g., *The Ladies Literary Cabinet* January 21, 1819, p. 119, "Lines written on the Battery," or ibid., New Series, vol. 2, p. 199 of October 28, 1820, a pseudonymous apostrophe "To M'Donald Clarke," beginning "Friend of my soul, I love thee well, . . . " answered by the apostrophized, p. 208 of November 4, 1820; more by him, vol. 3 p. 7 of November 11, 1820; then, p. 96 of January 27, 1821, "Mr. Ming of this city has issued proposals for publishing the works of M'Donald Clarke, subscriptions invited;" more poems, p. 143 of March 10, 1821; and so on. He appears to have begun his publishing career at the age of twenty, in the *Weekly Visitor & Ladies' Museum* for 1818 (and subsequent years to 1822), while also publishing verse in the *Ladies' Literary Cabinet* as above, and later in *The Minerva* of July 6, 1822 and July 13, *New York Mirror* (1823 and 1831), and Atkinson's Cabinet (1835). Eventually these pieces appeared as *The Elixir of Moonshine . . . by the Mad Poet* (Gotham 1822[1823]), as advertised, above; *The Gossip* (1823), promising in the subtitle "burlesques on Byron," with a second installment the next year; *Sketches* (1826, reprinted 1878); *Afara, a Poem* (1929); *Death in Disguise; a Temperance Poem* (1833); and *Poems* (1836, reprinted 1844). On his New York scenes, "Castle Garden" belongs to *Gossip No. II* pp. 5–7; "Broadway," to *Elixir* pp. 9–15; ibid, 39f., "To Lord Byron," and in *The Gossip*, pp. 34f., "Shakespeare" and "Sir Walter Scott." He addresses and is addressed by "Agnes," in *Elixir* pp. 40f., though it is not easy to picture Anna Fitch being much pleased by a love poem. On the other hand, the "Agnes" poem on pp. 70f., could well be hers. He also engages in an exchange with "Caroline," pp. 52–55 of December 1821, she being Caroline Matilda Thayer (below).

34. On Chavalier, see above, chapter 6, and *The Ladies' Literary Cabinet* of July 3, 1819, p. 63.

35. On Woodworth, see Duyckinck 1 pp. 764f.; chapter VI of H. B. Taft, "Samuel Woodworth," Diss. University of Chicago 1938, pp. 82 ff., 168; and the roster of his publications, including a second edition of his *Poems* in 1821, "Anniversary Poem delivered in New Haven for the Phi Beta Kappa Society" (1826), *The Rivals of Este* (1829, with his wife), and *Poetical Works* (1831).

36. See *The Ladies' Literary Cabinet* 3 p. 72, of January 1821, where Woodworth's "Harvest Home" was "written for inclusion in *Riley's Vocal Melodies*;" or again, *The New-York Mirror and Ladies' Literary Gazette* of August 23, 1823 (the periodical, edited by Woodworth at the time), advertising the sale of "Original poetry . . . ;'Love's Leger' set to music in Riley's *Vocal Melodies*, at No. 29 Chatham Street. Words by S. Woodworth;" and again, ibid. of October 4, 1823, announcing "that most of the lyric pieces which have appeared in this paper with the name of S. Woodworth have been published with music by E. Riley."

37. This poem, the more familiar title with "Oaken" added later, may be most conveniently seen in *American Poetry: The Nineteenth Century*, ed. J. Hollander (New York 1993) 1 p. 70. It appeared anonymously in *The Republican Chronicle* and *Weekly Visitor & Ladies' Museum* II pp. 172f., of July 11, 1818; next, under the author's (the editor's) name, in *The New-York Mirror and Ladies Literary Gazette* of October 4, 1823, p. 77, and in his *Poetical Works* of 1831, 1 pp. 31f. For a story on how it originated, see M. E. Phillips, *James Fenimore Cooper* (New York 1913) p. 94. Halleck's delineation of Woodworth can be found in J. G. Wilson, ed., *The Poetical Writings of Fitz-Greene Halleck* (New York 1869) p. 278, in 'To John Minshull, Esq.;" and the valedictory for the *Republican Chronicle* in Adkins, *Halleck* p. 58, in the poem of March 5, 1819, "To Mr. Simpson." On Woodworth's "benefits," see ibid. p. 26.

38. On Clarke's relation with Halleck "my poor friend McDonald Clarke," see Adkins, *Halleck* p. 243. Clarke died in an asylum in 1842.

39. Cf. Eliza and Mary on "Florio," especially his "Greece," in **nos. 122**f., **138**, and **168**; on Clarke, **166**, reference to "To a Female Artist" which, of March 15, 1822, was included in *The Elixir* pp. 89f.; general estimate in **168**; George Champlain's quoting of a line of Clarke in **150**; also, in *The Spectator* of January 1, 1822, p. 1, remarks in praise of "Florio," and excerpting of a poem of his from that periodical into the *Ladies Literary Cabinet* of June 8, 1822.

40. On the early days of this figure, see Adkins, *Halleck* pp. 24–39 and 45 (lyrics to Jessie), and Wilson, *The Life and Letters of Fitz-Greene Halleck* (New York 1869) pp. 64, 143ff., and 167; on the "Croaker" poems, Wilson, pp. 216–20, and Adkins, pp. 51f. and 78f.; on *Fanny* (1819), ibid. p. 126; on his "Address for the Opening of the New Theatre" of September 21, 1821, see ibid. p. 129, and J. G. Wilson, *The Poetical Writings of Fitz-Greene Halleck* (New York 1869) pp. 328f.; on his "Marco Bozzaris" recited in 1828, after its anonymous publication, Adkins, p. 165.

41. Drake died in 1820, cf. H. W. Boynton, *James Fenimore Cooper* (New York 1931) p. 108.

42. Connecticutters included Eliza, of course, but also her slightly older contemporary from New London, John G. Brainard, writing to his father in 1825 about his first sight of New York, "I came near seeing Mr. Halleck (Croaker as he call'd himself), the author of *Fanny*"–cf. the letter of February 20, 1825 in the New London County Historical Society.

43. On Clinch, see below, **no. 114**, Adkins, pp. 141ff., *The National Cyclopedia of American Biography* 22 (1932) p. 211, and especially E. R. Page, ed., *Metamora & Other Plays* (Princeton 1941) pp. 59ff., with brief biography and text of the play, which was onstage at the Park Theatre within ten weeks of the publication of the novel. In addition to *The Spy* he wrote "The First of May" for the Bowery theater (1830), the subject humorously treated in engravings and poems also–see above, chapter 4 note 17.

44. Wilson, *Life and Letters* p. 349.

45. Below, chapter 14 note 13.

46. Adkins, p. 151 (the date of Halleck's and Cooper's meeting controverted); M. E. Phillips, *James Fenimore Cooper* (New York 1913) pp. 89, Cooper's lodging and his consorting with Junius Brutus Booth and Irving as well as Halleck, and 94, his partnership with Woodworth and others in the early *Mirror*; and Wilson, *Life and Letters* 282, on the performance (at least the second, the first being May 17, 1819) of *Il Barbiere di Siviglia*.

47. See **no. 114** and Wilson, *Life and Letters* p. 228, on Halleck's abbreviated first name.

48. On the question of who wrote the *Waverley* novels, a matter continually ventilated in the *Ladies' Literary Cabinet* as elsewhere, see **nos. 148** (Eliza) and **213** (Anna).

49. In 1821 *Ladies' Literary Cabinet* of January 27, February 10 ("The hope of bliss in Heaven"), February 24, and March 3 ("The Evergreen. To Mrs. L . . . S . . . –Cherry-street"), Harriet Muzzy and Caroline Matilda Thayer contribute, and on February 24 issue under "Proposals" the project of a collection of Muzzy's past "poems moral and sentimental . . . collected and arranged by her friend," Thayer, the author being described as a deserving widow in poor health.

50. Mary Way was friends with Mrs. Clinch by 1818 (**no. 49**), evidently through her church, and brought Eliza in to the friendship (**114**, **119**). She later did his portrait and still later re-touched it (**186**); and Betsey did Clarke's in 1818 (**42**) and retouched it (**140**) in April of 1823.

51. Coleman of the *Evening Post* quoted in Wilson, *Life and Letters* p. 217. On the search for a native American literature, see for example R. B. Nye, *The Cultural Life of the New Nation 1776–1830* (New York 1960) chap. 11; ibid. p. 250 on the literacy rate; Isaiah Thomas' *History of Printing* (Barre 1810) II pp. 8f. on the number of newspapers, over 360 at the time he wrote.

52. The findings of this inventory of favorites among the correspondents, Shakespeare and scripture far in the lead, can be extended across the young nation: see L. W. Levine, *Highbrow/Lowbrow* (Cambridge 1988) pp. 16, 18; or compare Eliza's contemporary in *The Writings of Nancy M. Hyde, of Norwich, Conn.* (Norwich 1816), reading Blair, Collins, Crabbe, Shakespeare, Campbell, and the inevitable "Night Thoughts," plus Gibbon and a few biographies.

53. On these various connections, see above, notes 29–31 and 38, with Wilson, *Life and Letters* p. 352, for Halleck's anonymous edition of Byron, **nos. 29** and **42** (Byron, Clarke's favorite model), with Hart, *Popular Book* (cit. above, note 12) pp. 70ff., and W. E. Leonard, *Byron and Byronism in America* (New York 1905) passim, e.g. pp. 23, 29f. Byron was declared a favorite by George and Eliza, **nos. 50** and **247**; and Anna, Eliza, and a friend all painted miniature portraits of him (**19–21** and **27**). For Anna's portrait-pose, see **no. 133**.

54. Along with a couple of improving proverbs, Young's "Night-thoughts" 372ff., with "ray . . . day" wrongly for "rise . . . dawn," in the sampler, which survives in the editor's possession; the little girl, Lucinda MacMullen, grew up to marry Titian Ramsay Peale. For Woodworth, see the issue of August 23, 1823, p. 29; more broadly on Young's place, Hart, *Popular Book* p. 28.

55. On Pope, see W. Charvat, *Literary Publishing in America 1790–1850* (Philadelphia 1959) p. 32; A. M. Sibley, *Alexander Pope's Prestige in America* (New York 1949) pp. 3, 11, 23, 116

note 17, and passim, singling out "Whatever is . . . " and "A wit's a feather . . . " as most quoted, pp. 29 and 42.

56. For the place earned by these English authors, see Hart, *Popular Book* pp. 28, 59ff., 68ff., 72f., with Leonard, *Byron* p. 21, and any quantity of material in sales-lists, e.g. *The Spectator* of January 1, 1822, offering "the works of Campbell, Scott, Byron, Akenside, Cowper, Burns, Milton, Young, Thomson, Gray, Goldsmith . . . " as the first selection, or critical mentions in the popular press, e.g. *The Ladies' Literary Cabinet* of October 27, 1821, on *Lalla Rookh*. On the place earned by the American authors, see R. R. Wilson, *New York* pp. 287f., 290, and works by Hart, Charvat, and Leonard cited above.

57. See the critical mention in *The Republican Sentinel* of July 23, 1822, p. 3, specifying *Celadon and Amelia* of Thomson's "Spring," of which "a young lady, pupil of Alexander Robertson," also made a painting for exhibition in 1820, cf. M. B. Cowdrey, *American Academy of Fine Arts and American Art-Union* (New York 1953) 2 p. 305; **nos. 139**, **140**, and **142** for the New London paintings of the deranged, though it is not quite clear if Betsey or Eliza, or both, have done a *Crazy Jane*; and, for verse-analogies, **40** (Lockwood a Connecticut poet?), Whittier (cit. above, note 14) pp. 101f., and such efforts as "The lunatic lover" by "Harold" or "The maniac's grave" by "Horentius" in *The Ladies' Literary Cabinet* of June 15, 1822 and March 23, 1822.

58. The picture in the editor's possession is five and a half inches in diameter, water color on paper, the date to be guessed at only from the childish style, though the costume also indicates that year or so, a judgement I owe to the kindness of L. Thrift, Keeper of the American Portraits Catalogue in the National Portrait Gallery. The title on it, "Sterne's Maria," would hardly be needed by contemporaries, familiar as they would be with the extraordinarily popular depiction from which it is copied and simplified, by Angelica Kauffmann, with W. W. Ryland's print of 1778/9. See D. Alexander, "Kauffman and the print market in eighteenth century England," *Angelica Kaufman. A Continental Artist in Georgian England*, ed. W. W. Roworth (London 1992) p. 158 and Illus. 133, and M. F. Adams and M. Mauchline, "Kauffman's decorative work," ibid. pp. 128, 134f., and Fig. 107. For Inman's version, see J. Yarnell and W. H. Gerdts, *The National Museum of American Art's Index to American Art Exhibition Catalogues* 6 (Boston 1986) p. 1888; Victor Pelissier's opera of 1796 had the subtitle *The Vintage*. For depictions of "The Bucket," see R. F. Perkins and W. J. Gavin, *The Boston Athenaeum Art Exhibition Index* (Cambridge 1827–74) s.v. Woodworth, from 1835 on.

59. George Chalmer's *Life* of Mary came out in 1822 in Philadelphia, advertised in *The Spectator* of January 1, 1822; John Agg's *Mary of Scotland* some time previous to its mention in *The Minerva* of April 10, 1822, where it is noted for its "pondericity"; *The Money Diggers* in Cowdrey, *American Academy* 2 p. 292, matching the poem of 1827 written in New London, in Whittier pp. 66–8, cf. another painting by a young New York lady in 1827 also drawing from Washington Irving, Cowdrey p. 229. For other examples of literature inspiring art in examples from only the first decade of the Academy's exhibitions, see ibid. pp. 242 and 355 (Ossian, by Trumbull and an art student), 260 (James Miller's drama of 1809, *Mahomet*, drawn on by Samuel Morse), and 267 and 304 (Shakespeare and Spenser). Eliza too (**no. 182** of 1825) drew on Spenser for a depiction of nothing less than the Faery Queen herself. Beyond the Academy there is *A Scene from Lalla Rookh* by Mary Weston (1817–1894), cf. E. F. Ellet, *Women Artists in All Ages and Countries* (New York

1859) p. 342, or *King Lear in the Storm* by H. B. Bounetheau of ca. 1842, in R. Bolton-Smith, *Portrait Miniatures in the National Museum of American Art* (New York 1984) p. 22.

60. On this figure (1740s–1820), born in France, emigrating in 1792 to Philadelphia with his skills as a horn virtuoso, composer, and arranger, then to New York, a short return to Philadelphia, and back to New York, see E. E. Hipsher, *American Opera and Its Composers*[2] (New York 1978) p. 25; J. Mates, *America's Musical Stage. Two Hundred Years of Musical Theatre* (Westport 1985) p. 44; *The New Grove Dictionary of Opera*, ed. S. Sadie (New York 1992) 4 p. 933; G. Bordman, *American Musical Theatre. A Chronicle*[2] (New York 1992) p. 6; and especially S. L. Porter, *With an Air Debonair. Musical Theatre in America* 1785–1815 (Washington 1991) pp. 47, 380, 428, 489f., and passim. Notice Pelissier's collaboration with a Connecticut man, Elihu Hubbard, who did the libretto for the musical dramatization of a scene in Goldsmith's "Forgotten Village," under the title *Edwin and Angelina*, which has been called "the first opera" wholly made in America (Hipsher loc. cit.); also, an opera based on M. G. Lewis' *The Monk* (Porter p. 433, of 1798), another by Pelissier of 1800 based on Horace Walpole's *Castle of Otranto* (ibid. 438), a third based on Scott's long poem of 1808, "Marmion" (ibid. p. 470), with Wm. Dunlap the librettist, music by John Bray, and so forth.

61. The quotation is from Henry B. Fearon's *Sketches of America* of 1817, conveniently in B. Still, *Mirror for Gotham. New York as Seen By Contemporaries* (New York 1956) p. 102; on theaters and gardens, further, ibid. 60f.; V. B. Lawrence, *Strong on Music* 1: *Resonances 1836–1850* (New York 1988) pp. xxxif. and Index s.v. "Pleasure Gardens"; I. N. P. Stokes, *The Iconography of Manhattan Island* vol. 3 (New York 1918) pp. 976–85; and especially T. M. Garrett, "A History of Pleasure Gardens in New York City, 1700–1865" (Diss. New York University 1977) pp. 279, 284ff., 44off., and passim. In the correspondence, gardens figure especially in **nos. 43**, **49**, **98**, and **294**.

Notes to Chapter 10

1. An explanation for the very odd first name of the boy lies in either the "tragedy" by H. Brooke (New York, 1810 and 1824) or the "rhetorical opera" by W. Dimond (New York 1812), both titled *Gustavus Vasa*. As to the term for Hayden's friend, see the same colloquialism in **no. 114**, "friend and pitcher" = pal.

2. Spelt in different ways by the correspondents (e.g., below, in **no. 96**), and pieces of it protecting some ivory miniatures that have come down to the editor, this substance is mica (perhaps from Isinglass Mountain in New Hampshire); but (**no. 221**, below in chapter 14) Eliza also uses the word in the sense of gelatin, familiar under the same name in England.

3. See chapter 2 note 21.

4. John Barnes "literally 'did' Richard III" at his farewell performance before he left for England, as G. C. Odell puts it, in his *Annals of the New York Stage* 3 (New York 1928) p. 24, with more, pp. 137 and 433, on Barnes' "irresistible drollery," "possibly the most popular of comic geniuses." "*Richard III*, the most popular Shakespeare play in the nineteenth century, was lampooned frequently"–so, L. W. Levine, *Highbrow/Lowbrow* (Cambridge 1988) p. 14.

5. Ms. Mona Dearborn kindly identifies Augustus Burr as the painter of a miniature of ca. 1815 at the Edison Institute in the Ford Museum (Dearborn, Michigan), subject also of a note by A. Winchester in *Antiques* 40 (1941) p. 375, "The elusive Mr. Burr," on two miniatures of ca. 1825. Another with the artist's signature has recently surfaced in private hands.

6. The indication here that the portrait of the boy Walter Avery was easily portable but not a miniature in the ordinary sense of the time suggests something like the surviving portrait of Aunt Hannah, i.e. on paper and ca. 3 × 4 inches. Mary's portrait of Taber "hose and all" may have been of a like size? Cf. above, **no. 96**, and chapter 2 note 19.

7. The two quotations are from **nos. 20** and **21**, with further reference to **27**, Mary promising "to furnish you with beauxs as smart as any you leave behind," "you inquire about Giggins," etc., while Eliza indeed "inquires," e.g. toward the end of **nos. 43** and **48**. Betsey's view is quoted from **no. 42**, to be set against her flirting with the young Clarke toward the middle and end of the same letter, and Eliza's depiction of her as a flirtatious widow, in **no. 142**. Eliza's remark (**93**) that "single blessedness" is the wiser choice for Mary Ann Mason may apply only to the case at hand. For context and comparable views of marriage vs. old-maidism in Betsey's generation up to the 1830s, see C. N. Davidson, *Revolution and the Word* (New York 1986) pp. 113–23, while close parallels can be drawn to Eliza Champlain's views from those of Eliza Southgate (1783–1809). See *A Girl's Life Eighty Years Ago* (New York 1887) pp. 37f., and 51ff., 90, 102: at age fourteen she offers precocious opinions on women's roles and nature and doubts about marrying at all, sandwiched in among eager comments on beaux; and she marries gloriously, still a teenager. In her social class (below, chapter 12 note 25) and in her quite empty head she differs, however, from Eliza of this correspondence.

8. **No. 86**, with Mary's comment (**92**), "there is no doublet and hose in your disposition."

9. *The Vindication* was first published in 1792, but received especial attention after the author's husband in 1798 included in his account of her life much that shocked common opinion. Her philosophical rebellion, however, had been a limited one. For her scorn and disapproval of persons beneath her socially, see such remarks as she offers in J. M. Todd and M. Butler, *The Works of Mary Wollstonecraft* (New York 1989) 5 pp. 9, 23, 26, 57, 74, 130, and 211, in her *Thoughts on the Education of Daughters*, *Vindication of the Rights of Man* and *of Women*–inviting Dr. Johnson's remark about another female revolutionary (July 21, 1763), "your levellers wish to level *down* as far as themselves; but they cannot bear levelling *up* to themselves."

10. See above, chapter 9 note 40, regarding the competition for the honor of delivering an address at the opening of the rebuilt Park Theatre.

11. The man duly appears in the Directory, on Wall Street, "merchant tailor."

12. Leader of the second generation of Universalism, in some sense rival to John Murray, and based in Boston. See above, chapter 1 note 12 and chapter 3 note 2.

13. *Longworth's American Almanac, New-York Register, and City-Directory* for 1819–20 lists "Holt & Quinby flour merchants 229 Front St.," the same address to which Sam's mail is sent (**no. 105**).

14. Referred to by the first three of these names in **nos. 114** and **116**. Eliza's terminology is uncertain because the instrument was like Ben Franklin's invention, which did have several names. See G. Chase, *America's Music from the Pilgrims to the Present*[3] (Urbana 1987) 78ff.; but the fourth name is the right one, used in the *Diary of a Country Parson*. See the interesting description of it in S. Sadie, ed., *The New Grove Dictionary of Musical Instruments* (New York 1992) p. 454.

15. Parisen's portrait (see above, chapter 2 note 11) is signed and dated.

16. I find the advertisement in the *Republican Sentinel* of April 27, 1822 (but dated March 16), vol. I No. 108 fourth page, and May 4, 14, and 21, and June 1, 1822.

17. In *Longworth's*, "J. Slocomb teacher" appears at this date on Church Street.

18. On *The Spy*, see above, chapter 9 note 43. James Fenimore Cooper's name was not familar at this time, his first novel (*Precaution*) having only appeared in 1820 to no great stir, *The Spy* being new in 1821, and Cooper himself moved to New York in 1822.

19. Quoted in J. D. Hart, *The Popular Book. A History of American Taste* (Oxford 1950) p. 65.

20. On the perception of Freemasonry in the 1820s, see L. Benson, *The Concept of Jacksonian Democracy* (New York 1961) pp. 18ff., 24ff., e.g (p. 25), "Admittance to Masonic lodges apparently represented a distinction 'successful' Americans acquired to signify their passage to a higher social status," or the anonymous letter to a newspaper recounting how "the *newly initiated* among my neighbors soon became somewhat haughty in their manner." New London's first clearly attested Lodge dated back only to 1795, headed by William Judd and names like Perkins, Richards, Law and Lee, into the 1820s. See D. H. Hurd, *History of New London County, Connecticut* (Philadelphia 1882) p. 210.

21. In *Longworth's* directory for 1822–23 Francis Gross appears at this address.

22. On John Agg, see above, chapter 9 note 59. His publication of poetry began in London in 1813, to 1815, then Philadelphia, 1816–19, including two poems he alleged were Byron's; but Byron irritatedly denied them, cf. *The Works of Lord Byron* (New York 1836–37) 1 p. 836, of December 9, 1816. On the play *Lochiel*, a modest success, see G. C. D. Odell, *Annals of the New York Stage* 3 (New York 1928) p. 24.

23. Mary Way here refers to the Lascallas translation of *The Recluse* (above, chapter 9 note 10), and its praises sung by Eliza in **no. 122** of May 15th–so this part of her letter postdates that in turn and the "May 16th" that heads the page it is written on. Such are the confusions of these discontinuous Way letters.

24. It is clear from C. W. Drepperd, *American Drawing Books* (New York 1946) p. 6, that drawing books for students which showed flowers began in America with one of 1818 (Philadelphia, anonymous–it may be identified as John Hill's *A Series of Progressive Lessons intended to Elucidate the Art of Flower Painting*, cf. R. J. Koke, *A Checklist of the American Engravings of John Hill* [New York 1961] pp. 4, 10ff., and 26); but G. Brown's *A New Treatise on Flower Painting, or, Every Lady her own Drawing Master*, was already in its third edition in London by 1799–1803, and in its three sections are some hand-colored flowers (native to England) exactly in the technique of Eliza's. The author may be the "G. B. Brown" exhibiting in New York at least by 1816, to 1825, cf. M. B. Cowdrey, *American Academy of Fine Arts and American Art-Union, Exhibition Record 1816–1852* (New York 1953) 2 p. 45. Harriet Beecher Stowe's mother in East Hampton in 1805 was teaching flower-painting,

some from nature, cf. *The Autobiography of Lyman Beecher*, ed. B. M. Cross (Cambridge 1961) 1 p. 98; and flower-painting was advertised in a Boston school of 1819, *Columbian Centinel* of September 15, 1819, and in New York the next year, *The Ladies' Literary Cabinet* of April 1, 1820, specifying "from natural specimens." We see the Norwich teenager Nancy M. Hyde in 1809 "engaged in painting flowers" at her school, as her journal reads, in her *Writings* (Norwich 1816) p. 79; and work of the same sort is represented from the 1820s in T. and N. Sizer's *To Ornament Their Minds: Sarah Pierce's Litchfield Female Academy 1792–1833* (Litchfield 1993) pp. 95f. In the surviving score of her flower paintings Eliza shows then-common Connecticut varieties: Sweet William, Catchfly, heliotrope, Johnny jump-ups, etc., as kindly identified for me by M. Inman and S. M. Douglas of the Conn. Agricultural Station.

25. See above, chapter 9 note 10.

26. Francis Guy appears as an exhibitor at the Academy in 1822, cf. Cowdrey, *American Academy* 2 p. 163; but he had died in August of 1820. See G. C. Groce and D. H. Wallace, *The New-York Historical Society's Dictionary of Artists in America 1564–1860* (New Haven 1957) pp. 280f.

Notes to Chapter 11

1. Between mid-1818 and the turn of 1820, Betsey sent her verses to New York (**nos. 41**f., **42**, **54**f., **59**, **61**, **63**, and **67**), with one more piece in 1825, **no. 178**, and a variety composed and collected at an uncertain date, **327** which in part repeats poems separately sent; and from the collection she copied a selection for Ebb. Total, just over a thousand lines, most of them omitted from this book. A line of her poetry, quoted from **327**, "Eliza in Answer" (line 19), indicates her pleasure in playing. Her attachment to the guitar (Mary's) and flageolet appears early (**no. 43**, cf. **44**, **45**, **59**, **60**, **61**, and **107**) and lasts her life. She is continually plaguing Eliza to buy guitar strings in New York. For the harp and whistle, see **nos. 132–3**, and English octave flute, **125**, **130**, **131**, **132**, **139**, and **144**; Eliza's boast, **217**; the Whistlers, **178** and **217**; Ebb and Miss Stammers, **217**; and William's friends, **115**. The same social accomplishment was valued in their circle in New York: **nos. 93**, **97**, **98**, **124**, etc.
2. From Christopher Prince's *Autobiography* p. 111 (above, chapter 1 note 11).
3. Quoted from the *Minerviad* of March 30, 1822 by N. E. Tawa, "The performance of parlor songs in America, 1790–1860," *Anuario interamericano de investigacion musical* 11 (1975) p. 71.
4. To illustrate the pervasiveness of home music, notice the Philadelphia female miniaturist who with her guitar and singing entertained Charles Willson Peale, cf. his *Autobiography* in H. W. Sellers' transcription, p. 100; himself with friends in a spur-of-the-moment song-party in the Museum, ibid. p. 150, date in the 1780s; the Rev. Lyman Beecher "a fine singer and player on the violin," in S. Seabury, *Two Hundred and Seventy-Five Years of East Hampton* (East Hampton 1926) p. 75; admiration for a fine flute amateur, in *The Letters of James Kirke Paulding*, ed. R. A. Aderman (Madison 1962) pp. 20, 22; a range of further valuable illustrative anecdotes or scenes from various states and cities, 1785–1835, in N. E. Tawa, *Sweet Songs for Gentle Americans* (New York 1980) pp. 20–29; C. Moseley, "Music in a nineteenth century parlor," *Princeton Library Chronicle* 41 (1980) 233f.; J. Larkin,

The Reshaping of Everyday Life, 1790–1840 (New York 1988) pp. 237ff.; D. T. Deutsch, "The polite lady: American schoolgirls," *Antiques* 135 (1989) p.746, "it was the rare school that did not offer the study of . . . music" by 1820, and musical accomplishments considered essential in young ladies, pp. 747f.

5. On George Whitefield Champlain's dancing, see above, **no. 57**; on Aunt Champlain and Betsey, **nos. 43** and **47**; and on the prevalence of dancing generally, Larkin pp. 239ff.–an early show of it in New London at a ball in the Shaw house, cf. F. M. Caulkins, *History of Norwich, Connecticut* (Hartford 1866) p. 332 (1769, the date of Mary's birth).

6. See Dunlap's *Diary* p. 586. For background and Peale, see chapter 8 note 10; further, on Earl, E. M. Kornhauser and C. S. Schloss, "Painting and other pictorial arts," *The Great River: Art and Society in the Connecticut Valley*, eds. G. W. R. Ward and W. N. Hosley (Hartford 1985) p. 140; on William Dunlap (1766–1839), W. H. Gerdts and M. Thistlethwaite, *Grand Illusions. History Painting in America* (Fort Worth 1988) pp. 77f.; J. L. Yarnell and W. H. Gerdts, *The National Museum of American Art's Index to American Art Exhibition Catalogues* (Boston 1986) p. 1107; O. S. Coad, *William Dunlap* (New York 1962) pp. 101–11; and, adding little, R. H. Canary, *William Dunlap* (New York 1970) pp. 32f.

7. G. C. Groce and D. H. Wallace, *The New-York Historical Society's Dictionary of Artists in America 1564–1860* (New Haven 1957) p. 10, Betsey's letter giving the age of Andrews and confirming the guess that he is the "Andrus" of Stockbridge, 1801–ca. 1859. Further on this artist, D. Bolger, "Ambrose Andrews and his masterpiece, *The Children of Nathan Starr*," *American Art Journal* 22, 1 (1990) pp. 5ff.

8. Sir Martin Archer Shee (1769–1850), portrait painter, president of the Royal Academy (1830–), writes the second of his versified handbooks (London, 1805).

9. Among the reports, see Peter Neilson quoted in B. Still, *Mirror for Gotham. New York as Seen by Contemporaries* (New York 1956) pp. 103f.; G. B. Barnhill, " 'Extracts from the Journals of Ethan A. Greenwood'," *Proc. American Antiquarian Soc.* 103 (1993) p. 157; the onset noted by the Board of Health, *Republican Sentinel* of August 6, 1822, cf. September 7, 1822, etc.; suspension of daily activities, e.g. *The Minerva* of September 14, 1822, p. 183, or J. W. Francis, *Old New York* (New York 1958) pp. 240f.; *The Albion* of October 5, 1822 seeing the end of the epidemic but asking citizens not to return till the first frost; and summary accounts of recurrent epidemics in Still, loc. cit., and I. N. P. Stokes, *The Iconography of Manhattan Island, 1498–1909* vol. 1 (New York 1915) p. 635.

10. The death referred to is that of Dr. Nathaniel Allen, cf. F. M. Stoddard, *A Genealogical History of the Allen Family* (Boston 1891) p. 113. He was grandson to Pardon Taber (1712–1803), who was grandfather also to Mary and Betsey (Kin-chart B).

11. On the lovely big country house of the Drake family, see **nos. 62** and **131**.

12. On New Orleans' epidemic this year, see above, chapter 5 note 5.

13. On the Waldo-Jewett partnership, see William Dunlap's *History of the Rise and Progress of the Arts of Design*[2] (Boston 1918) 2 p. 358.

14. Betsey's lodging is indicated in **no. 34** of January 1818 (with Mrs. Bryant, then a stranger to her, later a friend); **42** of mid-1818; **75** of mid-1820, a rental for a year; etc. The Thatchers appear in **nos. 78**, **137**, **161**, **248**, and **327**: they are Anthony (1782–1844), a cashier of the New London Bank for 35 years, married by Rev. Charles Seabury to

Lucretia Christophers Mumford; his daughter Lucretia; also Daniel Thatcher (1767–1836) married to a Starr and sharing a grandfather Josiah with Anthony. See J. R. Totten, *Thacher-Thatcher* Genealogy (Boston 1910) pp. 323, 437, 445.

15. This Fig. 5 was begun seriously but never used. The bottom was cut off irregularly and the title and text done only in pencil, reading, "Harp of the North," and, in verse, "O minstrel Harp, still must thine accents sleep?/ Mid rustling leaves and fountains' murmurings,/ Still must thy sweeter sounds this silence keep,/ Nor bid a warrior smile, nor teach a maid to weep? Scott/'Lady of the Lake' " (Canto I, [preface] lines 6–9, published in Philadelphia in 1810, in New York by 1813). Eliza has reinforced the lines from behind in the manner used on ivory, see above, chapter 2 note 19.

16. Charles Matthews "celebrated" indeed: he arrived in the U.S. on his way to Baltimore in September (Francis, loc. cit. at n.9) and was being widely advertised in New York by the fall, e.g. in the *Republican Sentinel* of November 2, 1822, first appearing on February 24th of the next year. See e.g. F. C. Wemyss, *Twenty-six Years of the Life of an Actor and Manager* (New York 1847) pp. 82ff., or W. B. Wood, *Personal Recollections of the Stage* (Philadelphia 1854) pp. 282f.

17. See above, chapter 4 note 19.

18. Mrs. Maria Townshend had belonged to Spring's congregation until, through her evolving ideas of her faith which she communicated to the presbytery by a letter of January 3, 1822, she was excommunicated, and then found refuge with the Universalists; whereupon, on April 18th of 1823, Mitchell read to *his* congregation the documents in the case, including his own letter of protest to Spring on her behalf; and this most modest, pacific, and eloquent letter was added to make up his *Excommunication of Mrs. Maria Townshend* published by the *Gospel-Herald* offices in 1823 (I know only the second edition, of the same year). Spring, ordained in 1810, began his career of churchly publication in 1817 and produced thereafter many titles; but in the 641 pages of the *Personal Reminiscences of the Life and Times of Gardiner Spring* (New York 1866) he makes no mention of this encounter of 1822–23.

19. Asa Spencer writes to George Whitefield Champlain in 1819 (**no. 58**, quoted in chapters 1 and 9)–a jeweler on Bank Street (*New London Gazette* of May 29, 1805, etc.), an amusing man, intimate friend, father-in-law incidentally to Courtlandt Starr and so of the circle.

20. Ebenezer Way (1784–1849) served as an ensign of the Third Regiment in 1779, and was commissioned a lieutenant in the infantry in 1809, served with Gen. Hull until the latter's disgraceful surrender at Detroit, continued service as a captain in the Fourth Regiment with Harrison at Tippecanoe, and was assigned later to the garrison in Maine. See on the last assignment, **no. 14**; on Hull, S. Perkins, *History of Political and Military Events Between the U. S. and Great Britain* (New Haven 1825) pp. 81–91; and on other details, F. M. Caulkins, *Manuscript Copy: Green Oblong No. 6, S. T. U. V.* (n.d.) in the New London County Historical Society, p. 169, probably drawing on his obituary in the *New London Democrat* of February 3, 1849.

21. **No. 146** of August 18th, 1823, nine and a half by thirteen and a half inches, surviving in the editor's hands. On the extraordinary prevalence of fires, see rich descriptions in Still, *Mirror* pp. 97, 107f., of the 1820s and 1830s; G. G. Foster, *Celio* (New York 1850) p. 9,

and *New York in Slices* (New York 1849) pp. 48ff.; R. R. Wilson, *New York: Old and New*[2] (Philadelphia 1903) 345f.; and Stokes, *Iconography* p. 849.

22. On "Neutral-Tint" see below, chapter 12 note 41.

23. Toothbrushes were a rather new article, but for sale by 1820, see Larkin, *Reshaping* p. 92.

24. Jeremiah Halsey Goddard, son of Hezekiah (son of Calvin) and Phebe Halsey Goddard, was a ship-captain, enamored of Eliza (**no. 174**); but in 1824 he at last married someone else (**no. 154**). George quotes and asks after him, Oliver leaves a bequest to one of the family, another (mother?–Eliza Goddard) got Betsey some customers and lent her money (**21** and **67**). Halsey's sister Paulina is the "Paulinia" of **nos. 155** and **157**, below; and another sister? or cousin is the Mary Goddard related to Calvin Goddard, below (chapter 12 note 45).

Notes to Chapter 12

1. F. M. Caulkins, *History of New London, Connecticut* (New London 1895) pp. 656ff., surveys the newspapers, the main one, the *New London Gazette*, published throughout Mary's and Betsey's lifetime and beyond, but *The Bee* only from 1797 to 1802; on the *Gazette*'s marine list, above, chapter 1 at note 8; on the town's principal newsheet, "Green's paper," see **no. 142** and the ads by the firm in question, e.g., *Connecticut Gazette* of March 7, 1798, "New publications, to be sold by Thos. C. Green." The paper as the *New London Gazette* had been started by his ancestor Col. Timothy Green in 1763.

2. For these various offices, municipal and private, see the *Connecticut Gazette* of e.g. July 11, 1798 (and often), "2d P.M." = second postmaster; Caulkins, *History* pp. 619–67 passim; eadem, *Manuscript Copy: Town Offices, New London* (n.d., in the New London Country Historical Society); "Sea-drift from a New England Port," *Harper's Magazine* 60 (1879) p. 60, Sheriff Hempstead. On the banks, see R. O. Decker, *The Whaling City* (Chester 1976) pp. 95ff.; ibid. 264, 381, on schools, and, on court officers, idem, *The New London Merchants* (New York 1986) pp. 113f. On the population, see *Historical Statistics of the U.S., Colonial Times to 1970* (Washington 1975) pp. 12, 25; R. J. Purcell, *Connecticut in Transition 1775–1818* (Washington D.C. 1918) p. 151; and D. Hurd, *History of New London County, Connecticut* (Philadelphia 1882) p. 135.

3. On Ebb's line, far back, see the *New England Historical and Genealogical Register* 13 (1859) p. 235, the 1675 Uncas-bequest shared with John Allyn and others; on Ebb himself, Caulkins, *Manuscript Copy: Green Oblong No. 6: S. T. U. V. W.* (n.d.) pp. 165ff.; eadem, *History* p. 667, and Ebb's obituary of February 3, 1849 in the *New London Democrat*; on his wealth, notice close to eight thousand dollars in his estate in 1849, counting two houses on Main Street, a couple of dozen wine glasses and bottles of Madeira, not to mention two dining tables, mahogany chairs, five dozen bottles of claret, and other items in his estate expressive of a relatively rich household.

4. **No. 19** (Mary), "above all things keep in with your relations whatever you do;" **159**, "your brother George O. cannot engage in any [business] other than an honorable one;" and **187**, "there never was a Champlain or a Way that ever sold himself or forfeited his honour or ever will" (Sam).

5. For fears of mail being opened, see e.g. **nos. 142** and **147**, and J. D. and R. Buel, *The Way of Duty. A Woman and her Family in Revolutionary America* (New York 1984) p. 93, a woman writing, "I don't know how it is at Fairfield [Connecticut], but here [in New Haven] they take the freedom to open every letter that comes by the post, in search of news." On the town position of a postmaster, see below, chapter 16.

6. On the Starr line, aside from Kin-charts A and B, see Hurd, *History* pp. 158f. and 219, and B. P. Starr, *A History of the Starr Family* (Hartford 1879) pp. 14f. The ads for the Starr store, Jonathan and his brother Jared (later, the latter alone, or the former alone), appear regularly, e.g. *Connecticut Gazette* August 1, 1798, stationery, spices, etc., May 29, 1805, textiles, April 6, 1808, textiles again, May 5, 1808, lumber and bricks; location of the store on Bank Street between Lamphere and Tilley lots, in Caulkins, *Manuscript Copy: Harris, Chapman*, etc.; two Starrs on the health board, *Connecticut Gazette* of October 3, 1798; Jonathan on the board of the Union Bank, with Elias Perkins and Guy Richards, June 12, 1799, and himself alone as chairman of the New London and Lyme Turnpike Co., May 11, 1808. See also R. A. Hallam, *Annals of St. James's Church, New London* (Hartford 1873) p. 66, and Caulkins, *History* p. 592, where Jonathan as warden with a Saltonstall dedicates the new church in 1787, the old one having been burnt in 1781. On Jonathan Starr as selectman, see Caulkins, *Town Offices* for 1788–89. His portrait (Fig. 6) and that of his wife to be, Anna Morgan, are in the collection of the Wadsworth Athenaeum in Hartford, and are best dated to about 1822. Both might be by Betsey but are of a quality inferior to her two certain if unfinished works. Besides, it is very hard to imagine that she would never have referred to them at any point in the surviving letters if in fact she had had such prominent sitters.

7. On this artist, see E. M. Kornhauser, " 'Ralph Earl as an itinerant artist," *Itinerancy in New England and New York* (Boston 1986) pp. 172ff.; C. Heslip and H. Kellogg, "The Beardsley limner identified as Sarah Perkins," *Antiques* 126 (1984) p. 556

8. On the whaling company of Perkins, Shaw, and Smith, see Decker, *The Whaling City* pp. 76, 80; Perkins' leadership in the city's second bank, p. 97, with Hurd, *History* p. 219 (Anthony Thatcher the cashier, 1807–33); judicial career (1810 to his death) and political offices (1795–1832), Decker p. 161; on the son's career, Caulkins, *History* p. 662.

9. On the Lafayette reception (with a quotation on the Perkins house from the *New London Gazette*), see J. Foster's *Sketch of the Tour of General Lafayette* (Portland 1824) p. 82, E. E. Brandon's *Lafayette. Guest of the Nation* 1 (Oxford [Ohio] 1950) pp. 78–80, and E. E. Rogers, *Connecticut's Naval Office at New London* (New London 1933) pp. 135, 138; and friendship of Nathaniel Shaw Jr. (brother of Polly whose daughter married Elias Perkins) with Ebenezer Way implied by the circumstances of Shaw's death, ibid. p. 329.

10. On Bishop Seabury (1728–1796) and his sons Charles (1770–1845) and Samuel (1767–95), see Caulkins, *History* pp. 443f., 593, 670; eadem, *Manuscript Copy. Oblong No. 5. P. Q. R. S.* p. 103; Hallam, *Annals* pp. 66f.; Hurd, *History* p. 200; and the bishop's *Sermon to the Masons of New York* (publ. 1783). On the marriage of his son Samuel to Frances (Fanny) Taber, see the *New London Gazette* of May 18, 1789 and Caulkins, *Oblong No. 5* p. 103. On the funeral sermon, see Caulkins, *Manuscript Copy: Harris, Chapman* etc. (without pagination). In the third generation, Samuel Seabury (1801–68, son of Rev. Charles) published various works, including *Moneygripe's Apprentice*, cf. the edition by R. B. Mullin (New Haven 1989)

with the author identified and the book dated to 1831, on pages 4f. and 39; a further early publication, *The Study of the Classics on Christian Principles* (New York 1831); and *American Slavery* (New York 1861). On the family slaves, see the national Census of 1790.

11. Way-Champlain ties to the Starrs included not only Jonathan through his Taber wife but a number of other Ways (not, however, of the same New London branch with Ebenezer); as to ties with Seabury's, the second Samuel had married another granddaughter of Pardon Tillinghast Taber; and some acquaintance with Perkins is suggested by the young Ebb's presence with the hunting party on which Nathaniel Perkins Shaw Jr. died by tragic accident, cf. Rogers p. 329.

12. Dr. Samuel H. P. Lee, hero of New London's yellow fever epidemic of 1798, was sufficiently of the city's Establishment to be sought for endorsement of medicines and as board-member of the town's girls academy (of which Frances Caulkins was principal, 1829–32). See the *Connecticut Gazette* of May 8, 1805 etc.; Caulkins, *History* pp. 479, 584, and 641; and Decker, *Whaling City* pp. 75, 97, and 264. His pioneer entry into whaling in 1805 soon failed, and he opened instead a fashionable boarding house. His wife Eliza (Elizabeth) Sullivan (b.1773), his daughters Maria and Eliza and two doctor-sons Henry (with his wife Sarah) and Samuel recur in the correspondence, practicing in New York.

13. Anxiety or apologies for "defects in composition" feared from the "malicious criticism" of Jonathan Starr by Betsey (**no. 18**) or for faults in letters because of bad pen, bad light, no time for corrections, etc., by Eliza (**nos. 19**, **46**, **49**, **168**, **169**, or **202**), George (**nos. 35**, **66** and **78**), Amelia Taber (**47**), Hannah Way (**151**); first drafts of important letters, by Mary Way (**74**) or Sally as revealed by Ebb's postscript (**36**); and fear of writing at all, expressed by Maria Hayden (**103** and **142**). Outside of the Way-Champlain letters, see much the same on the part of a contemporary of another town, in R. L. Bushman, *The Refinement of America* (New York 1992) p. 215.

14. On Abel McEwen, pastor 1806–56, see Hurd, *History* p. 194; Caulkins, *History* p. 590; William's letter is **no. 115**, the mock-Latin matched by Betsey in **no. 18**, "In hoc vocus mutae quae in nulla alia editone hujus. Why don't you cry, you fool, don't you hear my Latin. You see I have rub'd my peticoat against the College, if not against a zealot's brains."

15. See Perkins Manuscript in the New London County Historical Society (five trustees of the Masonic Hall); on Freemasonry, above, chapter 10 note 20.

16. On "Pastor Seabury," see **nos. 23** and **31** (George) and **104** (Sam), quoted.

17. Seabury's *Monegripe* pp. 54f.

18. See Caulkins, *Oblong No. 6* pp. 76 (Taber wealth in 1803, $5,873), 78 (Tabers Baptists), and 80; and the fashionable congregation of Starrs, Allens, Trumans, Saltonstalls, Mumfords, Deshons, Manwarings, etc., ibid. passim, and Hurd, *History* chap. XIV. Add Jirah Isham to the congregation, cf. H. W. Brainard, *A Survey of the Ishams in England and America* (Rutland 1938) pp. 240f. But General Jedidiah Huntington was a Congregationalist, and the church building itself of 1787 had been largely paid for by a Shaw (Thomas, 1739–95), brother of Nathaniel, see Caulkins, *History* pp. 588ff. For the Taber-Arnold connection, Bendict Arnold (1741–1801) sharing a Westcott ancestor with Pardon Taber,

see R. L. Whitman, *History and Genealogy of the Ancestors and Some Descendants of Stukely Westcott* (n.p. 1932) pp. 126, 129.

19. **No. 15** is the credo of Samuel Taber (1723–1813), brother of the elder Pardon Taber (grandfather of Mary and Betsey). It was published in 1812. An understanding of it I owe to Caulkins, *Green Oblong No. 6* p. 77 (she had seen a copy, evidently) but especially to letters from my Yale colleague Jon Butler and from Nathan Hatch, both experts well known in the field. Taber emerged from a Baptist family (note 18 above), and declares beliefs which align him with John Murray against Hosea Ballou within the Universalist sect (above, chapter 1 note 12 and 3 note 2), though he departs from Universalism in some particulars (prohibition against singing, oath-taking, etc.). For his business connection with Samuel Hurlbut and the religion of that family, see Decker, *New London Merchants* p. 117, and Caulkins, *History* p. 628 note 1 (Samuel, Baptist) and 502 and 592 (other Hurlbuts, Congregationalists).

20. No Universalist church existed till 1843 when a disused Episcopalian church was taken over. Not many years later it was struck by lightning, a clear sign of *some*thing (Caulkins, *History* pp. 599, 606). References to Solomon Blakeslee, St. James rector from 1815 to 1818 (**nos. 29**, **36**, and **45**, with Caulkins p. 594), make clear that the Champlains saw him as their minister, and as to his successor Bethel Judd (to 1832), Ebb and Sally Way were guests at his daughter's wedding (**no. 289**), William watched at the deathbed of Judd's wife (**248**), and other references are most affectionate. As to church attendance, Hannah Way is quoted saying she went out of "good manners" (**no. 144**), and (**91** in chapter 8, above) Mary, "surrounded by Methodists" whom she does not fancy, attends at other churches, plural.

21. On class sense routinely inculcated in textbooks, see R. M. Elson, *Guardians of Tradition. American Schoolbooks of the Nineteenth Century* (Lincoln 1964) pp. 268ff., 280; and Decker, *Whaling City* p. 66 identifies one "most aristocratic block in" New London, while others seem to emerge in census lists.

22. See "black wench" in **no. 174** (Eliza's angry term), or a church "insulted" by blacks buying it (**53**); unthinkable that a brother should do work done by "coloured" (**66**, George); "sable clutches" (**225**, Anna Fitch's scornful phrase for clumsy hands, like Betsey's of **18**, where it's a white farm girl in question); a context in Bushman, *Refinement* p. xv, "The line that once [in the 18th century] divided gentry from the rest of society now dropped to a lower level and separated the middle class from workers and marginal persons"; and similar summing up of prejudice and hostility toward blacks in N. Weyl, *The Negro in American Civilization* (Washington, D.C., 1960) pp. 53ffl, or E. Ginzberg and A. S. Eichner, *The Troublesome Presence. American Democracy and the Negro* (London 1964) pp. 76ff. Notice, however, kindness shown by Anna Fitch and Eliza to the Fitch's black servant (**204**, **221**, etc.).

23. On the measures taken in New York to raise money for the Greeks, see the sources cited in I. N. P. Stokes, *The Iconography of Manhattan Island*, 1498–1909 vol.5 (1926) pp. 1634ff.: a civic resolution of December 2, 1823, a Bachelor's Ball of January 1, 1824 raising $266.44, and a Grand Military Ball of January 8, 1824 at the Park Theatre.

24. "Neutral-tint," see below, note 41.

25. *New York Genealogical and Biographical Record* 34 (1903) shows Amelia Laverty married in 1824 to Rufus Howard King, indeed "a splendid victory," grandson (it must be) of a namesake (1755–1827) who was a senator, ambassador to England, etc., and incidentally uncle to Eliza Southgate (above, chapter 10 note 7). When Eliza says the marriage was to Charles King, I think she is confusing the new husband (Rufus) with his father (Charles, son of Rufus Senior).

26. On Halsey Goddard, see chapter 11 note 24.

27. Above, note 25.

28. Of these various names, no less than three dozen of the Hallams may be traced through the index of Caulkins' *History*, throughout town offices and back to the mid 17th century and recently (John) on the reception committee; Dr. Lee, above at note 12; Thompson, presumably Isaac; and Anthony Thatcher (1782–1844) of Stratford, marrying into New London (in 1806–Lucretia Mumford), cashier of the New London City Bank from 1807 to 1833 (*Connecticut Gazette* of March 25, 1808, etc.; Caulkins, *History* p. 662; eadem, *Green Oblong No. 6* pp. 105f.; and Hurd, *History* p. 218), in business with Frink, *Gazette* of May 29, 1805 etc., Hurd p. 223, and **no. 128**, "the Frinks family–there cannot be better."

29. On the general difficulty of American viewers in valuing Rubens' art, because of its nudes, see W. R. Valentiner, "Rubens' paintings in America," *Art Quarterly* 9 (1946) p. 153; more specifically, in *The Selected Papers of Charles Willson Peale and His Family*, ed. L. B. Miller 3 (New Haven 1991) p. 499, Peale's indignation at a Titianesque nude shown to the public; or in Boston in 1831, marble cherubs in a sculpture exhibition diapered to assuage the citizens' outrage. See N. Wright, *Horatio Greenough. The First American Sculptor* (Philadelphia 1963) p. 72.

30. Henry Inman (1801–46) exhibited two portraits of "gentlemen" unnamed in 1824 (one, surely Edward Riley Sr.), cf. M. B. Cowdrey, *American Academy of Fine Arts and American Art-Union. Exhibition Record* (New York 1953) p. 201. He painted a number of prominent New York churchmen, cf. W. H. Gerdts, *The Art of Henry Inman* (Washington D.C. 1987) pp. 41, 44, or J. Yarnell and W. H. Gerdts, *The National Museum of American Art's Index to American Art Exhibition Catalogues* 6 (Boston 1986) p. 1886, on a portrait of the Swedenborgian society-head, Dr. Mott; Gerdts, *Art* p. 34 and passim, and T. Bolton, "Henry Inman, portrait painter," *Creative Art* 12 (1933) pp. 118ff., on Inman's great fame as a portraitist in the 1820s and 1830s, adding the tribute paid in anonymous verse to an Inman miniature of his sister, in the *New York Mirror and Ladies' Literary Gazette* of September 13, 1823 ; and on the 1817 portrait of his brother, Gerdts, *Art* p. 31.

31. The Irving portrait was surely the one by Jarvis shown in 1824, cf. Cowdrey, *American Academy* p. 207. Ibid. pp. 108, 119 for Dickenson's *Cupid*; and J. Bisbee's *Cleopatra*, p. 27. "The Broken Heart" appeared, e.g., in Irving's *Sketch Book of Geoffrey Crayon*[3] (London 1820) pp. 131–44.

32. On the New-York moments of Lafayette's visit, see Foster (cit. above, note 9) p. 58 and Brandon (cit. above, note 8) pp. 38f., 183f., and (on the Lafayette Ball on September 14th, when the General returned to the city) pp. 204ff. John MacMullen's presence in the crowds on August 16 he recalled in a couple of his later publications.

33. The marriage of Jonathan Starr Jr. to Anna Morgan is reported in the *Connecticut Gazette* of June 5, 1822; after she died in 1825, he married Catherine S. Sythoff on September 17, 1828.

34. In the vernacular of the day, any "fantastic ornament," cf. L. V. Berrey and M. Van Den Bark, *The American Thesaurus of Slang* (New York 1947) p. 37.

35. September 14, 1824, cf. above, note 32.

36. Among Thomas Moore's *National Airs* of 1818, "A Temple to Friendship" describes a shrine built in a garden by a young lady who bought for it a statue, not of Friendship–too cold in appearance–but of Love. "You're not the first maiden/ Who came but for Friendship and took away Love." I notice a puzzle here about **168**, undated, but which in my Transcription I attribute to October of 1824 for reasons which seem good to me, and to which I would add as a clincher the reference to the sculptured head of Byron here as in **163** of August 1824. In this **168** Eliza speaks of the *Temple* as just completed. However, back in January, Betsey praises the *Temple* she has just been sent (**154**, January 24 of a year unspecified, but which I give as 1824 in my Transcription, because of its ties to the wording in **155**). I can only suppose that Eliza painted two *Temple* versions, one on paper, the second on ivory, more carefully.

37. Above, **no. 162**, referring scornfully to the over-flow Universalist church called "the Price St. Church" in A. C. Thomas, *A Century of Universalism in Philadelphia and New York* (Philadelphia 1872) pp. 273, 335, headed briefly by Abner Kneeland (p. 80) and for a year 1824/5 by the Connecticutter Rev. Nehemiah Dodge (1770–1843). The Christology of both differed from Edward Mitchell's.

38. From **nos. 103** (November of 1821) and **107** it might be inferred that William had been found a job of some sort in the New London post-office, which is likely enough considering Uncle Ebb's position; more clearly, **126** (June of 1822) and **209** (1826).

39. On Rogers, see chapter 3 note 19.

40. In the sequence and numbering of my Transcription this letter, **no. 171**, should be placed after **172**, witness references in the former to "neck . . . a pipe-stem" and "Sam . . . the handsomest;" and re-reading of the date of **171** makes it November 2[4].

41. I owe to the kindness of C. Rebora the identification of "Neutral-Tint," well known to the sisters of the brush (**nos. 155**, **157**, and **184**, where he praises Eliza behind her back). He is John Rubens Smith (1775–1849). See her City-University-of-New-York dissertation, "The American Academy of the Fine Arts, New York 1802–1842" (1990) pp. 254, 259 ("Natural Squint," cf. **173**), and 293, with the illuminating if too-kind obituary in *The Crayon* (New York) of November 7, 1855, "Reminiscences of John R. Smith," which Dr. Rebora also supplied. His record may be seen also in Cowdrey, *American Academy* (cit. above, n. 30) pp. 330f.

42. This **no. 154** was wrongly placed in my Transcription; but the year can be corrected thanks to the mention of Halsey Goddard's marriage, which took place at just this time, cf. the *New London Gazette* of January 26, 1825. The Rev. Bethel Judd officiated.

43. This letter, **no. 174**, again I have misplaced in the sequence: the half-visible date cannot be the 6th, surely the 26th of February, since it is only received in New London on March 9th (**no. 177**); and further, Eliza reports the Kelly-performance as being "night before last,"

which was actually on the 28th. See W. B. Durham, *American Theatre Companies, 1749–1887* (New York 1986) p. 391. So the letter was completed in early March. Lydia Kelly's name appears in various records and accounts of Drury Lane, but for the American appearance of this "vivacious comedienne" at the Chatham Garden and her medium, described as "a Grand Asiatic Melodramatic Romance," see ibid.

44. In this **no. 178** there are interlinear additions and erasures which I have folded into the text as best I could (they are indicated more accurately in the Transcription). I omit five octaves of Betsey's verse, entitled "To a Friend who envied the Author's Perpetual Flow of High Spirits"–likely composed in answer to much earlier remarks of Eliza.

45. "Complete amateur," meaning of course "fully qualified lover of the art."

46. Mary Goddard's ?uncle Calvin Goddard of Norwich, "lawyer and statesman," became a business partner of Maj.-Gen. William Williams of Stonington in 1809 (who named a son Calvin Goddard Williams). See F. M. Caulkins, *History of Norwich, Connecticut* (Hartford 1866) p. 611; W. Haynes, *1649–1949 Stonington Chronology* (Stonington 1949) p. 49; and R. A. Wheeler, *History of the Town of Stonington* (Mystic 1966) p. 675.

Notes to Chapter 13

1. In this **no. 187** the month is hard to read, but in the light of what can be tracked regarding Sam's search for a bank-clerkship the date must be April 12, 1825 not "Au.12" (wrongly in my Transcription).

2. "S. Way" must be Ebb's "aged mother," who recovered remarkably, cf. **nos. 277** and **293**. As to Prudence [Champlin] Prentice, perhaps descended of Prudence (Thompson) Champlain (1716–50), her marriage to David Prentice is reported in the *Connecticut Gazette* of December 2, 1807.

3. Captain Pardon Tillinghast Taber (chapter 2 note 19; chapter 3 note 9) had a daughter Frances who in 1825 married James Coit (1786–).

4. **No. 182** of May 16, on which Eliza has written parts of a draft of **no. 186** and a partial description of a fancy piece reminiscent of what she described in **no. 174**: "or to express myself more *poeticaly* it is a slight imitation of Spenser's Fairy Queen. I thought if her drapery took the line of the waves from which she is rising it would not only be more proper but ten times more beautiful. I have endeavoured to make the folds cling to her form as well as I could without a pattern of a baptized Maria Tylher, as they must of course be saturated with wet and the shades proportionately dark, the ten thousand dies supposed to be reflected from her bright coral's waves."

5. Ethan Allen Brown (1766–1852) was governor 1818–22. He never married. See *The National Cyclopedia of American Biography* vol. 3 (1893) p. 138.

6. **No. 183**, which is misrepresented in my Transcription: from Eliza, and not from New London but New York (the postmark half-hidden by the address, but still certain).

7. *New London Gazette* of August 3, 1825. Hannah Way is referred to in the past tense in **no. 195**.

8. These letters are William's to Anna (**no. 192**), on which Anna drafts her letter of condolence; the latter itself (**194**); and Sam's to his brother (**193**)–all of October 26–28. To

these William offers his full account (**195**), matching others easily found in the times. For examples, see J. O. and J. C. Robertson, *All Our Yesterdays* (New York 1993) pp. 103ff.

9. Susanna Madelina Champlain (1778–1824) was born in Hesse (Germany). See **no. 329 I** and her headstone in the Grove Street cemetery. Her husband "never recovered from her death" (**no. 198**) and directed he should be buried in the same grave (**no. 301**). Among his effects were books and pamphlets "many of which are in an unknown language to the appraisers," presumably German (so, the probate record).
10. Roger Griswold, Connecticut governor 1811–13 (his brother Matthew, incidentally, chief judge of New London county). See the *National Cyclopedia* vol. 10 (1909) p. 329.
11. The success of this music-instruction appears in the *New London Gazette* of March 15, 1826 and later dates: "Miss Stammers respectfully informs the public she will remain one quarter more for the purpose of giving instruction upon the piano forte. . . . "
12. **No. 205** is undated, but as Eliza "grows more rational," etc., implying she has been under observation for a space of some weeks at least, her aunt should be writing around early February (Eliza having returned home about November 15, 1825). In the last paragraph, her "condition" which cannot be explained in a letter is her uncertainty about marrying, about which she has spoken now more frankly to her aunt. Reference to Mr. Mitchell's being "so low" in health would answer a mention in **no. 204** of February 4.
13. The reference is not to Eliza Lee but Eliza Champlain; and in the next paragraph, the "amanuensis" is, to judge from the hand, most likely Mary Prescott. This latter was a Champlain cousin of some sort (cf. "Aunt and Henry Prescott," **no. 206**).

Notes to Chapter 14

1. Riley Sr. hailed from Shropshire (**no. 329 I**, **K**, **M**, and **N**); for his dates and first wife (Susanna Jiggins) and second, Elizabeth Atkinson, see ibid. and Kin-chart B; concerning London, cf. a letter to Riley Sr. from his friend in 1798, **no. 9**, in which Riley is seen learning new songs and how to tune a piano; Riley's ad in the *New York Evening Post* of February 11, 1806; *Riley's Collection of 24 Country Dances . . .* (London, 1798); H. W. Hitchcock, ed., *Riley's Flute Melodies* (New York reprint of 1973), introduction; R. J. Wolfe, *Early American Music Engraving and Printing* (Urbana 1980) p. 55; the *New Grove Dictionary of American Music* (New York 1986) pp. 47f.; and N. Croce, *Musical Instrument Makers of New York* (Stuyvesant 1991) p. 131.
2. **No. 329 M**; *Longworth's American Almanac, New-York Register, and City Directory* of 1808–25; the places of publication on Riley's many works from 1811 on; the *Post* of February 11 and May 8, 1806, etc., especially March 27, 1816 (with his wife's school's ad, August 4, 1806); Wolfe and other sources cited in note 1; V. L. Redway, *Music Directory of Early New York City* (New York 1941) p. 51; and the concerts advertised from 1806 on, e.g. in the *Post* of January 5, 1807, February 15, 1808, March 27, 1810, and so into 1823, with a full pillage of the press made by G. C. D. Odell in the first three volumes of his *Annals of the New York Stage* (New York 1927–28)–most easily consulted through the Index s.v. "Riley" and, in vol. III, "Miss Riley." Further, S. L. Porter, *With an Air Debonair. Musical Theatre in America, 1785–1815* (Washington 1991) p. 489, on Riley's "Spanish Patriots" (with music by Charles Gilfert) of January 4, 1809, and subsequent publication from 1811, *Riley's New Instructions for the German Flute* etc. and Wolfe pp. 55, 130. His woodwinds can be found

in Yale University's Collection and (Wolfe, cit., pp. 55, 70) in the Library of Congress. For background, e.g. what stages looked like, or what reviews said, consult Odell's and Porter's excellent works.

3. On Woodworth and his collaboration with Riley, see above, chapter 6 note 2 and chapter 9 notes 35ff; V. B. Lawrence, by her very kind help to me pointing me to useful works, none more so than her own *Strong on Music . . .* , vol. 1, *Resonances 1836–1850* (Chicago 1988), e.g. p. 337 note, on the opera "The Forest Rose" of 1823; for Riley's publications, see the ads of the time, e.g. the *New York Columbian* of February 21, 1818, *New York Evening Post* of March 27, 1816, the *New York Mirror* of October 4, 1823, or (quoted) the *Ladies' Literary Cabinet* of November 11, 1820; the Library-of-Congress Pre-1956 catalogue vol. 495 pp. 260f. (with some confusion between elder and younger Riley); Hancock cit., on "Riley's immense anthology" of flute melodies of 1814–20; Wolfe pp. 72, 79–83, 187ff., 237f., 245 (Mrs. Bradish). The last-named ran a well-known boarding house with at least one even better-known guest, see *The Letters of James Kirke Paulding*, ed. R. M. Aderman (Madison 1962) pp. 9f., 14, 20, 23.

4. On Pleyel (1757–1831), see *The New Grove Dictionary of Music and Musicians* (New York 1980) 5 pp. 6ff.; Pleyel in ads collected by T. A. Garrett, "A History of Pleasure Gardens in New York City" (Diss. New York University 1977) pp. 162f., 179, 185, 211, 287, 308, etc.; a splendid account of the variety and vitality of "serious" music of the first twenty years of the century, in Lawrence pp. xxxi–xli; and Wolfe p. 177.

5. **No. 13** records Riley Sr.'s admission to the New Church in 1799, his wife's in 1802, "at which time there were 60 members;" accounts of the pre-Riley New-Church advocates in the U. S., whose activities collapsed, in *A Brief History. The New Church–Swedenborgian 115 East 35th Street, N.Y.* [no date, no pagination–and my thanks to the Rev. Robert E. McCluskey for making available this and the next document]; Margaret Sampson, *History of the Church* [n.d., typescript], "the real founder of the New York Society was Edward Riley;" "Extracts from the Journal of the . . . Convention . . . 1817," *Reprint of the Early Journals of the General Convention of the New Jerusalem* 1 (1817 [1888]) pp. 5ff.; "The Planting of the New Church in New York," an "Address delivered by the Rev. Charles H. Mann before the General Convention . . . 1884," *New-Jerusalem Messenger* of September 10, 1884, pp. 8, 46, 51, 104 (Riley a delegate in 1826), etc.; M. B. Block, *The New Church in the New World* (New York 1932) pp. 93f., on the failed efforts of the earlier 1790s, and pp. 95ff. on Riley, Woodworth, Mott, et al., with pp. 97ff. on the split of late 1821; I. N. P. Stokes, *The Iconography of Manhattan Island* vol.3 (New York 1918) p. 936, the move to Pearl Street in 1821; C. T. Odhner, *Annals of the New Church* 1 (Bryn Athyn 1904) p. 230; K. T. Jackson, ed., *Encyclopedia of New York* (New Haven 1995) p. 1144, the start of the church in 1805 at 16 Chamber Street, till 1807, then James Street for two years, followed by nine years on Broadway; occasional correspondence from Riley Sr., e.g. of September 20, 1817 in aid of missionizing; and the *New Jerusalem Magazine* 43 (1839) p. 31, delegates E. C. Riley and Samuel Waldo to the General Convention.

6. On Henry Riley (musical-instrument manufacturer from 1826 on) and Fredrick (only from 1844 on, though earlier at the old family location), see N. Croce, "Musical Instrument Making in New York During the Eighteenth and Nineteenth Centuries" (Diss. University of Michigan 1982) pp. 421f.; eadem, *Musical Instrument Makers* p. 131; and V. L. Redway, *Music Directory of Early New York City* (New York 1941) p. 51

7. On E. C. Riley's appearance, besides his portrait by Parisen (Pl. 8.18, in chapter 10), notice his nickname "Mr. Fox" (**nos. 230**, **232**, **234**); on his business and professional career, see **no. 200**, his business card without date but not later than 1826, listing all his many activities and wares; his "comic song," *Shopping* of 1848 and *Waterloo Waltz*; the two works by Croce, citt. (especially "Instrument Making" p. 421 on Edward's inventions); Odell, *Annals* vol. 2 p. 602, E. C. Riley as a band-conductor and flautist in concerts of 1821, and vol. 3 pp. 39, 113, 165, and 596, in the same roles along with choral-conducting in 1822–24 and 1832; Redway, *Directory* p. 51; *New Grove Dictionary* vol. 4; and H. Shanet, *Philharmonic: A History of New York's Orchestra* (Garden City 1975) pp. 48ff., 417, 426. On the 35th-Street church, a gift to the society in the 1850s, see Block, *New Church* pp. 97–99, the site being only a few blocks, as it happened, from where Edward's grandson Charles W. MacMullen later lived.

8. The New York society dismissed its pastor of twenty years, Charles Doughty, in 1838, electing Edward its head and later its delegate to the Convention, see the *Journal of the General Convention* (Boston 1839) pp. 405f., describing how he led services of 75–100 members in the room on Broadway, the Pearl-Street church having been leased to the Universalists. For his delegate-duties (with Samuel Waldo), see the *New Jerusalem Magazine* 43 (1839) p. 31.

9. This recommended song emerged to instant popularity in the early 1820s, first heard in New York in the opera *Clari* toward the end of 1823; cf. J. J. Fuld, *The Book of World-Famous Music*[3] (New York 1985) pp. 274f.

10. Isaac Marquand had a store on Pearl Street from 1813; his family were members of the Universalist church, and supplied pupils to Eliza's school (*Longworth's Directory* for 1813 through the 1820s; **nos. 97**, **109**, **117**, and **124**). The miniature titled *Mary* was likely of Mary Queen of Scots, and (**219**) fetched $5.

11. E. K. Rothman, *Hands and Hearts. A History of Courtship in America* (New York 1984) pp. 10ff.; R. L. Bushman, *The Refinement of America. Persons, Houses, Cities* (New York 1992) pp. 215, 220; and on New London as dull and confined, **no. 132** (Mary Way's description), earlier letters (Eliza's complaints), and the present complaint (quoted) from **no. 214**.

12. A Nathaniel Saltonstall's son Nathaniel (b.1776) of New London married one of the ubiquitous Lampheres, Lucretia, whose daughter Augusta (1804–51) married Peter Arcularius in 1826, as the newspapers report. In the following letter by Eliza, answering a lost one by Edward, it is clear that the Arcularius he thinks she speaks of is the prominent and detested Philip, see R. A. Mohl, *Poverty in New York 1783–1825* (New York 1971) p. 76. In **no. 219** Anna Fitch writes of seeing notice of the wedding.

13. Reference can only be to James Gates Percival (1795–1856), a Connecticut poet with New London kin, Yale graduate of 1815, publishing first in New Haven (a collection of his *Poems* in 1821), two other poetry volumes (*Clio* I and II in 1822), and much else in later years. He was very well received in New York, his verses excerpted in periodicals like the *Ladies' Literary Cabinet* of September 7, 1822, or set to music, and he himself shown around and introduced to James Fenimore Cooper and Bryant. He made several visits to the city on business. See J. H. Ward, *The Life and Letters of James Gates Percival* (Boston 1866) pp. 1, 3, 40, 100, 132, 138f., 213ff., 254ff., and 263f.

14. Captain Thomas Allen and wife Amelia Taber (1758–1838, Pardon Taber's daughter) spent 1812–16 and 1824–42 (his death) in Pomfret on the family farm. See M. A. Phinney, *A Brief History of Lewis Allen* (Rutland 1954) pp. 14ff.

15. Notice of the marriage in the *New London Gazette* of September 13, 1826; and **no. 316**, Mayor Jirah Isham's certification post-facto. Eliza's age for a first marriage was less unusual in her day than it would have been in the previous generation, see M. P. Ryan, *Womanhood in America*[3] (New York 1983) pp. 98f.

Notes to Chapter 15

1. The letter is **no. 229** of September 28th, 1826. In regard to William's new job, J. K. Owens, Director, National Archives, New England Region, kindly writes me that William "was an inspector in the New London customhouse from 1826 to 1831." For William's boss, the Collector Richard Law, see F. M. Caulkins, *History of New London, Connecticut* (New London 1895) p. 649.

2. See chap. 12 note 12 (probably Samuel Lee is meant, here).

3. Maria Hayden had suffered the loss of her husband (**no. 226**), and must quit New York for New Orleans.

4. On the Customs business with its various clearance forms through the New London port as elswhere, see Caulkins, *History of New London* pp. 648ff.; D. L. Stein, *American Maritime Documents 1776–1860* (Mystic 1992) pp. 59, 61, and passim; C. E. Prince and M. Keller, *The U. S. Customs Service* (Washington 1989) pp. 80 (on Jedidiah Huntington) and 62ff. and 102ff. (on the cronyism, politics, and partisanship in firings in the service of the 1820s and 1830s); on the city's economy from the 1790s on, R. J. Purcell, *Connecticut in Transition* (Washington 1918) pp. 115ff., 133; and R. O. Decker, *The New London Merchants* (New York 1986) pp. 115ff., 121.

5. The correspondence never explains what brush with the law bothered William. In the next letter Eliza congratulates him on getting out of it.

6. T. L. Gravell and G. Miller, *A Catalogue of American Watermarks 1690–1835* (New York 1979) help in the identifying of about fifty letters' American watermarks: some by R or A H Hubbard from 1825 on, mostly New York makers; iidem, *A Catalogue of Foreign Watermarks on Paper Used in America* (New York 1983) identifies **nos. 237**ff., "BATH SUPERFINE."

7. The Mary and Martha here (Lk 10.39ff.) are Eliza's term for the welcomers in the house.

8. Mrs. Amelia Opie (1769–1853) published a lot of fiction in the early 1800s, but just what it was in which of her works, to arouse the impatience of Mary Way (**no. 205**) and, here, of Edward, is not clear. Her popularity in America appears, for example, in the quotation of her poetry, *Albion* of October 30, 1822, or in the advertising of her *Tales of the Heart* through the *Commercial Advertiser* of January 15, 1823.

9. Something of George's life along these lines can be drawn from **nos. 175**, **182**, **18** (his fondness for the theatre), quoting of Shakespeare (above, chapter 9), **199**, **228**, and below, **245**, "evidence in the case" "in the marine court . . . detained me."

10. Solomon Smith quoted in S. M. Archer, *Junius Brutus Booth, Theatrical Prometheus* (Carbondale 1992) p. 108; visit by the troupe to Boston's Tremont Theatre at the end of August, pp. 108f., before heading south and west, and eventually (p. 112: June 1829) returning to New York; and further on Booth, out of an abundant literature, see F. C. Wemyss, *Twenty-Six Years of the Life of an Actor and Manager* (New York 1847) pp. 81–94; W. B. Wood, *Personal Recollections of the Stage* (Philadelphia 1854) pp. 271f., 281, 301ff.; and, for a selection of reactions to Booth's genius, G. Smith, *American Gothic* (New York 1992) p. 20.

11. Mary meant to call the music box after her great-nephew, but somehow erred: the first-born of Edward and Eliza was Edward *Champlain* Riley, born the day after Christmas of 1827 (**no. 329 I**; in **329 J** the year "1828" by error).

12. For Samuel Champlain's promotion, see **no. 255** of January 30, 1829; for William's rememberings, **no. 254** of January 24th. The summer trip may be inferred from his having seen his nephew to describe him to Mary (fourth paragraph of **253**).

13. Ebenezer Way was town clerk 1817–27, Recorder in 1817 etc., postmaster from March of 1816. See F. M. Caulkins, *Manuscript Copy: Green Oblong No. 6, S. T. U. V. W.* (in the New London County Historical Society) p. 169; eadem, *Manuscript Copy: Town Offices, New London*, second page (with Thomas Way mentioned as Assessor often throughout the 1820s, cf. also *New London Gazette* of October 5, 1825 etc.); on Ebb's work as town clerk in the probate court, ibid. e.g. of May 4, 1826. During the later 1820s, Thomas Mussey can be seen rising through New London officialdom, see Caulkins' *Town Offices* for 1826f.; and in the fall of 1830 he was elected to the state Assembly supported by the very new New London Mechanic's Association of Labouring Men–see R. O. Decker, *The Whaling City. A History of New London* (Chester 1976) p. 117–and later served as Collector in the Customs house (1846–49, see Caulkins, *History* p. 649). On the Jacksonian policies regarding federal appointments and their impact on Ebenezer Way and William Champlain, see below, chapter 16 note 15 and elsewhere.

14. On the "astounding" exodus from the state in the decades leading up to 1820, see Purcell, *Connecticut* p. 151; on the postmastership's social functions, J. O. and J. C. Robertson, *All Our Yesterdays* (New York 1993) pp. 147f., 164–68, describing the postmaster as "a social welfare worker" in Connecticut; its political nature, ibid., and that nature and its usefulness in forming a political base discussed in R. R. John, "Managing the Mails: The Postal System, Public Policy, and American Political Culture, 1823–1836" (Diss. Harvard University 1989) pp. 55f., 65, 93ff.; and open controversy on whether the job should be a political appointment seen especially well in the *New York Spectator* of Janaury 29, 1822 p.4, in a public exchange of letters. For the role of petitions, pressure on senators and contacts in Washington, etc., see the discussion and parallels by the Robertsons, pp. 171ff., and John, pp. 229ff., 240ff., 251ff. Ebb's story continues to unfold, below.

15. See **nos. 258**f. of March 14th and 31st, Richard Law nominating and the nomination approved by Samuel Delucenna Ingham (1779–1860), Treasury Sec. March 3, 1829–August 2, 1831.

16. Mrs. Duff indeed had a great reputation on the stage, from her New York debut in 1823 through the early 1830s. See G. C. D. Odell, *Annals of the New York Stage* 3 (New York 1928) pp. 87, 579f.

Notes to Chapter 16

1. William contemplated leaving the Way house almost a year prior (**no. 256** of February, 1829), actually making the move only in December (**no. 268**).
2. See above, chapter 5 note 7, and **no. 180**, the Perry family in New London, whose name crops up several times in the correspondence.
3. The desk (sold off by the family in the 1940s) was a handsome box of cherry sliced on the slant to open up and make a slanting writing surface, with drawers and pigeon holes, brass fittings, and so forth.
4. Mrs. Riley Sr. ran the store for a few years after her husband's death, as the Directories show. See V. L. Redway, *Music Directory of Early New York City* (New York 1941) p. 51.
5. Of these three paintings that Mary Way recalls, I can identify in M. B. Cowdrey, *American Academy of Fine Arts and American Art-Union, 2: Exhibition Record 1816 1852* (New York 1953) only Jarvis' "Portrait of an infant playing with a Bird" of 1818, p. 206, and the possibility of the third, Trumbull's "Saviour and St. John" of 1816, p. 355.
6. See E. S. Dodge, "Captain collectors," *Essex Institute Historical Collections* 81 (1945) pp. 27ff. (primacy of Salem and New Bedford) and especially 33; idem, *New England and the South Seas* (Cambridge 1965) pp. 25f., 43ff. (the first landings to the principal islands in 1819 and 1820).
7. At the death of Captain Hayden on June 10, 1826, his wife was on the eve of joining him at his post near New Orleans. There she stayed for some unknown time before returning to New York. On April 27, 1828 (**no. 250**), Mary refers without explanation to "the business she [Maria Hayden] is about to engage in," in New York.
8. Edward Mitchell (1768–1834) now fades out of the correspondence, unhappily. His son had died (**no. 260**) in April 1829, a daughter Susan not long afterwards (**no. 262**); but his daughter Cornelia recovered for a long life. His own health had been poor in 1824 (**nos. 162** and **168**) and 1826 (**no. 205**); again (**no. 271**), in April 1830; and in 1833 he gathered his sermons etc. into a valedictory work, *The Christian Universalist*. He had headed his church formally since 1803, informally since the originating group known as the Duane Street Society was formed in 1796. At his death, that church, Universalist but Trinitarian, declined rapidly, cf. the (hostile) mention by J. H. Allen and R. Eddy, *A History of the Unitarians and Universalists in the U. S.* (New York 1894) p. 399; E. Cassara, *Hosea Ballou* (Boston 1961) p. 31; and the fullest in his mentions of Mitchell, R. E. Miller, *The Larger Hope. The First Century of the Universalist Church* (Boston 1979) pp. 32, 42, 105, 674, 682, and 727.
9. John Way's daughter Sarah married Richard Douglass Starr (b.1775) in 1804, from whom was born the Marcus Aurelius Starr in question (1806–1865), marrying Elizabeth Starr Griffing grand-daughter of Jonathan Starr who married Elizabeth Taber. Etcetera–just to show the relation to Eliza, parts of which appear in Kin-chart B.
10. On the Groton Monument, see F. M. Caulkins, *History of New London, Connecticut* (New London 1895) pp. 571f. It recalled the victims of Benedict Arnold's attack on the city's fort. A heroic survivor, Stephen Hempstead (see Kin-chart C), in 1840 published with Rufus Avery *A Narrative* of the whole event, and in 1854 a *Description of the Monument* (both, in New London).

11. This **no. 279** is referred to as of "Sunday last," in **no. 280** (see next note).

12. For the "evacuation" or turn-out of the city on October 26th, see newspapers quoted in I. N. P. Stokes, *The Iconography of Manhattan Island* vol. 5 (New York 1926) p. 1696. **No. 280**, in referring to the event as of "the 26th of last month," dates itself to November–which contradicts the faded postmark of December [?]12; but a close reading shows the letter was set aside at mid-point, after mention of that "evacuation," and continued at a later moment.

13. J. De Angelis, Sam's fellow clerk in the Mechanics' Bank turned actor, was said in July of 1830 to have had "a successful debut last season," see G. C. D. Odell, *Annals of the New York Stage* 3 (New York 1928) p. 465. His career ended with a benefit in 1833, ibid. 648, and by 1836 at least he was back in the bank as First Teller, **no. 314**.

14. Is the answer to the riddle just Sam's jealousy at a clerk who attains fame?

15. Law's distinguished family and honorable career can be picked out of mentions in Caulkins' *History*, passim. **No. 278** of November 30, 1830 from Law in Washington shows him fighting for his office while handling its affairs by mail; next, this present letter from William, **no. 281** of December 17, 1830, indicating there had been other letters, not surviving, in the two-week interval. As to party allegiance, Ebb was a clear Jacksonian (**nos. 269** and **283**), Hannah Way was anti-Federalist (**no. 18**), Eliza a supporter of Monroe (evident in her enthusiasm for his reception, below, **no. 280**), but Betsey in her poem "Politics" (**no. 327** p. 7) is disgusted by the whole subject.

16. Samuel Burr Swartwout was a New York politician who ended his career a few years later in a storm of presidential anger for peculation on quite an extraordinary scale. He "was a precious scamp and a facile pander to the dispensers of patronage," J. S. Bassett sums up, in the *Correspondence of Andrew Jackson* 4 (Washington D.C. 1929) p. 130, apropos a fawning letter from S.; see idem, *The Life of Andrew Jackson* (New York 1911) pp. 452f., or J. Parton, *The Life of Andrew Jackson* (New York 1861) 1 pp. 209f., where is quoted a letter of S. in 1830 disclaiming any influence on the administration, anyway. As to "the venerable chairman Captain [Benjamin] Bailey" of the New York State Republican General Committee in 1828, see Bassett, *Correspondence* 3 p. 397; and on Henry Baldwin (1780–1844), a Connecticutter and Supreme Court justice of Jackson's appointing, see the *National Cyclopedia of American Biography* 2 (1891) pp. 257f. On the operation of the spoils system, see chapter XXI (esp. pp. 454f.) of Bassett's *Life*, cit., and H. L. Watson, *Liberty and Power. The Politics of Jacksonian America* (New York 1990) pp. 101ff. with bibliog.

17. Sheridan's play *The Critic* had a Boston edition in 1822, a New-York in 1824.

18. On whaling out of New London, see R. O. Decker, *The Whaling City. A History of New London* (Chester 1976) pp. 75 (organized whaling begun by Samuel H. P. Lee in 1804), 76–80, 95ff. (banks involved); idem, *The New London Merchants* (New York 1986) pp. 137, 143, 145, and Appendix XX passim.

19. On this figure (1795–1852), see C. M. Eckhardt, *Fanny Wright. Rebel in America* (Cambridge 1984). She lectured much in New York over the twenty years 1818–38 (e.g. in the Park Theatre, p. 185), attracting much attention to views which may be called proto-feminist, proto-socialist, and eventually indigestible among her countrymen. William's views are characteristically even-handed.

20. In **no. 296** of August 24th, Eliza tells William she cannot oblige him with a copy of a letter, which must be this **no. 295**. Yet a copy does survive (surely not later retrieved from the recipient). So, a puzzle.

21. Oliver Champlain's will (**no. 299**) specifies legacies of about $2500 among which Eliza is to get by far the largest amount, beyond Oliver's Harris- and Douglass-relatives, Nathaniel Shaw Perkins, and others; and she gets the remainder of his estate. Its inventory is on record in New London's court of probate.

22. These documents are **nos. 300**, the draft of Eliza's notification to Samuel, with a draft of her condolences to Anna; **302**, the notification to Samuel, evidently found in his effects after his death; and add Mary Prescott's postscript to **301**, "July 2nd," which seems of the date when news of Fitch's death reached New London. The *New-York Evening Post* gives his death as June 16, 1832.

23. See **no. 329 I** and **K**, where Grace L. MacMullen, daughter of the daughter of Eliza, writes to her kinsman John Denison Champlin (1834–1915), in 1898. On Champlin, see the *National Cyclopedia of American Biography* 8 (1924) pp. 357f. He shared an antecedent with Eliza only in the ninth generation back, to Geoffrey Champlin (1638–?95), but the actual acquaintance was much closer, cf. chapter 5 notes 7f. and other mentions of the wife of Commodore Perry.

24. Mary died in November of 1833, as appears in the *Connecticut Journal*, *New Haven Post-Boy* (of November 12, 1833), and *Hartford Courant* (of November 11, 1833). I have looked in vain in the Cedar Grove Cemetery for her grave or the Champlain lot–which was in any case full (**197**). The Curator of the New London County Historical Society, E. B. Knox, writes to W. L. Warren in 1979 that "Mary Way evidently didn't die in New London . . . not buried here." The likely burial place for Mary, New London's second cemetery, was disused and radically disturbed in 1885, cf. *Cedar Grove Cemetery* (New London) vol. 1, 1 (1936) pp. 50f.

Notes to Chapter 17

1. The letter is **no. 320** of November 1, 1843. In it, Albert Riley is Edward's brother (**no. 329 M**), "Uncle Albert" to little Edward, **no. 322**.

2. The son-in-law was John McMullen (as he spelt the name till at least his graduation from Columbia in 1837). He receives a letter of 1835 (**no. 311**) from Joseph Henry (1797–1878) supporting him for the librarianship of the Society Library. The "Prof. Gibbs" to whom Henry there refers is no doubt Josiah Willard G.(1790–1861). On MacMullen's relationship with Henry, see N. Reingold, ed., *The Papers of Joseph Henry* 2 (Washington 1975) pp. 6f., and M. Rothenberg, ed., 6 (ibid. 1992) p. 121. MacMullen (1818–96), who married Alice Fitch Riley, went on to become a famous schoolmaster; his sister Lucinda married Titian Peale in 1850 (**no. 329 C** and **D**). MacMullen only enters the correspondence twice again, writing to a stranger (**no. 330** of ?1853) and as a member of the Century Club in 1856, **no. 325**; but there is much other publication by and about him, from the 1830s on. He appears on the steps of his New York house with his family in one of the photos by T. R. Peale, in New York (the photos in the editor's possession).

3. By or to Sam, **nos. 306** and **308**f. of 1833, **312–4** of 1836, and **315** of 1837.

4. Anna Fitch's circumstances in the 1840s appear in **nos. 318–9** and **322**.
5. Ted Riley's letters: **nos. 321–3**. The edifying work (correctly, *The Constitution of Man* by George Combe, New York 1828, a 17th edition! by 1835) he reads aright, as showing the benign operation of the deity in the operation of physical laws, e.g. *re* intemperance.
6. E. C. Silver, *Sketches of the New Church in America* (Boston 1920) p. 191; for Edward as leader of the Swedenborgian society almost until his death in 1871, ibid.; also *Journal of the General Convention* [of the New Church] (1839) pp. 405–407; and **no. 329 R**, Edward's obituary.

Kin-charts

Concerning all this information, the most useful sources of information are the neatly bound and rudimentarily indexed volumes of C. D. Parkhurst's manuscript, "Early Families of New London and Vicinity" (Hartford, 1938), e.g., vol. 14, pp. 144, 147, 163; 23, pp. 102f. (Shapley); 28, pp. 63f. (Way), in the Connecticut State Library, and F. M. Caulkins' dozen or so "Manuscript Copy" volumes in the Shaw Mansion of the New London County Historical Society. In addition, in the Newport Historical Society, there is the typescript of J. D. Champlin's "Champlin Memorial" (n.d. [1903]). I have also drawn on such published sources as R. Canfield, *Rhode Island Descendants of Edward Perry* (Pacific Grove, 1988); F. W. Chapman, *The Coit Family* (Hartford, 1874); W. R. Cutter et al., *New England Families* (New York, 1913) 1 pp. 254 &c; D. S. Durrie, *Genealogical History of the Holt Family* (Albany, 1864); E. C. B. Jones, *The Brewster Genealogy* (New York, 1908); M. A. Phinney, *Allen Genealogy* (Rutland, n.d. [1954]); G. D. Phippen, *Pedigree of Saltonstalls* (Boston, 1871); F. A. Prince, *Genealogy of the Prince Family* (Danielson, 1899); G. Prince, *Elder John Prince of Hull* (Boston, 1888); C. E. Robinson, *The Hazard Family* (Boston, 1895); L. Saltonstall, *Ancestry and Descendants of Sir Richard Saltonstall* (New York, 1897); B. P. Starr, *History of the Starr Family of New England* (Hartford, 1879); F. M. Stoddard, *Genealogical History of the Allen Family* (Boston, 1891), with errors, p. 35; J. R. Totten, *Christophers Genealogy* (New York, n.d. [1921]); H. A. Way, *The Connecticut Way Family* (Charlestown, 1989); M. E. Way, *The Way Family* (Martinez, 1969); S. C. Wheat and H. L. Scranton, *Wheat Genealogy* (New York, 1903); and A. A. and A. H. Wright, *Descendants of Joseph and Philip, Sons of Philip Taber* (Ithaca, 1952).

Index

(Entries for the principal correspondents are extremely selective)